S0-FBV-147

# The Art of the Critic

# The Art of the Critic

## *Literary Theory and Criticism from the Greeks to the Present*

*Volume 6*
*Later Romantics*

EDITED WITH AN INTRODUCTION BY

HAROLD BLOOM
*Sterling Professor of the Humanities, Yale University*

1988
CHELSEA HOUSE PUBLISHERS
NEW YORK NEW HAVEN PHILADELPHIA

*Project Editor:* James Uebbing
*Editorial Coordinator:* Karyn Gullen Browne
*Copy Chief:* Richard Fumosa
*Editorial Staff:* Neal Dolan, Stephen Mudd
*Design:* Susan Lusk



Printed and bound in the United States of America

**Library of Congress Cataloging in Publication Data**
Main entry under title:

The Art of the Critic.

Includes bibliographies and index.
Contents: v. 1. Classical and medieval— —v. 6. Later Romantics—v. 7. Later nineteenth century.
1. Criticism—Collected works. 2. Literature—Philosophy—Collected works. I. Bloom, Harold.
PN86.A77 1985 809 84-15547
ISBN 0-87754-493-X (set)
0-87754-499-9 (v. 6)

# *Contents*

Index and Glossary are contained in Volume 11.

# *The Later Romantics: Shelley's Defense of the Imagination*

Harold Bloom

SHELLEY'S *Defence of Poetry* is hardly considered an indisputable classic of literary theory by the assorted formalists and historicists who proliferate among us. But then Shelley's *Defence,* as Paul H. Fry observes, is thoroughly Longinian in spirit, as Shelley perhaps did not know. Yeats proclaimed the *Defence* to be "the profoundest essay on the foundations of poetry in English," a judgment echoed by Croce and by Wilson Knight. I would go further, and place it with Longinus himself as the two central discourses upon poetry in Western critical tradition. It is from Longinus and from Shelley that sensitive readers, poets and critics, have learned the precise *use of inspiration* which, as Fry says, is to reproduce itself, to create by contagion.

Shelley's *Defence* was inspired, in this Longinian sense, by his close friend Thomas Love Peacock's splendidly ambivalent attack in *The Four Ages of Poetry* (1820). Peacock, a superb parodist, chose Wordsworth as target, but the exuberances of parody and the comprehensiveness of Wordsworth combined so as to make poetry itself appear the object of the Peacockian scorn. *The Four Ages of Poetry* has many delights, of which its most famous paragraph is perhaps the grandest:

> In the origin and perfection of poetry, all the associations of life were composed of poetical materials. With us it is decidedly the reverse. We know too that there are no Dryads in Hyde-park nor Naiads in the Regent's-canal. But barbaric manners and supernatural interventions are essential to poetry. Either in the scene, or in the time, or in both, it must be remote from our ordinary perceptions. While the historian and the philosopher are advancing in, and accelerating, the progress of knowledge, the poet is wallowing in the rubbish of departed ignorance, and raking up the ashes of dead savages to find gewgaws and rattles for the grown babies of the age. Mr. Scott digs up the poachers and cattle-stealers of the ancient border. Lord Byron cruizes for thieves and pirates on the shores of the Morea and among the Greek Islands. Mr. Southey wades through ponderous volumes of travels and old chronicles, from which he carefully selects all that is false, useless, and absurd, as being essentially poetical; and when he has a commonplace book full of monstrosities, strings them into an epic. Mr. Wordsworth picks up village legends from old women and sextons; and Mr. Coleridge, to the valuable information acquired from similar sources, superadds the dreams of crazy theologians and the mysticisms of

> German metaphysics, and favours the world with visions in verse, in which the quadruple elements of sexton, old woman, Jeremy Taylor, and Emanuel Kant, are harmonized into a delicious poetical compound. Mr. Moore presents us with a Persian, and Mr. Campbell with a Pennsylvanian tale, both formed on the same principle as Mr. Southey's epics, by extracting from a perfunctory and desultory perusal of a collection of voyages and travels, all that useful investigation would not seek for and that common sense would reject.

One is charmed to think of the grim and pompous Wordsworth having the patience to pick up village legends from old women and sextons, particularly when one remembers how the aged leech gatherer has to repeat himself in "Resolution and Independence." Peacock anticipates the two marvelous parodies of Wordsworth's habit of listening only to himself in Lewis Carroll's "The White Knight's Song" and Edward Lear's "Incidents in the Life of my Uncle Arly." "Frippery and barbarism," Peacock goes on to cry aloud, rejecting the Wordsworthian project for bringing the past alive into the present. That is hardly Peacock at his best, but this is: "Poetry is the mental rattle that awakened the attention of intellect in the infancy of society." It is the presence of apothegms of such quality that provoked Shelley to the sublimity of his reply.

M. H. Abrams reads the *Defence* as a Platonic aesthetic, but I cannot agree, except that Shelley's Plato, like Montaigne's, is a skeptic. Ironically, Peacock's *Four Ages* adopts something of *The Republic*'s stance toward poetry, whereas Shelley takes up the Homeric position that Plato attacked. This, to me, calls into question Abrams's contention that the *Defense* is not useful for the practical criticism of poems. Abrams asks: "For all its planetary music, has any critical essay of comparable scope and reputation ever contained less of specifically *literary* criticism?" The question is meant to be rhetorical, but is asked from a position partly historicist, partly formalist. Earl Wasserman, meeting Abrams's challenge, converted the *Defence* into historicism and formalism. Longinus and Shelley are Sublime theorists, and I myself find their essays supremely useful for a Sublime or antithetical practical criticism.

The cosmos, to Shelley as to Nietzsche after him, is the primordial poem of mankind. It is not accidental that Wallace Stevens's *Notes toward a Supreme Fiction* so agilely assimilates the Shelley of the *Defence* to Nietzsche as contemplating this invented world, the supreme fiction in which we dwell. Stevens's "inconceivable idea of the sun" follows Shelley's appropriation of the sun as the image of images, not so much Platonic as Shakespearean. Indeed, the sun in the *Defence* is at once a metaphor for the imagination and for poetic language as such. But this is the sun of each fresh day's creation of that particular day; it is not a Platonic sun beyond the sun. The imagination in Shelley's *Defence,* like the colors (tropes) of poetic language, is revising itself endlessly, revolving even as reality moves.

Innovation—in the heavens, in our institutions, in the new poem—is a Shelleyan synonym for imagination. The Shelleyan imagination, like the

Longinian or the Nietzschean, is agonistic in the extreme, a crucial truth that only Paul Fry among the exegetes of the *Defence* seems to have recovered. Poetry, Shelley knows, is always a response to prior poetry, a response that wavers dialectically between partial receptivity and partial opposition. Shelley, a superb critic of his own work, was telling the story of his relation to Dante, Shakespeare, and Milton, but above all the vexed tale of his immensely complex relations to Wordsworth. In some instances, poets write crucial essays on their precursors, as Browning and Yeats did on Shelley. But Shelley, subtly skeptical as an intellect, partly concealed, even from himself, that his *Defence of Poetry* was also a defense against Wordsworth.

There are paragraphs in the *Defence* that can be regarded as immensely eloquent prose reductions of Wordsworth, prophetic of moments to come in John Stuart Mill and George Eliot:

> We have more moral, political, and historical wisdom, than we know how to reduce into practice; we have more scientific and economical knowledge than can be accommodated to the just distribution of the produce which it multiplies. The poetry, in these systems of thought, is concealed by the accumulation of facts and calculating processes. There is no want of knowledge respecting what is wisest and best in morals, government, and political economy, or at least what is wiser and better than what men now practise and endure. But we let "*I dare not* wait upon *I would,* like the poor cat in the adage." We want the creative faculty to imagine that which we know; we want the generous impulse to act that which we imagine; we want the poetry of life: our calculations have outrun conception; we have eaten more than we can digest. The cultivation of those sciences which have enlarged the limits of the empire of man over the external world, has, for want of the poetical faculty, proportionally circumscribed those of the internal world; and man, having enslaved the elements, remains himself a slave. To what but a cultivation of the mechanical arts in a degree disproportioned to the presence of the creative faculty, which is the basis of all knowledge, is to be attributed the abuse of all invention for abridging and combining labour, to the exasperation of the inequality of mankind? From what other cause has it arisen that the discoveries which should have lightened, have added a weight to the curse imposed on Adam? Poetry, and principle of Self, of which money is the visible incarnation, are the God and Mammon of the world.

The Wordsworth of 1821 would not have endorsed the economic, social, and political radicalism of this passage, but it is pure Wordsworth of 1798. Shrewdly evading any mention of Wordsworth by name, Shelley has him in mind in the profound absolution granted to the great poets: "they have been washed in the blood of the mediator and redeemer, time." The great closing passage of the *Defence* centers itself upon Wordsworth, and to a lesser degree, Coleridge, defining both their glory and their fall into the quotidian, while also stating the credo for Shelley's life and work:

> For the literature of England, an energetic development of which has ever preceded or accompanied a great and free development of the national will, has arisen as it were from a new birth. In spite of the low-thoughted envy which would undervalue contemporary merit, our own will be a memorable age in intellectual achievements, and we live among such philosophers and poets as surpass beyond comparison any who have appeared since the last national struggle for civil and religious liberty. The most unfailing herald, companion, and follower of the awakening of a great people to work a beneficial change in opinion or institution, is poetry. At such periods there is an accumulation of the power of communicating and receiving intense and impassioned conceptions respecting man and nature. The persons in whom this power resides, may often, as far as regards many portions of their nature, have little apparent correspondence with that spirit of good of which they are the ministers. But even whilst they deny and abjure, they are yet compelled to serve, the power which is seated on the throne of their own soul. It is impossible to read the compositions of the most celebrated writers of the present day without being startled with the electric life which burns within their words. They measure the circumference and sound the depths of human nature with a comprehensive and all-penetrating spirit, and they are themselves perhaps the most sincerely astonished at its manifestations; for it is less their spirit than the spirit of the age. Poets are the hierophants of an unapprehended inspiration; the mirrors of the gigantic shadows which futurity casts upon the present; the words which express what they understand not; the trumpets which sing to battle and feel not what they inspire; the influence which is moved not, but moves. Poets are the unacknowledged legislators of the world.

Unquestionably, the poets of whom Shelley is speaking here are not himself, Byron, and Keats, but primarily Wordsworth and secondarily Coleridge. It does not matter, Shelley says, that as men Wordsworth and Coleridge have become Tories in politics, pillars of the established Church in religion, and mere time-servers in literature. "Even whilst they deny and abjure" the imagination, Wordsworth and Coleridge serve its power. Wordsworth is a hierophant or expounder of the mysterious, even though he himself cannot apprehend what he expounds. Wordsworth is a transumptive mirror of futurity, and sings Shelley on to the battle of poetry long after Wordsworth himself is uninspired. And then comes the beautifully summarizing formula: Wordsworth is the unmoved mover, as an *influence*. The famous, much misinterpreted last sentence, "Poets are the unacknowledged legislators of the world," clearly needs to be interpreted in the context of the paradox that Shelley himself calls poetic "influence." The late W. H. Auden had a passionate dislike of Shelley, and once went so far as to interpret the last sentence of the *Defence of Poetry* as meaning that Shelley thought that poets were in league with the secret police. An unacknowledged legislator is simply an unacknowledged influence, and since Shelley equates Wordsworth with the *Zeitgeist,* it is hardly an overestimate to say that Wordsworth's influence created a series of laws for a world of feeling and thinking that went beyond the domain of poetry. Very strong poet that he was, Shelley nevertheless had the wisdom and the sadness of knowing overtly what other poets since have evaded knowing, except in the involuntary patterns of their work. Wordsworth will legislate and go on legislating for your poem, no matter how you resist or evade or even unconsciously ignore him.

I do not want to end on such a tone of realistic sorrow and wisdom, even though the superbly intelligent Shelley is not ill-represented by such a tone. He knew that he could not escape the shadow of Wordsworth, and of and in that knowing he made his own poetry. I end by applying to him the last stanza of his own *Hymn of Apollo.* He would not have wanted us to think of him as the speaker of these lines, but he came as close, I think, as any poet since Wordsworth, down to our present day, to justifying our going beyond his intentions, and hearing the poet himself in this great declaration:

I am the eye with which the Universe
    Beholds itself and knows itself divine;
All harmony of instrument or verse,
    All prophecy, all medicine is mine,
All light of art or nature;—to my song
Victory and praise in its own right belong.

# The Art of the Critic

# *Friedrich Hölderlin*

1770–1843

Friedrich Hölderlin was born on March 29, 1770. His father died in 1772 and his step-father died when he was nine years old, early losses that were surely significant in the psychological development of this great poet of absence. Hölderlin's mother was a provincial parson's daughter who exerted considerable influence upon her gifted son, urging him to enter the ministry.

He yielded to her desires, and attended the Lutheran theological seminary at Tübingen from 1788 to 1793. He found contemporary Protestant theology lifeless, but he made the acquaintance of the philosophers Hegel and Schelling—fellow-students with whom Hölderlin formed close intellectual and emotional ties. He also read widely and intensely, particularly in the works of Kant and Rousseau, as well as Leibnitz, Spinoza, and Plato. He often became so absorbed in these books that he feared getting "lost in the realm of abstractions." By the time he passed his final examinations in theology in 1793, Hölderlin was certain that he would not enter the ministry; he had become more interested in the Romantic movement and in the culture of ancient Greece.

For eight years after his graduation Hölderlin devoted his energies to several projects motivated by his fervent love for ancient Greece. He worked strenuously on a translation of Pindar's odes, whose classical meter Hölderlin adapted for his own increasingly powerful lyrics. He also wrote several versions of *Hyperion,* an epistolary novel set in Greece that is now recognized as one of the greatest achievements of German Romanticism. And he began work on *Empedocles,* a Sophoclean verse tragedy. Although Goethe found his verses too "subjective," and "overstrained," Hölderlin was recognized as a poet, philosopher, and gifted classical scholar by most of the major Romantic figures in Germany. Hegel dedicated a long poem entitled *Eleusis* to Hölderlin, and Schiller helped him to find several of the tutorial positions by which he supported himself. In 1799 Hölderlin laid plans for a humanistic journal of poetry and criticism which was to include the work of Goethe, Schelling, Hegel, and Schiller, among others, but the project collapsed.

During this period Hölderlin fell passionately in love with Susette Gontard, the young wife of the wealthy Frankfurt banker whose children Hölderlin had been tutoring. She appears as "Diotima" in many of his poems, for which she became a central and lasting source of inspiration. He carried on a successful affair with her until his fateful trip to France in 1801.

In December of that year Hölderlin set off on foot from his mother's house to take up the post of tutor to a German burgher family living in Bordeaux. Although he left his beloved homeland reluctantly, neither Hegel, nor Fichtean philosophy, nor his radical political ties was to have a greater effect on his life than this trip. On the desolate road through rural France, Hölderlin began to believe that he was experiencing the primordial genius of southern Mediterranean culture firsthand. He felt that his studies of Greek culture were here being borne out, transmuted by some objective force into concrete reality. In a famous letter to his radical friend Casimir Ulrich Gohlendorff he wrote, "The mighty element, the fire of heaven and the silence of the people, their life in nature, their confinedness and contentment, moved me continually, and as one says of heroes, I can well say of myself, that Apollo has struck me." Fire frrom this vision poured into the fragmentary free-verse Hölderlin wrote soon upon his return to Germany, pushing lyric to a vatic intensity beyond anything German poetry had yet achieved.

But Hölderlin paid dearly for his direct encounter with the power or powers that he called variously "fire," the "Other," or "gods." He had always been remarkably intense and somewhat uncanny, often inspiring fear and concern in friends and acquaintances. But when he returned to Germany in June 1802, "pale as a corpse, emaciated, with hollow wild eyes, long hair and beard, and dressed like a beggar," his friends believed he had gone mad. The news that Diotima had died only aggravated his condition, and he spent the fall in the care of a local physician. For the next three years Hölderlin struggled with headaches, severe depression, and disorientation even as he wrote some of his greatest lyrics, including "Patmos," "Nightsongs," and several hymns.

In 1805 Hölderlin was implicated in an assassination plotted by a radical circle with which he had associated, but when the authorities questioned him he responded incoherently in a private language composed of a mixture of Greek, Latin, and German. He was judged mentally incompetent to stand trial, and placed under strict observation in a psychiatric clinic in Tübingen. In 1807 he was released into the care of a local carpenter who admired *Hyperion;* he lived alone in a tower in Tübingen for the next 40 years of his life—meditating, playing the flute, occasionally receiving friends, but writing little poetry. He died on June 7, 1843.

Hölderlin was a poetic genius so pure, so rhapsodic, as to question the limits of coherence. Richard Sieburth suggests that his life and work are best understood in terms of a dialogue with "otherness"—with an absent presence whose dialectical evasions could only be expressed lyrically. A distinguished Freudian critic, Jean La Planche, interprets Hölderlin's poetry more positively in relation to the psychic dilemma of the search for an absent father. According to La Planche, Hölderlin's personal search for figures of intellectual and spiritual authority (e.g., Hegel and Schiller) is echoed in the great religious longing of his poems. The fundamentally ambivalent nature of this search is dramatized by Hölderlin's elusive language, which finds itself only at the point where it slides over into silence, the realm where once again the poet has no authority whatsoever. Both in his central preoccupation with absence, and in his formal and metrical elaborations on the abyss, Hölderlin anticipates many of the major concerns of modern poetry, philosophy, and criticism. Wallace Stevens described modern poetry as "the poem, of the act of the mind / In the act of finding what will suffice," a poetry in which "exceeding music must take the place / Of empty heaven and its hymns." Hölderlin's essay "On the Processes of the Poetic Mind" stands as a singularly profound meditation upon the sufficiency of the poetic act of the mind.

# On the Process Of the Poetic Mind

If the poet has once mastered the mind; if he has felt and assimilated the common soul that is shared by all and is individual to everyone, has held it fast, has assured himself of it; if, further, he is certain of the free movement, of the harmonic interchange and advance in which the mind is inclined to reproduce itself in itself and in others; if he is certain of the fine progress prescribed in the ideal of the mind and of its poetic way of inference; if he has realized that a necessary conflict arises between the most primary demand of the mind, which aims at communality and some simultaneity of all parts, and between the other demand, which commands it to move outside of itself and to render itself in itself and in others in fine progress and interchange, if this conflict always holds him fast and draws him onward along the way towards fulfillment; if, further, he has realized that just that communality and relatedness of all parts, those mental contents, would not be tangible, if they were not different from the sensual contents, according to degree, even discounting the harmonic interchange, even with the similarity of the mental form (of simultaneity and association); further, that that harmonic interchange, that advance would, in turn, not be tangible but an empty, easy shadow play, if the interchanging parts, even with the difference in the sensual contents, do not remain the same in sensual form during the interchange and advance of the mind; if he has realized that that conflict between intellectual content (between the relatedness of all parts) and intellectual form (the interchange of all parts), between the pausing and the advance of the mind is solved by the form of the subject matter in all parts remaining identical in the very advance of the mind, in the interchange of intellectual form, and that it replaces just as much as must be lost of the original relatedness and unity of the parts in the harmonic interchange; that it constitutes objective contents in contrast to intellectual form and gives the latter its full significance; that, on the other hand, the material interchange of the subject matter, which accompanies what is eternal in the intellectual contents, the multiplicity of the same might satisfy the demands of the mind that it makes in its progress and that are retarded through the demands for unity and eternity in every moment; that precisely this material interchange constitutes the objective form, the shape, in contrast to the intellectual contents; if he has realized that, on the other hand, the conflict between the material interchange and the material identity is resolved by the loss of material identity, of passionate progress, wary of interruption, replaced by constantly resounding, all-equalizing intellectual content, and the loss of material multiplicity that comes about due to more rapid advance toward its goal and impression due to this material identity is replaced by constantly interchanging, ideal, intellectual mental form; if he has realized how, inversely, precisely the conflict between intellectual, peaceful content and intellectual interchanging form, as incompatible as they are, so too the conflict between material interchange and material, identical advance towards the principal moment, as incompatible as they are, makes the one as well as the other tangible; if he, finally, has realized that the conflict of the intellectual content and the ideal form, on the one hand, and of the material interchange and the identical advance, on the other hand, unite in the rest points and principal moments and, to the extent that they are not reconcilable in them, just here and just for this reason become tangible and are felt—if he has realized this, then for him everything depends on the receptivity of the subject matter to ideal content and to ideal form. If he is certain of and the master of the one as of the other, of the receptivity of the subject matter as of the mind, there can be no mistake in the principal moment.

And how must the subject matter be constituted that is chiefly receptive to the ideal, to its contents, for metaphor, and to its form, the transition?

The subject matter is either a series of occurrences or views describing or painting realities subjectively or objectively, or it is a series of efforts, ideas, thoughts, or passions denoting necessities subjectively or objectively, or a series of fantasies forming possibilities subjectively or objectively. In all three cases, it must be capable of ideal treatment, namely, if a genuine basis is present for the occurrences, for the views that are to be related, described, or for the fantasies that are to be formed, if the occurrences or views issue from real efforts, the thoughts and passions from a real circumstance, the fantasies from fine sensation. This basis of the poem, its significance, should form the transition between the expression, that which is depicted, the sensual subject matter, that which is actually expressed in the poem, and between the mind, the ideal treatment. The meaning of the poem can be twofold, just as the mind can, the ideal, just as the subject matter, too, the portrayal, can be twofold—namely, to the extent that it is understood as applied or unapplied. Unapplied, these words express nothing but the poetic process, as it is noticeable, genial, and governed by judgment, in every genuinely poetic enterprise; applied, these words indicate the adequacy of the circle of poetic effect in question to that process, the possibility lying in the element to realize that process, so that one can say that in every element in question, both objectively and actually real, something ideal faces that which is ideal, something living that which is living, something individual that which is individual, and the question is only what is to be understood by this circle of effect. It is that in which and on which the poetic enterprise and process in question is realized, the vehicle of the mind through which it reproduces itself in itself and in others. *In* itself the circle of effect is greater than the poetic mind, but not *for* itself. To the extent that it is observed in the context of the world, it is greater; to the extent that it is held fast by the poet and assimilated, it is subordinated. According to its tendency, according to the contents of its aspiration, it is opposed to the poetic enterprise, and the poet is led astray all too easily by his subject matter since, in that if it is taken out of the context of the living world it resists poetic restructuring, in that if it does not choose to serve the mind merely as a vehicle, in that even if it is chosen correctly, its initial and first development in regard to this is antithesis and a spur in regard to poetic fulfillment, so that its second development must be unfulfilled in part and fulfilled in part, as aforesaid.

But it must be shown how, regardless of this conflict, in that the poetic mind remains at its enterprise with the element and circle of effect in question, the latter would nevertheless favor the former; and how that conflict would be dissolved, how a receptivity for poetic enterprise would still inhere in the element that the poet chooses as vehicle; and how he would realize within it all the demands—the entire poetic process, in its metaphorical, its hyperbolic, its character in a mutual effect with the element that, to be sure, resists in its initial tendency and is even opposed, but unites with the former at the middle point.

Between the expression (the depiction) and the free, ideal treatment lies the foundation and the meaning of the poem. This is what gives the poem its seriousness, its stability, its truth; it protects the poem so that the free, ideal treatment will not become empty mannerism and the depiction became vanity. It is the intellectually sensual, the formally materialistic part of the poem; and if the ideal treatment is more unifying in its metaphors, its tradition, its episodes, whereas the expression, the depiction, is more divisive in its characters, its passion, its individualities, then the meaning should stand between the two; it distinguishes itself by being opposed to itself everywhere: instead of the mind comparing everything that is opposite in form, dividing everything united, holding fast everything free, generalizing everything specific, because according to the meaning, what is treated is not merely an individual whole, nor a whole bound together with its harmonic opposite into a whole, but rather a whole in general, and the connection with the harmonic opposite is also possible through an opposite in individual tendency, but not in form; that the meaning unites through opposition, through the contact of extremes, since these are comparable not according to contents but in the direction and the degree of their opposition, so that it also compares what is the most contradictory and is thoroughly hyperbolic, that it does not progress through opposition in form where the first is related to the second according to contents, but rather through opposition in content where the first is equal to the second according to form, so that naive and heroic and ideal tendencies contradict themselves in the object of their tendency but are comparable in the form of the conflict and aspiration and united according to the law of activity, thus united in what is most universal, in life.

So in this way, through this hyperbolic process, according to which the ideal, the harmonically opposed and connected, is considered not only as beautiful life but as life in general, thus also as capable of another condition, and specifically not of another harmonically opposite but one of a directly opposite one, of a most extreme one, so that this new condition is comparable to the previous one only through the idea of life in general—for that very reason, the poet gives the ideal a beginning, a direction, a meaning. The ideal in this shape is the subjective basis of the poem, the basis of departure and return, and since the inner, ideal life can be conceived of in various moods, can be observed as life in general, as something generalizable, as something transposable, as something separable, then there are also various kinds of subjective substantiations; either the ideal mood is conceived of as sensation—then it is the subjective basis of the poem, the principal mood of the poet in the whole enterprise, and precisely because it is grasped as a sensation, it is considered by means of substantiation as something generalizable—or it is grasped as an aspiration, then it becomes the principal mood of the poet in the entire enterprise; and since it is grasped as aspiration, this means that it is considered through substantiation as something fulfillable, or if it is grasped as intellectual contemplation, then this is the principal mood of the entire enterprise, and precisely because it was grasped as such means that it is considered as something realizable. And thus the subjective motivation demands and determines an objective one and prepares it. Thus, in the first case the subject matter is conceived of first as something general, in the second as fulfillable, in the third as what is happening.

If free, ideal, poetic life has been fixed, and if significance has been given to it, according to how it was fixed as something generalizable, as fulfillable, as realizable, if it is connected to its direct opposite, in this way, through the idea of life in general and if taken hyperbolically, then an important point is still lacking in the process of the poetic mind, through which it gives its enterprise not mood, tone, not even meaning and direction, but reality.

Considered as pure, poetic life, according to its contents, of course, this poetic life remains completely united with itself, as if by virtue of the harmonic in general and of temporal deficiency, a thing connected with the harmonic opposite; and only in the interchange of forms is it opposed; only in the manner, not in the base of its advance, is it wielded or aimed or, better, tossed; only coincidentally is it more or less interrupted; considered as life determined and founded through poetic reflection by virtue of the idea of life in general and of the lack of unity, it begins with an idealistically characteristic mood; it is no longer a thing connected with the harmonic opposite at all; it is present as such in a certain form and progresses in the interchange of moods, where each time the succeeding one is determined by the preceeding, and is opposed according to contents, that is, according to the organs by which it is comprehended, and to that extent is more individual, more general, fuller, so that the various moods are connected only where that which is pure finds its opposition, namely, in the manner of its advance, as life in general, so that purely poetic life can no longer be found; for in each of the changing moods, it is connected in a particular form with its direct opposite, thus is no longer pure; on the whole, it is present only as advance and, according to the laws of advance, only as life in general, and there prevails absolutely from this viewpoint a conflict of the individual (the material), the general (the formal), and the pure.

The pure, which is comprehended in every particular mood, conflicts with the organ by which it is comprehended; it conflicts with what is pure in the other organ; it conflicts with the interchange.

As a particular organ (form) has a characteristic mood, that which is general conflicts with the pure, which it comprehends in this mood; as advancement in totality, it conflicts with the pure that is comprehended within it; as characteristic mood, it conflicts with the next adjacent mood.

That which is individual conflicts with the pure that comprehends it, it conflicts with the next adjacent form; as something individual, it conflicts with that which is general in the interchange.

The process of the poetic mind in its enterprise thus cannot possibly end with this. If it is the true process, then something else must be detectable in it, and it must be shown that the manner of the process that gives the poem its meaning is only the transition from that which is pure to this detectable something, just as it is in reverse, from the latter to that which is pure. (Means of connecting mind and signs.)

Now, if that which is directly opposed to the mind, the organ in which it is contained and through which all opposition is possible, could be observed and comprehended not only as that through which the harmonically connected is formally opposed but also through which it is formally connected; if it could be observed and comprehended not only as that through which the various unharmonic moods are materially opposed and formally connected but through which they are also materially connected and formally opposed; if it could be observed and comprehended not only as that which as connective is merely formal life in general and as particular and material is not connective, only opposing and dividing; if it could be observed as something material that connects; if the organ of the mind could be observed as that one which, in order to make the harmonic opposite possible, must be receptive to the one as to the other harmonic opposite, so that to the extent that it is a formal opposition for the purely poetic life, it must also be a formal connection, so that, to the extent that it presents material opposition to certain poetic life and its moods, it must also be materially connecting, so that that which limits and determines is not just negative, that it is also positive, that, while it is considered isolated concerning harmonic connections, it is opposed to the one as well as the other, but both considered together are the union of both, then that act of the mind that in regard to the meaning had only one prevalent conflict as a result will be just as unifying as it was opposing.

But how is it understood in this quality? As possible and as necessary? Not merely through life in general, for it is rightly this to the extent it is considered merely as materially opposing and formally connecting, determining life directly. Also not merely through unity in general, for it is rightly this to the extent it is considered merely as formally opposing, but in the concept of the unity of the united, so that, of the harmonically connected, the *one* as well as the *other* is *present as regards opposition and unification,* and that, *in this regard, the mind in its infinity is tangible,* which appeared as something finite through opposition; that that which is pure, conflicting with the organ in itself, is present to itself in precisely this organ and thus here becomes alive; that, where it is present in different moods, the one following immediately after the basic mood is only the lengthened point, which leads thither, namely, to the middle point, where the harmonically opposed moods meet one another, so that precisely in the strongest contrast, in the contrast of the first ideal mood and the second artificially reflected mood, in the most material opposition (which lies between harmonically connected mind and life, meeting at the middle point, present in the middle point), that exists precisely in this most material opposition, which is opposed to itself (in regard to the point of unification towards which it is striving), in the conflicting, advancing acts of the mind, if they arise only from the reciprocal character of the harmonically opposed moods, that precisely there is the most infinite portrayed most tangibly, most negatively-positively and hyperbolically; that through this contrast in the depiction of that which is infinite in the conflicting advance to the point and its meeting at the point replaces the simultaneous inwardness and the differentiation of the harmonically opposed and living sensations lying at its base and, at the same time, is depicted more clearly by the free consciousness and more cultivated, more universally as a world of its own according to its form, as a world in the world, and thus as the voice of the eternal to the eternal.

Thus, the poetic mind, in the process it observes in its enterprise, cannot be satisfied with a harmonically opposite life, not even by comprehending or grasping it through hyperbolic opposition; if it has gone this far, if the enterprise is lacking neither in harmonic unity nor in meaning and energy, neither in harmonic spirit in general nor in harmonic interchange, then it is necessary, if the one (to the extent that it can be considered by itself) is not either to cancel itself out as something indistinguishable and become empty infinity, or if it is not to lose its identity in an interchange of antitheses, be these ever so harmonic, thus it no longer can by anything whole and unified but, on the contrary, will deteriorate into an infinity of isolated moments (like a series of atoms)—I say: It is necessary that the poetic mind with its unity and harmonic progress give itself also an infinite viewpoint in its enterprise, a unity where in the harmonic progress and interchange everything would go forward and backward and through its prevalent characteristic relationship to this unity gain not just objective context for the observer but also felt and tangible context and identity in the interchange of antitheses, and it is its last task to have a thread, a memory, in the harmonic interchange, so that the mind might never remain present to itself in the individual moment and then again in an individual moment but continue in one moment as in another and in the various moods, just as it is wholly present to itself *in the infinite unity,* which is now the separation point of the unified as unified but is then also the uniting point of the unified as opposites, finally, even both at the same time, so that that which is harmonically opposite in it is neither opposed as something unified nor unified as something opposed but rather as both in *one* is felt inseparably as something unifiedly opposed and indivisible and is discovered as felt. This sense is actually poetic character, neither genius nor art, poetic individuality, and to this alone is granted the identity of enthusiasm, to it the perfection of genius and of art, the realization of the infinite, the divine impetus.

So this is never merely the opposing of that which is unified, also never merely the relationship, unification of the opposing and the changing; what is opposed and unified is inseparable in it. If this is so, then it can be passive in its purity and subjective entirety, as primal sense, to be sure, in the acts of opposing and unifying, with which it is effective in harmonically opposed life, but in its last act, where the harmonically opposed is understood as that which is the opposed harmonic, that which is unified, as mutual effect, as one within it; in this act, it can and may by no means, understood through itself, become itself the object, if instead of an infinitely united and living unity it should be a dead and deadly unity, something that has become infinitely positive; for if unity and opposition are bound inseparably in it and are one, then it can appear to reflection neither as something opposable-unifiable nor as something unifiable-opposed, thus it cannot appear at all, or only in the character of a positive void, of an infinite stagnation; and the hyperbole of all hyperboles is the boldest and last attempt of the poetic mind, if in its process it ever makes the attempt to grasp original poetic individuality, the poetic ego, an attempt through which it might preserve this individuality and its pure object, that which is unified and living, harmonic, reciprocally effective life; yet it must; for since it is supposed to be freely everything that it is in its enterprise and must, by creating a world of its own—and instinct by nature belongs to that world of its own, in which it exists—since it thus should be everything freely, thus it must also assure itself of this, its individuality. But since it cannot perceive it through itself and by itself, an external object is necessary and, indeed, one through which pure individuality should be bound to take some one among various particular ones, neither solely an opposing one nor solely a relating one, but a poetic character that it can assume so that thus in pure individuality as well as in other characters the now chosen individuality and its character, now determined by the subject matter, is perceptible and can freely be held fast.

Within subjective nature, the ego can be perceived only as something opposing or as something relating; within subjective nature it cannot, however, be perceived as the poetic ego in a threefold characterization, for as it does appear within subjective nature and is differentiated from itself and differentiated by and through itself, then that which is perceived, always taken together only with that which perceives and the perception of both, must comprise that threefold nature of the poetic ego and neither grasped as the perceived by the perceiving, nor as the perceiving grasped by the perceiving, nor as the perceived and perceiving grasped by perception, nor as perception grasped by the perceiving; in none of these three abstractly assumed qualities is it conceived of as pure, poetic ego in its threefold nature, as opposing that which is harmonically opposite, as (formally) unifying that which is harmonically opposite, as perceiving as one that which is harmonically opposite, the opposition and the unification; on the contrary, it remains with and for itself in real contradiction. Thus, only to the extent that it is differentiated not from itself and in and through itself when it is made specifically differentiable by a third, and if this third, to the extent that it was freely chosen, to the extent also that it does not cancel pure individuality in its influences and determinants, but can be observed by it, where it then considers itself at the same time as something determined by choice, something empirically individualized and characterized, only then is it possible that the ego should appear in harmonically opposed life as unity, and conversely the harmonic opposite should appear as unity in the ego and become an object in beautiful individuality.

*a*. But how is it possible? Universally?

*b*. If it becomes possible in such a way that the ego may perceive itself and conduct itself in poetic individuality, what result arises from that for poetic portrayal? (It perceives in the threefold subjective and objective attempts the striving towards pure unity.)

*a*. If man, in this isolation, in this life with himself, in this contradictory middle condition between the natural context of a naturally present world and the higher context of a world also naturally present but chosen in advance with free choice in this sphere, known in advance, and in all its influences not determining him without his will—if he has lived in that middle condition between childhood and mature humanity, a beautiful life freely between the mechanically beautiful and the humanly beautiful, and has perceived and experienced this middle condition, how he must simply continue in contradiction with himself, in necessary conflict with (1) the aspiration for pure selfhood and identity, (2) the aspiration for significance and differentiation, (3) the aspiration for harmony; and how in this conflict each one of these aspirations must cancel itself out and show itself to be unrealizable; how he thus must be resigned, relapse into childhood, or exhaust himself in fruitless contradictions with himself; if he persists in this condition, then there is one thing that will draw him out of this sad alternative; and the problem of being free like a youth and of living in the world like a child, of the independence of a cultured man and the accommodation of an ordinary man, is solved by following this rule:

Place yourself by free choice in harmonic opposition to an external sphere, just as you are in harmonic opposition in yourself, by nature, but imperceptibly, as long as you remain within yourself.

For here, in following this rule, is an important difference from the behavior in the previous condition.

In the previous condition, namely, in that of isolation, harmonically opposed nature could not become perceptible unity for the reason that the ego, without canceling itself, could neither posit and perceive itself as an active unity without the reality of differentiation, thus canceling the reality of perception, nor as passive unity, without the reality of unity, its criterion of identity, namely, of canceling activity, and that the ego, by striving to perceive its unity in the harmonic opposite and the harmonic opposite in its unity, must posit itself absolutely and dogmatically as active unity, or as passive unity; it therefore comes into being because, in order to perceive itself through itself, it can replace the natural, intimate connection in which it stands to itself and through which differentiation is made difficult for it only through an unnatural (self-canceling) differentiation, because it is by nature one in its difference with itself, so that the difference necessary for perception, that it gives itself freely, is possible only in the extreme, thus only in striving, in attempts at thought that, realized in this manner, would only cancel themselves, because, in order to perceive its unity in the (subjective) harmonic opposite and the (subjective) harmonic opposite in its unity, it must necessarily abstract from itself to the extent that it is posited in the (subjective) harmonic opposite, and must reflect upon itself to the extent that it is not posited in the (subjective) harmonic opposite, and conversely; but since it cannot make this abstraction from its being in the (subjective) harmonic opposite or make this reflection upon nonbeing in it without canceling itself and the harmonic opposite and the subjective harmonic opposite and unity, then the attempts that it nevertheless makes in this fashion must be attempts such that, if they were realized in this manner, would cancel themselves.

This is thus the difference between the condition of isolation (the intuition of his being) and the new condition, where man places himself in harmonic opposition to the external sphere, through free choice, so that, precisely because he is not so intimately connected to it, he can abstract from it and from himself to the extent that he is posited in it, and can reflect on himself to the extent that he is not posited in it; this is the reason why he goes out from himself; this is the rule for his procedure in the external world. In this way, he reaches his destiny, which is: perception of the harmonic opposite in himself, in his unity and individuality, and again, perception of his identity, his unity and individuality in the harmonic opposite. This is the true freedom of his being, and if he is not too attached to this external, harmonically opposed sphere, does not become identical with it as with himself, so that he can never abstract from it, nor attaches himself too closely to himself, and can abstract too little from himself as an independent, if he neither reflects too much upon himself nor reflects too much on his sphere and his time, then he is on the right path to his destiny. The childhood of ordinary life, where he was identical with the world and could not abstract from it at all, was without freedom, therefore without perception of himself in the harmonic opposite, and of the harmonic opposite in himself, actually without stability, independence, actual identity in pure life; this time will be considered by him as the time of wishes, where man strives to perceive himself in the harmonic opposite and that in himself as unity by giving up entirely to the objective life, but where the impossibility of a perceptible identity in the harmonic opposite shows itself objectively, as it has already been shown subjectively. For, since in this condition he does not know himself at all in his subjective nature but is merely objective life in that which is objective, he can strive to perceive the unity in the harmonic opposite only by proceeding in his sphere, from which he can abstract just as little as the subjective man from his subjective sphere, just as the latter does in his. He is placed within it as within the harmonically opposed. He must strive to perceive himself, attempt to differentiate himself from himself within it, by making himself something opposing, to the extent that it is harmonic, and something unifying, to the extent that it is opposed. But if he strives to perceive himself in this diversity, then he must either deny to himself the reality of this conflict, by finding himself with himself, and consider this conflicting procedure an illusion and caprice, which expresses itself so that he perceives his identity in the harmonic opposite—but then also this, his identity, is, as something perceived, an illusion—or he may consider that distinction real, that, namely, he conduct himself as something unifying and differentiating according to whether he should find present in his objective sphere something to differentiate or to unite, thus posit himself as dependent as something unifying and as something differentiating; and because this is supposed to take place in his objective sphere, from which he, absolutely dependent, cannot abstract without canceling himself, so that he can recognize his act neither as something unifying nor as something opposing himself. In this case, he can again not perceive himself as identical, because the different acts in which he finds himself are not his acts. He cannot perceive himself at all, he is not something distinct; it is his sphere in which he conducts himself thus mechanically. But even if he now wanted to posit himself as identical with it, the conflict of life and personality, which he always strives and must strive to unify and to perceive as one, to dissolve in greatest intimacy, then it avails nothing, to the extent that he conducts himself in his sphere in such a way that he cannot abstract from it, for he can perceive himself precisely for this reason only in the extremes of antitheses of opposition and unification, because he lives too intimately within his sphere.

In a too subjective condition as in a too objective one man seeks in vain to attain his destiny, which consists of perceiving himself as a unity contained in the divine, harmonically opposed, as well as conversely, perceiving the divine, the unified, harmonically opposed contained as a unity within himself. For this is possible only in beautiful, sacred, divine sensation; in sensation that is beautiful because it is neither merely pleasant and happy nor merely noble and strong, nor merely unified and peaceful, but is all that at once and can be alone; in sensation that is sacred because it is neither merely devoted selflessly to its object, nor merely resting selflessly on its inner foundation, nor merely hovering selflessly between its inner foundation and its object, but is all that at once and can be alone; in sensation that is divine because it is neither mere consciousness, mere reflection (subjective or objective) with the loss of inner and outer life, nor mere striving (subjectively or objectively determined) with the loss of inner and outer harmony, nor mere harmony, like intellectual contemplation and its mythic, metaphorical subject, object, with the loss of consciousness and unity, but because it is all this at once and can be alone; in sensation that is therefore transcendental and can be this alone, because in the unification and mutual effect of the above-named characteristics it is neither too pleasant and sensual, nor too energetic and wild, not too intimate and enthusiastic, neither too selfless—that is, devoted too unselfishly to its object, nor too selfless—that is, too arbitrarily resting on its inner foundation, nor too selfish, that is, too undecided and empty and hovering uncertainly between its inner foundation and its object, neither too reflected, too conscious of it, too sharp and for this reason unconscious of its inner and outer foundation, nor too agitated, too contained within its inner and outer foundation, for this reason unconscious of its inner and outer harmony, nor too harmonic, for this reason too little conscious of its self and its inner and outer foundation, for this reason too undetermined, and less receptive of the real infinite, which is determined through it as a certain, real infinity, as lying external to it, and capable of less duration. In short, because it is present in its threefold characteristic and can be this alone, it is less exposed to partiality in any one of the three characteristics. On the contrary, all the forces originally grow out of it, which those characteristics possess certainly more determinedly and more perceptibly, but also more isolatedly, just as those forces and their characteristics and expressions concentrate within it again and through mutual context and living determination, enduring for itself, as organs of it, and gain freedom, as belonging to it and not limited to themselves in its limitation, and completeness, as comprised in its totality—those three characteristics may express themselves as efforts to perceive the harmonic opposite in the living unity, or the latter in the former, in the more subjective or more objective condition. For precisely these different conditions emanate from it as the unification of the same.

## *Suggestion for Representation and Language*

Is not language like perception, of which we were speaking and of which it was said that in it the unified was contained as unity and vice versa, and that it was of a threefold variety (see above)?

And must not the most beautiful moment for the one as for the other come where the actual expression, the most intellectual language, the most vital consciousness, where the transition from a specific infinity to a more general one is found?

Does not the strong point lie right here, through which the character and the degree of the sequence of sketches, their manner of relating, and the local color as well as its illumination are determined?

Will not all judgment of language be reduced to examining it for *the most certain and feasibly least treacherous criterion* of whether language is a genuine, beautifully described sensation?

Just as perception intuits language, thus does language remember perception.

Perception intuits language after (1) it was still unreflected, pure sensation of life, of the specific infinity in which it is contained, (2) after it had repeated itself in the dissonances of inward reflection and aspiration and composing of poetry, and now, after these vain attempts to find and to reproduce itself inwardly again, after these tacit intuitions, which must also have their time, goes out beyond itself and finds itself again in total infinity, that is, through insubstantial, pure mood, as if through the echo of the original, living sensation, which it gained and was able to gain through the total effect of all inner attempts, becomes master and possessor of its entire inner and outer life through this higher, divine receptivity. In precisely this instant, where the original, living sensation, now refined into the pure mood receptive of an infinity, finds itself as the intellectual whole in the living whole, in this instant one can say that language is intuited; and if now a reflection results, as in the original sensation, then it is no longer dissolving and generalizing, distributing and cultivating, even to pure mood, it returns to the heart everything that it took from it; it is invigorating art, just as previously it was intellectualizing art, and with one wave of the magic wand after another, it calls forth our lost life more beautifully, until it feels to be wholly itself, as it originally felt. And if it is the course and the destiny of life itself to develop to the highest form from original simplicity, where eternal life is present for man for just this reason, and where he takes in everything all the more intimately as something most abstract, then from this highest opposition and unification of what is living and intellectual, of the formal and material subject-object, to restore life to the intellectual, form to the living, love and heart to man, and gratitude to the world, and finally, after fulfilled intuition and hope, whenever, namely, in the expression of that highest point of cultivation the highest form was present in the highest life and not merely in itself, as at the beginning of the actual expression, nor in striving as in the continuation of the same; where expression evokes life from the mind and the mind from life, but rather where it has found original life in the highest form; where mind and life are equal on both sides and perceive their finding, the infinite in the infinite, after this third and last perfection of the heart and life, not simply original simplicity; where man feels uninhibited as in a limited infinity, also not merely achieved simplicity of the mind; where precisely that sensation, purified to a pure, formal mood, takes on the entire infinity of life (and is the ideal), but rather the mind, revived from infinite life, is not happiness, not the ideal but a successful work of a creation and can be found only in the expression and outside of the expression can only be hoped for in the ideal issuing from its specific, original sensation; how, finally, after his third perfection, where the specific infinity has been called so far into life, the infinite infinity has been so far intellectualized that one is equal to the other in mind and life, how after this third perfection the specific becomes more and more vital, the infinite becomes more and more intellectualized, until the original sensation ends up as life, just as it began in the expression as mind, and the higher infinity, from which it took its life, likewise is intellectualized, just as it was present in the expression as something alive—thus, if this seems to be the course and the destiny of man in general, then it is also the course and the destiny of all and any poetry, and as on that level of cultivation where man has issued forth from his original childhood and in opposed attempts struggled up to highest form, to pure echo of that first life and thus feels himself to be infinite mind within infinite life, as man on this level of cultivation really just begins to enter life and intuits his effect and his destiny, so the poet at that level has also struggled up from an original sensation through opposed attempts to the tone, to the highest, pure form of the same sensation and sees himself comprehended entirely in his entire inner and outer life by that tone, at that level he intuits his language, and with it actual perfection for existing and at the same time for all poetry.

It has already been said that a new reflection enters at that level, which restores to the heart everything that it has taken from it, which is invigorating art for the mind of the poet and the spirit of his future poetry, as it was intellectualizing art for the original sensation of the poet and his poem. The product of this creative reflection is language. While the poet, namely, feels himself comprehended by the pure tone of his original sensation in his entire inner and outer life and looks around in his world, it is for him just as new and unknown—the sum of all his experiences, of his knowledge, of his contemplation, of his thought, art, and nature as it is portrayed within him and outside of him; everything is as if for the first time, just for that reason uncomprehended, undetermined, dissolved into pure subject matter and life, present for him, and it is preeminently important that in this instant he assumes nothing as given, proceeds from nothing positive, that nature and art, as he has become acquainted with them and sees them, do not speak until a language is there for him, that is, until that which is now unknown and unnamed becomes known and named for him in his world in such a way that it has been compared and found in agreement with his mood; for if a specifically structured language of nature and art were there for him before reflection on the infinite subject matter and the infinite form, then he would not be within his circle of effect to that extent; and the language of nature or art, that *modus experimendi* of the one or of the other, would be, first, to the extent that it is not his language, not a product issuing from his mind and his life but the language of art, as soon as it is present to me in a specific form, already in advance a determining act of the creative reflection of the artist, which consisted in his taking from his world, from the sum of his outer and inner life that is more or less my own too, that he took the subject matter from this world to designate the tones of his mind, to call forth from his mood the life underlying it through this related sign; that he thus, to the extent that he names this sign to me, borrows the subject matter from my world, causes me to transpose this subject matter into the sign, where then the important difference is between me as something determined and him as something determining; that he, by making himself understandable and intelligible, progresses from lifeless, immaterial mood that for this reason is less opposable and more unconscious simply by explaining it (1) in its infinity of agreement a comparative totality of related subject matter, according to form as well as to substance, and through ideally interchanging world, (2) in its determination and actual finiteness through the depiction and enumeration of its own subject matter, (3) in its tendency, it generality in the particular, through the antithesis of its own subject matter to the infinite subject matter, (4) in its proportion, in the beautiful determination and unity and stability of its infinite agreement, in its infinite identity and individuality and bearing, in its poetic prose of an all-containing moment, in which and towards which all named pieces relate and are united negatively and for that reason expressly and sensually, namely, the infinite form with the infinite subject matter, so that through the moment the infinite form assumes a configuration, the interchange of the weaker and the stronger, the infinite subject matter assumes a resonance, an interchange of the shriller and the softer, and both finally unite negatively in the slowness and swiftness, in a standstill of motion, always through it and the activity underlying it, the infinite, beautiful reflection, which is universal limitation, is universally relating and unifying at the same time.

# *Heinrich von Kleist*

1777–1811

"With the best will in the world towards the poet, I have always been moved to horror and disgust by something in his works, as though here were a body well-planned by nature, tainted with an incurable disease." With these words Goethe described his reaction to the art of the younger poet, dramatist, and short story writer Heinrich von Kleist. In a certain sense Goethe's subjective reaction corresponds to a quality in Kleist's work and life that is nothing less than objective fact. Goethe, serene Olympian of German letters, perfecting the classical style in his country's literature after overcoming the artistic and personal struggle denoted by the words *Sturm und Drang,* saw in Kleist the horrible, demonic, and even titanic forces he himself had quelled and shaped into art.

Kleist's life may well be described as one long disease, a sickness unto death. In many respects his torturous existence resembles that of Kafka, who found in Kleist a kindred spirit and (to some extent) a literary model. Born into an old Prussian Junker family in Frankfurt on Oder in 1777, Kleist spent the early part of his life in military service. He later remarked that he regretted every moment he spent in the field and in the barracks. He became disillusioned with his subsequent university education in philosophy upon reading Kant, an encounter that left him feeling that the quest for knowledge and enlightenment was ultimately useless. He started to wander around Europe in 1801, and did not settle down until 1804, when he took a position as a Royal Clerk in Berlin.

In these tumultuous years he first met Goethe, with whom he suffered a relationship characterized by intense envy and barely-suppressed rage. Goethe misunderstood and mistreated this young and impetuous pretender to his literary throne; Kleist, in his turn, fit himself into a kind of masochistic relationship with the elder poet. He detested Goethe even as he absurdly claimed to be his only rival. Thomas Mann saw in this tortured relation some hidden equality between the two men, claiming for Kleist what Kleist never seriously believed about himself—the ability to outdo Goethe. "There is nothing in our literature as loftily beautiful as Goethe's *Iphigenia,*" wrote Mann. "Nevertheless, it is Kleist's plays alone, lacking as they are in harmonious proportion and decorum, that give us the archaic shudder of myth the way Sophocles and Aeschylus do."

Kleist, like Kafka, was a master of the short story. The remainder of his brief and tormented life was spent writing some of the most imaginative fiction in German literature. Stories like "Michael Kolhaas" and "The Foundling" are unmatched for their violence, dark vision, and expressive power. But Kleist's life ended as violently as any of his tales. Henriette von Vogel, a musician dying from an incurable disease, asked that Kleist put an end to her life. After shooting her he did away with himself on the shore of the Wannsee near Potsdam, on December 21, 1811.

In this essay "On the Marionette Theatre," a characteristically strange and whimsical fable, Kleist explores the dichotomy between innocence and experience, the state of grace and the state of sin. He draws an analogy between these conflicting states of the soul and the different levels of beauty in art. And he suggests a surprising means for their re-integration.

# On the Marionette Theater

One evening in M., where I was spending the winter of 1801, I met Mr. C. in a public park. He had recently been hired as the principal dancer at the opera and was enjoying immense popularity with the audiences.

I told him that I had been surprised to see him several times in a marionette theater that had been erected in the marketplace to entertain the populace with short dramatic burlesques interspersed with songs and dance.

He assured me that the pantomime of the puppets brought him much satisfaction and let it be known quite clearly that a dancer who wanted to perfect his art could learn a thing or two from them.

From the way in which he expressed himself, I could tell that it wasn't something he had just now thought up, so I sat down next to him to find out the reasons for such a remarkable claim.

He asked me if I hadn't, in fact, found some of the dance movements of the puppets, particularly of the smaller ones, very graceful.

I could not deny this. A group of four peasants dancing the rondo to a quick beat could not have been painted more delicately by Teniers.

I inquired about the mechanism of these figures. How was it possible to manipulate the individual limbs and extremities in the rhythm of movement or dance without having a myriad of strings on one's fingers?

He answered that I shouldn't imagine each limb as individually positioned and moved by the operator during various moments of the dance.

Each movement, he said, had its center of gravity: it would suffice to control this within the puppet; the limbs, which are only pendulums, follow mechanically of their own accord—without further help.

He added that this movement is very easy; whenever the center of gravity is moved in a *straight line,* the limbs describe *curves*. Often, when shaken in a rather haphazard manner, the entire puppet moves with a kind of rhythm which resembles dance.

This observation seemed to me to shed some light on the enjoyment he claimed to get from the marionette theater. But I was far from guessing the inferences which he would later draw from it.

I asked him if he thought that the operator who controlled these puppets would himself have to be a dancer or at least have some idea of the beauty in the dance.

He replied that if a job is mechanically simple, it doesn't follow that it can be done entirely without sensitivity.

The line which the center of gravity has to follow is indeed quite simple and in most cases, he believed, straight. In the cases in which it is curved, the law of its curvature seems to be at least of the first or at most of the second order; even in the latter case the line is only elliptical, a form of movement of the body's extremities (because of the joints) which is most natural, so this hardly demands great talent on the part of the operator.

But, seen from another point of view, this line could be something very mysterious, for it is nothing other than the *path taken by the dancer's soul;* and he doubted if this could be achieved unless the operator transposed himself into the marionette's center of gravity; that is to say, the operator *dances*.

I replied that the job of the operator had been presented to me as something done without sensitivity, somewhat like turning the handle of a barrel organ.

"Not at all," he answered. "In fact, there is a rather ingenious relationship between the movement of his fingers and the movements of the attached puppets, somewhat like that of numbers to their logarithms or the asymptotes to the hyperbola."

And yet he believed that even the last trace of human volition to which he had referred could be removed from the marionettes, that their dance could be transferred completely to the realm of mechanical forces and that it could be produced, as I had thought, by turning a handle.

I expressed my astonishment at the attention he was paying this species of an art form intended for the masses. It wasn't only that he thought a greater development possible; he himself seemed to be occupying his time with it.

He smiled and said he was confident that if a craftsman were to make a marionette according to his specifications, that he could perform a dance with it which neither he nor any other skilled dancer of his time, not even Vestris herself, could equal.

I said nothing and looked down at the ground. Then he said, "Have you ever heard of those artificial legs made by English craftsmen for those unfortunate individuals who have lost their limbs?"

I said that I hadn't seen anything of this kind.

"That's too bad," he replied, "because if I tell you that these unfortunate people can dance with them, I fear you won't believe me. What am I saying—dance? The range of their movements is rather limited, but those they can perform are executed with a calmness, ease, and grace which amazes any thinking observer."

I said, somewhat lightly, that he had, of course, found his man. A craftsman who could make such a remarkable limb could surely construct an entire marionette according to his specifications.

As he lowered his eyes, somewhat perplexed, I asked, "What are the specifications you are thinking of presenting to his artistic skill?"

"Nothing," he answered, "that isn't to be found here as well: symmetry, flexibility, lightness—but of a higher degree; and particularly a natural arrangement of the centers of gravity."

"And what advantage would this puppet have over living dancers?"

"Advantage? First of all a negative one, my dear friend; and that is that it would never behave *affectedly*. For affectation appears, as you know, when the soul (*vis motrix*) can be found at some point other than the center of gravity of movement. Because the operator controls only this point with the wire or thread, all the other limbs are what they should be: dead, mere pendulums, governed only by the law of gravity—an excellent quality hard to find in most of our dancers.

"Take, for example, P., the one who dances Daphne," he continued. "Pursued by Apollo, she turns to look at him. Her soul seems to be in the small of her back; she bends as if she's going to break, like a naiad after the school of Bernini. Or look at young F., who dances Paris. When he stands among the three goddesses and offers the apple to Venus, his soul is located (and it is a fright to perceive) in his elbow.

"Such mistakes are unavoidable," he said, "now that we have eaten from the Tree of Knowledge. But Paradise is locked and the cherubim behind us; we have to travel around the world to see if it is perhaps open again somewhere at the back."

I laughed. Certainly, I thought, the human spirit can't be in error when it doesn't exist. But I could see that he had more to tell me and asked him to continue.

"In addition," he said, "these puppets have the advantage of being practically weightless. The inertia of matter, that property most resistance to the dance, does not affect them, for the force which raises them into the air is greater than the one which draws them to the ground. What would our dear G. give to be sixty pounds lighter, or if a weight of this size came to her aid while she performed her entrechats and pirouettes? Puppets, like elves, need the ground only so that they can touch it lightly and renew the momentum of their limbs through this momentary delay. We need it to rest on, to recover from the exertions of the dance, a moment which is clearly not part of the dance. We can only do our best to make it as inconspicuous as possible."

I said that, regardless of how cleverly he might present his paradoxes, he would never make me believe that a mechanical puppet could be more graceful than the human body.

He said that it would be impossible for man to come anywhere near the puppet. Only a god could equal inanimate matter in this respect; and here is the point where the two ends of the circular world meet.

My wonderment increased, and I didn't know what to say to such extraordinary claims.

It seemed, he said as he took a pinch of snuff, that I had not read the third chapter of the Book of Genesis carefully enough; if a man wasn't familiar with that first period of all human development, it would be difficult to discuss the later ones, not to mention the final one.

I told him I was well aware of how consciousness could disturb the natural grace of man. Before my very eyes, one of my young acquaintances had lost his innocence, all because of a chance remark, and had never again, in spite of all conceivable efforts, been able to find his way back to its paradise. But what conclusions, I added, can you draw from that?

He asked me to which incident I was referring.

About three years ago, I related, I was at the baths with a young man who at the time was remarkably graceful in all respects of his education. He was about fifteen years old, and only faintly could one see in him the first traces of vanity—as a result of the favor shown him by women. It just so happened that in Paris we had seen a statue of a young boy pulling a thorn from his foot; the cast of the statue is well known and can be found in most German collections. Now, just as my young friend was lifting his foot on to a stool to dry it, he was reminded of the statue while he looked into a tall mirror; he smiled and told me what he had discovered. I had, in fact, noticed the same thing at the same moment. But—I don't know if it was to test the security of his grace or to provide a salutary counter to his vanity—I laughed and said that he must be seeing things! He blushed and raised his foot a second time in order to show me, but the attempt failed as anyone might have suspected it would. Somewhat confused, he raised his foot a third time and then a fourth; he raised it probably ten times: in vain! He was unable to reproduce the movement—what am I saying? The movements he made were of such a comical nature that I could barely contain my laughter.

From that day, beginning at that very moment, an inconceivable change came over the young man. He stood in front of the mirror for days. One attraction after the other left him. Like an iron net, an invisible and incomprehensible power enveloped the free play of his gestures. After a year had passed, nothing remained of the grace which has previously given pleasure to those who saw him. There's a man still alive who was a witness to that strange and unfortunate event. He can confirm it, just as I have described it, word for word.

"At this juncture," said Mr. C. amiably, "I have to tell you another story, and you'll easily see how it fits in here.

"While on my way to Russia, I spent some time on the estate of a Livonian nobleman, Mr. von G., whose sons were just then passionately interested in fencing. The elder in particular, who had just come back from the university, was somewhat of a virtuoso. One morning when I was in his room, he offered me a rapier. We parried, but it just so happened that I was better than he. His passion caused him to be confused. Almost every thrust I made found its mark, and finally his rapier flew into the corner of the room. As he picked it up, he half-jokingly, half-irritatedly, said that he had met his master. But then he added that there was a master for everyone and everything and that now he intended to lead me to mine. His brother laughed loudly and called out, 'Go ahead, go down to the stall!' Together they took me by the hand and led me out to a bear that their father, Mr. von G., was raising on the farm.

"Somewhat astounded, I walked up to the bear. He was standing on his hind legs, his back against the post to which he was chained, his right paw raised ready for a battle. He looked me straight in the eye. That was his fighting posture. I wasn't sure if I was dreaming, since I was standing face to face with such an opponent. 'Go ahead, attack,' said Mr. von G. 'See if you can hit him!' When I had recovered somewhat from my surprise, I lunged at him with my rapier. The bear moved slightly and warded off my thrust. I tried to mislead him by feinting thrusts, but the bear did not move. I attacked him again with all the skill at my command. I most certainly would have left my mark on a human breast, but the bear moved only slightly and warded off my thrust. I now felt the same as had the young Mr. von G. The bear's seriousness robbed me of my composure. I alternately thrust and feinted; sweat poured off me: all in vain! He not only averted my thrusts like the finest fencer in the world, but made no move when I feinted to deceive him. This was something that no fencer in the world could equal. He stood, his paw still raised for battle, his eye fixed on mine as if he could read my soul in it, and when my thrusts were not meant seriously, he didn't move.

"Do you believe this story?"

"Of course," I said, applauding joyfully. "I'd believe it from any stranger, it's so probable! And all the more so from you!"

"Now, my dear friend," said Mr. C., "you have everything you need to understand my argument. We see that in the organic world, as reflection grows darker and weaker, grace emerges more brilliantly and commandingly. But just as the section drawn through two lines suddenly appears on the other side of a point after passing through infinity, or just as the image of a concave mirror turns up before us again after having moved off into the endless distance, so too grace itself returns when knowledge has gone through an infinity. Grace appears purest in that human form which has either no consciousness or an infinite one, that is, in a puppet or in a god."

"Therefore," I said, somewhat bewildered, "we would have to eat again from the Tree of Knowledge in order to return to the state of innocence?"

"Quite right," he answered. "And that's the last chapter in the history of the world."

# *Stendhal*

1783–1842

Henri Beyle, later known as Stendhal, was born into a bourgeois family in Grenoble. As a child he experienced the effects of the French Revolution firsthand, and thus developed an acute political consciousness at a young age. He disdained the bourgeois atmosphere of his native town (he called it a "mudhole"), and sided with the common people. But he never forgot his aristocratic upbringing. As a result of his family's monarchist sympathies he "became a fanatical republican on the spot," but he also said that he "would do anything in his power to ensure the happiness of the common people, as long as [he didn't] have to live with them." Paradox occupied a central position in Stendhal's life and work.

At the age of fourteen Stendhal's mathematical talents won him the honor of admission to the famous École-Polytechnique. He chose instead to enroll at the École des Beaux-Arts. He soon became ill, however, and sought refuge with the Daru family, influential cousins who nursed him back to health and won him a post in Napoleon's Ministry of War. Stendhal thus became a civil servant enmeshed in the web of Napoleonic bureaucracy then being established in northern Italy. For the ambitious and brilliant young dandy, Italy came as a revelation to the senses and quickly became the stage of several amorous encounters. Women and the psychology of love became Stendhal's primary objects of study, but he did not neglect his growing interest in music, archeology, and painting. At the end of 1801 he obtained leave and travelled to Marseilles, where he read widely and began to write his journal.

In 1806 Stendhal moved to Paris. He boasted of his intention of becoming the new Molière, but spent most of that decade traveling, working in various capacities for Napoleon. Not until 1814 did he publish his first writing—biographies of Haydn, Mozart, and Metastasio. He then returned to Italy, where for the next seven years he embroiled himself in Milanese society and liberal politics—a Romantic milieu where Monti, Pellico, Rossini, and Lord Byron mingled and vied for the attention of society. It was during this time that Stendhal discovered his "great musical theme"—his painful love for Mathilde Voscontini Dombowsky, whom he called Methilde. He began to write a book about the feelings he was experiencing at the hands of Methilde; this became *De L' Amour*, one of his masterpieces. But before he could finish his book—or win the love of the increasingly cool Methilde—political pressure forced him to leave Milan.

In 1820 Stendhal returned once more to Paris. For the next ten years he frequented literary circles and wrote prolifically—publishing *De L' Amour* in 1822, *Vie de Rossini* and *Racine et Shakespeare* in 1823, *Racine et Shakespeare II* in 1825, *Armance* in 1827, and finally, in 1830, his great novel *Le Rouge et le noir*. This novel represented a new age for French fiction. In a plain, objective, colloquial style that anticipated the realism of Flaubert or Zola, Stendhal told the story of a "superior" individual at odds with the petty confinements of polite bourgeois society. Its theme and depth of insight placed Stendhal in the company of the great psychologists of the later nineteenth century—Dostoevsky and Nietzsche.

After the revolution of July 1830, which overthrew Charles X and established the citizen king Louis-Philippe and the Charter in France, Stendhal's liberalism and freethinking worked to his advantage; he obtained a position as French Consul at Civitàvecchia, the port city near Rome. He spent the rest of his life in his beloved Italy, though he often took prolonged leave in Paris. He published mostly autobiographical works in these years, including *Memoirs of an Egotist* and *La Vie de Henri Brulard*. In 1838 he wrote his third masterpiece, *La Chartreuse de Parma,* in fifty-two days. He died of a stroke on March 23, 1842.

In his critical writing no less than in his fiction, Stendhal is characterized above all by psychological acumen. He uses a witty, epigrammatic style to give voice to what is essentially an Epicurean synthesis. Politics, literature, and love are all analyzed as part of the quest for pleasure. This at once skeptical and optimistic outlook allows Stendhal both to stress the importance of pleasing the audience and to inveigh against the tyranny of fashion. Art, he argues, is never purely mimetic; it is a "charming lie" whose conventions are socially determined. He criticizes the rigidity of French classicism in favor of Romanticism, not because he thinks Shakespeare more "natural" than Racine, but rather because Romanticism occasionally allows the audience the irreplaceable pleasure of "complete illusion." In a similarly skeptical essay *On Laughter* he allows Hobbes his pessimistic theory of laughter as the result of a surprising perception of our superiority over others. But, typically, he embraces this dark pleasure and includes himself in "the spectacle of doting persons deceiving themselves, in a humorous way, on the path that leads to happiness."

FROM

# Racine and Shakespeare

## *Chapter I*

### *In Order to Write Tragedies Which Will Interest the Public of 1823, Should One Follow the Procedures of Racine or Those of Shakespeare?*

This question seems to have worn itself out in France; and yet we have heard the arguments of one side only. The newspapers that are the most opposed in their political opinions, both the *Quotidienne* and the *Constitutionnel*, agree on only one thing: they proclaim that French drama is not only the best drama in the world, but the only rational drama. If that poor thing, Romanticism, had a claim it wanted to publicize, all newspapers of all shades of opinion would be equally closed to it.

But this apparent disfavor in no way frightens us, because it is a matter of partisanship. We reply to this with a single fact.

What literary work has enjoyed the greatest success in France in the last ten years?

The novels of Sir Walter Scott.

What are the novels of Sir Walter Scott?

Romantic tragedy, intertwined with long descriptions.

By way of objection, our opponents will cite the success of *Les Vêpres siciliennes, Le Paria, Les Machabées,* and *Régulus*.

These plays provide a good deal of pleasure; but they do not provide a *dramatic pleasure*. The public—which, incidentally, does not enjoy any extreme freedom—likes to hear generous sentiments expressed in beautiful lines of poetry.

But this pleasure is of an *epic* nature, not a dramatic one. There is never that degree of illusion necessary for a profound emotion. It is for this reason—one of which the young public itself is unaware (because at the age of twenty, whatever is said to the contrary, one wants to enjoy things, not reason about them; and this is quite right)—it is for this secret reason that the young public of the second French theatre[1] puts so few demands upon the plot element in the plays that it applauds with the greatest transports. What, for example, is more ridiculous than the plot of *Le Paria*? It does not stand up to the least bit of analysis. Everybody has made this criticism; and yet this criticism has not had any effect. Why? Because the public wants only beautiful poetry. The public goes to the contemporary French theatre expecting to hear a series of very pompous odes which, incidentally, express forcefully some generous sentiments. If they are introduced by a few transitional lines of poetry, that suffices. It is like the ballets of the Rue Pelletier: the action must be gone through for the sole purpose of introducing some beautiful steps and in order to justify, after a fashion, some pleasant dances.

I address myself fearlessly to those misguided young people who believed they were being patriotic and defending the national honor when they hissed Shakespeare because he was English. Since I am full of esteem for hard-working young people, the hope of France, I shall talk to them in the severe language of truth.

The entire dispute between Racine and Shakespeare comes down to whether, while observing the two unities of *time* and *place*, one can write plays that vitally interest nineteenth-century audiences—plays that make them weep and shudder or, in other words, that give them *dramatic* pleasures rather than the *epic* pleasures that make us rush to the fiftieth performance of *Le Paria* or *Régulus*.

I maintain that adherence to the two unities of *time* and *place* is a French habit; a habit with very deep roots; a habit from which we shall free ourselves only with difficulty, because Paris is the salon of Europe and sets the fashion for Europe. But I also maintain that these unities are by no means necessary for producing profound emotion and the genuine dramatic effect.

Why, I will ask the partisans of *Classicism,* do you demand that the action depicted in a tragedy cover not more than twenty-four or thirty-six hours? And that the setting represented on the stage not change—or at any rate, as Voltaire says, that the changes of setting not extend beyond the different rooms of a palace?

THE ACADEMICIAN: Because it is not credible that an action represented in two hours should encompass a week or a month; or that in a few moments the actors should go from Venice to Cyprus, as in Shakespeare's *Othello,* or from Scotland to the English court, as in *Macbeth.*

THE ROMANTIC: Not only is that incredible and impossible; but it is likewise impossible that the action encompass twenty-four or thirty-six hours.[2]

THE ACADEMICIAN: Heaven forbid that we should be so absurd as to claim that the fictitious duration of the action should correspond exactly to the *material* time consumed by the performance. If this were the case, the rules would be actual fetters on genius. In the imitative arts, one must be strict but not rigorous. The spectator can easily imagine that several hours have passed during the interval of the intermissions—all the more so because he is diverted by the symphonies played by the orchestra.

THE ROMANTIC: Be careful of what you say, Monsieur. You are giving me a great advantage. You agree, then, that the spectator can *imagine* that more time is passing than that during which he is seated in the theatre. But tell me: Can he imagine a time passing that is double the real time, triple, quadruple, or a hundred times greater? Where shall we stop?

THE ACADEMICIAN: You are odd, you modern philosophers. You blame poetics because, so you say, it fetters genius. And now you want us to apply the rule of the *unity of time* with all the rigor and exactitude of mathematics, in order for it to be plausible. Is it not enough for you that it obviously contravenes all credibility for the spectator to imagine that a year, a month, or even a week has passed since he got his ticket and entered the theatre?

THE ROMANTIC: And who told you that the spectator cannot imagine that?

THE ACADEMICIAN: It is reason that tells me.

THE ROMANTIC: I beg your pardon. Reason cannot possibly teach you this. How could you know that the spectator can imagine that twenty-four hours have passed, whereas actually he has only been sitting in his box for two hours, unless experience had taught you this? How could you know that those hours that seem so long to a man who is bored, seem to fly when a person is being amused, unless experience had told you. In a word, it is *experience* alone that must settle the issue between you and me.

THE ACADEMICIAN: Yes, no doubt it is experience.

THE ROMANTIC: Well, experience has already spoken against you. In England, for two centuries now, and in Germany, during the past fifty years, they have been performing tragedies whose action covers entire months; and the spectators' imagination accomodates itself perfectly to this.

THE ACADEMICIAN: But now you are giving me the example of foreigners—and Germans at that!

THE ROMANTIC: Some other time we shall discuss this unquestionable superiority of the Frenchman in general, and the inhabitant of Paris in particular, over all the other peoples of the world. I shall be fair: this superiority is a *matter of feeling* with you. You are despots spoiled by two centuries of flattery. Fate willed that you Parisians should become responsible for making literary reputations in Europe. A woman of wit, known for her *enthusiasm* for the beauties of nature, once exclaimed, in order to please the Parisians: "The most beautiful stream in the world is the stream of the Rue du Bac!" All the genteel writers—not only in France but throughout Europe—have flattered you in order to obtain a bit of literary fame in return. And what you call *inner feeling* and *moral evidence* is nothing more than the moral evidence of a spoiled child; in other words, the habit of being flattered.

But let us get back to the point. Can you deny that the inhabitant of London or Edinburgh, the compatriots of Fox and Sheridan, who are perhaps not utter fools, see performances of tragedies like *Macbeth,* for example, without being shocked in the slightest? Now this play, which every year is applauded an infinite number of times in England and America, begins with the assassination of the king and the flight of his sons. And it ends with the return of these same princes at the head of an army that they have assembled in England in order to dethrone the bloody Macbeth. This series of actions necessarily requires several months.

THE ACADEMICIAN: Ah! You will never persuade me that the English and the Germans, even if they are foreigners, really imagine that entire months pass while they are at the theatre.

THE ROMANTIC: Just as you will never persuade me that the French spectators believe that twenty-four hours pass while they are watching a performance of *Iphigénie en Aulide*.

THE ACADEMICIAN (*impatient*): What a difference!

THE ROMANTIC: Let us not become incensed. And please observe carefully what is going on in your head. Try to draw aside for a moment the veil that habit has thrown over acts which take place so rapidly that you have lost the ability to follow them with your eye and see them *occur*. Let us come to an agreement on the word *illusion*. When one says that the spectator imagines that the time necessary for the events represented on the stage has passed, one does not mean that the spectator's illusion extends to the point of believing that all this time has really elapsed. The fact is that the spectator, caught up and carried along by the story, is not shocked by anything. He gives no thought whatsoever to the time that has passed. Your Parisian spectator sees Agamemnon awaken Arcas at exactly seven o'clock. He witnesses the arrival of Iphigenia; and he sees her led to the altar where the Jesuitic Calchas is waiting for her. If anyone asked him, he would of course reply that these events required several hours. And yet, if during the quarrel between Achilles and Agamemnon he were to take out his watch, it would show the hour of 8:15. What spectator would be surprised by this? Nonetheless, the play that he is applauding has already lasted for several hours.

The truth of the matter is that even your Parisian spectator is accustomed to seeing time move at different rates on the stage and in the other part of the theatre. This is a fact that you cannot deny. It is clear that even in Paris, even at the Théâtre-Français in the Rue de Richelieu, the spectator's imagination lends itself easily to the poet's suppositions. The spectator, quite naturally, pays no attention to the intervals of time required by the poet; just as in sculpture he does not take it into his head to reproach Dupaty or Bosio for the fact that their figures lack movement. This is one of the infirmities of art. The spectator, when he is not a pedant, is concerned only with the acts and developments of passions that are presented to his view. Precisely the same thing happens in the head of the Parisian who applauds *Iphigénie en Aulide* and in that of the Scotsman who admires the story of his former kings, Macbeth and Duncan. The only difference is that the Parisian, being a child of good family, has acquired the habit of mocking others.

THE ACADEMICIAN: In other words, according to you the theatrical illusion is the same for both?

THE ROMANTIC: To have illusions, to be in a state of *illusion*, means to deceive oneself, according to the *Dictionary* of the Academy. An *illusion*, M. Guizot says, is the effect of a thing or an idea that deceives us by its misleading appearance. Illusion therefore means the act of a man who believes a thing that does not exist—as in dreams, for example. Theatrical illusion would be the act of a man who believes that the things that take place on the stage really exist.

Last year (August 1822) a soldier who was standing guard in the theatre in Baltimore, upon seeing Othello, in the fifth act of the tragedy of that name, about to kill Desdemona, cried out: "It will never be said that in my presence a damned nigger killed a white woman." At the same moment the soldier shot at the actor who was playing Othello and broke his arm. Not one year passes but what the newspapers report similar incidents.

Now that soldier was entertaining an *illusion:* he believed in the reality of what was happening on the stage. But an ordinary spectator at the moment when his pleasure is most intense—at the moment when he is enthusiastically *applauding* Talma-Manlius[3] saying to his friend, "Do you recognize this writing?"—by virtue of the very fact that he applauds, does not have a *complete illusion,* because he is applauding Talma and not the Roman, Manlius. Manlius does nothing deserving of applause. His act is very simple and entirely in his own interest.

THE ACADEMICIAN: I beg your pardon, my friend, but what you have just said is a commonplace.

THE ROMANTIC: I beg your pardon, my friend, but what you have just said represents the defeat of a man made incapable of close reasoning by an ingrained habit of indulging in elegant phrases.

It is impossible for you not to agree that the illusion one seeks at the theatre is not a complete illusion. *Complete* illusion is the kind experienced by the soldier standing guard in the theatre in Baltimore. It is impossible for you not to agree that the spectators know very well that they are in a theatre and watching a work of art, not a real event.

THE ACADEMICIAN: Who would think of denying that?

THE ROMANTIC: Then you grant that there is *imperfect illusion*? You had better be on your guard.

Do you believe that from time to time—for example, two or three times in one act, and for only a second or two each time—the illusion is complete?

THE ACADEMICIAN: That is by no means clear. In order to give you an answer, I should have to go back to the theatre several times and observe my actions.

THE ROMANTIC: Ah! That is a charming reply, and one full of good faith. One can easily see that you belong to the Academy and that you no longer need the votes of your colleagues to be admitted. A man who had yet to make his reputation as a learned *littérateur* would take pains to avoid being so clear and reasoning in a manner so precise. You had better be on your guard: if you continue to be of good faith, we shall agree with each other.

It seems to me that these moments of *complete illusion* are more frequent than is generally supposed, especially than is admitted in literary discussions, as a matter of fact. But these moments are of infinitely brief duration—for example, a half-second or a quarter-second. One very quickly forgets Manlius and sees only Talma. Such moments last longer with young women, and that is why they cry so copiously at a tragedy.

But let us try to discover at what moments in a tragedy the spectator can hope to find these delicious instants of *complete illusion.*

Such charming instants do not occur when there is a change of scene; nor at the precise moment when the poet requires the spectator to skip over twelve or fifteen days; nor when the poet is obliged to give a long speech to one of his characters for the sole purpose of informing the spectator of a previous fact about which he must know; nor, again, when there are three or four lines which are admirable and remarkable as *poetry.*

These delicious and very rare instants of *complete illusion* are encountered only in the warmth of a lively scene when there is a rapid exchange of lines among the actors. For example, when Hermione says to Orestes, who has just assassinated Pyrrhus by her order:

Who told you?

One will never encounter these moments of *complete illusion* at the instant when a murder is committed on the stage or when the guards come to arrest a character and take him to prison. We cannot believe any of these things to be real, and they never produce an illusion. These bits are written only to introduce the scenes in which the spectators experience those half-seconds that are so delicious. *Now I maintain that these brief moments of complete illusion are found more often in the tragedies of Shakespeare than in the tragedies of Racine.*

All the pleasure one derives from the tragic spectacle depends upon the frequency of these brief moments of illusion *and upon the state of emotion in which the spectator is left during the intervals between them.*

One of the things most opposed to the birth of these moments of illusion is admiration—however well-founded it may be—for the beautiful poetic lines of a tragedy.

It is much worse if one decides he wants to judge the *poetic lines* of a tragedy. But this is precisely the state of soul of the Parisian spectator when he first goes to see that much-lauded tragedy *Le Paria*.

Here we have the question of *romanticism* reduced to its ultimate terms. If you are of bad faith, or if you lack sensitivity, or if you have been petrified by Laharpe, you will deny me my brief moments of perfect illusion.

And I admit that there is nothing I can say in reply to you. Your feelings are not something material that I can extract from your own heart and hold up in front of your eyes to confound you.

I say to you: You should have such and such a feeling at this moment. All men who are generally well organized experience such a feeling at this moment. And you will reply: Please pardon my use of the expression, *but that is not true.*

As for me, I have nothing further to add. I have arrived at the last confines of what logic can grasp in poetry.

THE ACADEMICIAN: Your metaphysics is abominably obscure. Do you hope, with that, to make people hiss Racine?

THE ROMANTIC: First of all, only charlatans claim that they can teach algebra or extract a tooth without some pain. The question we are discussing is one of the most difficult that the human mind can undertake.

As for Racine, I am pleased that you mentioned that great man. His name has been made an insult for us; but his glory is immortal. He will always be one of the greatest geniuses to stir the astonishment and admiration of men. Is Caesar less a great general because gunpowder has been invented since his campaigns against our ancestors, the Gauls? All we claim is that if Caesar were to return to the world, his first concern would be to have cannons in his army.

Would anyone say that Catinat or Luxembourg were greater generals than Caesar because they possessed a park of artillery, and because in three days they captured places that would have withstood the Roman legions for a month? It would have been a fine bit of reasoning if someone had said to Francis I at Marignan: "You must not use your artillery. Caesar had no cannons. Do you think you are more clever than Caesar?"

If persons of unquestionable talent like MM. Chénier, Lemercier, and Delavigne had dared to free themselves from rules whose absurdity has been recognized since Racine, they would have given us better plays than *Tibère, Agamemnon,* or *Les Vêpres siciliennes.* Is not *Pinto* a hundred times better than *Clovis, Orovèse, Cyrus,* or any other very correct tragedy of M. Lemercier?

Racine did not believe that tragedies could be written any other way. If he lived in our time and dared to follow the new rules, he would do a hundred times better than *Iphigénie.* Instead of arousing only admiration, a rather cold sentiment, he would cause torrents of tears to flow. Is there any man, of even a modicum of education, who does not derive more pleasure from seeing M. Lebrun's *Marie Stuart* at the Théâtre-Français than Racine's *Bajazet?* And yet M. Lebrun's lines of poetry are very weak. The great difference in the degree of pleasure is due to the fact that M. Lebrun has dared to be quasi-romantic.

THE ACADEMICIAN: You have talked a long time. You have perhaps spoken well, but you have not convinced me.

THE ROMANTIC: I was expecting that. But then, too, this rather lengthy intermission is going to end. The curtain is going up. I merely wanted to relieve the boredom by making you a bit angry. You must agree that I have succeeded.

This marks the end of the dialogue between the two adversaries—a dialogue that I actually heard in the pit of the theatre on the Rue Chantereine, and whose participants I could name if I wished.[4] The Romantic was polite and did not want to annoy the amiable Academician, who was much older than he. Otherwise he would have added: In order to be able still to read what is in one's own heart; in order that the veil of habit may be torn away; in order to be able to put oneself in a receptive state for the moments of *complete illusion* that we are discussing, one must have a soul susceptible to lively impressions; one must not be more than forty years old.

We are creatures of habit. If those habits are subjected to shock, we shall for a long time be aware only of the annoyances thrust upon us. Let us suppose that Talma comes on stage and plays Manlius with his hair powdered and arranged *en ailes de pigeon.* We would do nothing but laugh throughout the performance. Would it really be less sublime? No; but we would not see its sublime quality. Now Lekain would have produced *exactly the same effect in 1760* if he had come on stage *without* powdered hair to play this same role of Manlius. During the entire performance the audience would have been aware only of their *shocked habit.* This is precisely our situation in France with regard to Shakespeare. He disturbs a great many of those ridiculous habits that we have contracted from the assiduous reading of Laharpe and the other little perfumed rhetoricians of the eighteenth century. And what is worse, we have the vanity to maintain that these bad habits are rooted in nature.

The young people are still capable of recovering from this error of *amour-propre*. Since their souls are susceptible to lively impressions, pleasure can make them forget their vanity. But this cannot be demanded of a man older than forty. People of this age in Paris have taken their position on all things—even on things much more important than knowing whether, in order to write interesting tragedies in 1823, one should follow the system of Racine or that of Shakespeare.

## *Chapter II*

### *Laughter*

What will you do, Monsieur, with the nose of a churchwarden?

Regnard

A German prince known for his love of literature has recently offered a prize for the best philosophical dissertation on laughter. I hope that this prize will be won by a Frenchman. Wouldn't it be ridiculous if we were beaten in this competition? It seems to me that more jokes are made during one evening in Paris than in the whole of Germany during a month.

Nonetheless, this program on the subject of laughter has been drawn up in German. What we have to do is to understand its nature and its nuances. We have to reply clearly and concisely to that difficult question: *What is laughter?*

The great misfortune is that the judges are Germans. It is to be feared that a few pseudo thoughts, elegantly disseminated through twenty pages of academic phrases and learnedly cadenced periodic sentences, will strike these crude judges as only so much nothingness. This is a warning that I feel I must give to those young writers who are at once simple and so affected, natural and so mannered, eloquent but with so few ideas:

*La gloire du distique et l'espoir du quatrain.*

(The glory of the couplet and the hope of the quatrain.)

In this case it is necessary to find some ideas—something assuredly very impertinent. Those Germans are so barbarous!

What is laughter? Hobbes replies: *This physical convulsion, familiar to everyone, is produced by the unexpected sight of our superiority over someone else.*

Look at that young man passing by who has dressed himself up with such great care. He is walking on tiptoe. In the glad expression on his face, one can discern both self-satisfaction and the certitude of success. He is going to a ball.

Now he is already under the porte-cochere, in a clutter of lampions and lackeys. He is rushing toward pleasure. But he takes a fall, and when he gets up he is covered with mud from head to toe. His erstwhile white waistcoat, so skillfully tailored, and his tie, so elegantly knotted—all is covered with stinking black mud. From the carriages behind his own comes a general burst of laughter. The porter at the door holds his sides; the crowd of lackeys, laughing to the point of tears, form a circle around the unfortunate young man.

Comedy must be presented with clarity. Our superiority over someone else must be clearly seen.

But this superiority is something so trivial, and so easily destroyed by the least reflection, that we must see it unexpectedly.

Hence these two requirements for the comic: clarity and unexpected occurrence.

If the disadvantage of the person we are supposed to laugh at reminds us right away that we, too, might encounter that misfortune, there is no laughter.

If the handsome young man on his way to the ball is sly enough, after falling in the mud and getting up again, to limp and give the impression that he has been badly hurt, the laughter stops in a trice and gives way to fear.

The reason for this is very simple: there is no more enjoyment of our superiority. On the contrary, there is the spectacle of misfortune for us: I, too, in getting out of my carriage, might break my leg.

People have been making jokes in France for two hundred years, now. Hence a joke must be very clever; otherwise it is understood from the very beginning, and the element of the unexpected is lost.

One other thing. It is essential that I accord a certain degree of esteem to the person at whom I am supposed to laugh. I value very highly the talent of M. Picard. In some of his comedies, however, the characters intended to amuse us have such low morals that I do not admit any comparison between them and myself. As soon as they have spoken four lines, I hold them in utter contempt. There is nothing more of a ridiculous nature that I can, or need to, learn about these people.

A printer in Paris wrote a religious tragedy entitled *Joshua*. He printed it with the greatest possible luxury and sent it to his famous colleague, Bodoni, at Parma. Some time later the author-printer took a trip to Italy and went to see his friend Bodoni. "What do you think of my tragedy, *Joshua*?" "Ah, what beautiful things in it!" "Then you think the work will bring me some fame?" "Ah, my dear friend, it will make you immortal." "And the characters—what do you think of them?" "Sublime and perfectly sustained—especially the capital letters."

Bodoni, a devotee of his art, saw only the *typographical characters* in his friend's tragedy. This story made me laugh much more than it deserves. That was because I knew the author of *Joshua* and have the *very highest regard for him*. He is a sensible man with good manners and even intelligence, well endowed with talents for the book trade. All in all, the only fault I see in him is a bit of vanity—the same trait at which Bodoni's naïve reply made me laugh.

The *unrestrained laughter* provoked in us by Shakespeare's Falstaff when, in his account to Prince Henry (who later became the famous King Henry V), he gets started on the story of the twenty rogues who grew out of four rogues dressed in buckram—this laughter is delicious only because Falstaff is a most merry and infinitely witty man. By contrast, we hardly even laugh at the stupidities of Father Cassander.[5] Our superiority over him is a thing too well known in advance.

The laughter provoked in us by a fool like M. Maclou de Beaubuisson (of *Le Comédien d'etampes*) contains an element of vengeance for boredom.

I have noticed that in society, when a pretty woman says of another woman who is dancing, "Good Heavens, how ridiculous she is!" it is almost always said with an air of malice rather than one of gaiety. Translate "ricidulous" by "odious."

After having laughed like a fool tonight at M. Maclou de Beaubuisson, very well acted by Bernard-Léon, it occurred to me that I had realized, perhaps vaguely, that this ridiculous person had been able to arouse feelings of love in pretty women of the provinces—women who but for their lack of taste could have been completely captivating to me. The laughter of a very handsome young man who had many successes with women might not have had the nuance of vengeance that I thought I noticed in my own laughter.

Since ridicule is a great punishment among the French, they often laugh out of vengeance. This particular laughter is irrelevant to our discussion and should not enter into our analysis. It was merely necessary to take note of it in passing. Any laughter that is *affected* is, by that token alone, devoid of significance. It is like Father Morellet's opinion in favor of tithing and the priory of Thimer.

Everyone knows five or six excellent stories that circulate in society: one always laughs at *disappointed vanity*. If the story is told in a prolix manner—if the raconteur uses too many words and takes time to describe too many details—the listener surmises the end of the story, toward which he is being led too slowly. There is no laughter because there is no more surprise.

If, on the contrary, the raconteur skips over parts of his story and rushes toward the denouement, there is no laughter because the story lacks the extreme clarity it requires. Notice that very often the storyteller repeats twice the five or six words that make up the denouement of his story. If he knows what he is doing—if he has the charming art of being neither obscure nor too clear—the harvest of laughter is much greater at the second repetition than at the first.

*The absurd,* when carried to the extreme, often provokes laughter and provides a lively and delicious kind of merriment. This is the secret of Voltaire in the diatribe of Doctor Akakia and in his other pamphlets. Doctor Akakia (viz., Maupertuis) himself utters the absurdities that a shrewd fellow might employ to make light of his systems. On this point, I am well aware that I should offer some quotations; but I don't have a single French book in my retreat at Montmorency. I trust that my readers, if I have any, will be able to remember this charming volume of their edition of Voltaire, entitled *Facéties*, very pleasing imitations of which I often encounter in the *Miroir*.

In his plays, Voltaire employed this practice of putting into the mouths of the comic characters themselves a lively and brilliant description of the ridiculous ideas that obsessed them; and that great man must have been very surprised to see that no one laughed. This was because it is too much against nature for a man to mock himself so clearly. When, in social gatherings, we deliberately make ourselves ridiculous, it is still done out of an excess of vanity. We are stealing this pleasure from the malice of people whose envy we have excited.

But to fabricate a character like Fier-en-Fat is not to portray the foibles of the human heart. It is simply to have the burlesque phrases of a pamphlet uttered in the first person, and to give them life.

Is it not remarkable that Voltaire, who was so amusing in satire and in the philosophical novel, was never able to write a comic scene that made people laugh? Carmontelle, on the contrary, does not have a single skit in which this talent is not found. He had too much of a natural quality, as did Sedaine. They lacked the wit of Voltaire, who in this genre had only wit.

The foreign critics have observed that there is always an element of malice in the most amusing jokes of *Candide* and *Zadig*. Voltaire, himself richly endowed, took pleasure in parading before our eyes the inevitable misfortunes of poor human nature.

The reading of Schlegel and Dennis has taught me to scorn the French critics—Laharpe, Geoffroy, Marmontel—and to scorn all critics. These poor people, unable to create anything, lay a claim to intelligence, and they have no intelligence. For example, the French critics proclaim that Molière is the best of comic authors—present, past, and future. The only truth herein is the first assertion. There is no doubt that Molière, a man of genius, is superior to that moron admired in the courses of literature whose name is Destouches.

But Molière is inferior to Aristophanes.

Comedy, however, is like music: it is a thing whose beauty *does not last*. The comedy of Molière is too steeped in *satire* to give me very often the sensation of *gay laughter*, if I may so express it. When I go to the theatre for entertainment, I like to encounter a madcap imagination that makes me laugh like a child.

All Louis XIV's subjects prided themselves on imitating a certain model in order to be elegant and *de bon ton;* and Louis XIV himself was the god of that religion. There was a *sarcastic laugh* when one saw another person make a mistake in imitating the model. This accounts for all of the humor in the *Lettres* of Madame de Sévigné. In 1670 a man who, in comedy or in real life, decided to follow quite heedlessly the impulses of a madcap imagination, would not have provoked laughter in the society of the time; he would have passed for a fool.[6]

Molière, a man of genius if there ever was one, had the misfortune to work for that society.

Aristophanes, on the contrary, set out to evoke laughter in a society of amiable and light-hearted people who pursued happiness *in every possible way*. I should imagine that Alcibiades gave very little thought to imitating what was in style. He considered himself happy when he was laughing, and not when he was flushed with pride at feeling himself very similar to Lauzun, d'Antin, Villeroy, or some other famous courtier of Louis XIV.

Our courses in literature have taught us in school that one laughs at Molière; and we believe it, because in France, so far as literature is concerned, we remain schoolboys all our lives. I have undertaken to go to Paris whenever a comedy by Molière or another esteemed author is being performed at the Théâtre-Français. I note in pencil, on the copy of the play I am holding, the exact point at which the audience laughs, and the kind of laughter. For example, there is a laugh when they hear the word "enema" or "cuckolded husband." But this is laughter evoked by the scandalous, and is not the kind Laharpe tells us about.

On December 4, 1822, there was a performance of *Le Tartuffe*. Mlle Mars was appearing. Nothing was lacking for the occasion.

Well! During the whole of *Le Tartuffe* the audience laughed twice—no more. And at that, it was very slight laughter. Several times they applauded the vigor of the satire, or they applauded because of the allusions. But the only times they laughed, on December 4, were:

1. when Orgon, talking to his daughter Marianne about her marriage to Tartuffe (Act II), discovers Dorine nearby, who is listening;

2. during the scene of the quarrel and reconciliation between Valère and Marianne, at a malicious remark made by Dorine on the subject of love.

Astonished that the audience had laughed so little at this masterpiece by Molière, I related what I had observed to a group of intelligent persons. They told me I was mistaken.

Two weeks later I came back to Paris to see *Valérie*. They were also performing *Les Deux gendres,* the famous comedy by M. Etienne. I held my copy and my pencil ready in my hand. The audience laughed exactly *once*. That was when the son-in-law, who is a councilor of state and who is going to become a minister, tells his little cousin that he has read his petition. The spectator laughs because he has very plainly seen the little cousin tear up the petition, which he has seized from the hands of a lackey to whom the councilor of state had given it without reading it.

Unless I am mistaken, the spectator shares the urge toward wild laughter concealed by the little cousin, out of goodness, when he hears himself complimented on the contents of a petition which he knows very well has been torn up without having been read. I told the aforementioned intelligent people that the audience had laughed only this once at *Les Deux gendres*. Their answer was that it was a very good comedy that was excellently composed. So be it! But it therefore follows that laughter is not necessary in order to write a very good French comedy.

Could it be, by any chance, that all one needs is a little action of a very reasonable nature mixed with a rather strong dose of satire, the whole cut up into dialogue and translated into alexandrine lines that are witty, facile, and elegant? If *Les Deux gendres* had been written in vile prose, would it have managed to succeed?

Could it be that because our tragedy is only a series of *odes*[7] interspersed with *epic* narrations[8] that we like to hear declaimed on stage by Talma, in the same way our comedy, since Destouches and Collin d'Harleville, has been only a humorous, subtle, and witty *epistle* that we like to hear read, in the form of dialogue, by Mlle Mars and Damas?[9]

"You have taken us far afield from laughter," the reader will tell me. "You are writing an *ordinary* article on literature, like M.C. in the feuilleton of *Le Journal des débats*."

What do you expect? The trouble is that although I am not yet in the circle of Les Bonnes Lettres,[10] I am ignorant. Moreover, I have taken it upon myself to speak out in the absence of any idea. I hope that this noble audacity will cause me to be received in the circle of Les Bonnes Lettres.

As is very well stated in the German program, an understanding of laughter really requires a dissertation of one hundred and fifty pages. Furthermore, this dissertation must be written in the style of chemistry rather than the academic style.

Look at those young ladies in the boarding school whose garden can be seen from your windows. They laugh at everything. Is it not perhaps because they see happiness everywhere?

Look at that morose Englishman who has just finished his dinner at Tortoni's. With a bored air, and with the aid of a pince-nez, he is reading voluminous letters that he has received from Liverpool, which have brought him commissions of one hundred thousand francs. That is only half of his annual income; but he doesn't laugh at anything. The fact is that nothing in the world can give him a vision of happiness—not even his position as vice-president of a Bible society.

Regnard's genius is clearly inferior to that of Molière; but I shall make bold to say that he walked in the path of genuine comedy.

Our *student's attitude* toward literature has the result that when we see his comedies, instead of giving ourselves over to his genuinely madcap mirth, we think only of the terrible judgments that have relegated him to the second rank. If we did not know *by heart the very texts* of those severe judgments, we would tremble for our reputations as men of intelligence.

Is this, in all honesty, the proper state of mind for laughter?

As for Molière and his plays, why should I be concerned with the more or less successful imitation of the *bon ton* of the court and the impertinence of the *marquis*?

Today there is no more court. Or at any rate, I have as high an opinion of myself as I do of the persons who go there. And if, after visiting the Stock Exchange and then dining, I go to the theatre, I want somebody to make me laugh; and I never think of imitating anybody.

I want to see candid and brilliant images of all the passions of the human heart—not only and always the graces of the Marquis de Moncade.[11] Today, it is my daughter who is Mademoiselle Benjamine; and I know very well how to reject the marriage offer of a *marquis* if he does not have fifteen thousand *livres* income from landed property. As for his bills of exchange, if he makes them out and doesn't pay them, M. Mathieu, my brother-in-law, will send him to Sainte-Pélagie.[12] The mere use of the word "Sainte-Pélagie," for a titled man, makes Molière obsolete.

Finally, if they want to make me laugh in spite of the deeply serious state of mind produced in me by the Stock Exchange, politics, and the hatreds of political parties, I require the spectacle of doting persons deceiving themselves, in a humorous way, on the path that leads to happiness.

## *Chapter III*

### *What Romanticism Is*

*Romanticism* is the art of presenting to different peoples those literary works which, in the existing state of their habits and beliefs, are capable of giving them the greatest possible pleasure.

*Classicism,* on the contrary, presents to them that literature which gave the greatest possible pleasure to their great-grandfathers.

Sophocles and Euripides were eminently romantic. To the Greeks assembled in the theatre of Athens, they presented those tragedies which, in accordance with the moral usages of that people, its religion, and its prejudices in the matter of what constitutes the dignity of man, would provide for it the greatest possible pleasure.

To imitate Sophocles and Euripides today, and to maintain that these imitations will not cause a Frenchman of the nineteenth century to yawn with boredom, is classicism.[13]

I do not hesitate to state that Racine was a romantic. He gave the *marquis* of the court of Louis XIV a portrayal of the passions tempered by the *extreme formalism* then in style, which was such that a duke of 1670, even in the most tender effusions of paternal love, never failed to call his son *Monsieur*.

It was for this reason that the Pylades of *Andromaque* always calls Orestes *Seigneur*. And yet how great was the friendship between Orestes and Pylades!

That formalism did not exist at all among the Greeks; and it is because of that formalism, which today we find chilling, that Racine was romantic.

Shakespeare was romantic because he presented to the English of 1590, first, the bloody catastrophes brought on by the civil wars and then, by way of relief from those sad spectacles, a wealth of exact portrayals of the emotions and the most delicate nuances of feeling. A hundred years of civil wars and almost continuous troubles, with countless acts of treason, torturings, and generous acts of devotion, had prepared the subjects of Elizabeth for this kind of tragedy, which reproduces almost none of the *artificial* element in the court life and civilization of the tranquil nations. The English of 1590, fortunately very ignorant, loved to contemplate on the stage the image of those misfortunes that had recently been removed from real life thanks to the firm character of their queen. These same fresh details, which our alexandrine lines would repulse with disdain and which are so much appreciated today in *Ivanhoe* and *Rob Roy,* would have seemed to the proud *marquis* of Louis XIV to be lacking in dignity.

Those details would have mortally frightened the sentimental and perfumed dolls who, under Louis XV, could not see a spider without fainting. (This sentence, I realize, is most undignified.)

It requires courage to be a romantic, because one must *take a chance.*

The prudent *classicist,* on the contrary, never takes a step without being supported, secretly, by a line from Homer or by a philosophical comment made by Cicero in his treatise *De Senectute.*

It seems to me that the writer must have almost as much courage as the soldier: the former must give no more thought to the journalists than the latter gives to the hospital.

Lord Byron, the author of some heroic epistles that are sublime but always the same, and of many tragedies that are mortally boring, is not at all the leader of the romantics.

If there existed [sic] a man whose works were the object of strong competitive bidding by the translators in bulk at Madrid, Stuttgart, Paris, and Vienna alike, one could say that such a man had divined the moral trends of his age.[14]

In France, the popular Pigault-Lebrun is much more romantic than the sensitive author of *Trilby.*

Is there anybody in Brest or Perpignan who rereads *Trilby?*[15]

The romantic element in contemporary tragedy consists in the fact that the playwright always gives a fine role to the devil. He speaks with eloquence and is much admired. People love the opposition.

The antiromantic element is illustrated by M. Legouvé, who in his tragedy of *Henri IV* is unable to reproduce the finest saying of that patriotic king: "It is my wish that the poorest peasant in my kingdom should at least have a chicken in the pot on Sunday."

This truly French saying would have provided a touching scene for even the most poorly endowed student of Shakespeare. But the *Racinian* tragedy puts it much more nobly:

*Je veux enfin qu'au jour marqué pour le repos,*
*L'hôte laborieux des modestes hameaux*
*Sur sa table moins humble ait, par ma bienfaisance,*
*Quelques-uns de ces mets réservés à l'aisance.*

(Finally, it is my wish that on the day set aside for repose the laborious dweller in the modest hamlets should, through my beneficence, have on his less humble table some of those dishes reserved for comfortable living.)

*La Mort de Henri IV,* Act IV[16]

First of all, romantic comedy would not show us characters in embroidered coats. It would not perpetually have lovers and a marriage at the end of the play. The dramatis personae would not change in character precisely in the fifth act. One would sometimes get a glimpse of a love that could not be crowned with marriage. Marriage itself would not be called *hyménée* for the sake of rhyme. (Is there anyone who would not be a laughingstock if he used the word "hymen" in polite society?)

*Les Précepteurs,* by Fabre d'Eglantine, had opened up a way that censorship has closed. In his *Orange de Malte,* an E . . . [a bishop], they say, was preparing his niece to accept a position as the king's mistress.[17] The only vigorous situation we have seen in twenty years—the scene involving the folding screen in *Le Tartufe de moeurs*—we owe to English drama.[18] In France, anything *strong* is called *indecent.* The audience hissed Molière's *Avare* (February 7, 1823) because of the son's lack of respect for his father.

The most romantic thing in the comedy of our time is not the long plays in five acts, like *Les Deux gendres.* (Show me the person, today, who divests himself of his property.) It is quite simply *Le Solliciteur, Le Ci-devant jeune homme* (copied after Garrick's "Lord Ogleby"),[19] *Michel et Christine, Le Chevalier de canole, L'Etude du procureur, Les Calicots,* the songs of Béranger, etc. The romantic trend in the burlesque vein is represented by the interrogation in *L'Esturgeon,* from the charming vaudeville by M. Arnault, and by M. Beaufils. There we have the mania for reasoning and the literary Dandinism[20] of our age.

M. l'abbé Delille was eminently romantic for the age of Louis XV. His was, indeed, the kind of poetry suitable for the people who, at Fontenoy, took off their hats to the English column and said: "Fire first, gentlemen." This is assuredly very noble. But how do such people have the effrontery to say that they admire Homer?

The ancients would have had a good laugh at our sense of honor.

And they expect that this poetry will be to the liking of a Frenchman who participated in the retreat from Moscow![21]

No people in the memory of an historian has undergone a more rapid and complete change in its morals and pleasures than that from 1780 to 1823. And they want to give us the same literature as before!

Our solemn adversaries should take a look around them. The fool of 1780 produced stupid, flat jokes. He was always laughing. The fool of 1823 produces philosophical arguments that are vague, repetitious, and terribly dull. And he always wears a long face. Here we have a very important revolution. A society in which an element so essential and constant as the *fool* has changed to this extent can no longer put up with the same ridiculous things or the same pathetic ones. In those days everybody tried to make the other person laugh. Today everybody wants to deceive the other person.

An atheistic attorney buys the works of Bourdaloue[22] in a magnificent binding and says: "This is suitable for the clerks."

The romantic poet *par excellence* is Dante. He venerated Vergil; and yet he wrote *The Divine Comedy* and the episode of Ugolino, which of all things in the world least resembles *The Aeneid*. This was because he understood that in his time people were afraid of Hell.

The romantics do not advise anybody to imitate the plays of Shakespeare directly.

What one should imitate in that great man is his manner of studying the world we live in and the art of giving to our contemporaries precisely the kind of tragedy they need but do not have the boldness to demand, because they are so terrified by the reputation of the great Racine.

The new French tragedy might by chance bear a strong resemblance to that of Shakespeare.

But this would be only because our circumstances are the same as those of England in 1590. We, too, have factions, tortures, and plots. Someone who is now laughing, as he reads this pamphlet in a salon, will be in prison within a week. Another person, who is joking with him, will name the jury that will convict him.

We would soon have the *new French tragedy* that I am bold enough to predict if we had a strong enough feeling of security to take an active interest in literature. I say "feeling of security" because the trouble is especially in people's imaginations, which are given to fears. In the countryside and on the main roads, we have a physical security that would have been most astonishing to the England of 1590.

Because in the matter of intelligence, we are infinitely superior to the English of that age, our new tragedy will have more simplicity. Shakespeare employs rhetoric continually. This is because he had to make the situations in his drama comprehensible to an uncouth public with more courage than subtlety.

Our new tragedy will strongly resemble *Pinto*, the masterpiece of M. Lemercier.

The French mentality will especially reject the German bombast that many people today call romantic.

Schiller *copied* Shakespeare and his rhetoric. He lacked the intelligence to give his fellow countrymen the kind of tragedy required by their social usages.

I was forgetting the *unity of place*. It will be swept away in the rout of the alexandrine.

M. Picard's pleasant comedy *Le Conteur*, which only needs to have been written by Beaumarchais or Sheridan in order to be delicious, has given the public the good habit of realizing that there exist charming subjects for which changes of scenery are absolutely necessary.

We are almost as far advanced in the matter of tragedy. How does it happen that the Emilie of *Cinna* comes to the emperor's council chamber to do her conspiring? How can one imagine *Sylla* performed without changing the sets?

If M. Chénier had lived, that intelligent man would have rid us of the unity of place in tragedy and, consequently, of boring narrative speeches. He would have rid us of that unity of place that makes it forever impossible to dramatize great national subjects: the assassination of Montereau, the Etats de Blois, the death of Henri III.

*Henri III* requires absolutely, on the one hand Paris, the Duchess of Montpensier, and the cloister of the Jacobin friars, and on the other Saint-Cloud, the irresolution, the weakness, the sensual pleasures, and suddenly death, which puts an end to the whole thing.

Racinian tragedy can never use more than the thirty-six hours of an action; hence, there is never any development of the passions. What plot has the time to be hatched, or what movement of the people can develop, in thirty-six hours?

It is interesting, it is *beautiful,* to see Othello, so much in love in the first act, kill his wife in the fifth. If this change were to take place in thirty-six hours, it would be absurd, and I would have only contempt for Othello.

Macbeth, a good man in the first act, is enticed by his wife, murders his king and benefactor, and becomes a bloody monster. Either I am mistaken, or these changes of the passions in the human heart are the most magnificent thing that poetry can hold up to be viewed by the eyes of men, whom it at once moves and instructs.

## *The Naïveté of the* Journal des Débats *(Feuilleton of July 8, 1818)*

. . . O happy days when the theatre pit was occupied almost entirely by devoted and studious young people whose memory was *adorned in advance* with all the beautiful lines of Racine and Voltaire; young people who went to the theatre *only to round out the pleasure of their reading!*[23]

## *Résumé*

I am far from claiming that M. David ranks higher than the Lebruns and the Mignards. In my opinion, the modern artist, more remarkable for his strength of character than for his talent, remains inferior to the great painters of the age of Louis XIV. But what would MM. Gros, Girodet, Guérin, Prudhon, and all the distinguished painters produced by his school be today had it not been for M. David? Perhaps more or less ridiculous Vanloos and Buchers.

## *On Molière, Regnard, and Other Matters*[24]

*A few persons who had the kindness to read this pamphlet in its entirety have told the author that his ideas seemed to have particularly little relevance to Molière. It is quite possible that a man of genius writing works which are very pleasurable to people in one era of civilization should still give more pleasure to the people of a totally different era than do the mediocre artists of this latter age. These mediocre artists are boring chiefly because they slavishly copy the works of the great man. They are incapable of seeing either life as it exists before their very eyes, or life as it was when the great man gave us his sublime imitations of it.*

*I have deemed it more appropriate to write a new chapter on Molière; and I have entered into a few serious bits of reasoning, at the risk of seeming heavy.*

*This pamphlet has brought me an honor of which I am proud. A few of those men whose writings, and not their evening visions* [visits?], *have earned them a leading place in literature—a few of those men whose writings lend pleasure to my hours of leisure—have deigned to offer some objections to what I have said. I have taken the risk of replying to those objections with a new chapter. If I had allowed myself to voice my self-doubts as often as I feel how many reasons I have to be modest, this additional chapter would have been very long. I have so far respected my noble adversaries as to believe that they would have enough pride to love the truth without formulas. And I have therefore spoken simply, as one speaks to the immortals, saying in a plain way not what is true, perhaps, but what seems to me to be true.*

## *Chapter IV*

### *On the State of Society with Respect to Comedy in the Reign of Louis XIV*

To hate something is not a pleasure. In fact I believe many readers will agree with me that it is painful; and the more imagination or sensitivity one has, the greater the pain.

La Bruyère said: "To escape from the court for a single moment is to give it up. The courtier who has seen it in the morning sees it in the evening in order to recognize it the next day and in order that he himself be recognized there."

Even in 1670, in the best days of Louis XIV, the court was merely an assemblage of enemies and rivals. It was dominated by hatred and envy. How could true gaiety have shown itself there?

Those people who hated one another so cordially and who died after fifty years of hate still inquiring on their deathbed, "How is Monsieur So-and-So?"[25]—those people detested even more certain human beings of whom they never took notice except to oppress them or to be afraid of them. Their hatred was all the stronger in that it was preceded by contempt. There was nothing in the world that could shock them so much as the suspicion that they had something in common with such people. "What you have just said is very common," said Louis XIV one day when that great king deemed it appropriate to carry reprimand almost to the point of insult. In the eyes of

Louis XIV, Henri IV, or Louis XVIII there were never more than two classes of people in France: the nobles, who had to be governed by *honor* and recompensed with the *cordon bleu;*[26] and the *canaille,* to whom one threw sausages and hams on great occasions, but whom it was necessary to hang or massacre without pity the moment they took it into their heads to express their opinions.[27]

This state of civilization offered two sources of comedy for the courtiers: first, when a person made a mistake in imitating what was in good taste at court; second, when a person's manners or conduct showed some resemblance to a bourgeois. The letters of Madame de Sévigné prove all these things to the point of obviousness. She was a gentle, amiable, moderate woman, not at all malicious. (See her correspondence during her sojourns at her estate, Les Rochers, and the tone in which she talks about the hangings and other harsh measures employed by her good friend, the Duke of Chaulnes.)

These charming letters show above all that a courtier was always poor. He was poor because he could not have the same luxuries as his neighbor. And what was really *frightful* and painful for him was the favor of the court, which made it possible for that neighbor to display all this sumptuousness.

And so, in addition to the two sources of hatred mentioned above, the courtier also had (to contribute to his happiness) poverty plus vanity—the cruelest of all, because it is followed by contempt.[28]

At the court of Louis XIV, in 1670, among so many bitter sorrows, disappointed hopes, and betrayed friendships, one last resort remained for those vain and frivolous souls: the anxiety of the gamble, the raptures of winning, the horror of losing. Consider the profound desolation of a Vardes or a Bussy-Rabutin in the depths of this exile. To be no longer at court was to have all the misfortunes and sorrows, and to feel all the sharp edges, of the civilization of that day, without having the things that made them bearable. In exile, one had either to live with bourgeois (a horrible thing) or to see courtiers of the third and fourth rank who came to the province to discharge their duties, and who bestowed their pity upon one. The masterpiece of Louis XIV, the complement of the system of Richelieu, was to create this desolation of exile.

For anyone who knows how to view it, the court of Louis XIV was never anything more than a game of faro. It was people like this whom, in the intervals between games, Molière undertook to amuse. He succeeded like the great man that he was; that is, almost perfectly. The comedies that he produced for the courtiers of the *sun-king* were probably the best and the most amusing that one could write for such people. But, in 1825, we are no longer this kind of people. Public opinion is formed by people living in Paris, with more than ten thousand *livres* of income and less than one hundred.

Sometimes the formalism[29] of Louis XIV's courtiers was shocked even by the humorous imitation of what was most ridiculously odious in their eyes: a merchant of Paris. The *Bourgeois gentilhomme* struck them as frightful, not because of the role of Dorante, which today would give the chills to MM. Auger, Lémontey, and other censors, but quite simply because it was degrading and disgusting to have their eyes fixed for so long on a being so abject as M. Jourdain—on a merchant of Paris. Still, Louis XIV had better taste. That great king wanted to raise up those of his subjects engaged in industry. And by one remark he made them worthy of being mocked. "Molière," he said to his valet-upholsterer, who was plunged into sadness by the contempt of the court, "Molière, you never yet wrote anything which amused me so much. Your play is excellent."

I must confess that I am not deeply touched by this act of charity on the part of the great king.

When, about 1720, the dissipations of the great lords and the system devised by Law had finally created a bourgeoisie, a third source of comedy appeared: the imperfect and awkward imitation of those amiable courtiers. The son of M. Turcaret,[30] who took the disguise of a *nom de terre* and became a farmer-general of the king's revenues, must have led the kind of social life[31] for which there had been no model under Louis XIV, in that century when the ministers themselves had been only bourgeois to start with. A courtier could see M. Colbert only on business matters. Paris became filled with very wealthy bourgeois whose names you will find in the *Mémoires* of Collé: MM. d'Angivilliers, Turgot, Trudaine, Monticourt, Helvétius, d'Epinay, *et al.* Little by little these opulent and well-bred men, the sons of vulgar men like Turcaret, brought into being that fatal public opinion which finally spoiled everything in 1789. These farmers-general entertained men of letters at their *soupers,* and the latter emerged somewhat from the role of *buffoons* that they had played at the tables of the real *grands seigneurs.*

Duclos' *Considérations sur les moeurs* constitutes the Civil Code for this new order, a rather amusing description of which has been given to us in the *Mémoires* of Madame d'Epinay and Marmontel. We are told of a M. de Bellegarde who, despite his great name, is only a farmer-general. But he spends two hundred thousand francs a year. And his son, reared in the same luxury as the Duke of Fronsac, feels he is the latter's equal in manners.[32]

From this moment, Turcaret was without models. But this new society of the period between 1720 and 1790, this total change so important in history and politics, was of hardly any importance for comedy. During all this time, comedy produced no man of genius. Astonished at being able to reason, people pursued this altogether new pleasure at a furious pace. To reason on the existence of God seemed something fascinating, even to the ladies. The *parlements* and the archbishops, by means of their condemnations, added something piquant to this arid way of employing one's intelligence. Everybody was avidly reading *Emile,* the *Encyclopédie,* and *The Social Contract.*

One man of genius appeared at the very end of this period. The Academy, through the medium of M. Suard's publication, condemned Beaumarchais. But it was no longer a matter of amusing oneself in a salon. People were already thinking of rebuilding the house; and the architect Mirabeau won out over the decorator Beaumarchais. When a modicum of good faith in governmental power has brought the revolution to an end, everything will fall into place little by little. Heavy, philosophical, and unassailable reasoning will be left to the Chamber of Deputies. When this happens, comedy will be reborn, because people will have a wild urge to laugh.

The hypocrisy of the old Madame de Maintenon and of the old age of Louis XIV was followed by the orgies of the Regent. Likewise, when at last we emerge from this lugubrious farce and are permitted to dispense with passports, rifles, epaulettes, Jesuits' robes, and the whole revolutionary paraphernalia, we shall have an era of charming gaiety.

But let us abandon these political conjectures and return to comedy. In the mediocre comedies between 1720 and 1790, one was ridiculous when one did not imitate in the approved manner those usages of the court that M. de Monticourt or M. de Trudaine, who were wealthy men of Paris, could allow their vanity.[33]

But I am a Frenchman of 1825, who enjoys esteem in proportion to his wealth and pleasures in proportion to his wit. What does the more or less successful imitation of the *bon ton* of the court mean to me? It is still necessary, in order to be ridiculous, that a person make a false step on the road to happiness. But happiness no longer consists, for the French, merely in imitating (each according to established usages) the manners of the court.

Nonetheless, it should be noted that we have retained the habit of conforming, in our acts, to an accepted model. No people is so tenacious of its habit as the French. The key to this mystery is an excess of vanity: we abhor hidden dangers.

Still and all, we are no longer in the time of Louis XIV and his arrogant courtiers (so well depicted by another courtier, Dangeau), who were responsible for fabricating the *model* to which everyone, in accordance with the rules of decorum applicable to his station, was terribly anxious to conform.

It is the *opinion of the majority* that erects in the public square the model to which everyone scrupulously conforms. It is no longer enough to take a false step on the road that leads to the court. Count Alfieri, in his autobiography, relates the following. On New Year's Day, 1768, the aldermen of Paris lost their way and did not arrive at the gallery of Versailles in time to receive the glance that Louis XV deigned to throw in their direction. On that New Year's Day, on his way to Mass, the king asked what had become of the aldermen. A voice replied, "They are still stuck in the mud." And the king himself deigned to smile.[34]

Anecdotes of this kind are still told; and in the Faubourg Saint-Germain people laugh at them as they would at a fairy tale. They still have a bit of nostalgia for the fairy days. But there are two centuries between those poor aldermen of Paris, getting bogged down in the mud on the road to Versailles, and great lords coming to seek a bourgeois reputation for eloquence in the Chamber of Deputies, so that they can move on from there to a ministry.

# Chapter VII

## *Concerning Scenes Depicting Manners in Terms of Strong Situations, and the "Vis Comica"*

The court of Louis XIV put a heavy strain on the shrewdness of the courtier. Every morning he had to detect, from the look in the master's eyes, whether his favor was on the wane, or whether it would continue at all. Because the least gesture was decisive, the slightest nuance was observed.

The republic, on the contrary, has engendered the art of discussion, serious attacks, and the *eloquence of the rostrum* intended to stir up the masses. The knavery of a cabinet minister is always rather easy to see. The difficult thing is to make it tangible in the eyes of the people and arouse public indignation about it. It requires good sense and patience to detect a duplicated item in the friendly shade of a budget.[35] It required charming manners, a lively intellect, a high degree of tact attuned to the slightest nuance, and shrewdness at every moment to win or keep the favor of a despot who was bored and had a most refined taste,[36] because for fifty years he had been flattered by the most amiable men of Europe. Those courtiers who, every morning, went to read their fate in the eyes of the king, decided in their turn the fate of those who paid court to them and to whom they transmitted the same habits of perception. Before long this habit became general among all the French.

Molière, with his genius, was quick to note this deep shrewdness among the members of his audiences; and he made use of it for their pleasure and for his own fame. His plays are full of *testing* scenes, if I may so designate scenes which *test* the character or passions of the persons involved. Need I recall lines like "The poor man!" which is so fashionable today. Or "Oh God, forgive him his sins as I forgive him!"[37] Or Harpagon's "Without a dowry!" Or "How did he ever get into *that* fix?" from *Les Fourberies de Scapin*. Or "You are in the trade, Monsieur Josse." Or Orgon's "Get thee behind me, rascal!" to his son, Damis, who has just accused the good M. Tartuffe. These are celebrated witticisms which have enriched the language.

This is what many classical *littérateurs* call the *vis comica,* without stopping to realize that there is nothing comical in seeing Orgon curse and drive off his son, who has just accused Tartuffe of an obvious crime—and this because Tartuffe replies with phrases lifted from the Catechism, which prove nothing. The eye suddenly looks into one of the depths of the human heart—but a depth that is more curious than laughable. We see a good man, like Orgon, let himself be convinced by phrases that prove nothing. We are too attentive—I would even go so far as to say, too deeply moved—to laugh. We see that there is nothing so difficult to prove as the obvious, because the people who need to have it proven to them are blind. We see that the evident truth, our great support in acting on other men (because one must necessarily convince those whom one does not command) and the means of support by which we often move ahead to happiness, can suddenly fail us at the moment when we need it most urgently. A fact of this kind presages danger of a sort. And as soon as *danger* enters the picture, there is no longer any question of that frivolous comparison which produces laughter.[38]

This certainly represents strength, or *vis*. But why add the word *comica* (that which causes laughter) if no one laughs? *Vis comica* is one of the expressions of the old *classical* literature.

Shakespeare's "Misanthropist," entitled *Timon of Athens*, is full of very strong and very beautiful scenes. But no one laughs at them. This is because they are only *testing* scenes, if I may be permitted this expression. In those scenes the character of the misanthropist is established, for the spectator, in a manner superior to any objection—and not on hearsay or the accounts of men-servants, but on the basis of incontestable proofs: things that take place before the spectator's very eyes.

The bad-tempered Ménechme, in the comedy of that name, is the amusing misanthropist; and Regnard appropriated him for his own use. But poor Regnard, who was always gay, like the manners and morals of the Regency or of Venice, gives us scarcely any *testing* scenes. He would have found them boring or sad.

And so these scenes, which are strong but not comical, yield a very great philosophical pleasure. Old men like to quote them and then mentally classify all the events of their lives—which proves that Molière had accurate insight into the depths of the human heart. We often think of these immortal scenes, and we allude to them constantly. In conversation, they always cap our ideas. For the person who knows how to quote them apropos, they are by turns judgments, axioms, or jokes. No other scenes will ever penetrate so far into the French mentality. In this sense, they are like the religions: the time for creating them has passed. Finally, it is probably more difficult to write such scenes than to write the amusing scenes of Regnard. Orgon, seizing Tartuffe just when the latter, after having taken a good look around the entire room, has embraced Elmire, presents a spectacle full of genius but not comical. This scene strikes the spectator. It strikes him with helpless amazement, and it *avenges* him, if you will; but *it does not make him laugh*.

If someone will find another expression of admiration for Molière—for example: "He is the French poet with the 'most genius'"—I will gladly subscribe to it. And furthermore, I have always thought so. But let us not be dazzled by a great man. Let us not lend him qualities he does not possess. Should one admire base despotism because its throne has been adorned by a man like Napoleon?

However great Molière is, *Regnard is more comical*. He makes me laugh more often, and more heartily—and that despite the great inferiority of his genius. Imagine how far Molière would have gone if he had written for the court of the Regent, instead of living in the reign of Louis XIV! It is in vain that Boileau says:

*Dans le sac ridicule où Scapin s'enveloppe,*
*Je ne reconnais plus l'auteur du Misanthrope*

(In the ludicrous bag in which Scapin wraps himself, I no longer recognize the author of *Le Misanthrope*.)

I leave to poor Boileau, the poet of reason, his decorum of a bourgeois admitted to the court of Louis XIV, and his natural coldness.

The comedy of *Le Misanthrope* is like a splendid and magnificent palace built at great expense, where I grow bored—where time does not move. *Les Fourberies* is a pretty little country house, a charming cottage, where my heart is gladdened, and where I give no thought to anything grave.

On every occasion after I have laughed at *Le Ci-devant jeune homme* or *Le Solliciteur* at the Variétés, I leave the theatre in a rage against our petty rhetoricians who will not allow Ymbert and Scribe to write five-act comedies for the Théâtre-Français, and to develop at leisure those subjects of ridicule which today they can only touch upon in passing.

Will no one step forward to dethrone the pedants? Shall we once again let them falsify the taste of those fine young people who applaud with such noble enthusiasm the eloquent lessons of the Cousins and the Daunous? They are so little deceived by political disguises: will they always remain the dupes of literary disguises? Just once, before taking my leave of this world, I would like to laugh at a new play at the Théâtre-Français. Is this asking too much? And those gentlemen of the Academy, who constitute *a class* and whom one can no longer make fun of except at the risk of going to prison—will they always stop us from laughing, even when we are not in any way thinking of their brilliant qualities?

## *NOTES*

1. Le Théâtre de l'Odéon. [Translator's note.]
2. Dialogue of Ermeo Visconti in *Il Conciliatore*, Milan, 1818.
3. I.e., François-Joseph Talma, the famous tragic actor, in the leading role of *Manlius Capitolinus*, by Lafosse d'Aubigny, a playwright of the eighteenth century. [Translator's note.]
4. Much of the dialogue was in fact adopted from Ermeo Visconti. [Translator's note.]
5. "Pantaloon"; a stock character in popular French and Italian comedy: a foolish old man inevitably the butt of the clown's jokes. [Translator's note.]
6. The "marketplace theatre" of Regnard, Lesage, and Defresny has no rank in literature. Very few people have read these plays. The same applies to Scarron and Hauteroche.
7. The monologue of *Le Paria*, of *Régulus*, of *Les Machabées*.
8. The narrative speeches of Orestes in *Andromaque*. What nation does not have its literary prejudices? Look at the English, who condemn that dull schoolboy exaggeration entitled *Cain: A Mystery*, by Lord Byron, only because it is anti-aristocratic.
9. It is up to the Paris police to stop the decline of dramatic art. They should make

use of their unlimited powers to see that absolutely no free ticket is given out for the first two performances of new plays at the big theatres.

10. A group that combined political ultraconservatism with literary romanticism of the traditionalist variety. Its members included Chateaubriand, president of the society, and Victor Hugo. [Translator's note.]

11. Of *L'Ecole des bourgeois*.

12. The prison of Sainte-Pélagie, in Stendhal's day, housed debtors and writers who had been convicted of censorship violations. [Translator's note.]

13. See the analysis of Greek drama by Metastasio.

14. This success cannot be a matter of partisanship or personal enthusiasm. At the bottom of all parties there is always a monetary interest. In this case, I can discover only the interest of pleasure. The man himself is hardly deserving of enthusiasm. (His probable cooperation with the infamous *Beacon*, the ridiculous anecdote about the glass from which George IV had drunk.) [The reference is to Sir Walter Scott. Trans.]

15. By Charles Nodier (1780–1844), a leader of the French romantic school. [Translator's note.]

16. In English and Italian verse forms it is possible to say anything. Only the alexandrine line, created for a disdainful court, has all the ridiculous features of the latter.

17. It was customary, in speaking to Madame de Pompadour, to refer to the *position* that she occupied. See the *Mémoires* of Bézenval, Marmontel, and Madame d'Epinay. These *Mémoires* are replete with strong situations, in no way indecent, that our timid comedy does not dare to reproduce. See the story, *Le Spleen*, by Bézenval.

18. *Le Tartufe de moeurs*, by Louis-Claude Chéron (1758–1807) was an imitation of Sheridan's *School for Scandal*. [Translator's note.]

19. Presumably a reference to *The Clandestine Marriage*, by Garrick and Colman. [Translator's note.]

20. After Pierre Dandin, the judge in *Pantagruel*, who decides cases summarily and stupidly. [Translator's note.]

21. M. Lemercier's *Panhypocrisiade*, if it were not so badly written, would be the poem of the age. Just imagine the "Battlefield of Pavia" translated into French by Boileau or M. l'abbé Delille. In this poem of four hundred pages, there are forty verses more striking and more beautiful than any by Boileau.

22. A prominent churchman of Louis XIV's time, renowned for his skill as an orator and for the sermons that constitute his *Works*. [Translator's note.]

23. An excerpt from an article in the *Journal des débats*. [Translator's note.]

24. The chapters grouped under this heading were apparently intended by Stendhal to serve as a supplement to the three chapters of the first *Racine and Shakespeare* pamphlet (1823), *supra*, and were so treated by Colomb in his 1854 edition of the work. The "chapter" on French declamation (three paragraphs) has been omitted here. [Translator's note.]

25. Factual. See Saint-Simon.

26. The decoration worn by members of the order called "The Knights of the Holy Ghost." [Translator's note.]

27. The *Mémoires* of Bassompierre, de Gourville, *et al.*

28. The letters of Madame de Sévigné. Details on the life and projects of M. le marquis de Sévigné and MM. de Grignan, father and son.

29. In order to get an exact idea of this formalism, see the *Mémoires* of the Duchess of Orléans, the mother of the Regent. This sincere German woman casts a bit of doubt upon the countless lies of Madame de Genlis, M. de Lacretelle, and other persons of the same weight.

30. This evening my carriage was held up for a quarter of an hour on the Boulevard des Italiens by the descendants of Crusaders, who were standing in line in order to gain admission to a ball given by a Jewish banker (M. de Rothschild). The noble ladies of the Faubourg Saint-Germain had spent the early part of the day in all kinds of base maneuvers so that they might be invited.

31. The *Mémoires* of Collé.

32. Madame d'Epinay's morning reception: "The two liveried servants open the swinging doors so that I can pass through, and shout to the people in the reception room, 'Madame is coming, Messieurs. Madame is coming!' Everyone lines up. First in line is some young scamp who has come to bellow an aria. After having given him some lessons in good taste and having taught him what it is to sing French correctly, I grant him my patronage so that he can have entree into the Opéra. Then there are drapers, persons dealing in musical instruments, jewelers, peddlers, bootblacks, creditors, lackeys, etc. (*Mémoires et correspondance de Madame d'Epinay,* Vol. I, pp. 356–57.)

33. The role of Récard in a five-act prose comedy of Collé following his *Mémoires;* the Mondor of *Les Fausses infidélités,* etc.

34. *Vita di Alfieri,* Vol. I, p. 140.

35. Mr. Hume, in England, in the House of Commons, before Mr. Canning conceived the idea of resorting to good faith to keep himself in office.

36. The *Lettres* of Madame de Maintenon.

37. The death of the poor old man, Llorente, in 1823.

38. This is the sentiment whose lack makes kings into nitwits. They never, or only very rarely, *have to persuade anybody of anything.* Hence the difficulty in persuading themselves.

# WALTER SCOTT AND "LA PRINCESSE DE CLEVES"

These two names indicate the two extremes in the novel. Should the novelist describe the dress worn by the various characters, the landscape around them and their physiognomy, or would he do better to depict the passions and sentiments which agitate their souls? My reflections will not be welcome. An immense body of men of letters finds it in its own interest to praise Sir Walter Scott to the skies, together with his method of composition. The doublet and leather collar of a medieval serf are easier to describe than the movements of the human heart. One can either imagine or describe inaccurately medieval costume (we have only a half-knowledge of the customs and the dress worn in Cardinal Richelieu's ante-chamber); whereas we throw the book down in disgust if the author fails to describe the human heart, and ascribes, say, to an illustrious companion-in-arms of the son of Henri IV the ignoble sentiments of a lackey. Everyone recalls Voltaire's famous story. One day he was giving a lesson in tragic diction to a young actress, who recited a lively passage with the utmost coldness. 'But, my dear young lady', cried Voltaire, 'You ought to be acting as though the devil were in you. What would you do if a cruel tyrant had just separated you from your lover? 'I should take another', was her reply.

I do not wish to suggest that all the makers of historical novels think as reasonably as this prudent young pupil of Voltaire's; but even the most susceptible among them will not suspect me of calumny if I say that it is infinitely easier to describe in picturesque detail a character's dress than to say what he feels and to make him speak. Let us not forget another advantage which is offered by the school of Sir Walter Scott: the description of the costume and posture of a character, however minor he may be, takes at least two pages. The movements of the heart, which, to begin with, are so difficult to discern and so difficult to describe with precision and without either timidity or exaggeration, would scarcely furnish a few lines. Open at random ten pages from one of the volumes of *La Princesse de Clèves;* then compare them with ten pages from *Ivanhoe* or *Quentin Durward;* it will be found that the latter display a *historical merit*.

They teach those who know little or nothing about history a number of minor details concerning the past. Their historical merit has already given great pleasure. I do not wish to deny this, only it is the historical merit which will grow old the soonest. The century will move towards a more true and natural form of expression; and the mannered approximations of Sir Walter Scott will one day seem as distasteful as they at first seemed charming. Perhaps it would be wise if I were to develop these rapid hints and say something more of the future destiny of the fashionable novel.

See what a crowd of men and women have found it in their interest to maintain that Sir Walter Scott is a great man. Despite their numbers, I have no intention of borrowing the mask of hypocrisy which the nineteenth century finds so fashionable. I shall pronounce with all frankness my conviction that, in ten years time, the reputation of the Scottish novelist will have declined by half. Richardson's fame in France was equal to Scott's. Diderot used to say, 'In exile or prison I would ask for only three books: Homer, the Bible, and *Clarissa Harlowe*.' Like Sir Walter Scott, Richardson had a more distinguished reputation in Paris than in England.

Every work of art is a charming lie; anyone who has written knows this well. There is nothing more ridiculous than the advice commonly given to the writer in society: 'Imitate nature.' Confound it, I know that the writer should imitate nature, but to what extent? That is the whole question. Two men of equal genius, Racine and Shakespeare, have depicted, one of them Iphigenia at the moment when her father is about to sacrifice her in Aulis, the other the young Imogen at the moment when a husband she adores is about to have her stabbed somewhere in the mountain country near Milford Haven.

These great poets have both imitated nature; but one wished to amuse country gentlemen who still had the rough stern frankness which was the fruit of the long Wars of the Roses. The other sought the applause of the polite courtiers who, imitating the genteel forms established by Lauzun and the Marquis de Vardes, wished to win favour in the eyes of the king and the general approval of the ladies. 'Imitate nature' is therefore meaningless advice. To what extent must one imitate nature if one is to give pleasure to the reader? This is the main question.

I think that I should insist on one childish detail. If all that had been said at Aulis when Iphigenia was about to be murdered had been taken down on paper and preserved, we would possess five or six volumes, even if we confined ourselves to what was said by the principal characters of Racine's play. It was first necessary to reduce these six volumes to eighty pages. Furthermore, most of what was said by Agamemnon and Calchas would be unintelligible today and, even if we did understand it, would fill us with horror.

Art, then, is nothing more than a charming lie; only Sir Walter Scott has been too much of a liar. He would give greater pleasure to those higher natures who ultimately decide the fate of all literature, if, in his portrayal of the passions, he had admitted a greater number of natural traits. His characters, when they are moved by passion, seem ashamed of themselves, altogether like Mlle Mars when she is playing the part of a stupid, frivolous woman. When she comes on to the stage, this great actress glances meaningfully at the audience with a look that seems to say: 'Now don't go away thinking that I am nothing but a silly goose myself. I've got my wits about me just as much as you have. I merely want you to tell me one thing: in order to give you pleasure and deserve your applause, this being my greatest desire, I have chosen to impersonate this sort of woman. Have I succeeded or not?'

One would say of a painter who displayed this fault, which is to be found in both Scott and Mlle Mars, that his colours lacked freshness and were unnatural.

I will go even further. The more elevated the sentiments which Walter Scott's characters have to express, the less they are bold or confident. I am forced to confess this and it is this which I find most painful in what I have to say about the author and his work. One sees here all the experience and wiliness of an old judge. This is the man who, having been admitted to the table of George IV, when the latter was visiting Edinburgh, enthusiastically asked for the glass in which the King had just drunk the health of his people. Sir Walter Scott was given the precious goblet and placed it in his overcoat pocket. On returning home, however, forgetting this honour for an instant, he threw down his coat and broke the glass, an accident which threw him into despair. Would the elderly Corneille or the excellent Ducis have understood such feelings? In a hundred and forty-six years time, Scott will be less esteemed than Corneille still is a hundred and forty-six years after his death.

# *Leigh Hunt*

1784–1859

James Henry Leigh Hunt was born in Southgate, Middlesex, on October 19, 1784. The son of an Anglican minister, he was educated in London at Christ's Hospital School (1791–99). His first collection of verse, *Juvenilia,* appeared in 1801, and was followed in 1808 by a collection of theatre reviews, *Critical Essays on the Performers of the London Theatres* (dated 1807). Also in 1808 Hunt and his brother John founded the *Examiner,* which Hunt edited for twenty years. During this time he used his journal to campaign actively for liberal reform, and also did much to support the writing of his friends Shelley, Keats, Hazlitt, and Lamb. Lamb was also published in Hunt's short-lived paper, the *Reflector* (1810–11), a quarterly which lasted only four issues.

In 1813 Hunt and his brother were fined £500 and sentenced to two years' imprisonment for libeling the Prince Regent in the *Examiner.* Although he served his sentence, Hunt was able to continue writing and editing his paper from prison. In 1816, after his release, Hunt published his influential poem *The Story of Rimini,* based on Dante's story of Paolo and Francesca and written while he was in prison. This was followed in 1818 by *Foliage,* a collection of his verses, and in 1819 by his poems *Hero and Leander* and *Bacchus and Ariadne.* Also in 1819 Hunt founded the *Indicator,* a purely literary paper, which folded in 1821; with Byron he then started another journal, the *Liberal* (1822–24), in which appeared works by Byron, Shelley, Hazlitt, Hunt, Hogg, and others. The *Companion,* a magazine which contains some of Hunt's best work, appeared in 1828; his *Tatler* in 1830–32; and his *London Journal* in 1834–35.

In 1835 Hunt published his long anti-war poem *Captain Sword and Captain Pen,* followed in 1838 by the *Book of Gems,* an anthology containing one of his best-known poems, "Abou Ben Adhem." In 1840 Hunt's play *A Legend of Florence* was successfully produced at Covent Garden; he subsequently wrote many other plays, but none was well received. In 1844 he published *Poetical Works* and *Imagination and Fancy,* a critical study in which poetry and painting are compared. His later works include an anthology *Wit and Humour* (1846); *Stories from Italian Poets* (1846); *Men, Women, and Books* (1847); *A Jar of Honey from Mount Hybla* (1848); *The Town* (1848), about London; Hunt's *Autobiography* (1850); *Table Talk* (1851); *The Religion of the Heart* (1853); and *The Old Court Suburb* (1855), a collection of essays on Kensington.

Hunt, who married Marianne Kent in 1809, had seven children. He died in Putney on August 28, 1859. While his greatest desire was to be known as a poet, it is as an essayist and an associate of other writers that he is today best remembered.

# What Is Poetry?

Poetry, strictly and artistically so called, that is to say, considered not merely as poetic feeling, which is more or less shared by all the world, but as the operation of that feeling, such as we see it in the poet's book, is the utterance of a passion for truth, beauty and power, embodying and illustrating its conceptions by imagination and fancy, and modulating its language on the principle of variety in uniformity. Its means are whatever the universe contains; and its ends, pleasure and exaltation. Poetry stands between nature and convention, keeping alive among us the enjoyment of the external and spiritual world: it has constituted the most enduring fame of nations; and, next to Love and Beauty, which are its parents, is the greatest proof to man of the pleasure to be found in all things, and of the probable riches of infinitude.

Poetry is a passion, because it seeks the deepest impressions; and because it must undergo, in order to convey them.

It is a passion for truth, because without truth the impression would be false or defective.

It is a passion for beauty, because its office is to exalt and refine by means of pleasure, and because beauty is nothing but the loveliest form of pleasure.

It is a passion for power, because power is impression triumphant, whether over the poet, as desired by himself, or over the reader, as affected by the poet.

It embodies and illustrates its impressions by imagination, or images of the objects of which it treats, and other images brought in to throw light on those objects, in order that it may enjoy and impart the feeling of their truth in its utmost conviction and affluence.

It illustrates them by fancy, which is a lighter play of imagination, or the feeling of analogy coming short of seriousness, in order that it may laugh with what it loves, and show how it can decorate it with fairy ornament.

It modulates what it utters, because in running the whole round of beauty it must needs include beauty of sound; and because, in the height of its enjoyment, it must show the perfection of its triumph, and make difficulty itself become part of its facility and joy.

And lastly, Poetry shapes this modulation into uniformity for its outline, and variety for its parts, because it thus realizes the last idea of beauty itself, which includes the charm of diversity within the flowing round of habit and ease.

Poetry is imaginative passion. The quickest and subtlest test of the possession of its essence is in expression; the variety of things to be expressed shows the amount of its resources; and the continuity of the song completes the evidence of its strength and greatness. He who has thought, feeling, expression, imagination, action, character, and continuity, all in the largest amount and highest degree, is the greatest poet.

Poetry includes whatsoever of painting can be made visible to the mind's eye, and whatsoever of music can be conveyed by sound and proportion without singing or instrumentation. But it far surpasses those divine arts in suggestiveness, range, and intellectual wealth;—the first, in expression of thought, combination of images, and the triumph over space and time—the second, in all that can be done by speech, apart from the tones and modulations of pure sound. Painting and music, however, include all those portions of the gift of poetry that can be expressed and heightened by the visible and melodious. Painting, in a certain apparent manner, is things themselves; music, in a certain audible manner, is their very emotion and grace. Music and painting are proud to be related to poetry, and poetry loves and is proud of them.

Poetry begins where matter of fact or of science ceases to be merely such, and to exhibit a further truth; that is to say, the connexion it has with the world of emotion, and its power to produce imaginative pleasure. Inquiring of a gardener, for instance, what flower it is that we see yonder, he answers, "a lily." This is matter of fact. The botanist pronounces it to be of the order of "Hexandria Monogynia." This is matter of science. It is the "lady" of the garden, says Spenser; and here we begin to have a poetical sense of its fairness and grace. It is

The plant and flower of *light*,

says Ben Jonson; and poetry then shows us the beauty of the flower in all its mystery and splendor.

If it be asked, how we know perceptions like these to be true, the answer is, by the fact of their existence,—by the consent and delight of poetic readers. And as feeling is the earliest teacher, and perception the only final proof, of things the most demonstrable by science, so the remotest imaginations of the poets may often be found to have the closest connexion with matter of fact; perhaps might always be so, if the subtlety of our perceptions were a match for the causes of them. Consider this image of Ben Jonson's—of a lily being a flower of light. Light, undecomposed, is white; and as the lily is white, and light is white, and whiteness itself is nothing *but* light, the two things, so far, are not merely similar, but identical. A poet might add, by an analogy drawn from the connexion of light and color, and there is a "golden dawn" issuing out of the white lily, in the rich yellow of the stamens. I have no desire to push this similarity further than it may be worth. Enough has been stated to show that, in poetical as in other analogies, "the same feet of Nature," as Bacon says, may be seen "treading in different paths;" and that the most scornful, that is to say, dullest disciple of fact, should be cautious how he betrays the shallowness of his philosophy by discerning no poetry in its depths.

But the poet is far from dealing only with these subtle and analogical truths. Truth of every kind belongs to him, provided it can bud into any kind of beauty, or is capable of being illustrated and impressed by the poetic faculty. Nay, the simplest truth is often so beautiful and impressive of itself, that one of the greatest proofs of his genius consists in his leaving it to stand alone, illustrated by nothing but the light of its own tears or smiles, its own wonder, might, or playfulness. Hence the complete effect of many a simple passage in our old English ballads and romances, and of the passionate sincerity in general of the greatest early poets, such as Homer and Chaucer, who flourished before the existence of a "literary world," and were not perplexed by a heap of notions and opinions, or by doubts how emotion ought to be expressed. The greatest of their successors never write equally to the purpose, except when they can dismiss everything from their minds but the like simple truth. In the beautiful poem of "Sir Eger, Sir Graham, and Sir Gray-Steel" (see it in Ellis's *Specimens*, or Laing's *Early Metrical Tales*), a knight thinks himself disgraced in the eyes of his mistress:

Sir Eger said, "If it be so,
Then wot I well I must forego
Love-liking, and manhood, all clean!"
*The water rushed out of his een!*

Sir Gray-Steel is killed:

Gray-Steel into his death thus throws (throes?)
He *walters* (welters—throws himself about) *and the grass up draws;*

* * * * *

*A little while then lay he still*
*(Friends that him saw, liked full ill)*
*And bled into his armor bright.*

The abode of Chaucer's *Reve,* or Steward, in the *Canterbury Tales,* is painted in two lines, which nobody ever wished longer:

His wonning (dwelling) was full fair upon an heath,
With greeny trees yshadowed was his place.

Every one knows the words of Lear, "most *matter-of-fact,* most melancholy."

Pray do not mock me;
I am a very foolish fond old man
Fourscore and upwards:
Not an hour more, nor less; and to deal plainly
I fear I am not in my perfect mind

It is thus, by exquisite pertinence, melody, and the implied power of writing with exuberance, if need be, that beauty and truth become identical in poetry, and that pleasure, or at the very worst, a balm in our tears, is drawn out of pain.

It is a great and rare thing, and shows a lovely imagination, when the poet can write a commentary, as it were, of his own, on such sufficing passages of nature, and be thanked for the addition. There is an instance of this kind in

Warner, an old Elizabethan poet, than which I know nothing sweeter in the world. He is speaking of Fair Rosamond, and of a blow given her by Queen Eleanor.

> With that she dash'd her on the lips,
> *So dyed double red:*
> *Hard was the heart that gave the blow,*
> *Soft were those lips that bled.*

There are different kinds and degrees of imagination, some of them necessary to the formation of every true poet, and all of them possessed by the greatest. Perhaps they may be enumerated as follows: First, that which presents to the mind any object or circumstance in every-day life; as when we imagine a man holding a sword, or looking out of a window; Second, that which presents real, but not every-day circumstances; as King Alfred tending the loaves, or Sir Philip Sidney giving up the water to the dying soldier; Third, that which combines character and events directly imitated from real life, with imitative realities of its own invention; as the probable parts of the histories of Priam and Macbeth, or what may be called natural fiction as distinguished from supernatural; Fourth, that which conjures up things and events not to be found in nature; as Homer's gods, and Shakspeare's witches, enchanted horses and spears, Ariosto's hippogriff, &c.; Fifth, that which, in order to illustrate or aggravate one image, introduces another; sometimes in simile, as when Homer compares Apollo descending in his wrath at noon-day to the coming of night-time: sometimes in metaphor or simile comprised in a word, as in Milton's "motes that *people* the sunbeams;" sometimes in concentrating into a word the main history of any person or thing, past or even future, as in the "starry Galileo" of Byron, and that ghastly foregone conclusion of the epithet "murdered" applied to the yet living victim in Keats's story from Boccaccio

> So the two brothers and their *murder'd* man
> Rode towards fair Florence;

sometimes in the attribution of a certain representative quality which makes one circumstance stand for others; as in Milton's grey-fly winding its "*sultry* horn," which epithet contains the heat of a summer's day; Sixth, that which reverses this process, and makes a variety of circumstances take color from one, like nature seen with jaundiced or glad eyes, or under the influence of storm or sunshine; as when in "Lycidas," or the Greek pastoral poets, the flowers and the flocks are made to sympathize with a man's death; or, in the Italian poet, the river flowing by the sleeping Angelica seems talking of love

> *Parea che l' erba le fiorisse intorno,*
> *E d' amor ragionasse quella riva!*
> *Orlando Innamorato,* Canto iii

or in the voluptuous homage paid to the sleeping Imogen by the very light in the chamber and the reaction of her own beauty upon itself; or in the "witch element" of the tragedy of *Macbeth* and the May-day night of *Faust;* Seventh, and last, that which by a single expression, apparently of the vaguest kind, not only meets but surpasses in its effect the extremest force of the most particular description; as in that exquisite passage of Coleridge's *Christabel,* where the unsuspecting object of the witch's malignity is bidden to go to bed:

> Quoth Christabel, So let it be!
> And as the lady bade, did she.
> Her gentle limbs did she undress,
> *And lay down in her loveliness;*

a perfect verse surely, both for feeling and music. The very smoothness and gentleness of the limbs is in the series of the letter *l's*.

I am aware of nothing of the kind surpassing the most lovely inclusion of physical beauty in moral, neither can I call to mind any instances of the imagination that turns accompaniments into accessories, superior to those I have alluded to. Of the class of comparison, one of the most touching (many a tear must it have drawn from parents and lovers) is in a stanza which has been copied into the "Friar of Orders Grey," out of Beaumont and Fletcher:

> Weep no more, lady, weep no more,
>   Thy sorrow is in vain;
> *For violets pluck'd the sweetest showers*
>   *Will ne'er make grow again.*

And Shakspeare and Milton abound in the very grandest; such as Antony's likening his changing fortunes to the cloud-rack; Lear's appeal to the old age of the heavens; Satan's appearance in the horizon, like a fleet "hanging in the clouds;" and the comparisons of him with the comet and the eclipse. Nor unworthy of this glorious company, for its extraordinary combination of delicacy and vastness, is that enchanting one of Shelley's in the *Adonais:*

> Life, like a dome of many-colored glass,
> Stains the white radiance of eternity.

I multiply these particulars in order to impress upon the reader's mind the great importance of imagination in all its phases, as a constituent part of the highest poetic faculty.

The happiest instance I remember of imaginative metaphor is Shakspeare's moonlight "sleeping" on a bank; but half his poetry may be said to be made up of it, metaphor indeed being the common coin of discourse. Of imaginary creatures, none out of the pale of mythology and the East, are equal, perhaps, in point of invention, to Shakspeare's Ariel and Caliban; though poetry may grudge to prose the discovery of a Winged Woman, especially such as she has been described by her inventor in the story of Peter Wilkins; and in point of treatment, the Mammon and Jealousy of Spenser, some of the monsters in Dante, particularly his Nimrod, his interchangements of creatures into one another, and (if I am not presumptuous in anticipating what I think will be the verdict of posterity) the Witch in Coleridge's *Christabel,* may rank even with the creations of Shakspeare. It may be doubted, indeed, whether Shakspeare had bile and nightmare enough in him to have thought of such detestable horrors as those of the interchanging adversaries (now serpent, now man), or even of the huge, half-blockish enormity of Nimrod,—in Scripture, the "mighty hunter" and builder of the tower of Babel,—in Dante, a tower of a man in his own person, standing with some of his brother giants up to the middle in a pit in hell, blowing a horn to which a thunder-clap is a whisper, and hallooing after Dante and his guide in the jargon of the lost tongue! The transformations are too odious to quote: but of the towering giant we cannot refuse ourselves the "fearful joy" of a specimen. It was twilight, Dante tells us, and he and his guide Virgil were silently pacing through one of the dreariest regions of hell, when the sound of a tremendous horn made him turn all his attention to the spot from which it came. He there discovered through the dusk, what seemed to be the towers of a city. Those are no towers, said his guide; they are giants, standing up to the middle in one of these circular pits.

*Come quando la nibbia si dissipa,*
*Lo sguardo a poco a poco raffigura*
*Ciò che cela l' vapor che l' aere stipa;*
*Così forando l' aer grossa e scura*
*Più e più appressando in ver la sponda,*
*Fuggémi errore, e giugnemi paura:*
*Perocchè come in su la cerchia tonda*
*Montereggion di torri si corona,*
*Così la proda che 'l pozzo circonda*
*Torreggiavan di mezza la persona*
*Gli orribili giganti, cui minaccia*
*Giove del cielo ancora, quando tuona:*
*Ed io scorgeva già' d'alcun la faccia,*
*Le spalle e 'l petto, e del ventre gran parte,*
*E per le coste giù ambo le braccia.*

* * * *

*La faccia sua mi parea lunga e grossa*
*Come la pina di san Pietro a Roma:*
*E a sua proporzion eran l'altr' ossa.*

* * * *

*Rafel mai amech zabì almi*
*Cominciò a gridar la fiera bocca,*
*Cui non si convenien più dolci salmi.*
*E 'l duca mio ver lui: anima sciocca,*
*Tienti col corno, e con quel ti disfoga,*
*Quand' ira o altra passion ti tocca.*
*Cercati al collo, e troverai la soga*

*Che 'l tien legato, o anima confusa,*
*E vedi lui che 'l gran petto ti doga.*
*Poi disse a me: egli stesso s' accusa:*
*Questi è Nembrotto, per lo cui mal coto*
*Pure un linguaggio nel mondo non s' usa.*
*Lasciamlo stare, e non parliamo a voto:*
*Che così è a lui ciascun linguaggio,*
*Come 'l suo ad altrui ch' a nullo è noto.*
*Inferno,* Canto xxxi., ver. 34

I look'd again; and as the eye makes out,
By little and little, what the mist conceal'd
In which, till clearing up, the sky was steep'd;
So, looming through the gross and darksome air,
As we drew nigh, those mighty bulks grew plain,
And error quitted me, and terror join'd:
For in like manner as all round its height
Montereggione crowns itself with towers,
So tower'd above the circuit of that pit,
Though but half out of it, and half within,
The horrible giants that fought Jove, and still
Are threaten'd when he thunders. As we near'd
The foremost, I discern'd his mighty face,
His shoulders, breast, and more than half his trunk,
With both the arms down hanging by the sides.
His face appear'd to me, in length and breadth,
Huge as St. Peter's pinnacle at Rome,
And of a like proportion all his bones.
He open'd, as he went, his dreadful mouth,
Fit for no sweeter psalmody; and shouted
After us, in the words of some strange tongue,
Ràfel ma-èe amech zabèe almee!—
"Dull wretch!" my leader cried, "keep to thine born,
And so vent better whatsoever rage
Or other passion stuff thee. Feel thy throat
And find the chain upon thee, thou confusion!
Lo! what a hoop is clench'd about thy gorge."
Then turning to myself, he said, "His howl
Is its own mockery. This is Nimrod, he
Through whose ill thought it was that humankind
Were tongue-confounded. Pass him, and say naught:
For as he speaketh language known of none,
So none can speak save jargon to himself."

Assuredly it could not have been easy to find a fiction so uncouthly terrible as this in the hypochondria of Hamlet. Even his father had evidently seen no such ghost in the other world. All his phantoms were in the world he had left. Timon, Lear, Richard, Brutus, Prospero, Macbeth himself, none of Shakspeare's men had, in fact, any thought but of the earth they lived on, whatever supernatural fancy crossed them. The thing fancied was still a thing of this world, "in its habit as it lived," or no remoter acquaintance than a witch or a fairy. Its lowest depths (unless Dante suggested them) were the cellars under the stage. Caliban himself is a cross-breed between a witch and a clown. No offence to Shakspeare; who was not bound to be the greatest of healthy poets, and to have every morbid inspiration besides. What he might have done, had he set his wits to compete with Dante, I know not: all I know is, that in the infernal line he did nothing like him; and it is not to be wished he had. It is far better that, as a higher, more universal, and more beneficent variety of the genus Poet, he should have been the happier man he was, and left us the plump cheeks on his monument, instead of the carking visage of the great, but over-serious, and comparatively one-sided Florentine. Even the imagination of Spenser, whom we take to have been a "nervous gentleman" compared with Shakspeare, was visited with no such dreams as Dante. Or, if it was, he did not choose to make himself thinner (as Dante says *he* did) with dwelling upon them. He had twenty visions of nymphs and bowers, to one of the mud of Tartarus. Chaucer, for all he was "a man of this world" as well as the poets' world, and as great, perhaps a greater enemy of oppression than Dante, besides being one of the profoundest masters of pathos that ever lived, had not the heart to conclude the story of the famished father and his children, as finished by the inexorable anti-Pisan. But enough of Dante in this place. Hobbes, in order to daunt the reader from objecting to his friend Davenant's want of invention, says of these fabulous creations in general, in his letter prefixed to the poem of *Gondibert,* that "impenetrable armors, enchanted castles, invulnerable bodies, iron men, flying horses, and a thousand other such things, are easily feigned by them that dare." These are girds at Spenser and Ariosto. But, with leave of Hobbes (who translated Homer as if on purpose to show what execrable verses could be written by a philosopher), enchanted castles and flying horses are not easily feigned, as Ariosto and Spenser feigned them; and that just makes all the difference. For proof, see the accounts of Spenser's enchanted castle in Book the Third, Canto Twelfth, of the *Fairy Queen;* and let the reader of Italian open the *Orlando Furioso* at its first introduction of the Hippogriff (Canto iii., st. 4), where Bradamante, coming to an inn, hears a great noise, and sees all the people looking up at something in the air; upon which, looking up herself, she sees a knight in shining armor riding towards the sunset upon a creature with variegated wings, and then dipping and disappearing among the hills. Chaucer's steed of brass, that was

So horsly and so quick of eye,

is copied from the life. You might pat him and feel his brazen muscles. Hobbes, in objecting to what he thought childish, made a childish mistake. His criticism is just such as a boy might pique himself upon, who was educated on mechanical principles, and thought he had outgrown his Goody Two-shoes. With a wonderful dimness of discernment in poetic matters, considering his acuteness in others, he fancies he has settled the question by pronouncing such creations "impossible!" To the brazier they are impossible, no doubt; but not to the poet. Their possibility, if the poet wills it, is to be conceded; the problem is, the creature being given, how to square its actions with probability, according to the nature assumed of it. Hobbes did not see, that the skill and beauty of these fictions lay in bringing them within those very regions of truth and likelihood in which he thought they could not exist. Hence the serpent Python of Chaucer,

Sleeping against the sun upon a day,

when Apollo slew him. Hence the chariot-drawing dolphins of Spenser, softly swimming along the shore lest they should hurt themselves against the stones and gravel. Hence Shakspeare's Ariel, living under blossoms, and riding at evening on the bat; and his domestic namesake in the *Rape of the Lock* (the imagination of the drawing-room) saving a lady's petticoat from the coffee with his plumes, and directing atoms of snuff into a coxcomb's nose. In the *Orlando Furioso* (Canto xv., st. 65) is a wild story of a cannibal necromancer, who laughs at being cut to pieces, coming together again like quicksilver, and picking up his head when it is cut off, sometimes by the hair, sometimes by the nose! This, which would be purely childish and ridiculous in the hands of an inferior poet, becomes interesting, nay grand, in Ariosto's, from the beauties of his style, and its conditional truth to nature. The monster has a fated hair on his head,—a single hair,—which must be taken from it before he can be killed. Decapitation itself is of no consequence, without that proviso. The Paladin Astolfo, who has fought this phenomenon on horseback, and succeeded in getting the head and galloping off with it, is therefore still at a loss what to be at. How is he to discover such a needle in such a bottle of hay? The trunk is spurring after him to recover it, and he seeks for some evidence of the hair in vain. At length he bethinks himself of scalping the head. He does so; and the moment the operation arrives at the place of the hair, *the face of the head becomes pale, the eyes turn in their sockets,* and the lifeless pursuer tumbles from his horse.

*Si fece il viso allor pallido e brutto,*
*Travolse gli occhi, e dimostrò a 'l occaso*
*Per manifesti segni esser condutto.*
*E 'l busto che seguia troncato al collo,*
*Di sella cadde, e diè l' ultimo crollo*

Then grew the visage pale, and deadly wet;
The eyes turned in their sockets, drearily;
And all things show'd the villain's sun was set.
His trunk that was in chase, fell from its horse,
And giving the last shudder, was a corse.

It is thus, and thus only, by making Nature his companion wherever he goes, even in the most supernatural region, that the poet, in the words of a very instructive phrase, takes the world along with him. It is true, he must not (as the Platonists would say) humanize weakly or mistakenly in that region; otherwise he runs the chance of forgetting to be true to the supernatural itself, and so betraying a want of imagination from that quarter. His nymphs will have no taste of their woods and waters; his gods and goddesses be only so many fair or frowning ladies and gentlemen, such as we see in ordinary paintings; he will be in no danger of having his angels likened to a sort of wildfowl, as Rembrandt has made them in his Jacob's Dream. His Bacchus's will never remind us, like Titian's, of the force and fury, as well as of the graces, of wine. His Jupiter will reduce no females to ashes; his fairies be nothing fantastical; his gnomes not "of the earth, earthy." And this again will be wanting to Nature; for it will be wanting to the supernatural, as Nature would have made it, working in a supernatural direction. Nevertheless, the poet, even for imagination's sake, must not become a bigot to imaginative truth, dragging it down into the region of the mechanical and the limited, and losing sight of its paramount privilege, which is to make beauty, in a human sense, the lady and queen of the universe. He would gain nothing by making his ocean-nymphs mere fishy creatures, upon the plea that such only could live in the water: his wood-nymphs with faces of knotted oak; his angels without breath and song, because no lungs could exist between the earth's atmosphere and the empyrean. The Grecian tendency in this respect is safer than the Gothic; nay, more imaginative; for it enables us to imagine *beyond* imagination, and to bring all things healthily round to their only present final ground of sympathy—the human. When we go to heaven, we may idealize in a superhuman mode, and have altogether different notions of the beautiful; but till then, we must be content with the loveliest capabilities of earth. The sea-nymphs of Greece were still beautiful women, though they lived in the water. The gills and fins of the ocean's natural inhabitants were confined to their lowest semi-human attendants; or if Triton himself was not quite human, it was because he represented the fiercer part of the vitality of the seas, as they did the fairer.

To conclude this part of my subject, I will quote from the greatest of all narrative writers two passages;—one exemplifying the imagination which brings supernatural things to bear on earthly, without confounding them; the other, that which paints events and circumstances after real life. The first is where Achilles, who has long absented himself from the conflict between his countrymen and the Trojans, has had a message from heaven, bidding him re-appear in the enemy's sight, standing outside the camp-wall upon the trench, but doing nothing more; that is to say, taking no part in the fight. He is simply to be seen. The two armies down by the sea-side are contending which shall possess the body of Patroclus; and the mere sight of the dreadful Grecian chief—supernaturally indeed impressed upon them, in order that nothing may be wanting to the full effect of his courage and conduct upon courageous men—is to determine the question. We are to imagine a slope of ground towards the sea, in order to elevate the trench; the camp is solitary; the battle ("a dreadful roar of men," as Homer calls it) is raging on the sea-shore; and the goddess Iris has just delivered her message, and disappeared.

Αυταρ Αχιλλευς ωρτο Δυ φιλος· αμφι δ' Αθηνη
Ωμοις ιφθιμοισι βαλ' αιγιδα θυσσανοεσσαν·
Αμφι δε ὁι κεφαλη νεφος εστεφε δια θεαων
Χρυσεον, εκ δ' αυτου δαιε φλογα παμφανοωσαν.
'Ως δ' ὁτε καπνος ιων εξ αστεος αιθερ' ἱκηται
Τηλοθεν εκ νησου, την δηιοι αμφιμαχονται,
'Οιτε πανημεριοι στυγερω κρινονται Αρηι
Αστεος εκ σφετερου· ἁμα δ' ηελιω καταδυντι
Πυρσοι τε φλεγεθουσιν επητριμοι, ὑψοσε δ' αυγη
Γιγνεται αισσουσα, περικτιονεσσιν ιδεσθαι,
Αι κεν πως συν νηυσιν αρης αλκτηρες ἱκωνται·
'Ως απ' Αχιλληος κεφαλης σελας αιθεῤ ἱκανεν.

Στη δ' επι ταφρον ιων απο τειχεος· ουδ' ες Αχαιους
Μισγετο· μητρος γαρ πυκινην ωπιζετ' εφετμην.
Ενθα στας ηυσ'· απατερθε δε Παλλας Αθηνη
Φθεγξατ'· αταρ Τρωεσσιν εν ασπετον ωρσε κυδοιμον
'Ως δ' ὁτ αριζηλη φωνη, ὁτε τ' ιαχε σαλπιγξ
Αστυ περιπλομενων δηιων ὑπο θυμοραιστεων·
'Ως τοτ' αριζηλη φωνη γενετ' Αιακιδαο.
'Οι δ' ὡς ουν αιον οπα χαλκεον Αιακιδαο,
Πασιν ορινθη θυμος· αταρ καλλιτριχες ἱπποι
Αψ οχεα τροπεον· οσσοντο γαρ αλγεα θυμω.
'Ηνιοχοι δ' εκπληγεν, επει ιδον ακαματον πυρ
Δεινον ὑπερ κεφαλης μεγαθυμου Πηλειωνος
Δαιομενον· το δε δαιε θεα γλαυκωπις Αθηνη.
Τρις μεν ὑπερ ταφρου μεγαλ' ιαχε διος Αχιλλευς,
Τρις δε κυκηθησαν Τρωες, κλειτοι τ' επικουροι.
Ενθα δε και τοτ' ολοντο δυωδεκα φωτες αριστοι
Αμφι σφοις οχεεσσι και εγχεσιν.

*Iliad*, Lib. xviii., v. 903

But up Achilles rose, the lov'd of heaven;
And Pallas on his mighty shoulders cast
The shield of Jove; and round about his head
She put the glory of a golden mist,
From which there burnt a fiery-flaming light.
And as, when smoke goes heaven-ward from a town,
In some far island which its foes besiege,
Who all day long with dreadful martialness
Have pour'd from their own town; soon as the sun
Has set, thick lifted fires are visible,
Which, rushing upward, make a light in the sky,
And let the neighbors know, who may perhaps

Bring help across the sea; so from the head
Of great Achilles went up an effulgence.

Upon the trench he stood, without the wall,
But mix'd not with the Greeks, for he rever'd
His mother's word; and so, thus standing there,
He shouted; and Minerva, to his shout,
Added a dreadful cry; and there arose
Among the Trojans an unspeakable tumult.
And as the clear voice of a trumpet, blown
Against a town by spirit-withering foes,
So sprang the clear voice of Æacides.
And when they heard the brazen cry, their hearts
All leap'd within them; and the proud-maned horses
Ran with the chariots round, for they foresaw
Calamity; and the charioteers were smitten,
When they beheld the ever-active fire
Upon the dreadful head of the great-minded one
Burning; for bright-eyed Pallas made it burn.
Thrice o'er the trench divine Achilles shouted;
And thrice the Trojans and their great allies
Roll'd back; and twelve of all their noblest men
Then perished, crush'd by their own arms and chariots.

Of course there is no further question about the body of Patroclus. It is drawn out of the press, and received by the awful hero with tears.

The other passage is where Priam, kneeling before Achilles, and imploring him to give up the dead body of Hector, reminds him of his own father; who, whatever (says the poor old king) may be his troubles with his enemies, has the blessing of knowing that his son is still alive, and may daily hope to see him return. Achilles, in accordance with the strength and noble honesty of the passions in those times, weeps aloud himself at this appeal, feeling, says Homer, "desire" for his father in his very "limbs." He joins in grief with the venerable sufferer, and can no longer withstand the look of "his great head and his grey *chin*." Observe the exquisite introduction of this last word. It paints the touching fact of the chin's being imploringly thrown upward by the kneeling old man, and the very motion of his beard as he speaks.

'Ως αρα φωνησας απεβη προς μακρον Ολυμπον
'Ερμειας· Πριαμος δ' εξ ἱππων αλτο χαμαζε,
Ιδαιον δε κατ' αυθι λιπεν· ὁ δε μιμνεν ερυκων
'Ιππους ἡμιονους τε· γερων δ' ιθυς κιεν οικου,
Τη ῥ' Αχιλευς ἱζεσκε, Δυ φιλος· εν δε μιν αυτον
'Ευρ· ἑταροι δ' απανευθε καθειατο· τω δε δυ' οιω,
'Ηρως Αυτομεδων τε και Αλκιμος, οζος Αρηος,
Ποιπνυον παρεοντε· νεον δ' απεληγεν εδωδης

Εσθων και πινων, ετι και παρεκειτο τραπεζα.
Τους δ' ελαθ' εισελθων Πριαμος μεγας, αγχι δ' αρα στας
Χερσιν Αχιλληος λαβε γουνατα, και κυσε χειρας
Δεινας, ανδροφονους, αἵ οἱ πολεας κτανον υιας.
'Ως δ' όταν ανδρ' ατη πυκινη λαβη, όστ' ενι πατρη
Φωτα κατακτεινας, αλλων εξικετο δημον,
Ανδρος ες αφνειου, θαμβος δ' εχει εισορωωντας,
'Ως Αχιλευς θαμβησεν, ιδων Πριαμον θεοειδεα·
Θαμβησαν δε και αλλοι, ες αλληλους δε ιδοντο.
Τον και λισσομενος Πριαμος προς μυθον εειπεν·

Μνησαι πατρος σειο, θεοις επιεικελ' Αχιλλευ,
Τηλικου, ώσπερ εγων, ολοω επι γηραος ουδω.
Και μεν που κεινον περιναιεται αμφις εοντες
Τειρουσ', ουδε τις εστιν αρην και λοιγον αμυναι·
Αλλ' ήτοι κεινος γε, σεθεν ζωοντος ακουων,
Χαιρει τ' εν θυμω, επι τ' ελπεται ηματα παντα
Οψεσθαι φιλον ὑιον απο Τροιηθεν ιοντα·
Αυταρ εγω πανατοτμος, επει τεκον ὑιας αριστου
Τροιη εν ευρειη, των δ' ουτινα φημι λελειφθαι.
Πεντηκοντα μοι ησαν, ότ' ηλυθον υιες Αχαιων·
Εννεακαιδεκα μεν μοι ιης εκ νηδυος ησαν,
Τους δ' αλλους μοι ετικτον ενι μεγαροισι γυναικες.
Των μεν πολλων θουρος Αρης ὑπο γουνατ' ελυσεν·
'Ως δε μοι οιος εην, ειρυτο δε αστυ και αυτους,
Τον συ πρωην κτεινας, αμυνομενον περι πατρης,
'Εκτορα· του νυν έινεχ' ίκανω νηας Αχαιων,
Λυσομενος παρα σειο, φερω δ' απερεισί αποινα.
Αλλ' αιδειο θεους, Αχιλευ, αυτον τ' ελεησον,
Μνησαμενος σου πατρος· εγω δ' ελεεινοτερος περ,
Ετλην δ', όι ουπω τις επιχθονιος βροτος αλλος,
Ανδρος παιδοφονιο ποτι στομα χειρ' ορεγεσθαι.
'Ως φατο· τω δ' αρα πατρος ὑφ' ίμερον ωρσε γοοιο.
Αψαμενος δ' αρα χειρος, απωσατο ηκα γεροντα.
Τω δε μνησαμενω, ὁ μεν 'Εκτορος ανδροφονοιο,
Κλαι' αδινα, προπαροιθε ποδων Αχιληος ελυσθεις·
Αυταρ Αχιλλευς κλαιεν έον πατερ', αλλοτε δ' αυτε
Πατροκλον· των δε στοναχη κατα δωματ' ορωρει.
Αυταρ επει ῥα γοοιο τεταρπετο διος Αχιλλευς,
Και όι απο πραπιδων ηλθ' ίμερος ηδ' απο γυιων,
Αυτικ' απο θρονου ωρτο, γεροντα δε χειρος ανιστη,
Οικτειρων πολιον τε καρη, πολιον τε γενειον.
*Iliad*, Lib. xxiv., v. 468

So saying, Mercury vanished up to heaven:
And Priam then alighted from his chariot,

Leaving Idœus with it, who remain'd
Holding the mules and horses; and the old man
Went straight in-doors, where the belov'd of Jove
Achilles sat, and found him. In the room
Were others, but apart; and two alone,
The hero Automedon, and Alcimus,
A branch of Mars, stood by him. They had been
At meals, and had not yet removed the board.
Great Priam came, without their seeing him,
And kneeling down, he clasp'd Achilles' knees,
And kiss'd those terrible, homicidal hands,
Which had deprived him of so many sons.
And as a man who is press'd heavily
For having slain another, flies away
To foreign lands, and comes into the house
Of some great man, and is beheld with wonder,
So did Achilles wonder to see Priam;
And the rest wonder'd, looking at each other.
But Priam, praying to him, spoke these words:
"God-like Achilles, think of thine own father!
To the same age have we both come, the same
Weak pass; and though the neighboring chiefs may vex
Him also, and his borders find no help,
Yet when he hears that thou art still alive,
He gladdens inwardly, and daily hopes
To see his dear son coming back from Troy.
But I, bereav'd old Priam! I had once
Brave sons in Troy, and now I cannot say
That one is left me. Fifty children had I,
When the Greeks came; nineteen were of one womb;
The rest my women bore me in my house.
The knees of many of these fierce Mars has loosen'd;
And he who had no peer, Troy's prop and theirs,
Him has thou kill'd now, fighting for his country,
Hector; and for his sake am I come here
To ransom him, bringing a countless ransom.
But thou, Achilles, fear the gods, and think
Of thine own father, and have mercy on me;
For I am much more wretched, and have borne
What never mortal bore, I think, on earth,
To lift unto my lips the hand of him
Who slew my boys."
                He ceased; and there arose
Sharp longing in Achilles for his father;
And taking Priam by the hand, he gently
Put him away; for both shed tears to think

Of other times; the one, most bitter ones
For Hector, and with wilful wretchedness
Lay right before Achilles: and the other,
For his own father now, and now his friend;
And the whole house might hear them as they moan'd.
But when divine Achilles had refresh'd
His soul with tears, and sharp desire had left
His heart and limbs, he got up from his throne,
And rais'd the old man by the hand, and took
Pity on his grey head and his grey chin.

O lovely and immortal privilege of genius! that can stretch its hand out of the wastes of time, thousands of years back, and touch our eyelids with tears. In these passages there is not a word which a man of the most matter-of-fact understanding might not have written, *if he had thought of it*. But in poetry, feeling and imagination are necessary to the perception and presentation even of matters of fact. They, and they only, see what is proper to be told, and what to be kept back; what is pertinent, affecting, and essential. Without feeling, there is a want of delicacy and distinction; without imagination, there is no true embodiment. In poets, even good of their kind, but without a genius for narration, the action would have been encumbered or diverted with ingenious mistakes. The over-contemplative would have given us too many remarks; the over-lyrical, a style too much carried away; the over-fanciful, conceits and too many similes; the unimaginative, the facts without the feeling, and not even those. We should have been told nothing of the "grey chin," of the house hearing them as they moaned, or of Achilles gently putting the old man aside; much less of that yearning for his father, which made the hero tremble in every limb. Writers without the greatest passion and power do not feel in this way, nor are capable of expressing the feeling; though there is enough sensibility and imagination all over the world to enable mankind to be moved by it, when the poet strikes his truth into their hearts.

The reverse of imagination is exhibited in pure absence of ideas, in commonplaces, and, above all, in conventional metaphor, or such images and their phraseology as have become the common property of discourse and writing. Addison's *Cato* is full of them.

Passion unpitied and successless love
*Plant daggers in my breast.*

I've sounded my Numidians, man by man,
And find them *ripe for a revolt.*

The virtuous Marcia *towers above her sex.*

Of the same kind is his "courting the yoke"—"distracting my very heart"—"calling up all" one's "father" in one's soul—"working every nerve"—"copying a bright example;" in short, the whole play, relieved now and then with a smart sentence or turn of words. The following is a pregnant example of plagiarism and weak writing. It is from another tragedy of Addison's time,—the *Mariamne* of Fenton:

> Mariamne, *with superior charms,*
> *Triumphs o'er reason:* in her look she *bears*
> A paradise of ever-blooming sweets;
> Fair as the first idea beauty *prints*
> In her young lover's soul; a winning grace
> Guides every gesture, and obsequious love
> *Attends* on all her steps.

"Triumphing o'er reason" is an old acquaintance of everybody's. "Paradise in her look" is from the Italian poets through Dryden. "Fair as the first idea," &c., is from Milton spoilt; "winning grace" and "steps" from Milton and Tibullus, both spoilt. Whenever beauties are stolen by such a writer, they are sure to be spoilt; just as when a great writer borrows, he improves.

To come now to Fancy,—she is a younger sister of Imagination, without the other's weight of thought and feeling. Imagination indeed, purely so called, is all feeling; the feeling of the subtlest and most affecting analogies; the perception of sympathies in the natures of things, or in their popular attributes. Fancy is sporting with their resemblance, real or supposed, and with airy and fantastical creations.

> Rouse yourself; and the weak wanton Cupid
> Shall from your neck unloose his amorous fold,
> *And, like a dew-drop from the lion's mane,*
> *Be shook to air.*
>
> *Troilus and Cressida,* Act. iii., sc. 3

That is imagination;—the strong mind sympathizing with the strong beast, and the weak love identified with the weak dew-drop.

> Oh!—and I forsooth
> In love! I that have been love's whip!
> *A very beadle to a humorous sigh!—*
> A domineering pedant o'er the boy,—
> This whimpled, whining, purblind, wayward boy,—
> This senior-junior, giant-dwarf, Dan Cupid,
> *Regent of love-rhymes, lord of folded arms,*
> *The anointed sovereign of sighs and groans,* &c.
>
> *Love's Labor's Lost,* Act iii., sc. 1

That is fancy;—a combination of images not in their nature connected, or brought together by the feeling, but by the will and pleasure; and having just enough hold of analogy to betray it into the hands of its smiling subjector.

> Silent icicles
> *Quietly shining to the quiet moon.*
>
> Coleridge's *Frost at Midnight*

That, again, is imagination;—analogical sympathy; and exquisite of its kind it is.

> You are now sailed *into the north of my lady's opinion;* where you will hang *like an icicle on a Dutchman's beard,* unless you do redeem it by some laudable attempt.
>
> *Twelfth Night,* Act iii., sc. 2

And that is fancy;—one image capriciously suggested by another, and but half connected with the subject of discourse; nay, half opposed to it; for in the gaiety of the speaker's animal spirits, the "Dutchman's beard" is made to represent the lady!

Imagination belongs to Tragedy, or the serious muse; Fancy to the comic. *Macbeth, Lear, Paradise Lost,* the poem of Dante, are full of imagination: the *Midsummer Night's Dream* and the *Rape of the Lock,* of fancy: *Romeo and Juliet,* the *Tempest,* the *Fairy Queen,* and the *Orlando Furioso,* of both. The terms were formerly identical, or used as such; and neither is the best that might be found. The term Imagination is too confined: often too material. It presents too invariably the idea of a solid body;—of "images" in the sense of the plaster-cast cry about the streets. Fancy, on the other hand, while it means nothing but a spiritual image or apparition (appearance, *phantom*), has rarely that freedom from visibility which is one of the highest privileges of imagination. Viola, in *Twelfth Night,* speaking of some beautiful music, says:

> It gives a very echo to the seat,
> Where Love is throned.

In this charming thought, fancy and imagination are combined; yet the fancy, the assumption of Love's sitting on a throne, is the image of a solid body; while the imagination, the sense of sympathy between the passion of love and impassioned music, presents us no image at all. Some new term is wanting to express the more spiritual sympathies of what is called Imagination.

One of the teachers of Imagination is Melancholy; and like Melancholy, as Albert Durer has painted her, she looks out among the stars, and is busied with spiritual affinities and the mysteries of the universe. Fancy turns her sister's wizard instruments into toys. She takes a telescope in her hand, and puts a mimic star on her forehead, and sallies forth as an emblem of astronomy. Her tendency is to the child-like and sportive. She chases butterflies, while her sister takes flight with angels. She is the genius of fairies, of gallantries, of fashions; of whatever is quaint and light, showy and capricious; of the poetical part of wit. She adds wings and feelings to the images of wit; and delights as much to people nature with smiling ideal sympathies, as wit does to bring antipathies together, and make them strike light on absurdity. Fancy, however, is not incapable of sympathy with Imagination. She is often found in her company; always, in the case of the greatest poets; often in that of less, though with them she is the greater favorite. Spenser has great imagination and fancy too, but more of the latter; Milton both also, the very greatest, but with imagination predominant; Chaucer, the strongest imagination of real life, beyond any writers but Homer, Dante, and Shakspeare, and in comic painting inferior to none; Pope has hardly any imagination, but he has a great deal of fancy; Coleridge little fancy, but imagination exquisite. Shakspeare alone, of all poets that ever lived, enjoyed the regard of both in equal perfection. A whole fairy poem of his writing will be found in the present volume. See also his famous description of Queen Mab and her equipage, in *Romeo and Juliet:*

> Her waggon-spokes made of long spinners' legs;
> The cover, of the wings of grasshoppers;
> Her traces of the smallest spider's web;
> Her collars of the moonshine's watery beams, &c.

That is Fancy, in its playful creativeness. As a small but pretty rival specimen, less known, take the description of a fairy palace from Drayton's *Nymphidia:*

> This palace standeth in the air,
> By necromancy placèd there,
> That it no tempest needs to fear,
> Which way soe'er it blow it:
> And somewhat southward tow'rd the noon,
> Whence lies a way up to the moon,
> And thence the Fairy can as soon
> Pass to the earth below it.
> The walls of spiders' legs are made,
> Well morticèd and finely laid:
> He was the master of his trade,
> It curiously that builded:
> *The windows of the eyes of cats:*

(because they see best at night)

> And for the roof instead of slats
> Is cover'd with the skins of bats
> *With moonshine tint are gilded.*

Here also is a fairy bed, very delicate, from the same poet's *Muse's Elysium.*

> Of leaves of roses, *white and red,*
> Shall be the covering of the bed;
> The curtains, vallens, tester all,
> Shall be the flower imperial;
> And for the fringe it all along
> *With azure hare-bells shall be hung.*
> *Of lilies shall the pillows be*
> *With down stuft of the butterfly.*

Of fancy, so full of gusto as to border on imagination, Sir John Suckling, in his "Ballad on a Wedding," has given some of the most playful and charming specimens in the language. They glance like twinkles in the eye, or cherries bedewed:

*Her feet beneath her petticoat,*
*Like little mice stole in and out,*
  *As if they fear'd the light;*
But oh! she dances such a way!
*No sun upon an Easter day,*
  Is half so fine a sight.

It is very daring, and has a sort of playful grandeur, to compare a lady's dancing with the sun. But as the sun has it all to himself in the heavens, so she, in the blaze of her beauty, on earth. This is imagination fairly displacing fancy. The following has enchanted everybody:—

Her lips were red, *and one was thin,*
*Compared with that was next her chin,*
  *Some bee had stung it newly.*

Every reader has stolen a kiss at that lip, gay or grave.

With regard to the principle of Variety in Uniformity by which verse ought to be modulated, and one-ness of impression diversely produced, it has been contended by some, that Poetry need not be written in verse at all; that prose is as good a medium, provided poetry be conveyed through it; and that to think otherwise is to confound letter with spirit, or form with essence. But the opinion is a prosaical mistake. Fitness and unfitness for *song,* or metrical excitement, just make all the difference between a poetical and prosaical subject; and the reason why verse is necessary to the form of poetry, is, that the perfection of poetical spirit demands it; that the circle of enthusiasm, beauty, and power, is incomplete without it. I do not mean to say that a poet can never show himself a poet in prose; but that, being one, his desire and necessity will be to write in verse; and that, if he were unable to do so, he would not, and could not, deserve his title. Verse to the true poet is no clog. It is idly called a trammel and a difficulty. It is a help. It springs from the same enthusiasm as the rest of his impulses, and is necessary to their satisfaction and effect. Verse is no more a clog than the condition of rushing upward is a clog to fire, or than the roundness and order of the globe we live on is a clog to the freedom and variety that abound within its sphere. Verse is no dominator over the poet, except inasmuch as the bond is reciprocal, and the poet dominates over the verse. They are lovers playfully challenging each other's rules, and delighted equally to rule and to obey. Verse is the final proof to the poet that his mastery over his art is complete. It is the shutting up of his powers in "*measureful* content;" the answer of form to his spirit; of strength and ease to his guidance. It is the willing action, the proud and fiery happiness, of the winged steed on whose back he has vaulted,

To witch the world with wondrous horsemanship.

Verse, in short, is that finishing, and rounding, and "tuneful planetting" of the poet's creations, which is produced of necessity by the smooth tendencies of their energy or inward working, and the harmonious dance into which they are attracted round the orb of the beautiful. Poetry, in its complete sympathy with beauty, must, of necessity, leave no sense of the beautiful, and no power over its forms, unmanifested; and verse flows as inevitably from this condition of its integrity, as other laws of proportion do from any other kind of embodiment of beauty (say that of the human figure), however free and various the movements may be that play within their limits. What great poet ever wrote his poems in prose? or where is a good prose poem, of any length, to be found? The poetry of the Bible is understood to be in verse, in the original. Mr. Hazlitt has said a good word for those prose enlargements of some fine old song, which are known by the name of Ossian; and in passages they deserve what he said; but he judiciously abstained from saying anything about the form. Is Gesner's *Death of Abel* a poem? or Hervey's *Meditations*? The *Pilgrim's Progress* has been called one; and, undoubtedly, Bunyan had a genius which tended to make him a poet, and one of no mean order; and yet it was of as ungenerous and low a sort as was compatible with so lofty an affinity; and this is the reason why it stopped where it did. He had a craving after the beautiful, but not enough of it in himself to echo to its music. On the other hand, the possession of the beautiful will not be sufficient without force to utter it. The author of Telemachus had a soul full of beauty and tenderness. He was not a man who, if he had had a wife and children, would have run away from them, as Bunyan's hero did, to get a place by himself in heaven. He was "a little lower than the angels," like our own Bishop Jewells and Berkeleys; and yet he was no poet. He was too delicately, not to say feebly, absorbed in his devotions, to join in the energies of the seraphic choir.

Every poet, then, is a versifier; every fine poet an excellent one; and he is the best whose verse exhibits the greatest amount of strength, sweetness, straightforwardness, unsuperfluousness, *variety*, and *one-ness;* one-ness, that is to say, consistency, in the general impression, metrical and moral; and variety, or every pertinent diversity of tone and rhythm, in the process. *Strength* is the muscle of verse, and shows itself in the number and force of the marked syllables; as,

Sonòrous mètal blòwing màrtial sòunds.
*Paradise Lost*

Behèmoth, bìggest born of eàrth, ùphèav'd
His vàstness.
*Ibid*

Blòw wìnds and cràck your chèeks? ràge! blòw.
You càtăræ̀cts and hurricànoes, spòut,
Till you have drènch'd our stèeples, dròwn'd the còcks!
You sùlphurous and thoùght-èxecuting fìres,
Vaùnt coùriers of òak-clèaving thùnderbòlts,

Sìnge my white hèad! and thòu, àll-shàking thùnder,
Strìke flàt the thìck rotùndity o' the wòrld!
*Lear*

Unexpected locations of the accent double this force, and render its characteristic of passion and abruptness. And here comes into play the reader's corresponding fineness of ear, and his retardations and accelerations in accordance with those of the poet:

Then in the keyhole turns
The ìntrĭcăte wards, and every bolt and bar
Unfastens. On ă sŭddĕn òpen fly
Wĭth ĭmpètuous recoil and jarring sound
The infernal doors, and on their hinges grate
Harsh thunder.
*Par. Lost,* Book II

Abòmĭnăblĕ—unùttĕrăblĕ—and worse
Than fables yet have feigned.
*Ibid*

Wàllŏwĭng ŭnwìĕldy̆—ĕnòrmous in their gait.
*Ibid*

Of unusual passionate accent, there is an exquisite specimen in the *Fairy Queen,* where Una is lamenting her desertion by the Red-Cross Knight:

But he, my lion, and my noble lord,
How does he find in cruel heart to hate
Her that him lov'd, and ever most ador'd
*As the gòd of my lìfe?* Why hath he me abhorr'd?

See the whole stanza, with a note upon it, in the present volume.

The abuse of strength is harshness and heaviness; the reverse of it is weakness. There is a noble sentiment,—it appears both in Daniel's and Sir John Beaumont's works, but is most probably the latter's,—which is a perfect outrage of strength in the sound of the words:

Only the firmest and the *constant'st* hearts
God sets to act the *stout'st* and hardest parts.

*Stout'st* and *constant'st* for "stoutest" and "most constant!" It is as bad as the intentional crabbedness of the line in *Hudibras;*

He that hangs or *beats out's* brains,
The devil's in him if *he* feigns.

*Beats out's brains,* for "beats out his brains." Of heaviness, Davenant's *Gondibert* is a formidible specimen, almost throughout:

With sìlence (òrder's help, and màrk of càre)
  They chìde thàt nòise which hèedless yòuth affèct;
Stìll coùrse for ùse, for heàlth thèy clèarness wèar,
  And sàve in wèll-fìx'd àrms, all nìceness chèck'd.
Thèy thoùght, thòse that, unàrmed, expòs'd fràil lìfe,
  But nàked nàture vàliantly betrày'd;
Whò wàs, thoùgh nàked, sàfe, till prìde màde strìfe,
  But màde defènce must ùse, nòw dànger's màde.

And so he goes digging and lumbering on, like a heavy preacher thumping the pulpit in italics, and spoiling many ingenious reflections.

Weakness in versification is want of accent and emphasis. It generally accompanies prosaicalness, and is the consequence of weak thoughts, and of the affectation of a certain well-bred enthusiasm. The writings of the late Mr. Hayley were remarkable for it; and it abounds among the lyrical imitators of Cowley, and the whole of what is called our French school of poetry, when it aspired above its wit and "sense." It sometimes breaks down in a horrible, hopeless manner, as if giving way at the first step. The following ludicrous passage in Congreve, intended to be particularly fine, contains an instance:

  And lo! Silence himself is here;
Methinks I see the midnight god appear.
  In all his downy pomp array'd,
    Behold the reverend shade.
  *An ancient sigh he sits upon:!!*
Whose memory of sound is long since gone,
*And purposely annihilated for his throne!!*

*Ode on the singing of*
*Mrs. Arabella Hunt*

See also the would-be enthusiasm of Addison about music

  For ever consecrate the *day*
  To music and *Cecilia;*
Music, the greatest good that mortals know,
  And all of heaven we have below,
  Music can noble HINTS *impart!!!*

It is observable that the unpoetic masters of ridicule are apt to make the most ridiculous mistakes, when they come to affect a strain higher than the one they are accustomed to. But no wonder. Their habits neutralize the enthusiasm it requires.

*Sweetness,* though not identical with smoothness, any more than feeling is with sound, always includes it; and smoothness is a thing so little to be regarded for its own sake, and indeed so worthless in poetry but for some taste of sweetness, that I have not thought necessary to mention it by itself; though such an all-in-all in versification was it regarded not a hundred years back, that Thomas Warton himself, an idolator of Spenser, ventured to wish the following line in the *Fairy Queen,*

And was admirèd much of fools, *wòmen,* and boys

altered to

And was admirèd much of women, fools, and boys

thus destroying the fine scornful emphasis on the first syllable of "women!" (an ungallant intimation, by the way, against the fair sex, very startling in this no less woman-loving than great poet.) Any poetaster can be smooth. Smoothness abounds in all small poets, as sweetness does in the greater. Sweetness is the smoothness of grace and delicacy,—of the sympathy with the pleasing and lovely. Spenser is full of it,—Shakspeare—Beaumont and Fletcher—Coleridge. Of Spenser's and Coleridge's versification it is the prevailing characteristic. Its main secrets are a smooth progression between variety and sameness, and a voluptuous sense of the continuous,—"linked sweetness long drawn out." Observe the first and last lines of the stanza in the *Fairy Queen,* describing a shepherd brushing away the gnats;—the open and the close *e*'s in the one,

As gèntle shèpherd in swēēt ēventide-

and the repetition of the word *oft,* and the fall from the vowel *a,* into the two *u's* in the other,

She brusheth *oft,* and *oft* doth màr their mūrmŭrings

So in his description of two substances in the handling, both equally smooth;

*Each smoother seems than each, and each than each seems smoother.*

An abundance of examples from his poetry will be found in the volume before us. His beauty revolves on itself with conscious loveliness. And Coleridge is worthy to be named with him, as the reader will see also, and has seen already. Let him take a sample meanwhile from the poem called the "Day-Dream"! Observe both the variety and sameness of the vowels, and the repetition of the soft consonants:

My eyes make pictures when they're shut:
  I see a fountain, large and fair,
A willow and a ruin'd hut,
  And *thee* and *me* and Mary there.
*O Mary! make thy gentle lap our pillow;*
*Bend o'er us, like a bower, my beautiful green willow.*

By *Straightforwardness* is meant the flow of words in their natural order, free alike from mere prose, and from those inversions to which bad poets recur in order to escape the charge of prose, but chiefly to accommodate their rhymes. In Shadwell's play of *Psyche,* Venus gives the sisters of the heroine an answer, of which the following is the *entire* substance, literally, in so many words. The author had nothing better for her to say:

> I receive your prayers with kindness, and will give success to your hopes. I have seen, with anger, mankind adore your sister's beauty and deplore her scorn: which they shall do no more. For I'll so resent their idolatry, as shall content your wishes to the full.

Now in default of all imagination, fancy, and expression, how was the writer to turn these words into poetry or rhyme? Simply by diverting them from their natural order, and twisting the halves of the sentences each before the other.

> With kindness I your prayers receive,
> And to your hopes success will give.
> I have, with anger, seen mankind adore
> Your sister's beauty and her scorn deplore;
> Which they shall do no more.
> For their idolatry I'll so resent,
> As shall your wishes to the full content!!

This is just as if a man were to allow that there was no poetry in the words, "How do you find yourself?" "Very well, I thank you"; but to hold them inspired, if altered into

> Yourself how do you find?
> Very well, you I thank.

It is true, the best writers in Shadwell's age were addicted to these inversions, partly for their own reasons, as far as rhyme was concerned, and partly because they held it to be writing in the classical and Virgilian manner. What has since been called Artificial Poetry was then flourishing, in contradistinction to Natural; or Poetry seen chiefly through art and books, and not in its first sources. But when the artificial poet partook of the natural, or, in other words, was a true poet after his kind, his best was always written in the most natural and straightforward manner. Hear Shadwell's antagonist Dryden. Not a particle of inversion, beyond what is used for the sake of emphasis in common discourse, and this only in one line (the last but three), is to be found in his immortal character of the Duke of Buckingham:

> A man so various, that he seemed to be
> Not one, but all mankind's epitome:
> Stiff in opinions, *always in the wrong,*
> *Was everything by starts, and nothing long;*
> But in the course of one revolving moon
> Was chemist, fiddler, statesman, and buffoon:
> Then all for women, rhyming, dancing, drinking,
> *Besides ten thousand freaks that died in thinking*
> *Blest madman!* who could every hour employ
> *With something new to wish or to enjoy!*
> Railing and praising were his usual themes;

And both, to show his judgment, in extremes:
So over violent, or over civil,
*That every man with him was god or devil.*
In squandering wealth was his peculiar art;
*Nothing went unrewarded, but desert.*
Beggar'd by fools, whom still he found too late,
*He had his jest, and they had his estate.*

Inversion itself was often turned into a grace in these poets, and may be in others, by the power of being superior to it; using it only with a classical air, and as a help lying next to them, instead of a salvation which they are obliged to seek. In jesting passages also it sometimes gave the rhyme a turn agreeably wilful, or an appearance of choosing what lay in its way; as if a man should pick up a stone to throw at another's head, where a less confident foot would have stumbled over it. Such is Dryden's use of the word *might*—the mere sign of a tense—in his pretended ridicule of the monkish practice of rising to sing psalms in the night.

And much they griev'd to see so nigh their hall
The bird that warn'd St. Peter of his fall;
That he should raise his mitred crest on high,
And clap his wings and call his family
To sacred rites; and vex th' ethereal powers
With midnight matins at uncivil hours;
Nay more, his quiet neighbors should molest
*Just in the sweetness of their morning rest.*

(What a line full of "another doze" is that!)

*Beast of a bird!* supinely, when he *might*
Lie snug and sleep, to rise before the light!
What if his dull forefathers used that cry?
Could he not let a bad example die?

I the more gladly quote instances like those of Dryden, to illustrate the points in question, because they are specimens of the very highest kind of writing in the heroic couplet upon subjects not heroical. As to prosaicalness in general, it is sometimes indulged in by young writers on the plea of its being natural; but this is a mere confusion of triviality with propriety, and is usually the result of indolence.

*Unsuperfluousness* is rather a matter of style in general, than of the sound and order of words: and yet versification is so much strengthened by it, and so much weakened by its opposite, that it could not but come within the category of its requisites. When superfluousness of words is not occasioned by overflowing animal spirits, as in Beaumont and Fletcher, or by the very genius of luxury, as in Spenser (in which cases it is enrichment as well as overflow), there is no worse sign for a poet altogether, except pure barrenness. Every word that could be taken away from a poem, unreferable to either of the above reasons for it, is a damage; and many such are death; for there is nothing that posterity seems so determined to resent as this want of respect for its time and trouble. The world is too rich in books to endure it. Even true poets have died of this Writer's Evil. Trifling ones have survived, with scarcely any pretensions but the terseness of their trifles. What hope can remain for wordy mediocrity? Let the discerning reader take up any poem, pen in hand, for the purpose of discovering how many words he can strike out of it that give him no requisite ideas, no relevant ones that he cares for, and no reasons for the rhyme beyond its necessity, and he will see what blot and havoc he will make in many an admired production of its day,—what marks of its inevitable fate. Bulky authors in particular, however safe they may think themselves, would do well to consider what parts of their cargo they might dispense with in their proposed voyage down the gulfs of time; for many a gallant vessel, thought indestructible in its age, has perished;—many a load of words, expected to be in eternal demand, gone to join the wrecks of self-love, or rotted in the warehouses of change and vicissitude. I have said the more on this point, because in an age when the true inspiration has undoubtedly been re-awakened by Coleridge and his fellows, and we have so many new poets coming forward, it may be as well to give a general warning against that tendency to an accumulation and ostentation of *thoughts,* which is meant to be a refutation in full of the pretensions of all poetry less cogitabund, whatever may be the requirements of its class. Young writers should bear in mind, that even some of the very best materials for poetry are not poetry built; and that the smallest marble shrine, of exquisite workmanship, outvalues all that architect ever chipped away. Whatever can be dispensed with is rubbish.

*Variety* in versification consists in whatsoever can be done for the prevention of monotony, by diversity of stops and cadences, distribution of emphasis, and retardation and acceleration of time; for the whole real secret of versification is a musical secret, and is not attainable to any vital effect, save by the ear of genius. All the mere knowledge of feet and numbers, of accent and quantity, will no more impart it, than a knowledge of the "Guide to Music" will make a Beethoven or a Paisiello. It is a matter of sensibility and imagination; of the beautiful in poetical passion, accompanied by the musical; of the imperative necessity for a pause here, and a cadence there, and a quicker or slower utterance in this or that place, created by analogies of sound with sense, by the fluctuations of feeling, by the demands of the gods and graces that visit the poet's harp, as the winds visit that of Æolus. The same time and quantity which are occasioned by the spiritual part of this secret, thus become its formal ones,—not feet and syllables, long and short, iambics or trochees; which are the reduction of it to its *less* than dry bones. You might get, for instance, not only ten and eleven, but thirteen or fourteen syllables into a rhyming, as well as blank, heroical verse, if time and the feeling permitted; and in irregular measure this is often done; just as musicians put twenty notes in a bar instead of two, quavers instead of minims, according as the feeling they are expressing impels them to fill up the time with short and hurried notes, or with long; or as the choristers in a cathedral retard or precipitate the words of the chaunt, according as the quantity of its notes, and the colon which divides the verse of the psalm, conspire to demand it. Had the moderns borne this principle in mind when they settled the prevailing systems of verse, instead of learning them, as they appear to have done, from the first drawling and one-syllabled notation of the church hymns, we should have retained all the advantages of the more numerous versification of the ancients, without being compelled to fancy that there was no alternative for us between our syllabical uniformity and the hexameters or other special forms unsuited to our tongues. But to leave this question alone, we will present the reader with a few sufficing specimens of the difference between monotony and variety in versification, first from Pope, Dryden, and Milton, and next from Gay and Coleridge. The following is the boasted melody of the nevertheless exquisite poet of the *Rape of the Lock,*—exquisite in his wit and fancy, though not in his numbers. The reader will observe that it is literally *see-saw,* like the rising and falling of a plank, with a light person at one end who is jerked up in the briefer time, and a heavier one who is set down more leisurely at the other. It is in the otherwise charming description of the heroine of that poem:

On her white breast—a sparkling cross she wore,
Which Jews might kiss—and infidels adore;
Her lively looks—a sprightly mind disclose,
Quick as her eyes—and as unfix'd as those;
Favors to none—to all she smiles extends,
Oft she rejects—but never once offends;
Bright as the sun—her eyes the gazers strike,
And like the sun—they shine on all alike;
Yet graceful ease—and sweetness void of pride,
Might hide her faults—if belles had faults to hide;
If to her share—some female errors fall,
Look on her face—and you'll forget them all.

Compare with this the description of Iphigenia in one of Dryden's stories from Boccaccio:

It happen'd—on a summer's holiday,
That to the greenwood shade—he took his way,
For Cymon shunn'd the church—and used not much to pray,
His quarter-staff—which he could ne'er forsake,
Hung half before—and half behind his back:
He trudg'd along—not knowing what he sought,
And whistled as he went—for want of thought.

By chance conducted—or by thirst constrain'd,
The deep recesses of a grove he gain'd;—
Where—in a plain defended by a wood,
Crept through the matted grass—a crystal flood,
By which—an alabaster fountain stood;
And on the margent of the fount was laid—

Attended by her slaves—a sleeping maid;
Like Dian and her nymphs—when, tir'd with sport,
To rest by cool Eurotas they resort.—
The dame herself—the goddess well express'd
Not more distinguished by her purple vest—
Than by the charming features of the face—
And e'en in slumber—a superior grace:
Her comely limbs—compos'd with decent care,
Her body shaded—by a light cymarr,
Her bosom to the view—was only bare;
Where two beginning paps were scarcely spied—
For yet their places were but signified.—
The fanning wind upon her bosom blows—
To meet the fanning wind—the bosom rose;
The fanning wind—and purling stream—continue her repose.

For a further variety take, from the same author's "Theodore and Honoria," a passage in which the couplets are run one into the other, and all of it modulated, like the former, according to the feeling demanded by the occasion;

Whilst listening to the murmuring leaves he stood—
More than a mile immers'd within the wood—
At once the wind was laid.|—The whispering sound
Was dumb.|—A rising earthquake rock'd the ground.
With deeper brown the grove was overspread—
A sudden horror seiz'd his giddy head—
And his ears tinkled—and his color fled.
Nature was in alarm.—Some danger nigh
Seem'd threaten'd—though unseen to mortal eye.
Unus'd to fear—he summon'd all his soul,
And stood collected in himself—and whole:
Not long.—

But for a crowning specimen of variety of pause and accent, apart from emotion, nothing can surpass the account, in *Paradise Lost,* of the Devil's search for an accomplice;

There was a plàce,
Nòw not—though Sìn—not Tìme—fìrst wroùght the chànge,
Where Tìgris—at the foot of Pàradise,
Into a gùlf—shòt under ground—till pàrt
Ròse up a foùntain by the Trèe of Lìfe.
*In* with the river sunk—and *with* it *ròse*
Sàtan—invòlv'd in rìsing mìst—then soùght
Whère to lie hìd.—Sèa he had search'd—and lànd
From Eden over Pòntus—and the pòol
Mæòtis—*ùp* beyond the river *Ob;*

Dòwnward as fàr antàrctic;—and in lèngth
Wèst from Oròntes—to the òcean bàrr'd
At Dàriën—thènce to the lànd whère flòws
Gànges and Indus.—Thùs the òrb he ròam'd
With nàrrow sèarch;—and with inspèction dèep
Consìder'd èvery crèature—whìch of àll
Mòst opportùne mìght sèrve his wìles—and foùnd
The sèrpent—sùbtlest bèast of all the fièld.

If the reader cast his eye again over this passage, he will not find a verse in it which is not varied and harmonized in the most remarkable manner. Let him notice in particular that curious balancing of the lines in the sixth and tenth verses:—

*In* with the river sunk, &c.,

and

*Up* beyond the river *Ob*.

It might, indeed, be objected to the versification of Milton, that it exhibits too constant a perfection of this kind. It sometimes forces upon us too great a sense of consciousness on the part of the composer. We miss the first sprightly runnings of verse,—the ease and sweetness of spontaneity. Milton, I think, also too often condenses weight into heaviness.

Thus much concerning the chief of our two most popular measures. The other, called octosyllabic, or the measure of eight syllables, offered such facilities for *namby-pamby,* that it had become a jest as early as the time of Shakspeare, who makes Touchstone call it the "butterwoman's rate to market," and the "very false gallop of verses." It has been advocated, in opposition to the heroic measure, upon the ground that ten syllables lead a man into epithets and other superfluities, while eight syllables compress him into a sensible and pithy gentleman. But the heroic measure laughs at it. So far from compressing, it converts one line into two, and sacrifices everything to the quick and importunate return of the rhyme. With Dryden, compare Gay, even in the strength of Gay:

The wind was high—the window shakes
With sudden start the miser wakes;
Along the silent room he stalks,

(A miser never "stalks;" but a rhyme was desired for "walks")

Looks back, and trembles as he walks:
Each lock and every bolt he tries,
In every creek and corner pries.
Then opes the chest with treasure stor'd,
And stands in rapture o'er his hoard;

("Hoard" and "treasure stor'd" are just made for one another)

But now, with sudden qualms possess'd,
He wrings his hands, he beats his breast;
By conscience stung, he wildly stares,
And thus his guilty soul declares.

And so he denounces his gold, as miser never denounced it; and sighs, because

Virtue resides on earth no more!

Coleridge saw the mistake which had been made with regard to this measure, and restored it to the beautiful freedom of which it was capable, by calling to mind the liberties allowed its old musical professors the minstrels, and dividing it by *time* instead of *syllables;*—by the *beat of four* into which you might get as many syllables as you could, instead of allotting eight syllables to the poor time, whatever it might have to say. He varied it further with alternate rhymes and stanzas, with rests and omissions precisely analogous to those in music, and rendered it altogether worthy to utter the manifold thoughts and feelings of himself and his lady Christabel. He even ventures, with an exquisite sense of solemn strangeness and license (for there is witchcraft going forward), to introduce a couplet of blank verse, itself as mystically and beautifully modulated as anything in the music of Glück or Weber.

'Tis the middle of night by the castle clock,
And the owls have awaken'd the crowing cock;
Tu-whit!—Tu-whoo!
And hark, again! the crowing cock,
*How drowsily he crew.*
Sir Leoline, the baron rich,
Hath a toothless mastiff bitch;
From her kennel beneath the rock
She maketh answer to the clock
*Fòur fŏr thĕ qùartĕrs ănd twèlve fŏr thĕ hoùr,*
Ever and aye, by shine and shower,
Sixteen short howls, not over loud:
Some say, she sees my lady's shroud.

*Is the nìght chìlly and dàrk!*
*The nìght is chìlly, but nòt dàrk.*
The thin grey cloud is spread on high,
It covers, but not hides, the sky.
The moon is behind, and at the full,
And yet she looks both small and dull.
The night is chilly, the cloud is grey;

(These are not superfluities, but mysterious returns of importunate feeling)

*Tis a month before the month of May,*
*And the spring comes slowly up this way.*
The lovely lady, Christabel,
Whom her father loves so well,
What makes her in the wood so late,
A furlong from the castle-gate?
She had dreams all yesternight
Of her own betrothèd knight;
And shè ĭn thĕ midnight wood will pray
For the wèal ŏf hĕr lover that's far away.

She stole along, she nothing spoke,
The sighs she heav'd were soft and low
And naught was green upon the oak,
But moss and rarest misletoe;
She kneels beneath the huge oak tree,
And in silence prayeth she.

The lady sprang up suddenly,
The lovely lady, Christabel!
It moan'd as near as near can be,
But what it is, she cannot tell,
On the other side it seems to be
Of thĕ hùge, broàd-breàsted, òld oàk trèe

The night is chill, the forest bare;
Is it the wind that moaneth bleakly?

(This "bleak moaning" is a witch's)

There is not wind enough in the air
To move away the ringlet curl
From the lovely lady's cheek—
There is not wind enough to twirl
*The òne rèd lèaf, the làst ŏf ĭts clan,*
*That dàncĕs ăs òftĕn ăs dànce it càn,*
*Hàngĭng sŏ lìght and hàngĭng sŏ hìgh,*
*On thĕ tòpmost twìg thăt loŏks ùp ăt thè sky*

Hush, beating heart of Christabel!
Jesu Maria, shield her well!
She folded her arms beneath her cloak,
And stole to the other side of the oak.
        What sees she there?

There she sees a damsel bright,
Dressed in a robe of silken white,

That shadowy in the moonlight shone:
The neck that made that white robe wan,
Her stately neck and arms were bare:
Her blue-vein'd feet unsandall'd were;
And wildly glitter'd, here and there,
The gems entangled in her hair
I guess 'twas *frightful* there to see
*A lady so richly clad as she—*
*Beautiful exceedingly.*

The principle of Variety in Uniformity is here worked out in a style "beyond the reach of art." Every thing is diversified according to the demand of the moment, of the sounds, the sights, the emotions; the very uniformity of the outline is gently varied; and yet we feel that *the whole is one and of the same character,* the single and sweet unconsciousness of the heroine making all the rest seem more conscious, and ghastly, and expectant. It is thus that *versification itself becomes part of the sentiment of a poem,* and vindicates the pains that have been taken to show its importance. I know of no very fine versification unaccompanied with fine poetry; no poetry of a mean order accompanied with verse of the highest.

As to Rhyme, which might be thought too insignificant to mention, it is not at all so. The universal consent of modern Europe, and of the East in all ages, has made it one of the musical beauties of verse for all poetry but epic and dramatic, and even for the former with Southern Europe,—a sustainment for the enthusiasm, and a demand to enjoy. The mastery of it consists in never writing it for its own sake, or at least never appearing to do so; in knowing how to vary it, to give it novelty, to render it more or less strong, to divide it (when not in couplets) at the proper intervals, to repeat it many times where luxury or animal spirits demand it (see an instance in Titania's speech to the Fairies), to impress an affecting or startling remark with it, and to make it, in comic poetry, a new and surprising addition to the jest.

Large was his bounty and his soul sincere,
  Heav'n did a recompense as largely send;
He gave to misery all he had, *a tear,*
  He gain'd from heav'n ('twas all he wish'd) *a friend.*
Gray's *Elegy*

The fops are proud of scandal; for they cry
At every lewd, low character, "That's *I*"
Dryden's *Prologue to the Pilgrim*

What makes all doctrines plain and clear?
*About two hundred pounds a year.*
And that which was proved true before,
Prove false again? *Two hundred more.*
*Hudibras*

Compound for sins they are *inclin'd to,*
By damning thosc thcy havc *no mind to.*
*Ibid*

—Stor'd with deletery *med'cines,*
Which whosoever took is *dead since.*
*Ibid*

Sometimes it is a grace in a master like Butler to force his rhyme, thus showing a laughing wilful power over the most stubborn materials:

Win
The women, and make them draw in
The men, as Indians with a *fèmale*
Tame elephant inveigle *the* male.
*Hudibras*

He made an instrument to know
If the moon shines at full or no;
That would, as soon as e'er she *shone, straight*
Whether 'twere day or night *demonstrate;*
Tell what her diameter to an *inch is,*
And prove that she's not made of *green cheese.*
*Ibid*

Pronounce it, by all means, *grinches,* to make the joke more wilful. The happiest triple rhyme, perhaps, that ever was written, is in *Don Juan:*

But oh! ye lords of ladies *intellectual,*
Inform us truly,—haven't they *hen-peck'd you all?*

The sweepingness of the assumption completes the flowing breadth of effect.

Dryden confessed that a rhyme often gave him a thought. Probably the happy word "sprung," in the following passage from Ben Jonson, was suggested by it; but then the poet must have had the feeling in him.

—Let our trumpets sound,
And cleave both air and ground
With beating of our drums.
Let every lyre be strung,
Harp, lute, theorbo, *sprung*
*With touch of dainty thumbs.*

Boileau's trick for appearing to rhyme naturally was to compose the second line of his couplet first! which gives one the crowning idea of the "artificial school of poetry." Perhaps the most perfect master of rhyme, the easiest and most abundant, was the greatest writer of comedy that the world has seen,—Molière.

If a young reader should ask, after all, What is the quickest way of knowing bad poets from good, the best poets from the next best, and so on? the answer is, the only and two-fold way; first, the perusal of the best poets with the greatest attention; and, second, the cultivation of that love of truth and beauty which made them what they are. Every true reader of poetry partakes a more than ordinary portion of the poetic nature; and no one can be completely such, who does not love, or take an interest in, everything that interests the poet, from the firmament to the daisy,—from the highest heart of man to the most pitiable of the low. It is a good practice to read with pen in hand, marking what is liked or doubted. It rivets the attention, realizes the greatest amount of enjoyment, and facilitates reference. It enables the reader also, from time to time, to see what progress he makes with his own mind, and how it grows up towards the stature of its exalter.

If the same person should ask, What class of poetry is the highest? I should say, undoubtedly, the Epic; for it includes the drama, with narration besides; or the speaking and action of the characters, with the speaking of the poet himself, whose utmost address is taxed to relate all well for so long a time, particularly in the passages least sustained by enthusiasm. Whether this class has included the greatest poet, is another question still under trial; for Shakspeare perplexes all such verdicts, even when the claimant is Homer; though, if a judgment may be drawn from his early narratives (*Venus and Adonis*, and the *Rape of Lucrece*), it is to be doubted whether even Shakspeare could have told a story like Homer, owing to that incessant activity and superfœtation of thought, a little less of which might be occasionally desired even in his plays;—if it were possible, once possessing anything of his, to wish it away. Next to Homer and Shakspeare come such narrators as the less universal, but still intenser Dante; Milton, with his dignified imagination; the universal, profoundly simple Chaucer; and luxuriant, remote Spenser—immortal child in poetry's most poetic solitudes: then the great second-rate dramatists; unless those who are better acquainted with Greek tragedy than I am, demand a place for them before Chaucer: then the airy yet robust universality of Ariosto; the hearty, out-of-door nature of Theocritus, also a universalist; the finest lyrical poets (who only take short flights, compared with the narrators); the purely contemplative poets who have more thought than feeling; the descriptive, satirical, didactic, epigrammatic. It is to be borne in mind, however, that the first poet of an inferior class may be superior to followers in the train of a higher one, though the superiority is by no means to be taken for granted; otherwise Pope would be superior to Fletcher, and Butler to Pope. Imagination, teeming with action and character, makes the greatest poets; feeling and thought the next; fancy (by itself) the next; wit the last. Thought by itself makes no poet at all; for the mere conclusions of the understanding can at best be only so many intellectual matters of fact. Feeling, even destitute of conscious thought, stands a far better poetical chance; feeling being a sort of thought without the process of thinking,—a grasper of the truth without seeing it. And what is very remarkable, feeling seldom makes the blunders that thought does. An idle distinction has been made between taste and judgment. Taste is the very maker of judgment. Put an artificial fruit in your mouth, or only handle it, and you will soon perceive the difference between judging from taste or tact, and judging from the abstract figment called judgment. The latter does but throw you into guesses and doubts. Hence the conceits that astonish us in the gravest, and even subtlest thinkers, whose taste is not proportionate to their mental perceptions; men like Donne, for instance; who, apart from accidental personal impressions, seem to look at nothing as it really is, but only as to what may be thought of it. Hence, on the other hand, the delightfulness of those poets who never violate truth of feeling, whether in things real or imaginary; who are always consistent with their object and its requirements; and who run the great round of nature, not to perplex and be perplexed, but to make themselves and us happy. And luckily, delightfulness is not incompatible with greatness, willing soever as men may be in their present imperfect state to set the power to subjugate above the power to please. Truth, of any great kind whatsoever, makes great writing. This is the reason why such poets as Ariosto, though not writing with a constant detail of thought and feeling like Dante, are justly considered great as well as delightful. Their greatness proves itself by the same truth of nature, and sustained power, though in a different way. Their action is not so crowded and weighty; their sphere has more territories less fertile; but it has enchantments of its own, which excess of thought would spoil,—luxuries, laughing graces, animal spirits; and not to recognize the beauty and greatness of these, treated as they treat them, is simply to be defective in sympathy. Every planet is not Mars or Saturn. There is also Venus and Mercury. There is one genius of the south, and another of the north, and others uniting both. The reader who is too thoughtless or too sensitive to like intensity of any sort, and he who is too thoughtful or too dull to like anything but the greatest possible stimulus of reflection or passion, are equally wanting in complexional fitness for a thorough enjoyment of books. Ariosto occasionally says as fine things as Dante, and Spenser as Shakspeare; but the business of both is to enjoy; and in order to partake their enjoyment to its full extent, you must feel what poetry is in the general as well as the particular, must be aware that there are different songs of the spheres, some fuller of notes, and others of a sustained delight; and as the former keep you perpetually alive to thought or passion, so from the latter you receive a constant harmonious sense of truth and beauty, more agreeable perhaps on the whole, though less exciting. Ariosto, for instance, does not *tell a story* with the brevity and concentrated passion of Dante; every sentence is not so full of matter nor the style so removed from the indifference of prose; yet you are charmed with a truth of another sort, equally characteristic of the writer, equally drawn from nature, and substituting a healthy sense of enjoyment for intenser emotion. Exclusiveness of liking for this or that mode of truth, only shows, either that a reader's perceptions are limited, or that he would sacrifice truth itself to his favorite form of it. Sir Walter Raleigh, who was as tranchant with his pen as his sword, hailed the *Faerie Queene* of his friend Spenser in verses in which he said that "Petrarch" was thenceforward to be no more heard of; and that in all English poetry, there was nothing he counted "of any price" but the effusions of the new author. Yet Petrarch is still living; Chaucer was not abolished by Sir Walter; and Shakspeare is thought somewhat valuable. A botanist might as well have said, that myrtles and oaks were to disappear, because acacias had come up. It is with the poet's creations, as with nature's, great or small. Wherever truth and beauty, whatever their amount, can be worthily shaped into verse, and answer to some demand for it in our hearts, there poetry is to be found; whether in productions grand and beautiful as some great event, or some mighty, leafy solitude, or no bigger and more pretending than a sweet face or a bunch of violets; whether in Homer's epic or Gray's *Elegy,* in the enchanted gardens of Ariosto and Spenser, or the very pot-herbs of the *Schoolmistress* of Shenstone, the balms of the simplicity of a cottage. Not to know and feel this, is to be deficient in the universality of Nature herself, who is a poetess on the smallest as well as the largest scale, and who calls upon us to admire all her productions: not indeed with the same degree of admiration, but with no refusal of it, except to defect.

I cannot draw this essay towards its conclusion better than with three memorable words of Milton; who has said, that poetry, in comparison with science, is "simple, sensuous, and passionate." By simple, he means unperplexed and self-evident; by sensuous, genial and full of imagery; by passionate, excited and enthusiastic. I am aware that different constructions have been put on some of these words; but the context seems to me to necessitate those before us. I quote, however, not from the original, but from an extract in the *Remarks on "Paradise Lost"* by Richardson.

What the poet has to cultivate above all things is love and truth;—what he has to avoid, like poison, is the fleeting and the false. He will get no good by proposing to be "in earnest at the moment." His earnestness must be innate and habitual; born with him, and felt to be his most precious inheritance. "I expect neither profit nor general fame by my writings," says Coleridge, in the Preface to his Poems; "and I consider myself as having been amply repaid without either. Poetry has been to me its *'own exceeding great reward':* it has soothed my afflictions; it has multiplied and refined my enjoyments; it has endeared solitude; and it has given me the habit of wishing to discover the good and the beautiful in all that meets and surrounds me."—*Pickering's edition,* p. 10.

"Poetry," says Shelley, "lifts the veil from the hidden beauty of the world, *and makes familiar objects be as if they were not familiar.* It reproduces all that it represents; and the impersonations clothed in its Elysian light stand thenceforward in the minds of those who have once contemplated them, as memorials of that gentle and exalted content which extends itself over all thoughts and actions with which it co-exists. The great secret of morals is love, or a going out of our own nature, and an identification of ourselves with the beautiful which exists in thought, action, or person, not our own. A man, to be greatly good, must imagine intensely and comprehensively; he must put himself in the place of another, and of many others: the pains and pleasures of his species must become his own. The great instrument of moral good is imagination; and poetry administers to the effect by acting upon the cause." —*Essays and Letters,* vol i., p. 16.

I would not willingly say anything after perorations like these; but as treatises on poetry may chance to have auditors who think themselves called upon to vindicate the superiority of what is termed useful knowledge, it may be as well to add, that if the poet may be allowed to pique himself on any one thing more than another, compared with those who undervalue him, it is on that power of undervaluing nobody, and no attainments different from his own, which is given him by the very faculty of imagination they despise. The greater includes the less. They do not see that their inability to comprehend him argues the smaller capacity. No man recognizes the worth of utility more than the poet: he only desires that the meaning of the term may not come short of its greatness, and exclude the noblest necessities of his fellow-creatures. He is quite as much pleased, for instance, with the facilities for rapid conveyance afforded him by the railroad, as the dullest confiner of its advantages to that single idea, or as the greatest two-idead man who varies that single idea with hugging himself on his "buttons" or his good dinner. But he sees also the beauty of the country through which he passes, of the towns, of the heavens, of the steam-engine itself, thundering and fuming along like a magic horse, of the affections that are carrying, perhaps, half the passengers on their journey, nay, of those of the great two-idead man; and, beyond all this, he discerns the incalculable amount of good, and knowledge, and refinement, and mutual consideration, which this wonderful invention is fitted to circulate over the globe, perhaps to the displacement of war itself, and certainly to the diffusion of millions of enjoyments.

"And a button-maker, after all, invented it!" cries our friend.

Pardon me—it was a nobleman. A button-maker may be a very excellent, and a very poetical man, too, and yet not have been the first man visited by a sense of the gigantic powers of the combination of water and fire. It was a nobleman who first thought of this most poetical bit of science. It was a nobleman who first thought of it,—a captain who first tried it,—and a button-maker who perfected it. And he who put the nobleman on such thoughts, was the great philosopher, Bacon, who said that poetry had "something divine in it," and was necessary to the satisfaction of the human mind.

FROM

# WIT AND HUMOR

I confess I felt this [that "levity has as many tricks as the kitten."] so strongly when I began to reflect on the present subject, and found myself so perplexed with the demand, that I was forced to reject plan after plan, and feared I should never be able to give any tolerable account of the matter. I experienced no such difficulty with the concentrating seriousness and sweet attraction of the subject of "Imagination and Fancy;" but this laughing jade of a topic, with her endless whims and faces, and the legions of indefinable shapes that she brought about me, seemed to do nothing but scatter my faculties, or bear them off deridingly into pastime. I felt as if I was undergoing a Saint Anthony's Temptation reversed,—a laughable instead of a frightful one. Thousands of merry devils poured in upon me from all sides,—doubles of Similes, buffooneries of Burlesques, stalkings of Mock-heroics, stings in the tails of Epigrams, glances of Innuendos, dry looks of Ironies, corpulences of Exaggerations, ticklings of mad Fancies, claps on the back of Horse-plays, complacencies of *Unawarenesses,* flounderings of Absurdities, irresistibilities of Iterations, significances of Jargons, wailings of Pretended Woes, roarings of Laughters, and hubbubs of Animal Spirits;—all so general yet particular, so demanding distinct recognition, and yet so baffling the attempt with their numbers and their confusion, that a thousand masquerades in one would have seemed to threaten less torment to the pen of a reporter. . . .

[It is not to be supposed] that everything witty or humorous excites laughter. It may be accompanied with a sense of too many other things to do so; with too much thought, with too great a perfection even, or with pathos and sorrow. All extremes meet; excess of laughter itself runs into tears, and mirth becomes heaviness. Mirth itself is too often but melancholy in disguise. The jests of the fool in "Lear" are the sighs of knowledge. But as far as Wit and Humor affect us on their own accounts, or unmodified by graver considerations, laughter is their usual result and happy ratification. . . .

Wit is the clash and reconcilement of incongruities; the meeting of extremes round a corner; the flashing of an artificial light from one object to another, disclosing some unexpected resemblance or connection. It is the detection of likeness in unlikeness, of sympathy in antipathy, or of the extreme points of antipathies themselves, made friends by the very merriment of their introduction. The mode, or form, is comparatively of no consequence, provided it give no trouble to the apprehension: and you may bring as many ideas together as can pleasantly assemble. But a single one is nothing. Two ideas are as necessary to Wit, as couples are to marriages; and the union is happy in proportion to the agreeableness of the offspring. . . .

*Humor,* considered as the object treated of by the humorous writer, and not as the power of treating it, derives its name from the prevailing quality of *moisture* in the bodily temperament; and is *a tendency of the mind to run in particular directions of thought or feeling more amusing than accountable;* at least in the opinion of society. It is, therefore, either in reality or appearance, a thing inconsistent. It deals in incongruities of character and circumstance, as Wit does in those of arbitrary ideas. The more the incongruities the better, provided they are all in nature; but two, at any rate, are as necessary to Humor, as the two ideas are to Wit; and the more strikingly they differ yet harmonize, the more amusing the result. Such is the melting together of the propensities to love and war in the person of exquisite Uncle Toby; of the gullible and the manly in Parson Adams; of the professional and the individual, or the accidental and the permanent, in the Canterbury Pilgrims; of the objectionable and the agreeable, the fat and the sharp-witted, in Falstaff; of honesty and knavery in Gil Blas; of pretension and non-performance in the Bullies of the dramatic poets; of folly and wisdom in Don Quixote; of shrewdness and doltishness in Sancho Panza; and, it may be added, in the discordant yet harmonious co-operation of Don Quixote and his attendant, considered as a pair. . . .

# *Thomas De Quincey*

1785–1859

Master and apostle of visionary literature, economist, novelist and opium addict, Thomas De Quincey was certainly one of the most brilliant essayists of his time. He was born at Freenheys, Manchester, on August 15, 1785; his father was a reputable merchant and his mother a woman of strict religious principles. De Quincey was a sensitive, effeminate and precocious child. He also showed himself to be a brilliant, if somewhat unruly, pupil at the various schools to which he was sent after the death of his father. He ran away from the Manchester Grammar School in 1802, and after roaming for some time in the Welsh mountains, went to London, hoping to raise enough money to live independently of his family and continue his studies. In London, however, he suffered financial hardships that would affect his health as well as his temperament for the rest of his life. Some of the most moving chapters of *The Confessions of an English Opium Eater* come from reminiscences of this period.

De Quincey went to Oxford to finish his education. Here he formed his first link with the Romantics, especially the "Lake School." He began a correspondence with Wordsworth in 1803 and met Coleridge in 1807. Oxford was also the place where, suffering from ailments probably contracted during his impoverished London years, De Quincey followed the advice of a friend and began to take opium to relieve the pain. This became a habit which brought him great suffering, but also relief and inspiration; it created his fame both as an "Opium Eater" and as a writer of visionary prose, of which he is considered the unrivalled master. From here on his life vacillated between periods of literary prolixity, remarkable for their eclecticism and diversity of subject, and periods of great depression. His low spirits were often caused by withdrawal from opium, but also by the death of both his wife and his daughter in 1837.

De Quincey's works, many of them fragmentary, range from literary criticism to history, biography, journalism, and economics. He wrote on Shakespeare and Pope, and, reacting against the literary principles dominant in the 18th-century, brought a new light to the tradition of the great prose stylists of the 17th-century—figures such as Jeremy Taylor and Sir Thomas Browne. John Stuart Mill himself quoted from "The Logic of Political Economy," which De Quincey wrote in 1844, and such pamphlets as "Of Murder Considered as One of the Fine Arts" brought early 19th-century journalism to some of its stylistic peaks.

A picturesque character, De Quincey was also renowned among his friends for his generosity, which amounted to a reckless indifference to money, and his habits of procrastination. He would accumulate papers and books until he was, in his own words, "snowed up," and then move to another apartment; he left six of them behind at his death. De Quincey also had a major influence on French literature through Musset, who translated the *Confessions;* Baudelaire took inspiration from this work to compose the "Paradis Artificiels," as did Balzac for "La Peau de Chagrin." When De Quincey died, on December 8, 1859, near Edinburgh, he was already considered the author of some of the most beautiful prose in modern English.

# On the Knocking At the Gate in "Macbeth"

From my boyish days I had always felt a great perplexity on one point in *Macbeth*. It was this: The knocking at the gate which succeeds to the murder of Duncan produced to my feelings an effect for which I never could account. The effect was that it reflected back upon the murderer a peculiar awfulness and a depth of solemnity; yet, however obstinately I endeavoured with my understanding to comprehend this, for many years I never could see *why* it should produce such an effect.

Here I pause for one moment, to exhort the reader never to pay any attention to his understanding when it stands in opposition to any other faculty of his mind. The mere understanding, however useful and indispensable, is the meanest faculty in the human mind, and the most to be distrusted; and yet the great majority of people trust to nothing else—which may do for ordinary life, but not for philosophical purposes. Of this out of ten thousand instances that I might produce I will cite one. Ask of any person whatsoever who is not previously prepared for the demand by a knowledge of the perspective to draw in the rudest way the commonest appearance which depends upon the laws of that science—as, for instance, to represent the effect of two walls standing at right angles to each other, or the appearance of the houses on each side of a street as seen by a person looking down the street from one extremity. Now, in all cases, unless the person has happened to observe in pictures how it is that artists produce these effects, he will be utterly unable to make the smallest approximation to it. Yet why? For he has actually seen the effect every day of his life. The reason is that he allows his understanding to overrule his eyes. His understanding, which includes no intuitive knowledge of the laws of vision, can furnish him with no reason why a line which is known and can be proved to be a horizontal line should not *appear* a horizontal line: a line that made any angle with the perpendicular less than a right angle would seem to him to indicate that his houses were all tumbling down together. Accordingly, he makes the line of his houses a horizontal line, and fails, of course, to produce the effect demanded. Here, then, is one instance out of many in which not only the understanding is allowed to overrule the eyes, but where the understanding is positively allowed to obliterate the eyes, as it were; for not only does the man believe the evidence of his understanding in opposition to that of his eyes, but (what is monstrous) the idiot is not aware that his eyes ever gave such evidence. He does not know that he has seen (and therefore *quoad* his consciousness has *not* seen) that which he *has* seen every day of his life.

But to return from this digression. My understanding could furnish no reason why the knocking at the gate in *Macbeth* should produce any effect, direct or reflected. In fact, my understanding said positively that it could *not* produce any effect. But I knew better; I felt that it did; and I waited and clung to the problem until further knowledge should enable me to solve it. At length, in 1812, Mr. Williams made his *début* on the stage of Ratcliffe Highway, and executed those unparalleled murders which have procured for him such a brilliant and undying reputation. On which murders, by the way, I must observe that in one respect they have had an ill effect, by making the connoisseur in murder very fastidious in his taste, and dissatisfied by anything that has been since done in that line. All other murders look pale by the deep crimson of his; and, as an amateur once said to me in a querulous tone, "There has been absolutely nothing *doing* since his time, or nothing that's worth speaking of." But this is wrong; for it is unreasonable to expect all men to be great artists, and born with the genius of Mr. Williams. Now, it will be remembered that in the first of these murders (that of the Marrs) the same incident (of a knocking at the door soon after the work of extermination was complete) did actually occur which the genius of Shakespeare has invented; and all good judges, and the most eminent dilettanti, acknowledged the felicity of Shakespeare's suggestion as soon as it was actually realized. Here, then, was a fresh proof that I was right in relying on my own feeling, in opposition to my understanding; and I again set myself to study the problem. At length I solved it to my own satisfaction; and my solution is this: Murder, in ordinary cases, where the sympathy is wholly directed to the case of the murdered person, is an incident of coarse and vulgar horror; and for this reason—that it flings the interest exclusively upon the natural but ignoble instinct by which we cleave to life: an instinct which, as being indispensable to the primal law of self-preservation, is the same in kind (though different in degree) amongst all living creatures. This instinct, therefore, because it annihilates all distinctions, and degrades the greatest of men to the level of "the poor beetle that we tread on," exhibits human nature in its most abject and humiliating attitude. Such an attitude would little suit the purposes of the poet. What then must he do? He must throw the interest on the murderer. Our sympathy must be with *him* (of course I mean a sympathy of comprehension, a sympathy by which we enter into his feelings, and are made to understand them—not a sympathy of pity or approbation).[1] In the murdered person, all strife of thought, all flux and reflux of passion and of purpose, are crushed by one overwhelming panic; the fear of instant death smites him "with its petrific mace." But in the murderer, such a murderer as a poet will condescend to, there must be raging some great storm of passion—jealousy, ambition, vengeance, hatred—which will create a hell within him; and into this hell we are to look.

In *Macbeth,* for the sake of gratifying his own enormous and teeming faculty of creation, Shakespeare has introduced two murderers: and, as usual in his hands, they are remarkably discriminated: but—though in Macbeth the strife of mind is greater than in his wife, the tiger spirit not so awake, and his feelings caught chiefly by contagion from her—yet, as both were finally involved in the guilt of murder, the murderous mind of necessity is finally to be presumed in both. This was to be expressed; and, on its own account, as well as to make it a more proportionable antagonist to the unoffending nature of their victim, "the gracious Duncan," and adequately to expound "the deep damnation of his taking off," this was to be expressed with peculiar energy. We were to be made to feel that the human nature—*i.e.* the divine nature of love and mercy, spread through the hearts of all creatures, and seldom utterly withdrawn from man—was gone, vanished, extinct, and that the fiendish nature had taken its place. And, as this effect is marvellously accomplished in the *dialogues* and *soliloquies* themselves, so it is finally consummated by the expedient under consideration; and it is to this that I now solicit the reader's attention. If the reader has ever witnessed a wife, daughter, or sister in a fainting fit, he may chance to have observed that the most affecting moment in such a spectacle is *that* in which a sigh and a stirring announce the recommencement of suspended life. Or, if the reader has ever been present in a vast metropolis on the day when some great national idol was carried in funeral pomp to his grave, and, chancing to walk near the course through which it passed, has felt powerfully, in the silence and desertion of the streets, and in the stagnation of ordinary business, the deep interest which at that moment was possessing the heart of man—if all at once he should hear the death-like stillness broken up by the sound of wheels rattling away from the scene, and making known that the transitory vision was dissolved, he will be aware that at no moment was his sense of the complete suspension and pause in ordinary human concerns so full and affecting as at that moment when the suspension ceases, and the goings-on of human life are suddenly resumed. All action in any direction is best expounded, measured, and made apprehensible, by reaction. Now, apply this to the case in *Macbeth*. Here, as I have said, the retiring of the human heart and the entrance of the fiendish heart was to be expressed and made sensible. Another world has stepped in; and the murderers are taken out of the region of human things, human purposes, human desires. They are transfigured: Lady Macbeth is "unsexed"; Macbeth has forgot that he was born of woman; both are conformed to the image of devils; and the world of devils is suddenly revealed. But how shall this be conveyed and made palpable? In order that a new world may step in, this world must for a time disappear. The murderers and the murder must be insulated—cut off by an immeasurable gulf from the ordinary tide and succession of human affairs—locked up and sequestered in some deep recess; we must be made sensible that the world of ordinary life is suddenly arrested, laid asleep, tranced, racked into a dread armistice; time must be annihilated, relation to things without abolished; and all must pass self-withdrawn into a deep syncope and suspension of earthly passion. Hence it is that, when the deed is done, when the work of darkness is perfect, then the world of darkness passes away like a pageantry in the clouds: the knocking at the gate is heard, and it makes known audibly that the reaction has commenced; the human has made its reflux upon the fiendish; the pulses of life are beginning to beat again; and the re-establishment of the goings-on of the world in which we live first makes us profoundly sensible of the awful parenthesis that had suspended them.

O mighty poet! Thy works are not as those of other men, simply and merely great works of art, but are also like the phenomena of nature, like the sun and the sea, the stars and the flowers, like frost and snow, rain and dew, hail-storm and thunder, which are to be studied with entire submission of our own faculties, and in the perfect faith that in them there can be no too much or too little, nothing useless or inert, but that, the farther we press in our discoveries, the more we shall see proofs of design and self-supporting arrangement where the careless eye had seen nothing but accident!

## *Note*

1. It seems almost ludicrous to guard and explain my use of a word in a situation where it would naturally explain itself. But it has become necessary to do so, in consequence of the unscholarlike use of the word sympathy, at present so general, by which, instead of taking it in its proper sense, as the act of reproducing in our minds the feelings of another, whether for hatred, indignation, love, pity, or approbation, it is made a mere synonym of the word *pity;* and hence, instead of saying "sympathy *with* another," many writers adopt the monstrous barbarism of "sympathy *for* another."

FROM

# Suspiria de Profundis

## *DREAMING*

In 1821, as a contribution to a periodical work—in 1822, as a separate volume—appeared the *Confessions of an English Opium-Eater*. The object of that work was to reveal something of the grandeur which belongs *potentially* to human dreams. Whatever may be the number of those in whom this faculty of dreaming splendidly can be supposed to lurk, there are not, perhaps, very many in whom it is developed. He whose talk is of oxen will probably dream of oxen; and the condition of human life which yokes so vast a majority to a daily experience incompatible with much elevation of thought oftentimes neutralizes the tone of grandeur in the reproductive faculty of dreaming, even for those whose minds are populous with solemn imagery. Habitually to dream magnificently, a man must have a constitutional determination to reverie. This in the first place; and even this, where it exists strongly, is too much liable to disturbance from the gathering agitation of our present English life. Already, what by the procession through fifty years of mighty revolutions amongst the kingdoms of the earth, what by the continual development of vast physical agencies—steam in all its applications, light getting under harness as a slave for man, powers from heaven descending upon education and accelerations of the press, powers from hell (as it might seem, but these also celestial) coming round upon artillery and the forces of destruction—the eye of the calmest observer is troubled; the brain is haunted as if by some jealousy of ghostly beings moving amongst us; and it becomes too evident that, unless this colossal pace of advance can be retarded (a thing not to be expected), or, which is happily more probable, can be met by counterforces of corresponding magnitude—forces in the direction of religion or profound philosophy that shall radiate centrifugally against this storm of life so perilously centripetal towards the vortex of the merely human—left to itself, the natural tendency of so chaotic a tumult must be to evil; for some minds to lunacy, for others a reagency of fleshly torpor. How much this fierce condition of eternal hurry upon an arena too exclusively human in its interests is likely to defeat the grandeur which is latent in all men, may be seen in the ordinary effect from living too constantly in varied company. The word *dissipation,* in one of its uses, expresses that effect; the action of thought and feeling is consciously dissipated and squandered. To reconcentrate them into meditative habits, a necessity is felt by all observing persons for sometimes retiring from crowds. No man ever will unfold the capacities of his own intellect who does not at least checker his life with solitude. How much solitude, so much power. Or, if not true in that rigour of expression, to this formula undoubtedly it is that the wise rule of life must approximate.

Among the powers in man which suffer by this too intense life of the *social* instincts, none suffers more than the power of dreaming. Let no man think this a trifle. The machinery for dreaming planted in the human brain was not planted for nothing. That faculty, in alliance with the mystery of darkness, is the one great tube through which man communicates with the shadowy. And the dreaming organ, in connexion with the heart, the eye, and the ear, composes the magnificent apparatus which forces the infinite into the chambers of a human brain, and throws dark reflections from eternities below all life upon the mirrors of that mysterious *camera obscura*—the sleeping mind.

But, if this faculty suffers from the decay of solitude, which is becoming a visionary idea in England, on the other hand it is certain that some merely physical agencies can and do assist the faculty of dreaming almost preternaturally. Amongst these is intense exercise—to some extent at least, for some persons; but beyond all others is opium: which indeed seems to possess a *specific* power in that direction; not merely for exalting the colours of dream-scenery, but for deepening its shadows, and, above all, for strengthening the sense of its fearful *realities*.

The *Opium Confessions* were written with some slight secondary purpose of exposing this specific power of opium upon the faculty of dreaming, but much more with the purpose of displaying the faculty itself; and the outline of the work travelled in this course—Supposing a reader acquainted with the true object of the *Confessions* as here stated—namely, the revelation of dreaming—to have put this question:

"But how came you to dream more splendidly than others?"

The answer would have been—

"Because *(prœmissis præmittendis)* I took excessive quantities of opium."

Secondly, suppose him to say, "But how came you to take opium in this excess?"

The answer to *that* would be, "Because some early events in my life had left a weakness in one organ which required (or seemed to require) that stimulant."

Then, because the opium dreams could not always have been understood without a knowledge of these events, it became necessary to relate them. Now, these two questions and answers exhibit the *law* of the work—that is, the principle which determined its form—but precisely in the inverse or regressive order. The work itself opened with the narration of my early adventures. These, in the natural order of succession, led to the opium as a resource for healing their consequences; and the opium as naturally led to the dreams. But, in the synthetic order of presenting the facts, what stood last in the succession of development stood first in the order of my purposes.

At the close of this little work, the reader was instructed to believe, and *truly* instructed, that I had mastered the tyranny of opium. The fact is that *twice* I mastered it, and by efforts even more prodigious in the second of these cases than in the first. But one error I committed in both. I did not connect with the abstinence from opium, so trying to the fortitude under *any* circumstances, that enormity of exercise which (as I have since learned) is the one sole resource for making it endurable. I overlooked, in those days, the one *sine qua non* for making the triumph permanent. Twice I sank, twice I rose again. A third time I sank; partly from the cause mentioned (the oversight as to exercise), partly from other causes, on which it avails not now to trouble the reader. I could moralize, if I chose; and perhaps *he* will moralize, whether I choose it or not. But, in the meantime, neither of us is acquainted properly with the circumstances of the case: I, from natural bias of judgement, not altogether acquainted; and he (with his permission) not at all.

During this third prostration before the dark idol, and after some years, new and monstrous phenomena began slowly to arise. For a time, these were neglected as accidents, or palliated by such remedies as I knew of. But, when I could no longer conceal from myself that these dreadful symptoms were moving forward for ever, by a pace steadily, solemnly, and equably increasing, I endeavoured, with some feeling of panic, for a third time to retrace my steps. But I had not reversed my motions for many weeks before I became profoundly aware that this was impossible. Or, in the imagery of my dreams, which translated everything into their own language, I saw, through vast avenues of gloom, those towering gates of ingress which hitherto had always seemed to stand open now at last barred against my retreat, and hung with funeral crape. I, upon seeing those awful gates closed and hung with draperies of woe, as for a death already past, spoke not, nor started, nor groaned. One profound sigh ascended from my heart, and I was silent for days.

* * *

In the *Opium Confessions* I touched a little upon the extraordinary power connected with opium (after long use) of amplifying the dimensions of time. Space, also, it amplifies by degrees that are sometimes terrific. But time it is upon which the exalting and multiplying power of opium chiefly spends its operation. Time becomes infinitely elastic, stretching out to such immeasurable and vanishing termini that it seems ridiculous to compute the sense of it, on waking, by expressions commensurate to human life. As in starry fields one computes by diameters of the Earth's orbit, or of Jupiter's, so, in valuing the *virtual* time lived during some dreams, the measurement by generations is ridiculous—by millennia is ridiculous; by æons, I should say, if æons were more determinate, would be also ridiculous.

* * *

Here pause, reader! Imagine yourself seated in some cloud-scaling swing, oscillating under the impulse of lunatic hands; for the strength of lunacy may belong to human dreams, the fearful caprice of lunacy, and the malice of lunacy, whilst the *victim* of those dreams may be all the more certainly removed from lunacy; even as a bridge gathers cohesion and strength from the increasing resistance into which it is forced by increasing pressure. Seated in such a swing, fast as you reach the lowest point of depression, may you rely on racing up to a starry altitude of corresponding ascent. Ups and downs you will see, heights and depths, in our fiery course together, such as will sometimes tempt you to look shyly and suspiciously at me, your guide, and the ruler of the oscillations. Here, at the point where I have called a halt, the reader has reached the lowest depths in my nursery afflictions. From that point according to the principles of *art* which govern the movement of these *Confessions,* I had meant to launch him upwards through the whole arch of ascending visions which seemed requisite to balance the sweep downwards, so recently described in his course. But accidents of the press have made it impossible to accomplish this purpose. There is reason to regret that the advantages of position which were essential to the full effect of passages planned for the equipoise and mutual resistance have thus been lost. Meantime, upon the principle of the mariner who rigs a *jury*-mast in default of his regular spars, I find my resource in a sort of "jury" peroration, not sufficient in the way of a balance by its *proportions,* but sufficient to indicate the *quality* of the balance which I had contemplated. He who has *really* read the preceding parts of these present *Confessions* will be aware that a stricter scrutiny of the past, such as was natural after the whole economy of the dreaming faculty had been convulsed beyond all precedents on record, led me to the conviction that not one agency, but two agencies had cooperated to the tremendous result. The nursery experience had been the ally and the natural coefficient of the opium. For that reason it was that the nursery experience has been narrated. Logically it bears the very same relation to the convulsions of the dreaming faculty as the opium. The idealizing tendency existed in the dream-theatre of my childhood; but the preternatural strength of its action and colouring was first developed after the confluence of the *two* causes. The reader must suppose me at Oxford; twelve years and a half are gone by; I am in the glory of youthful happiness: but I have now first tampered with opium; and now first the agitations of my childhood reopened in strength; now first they swept in upon the brain with power and the grandeur of recovered life under the separate and the concurring inspirations of opium.

## *THE PALIMPSEST OF THE HUMAN BRAIN*

You know perhaps, masculine reader, better than I can tell you, what is a *Palimpsest.* Possibly you have one in your own library. But yet, for the sake of others who may *not* know, or may have forgotten, suffer me to explain it here, lest any female reader who honours these papers with her notice should tax me with explaining it once too seldom; which would be worse to bear than a simultaneous complaint from twelve proud men that I had explained it three times too often. You, therefore, fair reader, understand that for *your* accommodation exclusively I explain the meaning of this word. It is Greek; and our sex enjoys the office and privilege of standing counsel to yours in all questions of Greek. We are, under favour, perpetual and hereditary dragomans to you. So that if, by accident, you know the meaning of a Greek word, yet by courtesy to us, your counsel learned in that matter, you will always seem *not* to know it.

A palimpsest, then, is a membrane or roll cleansed of its manuscript by reiterated successions.

What was the reason that the Greeks and the Romans had not the advantage of printed books? The answer will be, from ninety-nine persons in a hundred—Because the mystery of printing was not then discovered. But this is altogether a mistake. The secret of printing must have been discovered many thousands of times before it was used, or *could* be used. The inventive powers of man are divine; and also his stupidity is divine, as Cowper so playfully illustrates in the slow development of the *sofa* through successive generations of immortal dulness. It took centuries of blockheads to raise a joint stool into a chair; and it required something like a miracle of genius, in the estimate of elder generations, to reveal the possibility of lengthening a chair into a *chaise-longue*, or a sofa. Yes, these were inventions that cost mighty throes of intellectual power. But still, as respects printing, and admirable as is the stupidity of man, it was really not quite equal to the task of evading an object which stared him in the face with so broad a gaze. It did not require an Athenian intellect to read the main secret of printing in many scores of processes which the ordinary uses of life were *daily* repeating. To say nothing of analogous artifices amongst various mechanic artisans, all that is essential in printing must have been known to every nation that struck coins and medals. Not, therefore, any want of a printing art—that is, of an art for multiplying impressions—but the want of a cheap material for *receiving* such impressions, was the obstacle to an introduction of printed books even as early as Pisistratus. The ancients *did* apply printing to records of silver and gold; to marble, and many other substances cheaper than gold or silver, they did *not*, since each monument required a *separate* effort of inscription. Simply this defect it was of a cheap material for receiving impresses which froze in its very fountains the early resources of printing.

Some twenty years ago this view of the case was luminously expounded by Dr. Whately, and with the merit, I believe, of having first suggested it. Since then, this theory has received indirect confirmation. Now, out of that original scarcity affecting all materials proper for durable books, which continued up to times comparatively modern, grew the opening for palimpsests. Naturally, when once a roll of parchment or of vellum had done its office, by propagating through a series of generations what once had possessed an interest for *them*, but which, under changes of opinion or of taste, had faded to their feelings or had become obsolete for their undertakings, the whole *membrana* or vellum skin, the twofold product of human skill and costly material, and the costly freight of thought which it carried, drooped in value concurrently—supposing that each were inalienably associated to the other. Once it had been the impress of a human mind which stamped its value upon the vellum; the vellum, though costly, had contributed but a secondary element of value to the total result. At length, however, this relation between the vehicle and its freight has gradually been undermined. The vellum, from having been the setting of the jewel, has risen at length to be the jewel itself; and the burden of thought, from having given the chief value to the vellum, has now become the chief obstacle to its value; nay, has totally extinguished its value, unless it can be dissociated from the connexion. Yet, if this unlinking *can* be effected, then, fast as the inscription upon the membrane is sinking into rubbish, the membrane itself is reviving in its separate importance; and, from bearing a ministerial value, the vellum has come at last to absorb the whole value.

Hence the importance for our ancestors that the separation *should* be effected. Hence it arose in the Middle Ages as a considerable object for chemistry to discharge the writing from the roll, and thus to make it available for a new succession of thoughts. The soil, if cleansed from what once had been hot-house plants, but now were held to be weeds would be ready to receive a fresh and more appropriate crop. In that object the monkish chemists succeeded; but after a fashion which seems almost incredible—incredible not as regards the extent of their success, but as regards the delicacy of restraints under which it moved—so equally adjusted was their success to the immediate interests of that period, and to the reversionary objects of our own. They did the thing; but not so radically as to prevent us, their posterity, from *un*doing it. They expelled the writing sufficiently to leave a field for the new manuscript, and yet not sufficiently to make the traces of the elder manuscript irrecoverable for us. Could magic, could Hermes Trismegistus, have done more? What would you think, fair reader, of a problem such as this: to write a book which should be sense for your own generation, nonsense for the next; should revive into sense for the next after that, but again become nonsense for the fourth; and so on by alternate successions sinking into night or blazing into day, like the Sicilian river Arethusa and the English river Mole, or like the undulating motions of a flattened stone which children cause to skim the breast of a river, now diving below the water, now grazing its surface, sinking heavily into darkness, rising buoyantly into light, through a long vista of alternations? Such a problem, you say, is impossible. But really it is a problem not harder apparently than to bid a generation kill, so that a subsequent generation may call back into life; bury, so that posterity may command to rise again. Yet *that* was what the rude chemistry of past ages effected when coming into combination with the reaction from the more refined chemistry of our own. Had *they* been better chemists, had *we* been worse, the mixed result—namely, that, dying for *them*, the flower should revive for *us*—could not have been effected. They did the thing proposed to them: they did it effectually, for they founded upon it all that was wanted: and yet ineffectually, since we unravelled their work, effacing all above which they had superscribed, restoring all below which they had effaced.

Here, for instance, is a parchment which contained some Grecian tragedy—the *Agamemnon* of Æschylus, or the *Phœnissæ* of Euripides. This had possessed a value almost inappreciable in the eyes of accomplished scholars, continually growing rarer through generations. But four centuries are gone by since the destruction of the Western Empire. Christianity, with towering grandeurs of another class, has founded a different empire; and some bigoted, yet perhaps holy monk has washed away (as he persuades himself) the heathen's tragedy, replacing it with a monastic legend; which legend is disfigured with fables in its incidents, and yet in a higher sense is true, because interwoven with Christian morals, and with the sublimest of Christian revelations. Three, four, five, centuries more find man still devout as ever; but the language has become obsolete; and even for Christian devotion a new era has arisen, throwing it into the channel of crusading zeal or of chivalrous enthusiasm. The *membrana* is wanted now for a knightly romance—for *My Cid* or *Cœur de Lion*, for *Sir Tristram* or *Lybæus Disconus*. In this way, by means of the imperfect chemistry known to the medieval period, the same roll has served as a conservatory for three separate generations of flowers and fruits, all perfectly different, and yet all specially adapted to the wants of the successive possessors. The Greek tragedy, the monkish legend, the knightly romance, each has ruled its own period. One harvest after another has been gathered into the garners of man through ages far apart. And the same hydraulic machinery has distributed, through the same marble fountains, water, milk, or wine, according to the habits and training of the generations that came to quench their thirst.

Such were the achievements of rude monastic chemistry. But the more elaborate chemistry of our own days has reversed all these motions of our simple ancestors, with results in every stage that to *them* would have realized the most fantastic amongst the promises of thaumaturgy. Insolent vaunt of Paracelsus, that he would restore the original rose or violet out of the ashes settling from its combustion—*that* is now rivalled in this modern achievement. The traces of each successive handwriting, regularly effaced, as had been imagined, have, in the inverse order, been regularly called back: the footsteps of the game pursued, wolf or stag, in each several chase, have been unlinked, and hunted back through all their doubles; and, as the chorus of the Athenian stage unwove through the antistrophe every step that had been mystically woven through the strophe, so, by our modern conjurations of science, secrets of ages remote from each other have been exorcized[1] from the accumulated shadows of centuries. Chemistry, a witch as potent as the Erichtho of Lucan (*Pharsalia*, lib. vi or vii), has extorted by her torments, from the dust and ashes of forgotten centuries, the secrets of a life extinct for the general eye, but still glowing in the embers. Even the fable of the Phœnix, that secular bird who propagated his solitary existence, and his solitary births, along the line of centuries, through eternal relays of funeral mists, is but a type of what we have done with palimpsests. We have backed upon each phœnix in the long *regressus*, and forced him to expose his ancestral phœnix, sleeping in the ashes below his own ashes. Our good old forefathers would have been aghast at our sorceries; and, if they speculated on the propriety of burning Dr. Faustus, *us* they would have burned by acclamation. Trial there would have been none; and they could not otherwise have satisfied their horror of the brazen profligacy marking our modern magic than by ploughing up the houses of all who had been parties to it, and sowing the ground with salt.

Fancy not, reader, that this tumult of images, illustrative or allusive, moves under any impulse or purpose of mirth. It is but the coruscation of a restless understanding, often made ten times more so by irritation of the nerves, such as you will first learn to comprehend (its *how* and its *why*) some stage or two ahead. The image, the memorial, the record, which for me is derived from a palimpsest as to one great fact in our human being, and which immediately I will show you, is but too repellent of laughter; or, even if laughter *had* been possible, it would have been such laughter as oftentimes is thrown off from the fields of ocean,[2] laughter that hides, or that seems to evade, mustering tumult; foam-bells that weave garlands of phosphoric radiance for one moment round the eddies of gleaming abysses; mimicries of earthborn flowers that for the eye raise phantoms of gaiety, as oftentimes for the ear they raise the echoes of fugitive laughter, mixing with the ravings and choir-voices of an angry sea.

What else than a natural and mighty palimpsest is the human brain? Such a palimpsest is my brain; such a palimpsest, oh reader! is yours. Everlasting layers of ideas, images, feelings, have fallen upon your brain softly as light. Each succession has seemed to bury all that went before. And yet, in reality, not one has been extinguished. And, if in the vellum palimpsest, lying amongst the other *diplomata* of human archives or libraries, there is anything fantastic or which moves to laughter, as oftentimes there is in the grotesque collisions of those successive themes, having no natural connexion, which by pure accident have consecutively occupied the roll, yet, in our own heaven-created palimpsest, the deep memorial palimpsest of the brain, there are not and cannot be such incoherencies. The fleeting accidents of a man's life, and its external shows, may indeed be irrelate and incongruous; but the organizing principles which fuse into harmony, and gather about fixed predetermined centres, whatever heterogeneous elements life may have accumulated from without, will not permit the grandeur of human unity greatly to be violated, or its ultimate repose to be troubled, in the retrospect from dying moments, or from other great convulsions.

Such a convulsion is the struggle of gradual suffocation, as in drowning; and in the original *Opium Confessions* I mentioned a case of that nature communicated to me by a lady from her own childish experience. The lady was then still living, though of unusually great age; and I may mention that amongst her faults never was numbered any levity of principle, or carelessness of the most scrupulous veracity, but, on the contrary, such faults as arise from austerity, too harsh, perhaps, and gloomy, indulgent neither to others nor herself. And, at the time of relating this incident, when already very old, she had become religious to asceticism. According to my present belief, she had completed her ninth year when, playing by the side of a solitary brook, she fell into one of its deepest pools. Eventually, but after what lapse of time nobody ever knew, she was saved from death by a farmer, who, riding in some distant lane, had seen her rise to the surface; but not until she had descended within the abyss of death and looked into its secrets, as far, perhaps, as ever human eye *can* have looked that had permission to return. At a certain stage of this descent, a blow seemed to strike her; phosphoric radiance sprang forth from her eyeballs; and immediately a mighty theatre expanded within her brain. In a moment, in the twinkling of an eye, every act, every design of her past life, lived again, arraying themselves not as a succession, but as parts of a coexistence. Such a light fell upon the whole path of her life backwards into the shades of infancy as the light, perhaps, which wrapt the destined Apostle on his road to Damascus. Yet that light blinded for a season; but hers poured celestial vision upon the brain, so that her consciousness became omnipresent at one moment to every feature in the infinite review.

This anecdote was treated sceptically at the time by some critics. But, besides that it has since been confirmed by other experiences essentially the same, reported by other parties in the same circumstances, who had never heard of each other, the true point for astonishment is not the *simultaneity* of arrangement under which the past events of life, though in fact successive, had formed their dread line of revelation. This was but a secondary phenomenon; the deeper lay in the resurrection itself, and the possibility of resurrection for what had so long slept in the dust. A pall, deep as oblivion, had been thrown by life over every trace of these experiences; and yet suddenly, at a silent command, at the signal of a blazing rocket sent up from the brain, the pall draws up, and the whole depths of the theatre are exposed. Here was the greater mystery. Now, this mystery is liable to no doubt; for it is repeated, and ten thousand times repeated, by opium, for those who are its martyrs.

Yes, reader, countless are the mysterious handwritings of grief or joy which have inscribed themselves successively upon the palimpsest of your brain; and, like the annual leaves of aboriginal forests, or the undissolving snows on the Himalayas, or light falling upon light, the endless strata have covered up each other in forgetfulness. But by the hour of death, but by fever, but by the searchings of opium, all these can revive in strength. They are not dead, but sleeping. In the illustration imagined by myself from the case of some individual palimpsest, the Grecian tragedy had seemed to be displaced, but was *not* displaced, by the monkish legend; and the monkish legend had seemed to be displaced, but was *not* displaced, by the knightly romance. In some potent convulsion of the system, all wheels back into its earliest elementary stage. The bewildering romance, light tarnished with darkness, the semi-fabulous legend, truth celestial mixed with human falsehoods, these fade even of themselves as life advances. The romance has perished that the young man adored; the legend has gone that deluded the boy; but the deep, deep tragedies of infancy, as when the child's hands were unlinked for ever from his mother's neck, or his lips for ever from his sister's kisses, these remain lurking below all, and these lurk to the last.

## *VISION OF LIFE*

Upon me, as upon others scattered thinly by tens and twenties over every thousand years, fell too powerfully and too early the vision of life. The horror of life mixed itself already in earliest youth with the heavenly sweetness of life; that grief which one in a hundred has sensibility enough to gather from the sad retrospect of life in its closing stage for *me* shed its dews as a prelibation upon the fountains of life whilst yet sparkling to the morning sun. I saw from afar and from before what I was to see from behind. Is this the description of an early youth passed in the shades of gloom? No; but of a youth passed in the divinest happiness. And, if the reader has (which so few have) the passion without which there is no reading of the legend and superscription upon man's brow, if he is not (as most are) deafer than the grave to every *deep* note that sighs upwards from the Delphic caves of human life, he will know that the rapture of life (or anything which by approach can merit that name) does not arise, unless as perfect music arises, music of Mozart or Beethoven, by the confluence of the mighty and terrific discords with the subtle concords. Not by contrast, or as reciprocal foils, do these elements act—which is the feeble conception of many—but by union. They are the sexual forces in music: "male and female created he them"; and these mighty antagonists do not put forth their hostilities by repulsion, but by deepest attraction.

As "in today already walks tomorrow," so in the past experience of a youthful life may be seen dimly the future. The collisions with alien interests or hostile views of a child, boy, or very young man, so insulated as each of these is sure to be—those aspects of opposition which such a person *can* occupy—are limited by the exceedingly few and trivial lines of connexion along which he is able to radiate any essential influence whatever upon the fortunes or happiness of others. Circumstances may magnify his importance for the moment; but, after all, any cable which he carries out upon other vessels is easily slipped upon a feud arising. Far otherwise is the state of relations connecting an adult or responsible man with the circles around him as life advances. The network of these relations is a thousand times more intricate, the jarring of these intricate relations a thousand times more frequent, and the vibrations a thousand times harsher which these jarrings diffuse. This truth is felt beforehand, misgivingly and in troubled vision, by a young man who stands upon the threshold of manhood. One earliest instinct of fear and horror would darken his spirit if it could be revealed to itself and self-questioned at the moment of birth: a second instinct of the same nature would again pollute that tremulous mirror if the moment were as punctually marked as physical birth is marked which dismisses him finally upon the tides of absolute self-control. A dark ocean would seem the total expanse of life from the first; but far darker and more appalling would seem that inferior and second chamber of the ocean which called him away for ever from the direct accountability of others. Dreadful would be the morning which should say, "Be thou a human child incarnate"; but more dreadful the morning which should say, "Bear thou henceforth the sceptre of thy self-dominion through life, and the passion of life!" Yes, dreadful would be both; but without a basis of the dreadful there is no perfect rapture. It is in part through the sorrow of life, growing out of dark events, that this basis of awe and solemn darkness slowly accumulates. *That* I have illustrated. But, as life expands, it is more through the *strife* which besets us, strife from conflicting opinions, positions, passions, interests, that the funereal ground settles and deposits itself which sends upward the dark lustrous brilliancy through the jewel of life, else revealing a pale and superficial glitter. Either the human being must suffer and struggle, as the price of a more searching vision, or his gaze must be shallow and without intellectual revelation.

# *THE DARK INTERPRETER*

Oh, eternity with outstretched wings, that broodest over the secret truths in whose roots lie the mysteries of man—his whence, his whither—have I searched thee, and struck a right key on thy dreadful organ!

Suffering is a mightier agency in the hands of nature, as a Demiurgus creating the intellect, than most people are aware of.

The truth I heard often in sleep from the lips of the Dark Interpreter. Who is he? He is a shadow, reader, but a shadow with whom you must suffer me to make you acquainted. You need not be afraid of him, for when I explain his nature and origin you will see that he is essentially inoffensive; or if sometimes he menaces with his countenance, that is but seldom: and then, as his features in those moods shift as rapidly as clouds in a gale of wind, you may always look for the terrific aspects to vanish as fast as they have gathered. As to his origin—what it is, I know exactly, but cannot without a little circuit of preparation make *you* understand. Perhaps you are aware of that power in the eye of many children by which in darkness they project a vast theatre of phantasmagorical figures moving forwards or backwards between their bed-curtains and the chamber walls. In some children this power is semi-voluntary—they can control or perhaps suspend the shows; but in others it is altogether automatic. I myself, at the date of my last confessions, had seen in this way more processions—generally solemn, mournful, belonging to eternity, but also at times glad, triumphal pomps, that seemed to enter the gates of Time—than all the religions of paganism, fierce or gay, ever witnessed. Now, there is in the dark places of the human spirit—in grief, in fear, in vindictive wrath—a power of self-projection not unlike to this. Thirty years ago, it may be, a man called Symons committed several murders in a sudden epilepsy of planet-struck fury. According to my recollection, this case happened at Hoddesdon, which is in Middlesex. "Revenge is sweet!" was his hellish motto on that occasion, and that motto itself records the abysses which a human will can open. Revenge is *not* sweet, unless by the mighty charm of a charity that seeketh not her own it has become benignant. And what he had to revenge was woman's scorn. He had been a plain farm-servant; and, in fact, he was executed, as such men often are, on a proper point of professional respect to their calling, in a smock-frock, or blouse, to render so ugly a clash of syllables. His young mistress was every way and by much his superior, as well in prospects as in education. But the man, by nature arrogant, and little acquainted with the world, presumptuously raised his eyes to one of his young mistresses. Great was the scorn with which she repulsed his audacity, and her sisters participated in her disdain. Upon this affront he brooded night and day; and, after the term of his service was over, and he, in effect, forgotten by the family, one day he suddenly descended amongst the women of the family like an Avatar of vengeance. Right and left he threw out his murderous knife without distinction of person, leaving the room and the passage floating in blood.

The final result of this carnage was not so terrific as it threatened to be. Some, I think, recovered; but, also, one, who *did* not recover, was unhappily a stranger to the whole cause of his fury. Now, this murderer always maintained, in conversation with the prison chaplain, that, as he rushed on in his hellish career, he perceived distinctly a dark figure on his right hand, keeping pace with himself. Upon *that* the superstitious, of course, supposed that some fiend had revealed himself, and associated his superfluous presence with the dark atrocity. Symons was not a philosopher, but my opinion is, that he was too much so to tolerate that hypothesis, since, if there was one man in all Europe that needed no tempter to evil on that evening, it was precisely Mr. Symons, as nobody knew better than Mr. Symons himself. I had not the benefit of his acquaintance, or I would have explained it to him. The fact is, in point of awe a fiend would be a poor, trivial *bagatelle* compared to the shadowy projections, *umbras* and *penumbras,* which the unsearchable depths of man's nature is capable, under adequate excitement, of throwing off, and even into stationary forms. I shall have occasion to notice this point again. There are creative agencies in every part of human nature, of which the thousandth part could never be revealed in one life.

* * *

You have heard, reader, in the vision which describes Our Ladies of Sorrow, particularly in the dark admonition of Madonna, to her wicked sister that hateth and tempteth, what root of dark uses may lie in moral convulsions; not the uses hypocritically vaunted by theatrical devotion which affronts the majesty of God, that ever and in all things loves Truth—prefers sincerity that is erring to piety that cants. Rebellion which is the sin of witch-craft is more pardonable in His sight than speechifying resignation, listening with complacency to its own self-conquests. Show always as much neighbourhood as thou canst to grief that abases itself, which will cost thee but little effort if thine own grief hath been great. But God, who sees thy efforts in secret, will slowly strengthen those efforts, and make that to be a real deed, bearing tranquillity for thyself, which at first was but a feeble wish breathing homage to *Him*.

In after-life, from twenty to twenty-four, on looking back to those struggles of my childhood, I used to wonder exceedingly that a child could be exposed to struggles on such a scale. But two views unfolded upon me as my experience widened, which took away that wonder. The first was the vast scale upon which the sufferings of children are found everywhere expanded in the realities of life. The generation of infants which you see is but part of those who belong to it; were born in it; and make, the world over, not one half of it. The missing half, more than an equal number to those of any age that are now living, have perished by every kind of torments. Three thousand children per annum—that is, three hundred thousand per century; that is (omitting Sundays), about ten every day—pass to heaven through flames[3] in this very island of Great Britain. And of those who survive to reach maturity what multitudes have fought with fierce pangs of hunger, cold, and nakedness! When I came to know all this, then reverting my eye to *my* struggle, I said oftentimes it was nothing! Secondly, in watching the infancy of my own children, I made another discovery—it is well known to mothers, to nurses, and also to philosophers—that the tears and lamentations of infants during the year or so when they have no *other* language of complaint run through a gamut that is as inexhaustible as the Cremona of Paganini. An ear but moderately learned in that language cannot be deceived as to the rate and *modulus* of the suffering which it indicates. A fretful or peevish cry cannot by any efforts make itself impassioned. The cry of impatience, of hunger, of irritation, of reproach, of alarm, are all different—different as a chorus of Beethoven from a chorus of Mozart. But if ever you saw an infant suffering for an hour, as sometimes the healthiest does, under some attack of the stomach, which has the tiger-grasp of the Oriental cholera, then you will hear moans that address to their mothers an anguish of supplication for aid such as might storm the heart of Moloch. Once hearing it, you will not forget it. Now, it was a constant remark of mine, after any storm of that nature (occurring, suppose, once in two months), that always on the following day, when a long, long sleep had chased away the darkness, and the memory of the darkness from the little creature's brain, a sensible expansion had taken place in the intellectual faculties of attention, observation, and animation. It renewed the case of our great modern poet, who, on listening to the raving of the midnight storm, and the crashing which it was making in the mighty woods, reminded himself that all this hell of trouble

Tells also of bright calms that shall succeed.

Pain driven to agony, or grief driven to frenzy, is essential to the ventilation of profound natures. A sea which is deeper than any that Count Massigli[4] measured cannot be searched and torn up from its sleeping depths without a levanter or a monsoon. A nature which is profound in excess, but also introverted and abstracted in excess, so as to be in peril of wasting itself in interminable reverie, cannot be awakened sometimes without afflictions that go to the very foundations, heaving, stirring, yet finally harmonizing; and it is in such cases that the Dark Interpreter does his work, revealing the worlds of pain and agony and woe possible to man—possible even to the innocent spirit of a child.

## *Notes*

1. Some readers may be apt to suppose, from all English experience, that the word *exorcize* means properly banishment to the shades. Not so. Citation *from* the shades, or sometimes the torturing coercion of mystic adjurations, is more truly the primary sense.

2. Many readers will recall, though, at the moment of writing, my own thoughts did *not* recall, the well-known passage in the *Prometheus*—

—ποντιων τε κυματων
Ανηριϑμον γελασμα.

"O multitudinous laughter of the ocean billows!" It is not clear whether Æschylus contemplated the laughter as addressing the ear or the eye.

3. Three thousand children are annually burnt to death in the nations of England and Scotland, chiefly through the carelessness of parents. I shudder to add another and darker cause, which is a deep disgrace to the present age.

4. Count Massigli (an Austrian officer in the imperial service) about sixty years ago fathomed and attempted to fathom many parts of the Mediterranean and the Atlantic. If I remember rightly, he found the bottom within less than an English mile.

# The Literature of Knowledge and the Literature of Power

Every great classic in our native language should from time to time be reviewed anew; and especially if he belongs in any considerable extent to that section of the literature which connects itself with manners, and if his reputation originally, or his style of composition, is likely to have been much influenced by the transient fashions of his own age. The withdrawal, for instance, from a dramatic poet, or a satirist, of any false lustre which he has owed to his momentary connexion with what we may call the *personalities* of a fleeting generation, or of any undue shelter to his errors which may have gathered round them from political bias, or from intellectual infirmities amongst his partisans, will sometimes seriously modify, after a century or so, the fairest *original* appreciation of a fine writer. A window composed of Claude Lorraine glasses spreads over the landscape outside a disturbing effect, which not the most practised eye can evade. The *eidola theatri* affect us all. No man escapes the contagion from his contemporary bystanders.

As books multiply to an unmanageable excess, selection becomes more and more a necessity for readers, and the power of selection more and more a desperate problem for the busy part of readers. The possibility of selecting wisely is becoming continually more hopeless as the necessity for selection is becoming continually more pressing. Exactly as the growing weight of books overlays and stifles the power of comparison, *pari passu* is the call for comparison the more clamorous; and thus arises a duty correspondingly more urgent of searching and revising until everything spurious has been weeded out from amongst the Flora of our highest literature, and until the waste of time for those who have so little at their command is reduced to a *minimum*. For, where the good cannot be read in its twentieth part, the more requisite it is that no part of the bad should steal an hour of the available time; and it is not to be endured that people without a minute to spare should be obliged first of all to read a book before they can ascertain whether in fact it is *worth* reading. The public cannot read by proxy as regards the good which it is to appropriate, but it *can* as regards the poison which it is to escape. And thus, as literature expands, becoming continually more of a household necessity, the duty resting upon critics (who are the vicarious readers for the public) becomes continually more urgent—of reviewing all works that may be supposed to have benefited too much or too indiscriminately by the superstition of a name. The *prægustatores* should have tasted of every cup, and reported its quality, before the public call for it; and, above all, they should have done this in all cases of the higher literature—that is, of literature properly so called.

What is it that we mean by *literature*? Popularly, and amongst the thoughtless, it is held to include everything that is printed in a book. Little logic is required to disturb *that* definition. The most thoughtless person is easily made aware that in the idea of *literature* one essential element is some relation to a general and common interest of man—so that what applies only to a local, or professional, or merely personal interest, even though presenting itself in the shape of a book, will not belong to literature. So far the definition is easily narrowed; and it is as easily expanded. For not only is much that takes a station in books not literature; but inversely, much that really *is* literature never reaches a station in books. The weekly sermons of Christendom, that vast pulpit literature which acts so extensively upon the popular mind—to warn, to uphold, to renew, to comfort, to alarm—does not attain the sanctuary of libraries in the ten-thousandth part of its extent. The drama again—as, for instance, the finest of Shakespeare's plays in England, and all leading Athenian plays in the noontide of the Attic stage—operated as a literature on the public mind, and were (according to the strictest letter of that term) *published* through the audiences that witnessed[1] their representation some time before they were published as things to be read; and they were published in this scenical mode of publication with much more effect than they could have had as books during ages of costly copying or of costly printing.

Books, therefore, do not suggest an idea coextensive and interchangeable with the idea of literature; since much literature, scenic, forensic, or didactic (as from lecturers and public orators), may never come into books, and much that *does* come into books may connect itself with no literary interest.[2] But a far more important correction, applicable to the common vague idea of literature, is to be sought not so much in a better definition of literature as in a sharper distinction of the two functions which it fulfils. In that great social organ which, collectively, we call literature, there may be distinguished two separate offices that may blend and often *do* so, but capable, severally, of a severe insulation, and naturally fitted for reciprocal repulsion. There is, first, the Literature of *Knowledge;* and, secondly, the Literature of *Power*. The function of the first is—to *teach;* the function of the second is—to *move:* the first is a rudder; the second, an oar or a sail. The first speaks to the *mere* discursive understanding; the second speaks ultimately, it may happen, to the higher understanding or reason, but always *through* affections of pleasure and sympathy. Remotely, it may travel towards an object seated in what Lord Bacon calls *dry* light; but, proximately, it does and must operate—else it ceases to be a Literature of *Power*—on and through that *humid* light which clothes itself in the mists and glittering *iris* of human passions, desires, and genial emotions. Men have so little reflected on the higher functions of literature as to find it a paradox if one should describe it as a mean or subordinate purpose of books to give information. But this is a paradox only in the sense which makes it honourable to be paradoxical. Whenever we talk in ordinary language of seeking information or gaining knowledge, we understand the words as connected with something of absolute novelty. But it is the grandeur of all truth which *can* occupy a very high place in human interests that it is never absolutely novel to the meanest of minds: it exists eternally by way of germ or latent principle in the lowest as in the highest, needing to be developed, but never to be planted. To be capable of transplantation is the immediate criterion of a truth that ranges on a lower scale. Besides which, there is a rarer thing than truth—namely, *power*, or deep sympathy with truth. What is the effect, for instance, upon society, of children? By the pity, by the tenderness, and by the peculiar modes of admiration, which connect themselves with the helplessness, with the innocence, and with the simplicity of children, not only are the primal affections strengthened and continually renewed, but the qualities which are dearest in the sight of heaven—the frailty, for instance, which appeals to forbearance, the innocence which symbolizes the heavenly, and the simplicity which is most alien from the worldly—are kept up in perpetual remembrance, and their ideals are continually refreshed. A purpose of the same nature is answered by the higher literature, viz. the Literature of Power. What do you learn from *Paradise Lost*? Nothing at all. What do you learn from a cookery-book? Something new, something that you did not know before, in every paragraph. But would you therefore put the wretched cookery-book on a higher level of estimation than the divine poem? What you owe to Milton is not any knowledge, of which a million separate items are still but a million of advancing steps on the same earthly level; what you owe is *power*—that is, exercise and expansion to your own latent capacity of sympathy with the infinite, where every pulse and each separate influx is a step upwards, a step ascending as upon a Jacob's ladder from earth to mysterious altitudes above the earth. *All* the steps of knowledge, from first to last, carry you further on the same plane, but could never raise you one foot above your ancient level of earth: whereas the very *first* step in power is a flight—is an ascending movement into another element where earth is forgotten.

Were it not that human sensibilities are ventilated and continually called out into exercise by the great phenomena of infancy, or of real life as it moves through chance and change, or of literature as it recombines these elements in the mimicries of poetry, romance, &c., it is certain that, like any animal power or muscular energy falling into disuse, all such sensibilities would gradually droop and dwindle. It is in relation to these great *moral* capacities of man that the Literature of Power, as contradistinguished from that of knowledge, lives and has its field of action. It is concerned with what is highest in man; for the Scriptures themselves never condescended to deal by suggestion or co-operation with the mere discursive understanding: when speaking of man in his intellectual capacity, the Scriptures speak not of the understanding, but of "*the understanding heart*"—making the heart, *i.e.* the great *intuitive* (or non-discursive) organ, to be the interchangeable formula for man in his highest state of capacity for the infinite. Tragedy, romance, fairy tale, or epopee, all alike restore to man's mind the ideals of justice, of hope, of truth, of mercy, of retribution, which else (left to the support of daily life in its realities) would languish for want of sufficient illustration. What is meant, for instance, by *poetic justice*?—It does not mean a justice that differs by its object from the ordinary justice of human jurisprudence; for then it must be confessedly a very bad kind of justice; but it means a justice that differs from common forensic justice by the degree in which it *attains* its object, a justice that is more omnipotent over its own ends, as dealing—not with the refractory elements of earthly life, but with the elements of its own creation, and with materials flexible to its own purest preconceptions. It is certain that, were it not for the Literature of Power, these ideals would often remain amongst us as mere arid notional forms; whereas, by the creative forces of man put forth in literature, they gain a vernal life of restoration, and germinate into vital activities. The commonest novel, by moving in alliance with human fears and hopes, with human instincts of wrong and right, sustains and quickens those affections. Calling them into action, it rescues them from torpor. And hence the pre-eminency over all authors that merely *teach* of the meanest that *moves,* or that teaches, if at all, indirectly *by* moving. The very highest work that has ever existed in the Literature of Knowledge is but a *provisional* work: a book upon trial and sufferance, and *quamdiu bene se gesserit*. Let its teaching be even partially revised, let it be but expanded—nay, even let its teaching be but placed in a better order—and instantly it is superseded. Whereas the feeblest works in the Literature of Power, surviving at all, survive as finished and unalterable amongst men. For instance, the *Principia* of Sir Isaac Newton was a book *militant* on earth from the first. In all stages of its progress it would have to fight for its existence: first, as regards absolute truth; secondly, when that combat was over, as regards its form or mode of presenting the truth. And as soon as a Laplace, or anybody else, builds higher upon the foundations laid by this book, effectually he throws it out of the sunshine into decay and darkness; by weapons won from this book he superannuates and destroys this book, so that soon the name of Newton remains as a mere *nominis umbra,* but his book, as a living power, has transmigrated into other forms. Now, on the contrary, the Iliad, the *Prometheus* of Æschylus, the *Othello* or *King Lear,* the *Hamlet* or *Macbeth,* and the *Paradise Lost*, are not militant, but triumphant for ever as long as the languages exist in which they speak or can be taught to speak. They never *can* transmigrate into new incarnations. To reproduce *these* in new forms, or variations, even if in some things they should be improved, would be to plagiarize. A good steam-engine is properly superseded by a better. But one lovely pastoral valley is not superseded by another, nor a statue of Praxiteles by a statue of Michael Angelo. These things are separated not by imparity, but by disparity. They are not thought of as unequal under the same standard, but as different in *kind,* and, if otherwise equal, as equal under a different standard. Human works of immortal beauty and works of nature in one respect stand on the same footing: they never absolutely repeat each other, never approach so near as not to differ; and they differ not as better and worse, or simply by more and less: they differ by undecipherable and incommunicable differences, that cannot be caught by mimicries, that cannot be reflected in the mirror of copies, that cannot become ponderable in the scales of vulgar comparison.

All works in this class, as opposed to those in the Literature of Knowledge, first, work by far deeper agencies, and, secondly, are more permanent; in the strictest sense they are κτηματα ἐς ἀει: and what evil they do, or what good they do, is commensurate with the national language, sometimes long after the nation has departed. At this hour, five hundred years since their creation, the tales of Chaucer, never equalled on this earth for their tenderness, and for life of picturesqueness, are read familiarly by many in the charming language of their natal day, and by others in the modernizations of Dryden, of Pope, and Wordsworth. At this hour, one thousand eight hundred years since their creation, the Pagan tales of Ovid, never equalled on this earth for the gaiety of their movement and the capricious graces of their narrative, are read by all Christendom. This man's people and their monuments are dust; but *he* is alive: he has survived them, as he told us that he had it in his commission to do, by a thousand years; "and *shall* a thousand more."

All the Literature of Knowledge builds only groundnests, that are swept away by floods, or confounded by the plough; but the Literature of Power builds nests in aerial altitudes of temples sacred from violation, or of forests inaccessible to fraud. *This* is a great prerogative of the *power* literature; and it is a greater which lies in the mode of its influence. The *knowledge* literature, like the fashion of this world, passeth away. An encyclopædia is its abstract; and, in this respect, it may be taken for its speaking symbol—that before one generation has passed an encyclopædia is superannuated; for it speaks through the dead memory and unimpassioned understanding, which have not the repose of higher faculties, but are continually enlarging and varying their phylacteries. But all literature properly so called—literature κατ' ἐξοχην—for the very same reason that it is so much more durable than the Literature of Knowledge, is (and by the very same proportion it is) more intense and electrically searching in its impressions. The directions in which the tragedy of this planet has trained our human feelings to play, and the combinations into which the poetry of this planet has thrown our human passions of love and hatred, of admiration and contempt, exercise a power for bad or good over human life that cannot be contemplated, when stretching through many generations, without a sentiment allied to awe.[3] And of this let every one be assured—that he owes to the impassioned books which he has read many a thousand more of emotions than he can consciously trace back to them. Dim by their origination, these emotions yet arise in him, and mould him through life, like forgotten incidents of his childhood.

## *NOTES*

1. Charles I, for example, when Prince of Wales, and many others in his father's court, gained their known familiarity with Shakespeare not through the original quartos, so slenderly diffused, nor through the first folio of 1623, but through the court representations of his chief dramas at Whitehall.

2. What are called *The Blue Books*—by which title are understood the folio Reports issued every session of Parliament by committees of the two Houses, and stitched into blue covers—though often sneered at by the ignorant as so much waste paper, will be acknowledged gratefully by those who have used them diligently as the main well-heads of all accurate information as to the Great Britain of this day. As an immense depository of faithful *(and not superannuated)* statistics, they are indispensable to the honest student. But no man would therefore class *The Blue Books* as literature.

3. The reason why the broad distinctions between the two literatures of power and knowledge so little fix the attention lies in the fact that a vast proportion of books—history, biography, travels, miscellaneous essays, &c.—lying in a middle zone, confound these distinctions by interblending them. All that we call "amusement" or "entertainment" is a diluted form of the power belonging to passion, and also a mixed form; and, where threads of direct *instruction* intermingle in the texture with these threads of *power,* this absorption of the duality into one representative *nuance* neutralizes the separate perception of either. Fused into a *tertium quid,* or neutral state, they disappear to the popular eye as the repelling forces which, in fact, they are.

# *Thomas Love Peacock*

1785–1866

Thomas Love Peacock can perhaps be best understood as a minor English Romantic whose novels poke fun at major English Romantics. These novels, or "comic romances" (the term is his own), typically display a preponderance of witty conversation combined with a paucity of plot and character development. The conversations take place over dinner tables; much learned verbiage is thrown about as the conversationalists—closely modeled on Peacock's friends Coleridge, Byron, and Shelley—are gently made to look ridiculous. This particular genre, which represents one of the most cultivated examples of the *roman à clef* in English literature, not only reveals Peacock's intimate acquaintance with his more illustrious friends, but also subtly underscores his admiration for them.

Peacock's friendship with Shelley was of particular importance for both men. *The Four Ages of Poetry* (1820) provoked Shelley to respond with his celebrated *Defence of Poetry* (written 1821, published 1840). Although Peacock displayed great business acumen (he worked for the British East India Company for at least 20 years as its Chief Examiner), he seems to have been financially dependent on Shelley for a period of his life and became the executor of his will. In Peacock's *Headlong Hall* (1816), Shelley might be said to play a prominent—if disguised—role; in *Nightmare Abbey* (1818), a satiric *tour de force* in which the conventions of Romantic melancholy are made to appear benignly ridiculous, he appears as the poet Scythrop. Peacock, as his name suggests, was something of a gaudy creature, but a light, genial, and wholly gentle one. As Edward Strachey said of this kindly bird who joyfully mixed life with art, he was "a friendly man, who loved to share his enjoyment of life with all around him, and self-indulgent without being selfish."

# The Four Ages of Poetry

*Qui inter hæc nutriuntur non magis sapere possunt, quam bene olere qui in culinâ habitant.*

Petronius

Poetry, like the world, may be said to have four ages, but in a different order: the first age of poetry being the age of iron; the second, of gold; the third of silver; and the fourth of brass.

The first, or iron age of poetry, is that in which rude bards celebrate in rough numbers the exploits of ruder chiefs, in days when every man is a warrior, and when the great practical maxim of every form of society, "to keep what we have and to catch what we can," is not yet disguised under names of justice and forms of law, but is the naked motto of the naked sword, which is the only judge and jury in every question of *meum* and *tuum*. In these days, the only three trades flourishing (besides that of priest, which flourishes always) are those of king, thief, and beggar: the beggar being, for the most part, a king deject, and the thief a king expectant. The first question asked of a stranger is, whether he is a beggar or a thief: the stranger, in reply, usually assumes the first, and awaits a convenient opportunity to prove his claim to the second appellation.

The natural desire of every man to engross to himself as much power and property as he can acquire by any of the means which might makes right, is accompanied by the no less natural desire of making known to as many people as possible the extent to which he has been a winner in this universal game. The successful warrior becomes a chief; the successful chief becomes a king: his next want is an organ to disseminate the fame of his achievements and the extent of his possessions; and this organ he finds in a bard, who is always ready to celebrate the strength of his arm, being first duly inspired by that of his liquor. This is the origin of poetry, which, like all other trades, takes its rise in the demand for the commodity, and flourishes in proportion to the extent of the market.

Poetry is thus in its origin panegyrical. The first rude songs of all nations appear to be a sort of brief historical notices, in a strain of tumid hyperbole, of the exploits and possessions of a few pre-eminent individuals. They tell us how many battles such an one has fought, how many helmets he has cleft, how many breastplates he has pierced, how many widows he has made, how much land he has appropriated, how many houses he has demolished for other people, what a large one he has built for himself, how much gold he has stowed away in it, and how liberally and plentifully he pays, feeds, and intoxicates the divine and immortal bards, the sons of Jupiter, but for whose everlasting songs the names of heroes would perish.

This is the first stage of poetry before the invention of written letters. The numerical modulation is at once useful as a help to memory, and pleasant to the ears of uncultured men, who are easily caught by sound: and, from the exceeding flexibility of the yet unformed language, the poet does no violence to his ideas in subjecting them to the fetters of number. The savage, indeed, lisps in numbers, and all rude and uncivilized people express themselves in the manner which we call poetical.

The scenery by which he is surrounded, and the superstitions which are the creed of his age, form the poet's mind. Rocks, mountains, seas, unsubdued forests, unnavigable rivers, surround him with forms of power and mystery, which ignorance and fear have peopled with spirits, under multifarious names of gods, goddesses, nymphs, genii, and dæmons. Of all these personages marvellous tales are in existence: the nymphs are not indifferent to handsome young men, and the gentlemen-genii are much troubled and very troublesome with a propensity to be rude to pretty maidens: the bard, therefore, finds no difficulty in tracing the genealogy of his chief to any of the deities in his neighbourhood with whom the said chief may be most desirous of claiming relationship.

In this pursuit, as in all others, some, of course, will attain a very marked pre-eminence; and these will be held in high honour, like Demodocus in the Odyssey, and will be consequently inflated with boundless vanity, like Thamyris in the Iliad. Poets are as yet the only historians and chroniclers of their time, and the sole depositories of all the knowledge of their age; and though this knowledge is rather a crude congeries of traditional phantasies than a collection of useful truths, yet, such as it is, they have it to themselves. They are observing and thinking, while others are robbing and fighting: and though their object be nothing more than to secure a share of the spoil, yet they accomplish this end by intellectual, not by physical power: their success excites emulation to the attainment of intellectual eminence: thus they sharpen their own wits and awaken those of others, at the same time that they gratify vanity and amuse curiosity. A skilful display of the little knowledge they have gains them credit for the possession of much more which they have not. Their familiarity with the secret history of gods and genii obtains for them, without much difficulty, the reputation of inspiration; thus they are not only historians, but theologians, moralists, and legislators: delivering their oracles *ex cathedrâ,* and being indeed often themselves (as Orpheus and Amphion) regarded as portions and emanations of divinity: building cities with a song, and leading brutes with a symphony; which are only metaphors for the faculty of leading multitudes by the nose.

The golden age of poetry finds its materials in the age of iron. This age begins when poetry begins to be retrospective; when something like a more extended system of civil polity is established; when personal strength and courage avail less to the aggrandizing of their possessor, and to the making and marring of kings and kingdoms, and are checked by organized bodies, social institutions, and hereditary successions. Men also live more in the light of truth and within the interchange of observation; and thus perceive that the agency of gods and genii is not so frequent among themselves as, to judge from the songs and legends of the past time, it was among their ancestors. From these two circumstances, really diminished personal power, and apparently diminished familiarity with gods and genii, they very easily and naturally deduce two conclusions: 1st, That men are degenerated, and 2nd, That they are less in favour with the gods. The people of the petty states and colonies, which have now acquired stability and form, which owed their origin and first prosperity to the talents and courage of a single chief, magnify their founder through the mists of distance and tradition, and perceive him achieving wonders with a god or goddess always at his elbow. They find his name and his exploits thus magnified and accompanied in their traditionary songs, which are their only memorials. All that is said of him is in this character. There is nothing to contradict it. The man and his exploits and his tutelary deities are mixed and blended in one invariable association. The marvellous, too, is very much like a snow-ball: it grows as it rolls downward, till the little nucleus of truth, which began its descent from the summit, is hidden in the accumulation of superinduced hyperbole.

When tradition, thus adorned and exaggerated, has surrounded the founders of families and states with so much adventitious power and magnificence, there is no praise which a living poet can, without fear of being kicked for clumsy flattery, address to a living chief, that will not still leave the impression that the latter is not so great a man as his ancestors. The man must, in this case, be praised through his ancestors. Their greatness must be established, and he must be shown to be their worthy descendant. All the people of a state are interested in the founder of their state. All states that have harmonized into a common form of society, are interested in their respective founders. All men are interested in their ancestors. All men love to look back into the days that are past. In these circumstances traditional national poetry is reconstructed and brought, like chaos, into order and form. The interest is more universal: understanding is enlarged: passion still has scope and play: character is still various and strong: nature is still unsubdued and existing in all her beauty and magnificence, and men are not yet excluded from her observation by the magnitude of cities, or the daily confinement of civic life: poetry is more an art: it requires greater skill in numbers, greater command of language, more extensive and various knowledge, and greater comprehensiveness of mind. It still exists without rivals in any other department of literature; and even the arts, painting and sculpture certainly, and music probably, are comparatively rude and imperfect. The whole field of intellect is its own. It has no rivals in history, nor in philosophy, nor in science. It is cultivated by the greatest intellects of the age, and listened to by all the rest. This is the age of Homer, the golden age of poetry. Poetry has now attained its perfection: it has attained the point which it cannot pass: genius therefore seeks new forms for the treatment of the same subjects: hence the lyric poetry of Pindar and Alcæus, and the tragic poetry of Æschylus and Sophocles. The favour of kings, the honour of the Olympic crown, the applause of present multitudes, all that can feed vanity and stimulate rivalry, await the successful cultivator of this art, till its forms become exhausted, and new rivals arise around it in new fields of literature, which gradually acquire more influence as, with the progress of reason and civilization, facts become more interesting than fiction: indeed, the maturity of poetry may be considered the infancy of history. The transition from Homer to Herodotus is scarcely more remarkable than that from Herodotus to Thucydides: in the gradual dereliction of fabulous incident and ornamented language. Herodotus is as much a poet, in relation to Thucydides as Homer is in relation to Herodotus. The history of Herodotus is half a poem: it was written while the whole field of literature yet belonged to the Muses, and the nine books of which it was composed were therefore of right, as well of courtesy, superinscribed with their nine names.

Speculations, too, and disputes, on the nature of man and of mind; on moral duties and on good and evil; on the animate and inanimate components of the visible world; begin to share attention with the eggs of Leda and the horns of Io, and to draw off from poetry a portion of its once undivided audience.

Then comes the silver age, or the poetry of civilized life. This poetry is of two kinds, imitative and original. The imitative consists in recasting, and giving an exquisite polish to the poetry of the age of gold: of this Virgil is the most obvious and striking example. The original is chiefly comic, didactic, or satiric: as in Menander, Aristophanes, Horace, and Juvenal. The poetry of this age is characterized by an exquisite and fastidious selection of words, and a laboured and somewhat monotonous harmony of expression: but its monotony consists in this, that experience having exhausted all the varieties of modulation, the civilized poetry selects the most beautiful, and prefers the repetition of these to ranging through the variety of all. But the best expression being that into which the idea naturally falls, it requires the utmost labour and care so to reconcile the inflexibility of civilized language and the laboured polish of versification with the idea intended to be expressed, that sense may not appear to be sacrificed to sound. Hence numerous efforts and rare success.

This state of poetry is, however, a step towards its extinction. Feeling and passion are best painted in, and roused by, ornamental and figurative language; but the reason and the understanding are best addressed in the simplest and most unvarnished phrase. Pure reason and dispassionate truth would be perfectly ridiculous in verse, as we may judge by versifying one of Euclid's demonstrations. This will be found true of all dispassionate reasoning whatever, and of all reasoning that requires comprehensive views and enlarged combinations. It is only the more tangible points of morality, those which command assent at once, those which have a mirror in every mind, and in which the severity of reason is warmed and rendered palatable by being mixed up with feeling and imagination, that are applicable even to what is called moral poetry: and as the sciences of morals and of mind advance towards perfection, as they become more enlarged and comprehensive in their views, as reason gains the ascendancy in them over imagination and feeling, poetry can no longer accompany them in their progress, but drops into the background, and leaves them to advance alone.

Thus the empire of thought is withdrawn from poetry, as the empire of facts had been before. In respect of the latter, the poet of the age of iron celebrates the achievements of his contemporaries; the poet of the age of gold celebrates the heroes of the age of iron; the poet of the age of silver re-casts the poems of the age of gold: we may here see how very slight a ray of historical truth is sufficient to dissipate all the illusions of poetry. We know no more of the men than of the gods of the Iliad; no more of Achilles than we do of Thetis; no more of Hector and Andromache than we do of Vulcan and Venus: these belong altogether to poetry; history has no share in them: but Virgil knew better than to write an epic about Cæsar; he left him to Livy; and travelled out of the confines of truth and history into the old regions of poetry and fiction.

Good sense and elegant learning, conveyed in polished and somewhat monotonous verse, are the perfection of the original and imitative poetry of civilized life. Its range is limited, and when exhausted, nothing remains but the *crambe repetita* of commonplace, which at length becomes thoroughly wearisome, even to the most indefatigable readers of the newest new nothings.

It is now evident that poetry must either cease to be cultivated, or strike into a new path. The poets of the age of gold have been imitated and repeated till no new imitation will attract notice: the limited range of ethical and didactic poetry is exhausted: the associations of daily life in an advanced state of society are of very dry, methodical, unpoetical matters-of-fact: but there is always a multitude of listless idlers, yawning for amusement, and gaping for novelty: and the poet makes it his glory to be foremost among their purveyors.

Then comes the age of brass, which, by rejecting the polish and the learning of the age of silver, and taking a retrograde stride to the barbarisms and crude traditions of the age of iron, professes to return to nature and revive the age of gold. This is the second childhood of poetry. To the comprehensive energy of the Homeric Muse, which, by giving at once the grand outline of things, presented to the mind a vivid picture in one or two verses, inimitable alike in simplicity and magnificence, is substituted a verbose and minutely-detailed description of thoughts, passions, actions, persons, and things, in that loose rambling style of verse, which any one may write, *stans pede in uno,* at the rate of two hundred lines in an hour. To this age may be referred all the poets who flourished in the decline of the Roman Empire. The best specimen of it, though not the most generally known, is the Dionysiaca of Nonnus, which contains many passages of exceeding beauty in the midst of masses of amplification and repetition.

The iron age of classical poetry may be called the bardic; the golden, the Homeric; the silver, the Virgilian; and the brass, the Nonnic.

Modern poetry has also its four ages: but "it wears its rue with a difference."

To the age of brass in the ancient world succeeded the dark ages, in which the light of the Gospel began to spread over Europe, and in which, by a mysterious and inscrutable dispensation, the darkness thickened with the progress of the light. The tribes that overran the Roman Empire brought back the days of barbarism, but with this difference, that there were many books in the world, many places in which they were preserved, and occasionally some one by whom they were read, who indeed (if he escaped being burned *pour l'amour de Dieu*) generally lived an object of mysterious fear, with the reputation of magician, alchymist, and astrologer. The emerging of the nations of Europe from this superinduced barbarism, and their settling into new forms of polity, was accompanied, as the first ages of Greece had been, with a wild spirit of adventure, which, co-operating with new manners and new superstitions, raised up a fresh crop of chimæras, not less fruitful, though far less beautiful, than those of Greece. The semi-deification of women by the maxims of the age of chivalry, combining with these new fables, produced the romance of the middle ages. The founders of the new line of heroes took the place of the demi-gods of Grecian poetry. Charlemagne and his Paladins, Arthur and his knights of the round table, the heroes of the iron age of chivalrous poetry, were seen through the same magnifying mist of distance, and their exploits were celebrated with even more extravagant hyperbole. These legends, combined with the exaggerated love that pervades the songs of the troubadours, the reputation of magic that attached to learned men, the infant wonders of natural philosophy, the crazy fanaticism of the crusades, the power and privileges of the great feudal chiefs, and the holy mysteries of monks and nuns, formed a state of society in which no two laymen could meet without fighting, and in which the three staple ingredients of lover, prize-fighter, and fanatic, that composed the basis of the character of every true man, were mixed up and diversified, in different individuals and classes, with so many distinctive excellences, and under such an infinite motley variety of costume, as gave the range of a most extensive and picturesque field to the two great constituents of poetry, love and battle.

From these ingredients of the iron age of modern poetry, dispersed in the rhymes of minstrels and the songs of the troubadours, arose the golden age, in which the scattered materials were harmonized and blended about the time of the revival of learning; but with this peculiar difference, that Greek and Roman literature pervaded all the poetry of the golden age of modern poetry, and hence resulted a heterogeneous compound of all ages and nations in one picture; an infinite licence, which gave to the poet the free range of the whole field of imagination and memory. This was carried very far by Ariosto, but farthest of all by Shakspeare and his contemporaries, who used time and locality merely because they could not do without them, because every action must have its when and where: but they made no scruple of deposing a Roman Emperor by an Italian Count, and sending him off in the disguise of a French pilgrim to be shot with a blunderbuss by an English archer. This makes the old English drama very picturesque, at any rate, in the variety of costume, and very diversified in action and character; though it is a picture of nothing that ever was seen on earth except a Venetian carnival.

The greatest of English poets, Milton, may be said to stand alone between the ages of gold and silver, combining the excellences of both; for with all the energy, and power, and freshness of the first, he united all the studied and elaborate magnificence of the second.

The silver age succeeded; beginning with Dryden, coming to perfection with Pope, and ending with Goldsmith, Collins, and Gray.

Cowper divested verse of its exquisite polish; he thought in metre, but paid more attention to his thoughts than his verse. It would be difficult to draw the boundary of prose and blank verse between his letters and his poetry.

The silver age was the reign of authority; but authority now began to be shaken, not only in poetry but in the whole sphere of its dominion. The contemporaries of Gray and Cowper were deep and elaborate thinkers. The subtle scepticism of Hume, the solemn irony of Gibbon, the daring paradoxes of Rousseau, and the biting ridicule of Voltaire, directed the energies of four extraordinary minds to shake every portion of the reign of authority. Inquiry was roused, the activity of intellect was excited, and poetry came in for its share of the general result. The changes had been rung on lovely maid and sylvan shade, summer heat and green retreat, waving trees and sighing breeze, gentle swains and amorous pains, by versifiers who took them on trust, as meaning something very soft and tender, without much caring what: but with this general activity of intellect came a necessity for even poets to appear to know something of what they professed to talk of. Thomson and Cowper looked at the trees and hills which so many ingenious gentlemen had rhymed about so long without looking at them at all, and the effect of the operation on poetry was like the discovery of a new world. Painting shared the influence, and the principles of picturesque beauty were explored by adventurous essayists with indefatigable pertinacity. The success which attended these experiments, and the pleasure which resulted from them, had the usual effect of all new enthusiasms, that of turning the heads of a few unfortunate persons, the patriarchs of the age of brass, who, mistaking the prominent novelty for the all-important totality, seem to have ratiocinated much in the following manner: "Poetical genius is the finest of all things, and we feel that we have more of it than any one ever had. The way to bring it to perfection is to cultivate poetical impressions exclusively. Poetical impressions can be received only among natural scenes: for all that is artificial is anti-poetical. Society is artificial, therefore we will live out of society. The mountains are natural, therefore we will live in the mountains. There we shall be shining models of purity and virtue, passing the whole day in the innocent and amiable occupation of going up and down hill, receiving poetical impressions, and communicating them in immortal verse to admiring generations." To some such perversion of intellect we owe that egregious confraternity of rhymesters, known by the name of the Lake Poets; who certainly did receive and communicate to the world some of the most extraordinary poetical impressions that ever were heard of, and ripened into models of public virtue, too splendid to need illustration. They wrote verses on a new principle; saw rocks and rivers in a new light; and remaining studiously ignorant of history, society, and human nature, cultivated the phantasy only at the expense of the memory and the reason; and contrived, though they had retreated from the world for the express purpose of seeing nature as she was, to see her only as she was not, converting the land they lived in into a sort of fairy-land, which they peopled with mysticisms and chimæras. This gave what is called a new tone to poetry, and conjured up a herd of desperate imitators, who have brought the age of brass prematurely to its dotage.

The descriptive poetry of the present day has been called by its cultivators a return to nature. Nothing is more impertinent than this pretension. Poetry cannot travel out of the regions of its birth, the uncultivated lands of semi-civilized men. Mr. Wordsworth, the great leader of the returners to nature, cannot describe a scene under his own eyes without putting into it the shadow of a Danish boy or the living ghost of Lucy Gray, or some similar phantastical parturition of the moods of his own mind.

In the origin and perfection of poetry, all the associations of life were composed of poetical materials. With us it is decidedly the reverse. We know too that there are no Dryads in Hyde-park nor Naiads in the Regent's-canal. But barbaric manners and supernatural interventions are essential to poetry. Either in the scene, or in the time, or in both, it must be remote from our ordinary perceptions. While the historian and the philosopher are advancing in, and accelerating, the progress of knowledge, the poet is wallowing in the rubbish of departed ignorance, and raking up the ashes of dead savages to find gewgaws and rattles for the grown babies of the age. Mr. Scott digs up the poachers and cattle-stealers of the ancient border. Lord Byron cruises for thieves and pirates on the shores of the Morea and among the Greek islands. Mr. Southey wades through ponderous volumes of travels and old chronicles, from which he carefully selects all that is false, useless, and absurd, as being essentially poetical; and when he has a commonplace book full of monstrosities, strings them into an epic. Mr. Wordsworth picks up village legends from old women and sextons; and Mr. Coleridge, to the valuable information acquired from similar sources, superadds the dreams of crazy theologians and the mysticisms of German metaphysics, and favours the world with visions in verse, in which the quadruple elements of sexton, old woman, Jeremy Taylor, and Emanuel Kant are harmonized into a delicious poetical compound. Mr. Moore presents us with a Persian, and Mr. Campbell with a Pennsylvanian tale, both formed on the same principle as Mr. Southey's epics, by extracting from a perfunctory and desultory perusal of a collection of voyages and travels, all that useful investigation would not seek for and that common sense would reject.

These disjointed relics of tradition and fragments of secondhand observation, being woven into a tissue of verse, constructed on what Mr. Coleridge calls a new principle (that is, no principle at all), compose a modern-antique compound of frippery and barbarism, in which the puling sentimentality of the present time is grafted on the misrepresented ruggedness of the past into a heterogeneous congeries of unamalgamating manners, sufficient to impose on the common readers of poetry, over whose understandings the poet of this class possesses that commanding advantage, which, in all circumstances and conditions of life, a man who knows something, however little, always possesses over one who knows nothing.

A poet in our times is a semi-barbarian in a civilized community. He lives in the days that are past. His ideas, thoughts, feelings, associations, are all with barbarous manners, obsolete customs, and exploded superstitions. The march of his intellect is like that of a crab, backward. The brighter the light diffused around him by the progress of reason, the thicker is the darkness of antiquated barbarism, in which he buries himself like a mole, to throw up the barren hillocks of his Cimmerian labours. The philosophic mental tranquillity which looks round with an equal eye on all external things, collects a store of ideas, discriminates their relative value, assigns to all their proper place, and from the materials of useful knowledge thus collected, appreciated, and arranged, forms new combinations that impress the stamp of their power and utility on the real business of life, is diametrically the reverse of that frame of mind which poetry inspires, or from which poetry can emanate. The highest inspirations of poetry are resolvable into three ingredients: the rant of unregulated passion, the whining of exaggerated feeling, and the cant of factitious sentiment: and can therefore serve only to ripen a splendid lunatic like Alexander, a puling driveller like Werter, or a morbid dreamer like Wordsworth. It can never make a philosopher, nor a statesman, nor in any class of life an useful or rational man. It cannot claim the slightest share in any one of the comforts and utilities of life of which we have witnessed so many and so rapid advances. But though not useful, it may be said it is highly ornamental, and deserves to be cultivated for the pleasure it yields. Even if this be granted, it does not follow that a writer of poetry in the present state of society is not a waster of his own time, and a robber of that of others. Poetry is not one of those arts which, like painting, require repetition and multiplication, in order to be diffused among society. There are more good poems already existing than are sufficient to employ that portion of life which any mere reader and recipient of poetical impressions should devote to them, and these having been produced in poetical times, are far superior in all the characteristics of poetry to the artificial reconstructions of a few morbid ascetics in unpoetical times. To read the promiscuous rubbish of the present time to the exclusion of the select treasures of the past, is to substitute the worse for the better variety of the same mode of enjoyment.

But in whatever degree poetry is cultivated, it must necessarily be to the neglect of some branch of useful study: and it is a lamentable spectacle to see minds, capable of better things, running to seed in the specious indolence of these empty aimless mockeries of intellectual exertion. Poetry was the mental rattle that awakened the attention of intellect in the infancy of civil society: but for the maturity of mind to make a serious business of the playthings of its childhood, is as absurd as for a full grown man to rub his gums with coral, and cry to be charmed to sleep by the jingle of silver bells.

As to that small portion of our contemporary poetry, which is neither descriptive, nor narrative, nor dramatic, and which, for want of a better name, may be called ethical, the most distinguished portion of it, consisting merely of querulous, egotistical rhapsodies, to express the writer's high dissatisfaction with the world and everything in it, serves only to confirm what has been said of the semi-barbarous character of poets, who from singing dithyrambics and "Io Triumphe," while society was savage, grow rabid, and out of their element, as it becomes polished and enlightened.

Now when we consider that it is not to the thinking and studious, and scientific and philosophical part of the community, not to those whose minds are bent on the pursuit and promotion of permanently useful ends and aims, that poets must address their minstrelsy, but to that much larger portion of the reading public, whose minds are not awakened to the desire of valuable knowledge, and who are indifferent to anything beyond being charmed, moved, excited, affected, and exalted: charmed by harmony, moved by sentiment, excited by passion, affected by pathos, and exalted by sublimity: harmony, which is language on the rack of Procrustes; sentiment, which is canting egotism in the mask of refined feeling; passion, which is the commotion of a weak and selfish mind; pathos, which is the whining of an unmanly spirit; and sublimity, which is the inflation of an empty head: when we consider that the great and permanent interests of human society become more and more the main-spring of intellectual pursuit; that in proportion as they become so, the subordinacy of the ornamental to the useful will be more and more seen and acknowledged; and that therefore the progress of useful art and science, and of moral and political knowledge, will continue more and more to withdraw attention from frivolous and unconducive, to solid and conducive studies: that therefore the poetical audience will not only continually diminish in the proportion of its number to that of the rest of the reading public, but will also sink lower and lower in the comparison of intellectual acquirement: when we consider that the poet must still please his audience, and must therefore continue to sink to their level, while the rest of the community is rising above it: we may easily conceive that the day is not distant, when the degraded state of every species of poetry will be as generally recognized as that of dramatic poetry has long been: and this not from any decrease either of intellectual power, or intellectual acquisition, but because intellectual power and intellectual acquisition have turned themselves into other and better channels, and have abandoned the cultivation and the fate of poetry to the degenerate fry of modern rhymesters, and their olympic judges, the magazine critics, who continue to debate and promulgate oracles about poetry, as if it were still what it was in the Homeric age, the all-in-all of intellectual progression, and as if there were no such things in existence as mathematicians, astronomers, chemists, moralists, metaphysicians, historians, politicians, and political economists, who have built into the upper air of intelligence a pyramid, from the summit of which they see the modern Parnassus far beneath them, and, knowing how small a place it occupies in the comprehensiveness of their prospect, smile at the little ambition and the circumscribed perceptions with which the drivellers and mountebanks upon it are contending for the poetical palm and the critical chair.

# *Arthur Schopenhauer*

1788–1860

Arthur Schopenhauer was born on February 22, 1788 in Danzig (now Gdansk), the son of a wealthy liberal businessman, Heinrich Floris Schopenhauer. The boy's father was of such staunch republican sentiment that when Danzig was incorporated into Prussia in 1793, he chose to move to Hamburg at some cost to his business rather than remain under Prussian rule. This was not to be the last of young Arthur's travels; at the age of nine he was sent to live for two years with a family in Le Havre to perfect his French—for the future philosopher's father wanted him to become a cosmopolitan "world citizen" in preparation for his presumed career as a businessman. Thus, when Arthur pleaded with his father to allow him to enter a *Gymnasium* for humanistic studies, he was offered a choice: either an education in the humanities or a two-year period of travel to be followed by a business apprenticeship. It is a measure of the young Schopenhauer's already unconventional mind that he chose the latter, and thus spent the allotted time in France, Holland, Switzerland, and England, where some of his earliest critical reflections were written; they already betray, for all the worldly experience of the fifteen-year-old, the pessimistic tone that was to be so characteristic of the mature thinker. Upon the family's return to Hamburg in 1805, Arthur entered upon the promised apprenticeship, although he could not muster much enthusiasm for the work. The assignment was not, however, to last for long, for Schopenhauer's father died in an accident that April; Arthur, who greatly loved his father, was embittered to see his mother, a confirmed society woman, going to fashionable parties while his father lay dying. The experience was to instill in Schopenhauer a life-long distrust of women.

Even after his father's death, when his mother and sister had left Hamburg for Weimar, Schopenhauer felt obliged to remain at his hated apprenticeship for some time. In 1807, after receiving his paternal inheritance, he finally went to study, first at the Gotha *Gymnasium*, where he studied philology; then the University of Göttingen, where he enrolled as a student of medicine; and finally, in 1811, the University of Berlin, where he rapidly became disillusioned with the lectures of Fichte and Schleiermacher, finding the then-current vogue for systematic idealism not to his liking. The renewed outbreak of war forced him to leave Berlin in 1813 before he could finish his degree. He went next to Weimar where his contacts with his mother were uncomfortable for both parties; the chilly indifference and lack of understanding shown in the mother's letters to her son are exceptional by any standards. Schopenhauer was consoled by his frequent contacts with Goethe, then at work on his studies in color and optical theory, in which the younger man took a lively interest. It was at this time that Schopenhauer began work on the first part of what was to become *The World as Will and Idea*, and Goethe was one of its first readers; although he had great respect for his younger friend, he nonetheless admonished him to "have greater regard for the world," that is, to be less withdrawn, less harshly critical of life and of society. The advice was to be ignored, however, for it was at this same time (1813–14) that Schopenhauer first became acquainted with Hindu philosophy, which became, in his own words, "the consolation of my life and of my death." The discovery was not only decisive for his own later development but also typical of his time; in a sense, that encounter with the East which has been so important for the 19th- and 20th-century West began with Schopenhauer.

By 1814, Schopenhauer's difficulties with his mother became so intolerable that he moved to Dresden, where he spent four years in intensive work, the first fruit of which was the essay *On Vision and Color*, published in 1816. Goethe, jealous and domineering as ever, gave a cool reception to a work he doubtless felt too independent of his own. In 1818 Schopenhauer finished the first volume of *The World as Will and Idea*. It was published the next year, but was completely ignored by the larger public, which was more interested in the grand systematic synthesis of Hegel, still teaching in Berlin, than in Schopenhauer's soberly analytical and critical work.

After the completion of this first volume Schopenhauer traveled to Italy to rest. In Venice he became deeply involved with a young woman in what was to be probably his closest approach to married life. Although Goethe had given him a letter of introduction to Byron, who was living there at the time, Schopenhauer missed the occasion, only seeing the poet ride by one evening on the Lido. While in Italy, Schopenhauer received the unpleasant news of the failure of the Danzig firm in which he had invested most of his inheritance; the resultant financial insecurity forced him finally to seek the academic post he had always sought to avoid, preferring a life as independent thinker and private citizen. His extraordinary stubbornness—one could even say perversity—showed itself in his decision not only to teach in Berlin, then dominated by the man who was philosophically his polar opposite (Hegel), but also to give his own lectures at the same time as Hegel's. It was inevitable that the younger man, whose work was so alien to the tenor of his time, could hardly compete with his older rival, and Schopenhauer had so few listeners that he eventually abandoned the lectures altogether. This was his second failure, the first being the complete lack of response to the publication of *The World as Will and Idea.* Schopenhauer became so quickly discouraged by his lack of success in Berlin that within two years of his arrival there he left again for Italy, thus beginning a period of wandering and prolonged sickness. He returned to Berlin in 1825 and had no more success than before with his lectures; in 1831 he fled an epidemic of cholera which was to end Hegel's life, and in 1833 settled finally in Frankfurt, where he lived until his death. Curiously enough, one of the reasons for the choice of Frankfurt was the presence of many Englishmen there: Schopenhauer had enjoyed their company in Italy, and sought their companionship as consolation for the "provincial stiffness" he felt in the native residents of the city.

At the time that he settled in Frankfurt, Schopenhauer was 45 years old and ready to begin the final gathering in and formulation of the ideas he had discovered in his youth. The years of travel were behind him—he wrote, "I have become like a mushroom rooted to the spot, out of pure aversion to travel"—and it is the Schopenhauer of these years, the aging, lonely, local eccentric going on walks with his poodle, who has remained fixed in the collective memory. He began at last to publish again: *On the Will in Nature* (1836), an attempt to underpin the speculative ideas of *The World as Will and Idea* with reference to positive science; *The Two Fundamental Problems of Ethics* (1841), a systematic rebuttal of Kant's ethics, which Schopenhauer saw as "disguised theology"; the second half of *The World as Will and Idea* (1844); and finally, his most popular work, which he considered only a by-product, *Parerga and Paralipomena* (1851), a collection of aphorisms and studies on human character and experience. This last book finally gave Schopenhauer the recognition he had so long awaited, and in the years until his death in 1860, he was increasingly sought after and honored. His admirers included the playwright Friedrich Hebbel and Richard Wagner, who in 1854 sent him the text for his opera *The Ring of the Nibelungen* (Schopenhauer thought Wagner "more talented as poet than as composer").

Schopenhauer's entire work is characterized by a radically pessimistic dualism, in the sharpest contrast to Hegel's optimistic monism. The younger thinker pushed the idealism of his great predecessors—especially Kant's notion of the thing-in-itself—so far that he returned to a Platonic doctrine of the separation of transcendent Ideas from all appearances; but for Schopenhauer, what lay beneath the surface of the senses was not a static Form, but rather the *will to life*. The thinking subject is thus given not only the world of "representation" (*Vorstellung*, usually mistranslated as "idea" in the title of *The World as Will and Idea*), but also his own *body* as immediate objectification of the will to life. Knowledge consists in the recognition of the illusory nature of appearances—for all individuals, human and non-human, are only temporary manifestations of the universal will—and thus the liberation of the subject from the blind impulses of the will in favor of selfless quietistic contemplation. Ethics similarly depend on seeing through the illusion of individuality to the deeper identity of all life. Aesthetic pleasure is also, as it was for Kant, essentially disinterested contemplation. Most interesting is the privileged role accorded art in Schopenhauer's thought: because true knowledge is always the result of exceptional and distinct experience, not of systematic deduction, it finds its purest form in the exceptional production that is the work of art. The appeal this idea had to the genius-worshipping later 19th century was understandably immense—as was Schopenhauer's belief in the primacy of music, as the direct artistic manifestation of the world-will, over the other arts, which can only imitate appearances: this points directly ahead to Symbolism.

Unfortunately, Schopenhauer's immense popularity and influence in the latter half of the 19th century has been matched by his near-total neglect in our own; this is true not only of his speculative thought, always suspect to academic philosophers, but also of his more accessible ethical reflections, for the sharp pessimism of which the ever more crudely health- and power-obsessed 20th century has no use. Yet Schopenhauer belongs unquestionably with Kierkegaard and Nietzsche as one of those lonely few who broke apart the grand Hegelian synthesis to release a polemically unsystematic, subjective and open-ended thought where independent motives are not, as with Hegel, forced into a totality, but rather allowed to extend themselves in flexible coordination with each other. Schopenhauer has become less popular than either Nietzsche or Kierkegaard mostly because his language has not the poetically-figured opacity of their work; it must also be admitted that he was perhaps less consistent than they, in that he retained more of traditional metaphysics, was less daring and virtuosic in allowing his thought to work on deciphering the surfaces and appearances of the sensible world for their own sake. Nietzsche, though, himself not exactly an uncritical mind, knew well how much he owed Schopenhauer and acknowledged it in an early essay, "Schopenhauer as Educator." Many of Nietzsche's most characteristic thoughts have their precedent, if in less clear formulation, in Schopenhauer—the most obvious being the stress on the independence of the will from rational order, thus the will's "groundlessness," or uncaused nature. Finally one must recognize in Schopenhauer not only a great observer of human character but also a master of prose style; in these two virtues he will endure, even if his own larger metaphysics may no longer be of interest.

# On Books and Reading

Ignorance is degrading only when found in company with riches. The poor man is restrained by poverty and need: labor occupies his thoughts, and takes the place of knowledge. But rich men who are ignorant live for their lusts only, and are like the beasts of the field; as may be seen every day: and they can also be reproached for not having used wealth and leisure for that which gives them their greatest value.

When we read, another person thinks for us: we merely repeat his mental process. In learning to write, the pupil goes over with his pen what the teacher has outlined in pencil: so in reading; the greater part of the work of thought is already done for us. This is why it relieves us to take up a book after being occupied with our own thoughts. And in reading, the mind is, in fact, only the playground of another's thoughts. So it comes about that if anyone spends almost the whole day in reading, and by way of relaxation devotes the intervals to some thoughtless pastime, he gradually loses the capacity for thinking; just as the man who always rides, at last forgets how to walk. This is the case with many learned persons: they have read themselves stupid. For to occupy every spare moment in reading, and to do nothing but read, is even more paralyzing to the mind than constant manual labor, which at least allows those engaged in it to follow their own thoughts. A spring never free from the pressure of some foreign body at last loses its elasticity; and so does the mind if other people's thoughts are constantly forced upon it. Just as you can ruin the stomach and impair the whole body by taking too much nourishment, so you can overfill and choke the mind by feeding it too much. The more you read, the fewer are the traces left by what you have read: the mind becomes like a tablet crossed over and over with writing. There is no time for ruminating, and in no other way can you assimilate what you have read. If you read on and on without setting your own thoughts to work, what you have read cannot strike root, and is generally lost. It is, in fact, just the same with mental as with bodily food: hardly the fifth part of what one takes is assimilated. The rest passes off in evaporation, respiration and the like.

The result of all this is that thoughts put on paper are nothing more than footsteps in the sand: you see the way the man has gone, but to know what he saw on his walk, you want his eyes.

There is no quality of style that can be gained by reading writers who possess it; whether it be persuasiveness, imagination, the gift of drawing comparisons, boldness, bitterness, brevity, grace, ease of expression or wit, unexpected contrasts, a laconic or naïve manner, and the like. But if these qualities are already in us, exist, that is to say, potentially, we can call them forth and bring them to consciousness; we can learn the purposes to which they can be put; we can be strengthened in our inclination to use them, or get courage to do so; we can judge by examples the effect of applying them, and so acquire the correct use of them; and of course it is only when we have arrived at that point that we actually possess these qualities. The only way in which reading can form style is by teaching us the use to which we can put our own natural gifts. We must have these gifts before we begin to learn the use of them. Without them, reading teaches us nothing but cold, dead mannerisms and makes us shallow imitators.

The strata of the earth preserve in rows the creatures which lived in former ages; and the array of books on the shelves of a library stores up in like manner the errors of the past and the way in which they have been exposed. Like those creatures, they too were full of life in their time, and made a great deal of noise; but now they are stiff and fossilized, and an object of curiosity to the literary palæontologist alone.

Herodotus relates that Xerxes wept at the sight of his army, which stretched further than the eye could reach, in the thought that of all these, after a hundred years, not one would be alive. And in looking over a huge catalogue of new books, one might weep at thinking that, when ten years have passed, not one of them will be heard of.

It is in literature as in life: wherever you turn, you stumble at once upon the incorrigible mob of humanity, swarming in all directions, crowding and soiling everything, like flies in summer. Hence the number, which no man can count, of bad books, those rank weeds of literature, which draw nourishment from the corn and choke it. The time, money and attention of the public, which rightfully belong to good books and their noble aims, they take for themselves: they are written for the mere purpose of making money or procuring places. So they are not only useless; they do positive mischief. Nine-tenths of the whole of our present literature has no other aim than to get a few shillings out of the pockets of the public; and to this end author, publisher and reviewer are in league.

Let me mention a crafty and wicked trick, albeit a profitable and successful one, practised by littérateurs, hack writers, and voluminous authors. In complete disregard of good taste and the true culture of the period, they have succeeded in getting the whole of the world of fashion into leading strings, so that they are all trained to read in time, and all the same thing, viz., *the newest books;* and that for the purpose of getting food for conversation in the circles in which they move. This is the aim served by bad novels, produced by writers who were once celebrated, as Spindler, Bulwer Lytton, Eugene Sue. What can be more miserable than the lot of a reading public like this, always bound to peruse the latest works of extremely commonplace persons who write for money only, and who are therefore never few in number? and for this advantage they are content to know by name only, the works of the few superior minds of all ages and all countries. Literary newspapers, too, are a singularly cunning device for robbing the reading public of the time which, if culture is to be attained, should be devoted to the genuine productions of literature, instead of being occupied by the daily bungling commonplace persons.

Hence, in regard to reading, it is a very important thing to be able to refrain. Skill in doing so consists in not taking into one's hands any book merely because at the time it happens to be extensively read; such as political or religious pamphlets, novels, poetry, and the like, which make a noise, and may even attain to several editions in the first and last year of their existence. Consider, rather, that the man who writes for fools is always sure of a large audience; be careful to limit your time for reading, and devote it exclusively to the works of those great minds of all times and countries, who o'ertop the rest of humanity, those whom the voice of fame points to as such. These alone really educate and instruct. You can never read bad literature too little, nor good literature too much. Bad books are intellectual poison; they destroy the mind. Because people always read what is new instead of the best of all ages, writers remain in the narrow circle of the ideas which happen to prevail in their time; and so the period sinks deeper and deeper into its own mire.

There are at all times two literatures in progress, running side by side, but little known to each other; the one real, the other only apparent. The former grows into permanent literature; it is pursued by those who live *for* science or poetry; its course is sober and quiet, but extremely slow; and it produces in Europe scarcely a dozen works in a century; these, however, are permanent. The other kind is pursued by persons who live *on* science or poetry; it goes at a gallop with much noise and shouting of partisans; and every twelve-month puts a thousand works on the market. But after a few years one asks, Where are they? where is the glory which came so soon and made so much clamor? This kind may be called fleeting, and the other, permanent literature.

In the history of politics, half a century is always a considerable time; the matter which goes to form them is ever on the move; there is always something going on. But in the history of literature there is often a complete standstill for the same period; nothing has happened, for clumsy attempts don't count. You are just where you were fifty years previously.

To explain what I mean, let me compare the advance of knowledge among mankind to the course taken by a planet. The false paths on which humanity usually enters after every important advance are like the epicycles in the Ptolemaic system, and after passing through one of them, the world is just where it was before it entered it. But the great minds, who really bring the race further on its course do not accompany it on the epicycles it makes from time to time. This explains why posthumous fame is often bought at the expense of contemporary praise, and *vice versa*. An instance of such an epicycle is the philosophy started by Fichte and Schelling, and crowned by Hegel's caricature of it. This epicycle was a deviation from the limit to which philosophy had been ultimately brought by Kant; and at that point I took it up again afterwards, to carry it further. In the intervening period the sham philosophers I have mentioned and some others went through their epicycle, which had just come to an end; so that those who went with them on their course are conscious of the fact that they are exactly at the point from which they started.

This circumstance explains why it is that, every thirty years or so, science, literature, and art, as expressed in the spirit of the time, are declared bankrupt. The errors which appear from time to time mount to such a height in that period that the mere weight of their absurdity makes the fabric fall; whilst the opposition to them has been gathering force at the same time. So an upset takes place, often followed by an error in the opposite direction. To exhibit these movements in their periodical return would be the true practical aim of the history of literature: little attention, however, is paid to it. And besides, the comparatively short duration of these periods makes it difficult to collect the data of epochs long gone by, so that it is most convenient to observe how the matter stands in one's own generation. An instance of this tendency, drawn from physical science, is supplied in the Neptunian geology of Werter.

But let me keep strictly to the example cited above, the nearest we can take. In German philosophy, the brilliant epoch of Kant was immediately followed by a period which aimed rather at being imposing than at convincing. Instead of being thorough and clear, it tried to be dazzling, hyperbolical, and, in a special degree, unintelligible: instead of seeking truth, it intrigued. Philosophy could make no progress in this fashion; and at last the whole school and its method became bankrupt. For the effrontery of Hegel and his fellows came to such a pass,—whether because they talked such sophisticated nonsense, or were so unscrupulously puffed, or because the entire aim of this pretty piece of work was quite obvious,—that in the end there was nothing to prevent charlatanry of the whole business from becoming manifest to everybody: and when, in consequence of certain disclosures, the favor it had enjoyed in high quarters was withdrawn, the system was openly ridiculed. This most miserable of all the meagre philosophies that have ever existed came to grief, and dragged down with it into the abysm of discredit, the systems of Fichte and Schelling which had preceded it. And so, as far as Germany is concerned, the total philosophical incompetence of the first half of the century following upon Kant is quite plain: and still the Germans boast of their talent for philosophy in comparison with foreigners, especially since an English writer has been so maliciously ironical as to call them "a nation of thinkers."

For an example of the general system of epicycles drawn from the history of art, look at the school of sculpture which flourished in the last century and took its name from Bernini, more especially at the development of it which prevailed in France. The ideal of this school was not antique beauty, but commonplace nature: instead of the simplicity and grace of ancient art, it represented the manners of a French minuet.

This tendency became bankrupt when, under Wincklemann's direction, a return was made to the antique school. The history of painting furnishes an illustration in the first quarter of the century, when art was looked upon merely as a means and instrument of mediæval religious sentiment, and its themes consequently drawn from ecclesiastical subjects alone: these, however, were treated by painters who had none of the true earnestness of faith, and in their delusion they followed Francesco Francia, Pietro Perugino, Angelico da Fiesole and others like them, rating them higher even than the really great masters who followed. It was in view of this terror, and because in poetry an analogous aim had at the same time found favor, that Goethe wrote his parable *Pfaffenspiel*. This school, too, got the reputation of being whimsical, became bankrupt, and was followed by a return to nature, which proclaimed itself in *genre* pictures and scenes of life of every kind, even though it now and then strayed into what was vulgar.

The progress of the human mind in literature is similar. The history of literature is for the most part like the catalogue of a museum of deformities; the spirit in which they keep best is pigskin. The few creatures that have been born in goodly shape need not be looked for there. They are still alive, and are everywhere to be met with in the world, immortal, and with their years ever green. They alone form what I have called real literature; the history of which, poor as it is in persons, we learn from our youth up out of the mouths of all educated people, before compilations recount it for us.

As an antidote to the prevailing monomania for reading literary histories, in order to be able to chatter about everything, without having any real knowledge at all, let me refer to a passage in Lichtenberg's works (vol. II., p. 302), which is well worth perusal.

> I believe that the over-minute acquaintance with the history of science and learning, which is such a prevalent feature of our day, is very prejudicial to the advance of knowledge itself. Thcrc is plcasure in following up this history; but as a matter of fact, it leaves the mind, not empty indeed, but without any power of its own, just because it makes it so full. Whoever has felt the desire, not to fill up his mind, but to strengthen it, to develop his faculties and aptitudes, and generally, to enlarge his powers, will have found that there is nothing so weakening as intercourse with a so-called littérateur, on a matter of knowledge on which he has not thought at all, though he knows a thousand little facts appertaining to its history and literature. It is like reading a cookery-book when you are hungry. I believe that so-called literary history will never thrive amongst thoughtful people, who are conscious of their own worth and the worth of real knowledge. These people are more given to employing their own reason than to troubling themselves to know how others have employed theirs. The worst of it is that, as you will find, the more knowledge takes the direction of literary research, the less the power of promoting knowledge becomes; the only thing that increases is pride in the possession of it. Such persons believe that they possess knowledge in a greater degree than those who really possess it. It is surely a well-founded remark, that knowledge never makes its possessor proud. Those alone let themselves be blown out with pride, who incapable of extending knowledge in their own persons, occupy themselves with clearing up dark points in its history, or are able to recount what others have done. They are proud, because they consider this occupation, which is mostly of a mechanical nature, the practice of knowledge. I could illustrate what I mean by examples, but it would be an odious task.

Still, I wish some one would attempt a *tragical* history of literature, giving the way in which the writers and artists, who form the proudest possession of the various nations which have given them birth, have been treated by them during their lives. Such a history would exhibit the ceaseless warfare, which what was good and genuine in all times and countries has had to wage with what was bad and perverse. It would tell of the martyrdom of almost all those who truly enlightened humanity, of almost all the great masters of every kind of art: it would show us how, with few exceptions, they were tormented to death, without recognition, without sympathy, without followers; how they lived in poverty and misery, whilst fame, honor, and riches, were the lot of the unworthy; how their fate was that of Esau, who, while he was hunting and getting venison for his father, was robbed of the blessing by Jacob, disguised in his brother's clothes, how, in spite of all, they were kept up by the love of their work, until at last the bitter fight of the teacher of humanity is over, until the immortal laurel is held out to him, and the hour strikes when it can be said:

*Der schwere Panzer wird zum Flügelkleid*
*Kurz ist der Schmerz, unendlich ist die Freude.*

The heavy armor seems like wings in flight;
Brief is the pain, unending the delight.

FROM

# The World as Will and Idea

## *Chapter XXXI*

### *On Genius*

What is properly denoted by the name genius is the predominating capacity for that kind of knowledge which has been described in the two preceding chapters, the knowledge from which all genuine works of art and poetry, and even of philosophy, proceed. Accordingly, since this has for its objects the Platonic Ideas, and these are not comprehended in the abstract, but *only perceptibly,* the essence of genius must lie in the perfection and energy of the knowledge of *perception.* Corresponding to this, the works which we hear most decidedly designated works of genius are those which start immediately from perception and devote themselves to perception; thus those of plastic and pictorial art, and then those of poetry, which gets its perceptions by the assistance of the imagination. The difference between genius and mere talent makes itself noticeable even here. For talent is an excellence which lies rather in the greater versatility and acuteness of discursive than of intuitive knowledge. He who is endowed with talent thinks more quickly and more correctly than others; but the genius beholds another world from them all, although only because he has a more profound perception of the world which lies before them also, in that it presents itself in his mind more objectively, and consequently in greater purity and distinctness.

The intellect is, according to its destination, merely the medium of motives; and in accordance with this it originally comprehends nothing in things but their relations to the will, the direct, the indirect, and the possible. In the case of the brutes, where it is almost entirely confined to the direct relations, the matter is just on that account most apparent: what has no relation to their will does not exist for them. Therefore we sometimes see with surprise that even clever animals do not observe at all something conspicuous to them; for example, they show no surprise at obvious alterations in our person and surroundings. In the case of normal men the indirect, and even the possible, relations to the will are added, the sum of which make up the total of useful knowledge; but here also knowledge remains confined to the relations. Therefore the normal mind does not attain to an absolutely pure, objective picture of things, because its power of perception, whenever it is not spurred on by the will and set in motion, at once becomes tired and inactive, because it has not enough energy of its own elasticity and without an *end* in view to apprehend the world in a purely objective manner. Where, on the other hand, this takes place—where the brain has such a surplus of the power of ideation that a pure, distinct, objective image of the external world exhibits itself *without any aim;* an image which is useless for the intentions of the will, indeed, in the higher degrees, disturbing, and even injurious to them—there, the natural disposition, at least, is already present for that abnormity which the name genius denotes, which signifies that here a *genius* foreign to the will, *i. e.,* to the I proper, as it were coming from without, seems to be active. But to speak without a figure: genius consists in this, that the knowing faculty has received a considerably greater development than the *service of the will,* for which alone it originally appeared, demands. Therefore, strictly speaking, physiology might to a certain extent class such a superfluity of brain activity, and with it of brain itself, among the *monstra per excessum,* which, it is well known, it co-ordinates with *monstra per defectum* and those *per situm mutatum.*[1] Thus genius consists in an abnormally large measure of intellect, which can only find its use by being applied to the universal of existence, whereby it then devotes itself to the service of the whole human race, as the normal intellect to that of the individual. In order to make this perfectly comprehensible one might say: If the normal man consists of two-thirds will and one-third intellect, the genius, on the contrary, has two-thirds intellect and one-third will. This might, then, be further illustrated by a chemical simile: the base and the acid of a neutral salt are distinguished by the fact that in each of the two the radical has the converse relation to oxygen to that which it has in the other. The base or the alkali is so because in it the radical predominates with reference to oxygen, and the acid is so because in it oxygen predominates. In the same way now the normal man and the genius are related in respect of will and intellect. From this arises a thorough distinction between them, which is visible even in their whole nature and behaviour, but comes out most clearly in their achievements. One might add the difference that while that total opposition between the chemical materials forms the strongest affinity and attraction between them, in the human race the opposite is rather wont to be found.

The first manifestation which such a superfluity of the power of knowledge calls forth shows itself for the most part in the most original and fundamental knowledge, *i. e.,* in knowledge of *perception,* and occasions the repetition of it in an image; hence arise the painter and the sculptor. In their case, then, the path between the apprehension of genius and the artistic production is the shortest; therefore the form in which genius and its activity here exhibits itself is the simplest and its description the easiest. Yet here also the source is shown from which all genuine productions in every art, in poetry, and indeed in philosophy, have their origin, although in the case of these the process is not so simple.

Let the result arrived at in the first book be here borne in mind, that all perception is intellectual and not merely sensuous. If one now adds the exposition given here, and, at the same time, in justice considers that the philosophy of the last century denoted the perceptive faculty of knowledge by the name "lower powers of the soul," we will not think it so utterly absurd nor so deserving of the bitter scorn with which Jean Paul quotes it in his "*Vorschule der Æsthetik,*" that Adelung, who had to speak the language of his age, placed genius in "a remarkable strength of the lower powers of the soul." The work just referred to of this author, who is so worthy of our admiration, has great excellences, but yet I must remark that all through, whenever a theoretical explanation and, in general, instruction is the end in view, a style of exposition which is constantly indulging in displays of wit and hurrying along in mere similes cannot be well adapted to the purpose.

It is, then, *perception* to which primarily the peculiar and true nature of things, although still in a conditioned manner, discloses and reveals itself. All conceptions and everything thought are mere abstractions, consequently partial ideas taken from perception, and have only arisen by thinking away. All profound knowledge, even wisdom properly so called, is rooted in the *perceptive* apprehension of things, as we have fully considered in the supplements to the first book. A *perceptive* apprehension has always been generative process in which every genuine work of art, every immortal thought, received the spark of life. All primary thought takes place in pictures. From conceptions, on the other hand, arise the works of mere talent, the merely rational thoughts, imitations, and indeed all that is calculated merely with reference to the present need and contemporary conditions.

But if now our perception were constantly bound to the real present of things, its material would be entirely under the dominion of chance, which seldom produces things at the right time, seldom arranges them for an end and for the most part presents them to us in very defective examples. Therefore the *imagination* is required in order to complete, arrange, give the finishing touches to, retain, and repeat at pleasure all those significant pictures of life, according as the aims of a profoundly penetrating knowledge and of the significant work whereby they are to be communicated may demand. Upon this rests the high value of imagination, which is an indispensable tool of genius. For only by virtue of imagination can genius ever, according to the requirements of the connection of its painting or poetry or thinking, call up to itself each object or event in a lively image, and thus constantly draw fresh nourishment from the primary source of all knowledge, perception. The man who is endowed with imagination is able, as it were, to call up spirits, who at the right time reveal to him the truths which the naked reality of things exhibits only weakly, rarely, and then for the most part at the wrong time. Therefore the man without imagination is related to him, as the mussel fastened to its rock, which must wait for what chance may bring it, is related to the freely moving or even winged animal. For such a man knows nothing but the actual perception of the senses: till it comes he gnaws at conceptions and abstractions which are yet mere shells and husks, not the kernel of knowledge. He will never achieve anything great, unless it be in calculating and mathematics. The works of plastic and pictorial art of poetry, as also the achievements of mimicry, may also be regarded as means by which those who have no imagination may make up for this defect as far as possible, and those who are gifted with it may facilitate the use of it.

Thus, although the kind of knowledge which is peculiar and essential to genius is knowledge of *perception,* yet the special object of this knowledge by no means consists of the particular things, but of the Platonic Ideas which manifest themselves in these, as their apprehension was analyzed above. Always to see the universal in the particular is just the fundamental characteristic of genius, while the normal man knows in the particular only the particular as such, for only as such does it belong to the actual which alone has interests for him, *i.e.*, relations to the *will.* The degree in which every one not merely thinks, but actually perceives, in the particular thing, only the particular, or a more or less universal up to the most universal of the species, is the measure of his approach to genius. And corresponding to this, only the nature of things generally, the universal in them, the whole, is the special object of genius. The investigation of the particular phenomena is the field of the talents, in the real sciences, whose special object is always only the relations of things to each other.

What was fully shown in the preceding chapter, that the apprehension of the Ideas is conditioned by the fact that the knower is the *pure subject* of knowledge, *i. e.*, that the will entirely vanishes from consciousness, must be borne in mind here. The pleasure which we have in many of Goethe's songs which bring the landscape before our eyes, or in Jean Paul's sketches of nature, depends upon the fact that we thereby participate in the objectivity of those minds, *i. e.,* the purity with which in them the world as idea separated from the world as will, and, as it were, entirely emancipated itself from it. It also follows from the fact that the kind of knowledge peculiar to genius is essentially that which is purified from all will and its relations, that the works of genius do not proceed from intention or choice, but it is guided in them by a kind of instinctive necessity. What is called the awaking of genius, the hour of initiation, the moment of inspiration, is nothing but the attainment of freedom by the intellect, when, delivered for a while from its service under the will, it does not now sink into inactivity or lassitude, but is active for a short time entirely alone and spontaneously. Then it is of the greatest purity, and becomes the clear mirror of the world; for, completely severed from its origin, the will, it is now the world as idea itself, concentrated in *one* consciousness. In such moments, as it were, the souls of immortal works are begotten. On the other hand, in all intentional reflection the intellect is not free, for indeed the will guides it and prescribes it its theme.

The stamp of commonness, the expression of vulgarity, which is impressed on the great majority of countenances consists really in this, that in them becomes visible the strict subordination of their knowledge to their will, the firm chain which binds these two together, and the impossibility following from this of apprehending things otherwise than in their relation to the will and its aims. On the other hand, the expression of genius which constitutes the evident family likeness of all highly gifted men consists in this, that in it we distinctly read the liberation, the manumission of the intellect from the service of the will, the predominance of knowledge over volition; and because all anxiety proceeds from the will, and knowledge, on the contrary, is in and for itself painless and serene, this gives to their lofty brow and clear, perceiving glance, which are not subject to the service of the will and its wants, that look of great, almost supernatural serenity which at times breaks through, and consists very well with the melancholy of their other features, especially the mouth, and which in this relation may be aptly described by the motto of Giordano Bruno: *In tristitia hilaris, in hilaritate tristis.*[2]

The will, which is the root of the intellect, opposes itself to any activity of the latter which is directed to anything else but its own aims. Therefore the intellect is only capable of a purely objective and profound comprehension of the external world when it had freed itself at least for a while from this its root. So long as it remains bound to the will, it is of its own means capable of no activity, but sleeps in a stupor, whenever the will (the interests) does not awake it, and set it in motion. If, however, this happens, it is indeed very well fitted to recognize the relations of things according to the interest of the will, as the prudent mind does, which, however, must always be an awakened mind, *i. e.*, a mind actively aroused by volition; but just on this account it is not capable of comprehending the purely objective nature of things. For the willing and the aims make it so one-sided that it sees in things only that which relates to these, and the rest either disappears or enters consciousness in a falsificd form. For cxample, the traveller in anxiety and haste will see the Rhine and its banks only as a line, and the bridges over it only as lines cutting it. In the mind of the man who is filled with his own aims the world appears as a beautiful landscape appears on the plan of a battlefield. Certainly these are extremes, taken for the sake of distinctness; but every excitement of the will, however slight, will have as its consequence a slight but constantly proportionate falsification of knowledge. The world can only appear in its true colour and form, in its whole and correct significance, when the intellect, devoid of willing, moves freely over the objects, and without being driven on by the will is yet energetically active. This is certainly opposed to the nature and determination of the intellect, thus to a certain extent unnatural, and just on this account exceedingly rare; but it is just in this that the essential nature of genius lies, in which alone that condition takes place in a high degree and is of some duration, while in others it only appears approximately and exceptionally. I take it to be in the sense expounded here that Jean Paul (*Vorschule der Æsthetik,* § 12) places the essence of genius in *reflectiveness*. The normal man is sunk in the whirl and tumult of life, to which he belongs through his will; his intellect is filled with the things and events of life; but he does not know these things nor life itself in their objective significance; as the merchant on 'Change in Amsterdam apprehends perfectly what his neighbour says, but does not hear the hum of the whole Exchange, like the sound of the sea, which astonishes the distant observer. From the genius, on the contrary, whose intellect is delivered from the will, and thus from the person, what concerns these does not conceal the world and things themselves; but he becomes distinctly conscious of them, he apprehends them in and for themselves in objective perception; in this sense he is *reflective*.

It is *reflectiveness* which enables the painter to repeat the natural objects which he contemplates faithfully upon the canvas, and the poet accurately to call up again the concrete present, by means of abstract conceptions, by giving it utterance and so bringing it to distinct consciousness, and also to express everything in words which others only feel. The brute lives entirely without reflection. It has consciousness, *i. e.*, it knows itself and its good and ill, also the objects which occasion these. But its knowledge remains always subjective, never becomes objective; everything that enters it seems a matter of course, and therefore can never become for it a theme (an object of exposition) nor a problem (an object of meditation). Its consciousness is thus entirely *immanent*. Not certainly the same, but yet of kindred nature, is the consciousness of the common type of man, for his apprehension also of things and the world is predominantly subjective and remains prevalently immanent. It apprehends the things in the world, but not the world; its own action and suffering, but not itself. As now in innumerable gradations the distinctness of consciousness rises, reflectiveness appears more and more; and thus it is brought about little by little that sometimes, though rarely, and then again in very different degrees of distinctness, the question passes through the mind like a flash, "What is all this?" or again, "How is it really fashioned?" The first question, if it attains great distinctness and continued presence, will make the philosopher, and the other, under the same conditions, the artist or the poet. Therefore, then, the high calling of both of these has its root in the reflectiveness which primarily springs from the distinctness with which they are conscious of the world and their own selves, and thereby come to reflect upon them. But the whole process springs from the fact that the intellect through its preponderance frees itself for a time from the will, to which it is originally subject.

The considerations concerning genius here set forth are connected by way of supplement with the exposition of the *ever wider separation of the will and the intellect,* which can be traced in the whole series of existences. This reaches its highest grade in genius, where it extends to the entire liberation of the intellect from its root the will, so that here the intellect becomes perfectly free, whereby the *world as idea* first attains to complete objectification.

A few remarks now concerning the individuality of genius. Aristotle has already said, according to Cicero (*Tusc.*, i., 33), *"Omnes ingeniosos melancholicos esse";*[3] which without doubt is connected with the passage of Aristotle's *"Problemata"* (xxx.) I. Goethe also says: "My poetic rapture was very small, so long as I only encountered good; but it burnt with a bright flame when I fled from threatening evil. The tender poem, like the rainbow, is only drawn on a dark ground; hence the genius of the poet loves the element of melancholy."

This is to be explained from the fact that since the will constantly re-establishes its original sway over the intellect, the latter more easily withdraws from this under unfavourable personal relations; because it gladly turns from adverse circumstances, in order to a certain extent to divert itself, and now directs itself with so much the greater energy to the foreign external world, thus more easily becomes purely objective. Favourable personal relations act conversely. Yet as a whole and in general the melancholy which accompanies genius depends upon the fact that the brighter the intellect which enlightens the will to live, the more distinctly does it perceive the misery of its condition. The melancholy disposition of highly gifted minds which has so often been observed has its emblem in Mont Blanc, the summit of which is for the most part lost in clouds; but when sometimes, especially in the early morning, the veil of clouds is rent and now the mountain looks down on Chamounix from its height in the heavens above the clouds, then it is a sight at which the heart of each of us swells from its profoundest depths. So also the genius, for the most part melancholy, shows at times that peculiar serenity already described above, which is possible only for it, and springs from the most perfect objectivity of the mind. It floats like a ray of light upon his lofty brow: *In tristitia hilaris, in hilaritate tristis.*

All bunglers are so ultimately because their intellect, still too firmly bound to the will, only becomes active when spurred on by it, and therefore remains entirely in its service. They are accordingly only capable of personal aims. In conformity with these they produce bad pictures, insipid poems, shallow, absurd, and very often dishonest philosophemes, when it is to their interest to recommend themselves to high authorities by a pious disingenuousness. Thus all their action and thought is personal. Therefore they succeed at most in appropriating what is external, accidental, and arbitrary in the genuine works of others as mannerisms, in doing which they take the shell instead of the kernel, and yet imagine they have attained to everything, nay, have surpassed those works. If, however, the failure is patent, yet many hope to attain success in the end through their good intentions. But it is just this good will which makes success impossible; because this only pursues personal ends, and with these neither art nor poetry nor philosophy can ever be taken seriously. Therefore the saying is peculiarly applicable to such persons: "They stand in their own light." They have no idea that it is only the intellect delivered from the government of the will and all its projects, and therefore freely active, that makes one capable of genuine productions, because it alone imparts true seriousness; and it is well for them that they have not, otherwise they would leap into the water. The *good will* is in *morality* everything; but in art it is nothing. In art, as the word itself indicates (*Kunst*), what alone is of consequence is ability (*Können*). It all amounts ultimately to this, where the true *seriousness* of the man lies. In almost all it lies exclusively in their own well-being and that of their families; therefore they are in a position to promote this and nothing else; for no purpose, no voluntary and intentional effort, imparts the true, profound, and proper seriousness, or makes up for it, or more correctly, takes its place. For it always remains where nature has placed it; and without it everything is only half performed. Therefore, for the same reason, persons of genius often manage so badly for their own welfare. As a leaden weight always brings a body back to the position which its centre of gravity thereby determines demands, so the true seriousness of the man always draws the strength and attention of the intellect back to that in which it lies; everything else the man does *without true seriousness*. Therefore only the exceedingly rare and abnormal men whose true seriousness does not lie in the personal and practical, but in the objective and theoretical, are in a position to apprehend what is essential in the things of the world, thus the highest truths, and reproduce them in any way. For such a seriousness of the individual, falling outside himself in the objective, is something foreign to the nature of man, something unnatural, or really supernatural: yet on account of this alone is the man *great;* and therefore what he achieves is then ascribed to a *genius* different from himself, which takes possession of him. To such a man his painting, poetry, or thinking is an *end;* to others it is a *means*. The latter thereby seek their own things, and, as a rule, they know how to further them, for they flatter their contemporaries, ready to serve their wants and humours; therefore for the most part they live in happy circumstances; the former often in very miserable circumstances. For he sacrifices his personal welfare to his *objective end;* he cannot indeed do otherwise, because his seriousness lies there. They act conversely; therefore they are *small,* but he is *great*. Accordingly his work is for all time, but the recognition of it generally only begins with posterity: they live and die with their time. In general he only is great who in his work, whether it is practical or theoretical, seeks *not his own concerns,* but pursues an *objective end* alone; he is so, however, even when in the practical sphere this end is a misunderstood one, and even if in consequence of this it should be a crime. *That he seeks not himself and his own concerns,* this makes him under all circumstances *great*. *Small,* on the other hand, is all action which is directed to personal ends; for whoever is thereby set in activity knows and finds himself only in his own transient and insignificant person. He who is great, again, finds himself in all, and therefore in the whole: he lives not, like others, only in the microcosm, but still more in the macrocosm. Hence the whole interests him, and he seeks to comprehend it in order to represent it, or to explain it, or to act practically upon it. For it is not strange to him; he feels that it concerns him. On account of this extension of his sphere he is called *great*. Therefore that lofty predicate belongs only to the true hero, in some sense, and to genius: it signifies that they, contrary to human nature, have not sought their own things, have not lived for themselves, but for all. As now clearly the great majority must *constantly* be small, and can *never* become great, the converse of this, that one should be great throughout, that is, constantly and every moment, is yet not possible—

For man is made of common clay,
And custom is his nurse.

Every great man must often be only the individual, have only himself in view, and that means he must be small. Upon this depends the very true remark, that no man is a hero to his valet, and not upon the fact that the valet cannot appreciate the hero; which Goethe, in the "*Wahlverwandhschaften*" (vol. ii., chap. 5), serves up as an idea of Ottilie's.

Genius is its own reward: for the best that one is, one must necessarily be for oneself. "Whoever is born with a talent, to a talent, finds in this his fairest existence," says Goethe. When we look back at a great man of former times, we do not think, "How happy is he to be still admired by all of us!" but, "How happy must he have been in the immediate enjoyment of a mind at the surviving traces of which centuries revive themselves!" Not in the fame, but in that whereby it is attained, lies the value, and in the production of immortal children the pleasure. Therefore those who seek to show the vanity of posthumous fame from the fact that he who obtains it knows nothing of it, may be compared to the wiseacre who very learnedly tried to demonstrate to the man who cast envious glances at a heap of oyster-shells in his neighbour's yard the absolute uselessness of them.

According to the exposition of the nature of genius which has been given, it is so far contrary to nature, inasmuch as it consists in this, that the intellect, whose real destination is the service of the will, emancipates itself from this service in order to be active on its own account. Accordingly genius is an intellect which has become untrue to its destination. Upon this depend the *disadvantages* connected with it, for the consideration of which we shall now prepare the way by comparing genius with the less decided predominance of the intellect.

The intellect of the normal man, strictly bound to the service of the will, and therefore really only occupied with the apprehension of motives, may be regarded as a complex system of wires, by means of which each of these puppets is set in motion in the theatre of the world. From this arises the dry, grave seriousness of most people, which is only surpassed by that of the brutes, who never laugh. On the other hand, we might compare the genius, with his unfettered intellect, to a living man playing along with the large puppets of the famous puppet-show at Milan, who would be the only one among them who would understand everything, and would therefore gladly leave the stage for a while to enjoy the play from the boxes;—that is the reflectiveness of genius. But even the man of great understanding and reason, whom one might almost call wise, is very different from the genius, and in this way, that his intellect retains a *practical* tendency, is concerned with the choice of the best ends and means, therefore remains in the service of the will, and accordingly is occupied in a manner that is thoroughly in keeping with nature. The firm, practical seriousness of life which the Romans denoted *gravitas* presupposes that the intellect does not forsake the service of the will in order to wander away after that which does not concern the will; therefore it does not admit of that separation of the will and the intellect which is the condition of genius. The able, nay, eminent man, who is fitted for great achievements in the practical sphere, is so precisely because objects rouse his will in a lively manner, and spur him on to the ceaseless investigation of their relations and connections. Thus his intellect has grown up closely connected with his will. Before the man of genius, on the contrary, there floats in his objective comprehension the phenomenon of the world, as something foreign to him, an object of contemplation, which expels his will from consciousness. Round this point turns the distinction between the capacity for *deeds* and for *works*. The latter demand objectivity and depth of knowledge, which presupposes entire separation of the intellect from the will; the former, on the other hand, demands the application of knowledge, presence of mind, and decision, which required that the intellect should uninterruptedly attend to the service of the will. Where the bond between the intellect and the will is loosened, the intellect, turned away from its natural destination, will neglect the service of the will; it will, for example, even in the need of the moment, preserve its emancipation, and perhaps be unable to avoid taking in the picturesque impression of the surroundings, from which danger threatens the individual. The intellect of the reasonable and understanding man, on the other hand, is constantly at its post, is directed to the circumstances and their requirements. Such a man will therefore in all cases determine and carry out what is suitable to the case, and consequently will by no means fall into those eccentricities, personal slips, nay, follies, to which the genius is exposed, because his intellect does not remain exclusively the guide and guardian of his will, but sometimes more, sometimes less, is laid claim to by the purely objective. In the contrast of Tasso and Antonio, Goethe has illustrated the opposition, here explained in the abstract, in which these two entirely different kinds of capacity stand to each other. The kinship of genius and madness, so often observed, depends chiefly upon that separation of the intellect from the will which is essential to genius, but is yet contrary to nature. But this separation itself is by no means to be attributed to the fact that genius is accompanied by less intensity of will; for it is rather distinguished by a vehement and passionate character; but it is to be explained from this, that the practically excellent person, the man of deeds, has merely the whole, full measure of intellect required for an energetic will while most men lack even this; but genius consists in a completely abnormal, actual superfluity of intellect, such as is required for the service of no will. On this account the men of genuine works are a thousand times rarer than the men of deeds. It is just that abnormal superfluity of intellect by virtue of which it obtains the decided preponderance, sets itself free from the will, and now, forgetting its origin, is freely active from its own strength and elasticity; and from this the creations of genius proceed.

Now further, just this, that genius in working consists of the free intellect, *i. e.*, of the intellect emancipated from the service of the will, has as a consequence that its productions serve no useful ends. The work of genius is music, or philosophy, or paintings, or poetry; it is nothing to use. To be of no use belongs to the character of the works of genius; it is their patent of nobility. All other works of men are for the maintenance or easing of our existence; only those we are speaking of are not; they alone exist for their own sake, and are in this sense to be regarded as the flower or the net profit of existence. Therefore our heart swells at the enjoyment of them, for we rise out of the heavy earthly atmosphere of want. Analogous to this, we see the beautiful, even apart from these, rarely combined with the useful. Lofty and beautiful trees bear no fruit; the fruit-trees are small, ugly cripples. The full garden rose is not fruitful, but the small, wild, almost scentless roses are. The most beautiful buildings are not the useful ones; a temple is no dwelling-house. A man of high, rare mental endowments compelled to apply himself to a merely useful business, for which the most ordinary man would be fitted, is like a costly vase decorated with the most beautiful painting which is used as a kitchen pot; and to compare useful people with men of genius is like comparing building-stone with diamonds.

Thus the merely practical man uses his intellect that for which nature destined it, the comprehension of the relations of things, partly to each other, partly to the will of the knowing individual. The genius, on the other hand, uses it, contrary to its destination, for the comprehension of the objective nature of things. His mind, therefore, belongs not to himself, but to the world, to the illumination of which, in some sense, it will contribute. From this must spring manifold *disadvantages* to the individual favoured with genius. For his intellect will in general show those faults which are rarely wanting in any tool which is used for that for which it has not been made. First of all, it will be, as it were, the servant of two masters, for on every opportunity it frees itself from the service to which it was destined in order to follow its own ends, whereby it often leaves the will very inopportunely in a fix, and thus the individual so gifted becomes more or less useless for life, nay, in his conduct sometimes reminds us of madness. Then, on account of its highly developed power of knowledge, it will see in things more the universal than the particular; while the service of the will principally requires the knowledge of the particular. But, again, when, as opportunity offers, that whole abnormally heightened power of knowledge directs itself with all its energy to the circumstances and miseries of the will, it will be apt to apprehend these too vividly, to behold all in too glaring colours, in too bright a light, and in a fearfully exaggerated form, whereby the individual falls into mere extremes. The following may serve to explain this more accurately. All great theoretical achievements, in whatever sphere they may be, are brought about in this way: Their author directs all the forces of his mind upon one point, in which he lets them unite and concentrate so strongly, firmly, and exclusively that now the whole of the rest of the world vanishes for him, and his object fills all reality. Now this great and powerful concentration which belongs to the privileges of genius sometimes appears for it also in the case of objects of the real world and the events of daily life, which then, brought under such a focus, are magnified to such a monstrous extent that they appear like the flea, which under the solar miscroscope assumes the stature of an elephant. Hence it arises that highly gifted individuals sometimes are thrown by trifles into violent emotions of the most various kinds, which are incomprehensible to others, who see them transported with grief, joy, care, fear, anger, &c., by things which leave the everyday man quite composed. Thus, then, the genius lacks *soberness,* which simply consists in this, that one sees in things nothing more than actually belongs to them, especially with reference to our possible ends; therefore no soberminded man can be a genius. With the disadvantages which have been enumerated there is also associated hyper-sensibility, which an abnormally developed nervous and cerebral system brings with it, and indeed in union with the vehemence and passionateness of will which is certainly characteristic of genius, and which exhibits itself physically as energy of the pulsation of the heart. From all this very easily arises that extravagance of disposition, that vehemence of the emotions, that quick change of mood under prevailing melancholy, which Goethe has presented to us in Tasso. What reasonableness, quiet composure, finished surveyal, certainty and proportionateness of behaviour is shown by the well-endowed normal man in comparison with the now dreamy absentness, and now passionate excitement of the man of genius, whose inward pain is the mother's lap of immortal works! To all this must still be added that genius lives essentially alone. It is too rare to find its like with ease, and too different from the rest of men to be their companion. With them it is the will, with him it is knowledge, that predominates; therefore their pleasures are not his, and his are not theirs. They are merely moral beings, and have merely personal relations; he is at the same time a pure intellect, and as such belongs to the whole of humanity. The course of thought of the intellect which is detached from its mother soil, the will, and only returns to it periodically, will soon show itself entirely different from that of the normal intellect, still cleaving to its stem. For this reason, and also on account of the dissimilarity of the pace, the former is not adapted for thinking in common, *i. e.*, for conversation with the others: they will have as little pleasure in him and his oppressive superiority as he will in them. They will therefore feel more comfortable with their equals, and he will prefer the entertainment of his equals, although, as a rule, this is only possible through the works they have left behind them. Therefore Chamfort says very rightly: *"Il y a peu de vices qui empêchent un homme d'avoir beaucoup d'amis, autant que peuvent le faire de trop grandes qualitiés."*[4] The happiest lot that can fall to the genius is release from action, which is not his element, and leisure for production. From all this it results that although genius may highly bless him who is gifted with it, in the hours in which, abandoned to it, he revels unhindered in its delight, yet it is by no means fitted to procure for him a happy course of life; rather the contrary. This is also confirmed by the experience recorded in biographies. Besides this there is also an external incongruity, for the genius, in his efforts and achievements themselves, is for the most part in contradiction and conflict with his age. Mere men of talent come always at the right time; for as they are roused by the spirit of their age, and called forth by its needs, they are also capable only of satisfying these. They therefore go hand in hand with the advancing culture of their contemporaries or with the gradual progress of a special science: for this they reap reward and approval. But to the next generation their works are no longer enjoyable; they must be replaced by others, which again are not permanent. The genius, on the contrary, comes into his age like a comet into the paths of the planets, to whose well-regulated and comprehensible order his entirely eccentric course is foreign. Accordingly he cannot go hand in hand with the existing, regular progress of the culture of the age, but flings his works far out on to the way in front (as the dying emperor flung his spear among the enemy), upon which time has first to overtake them. The man of talent can achieve what is beyond the power of achievement of other men, but not what is beyond their power of apprehension: therefore he at once finds those who prize him. But the achievement of the man of genius, on the contrary, transcends not only the power of achievement, but also the power of apprehension of others; therefore they do not become directly conscious of him. The man of talent is like the marksman who hits a mark the others cannot hit; the man of genius is like the marksman who hits a mark they cannot even see to; therefore they get news of him only indirectly, and thus late; and even this they accept only upon trust and faith. Accordingly Goethe says in one of his letters, "Imitation is inborn in us; what to imitate is not easily recognized. Rarely is what is excellent found; still more rarely is it prized." And Chamfort says: *"Il en est de la valeur des hommes comme de celle des diamans, qui à une certaine mesure de grosseur, de pureté, de perfection, ont un prix fixe et marqué, mais qui, par-delà cette mesure, restent sans prix, et ne trouvent point d'acheteurs."*[5] And Bacon of Verulam has also expressed it: *"Infirmarum virtutum, apud vulgus, laus est, mediarum admiratio, supremarum sensus nullus"* (*De augm. sc.*, L. vi., c. 3).[6] Indeed, one might perhaps reply, *Apud vulgus!* But I must then come to his assistance with Machiavelli's assurance: *"Nel monde non è se non volgo"*;[7] as also Thilo (*Ueber den Ruhm*) remarks, that to the vulgar herd there generally belongs one more than each of us believes. It is a consequence of this late recognition of the works of the man of genius that they are rarely enjoyed by their contemporaries, and accordingly in the freshness of colour which synchronism and presence imparts, but, like figs and dates, much more in a dry than in a fresh state.

If, finally, we consider genius from the somatic side, we find it conditioned by several anatomical and physiological qualities, which individually are seldom present in perfection, and still more seldom perfect together, but which are yet all indispensably required; so that this explains why genius only appears as a perfectly isolated and almost portentous exception. The fundamental condition is an abnormal predominance of sensibility over irritability and reproductive power; and what makes the matter more difficult, this must take place in a male body. (Women may have great talent, but no genius, for they always remain subjective.) Similarly the cerebral system must be perfectly separated from the ganglion system by complete isolation, so that it stands in complete opposition to the latter; and thus the brain pursues its parasitic life on the organism in a very decided, isolated, powerful, and independent manner. Certainly it will thereby very easily affect the rest of the organism injuriously, and through its heightened life and ceaseless activity wear it out prematurely, unless it is itself possessed of energetic vital force and a good constitution: thus the latter belong to the conditions of genius. Indeed even a good stomach is a condition on account of the special and close agreement of this part with the brain. But chiefly the brain must be of unusual development and magnitude, especially broad and high. On the other hand, its depth will be inferior, and the cerebrum will abnormally preponderate in proportion to the cerebellum. Without doubt much depends upon the configuration of the brain as a whole and in its parts;

but our knowledge is not yet sufficient to determine this accurately, although we easily recognize the form of skull that indicates a noble and lofty intelligence. The texture of the mass of the brain must be of extreme fineness and perfection, and consist of the purest, most concentrated, tenderest, and most excitable nervesubstance; certainly the quantitative proportion of the white to the grey matter has a decided influence, which, however, we are also unable as yet to specify. However, the report of the *postmortem* on the body of Byron[8] shows that in his case the white matter was in unusually large proportion to the grey, and also that his brain weighed six pounds. Cuvier's brain weighed five pounds; the normal weight is three pounds. In contrast to the superior size of the brain, the spinal cord and nerves must be unusually thin. A beautifully arched, high and broad skull of thin bone must protect the brain without in any way cramping it. This whole quality of the brain and nervous system is the inheritance from the mother, to which we shall return in the following book. But it is quite insufficient to produce the phenomenon of genius if the inheritance from the father is not added, a lively, passionate temperament, which exhibits itself somatically as unusual energy of the heart, and consequently of the circulation of the blood, especially towards the head. For, in the first place, that turgescence peculiar to the brain on account of which it presses against its walls is increased by this; therefore it forces itself out of any opening in these which has been occasioned by some injury; and secondly, from the requisite strength of the heart the brain receives that internal movement different from its constant rising and sinking at every breath, which consists in a shaking of its whole mass at every pulsation of the four cerebral arteries, and the energy of which must correspond to the here increased quantity of the brain, as this movement in general is an indispensable condition of its activity. To this, therefore, small stature and especially a short neck is favourable, because by the shorter path the blood reaches the brain with more energy; and on this account great minds have seldom large bodies. Yet that shortness of the distance is not indispensable; for example, Goethe was of more than middle height. If, however, the whole condition connected with the circulation of the blood, and therefore coming from the father is wanting, the good quality of the brain coming from the mother, will at most produce a man of talent, a fine understanding, which the phlegmatic temperament thus introduced supports; but a phlegmatic genius is impossible. This condition coming from the father explains many faults of temperament described above. But, on the other hand, if this condition exists without the former, thus with an ordinarily or even badly constructed brain, it gives vivacity without mind, heat without light, hot-headed persons, men of unsupportable restlessness and petulance. That of two brothers only one has genius, and that one generally the elder, as, for example, in Kant's case, is primarily to be explained from the fact that the father was at the age of strength and passion only when he was begotten; although also the other condition originating with the mother may be spoiled by unfavourable circumstances.

I have further to add here a special remark on the *childlike* character of the genius, *i. e.*, on a certain resemblance which exists between genius and the age of childhood. In childhood, as in the case of genius, the cerebral and nervous system decidedly preponderates, for its development hurries far in advance of that of the rest of the organism; so that already at the seventh year the brain has attained its full extension and mass. On the other hand, the development of the genital system begins latest, and irritability, reproduction, and genital function are in full force only at the age of manhood, and then, as a rule, they predominate over the brain function. Hence it is explicable that children, in general, are so sensible, reasonable, desirous of information, and teachable, nay, on the whole, are more disposed and fitted for all theoretical occupation than grown-up people. They have, in consequence of that course of development, more intellect than will, *i. e.*, than inclinations, desire, and passion. For intellect and brain are one, and so also is the genital system one with the most vehement of all desires: therefore I have called the latter the focus of the will. Just because the fearful activity of this system still slumbers, while that of the brain has already full play, childhood is the time of innocence and happiness, the paradise of life, the lost Eden on which we look longingly back through the whole remaining course of our life. But the basis of that happiness is that in childhood our whole existence lies much more in knowing than in willing—a condition which is also supported from without by the novelty of all objects. Hence in the morning sunshine of life the world lies before us so fresh, so magically gleaming, so attractive. The small desires, the weak inclinations, and trifling cares of childhood are only a weak counterpoise to that predominance of intellectual activity. The innocent and clear glance of children, at which we revive ourselves, and which sometimes in particular cases reaches the sublime contemplative expression with which Raphael has glorified his cherubs, is to be explained from what has been said. Accordingly the mental powers develop much earlier than the needs they are destined to serve; and here, as everywhere, nature proceeds very designedly. For in this time of predominating intelligence the man collects a great store of knowledge for future wants which at the time are foreign to him. Therefore his intellect, now unceasingly active, eagerly apprehends all phenomena, broods over them and stores them up carefully for the coming time,—like the bees, who gather a great deal more honey than they can consume, in anticipation of future need. Certainly what a man acquires of insight and knowledge up to the age of puberty is, taken as a whole, more than all that he afterwards learns, however learned he may become; for it is the foundation of all human knowledge. Up till the same time plasticity predominates in the child's body, and later, by a metastasis, its forces throw themselves into the system of generation; and thus with puberty the sexual passion appears, and now, little by little, the will gains the upper hand. Then childhood, which is prevailingly theoretical and desirous of learning, is followed by the restless, now stormy, now melancholy, period of youth, which afterwards passes into the vigorous and earnest age of manhood. Just because that impulse pregnant with evil is wanting in the child is its volition so adapted and subordinated to knowledge, whence arises that character of innocence, intelligence, and reasonableness which is peculiar to the age of childhood. On what, then, the likeness between childhood and genius depends I scarcely need to express further: upon the surplus of the powers of knowledge over the needs of the will, and the predominance of the purely intellectual activity which springs from this. Really every child is to a certain extent a genius, and the genius is to a certain extent a child. The relationship of the two shows itself primarily in the naïveté and sublime simplicity which is characteristic of true genius; and besides this it appears in several traits, so that a certain childishness certainly belongs to the character of the genius. In Riemer's *"Mittheilungen über Goethe"* (vol. i., p. 184) it is related that Herder and others found fault with Goethe, saying he was always a big child. Certainly they were right in what they said, but they were not right in finding fault with it. It has also been said of Mozart that all his life he remained a child (Nissen's Biography of Mozart, pp. 2 and 529). Schlichtegrolls *"Nekrology"* (for 1791, vol. ii., p. 109) says of him: "In his art he early became a man, but in all other relations he always remained a child." Every genius is even for this reason a big child; he looks out into the world as into something strange, a play, and therefore with purely objective interest. Accordingly he has just as little as the child that dull gravity of ordinary men, who, since they are capable only of subjective interests, always see in things mere motives for their action. Whoever does not to a certain extent remain all his life a big child, but becomes a grave, sober, thoroughly composed, and reasonable man, may be a very useful and capable citizen of this world; but never a genius. In fact, the genius is so because that predominance of the sensible system and of intellectual activity which is natural to childhood maintains itself in him in an abnormal manner through his whole life, thus here becomes perennial. A trace of this certainly shows itself in many ordinary men up to the period of their youth; therefore, for example, in many students a purely intellectual tendency and an eccentricity suggestive of genius is unmistakable. But nature returns to her track; they assume the chrysalis form and reappear at the age of manhood, as incarnate Philistines, at whom we are startled when we meet them again in later years. Upon all this that has been expounded here depends Goethe's beautiful remark: "Children do not perform what they promise; young people very seldom; and if they do keep their word, the world does not keep its word with them" (*Wahlverwandtschaften,* Pt. i., ch. 10)—the world which afterwards bestows the crowns which it holds aloft for merit on those who are the tools of its low aims or know how to deceive it. In accordance with what has been said, as there is a mere beauty of youth, which almost every one at some time possesses *(beauté du diable),* so there is a mere intellectuality of youth, a certain mental nature disposed and adapted for apprehending, understanding, and learning, which every one has in childhood, and some have still in youth, but which is afterwards lost, just like that beauty. Only in the case of a very few, the chosen, the one, like the other, lasts through the whole life; so that even in old age a trace of it still remains visible; these are the truly beautiful and the men of true genius.

## *NOTES*

1. "Monsters by excess, defect, or abnormal position."
2. "Hilarious in sadness, sad in hilarity."
3. "All men of genius are melancholy."
4. "There are few vices that can so hinder a man from having many friends, as can the possession of superior qualities."
5. "It is with the value of men as with that of diamonds, which, up to a certain degree of size, purity, and perfection, have a fixed and marked price, but which, beyond that degree, remain without price and find no buyers."
6. "Among the people there is praise for the smaller virtues, administration for the middling ones, but no sense of the greatest."
7. "There is nothing else in the world but the vulgar."
8. In Medwin's "Conversations of Lord Byron," p. 333.

# Percy Bysshe Shelley

1792–1822

Percy Bysshe Shelley was born in Sussex in 1792. One side of his family was of noble descent, and he spent his boyhood years on the ample grounds of his family's mansion. He was the oldest of seven, and seems to have been worshipped by his four younger sisters; he delighted in telling them gothic stories spun from his already-fecund imagination. Sent to Eton at the age of twelve, he exhibited a tendency towards nonconformism from the very start. His strangeness, gentleness, and solitariness made him vulnerable to the mockery of his classmates, but Shelley was fierce in his own defense, and he was a superior student. He became known as "Mad Shelley" and "Shelley the Atheist," and in 1810 he was expelled from Oxford for writing a tract against religion called "The Necessity of Atheism." Outsidc thc stifling university environment, Shelley continued to read deeply in Platonic philosophy and was swept up by the radical intellectual currents unleashed by the French Revolution. Although he originally planned to inherit his father's seat as a Whig member of Parliament, his growing radicalism caused him to reject his patrimony. Among the crucial influences upon his moral vision and conduct was the philosophy of Godwin, a freethinking rationalist whose waking dreams envisioned a utopian society free from ignorance, marriage, and poverty. Shelley embraced both Godwin's thought and his daughter, Mary Wollstonecraft, who became his second wife.

Shelley's emotional life, like his poetry, was characterized by the clash between ideality and the reality of loss. His first wife, Harriet Westbrook, did not permit him the luxury of Godwin's freethinking, and may have induced him into marriage against his will and philosophy. During this first marriage he wrote the virulently anti-religious *Queen Mab,* a poem whose attack on conventional morality earned him the fully deserved reputation of a renegade. This marriage was destined to fail; Westbrook, in Shelley's own estimation, did not "understand" poetry. He fell in love with Mary Wollstonecraft, but did not marry her until after Westbrook's suicide. Settling first in London, and then in the country, Shelley broke through to his mature style with *Alastor, or the Spirit of Solitude,* in 1816.

In subsequent years of nomadic wandering on the Continent, and especially in Italy, Shelley conceived his finest verse. In Switzerland in the summer of 1816 he wrote the transcendental *Hymn to Intellectual Beauty*—a lyrical record of an ecstatic moment in Shelley's school days when he felt for the first time "the awful shadow of some unseen power."

That same summer, in the vale of Chamounix, he wrote *Mont Blanc,* one of the central Romantic meditations on the relationship of man to nature. In 1817 he wrote *Laon and Cythna, or The Revolt of Islam,* a political romance which set forth once again Shelley's extreme political idealism. In 1818 he journeyed to Italy where for the next four years he led an almost unbelievably hectic life, moving constantly from city to city with his sometimes pregnant wife, his children, servants, and Mary's half-sister Claire Clarmont, who had recently given birth out of wedlock to a daughter of Shelley's close friend Lord Byron. "I go until I am stopped," Shelley said, "and I am never stopped." Indeed, during these years Shelley also wrote many of the greatest visionary lyrics in English: *Prometheus Unbound* (1818–19)—a mythopoeic dramatization of the regenerative power of love, which Yeats would later recommend as "the bible" to students of poetry; *Adonais* (1821)—the passionate lament for Keats which is rivalled only by *Lycidas* in the history of English elegy; *Epipsychidion* (1821)—a dream vision of love inspired by Emilia Viviani, a beautiful 17-year-old heiress "tyrannized" in a convent in Pisa; and in 1822 *The Triumph of Life*—a fragment in Dantesque *terza rima* which attempted a kind of spiritual history of the Western tradition. Before he finished this last work, however, Shelley died in a boating accident in the Bay of Spezia, July 12, 1822.

During the years in Italy Shelley also wrote his *Defence of Poetry,* the prose work which Yeats declared to be "the profoundest essay on the foundations of poetry in English." In this essay Shelley defends the imagination against the recent attack of his friend Thomas Love Peacock, who had asserted in his *Four Ages of Poetry* that imagination was an anachronistic vestige from the days of the savages, and only reason would remain useful and relevant to the progress of modern, scientific society. Shelley grants Peacock's claim that imagination preceded reason in human thinking, but he does not submit to his rationalist myth of progress. He defines poetry broadly as the expression of imagination, and asserts that imagination is actively at work in virtually every sphere of human activity, including ethics, religion, science, and philosophy as well as the innumerable forms of beauty. Especially in the struggle for civil and religious liberty, he argues, "the most unfailing herald, companion, and follower of the awakening of a great people to work a beneficial change in opinion or institution, is Poetry." As Paul Fry points out in his article "On Shelley's Defense of Poetry in Our Time," Shelley's essay is not merely the idealistic polemic of a visionary, but is rather a shrewd and closely-reasoned argument based upon an epistemological insight into the figurative nature of knowledge itself. Shelley defends poetry against science by showing that "science" is a type of poetry, that invention or projection of possibility is intrinsic to all modes of thought, and that all thought requires the "colors" or "music" of representation: "He agrees that imagination precedes reason in the development of thought, but he goes on to insist that the imagination has not therefore been left behind by the grand march of intellect. On the contrary, imagination must pave the way for reason in every new venture of thought or else the mind will atrophy and fail to keep pace with the need for change in society. Moreover, reason has no useful function that is independent of, or different from, the function of imagination. Insofar as it is valuable, reason 'in her most exalted mood' simply is the imagination. Hence for any praiseworthy human endeavor there is only one faculty, not two of them dividing the labor." If Fry and other modern theorists are correct in suggesting that all knowledge is linguistic, or figurative, or rhetorical, then Shelley's exalted defense of poetry comes to seem not only beautiful but persuasive.

FROM

# THE FALL OF ISLAM

## *PREFACE*

The Poem which I now present to the world, is an attempt from which I scarcely dare to expect success, and in which a writer of established fame might fail without disgrace. It is an experiment on the temper of the public mind, as to how far a thirst for a happier condition of moral and political society survives, among the enlightened and refined, the tempests which have shaken the age in which we live. I have sought to enlist the harmony of metrical language, the etherial combinations of the fancy, the rapid and subtle transitions of human passion, all those elements which essentially compose a Poem, in the cause of a liberal and comprehensive morality: and in the view of kindling within the bosoms of my readers, a virtuous enthusiasm for those doctrines of liberty and justice, that faith and hope in something good, which neither violence, nor misrepresentation, nor prejudice, can ever totally extinguish among mankind.

For this purpose I have chosen a story of human passion in its most universal character, diversified with moving and romantic adventures, and appealing, in contempt of all artificial opinions or institutions, to the common sympathies of every human breast. I have made no attempt to recommend the motives which I would substitute for those at present governing mankind by methodical and systematic argument. I would only awaken the feelings, so that the reader should see the beauty of true virtue, and be incited to those inquiries which have led to my moral and political creed, and that of some of the sublimest intellects in the world. The Poem, therefore (with the exception of the first Canto, which is purely introductory), is narrative, not didactic. It is a succession of pictures illustrating the growth and progress of individual mind aspiring after excellence, and devoted to the love of mankind; its influence in refining and making pure the most daring and uncommon impulses of the imagination, the understanding, and the senses; its impatience at "all the oppressions which are done under the sun;" its tendency to awaken public hope and to enlighten and improve mankind; the rapid effects of the application of that tendency; the awakening of an immense nation from their slavery and degradation to a true sense of moral dignity and freedom; the bloodless dethronement of their oppressors, and the unveiling of the religious frauds by which they had been deluded into submission; the tranquillity of successful patriotism, and the universal toleration and benevolence of true philanthropy; the treachery and barbarity of hired soldiers; vice not the object of punishment and hatred, but kindness and pity; the faithlessness of tyrants; the confederacy of the Rulers of the World, and the restoration of the expelled Dynasty by foreign arms; the massacre and extermination of the Patriots, and the victory of established power; the consequences of legitimate despotism, civil war, famine, plague, superstition, and an utter extinction of the domestic affections; the judicial murder of the advocates of Liberty; the temporary triumph of oppression, that secure earnest of its final and inevitable fall; the transient nature of ignorance and error, and the eternity of genius and virtue. Such is the series of delineations of which the Poem consists. And if the lofty passions with which it has been my scope to distinguish this story, shall not excite in the reader a generous impulse, an ardent thirst for excellence, an interest profound and strong, such as belongs to no meaner desires—let not the failure be imputed to a natural unfitness for human sympathy in these sublime and animating themes. It is the business of the Poet to communicate to others the pleasure and the enthusiasm arising out of those images and feelings, in the vivid presence of which within his own mind, consists at once his inspiration and his reward.

The panic which, like an epidemic transport, seized upon all classes of men during the excesses consequent upon the French Revolution, is gradually giving place to sanity. It has ceased to be believed, that whole generations of mankind ought to consign themselves to a hopeless inheritance of ignorance and misery, because a nation of men who had been dupes and slaves for centuries, were incapable of conducting themselves with the wisdom and tranquillity of freemen so soon as some of their fetters were partially loosened. That their conduct could not have been marked by any other characters than ferocity and thoughtlessness, is the historical fact from which liberty derives all its recommendations, and falsehood the worst features of its deformity. There is a reflux in the tide of human things which bears the shipwrecked hopes of men into a secure haven, after the storms are past. Methinks, those who now live have survived an age of despair.

The French Revolution may be considered as one of those manifestations of a general state of feeling among civilized mankind, produced by a defect of correspondence between the knowledge existing in society and the improvement or gradual abolition of political institutions. The year 1788 may be assumed as the epoch of one of the most important crises produced by this feeling. The sympathies connected with that event extended to every bosom. The most generous and amiable natures were those which participated the most extensively in these sympathies. But such a degree of unmingled good was expected, as it was impossible to realize. If the Revolution had been in every respect prosperous, then misrule and superstition would lose half their claims to our abhorrence, as fetters which the captive can unlock with the slightest motion of his fingers, and which do not eat with poisonous rust into the soul. The revulsion occasioned by the atrocities of the demagogues and the re-establishment of successive tyrannies in France was terrible, and felt in the remotest corner of the civilized world. Could they listen to the plea of reason who had groaned under the calamities of a social state, according to the provisions of which, one man riots in luxury whilst another famishes for want of bread. Can he who the day before was a trampled slave, suddenly become liberal-minded, forbearing, and independent? This is the consequence of the habits of a state of society to be produced by resolute perseverance and indefatigable hope, and long-suffering and long believing courage, and the systematic efforts of generations of men of intellect and virtue. Such is the lesson which experience teaches now. But on the first reverses of hope in the progress of French liberty, the sanguine eagerness for good overleapt the solution of these questions, and for a time extinguished itself in the unexpectedness of their result. Thus many of the most ardent and tender-hearted of the worshippers of public good have been morally ruined by what a partial glimpse of the events they deplored, appeared to shew as the melancholy desolation of all their cherished hopes. Hence gloom and misanthropy have become the characteristics of the age in which we live, the solace of a disappointment that unconsciously finds relief only in the wilful exaggeration of its own despair. This influence has tainted the literature of the age with the hopelessness of the minds from which it flows. Metaphysics,[1] and enquiries into moral and political science, have become little else than vain attempts to revive exploded superstitions, or sophisms like those[2] of Mr. Malthus, calculated to lull the oppressors of mankind into a security of everlasting triumph. Our works of fiction and poetry have been overshadowed by the same infectious gloom. But mankind appear to me to be emerging from their trance. I am aware, methinks, of a slow, gradual, silent change. In that belief I have composed the following Poem.

I do not presume to enter into competition with our greatest contemporary Poets. Yet I am unwilling to tread in the footsteps of any who have preceded me. I have sought to avoid the imitation of any style of language or versification peculiar to the original minds of which it is the character, designing that even if what I have produced be worthless, it should still be properly my own. Nor have I permitted any system relating to mere words, to divert the attention of the reader from whatever interest I may have succeeded in creating, to my own ingenuity in contriving to disgust them according to the rules of criticism. I have simply clothed my thoughts in what appeared to me the most obvious and appropriate language. A person familiar with nature, and with the most celebrated productions of the human mind, can scarcely err in following the instinct, with respect to selection of language, produced by that familiarity.

There is an education peculiarly fitted for a Poet, without which, genius and sensibility can hardly fill the circle of their capacities. No education indeed can entitle to this appellation a dull and unobservant mind, or one, though neither dull nor unobservant, in which the channels of communication between thought and expression have been obstructed or closed. How far it is my fortune to belong to either of the latter classes, I cannot know. I aspire to be something better. The circumstances of my accidental education have been favourable to this ambition. I have been familiar from boyhood with mountains and lakes, and the sea, and the solitude of forests: Danger, which sports upon the brink of precipices, has been my playmate. I have trodden the glaciers of the Alps, and lived under the eye of Mont Blanc. I have been a wanderer among distant fields. I have sailed down mighty rivers, and seen the sun rise and set, and the stars come forth, whilst I have sailed night and day down a rapid stream among mountains. I have seen populous cities, and have watched the passions which rise and spread, and sink and change, amongst assembled multitudes of men. I have seen the theatre of the more visible ravages of tyranny and war, cities and villages reduced to scattered groups of black and roofless houses, and the naked inhabitants sitting famished upon their desolated thresholds. I have conversed with living men of genius. The poetry of antient Greece and Rome, and modern Italy, and our own country, has been to me like external nature, a passion and an enjoyment. Such are the sources from which the materials for the imagery of my Poem have been drawn. I have considered Poetry in its most comprehensive sense, and have read the Poets and the Historians, and thc Mctaphysicians[3] whose writings have been accessible to me, and have looked upon the beautiful and majestic scenery of the earth as common sources of those elements which it is the province of the Poet to embody and combine. Yet the experience and the feelings to which I refer, do not in themselves constitute men Poets, but only prepare them to be the auditors of those who are. How far I shall be found to possess that more essential attribute of Poetry, the power of awakening in others sensations like those which animate my own bosom, is that which, to speak sincerely, I know not; and which with an acquiescent and contented spirit, I expect to be taught by the effect which I shall produce upon those whom I now address.

I have avoided, as I have said before, the imitation of any contemporary style. But there must be a resemblance which does not depend upon their own will, between all the writers of any particular age. They cannot escape from subjection to a common influence which arises out of an infinite combination of circumstances belonging to the times in which they live, though each is in a degree the author of the very influence by which his being is thus pervaded. Thus, the tragic Poets of the age of Pericles; the Italian revivers of ancient learning; those mighty intellects of our own country that succeeded the Reformation, the translators of the Bible, Shakspeare, Spenser, the Dramatists of the reign of Elizabeth, and Lord Bacon[4]; the colder spirits of the interval that succeeded;—all resemble each other, and differ from every other in their several classes. In this view of things, Ford can no more be called the imitator of Shakspeare, than Shakspeare the imitator of Ford. There were perhaps few other points of resemblance between these two men, than that which the universal and inevitable influence of their age produced. And this is an influence which neither the meanest scribbler, nor the sublimest genius of any æra, can escape; and which I have not attempted to escape.

I have adopted the stanza of Spenser ( a measure inexpressibly beautiful) not because I consider it a finer model of poetical harmony than the blank verse of Shakspeare and Milton, but because in the latter there is no shelter for mediocrity; you must either succeed or fail. This perhaps an aspiring spirit should desire. But I was enticed also, by the brilliancy and magnificence of sound which a mind that has been nourished upon musical thoughts, can produce by a just and harmonious arrangement of the pauses of this measure. Yet there will be found some instances where I have completely failed in this attempt, and one, which I here request the reader to consider as an erratum, where there is left most inadvertently an alexandrine in the middle of a stanza.

But in this, as in every other respect, I have written fearlessly. It is the misfortune of this age, that its Writers, too thoughtless of immortality, are exquisitely sensible to temporary praise or blame. They write with the fear of Reviews before their eyes. This system of criticism sprang up in that torpid interval when Poetry was not. Poetry, and the art which professes to regulate and limit its powers, cannot subsist together. Longinus could not have been the contemporary of Homer, nor Boileau of Horace. Yet this species of criticism never presumed to assert an understanding of its own: it has always, unlike true science, followed, not preceded the opinion of mankind, and would even now bribe with worthless adulation some of our greatest Poets to impose gratuitous fetters on their own imaginations, and become unconscious accomplices in the daily murder of all genius either not so aspiring or not so fortunate as their own. I have sought therefore to write, as I believe that Homer, Shakspeare, and Milton wrote, with an utter disregard of anonymous censure. I am certain that calumny and misrepresentation, though it may move me to compassion, cannot disturb my peace. I shall understand the expressive silence of those sagacious enemies who dare not trust themselves to speak. I shall endeavour to extract from the midst of insult, and contempt, and maledictions, those admonitions which may tend to correct whatever imperfections such censurers may discover in this my first serious appeal to the Public. If certain Critics were as clear-sighted as they are malignant, how great would be the benefit to be derived from their virulent writings! As it is, I fear I shall be malicious enough to be amused with their paltry tricks and lame invectives. Should the Public judge that my composition is worthless, I shall indeed bow before the tribunal from which Milton received his crown of immortality, and shall seek to gather, if I live, strength from that defeat, which may nerve me to some new enterprise of thought which may *not* be worthless. I cannot conceive that Lucretius, when he meditated that poem whose doctrines are yet the basis of our metaphysical knowledge, and whose eloquence has been the wonder of mankind, wrote in awe of such censure as the hired sophists of the impure and superstitious noblemen of Rome might affix to what he should produce. It was at the period when Greece was led captive, and Asia made tributary to the Republic, fast verging itself to slavery and ruin, that a multitude of Syrian captives, bigotted to the worship of their obscene Ashtaroth, and the unworthy successors of Socrates and Zeno, found there a precarious subsistence by administering, under the name of freedmen, to the vices and vanities of the great. These wretched men were skilled to plead, with a superficial but plausible set of sophisms, in favour of that contempt for virtue which is the portion of slaves, and that faith in portents, the most fatal substitute for benevolence in the imaginations of men, which, arising from the enslaved communities of the East, then first began to overwhelm the western nations in its stream. Were these the kind of men whose disapprobation the wise and lofty-minded Lucretius should have regarded with a salutary awe? The latest and perhaps the meanest of those who follow in his footsteps, would disdain to hold life on such conditions.

The Poem now presented to the Public occupied little more than six months in the composition. That period has been devoted to the task with unremitting ardour and enthusiasm. I have exercised a watchful and earnest criticism on my work as it grew under my hands. I would willingly have sent it forth to the world with that perfection which long labour and revision is said to bestow. But I found that if I should gain something in exactness by this method, I might lose much of the newness and energy of imagery and language as it flowed afresh from my mind. And although the mere composition occupied no more than six months, the thoughts thus arranged were slowly gathered in as many years.

I trust that the reader will carefully distinguish between those opinions which have a dramatic propriety in reference to the characters which they are designed to elucidate and such as are properly my own. The erroneous and degrading idea which men have conceived of a Supreme Being, for instance, is spoken against, but not the Supreme Being itself. The belief which some superstitious persons whom I have brought upon the stage entertain of the Deity, as injurious to the character of his benevolence, is widely different from my own. In recommending also a great and important change in the spirit which animates the social institutions of mankind, I have avoided all flattery to those violent and malignant passions of our nature, which are ever on the watch to mingle with and to alloy the most beneficial innovations. There is no quarter given to Revenge, or Envy, or Prejudice. Love is celebrated every where as the sole law which should govern the moral world.

In the personal conduct of my Hero and Heroine, there is one circumstance which was intended to startle the reader from the trance of ordinary life. It was my object to break through the crust of those outworn opinions on which established institutions depend. I have appealed therefore to the most universal of all feelings, and have endeavoured to strengthen the moral sense, by forbidding it to waste its energies in seeking to avoid actions which are only crimes of convention. It is because there is so great a multitude of artificial vices, that there are so few real virtues. Those feelings alone which are benevolent or malevolent, are essentially good or bad. The circumstance of which I speak, was introduced, however, merely to accustom men to that charity and toleration which the exhibition of a practice widely differing from their own, has a tendency to promote.[5] Nothing indeed can be more mischievous, than many actions innocent in themselves, which might bring down upon individuals the bigotted contempt and rage of the multitude.

## *NOTES*

1. I ought to except Sir W. Drummond's "Academical Questions;" a volume of very acute and powerful metaphysical criticism. [Shelley's note.]

2. It is remarkable, as a symptom of the revival of public hope, that Mr. Malthus has assigned, in the later editions of his work, an indefinite dominion to moral restraint

over the principle of population. This concession answers all the inferences from his doctrine unfavourable to human improvement, and reduces the "ESSAY ON POPULATION," to a commentary illustrative of the unanswerableness of "POLITICAL JUSTICE." [Shelley's note.]

3. In this sense there may be such a thing as perfectibility in works of fiction, notwithstanding the concession often made by the advocates of human improvement, that perfectibility is a term applicable only to science. [Shelley's note.]

4. Milton stands alone in the stage which he illumined.

5. The sentiments connected with and characteristic of this circumstance, have no personal reference to the Writer. [Shelley's note.]

FROM

# PROMETHEUS UNBOUND

## *PREFACE*

The Greek tragic writers, in selecting as their subject any portion of their national history or mythology, employed in their treatment of it a certain arbitrary discretion. They by no means conceived themselves bound to adhere to the common interpretation or to imitate in story as in title their rivals and predecessors. Such a system would have amounted to a resignation of those claims to preference over their competitors which incited the composition. The Agamemnonian story was exhibited on the Athenian theatre with as many variations as dramas.

I have presumed to employ a similar licence. The "Prometheus Unbound" of Æschylus supposed the reconciliation of Jupiter with his victim as the price of the disclosure of the danger threatened to his empire by the consummation of his marriage with Thetis. Thetis, according to this view of the subject, was given in marriage to Peleus, and Prometheus, by the permission of Jupiter, delivered from his captivity by Hercules. Had I framed my story on this model, I should have done no more than have attempted to restore the lost drama of Æschylus; an ambition, which, if my preference to this mode of treating the subject had incited me to cherish, the recollection of the high comparison such an attempt would challenge might well abate. But, in truth, I was averse from a catastrophe so feeble as that of reconciling the Champion with the Oppressor of mankind. The moral interest of the fable, which is so powerfully sustained by the sufferings and endurance of Prometheus, would be annihilated if we could conceive of him as unsaying his high language and quailing before his successful and perfidious adversary. The only imaginary being resembling in any degree Prometheus, is Satan; and Prometheus is, in my judgment, a more poetical character than Satan, because, in addition to courage, and majesty, and firm and patient opposition to omnipotent force, he is susceptible of being described as exempt from the taints of ambition, envy, revenge, and a desire for personal aggrandisement, which, in the Hero of Paradise Lost, interfere with the interest. The character of Satan engenders in the mind a pernicious casuistry which leads us to weigh his faults with his wrongs, and to excuse the former because the latter exceed all measure. In the minds of those who consider that magnificent fiction with a religious feeling it engenders something worse. But Prometheus is, as it were, the type of the highest perfection of moral and intellectual nature, impelled by the purest and the truest motives to the best and noblest ends.

This Poem was chiefly written upon the mountainous ruins of the Baths of Caracalla, among the flowery glades, and thickets of odoriferous blossoming trees, which are extended in ever winding labyrinths upon its immense platforms and dizzy arches suspended in the air. The bright blue sky of Rome, and the effect of the vigorous awakening spring in that divinest climate, and the new life with which it drenches the spirits even to intoxication, were the inspiration of this drama.

The imagery which I have employed will be found, in many instances, to have been drawn from the operations of the human mind, or from those external actions by which they are expressed. This is unusual in modern poetry, although Dante and Shakspeare are full of instances of the same kind: Dante indeed more than any other poet, and with greater success. But the Greek poets, as writers to whom no resource of awakening the sympathy of their contemporaries was unknown, were in the habitual use of this power; and it is the study of their works, (since a higher merit would probably be denied me,) to which I am willing that my readers should impute this singularity.

One word is due in candour to the degree in which the study of contemporary writings may have tinged my composition, for such has been a topic of censure with regard to poems far more popular, and indeed more deservedly popular, than mine. It is impossible that any one who inhabits the same age with such writers as those who stand in the foremost ranks of our own, can conscientiously assure himself that his language and tone of thought may not have been modified by the study of the productions of those extraordinary intellects. It is true, that, not the spirit of their genius, but the forms in which it has manifested itself, are due less to the peculiarities of their own minds than to the peculiarity of the moral and intellectual condition of the minds among which they have been produced. Thus a number of writers possess the form, whilst they want the spirit of those whom, it is alleged, they imitate; because the former is the endowment of the age in which they live, and the latter must be the uncommunicated lightning of their own mind.

The peculiar style of intense and comprehensive imagery which distinguishes the modern literature of England, has not been, as a general power, the product of the imitation of any particular writer. The mass of capabilities remains at every period materially the same; the circumstances which awaken it to action perpetually change. If England were divided into forty republics, each equal in population and extent to Athens, there is no reason to suppose but that, under institutions not more perfect than those of Athens, each would produce philosophers and poets equal to those who (if we except Shakspeare) have never been surpassed. We owe the great writers of the golden age of our literature to that fervid awakening of the public mind which shook to dust the oldest and most oppressive form of the Christian religion. We owe Milton to the progress and development of the same spirit: the sacred Milton was, let it ever be remembered, a republican, and a bold inquirer into morals and religion. The great writers of our own age are, we have reason to suppose, the companions and forerunners of some unimagined change in our social condition, or the opinions which cement it. The cloud of mind is discharging its collected lightning, and the equilibrium between institutions and opinions is now restoring, or is about to be restored.

As to imitation, poetry is a mimetic art. It creates, but it creates by combination and representation. Poetical abstractions are beautiful and new, not because the portions of which they are composed had no previous existence in the mind of man or in nature, but because the whole produced by their combination has some intelligible and beautiful analogy with those sources of emotion and thought, and with the contemporary condition of them: one great poet is a masterpiece of nature which another not only ought to study but must study. He might as wisely and as easily determine that his mind should no longer be the mirror of all that is lovely in the visible universe, as exclude from his contemplation the beautiful which exists in the writings of a great contemporary. The pretence of doing it would be a presumption in any but the greatest; the effect, even in him, would be strained, unnatural, and ineffectual. A poet is the combined product of such internal powers as modify the nature of others; and of such external influences as excite and sustain these powers; he is not one, but both. Every man's mind is, in this respect, modified by all the objects of nature and art; by every word and every suggestion which he ever admitted to act upon his consciousness; it is the mirror upon which all forms are reflected, and in which they compose one form. Poets, not otherwise than philosophers, painters, sculptors, and musicians, are, in one sense, the creators, and, in another, the creations, of their age. From this subjection the loftiest do not escape. There is a similarity between Homer and Hesiod, between Æschylus and Euripides, between Virgil and Horace, between Dante and Petrarch, between Shakspeare and Fletcher, between Dryden and Pope; each has a generic resemblance under which their specific distinctions are arranged. If this similarity be the result of imitation, I am willing to confess that I have imitated.

Let this opportunity be conceded to me of acknowledging that I have, what a Scotch philosopher characteristically terms, "a passion for reforming the world:" what passion incited him to write and publish his book, he omits to explain. For my part, I had rather be damned with Plato and Lord Bacon, than go to Heaven with Paley and Malthus. But it is a mistake to suppose that I dedicate my poetical compositions solely to the direct enforcement of reform, or that I consider them in any degree as containing a reasoned system on the theory of human life. Didactic poetry is my abhorrence; nothing can be equally well expressed in prose that is not tedious and supererogatory in verse. My purpose has hitherto been simply to familiarize the highly refined imagination of the more select classes of poetical readers with beautiful idealisms of moral excellence; aware that until the mind can love, and admire, and trust, and hope, and endure, reasoned principles of moral conduct are seeds cast upon the highway of life which the unconscious passenger tramples into dust, although they would bear the harvest of his happiness. Should I live to accomplish what I purpose, that is, produce a systematical history of what appear to me to be the genuine elements of human society, let not the advocates of injustice and superstition flatter themselves that I should take Æschlyus rather than Plato as my model.

The having spoken of myself with unaffected freedom will need little apology with the candid; and let the uncandid consider that they injure me less than their own hearts and minds by misrepresentation. Whatever talents a person may possess to amuse and instruct others, be they ever so inconsiderable, he is yet bound to exert them: if his attempt be ineffectual, let the punishment of an unaccomplished purpose have been sufficient; let none trouble themselves to heap the dust of oblivion upon his efforts; the pile they raise will betray his grave which might otherwise have been unknown.

# On Love

What is love? Ask him who lives, what is life? ask him who adores, what is God?

I know not the internal constitution of other men, nor even thine, whom I now address. I see that in some external attributes they resemble me, but when, misled by that appearance, I have thought to appeal to something in common, and unburthen my inmost soul to them, I have found my language misunderstood, like one in a distant and savage land. The more opportunities they have afforded me for experience, the wider has appeared the interval between us, and to a greater distance have the points of sympathy been withdrawn. With a spirit ill fitted to sustain such proof, trembling and feeble through its tenderness, I have everywhere sought sympathy, and have found only repulse and disappointment.

*Thou* demandest what is love? It is that powerful attraction towards all that we conceive, or fear, or hope beyond ourselves, when we find within our own thoughts the chasm of an insufficient void, and seek to awaken in all things that are, a community with what we experience within ourselves. If we reason, we would be understood; if we imagine, we would that the airy children of our brain were born anew within another's; if we feel, we would that another's nerves should vibrate to our own, that the beams of their eyes should kindle at once and mix and melt into our own, that lips of motionless ice should not reply to lips quivering and burning with the heart's best blood. This is Love. This is the bond and the sanction which connects not only man with man, but with every thing which exists. We are born into the world, and there is something within us which, from the instant that we live, more and more thirsts after its likeness. It is probably in correspondence with this law that the infant drains milk from the bosom of its mother; this propensity develops itself with the development of our nature. We dimly see within our intellectual nature a miniature as it were of our entire self, yet deprived of all that we condemn or despise, the ideal prototype of every thing excellent or lovely that we are capable of conceiving as belonging to the nature of man. Not only the portrait of our external being, but an assemblage of the minutest particles of which our nature is composed[1]; a mirror whose surface reflects only the forms of purity and brightness; a soul within our soul that describes a circle around its proper paradise, which pain, and sorrow, and evil dare not overleap. To this we eagerly refer all sensations, thirsting that they should resemble or correspond with it. The discovery of its antitype; the meeting with an understanding capable of clearly estimating our own; an imagination which should enter into and seize upon the subtle and delicate peculiarities which we have delighted to cherish and unfold in secret; with a frame whose nerves, like the chords of two exquisite lyres, strung to the accompaniment of one delightful voice, vibrate with the vibrations of our own; and of a combination of all these in such proportion as the type within demands; this is the invisible and unattainable point to which Love tends; and to attain which, it urges forth the powers of man to arrest the faintest shadow of that, without the possession of which there is no rest nor respite to the heart over which it rules. Hence in solitude, or in that deserted state when we are surrounded by human beings, and yet they sympathise not with us, we love the flowers, the grass, and the waters, and the sky. In the motion of the very leaves of spring, in the blue air, there is then found a secret correspondence with our heart. There is eloquence in the tongueless wind, and a melody in the flowing brooks and the rustling of the reeds beside them, which by their inconceivable relation to something within the soul, awaken the spirits to a dance of breathless rapture, and bring tears of mysterious tenderness to the eyes, like the enthusiasm of patriotic success, or the voice of one beloved singing to you alone. Sterne says that, if he were in a desert, he would love some cypress. So soon as this want or power is dead, man becomes the living sepulchre of himself, and what yet survives is the mere husk of what once he was.

## *NOTES*

1. These words are ineffectual and metaphorical. Most words are so—No help! [Shelley's Note.]

# A Defence of Poetry

## *Part I*

According to one mode of regarding those two classes of mental action, which are called reason and imagination, the former may be considered as mind contemplating the relations borne by one thought to another, however produced; and the latter, as mind acting upon those thoughts so as to colour them with its own light, and composing from them, as from elements, other thoughts, each containing within itself the principle of its own integrity. The one is the τὸ ποιειν, or the principle of synthesis, and has for its objects those forms which are common to universal nature and existence itself; the other is the τὸ λογιζεν, or principle of analysis, and its action regards the relations of things, simply as relations; considering thoughts, not in their integral unity, but as the algebraical representations which conduct to certain general results. Reason is the enumeration of quantities already known; imagination is the perception of the value of those quantities, both separately and as a whole. Reason respects the differences, and imagination the similitudes of things. Reason is to imagination as the instrument to the agent, as the body to the spirit, as the shadow to the substance.

Poetry, in a general sense, may be defined to be "the expression of the imagination": and poetry is connate with the origin of man. Man is an instrument over which a series of external and internal impressions are driven, like the alternations of an everchanging wind over an Æolian lyre, which move it by their motion to ever-changing melody. But there is a principle within the human being, and perhaps within all sentient beings, which acts otherwise than in the lyre, and produces not melody, alone, but harmony, by an internal adjustment of the sounds or motions thus excited to the impressions which excite them. It is as if the lyre could accommodate its chords to the motions of that which strikes them, in a determined proportion of sound; even as the musician can accommodate his voice to the sound of the lyre. A child at play by itself will express its delight by its voice and motions; and every inflexion of tone and every gesture will bear exact relation to a corresponding antitype in the pleasurable impressions which awakened it; it will be the reflected image of that impression; and as the lyre trembles and sounds after the wind has died away, so the child seeks, by prolonging in its voice and motions the duration of the effect, to prolong also a consciousness of the cause. In relation to the objects which delight a child, these expressions are, what poetry is to higher objects. The savage (for the savage is to ages what the child is to years) expresses the emotions produced in him by surrounding objects in a similar manner; and language and gesture, together with plastic or pictorial imitation, become the image of the combined effect of those objects, and of his apprehension of them. Man in society, with all his passions and his pleasures, next becomes the object of the passions and pleasures of man; an additional class of emotions produces an augmented treasure of expressions; and language, gesture, and the imitative arts, become at once the representation and the medium, the pencil and the picture, the chisel and the statue, the chord and the harmony. The social sympathies, or those laws from which, as from its elements, society results, begin to develop themselves from the moment that two human beings coexist; the future is contained within the present, as the plant within the seed; and equality, diversity, unity, contrast, mutual dependence, become the principles alone capable of affording the motives according to which the will of a social being is determined to action, inasmuch as he is social; and constitute pleasure in sensation, virtue in sentiment, beauty in art, truth in reasoning, and love in the intercourse of kind. Hence men, even in the infancy of society, observe a certain order in their words and actions, distinct from that of the objects and the impressions represented by them, all expression being subject to the laws of that from which it proceeds. But let us dismiss those more general considerations which might involve an inquiry into the principles of society itself, and restrict our view to the manner in which the imagination is expressed upon its forms.

In the youth of the world, men dance and sing and imitate natural objects, observing in these actions, as in all others, a certain rhythm or order. And, although all men observe a similar, they observe not the same order, in the motions of the dance, in the melody of the song, in the combinations of language, in the series of their imitations of natural objects. For there is a certain order or rhythm belonging to each of these classes of mimetic representation, from which the hearer and the spectator receive an intenser and purer pleasure than from any other: the sense of an approximation to this order has been called taste by modern writers. Every man in the infancy of art, observes an order which approximates more or less closely to that from which this highest delight results: but the diversity is not sufficiently marked, as that its gradations should be sensibie, except in those instances where the predominance of this faculty of approximation to the beautiful (for so we may be permitted to name the relation between this highest pleasure and its cause) is very great. Those in whom it exists in excess are poets, in the most universal sense of the word; and the pleasure resulting from the manner in which they express the influence of society or nature upon their own minds, communicates itself to others, and gathers a sort of reduplication from that community. Their language is vitally metaphorical; that is, it marks the before unapprehended relations of things and perpetuates their apprehension, until the words which represent them, become, through time, signs for portions or classes of thoughts instead of pictures of integral thoughts; and then if no new poets should arise to create afresh the associations which have been thus disorganised, language will be dead to all the nobler purposes of human intercourse. These similitudes or relations are finely said by Lord Bacon to be "the same footsteps of nature impressed upon the various subjects of the world[1]"—and he considers the faculty which perceives them as the storehouse of axioms common to all knowledge. In the infancy of society every author is necessarily a poet, because language itself is poetry; and to be a poet is to apprehend the true and the beautiful, in a word, the good which exists in the relation, subsisting, first between existence and perception, and secondly between perception and expression. Every original language near to its source is in itself the chaos of a cyclic poem: the copiousness of lexicography and the distinctions of grammar are the works of a later age, and are merely the catalogue and the form of the creations of poetry.

But poets, or those who imagine and express this indestructible order, are not only the authors of language and of music, of the dance and architecture, and statuary, and painting; they are the institutors of laws, and the founders of civil society, and the inventors of the arts of life, and the teachers, who draw into a certain propinquity with the beautiful and the true, that partial apprehension of the agencies of the invisible world which is called religion. Hence all original religions are allegorical, or susceptible of allegory, and, like Janus, have a double face of false and true. Poets, according to the circumstances of the age and nation in which they appeared, were called, in the earlier epochs of the world, legislators, or prophets: a poet essentially comprises and unites both these characters. For he not only beholds intensely the present as it is, and discovers those laws according to which present things ought to be ordered, but he beholds the future in the present, and his thoughts are the germs of the flower and the fruit of latest time. Not that I assert poets to be prophets in the gross sense of the word, or that they can foretell the form as surely as they foreknow the spirit of events: such is the pretence of superstition, which would make poetry an attribute of prophecy, rather than prophecy an attribute of poetry. A poet participates in the eternal, the infinite, and the one; as far as relates to his conceptions, time and place and number are not. The grammatical forms which express the moods of time, and the difference of persons, and the distinction of place, are convertible with respect to the highest poetry without injuring it as poetry; and the choruses of Æschylus, and the book of Job, and Dante's Paradise, would afford, more than any other writings, examples of this fact, if the limits of this essay did not forbid citation. The creations of sculpture, painting, and music, are illustrations still more decisive.

Language, colour, form, and religious and civil habits of action, are all the instruments and materials of poetry; they may be called poetry by that figure of speech which considers the effect as a synonyme of the cause. But poetry in a more restricted sense expresses those arrangements of language, and especially metrical language, which are created by that imperial faculty, whose throne is curtained within the invisible nature of man. And this springs from the nature itself of language, which is a more direct representation of the actions and passions of our internal being, and is susceptible of more various and delicate combinations, than colour, form, or motion, and is more plastic and obedient to the control of that faculty of which it is the creation. For language is arbitrarily produced by the imagination, and has relation to thoughts alone; but all other materials, instruments, and conditions of art, have relations among each other, which limit and interpose between conception and expression. The former is as a mirror which reflects, the latter as a cloud which enfeebles, the light of which both are mediums of communication. Hence the fame of sculptors, painters, and musicians, although the intrinsic powers of the great masters of these arts may yield in no degree to that of those who have employed language as the hieroglyphic of their thoughts, has never equalled that of poets in the restricted sense of the term; as two performers of equal skill will produce unequal effects from a guitar and a harp. The fame of legislators and founders of religions, so long as their institutions last, alone seems to exceed that of poets in the restricted sense; but it can scarcely be a question, whether, if we deduct the celebrity which their flattery of the gross opinions of the vulgar usually conciliates, together with that which belonged to them in their higher character of poets, any excess will remain.

We have thus circumscribed the meaning of the word Poetry within the limits of that art which is the most familiar and the most perfect expression of the faculty itself. It is necessary, however, to make the circle still narrower, and to determine the distincton between measured and unmeasured language; for the popular division into prose and verse is inadmissible in accurate philosophy.

Sounds as well as thoughts have relation both between each other and towards that which they represent, and a perception of the order of those relations has always been found connected with a perception of the order of those relations of thoughts. Hence the language of poets has ever affected a certain uniform and harmonious recurrence of sound, without which it were not poetry, and which is scarcely less indispensable to the communication of its action, than the words themselves, without reference to that peculiar order. Hence the vanity of translation; it were as wise to cast a violet into a crucible that you might discover the formal principle of its colour and odour, as seek to transfuse from one language into another the creations of a poet. The plant must spring again from its seed, or it will bear no flower—and this is the burthen of the curse of Babel.

An observation of the regular mode of the recurrence of this harmony in the language of poetical minds, together with its relation to music, produced metre, or a certain system of traditional forms of harmony of language. Yet it is by no means essential that a poet should accommodate his language to this traditional form, so that the harmony, which is its spirit, be observed. The practice is indeed convenient and popular, and to be preferred, especially in such composition as includes much form and action: but every great poet must inevitably innovate upon the example of his predecessors in the exact structure of his peculiar versification. The distinction between poets and prose writers is a vulgar error. The distinction between philosophers and poets has been anticipated. Plato was essentially a poet—the truth and splendour of his imagery, and the melody of his language, is the most intense that it is possible to conceive. He rejected the measure of the epic, dramatic, and lyrical forms, because he sought to kindle a harmony in thoughts divested of shape and action, and he forbore to invent any regular plan of rhythm which should include, under determinate forms, the varied pauses of his style. Cicero sought to imitate the cadence of his periods, but with little success. Lord Bacon was a poet.[2] His language has a sweet and majestic rhythm, which satisfies the sense, no less than the almost superhuman wisdom of his philosophy satisfies the intellect; it is a strain which distends, and then bursts the circumference of the hearer's mind, and pours itself forth together with it into the universal element with which it has perpetual sympathy. All the authors of revolutions in opinion are not only necessarily poets as they are inventors, nor even as their words unveil the permanent analogy of things by images which participate in the life of truth; but as their periods are harmonious and rhythmical, and contain in themselves the elements of verse; being the echo of the eternal music. Nor are those supreme poets, who have employed traditional forms of rhythm on account of the form and action of their subjects, less capable of perceiving and teaching the truth of things, than those who have omitted that form. Shakspeare, Dante, and Milton (to confine ourselves to modern writers) are philosophers of the very loftiest power.

A poem is the image of life expressed in its eternal truth. There is this difference between a story and a poem, that a story is a catalogue of detached facts, which have no other bond of connexion than time, place, circumstance, cause and effect; the other is the creation of actions according to the unchangeable forms of human nature, as existing in the mind of the creator, which is itself the image of all other minds. The one is partial, and applies only to a definite period of time, and a certain combination of events which can never again recur; the other is universal, and contains within itself the germ of a relation to whatever motives or actions have place in the possible varieties of human nature. Time, which destroys the beauty and the use of the story of particular facts, stript of the poetry which should invest them, augments that of Poetry, and for ever develops new and wonderful applications of the eternal truth which it contains. Hence epitomes have been called the moths of just history; they eat out the poetry of it. The story of particular facts is as a mirror which obscures and distorts that which should be beautiful: Poetry is a mirror which makes beautiful that which is distorted.

The parts of a composition may be poetical, without the composition as a whole being a poem. A single sentence may be considered as a whole, though it be found in a series of unassimilated portions; a single word even may be a spark of inextinguishable thought. And thus all the great historians, Herodotus, Plutarch, Livy, were poets; and although the plan of these writers, especially that of Livy, restrained them from developing this faculty in its highest degree, they make copious and ample amends for their subjection, by filling all the interstices of their subjects with living images.

Having determined what is poetry, and who are poets, let us proceed to estimate its effects upon society.

Poetry is ever accompanied with pleasure: all spirits on which it falls open themselves to receive the wisdom which is mingled with its delight. In the infancy of the world, neither poets themselves nor their auditors are fully aware of the excellence of poetry: for it acts in a divine and unapprehended manner, beyond and above consciousness; and it is reserved for future generations to contemplate and measure the mighty cause and effect in all the strength and splendour of their union. Even in modern times, no living poet ever arrived at the fulness of his fame; the jury which sits in judgment upon a poet, belonging as he does to all time, must be composed of his peers: it must be impanneled by Time from the selectest of the wise of many generations. A Poet is a nightingale, who sits in darkness and sings to cheer its own solitude with sweet sounds; his auditors are as men entranced by the melody of an unseen musician, who feel that they are moved and softened, yet know not whence or why. The poems of Homer and his contemporaries were the delight of infant Greece; they were the elements of that social system which is the column upon which all succeeding civilization has reposed. Homer embodied the ideal perfection of his age in human character; nor can we doubt that those who read his verses were awakened to an ambition of becoming like to Achilles, Hector, and Ulysses: the truth and beauty of friendship, patriotism, and persevering devotion to an object, were unveiled to the depths in these immortal creations: the sentiments of the auditors must have been refined and enlarged by a sympathy with such great and lovely impersonations, until from admiring they imitated, and from imitation they identified themselves with the objects of their admiration. Nor let it be objected, that these characters are remote from moral perfection, and that they can by no means be considered as edifying patterns for general imitation. Every epoch, under names more or less specious, has deified its peculiar errors; Revenge is the naked Idol of the worship of a semi-barbarous age; and Self-deceit is the veiled Image of unknown evil, before which luxury and satiety he prostrate. But a poet considers the vices of his contemporaries as the temporary dress in which his creations must be arrayed, and which cover without concealing the eternal proportions of their beauty. An epic or dramatic personage is understood to wear them around his soul, as he may the antient armour or the modern uniform around his body; whilst it is easy to conceive a dress more graceful than either. The beauty of the internal nature cannot be so far concealed by its accidental vesture, but that the spirit of its form shall communicate itself to the very disguise, and indicate the shape it hides from the manner in which it is worn. A majestic form and graceful motions will express themselves through the most barbarous and tasteless costume. Few poets of the highest class have chosen to exhibit the beauty of their conceptions in its naked truth and splendour; and it is doubtful whether the alloy of costume, habit, &c., be not necessary to temper this planetary music for mortal ears.

The whole objection, however, of the immorality of poetry rests upon a misconception of the manner in which poetry acts to produce the moral improvement of man. Ethical science arranges the elements which poetry has created, and propounds schemes and proposes examples of civil and domestic life: nor is it for want of admirable doctrines that men hate, and despise, and censure, and deceive, and subjugate one another. But Poetry acts in another and diviner manner. It awakens and enlarges the mind itself by rendering it the receptacle of a thousand unapprehended combinations of thought. Poetry lifts the veil from the hidden beauty of the world, and makes familiar objects be as if they were not familiar; it reproduces all that it represents, and the impersonations clothed in its Elysian light stand thenceforward in the minds of those who have once contemplated them, as memorials of that gentle and exalted content which extends itself over all thoughts and actions with which it coexists. The great secret of morals is love; or a going out of our own nature, and an identification of ourselves with the beautiful which exists in thought, action, or person, not our own. A man, to be greatly good, must imagine intensely and comprehensively; he must put himself in the place of another and of many others; the pains and pleasures of his species must become his own. The great instrument of moral good is the imagination; and poetry administers to the effect by acting upon the cause. Poetry enlarges the circumference of the imagination by replenishing it with thoughts of ever new delight, which have the power of attracting and assimilating to their own nature all other thoughts, and which form new intervals and interstices whose void for ever craves fresh food. Poetry strengthens that faculty which is the organ of the moral nature of man, in the same manner as exercise strengthens a limb. A Poet therefore would do ill to embody his own conceptions of right and wrong, which are usually those of his place and time, in his poetical creations, which participate in neither. By this assumption of the inferior office of interpreting the effect, in which perhaps after all he might acquit himself but imperfectly, he would resign the glory in a participation in the cause. There was little danger that Homer, or any of the eternal Poets, should have so far misunderstood themselves as to have abdicated this throne of their widest dominion. Those in whom the poetical faculty, though great, is less intense, as Euripides, Lucan, Tasso, Spenser, have frequently affected a moral aim, and the effect of their poetry is diminished in exact proportion to the degree in which they compel us to advert to this purpose.

Homer and the cyclic poets were followed at a certain interval by the dramatic and lyrical Poets of Athens, who flourished contemporaneously with all that is most perfect in the kindred expressions of the poetical faculty; architecture, painting, music, the dance, sculpture, philosophy, and we may add, the forms of civil life. For although the scheme of Athenian society was deformed by many imperfections which the poetry existing in Chivalry and Christianity have erased from the habits and institutions of modern Europe; yet never at any other period has so much energy, beauty, and virtue, been developed; never was blind strength and stubborn form so disciplined and rendered subject to the will of man, or that will less repugnant to the dictates of the beautiful and the true, as during the century which preceded the death of Socrates. Of no other epoch in the history of our species have we records and fragments stamped so visibly with the image of the divinity in man. But it is Poetry alone, in form, in action, or in language, which has rendered this epoch memorable above all others, and the storehouse of examples to everlasting time. For written poetry existed at that epoch simultaneously with the other arts, and it is an idle enquiry to demand which gave and which received the light, which all, as from a common focus, have scattered over the darkest periods of succeeding age. We know no more of cause and effect than a constant conjunction of events: Poetry is ever found to coexist with whatever other arts contribute to the happiness and perfection of man. I appeal to what has already been established to distinguish between the cause and the effect.

It was at the period here adverted to, that the Drama had its birth; and however a succeeding writer may have equalled or surpassed those few great specimens of the Athenian drama which have been preserved to us, it is indisputable that the art itself never was understood or practised according to the true philosophy of it, as at Athens. For the Athenians employed language, action, music, painting, the dance, and religious institutions, to produce a common effect in the representation of the loftiest idealisms of passion and of power; each division in the art was made perfect in its kind by artists of the most consummate skill, and was disciplined into a beautiful proportion and unity one towards another. On the modern stage a few only of the elements capable of expressing the image of the poet's conception are employed at once. We have tragedy without music and dancing; and music and dancing without the high impersonations of which they are the fit accompaniment, and both without religion and solemnity; religious institution has indeed been usually banished from the stage. Our system of divesting the actor's face of a mask, on which the many expressions appropriated to his dramatic character might be moulded into one permanent and unchanging expression, is favourable only to a partial and inharmonious effect; it is fit for nothing but a monologue, where all the attention may be directed to some great master of ideal mimicry. The modern practice of blending comedy with tragedy, though liable to great abuse in point of practice, is undoubtedly an extension of the dramatic circle; but the comedy should be as in King Lear, universal, ideal, and sublime. It is perhaps the intervention of this principle which determines the balance in favour of King Lear against the Œdipus Tyrannus or the Agamemnon, or, if you will the trilogies with which they are connected; unless the intense power of the choral poetry, especially that of the latter, should be considered as restoring the equilibrium. King Lear, if it can sustain this comparison, may be judged to be the most perfect specimen of the dramatic art existing in the world; in spite of the narrow conditions to which the poet was subjected by the ignorance of the philosophy of the drama which has prevailed in modern Europe. Calderon, in his religious Autos, has attempted to fulfil some of the high conditions of dramatic representation neglected by Shakspeare; such as the establishing a relation between the drama and religion, and the accommodating them to music and dancing; but he omits the observation of conditions still more important, and more is lost than gained by a substitution of the rigidly-defined and ever-repeated idealisms of a distorted superstition for the living impersonations of the truth of human passion.

But we disgress.—The Author of the Four Ages of Poetry has prudently omitted to dispute on the effect of the Drama upon life and manners. For, if I know the Knight by the device of his shield, I have only to inscribe Philoctetes or Agamemnon or Othello upon mine to put to flight the giant sophisms which have enchanted him, as the mirror of intolerable light though on the arm of one of the weakest of the Paladines could blind and scatter whole armies of necromancers and pagans. The connexion of scenic exhibitions with the improvement or corruption of the manners of men, has been universally recognised: in other words, the presence or absence of poetry in its most perfect and universal form, has been found to be connected with good and evil in conduct and habit. The corruption which has been imputed to the drama as an effect, begins, when the poetry employed in its constitution ends: I appeal to the history of manners whether the gradations of the growth of the one and the decline of the other have not corresponded with an exactness equal to any other example of moral cause and effect.

The drama at Athens, or wheresoever else it may have approached to its perfection, coexisted with the moral and intellectual greatness of the age. The tragedies of the Athenian poets are as mirrors in which the spectator beholds himself, under a thin disguise of circumstance, stript of all but that ideal perfection and energy which every one feels to be the internal type of all that he loves, admires, and would become. The imagination is enlarged by a sympathy with pains and passions so mighty, that they distend in their conception the capacity of that by which they are conceived; the good affections are strengthened by pity, indignation, terror and sorrow; and an exalted calm is prolonged from the satiety of this high exercise of them into the tumult of familiar life: even crime is disarmed of half its horror and all its contagion by being represented as the fatal consequence of the unfathomable agencies of nature; error is thus divested of its wilfulness; men can no longer cherish it as the creation of their choice. In a drama of the highest order there is little food for censure or hatred; it teaches rather self-knowledge and self-respect. Neither the eye nor the mind can see itself, unless reflected upon that which it resembles. The drama, so long as it continues to express poetry, is as a prismatic and many-sided mirror, which collects the brightest rays of human nature and divides and reproduces them from the simplicity of these elementary forms, and touches them with majesty and beauty, and multiplies all that it reflects, and endows it with the power of propagating its like wherever it may fall.

But in periods of the decay of social life, the drama sympathises with that decay. Tragedy becomes a cold imitation of the form of the great masterpieces of antiquity, divested of all harmonious accompaniment of the kindred arts; and often the very form misunderstood, or a weak attempt to teach certain doctrines, which the writer considers as moral truths; and which are usually no more than specious flatteries of some gross vice or weakness, with which the author, in common with his auditors, are infected. Hence what has been called the classical and domestic drama. Addison's "Cato" is a specimen of the one; and would it were not superfluous to cite examples of the other! To such purposes poetry cannot be made subservient. Poetry is a sword of lightning, ever unsheathed, which consumes the scabbard that would contain it. And thus we observe that all dramatic writings of this nature are unimaginative in a singular degree; they affect sentiment and passion, which, divested of imagination, are other names for caprice and appetite. The period in our own history of the grossest degradation of the drama is the reign of Charles II., when all forms in which poetry had been accustomed to be expressed became hymns to the triumph of kingly power over liberty and virtue. Milton stood alone illuminating an age unworthy of him. At such periods the calculating principle pervades all the forms of dramatic exhibition, and poetry ceases to be expressed upon them. Comedy loses its ideal universality: wit succeeds to humour; we laugh from self complacency and triumph, instead of pleasure; malignity, sarcasm and contempt, succeed to sympathetic merriment; we hardly laugh, but we smile. Obscenity, which is ever blasphemy against the divine beauty in life, becomes, from the very veil which it assumes, more active if less disgusting: it is a monster for which the corruption of society for ever brings forth new food, which it devours in secret.

The drama being that form under which a greater number of modes of expression of poetry are susceptible of being combined than any other, the connexion of poetry and social good is more observable in the drama than in whatever other form. And it is indisputable that the highest perfection of human society has ever corresponded with the highest dramatic excellence; and that the corruption or the extinction of the drama in a nation where it has once flourished, is a mark of a corruption of manners, and an extinction of the energies which sustain the soul of social life. But, as Machiavelli says of political institutions, that life may be preserved and renewed, if men should arise capable of bringing back the drama to its principles. And this is true with respect to poetry in its most extended sense; all language institution and form, require not only to be produced but to be sustained: the office and character of a poet participates in the divine nature as regards providence, no less than as regards creation.

Civil war, the spoils of Asia, and the fatal predominance first of the Macedonian, and then of the Roman arms, were so many symbols of the extinction or suspension of the creative faculty in Greece. The bucolic writers, who found patronage under the lettered tyrants of Sicily and Egypt, were the latest representatives of its most glorious reign. Their poetry is intensely melodious; like the odour of the tuberose, it overcomes and sickens the spirit with excess of sweetness; whilst the poetry of the preceding age was as a meadow-gale of June, which mingles the fragrance of all the flowers of the field, and adds a quickening and harmonising spirit of its own which endows the sense with a power of sustaining its extreme delight. The bucolic and erotic delicacy in written poetry is correlative with that softness in statuary, music, and the kindred arts, and even in manners and institutions, which distinguished the epoch to which we now refer. Nor is it the poetical faculty itself, or any misapplication of it, to which this want of harmony is to be imputed. An equal sensibility to the influence of the senses and the affections is to be found in the writings of Homer and Sophocles: the former, especially, has clothed sensual and pathetic images with irresistible attractions. Their superiority over these succeeding writers consists in the presence of those thoughts which belong to the inner faculties of our nature, not in the absence of those which are connected with the external: their incomparable perfection consists in an harmony of the union of all. It is not what the erotic writers have, but what they have not, in which their imperfection consists. It is not inasmuch as they were Poets, but inasmuch as they were not Poets, that they can be considered with any plausibility as connected with the corruption of their age. Had that corruption availed so as to extinguish in them the sensibility to pleasure, passion, and natural scenery, which is imputed to them as an imperfection, the last triumph of evil would have been achieved. For the end of social corruption is to destroy all sensibility to pleasure; and, therefore, it is corruption. It begins at the imagination and the intellect as at the core, and distributes itself thence as a paralysing venom, through the affections into thc vcry appetites, till all become a torpid mass in which sense hardly survives. At the approach of such a period, Poetry ever addresses itself to those faculties which are the last to be destroyed, and its voice is heard, like the footsteps of Astræa, departing from the world. Poetry ever communicates all the pleasure which men are capable of receiving: it is ever still the light of life; the source of whatever of beautiful or generous or true can have place in an evil time. It will readily be confessed that those among the luxurious citizens of Syracuse and Alexandria, who were delighted with the poems of Theocritus, were less cold, cruel, and sensual than the remnant of their tribe. But corruption must have utterly destroyed the fabric of human society before poetry can ever cease. The sacred links of that chain have never been entirely disjoined, which descending through the minds of many men is attached to those great minds, whence as from a magnet the invisible effluence is sent forth, which at once connects, animates and sustains the life of all. It is the faculty which contains within itself the seeds at once of its own and of social renovation. And let us not circumscribe the effects of the bucolic and erotic poetry within the limits of the sensibility of those to whom it was addressed. They may have perceived the beauty of those immortal compositions, simply as fragments and isolated portions: those who are more finely organised, or born in a happier age, may recognise them as episodes to that great poem, which all poets, like the co-operating thoughts of one great mind, have built up since the beginning of the world.

The same revolutions within a narrower sphere had place in antient Rome; but the actions and forms of its social life never seem to have been perfectly saturated with the poetical element. The Romans appear to have considered the Greeks as the selectest treasuries of the selectest forms of manners and of nature, and to have abstained from creating in measured language, sculpture, music, or architecture, any thing which might bear a particular relation to their own condition, whilst it might bear a general one to the universal constitution of the world. But we judge from partial evidence, and we judge perhaps partially. Ennius, Varro, Pacuvius, and Accius, all great poets, have been lost. Lucretius is in the highest, and Virgil in a very high sense, a creator. The chosen delicacy of the expressions of the latter, are as a mist of light which conceal from us the intense and exceeding truth of his conceptions of nature. Livy is instinct with poetry. Yet Horace, Catullus, Ovid, and generally the other great writers of the Virgilian age, saw man and nature in the mirror of Greece. The institutions also, and the religion of Rome, were less poetical than those of Greece, as the shadow is less vivid than the substance. Hence poetry in Rome, seemed to follow, rather than accompany, the perfection of political and domestic society. The true poetry of Rome lived in its institutions; for whatever of beautiful, true, and majestic, they contained, could have sprung only from the faculty which creates the order in which they consist. The life of Camillus, the death of Regulus; the expectation of the Senators, in their godlike state, of the victorious Gauls; the refusal of the Republic to make peace with Hannibal, after the battle of Cannæ, were not the consequences of a refined calculation of the probable personal advantage to result from such a rhythm and order in the shews of life, to those who were at once the poets and the actors of these immortal dramas. The imagination beholding the beauty of this order, created it out of itself according to its own idea; the consequence was empire, and the reward ever-living fame. These things are not the less poetry, *quia carent vate sacro*. They are the episodes of that cyclic poem written by Time upon the memories of men. The Past, like an inspired rhapsodist, fills the theatre of everlasting generations with their harmony.

At length the antient system of religion and manners had fulfilled the circle of its revolution. And the world would have fallen into utter anarchy and darkness, but that there were found poets among the authors of the Christian and Chivalric systems of manners and religion, who created forms of opinion and action never before conceived; which, copied into the imaginations of men, became as generals to the bewildered armies of their thoughts. It is foreign to the present purpose to touch upon the evil produced by these systems: except that we protest, on the ground of the principles already established, that no portion of it can be imputed to the poetry they contain.

It is probable that the astonishing poetry of Moses, Job, David, Solomon, and Isaiah, had produced a great effect upon the mind of Jesus and his disciples. The scattered fragments preserved to us by the biographers of this extraordinary person, are all instinct with the most vivid poetry. But his doctrines seem to have been quickly distorted. At a certain period after the prevalence of doctrines founded upon those promulgated by him, the three forms into which Plato had distributed the faculties of mind underwent a sort of apotheosis, and became the object of the worship of Europe. Here it is to be confessed that "Light seems to thicken," and

> The crow makes wing to the rooky wood,
> Good things of day begin to droop and drowse,
> And night's black agents to their preys do rouse.

But mark how beautiful an order has sprung from the dust and blood of this fierce chaos! how the World, as from a resurrection, balancing itself on the golden wings of knowledge and of hope, has reassumed its yet unwearied flight into the Heaven of time. Listen to the music, unheard by outward ears, which is as a ceaseless and invisible wind, nourishing its everlasting course with strength and swiftness.

The poetry in the doctrines of Jesus Christ, and the mythology and institutions of the Celtic conquerors of the Roman empire, outlived the darkness and the convulsions connected with their growth and victory, and blended themselves into a new fabric of manners and opinion. It is an error to impute the ignorance of the dark ages to the Christian doctrines or the predominance of the Celtic nations. Whatever of evil their agencies may have contained sprang from the extinction of the poetical principle, connected with the progress of despotism and superstition. Men, from causes too intricate to be here discussed, had become insensible and selfish: their own will had become feeble, and yet they were its slaves, and thence the slaves of the will of others: lust, fear, avarice, cruelty, and fraud, characterised a race amongst whom no one was to be found capable of *creating* in form, language, or institution. The moral anomalies of such a state of society are not justly to be charged upon any class of events immediately connected with them, and those events are most entitled to our approbation which could dissolve it most expeditiously. It is unfortunate for those who cannot distinguish words from thoughts, that many of these anomalies have been incorporated into our popular religion.

It was not until the eleventh century that the effects of the poetry of the Christian and Chivalric systems began to manifest themselves. The principle of equality had been discovered and applied by Plato in his Republic, as the theoretical rule of the mode in which the materials of pleasure and of power produced by the common skill and labour of human beings ought to be distributed among them. The limitations of this rule were asserted by him to be determined only by the sensibility of each, or the utility to result to all. Plato, following the doctrines of Timæus and Pythagoras, taught also a moral and intellectual system of doctrine, comprehending at once the past, the present, and the future condition of man. Jesus Christ divulged the sacred and eternal truths contained in these views to mankind, and Christianity, in its abstract purity, became the exoteric expression of the esoteric doctrines of the poetry and wisdom of antiquity. The incorporation of the Celtic nations with the exhausted population of the south, impressed upon it the figure of the poetry existing in their mythology and institutions. The result was a sum of the action and reaction of all the causes included in it; for it may be assumed as a maxim that no nation or religion can supersede any other without incorporating into itself a portion of that which it supersedes. The abolition of personal and domestic slavery, and the emancipation of women from a great part of the degrading restraints of antiquity, were among the consequences of these events.

The abolition of personal slavery is the basis of the highest political hope that it can enter into the mind of man to conceive. The freedom of women produced the poetry of sexual love. Love became a religion, the idols of whose worship were ever present. It was as if the statues of Apollo and the Muses had been endowed with life and motion, and had walked forth among their worshippers; so that earth became peopled by the inhabitants of a diviner world. The familiar appearance and proceedings of life became wonderful and heavenly; and a paradise was created as out of the wrecks of Eden. And as this creation itself is poetry, so its creators were poets; and language was the instrument of their art: "Galeotto fù il libro, e chi lo scrisse." The Provençal Trouveurs, or inventors, preceded Petrarch, whose verses are as spells, which unseal the inmost enchanted fountains of the delight which is in the grief of love. It is impossible to feel them without becoming a portion of that beauty which we contemplate: it were superfluous to explain how the gentleness and the elevation of mind connected with these sacred emotions can render men more amiable, and generous and wise, and lift them out of the dull vapours of the little world of self. Dante understood the secret things of love even more than Petrarch. His *Vita Nuova* is an inexhaustible fountain of purity of sentiment and language: it is the idealised history of that period, and those intervals of his life which were dedicated to love. His apotheosis of Beatrice in Paradise, and the gradations of his own love and her loveliness, by which as by steps he feigns himself to have ascended to the throne of the Supreme Cause, is the most glorious imagination of modern poetry. The acutest critics have justly reversed the judgment of the vulgar, and the order of the great acts of the "Divine Drama," in the measure of the admiration which they accord to the Hell, Purgatory, and Paradise. The latter is a perpetual hymn of everlasting Love. Love, which found a worthy poet in Plato alone of all the antients, has been celebrated by a chorus of the greatest writers of the renovated world; and the music has penetrated the caverns of society, and its echoes still drown the dissonance of arms and superstition. At successive intervals, Ariosto, Tasso, Shakspeare, Spenser, Calderon, Rousseau, and the great writers of our own age, have celebrated the dominion of love, planting as it were trophies in the human mind of that sublimest victory over sensuality and force. The true relation borne to each other by the sexes into which human kind is distributed, has become less misunderstood; and if the error which confounded diversity with inequality of the powers of the two sexes has become partially recognised in the opinions and institutions of modern Europe, we owe this great benefit to the worship of which Chivalry was the law, and poets the prophets.

The poetry of Dante may be considered as the bridge thrown over the stream of time, which unites the modern and antient World. The distorted notions of invisible things which Dante and his rival Milton have idealised, are merely the mask and the mantle in which these great poets walk through eternity enveloped and disguised. It is a difficult question to determine how far they were conscious of the distinction which must have subsisted in their minds between their own creeds and that of the people. Dante at least appears to wish to mark the full extent of it by placing Riphæus, whom Virgil calls *justissimus unus,* in Paradise, and observing a most heretical caprice in his distribution of rewards and punishments. And Milton's poem contains within itself a philosophical refutation of that system, of which, by a strange and natural antithesis, it has been a chief popular support. Nothing can exceed the energy and magnificence of the character of Satan as expressed in "Paradise Lost." It is a mistake to suppose that he could ever have been intended for the popular personification of evil. Implacable hate, patient cunning and a sleepless refinement of device to inflict the extremest anguish on an enemy, these things are evil; and, although venial in a slave, are not to be forgiven in a tyrant; although redeemed by much that ennobles his defeat in one subdued, are marked by all that dishonours his conquest in the victor. Milton's Devil as a moral being is as far superior to his God, as One who perseveres in some purpose which he has conceived to be excellent in spite of adversity and torture, is to One who in the cold security of undoubted triumph inflicts the most horrible revenge upon his enemy, not from any mistaken notion of inducing him to repent of a perseverance in enmity, but with the alleged design of exasperating him to deserve new torments. Milton has so far violated the popular creed (if this shall be judged to be a violation) as to have alleged no superiority of moral virtue to his God over his Devil. And this bold neglect of a direct moral purpose is the most decisive proof of the supremacy of Milton's genius. He mingled as it were the elements of human nature as colours upon a single pallet, and arranged them in the composition of his great picture according to the laws of epic truth; that is, according to the laws of that principle by which a series of actions of the external universe and of intelligent and ethical beings is calculated to excite the sympathy of succeeding generations of mankind. The Divina Commedia and Paradise Lost have conferred upon modern mythology a systematic form; and when change and time shall have added one more superstition to the mass of those which have arisen and decayed upon the earth, commentators will be learnedly employed in elucidating the religion of ancestral Europe, only not utterly forgotten because it will have been stamped with the eternity of genius.

Homer was the first and Dante the second epic poet: that is, the second poet, the series of whose creations bore a defined and intelligible relation to the knowledge and sentiment and religion and political conditions of the age in which he lived, and of the ages which followed it: developing itself in correspondence with their development. For Lucretius had limed the wings of his swift spirit in the dregs of the sensible world; and Virgil, with a modesty which ill became his genius, had affected the fame of an imitator, even whilst he created anew all that he copied; and none among the flock of Mock-birds, though their notes were sweet, Apollonius Rhodius, Quintus Calaber Smyrnetheus, Nonnus, Lucan, Statius, or Claudian, have sought even to fulfil a single condition of epic truth. Milton was the third epic poet. For if the title of epic in its highest sense be refused to the Æneid, still less can it be conceded to the Orlando Furioso, the Gerusalemme Liberata, the Lusiad, or the Fairy Queen.

Dante and Milton were both deeply penetrated with the antient religion of the civilized world; and its spirit exists in their poetry probably in the same proportion as its forms survived in the unreformed worship of modern Europe. The one preceded and the other followed the Reformation at almost equal intervals. Dante was the first religious reformer, and Luther surpassed him rather in the rudeness and acrimony, than in the boldness of his censures of papal usurpation. Dante was the first awakener of entranced Europe; he created a language, in itself music and persuasion, out of a chaos of inharmonious barbarisms. He was the congregator of those great spirits who presided over the resurrection of learning; the Lucifer of that starry flock which in the thirteenth century shone forth from republican Italy, as from a heaven, into the darkness of the benighted world. His very words are instinct with spirit; each is as a spark, a burning atom of inextinguishable thought; and many yet lie covered in the ashes of their birth, and pregnant with a lightning which has yet found no conductor. All high poetry is infinite; it is as the first acorn, which contained all oaks potentially. Veil after veil may be undrawn, and the inmost naked beauty of the meaning never exposed. A great poem is a fountain for ever overflowing with the waters of wisdom and delight; and after one person and one age has exhausted all its divine effluence which their peculiar relations enable them to share, another and yet another succeeds, and new relations are ever developed, the source of an unforeseen and an unconceived delight.

The age immediately succeeding to that of Dante, Petrarch, and Boccaccio, was characterized by a revival of painting, sculpture, music, and architecture. Chaucer caught the sacred inspiration, and the superstructure of English literature is based upon the materials of Italian invention.

But let us not be betrayed from a defence into a critical history of Poetry and its influence on Society. Be it enough to have pointed out the effects of poets, in the large and true sense of the word, upon their own and all succeeding times, and to revert to the partial instances cited as illustrations of an opinion the reverse of that attempted to be established by the Author of the Four Ages of Poetry.

But poets have been challenged to resign the civic crown to reasoners and mechanists on another plea. It is admitted that the exercise of the imagination is most delightful, but it is alleged, that that of reason is more useful. Let us examine as the grounds of this distinction, what is here meant by utility. Pleasure or good, in a general sense, is that which the consciousness of a sensitive and intelligent being seeks, and in which, when found, it acquiesces. There are two modes or degrees of pleasure, one durable, universal and permanent; the other transitory and particular. Utility may either express the means of producing the former or the latter. In the former sense, whatever strengthens and purifies the affections, enlarges the imagination, and adds spirit to sense, is useful. But the meaning in which the Author of the Four Ages of Poetry seems to have employed the word utility is the narrower one of banishing the importunity of the wants of our animal nature, the surrounding men with security of life, the dispersing the grosser delusions of superstition, and the conciliating such a degree of mutual forbearance among men as may consist with the motives of personal advantage.

Undoubtedly the promoters of utility, in this limited sense, have their appointed office in society. They follow the footsteps of poets, and copy the sketches of their creations into the book of common life. They make space, and give time. Their exertions are of the highest value, so long as they confine their administration of the concerns of the inferior powers of our nature within the limits due to the superior ones. But whilst the sceptic destroys gross superstitions, let him spare to deface, as some of the French writers have defaced, the eternal truths charactered upon the imaginations of men. Whilst the mechanist abridges, and the political economist combines, labour, let them beware that their speculations, for want of correspondence with those first principles which belong to the imagination, do not tend, as they have in modern England, to exasperate at once the extremes of luxury and want. They have exemplified the saying, "To him that hath, more shall be given; and from him that hath not, the little that he hath shall be taken away." The rich have become richer, and the poor have become poorer; and the vessel of the state is driven between the Scylla and Charybdis of anarchy and despotism. Such are the effects which must ever flow from an unmitigated exercise of the calculating faculty.

It is difficult to define pleasure in its highest sense; the definition involving a number of apparent paradoxes. For, from an inexplicable defect of harmony in the constitution of human nature, the pain of the inferior is frequently connected with the pleasures of the superior portions of our being. Sorrow, terror, anguish, despair itself, are often the chosen expressions of an approximation to the highest good. Our sympathy in tragic fiction depends on this principle; tragedy delights by affording a shadow of the pleasure which exists in pain. This is the source also of the melancholy which is inseparable from the sweetest melody. The pleasure that is in sorrow is sweeter than the pleasure of pleasure itself. And hence the saying, "It is better to go to the house of mourning, than to the house of mirth." Not that this highest species of pleasure is necessarily linked with pain. The delight of love and friendship, the ecstasy of the admiration of nature, the joy of the perception and still more of the creation of poetry is often wholly unalloyed.

The production and assurance of pleasure in this highest sense is true utility. Those who produce and preserve this pleasure are Poets or poetical philosophers.

The exertions of Locke, Hume, Gibbon, Voltaire, Rousseau,[3] and their disciples, in favour of oppressed and deluded humanity, are entitled to the gratitude of mankind. Yet it is easy to calculate the degree of moral and intellectual improvement which the world would have exhibited, had they never lived. A little more nonsense would have been talked for a century or two; and perhaps a few more men, women, and children, burnt as heretics. We might not at this moment have been congratulating each other on the abolition of the Inquisition in Spain. But it exceeds all imagination to conceive what would have been the moral condition of the world if neither Dante, Petrarch, Boccaccio, Chaucer, Shakspeare, Calderon, Lord Bacon, nor Milton, had ever existed; if Raphael and Michael Angelo had never been born; if the Hebrew poetry had never been translated; if a revival of the study of Greek literature had never taken place; if no monuments of antient sculpture had been handed down to us; and if the poetry of the religion of the antient world had been extinguished together with its belief. The human mind could never, except by the intervention of these excitements, have been awakened to the invention of the grosser sciences, and that application of analytical reasoning to the aberrations of society, which it is now attempted to exalt over the direct expression of the inventive and creative faculty itself.

We have more moral, political and historical wisdom, than we know how to reduce into practice; we have more scientific and economical knowledge than can be accommodated to the just distribution of the produce which it multiplies. The poetry in these systems of thought, is concealed by the accumulation of facts and calculating processes. There is no want of knowledge respecting what is wisest and best in morals, government, and political economy, or at least, what is wiser and better than what men now practise and endure. But we let "*I dare not* wait upon *I would,* like the poor cat i' the adage." We want the creative faculty to imagine that which we know; we want the generous impulse to act that which we imagine; we want the poetry of life: our calculations have outrun conception; we have eaten more than we can digest. The cultivation of those sciences which have enlarged the limits of the empire of man over the external world, has, for want of the poetical faculty, proportionally circumscribed those of the internal world; and man, having enslaved the elements, remains himself a slave. To what but a cultivation of the mechanical arts in a degree disproportioned to the presence of the creative faculty, which is the basis of all knowledge, is to be attributed the abuse of all invention for abridging and combining labour, to the exasperation of the inequality of mankind? From what other cause has it arisen that these inventions which should have lightened, have added a weight to the curse imposed on Adam? Thus Poetry, and the principle of Self, of which Money is the visible incarnation, are the God and Mammon of the world.

The functions of the poetical faculty are twofold; by one it creates new materials for knowledge, and power and pleasure; by the other it engenders in the mind a desire to reproduce and arrange them according to a certain rhythm and order which may be called the beautiful and the good. The cultivation of poetry is never more to be desired than at periods when, from an excess of the selfish and calculating principle, the accumulation of the materials of external life exceed the quantity of the power of assimilating them to the internal laws of human nature. The body has then become too unwieldy for that which animates it.

Poetry is indeed something divine. It is at once the centre and circumference of knowledge; it is that which comprehends all science, and that to which all science must be referred. It is at the same time the root and blossom of all other systems of thought; it is that from which all spring, and that which adorns all; and that which, if blighted, denies the fruit and the seed, and withholds from the barren world the nourishment and the succession of the scions of the tree of life. It is the perfect and consummate surface and bloom of things; it is as the odour and the colour of the rose to the texture of the elements which compose it, as the form and the splendour of unfaded beauty to the secrets of anatomy and corruption. What were Virtue, Love, Patriotism, Friendship—what were the scenery of this beautiful Universe which we inhabit; what were our consolations on this side of the grave, and what were our aspirations beyond it, if Poetry did not ascend to bring light and fire from those eternal regions where the owl-winged faculty of calculation dare not ever soar? Poetry is not like reasoning, a power to be exerted according to the determination of the will. A man cannot say, "I will compose poetry." The greatest poet even cannot say it: for the mind in creation is as a fading coal, which some invisible influence, like an inconstant wind, awakens to transitory brightness: this power arises from within, like the colour of a flower which fades and changes as it is developed, and the conscious portions of our natures are unprophetic either of its approach or its departure. Could this influence be durable in its original purity and force, it is impossible to predict the greatness of the results; but when composition begins, inspiration is already on the decline, and the most glorious poetry that has ever been communicated to the world is probably a feeble shadow of the original conception of the Poet. I appeal to the great poets of the present day, whether it be not an error to assert that the finest passages of poetry are produced by labour and study. The toil and the delay recommended by critics, can be justly interpreted to mean no more than a careful observation of the inspired moments, and an artificial connexion of the spaces between their suggestions by the intertexture of conventional expressions; a necessity only imposed by the limitedness of the poetical faculty itself. For Milton conceived the Paradise Lost as a whole before he executed it in portions. We have his own authority also for the Muse having "dictated" to him the "unpremeditated song," and let this be an answer to those who would allege the fifty-six various readings of the first line of the Orlando Furioso. Compositions so produced are to poetry what mosaic is to painting. This instinct and intuition of the poetical faculty is still more observable in the plastic and pictorial arts; a great statue or picture grows under the power of the artist as a child in the mother's womb; and the very mind which directs the hands in formation is incapable of accounting to itself for the origin, the gradations, or the media of the process.

Poetry is the record of the best and happiest moments of the happiest and best minds. We are aware of evanescent visitations of thought and feeling sometimes associated with place or person, sometimes regarding our own mind alone, and always arising unforeseen and departing unbidden, but elevating and delightful beyond all expression: so that even in the desire and the regret they leave, there cannot but be pleasure, participating as it does in the nature of its object. It is as it were the interpenetration of a diviner nature through our own; but its footsteps are like those of a wind over a sea, which the coming calm erases, and whose traces remain only, as on the wrinkled sand which paves it. These and corresponding conditions of being are experienced principally by those of the most delicate sensibility and the most enlarged imagination; and the state of mind produced by them is at war with every base desire. The enthusiasm of virtue, love, patriotism, and friendship, is essentially linked with these emotions; and whilst they last, self appears as what it is, an atom to a Universe. Poets are not only subject to these experiences as spirits of the most refined organisation, but they can colour all that they combine with the evanescent hues of this ethereal world; a word, or a trait in the representation of a scene or a passion, will touch the enchanted chord, and reanimate, in those who have ever experienced these emotions, the sleeping, the cold, the buried image of the past. Poetry thus makes immortal all that is best and most beautiful in the world; it arrests the vanishing apparitions which haunt the interlunations of life, and veiling them, or in language or in form, sends them forth among mankind, bearing sweet news of kindred joy to those with whom their sisters abide—abide, because there is no portal of expression from the caverns of the spirit which they inhabit into the universe of things. Poetry redeems from decay the visitations of the divinity in Man.

Poetry turns all things to loveliness; it exalts the beauty of that which is most beautiful, and it adds beauty to that which is most deformed; it marries exultation and horror, grief and pleasure, eternity and change; it subdues to union under its light yoke, all irreconcilable things. It transmutes all that it touches, and every form moving within the radiance of its presence is changed by wondrous sympathy to an incarnation of the spirit which it breathes; its secret alchemy turns to potable gold the poisonous waters which flow from death through life; it strips the veil of familiarity from the world, and lays bare the naked and sleeping beauty, which is the spirit of its forms.

All things exist as they are perceived; at least in relation to the percipient. "The mind is its own place, and of itself can make a Heaven of Hell, a Hell of Heaven." But poetry defeats the curse which binds us to be subjected to the accident of surrounding impressions. And whether it spreads its own figured curtain, or withdraws life's dark veil from before the scene of things, it equally creates for us a being within our being. It makes us the inhabitants of a world to which the familiar world is a chaos. It reproduces the common Universe of which we are portions and percipients, and it purges from our inward sight the film of familiarity which obscures from us the wonder of our being. It compels us to feel that which we perceive, and to imagine that which we know. It creates anew the universe, after it has been annihilated in our minds by the recurrence of impressions blunted by reiteration. It justifies that bold and true word of Tasso: *Non merita nome di creatore, se non Iddio ed il Poeta.*

A poet, as he is the author to others of the highest wisdom, pleasure, virtue and glory, so he ought personally to be the happiest, the best, the wisest, and the most illustrious of men. As to his glory, let Time be challenged to declare whether the fame of any other institutor of human life be comparable to that of a poet. That he is the wisest, the happiest, and the best, inasmuch as he is a poet, is equally incontrovertible: the greatest Poets have been men of the most spotless virtue, of the most consummate prudence, and, if we could look into the interior of their lives, the most fortunate of men: and the exceptions, as they regard those who possessed the imaginative faculty in a high yet inferior degree, will be found on consideration to confirm rather than destroy the rule. Let us for a moment stoop to the arbitration of popular breath, and usurping and uniting in our own persons the incompatible characters of accuser, witness, judge and executioner, let us without trial, testimony, or form, determine that certain motives of those who are "there sitting where we dare not soar," are reprehensible. Let us assume that Homer was a drunkard, that Virgil was a flatterer, that Horace was a coward, that Tasso was a madman, that Lord Bacon was a peculator, that Raphael was a libertine, that Spenser was a poet laureate. It is inconsistent with this division of our subject to cite living poets, but Posterity has done ample justice to the great names now referred to. Their errors have been weighed and found to have been dust in the balance; if their sins were as scarlet, they are now white as snow: they have been washed in the blood of the mediator and the redeemer, Time. Observe in what a ludicrous chaos the imputations of real or fictitious crime have been confused in the contemporary calumnies against poetry and poets; consider how little is, as it appears—or appears, as it is; look to your own motives, and judge not, lest ye be judged.

Poetry, as has been said, in this respect differs from logic, that it is not subject to the controul of the active powers of the mind, and that its birth and recurrence has no necessary connexion with consciousness or will. It is presumptuous to determine that these are the necessary conditions of all mental causation, when mental effects are experienced insusceptible of being referred to them. The frequent recurrence of the poetical power, it is obvious to suppose, may produce in the mind an habit of order and harmony correlative with its own nature and with its effects upon other minds. But in the intervals of inspiration, and they may be frequent without being durable, a Poet becomes a man, and is abandoned to the sudden reflux of the influences under which others habitually live. But as he is more delicately organized than other men, and sensible to pain and pleasure, both his own and that of others, in a degree unknown to them, he will avoid the one and pursue the other with an ardour proportioned to this difference. And he renders himself obnoxious to calumny, when he neglects to observe the circumstances under which these objects of universal pursuit and flight have disguised themselves in one another's garments.

But there is nothing necessarily evil in this error, and thus cruelty, envy, revenge, avarice, and the passions purely evil, have never formed any portion of the popular imputations on the lives of poets.

I have thought it most favourable to the cause of truth to set down these remarks according to the order in which they were suggested to my mind, by a consideration of the subject itself, instead of following that of the treatise that excited me to make them public. Thus although devoid of the formality of a polemical reply; if the view they contain be just, they will be found to involve a refutation of the doctrines of the Four Ages of Poetry, so far at least as regards the first division of the subject. I can readily conjecture what should have moved the gall of the learned and intelligent author of that paper; I confess myself, like him, unwilling to be stunned by the Theseids of the hoarse Codri of the day. Bavius and Mævius undoubtedly are, as they ever were, insufferable persons. But it belongs to a philosophical critic to distinguish rather than confound.

The first part of these remarks has related to Poetry in its elements and principles; and it has been shewn, as well as the narrow limits assigned them would permit, that what is called poetry, in a restricted sense, has a common source with all other forms of order and of beauty, according to which the materials of human life are susceptible of being arranged, and which is Poetry in an universal sense.

The second part will have for its object an application of these principles to the present state of the cultivation of Poetry, and a defence of the attempt to idealize the modern forms of manners and opinions, and compel them into a subordination to the imaginative and creative faculty. For the literature of England, an energetic development of which has ever preceded or accompanied a great and free development of the national will, has arisen as it were from a new birth. In spite of the low-thoughted envy which would undervalue contemporary merit, our own will be a memorable age in intellectual achievements, and we live among such philosophers and poets as surpass beyond comparison any who have appeared since the last national struggle for civil and religious liberty. The most unfailing herald, companion, and follower of the awakening of a great people to work a beneficial change in opinion or institution, is Poetry. At such periods there is an accumulation of the power of communicating and receiving intense and impassioned conceptions respecting man and nature. The persons in whom this power resides, may often as far as regards many portions of their nature, have little apparent correspondence with that spirit of good of which they are the ministers. But even whilst they deny and abjure, they are yet compelled to serve, the Power which is seated upon the throne of their own soul. It is impossible to read the compositions of the most celebrated writers of the present day without being startled with the electric life which burns within their words. They measure the circumference and sound the depths of human nature with a comprehensive and all-penetrating spirit, and they are themselves perhaps the most sincerely astonished at its manifestations; for it is less their spirit than the spirit of the age. Poets are the hierophants of an unapprehended inspiration; the mirrors of the gigantic shadows which futurity casts upon the present; the words which express what they understand not; the trumpets which sing to battle, and feel not what they inspire; the influence which is moved not, but moves. Poets are the unacknowledged legislators of the world.

## *NOTES*

1. *De Augment. Scient.*, cap. 1, lib. iii.
2. See the *Filum Labyrinthi* and the *Essay on Death* particularly.
3. I follow the classification adopted by the Author of the Four Ages of Poetry; but he was essentially a Poet. The others, even Voltaire, were mere reasoners. [Shelley's note.]

# *John Keble*

1792–1866

# *John Henry Newman*

1801–1890

John Keble was the son of a clergyman, destined to become a clergyman himself. Born on April 25, 1792 in Fairford, Gloucestershire, he was a clever boy who grew up in a literate household, an atmosphere in which piety could not have been seen as any impediment to erudition. At Oxford, Keble distinguished himself by taking a double first-class degree—highest honors in two subjects, an almost unprecedented feat of brilliance—and was elected a Fellow of Oriel College in 1811. At the time, Oriel's brilliance far outshone that of the other colleges, and it was here that Keble came into contact with such figures as Coplestone, Whately, Arnold, Pusey, and—above all—Newman.

Newman's route had been somewhat different. The son of a comfortable banker, Newman's upbringing had been conventional in the narrowest and unhappiest sense of the term. Religious observance in his family was punctilious but vapid, and the young boy's reaction to this devotional charade was a cynicism that expressed itself as a sluggish indifference to all spiritual concepts. Shortly before going up to Oxford, however, Newman underwent a "profound change of thought" as a result of reading evangelical literature, and made a conscious decision in favor of Christianity. The next year, he entered Trinity College, and, after a distinguished undergraduate career, was elected to an Oriel fellowship in 1822.

Both Keble and Newman took Orders in the Church of England. At the time, the Church was in a highly decrepit state, functioning almost as a department of the Civil Service. Doctrinal and ecclesiastical disputes were settled by act of Parliament. When the government of Earl Grey suppressed ten bishoprics in Ireland in 1833, Keble preached his famous "National Apostasy" sermon denouncing the measure from the pulpit of Newman's parish—St. Mary's, Oxford. "I have ever considered and kept [that] day as the start of the religious movement of 1833," Newman wrote later.

This movement—the Oxford Movement, as it soon became known—was an attempt to revivify the Church of England. Newman and Keble were its leaders, and their starting-point was the proposition that the Church is a divine institution, expressly founded by Christ, and thus in no way subject—at least as far as matters of faith and morals are concerned—to civil authority. One of the goals of the movement was the re-incorporation into Anglicanism of many liturgical, theological, and ecclesiastical forms that had been discarded with the Reformation.

The resistance was very great. As a means of disseminating their ideas, Newman and Keble wrote a series of pamphlets called *Tracts for the Times*. When Newman attempted, in *Tract 90* (1841), to reconcile the 39 Articles of Anglicanism with the propositions of the Council of Trent, the furor overwhelmed him, and made him understand—possibly for the first time—just how radical his conception of a "Catholic Anglicanism" had been. The movement came under official censure, and Newman retired to the village of Littlemore, where he lived in a semi-monastic community with some of his followers. In 1844 he was received into the Catholic Church, travelled to Rome, and was ordained a priest.

Keble never forgave Newman for what was widely seen as a desertion. Not only did Newman's step split the Oxford Movement badly, it called into dispute the sincerity of its spokesmen. If the movement was a genuinely Anglican attempt at reform, why were so many of the Tractarians making their submission to Rome?

The charges of dishonesty and hypocrisy rankled Newman, and when Charles Kingsley impugned his integrity in print, Newman responded by publishing a lengthy history of his religious opinions, his mighty *Apologia Pro Vita Sua* (1864). A brilliant, lucidly-written, carefully-argued polemic, it succeeded in restoring to Newman the public goodwill he had enjoyed before the debacle of *Tract 90,* and almost single-handedly instilled in the minds of educated Englishmen a respect for Catholicism which had not existed since the time of Henry VIII. The book also had the effect of satisfying those Catholics who had reservations concerning Newman's theological orthodoxy. It was indicative of the new respect in which Newman was held in both Anglican and Catholic circles that he was made an honorary fellow of Trinity College in 1878, and elevated to the College of Cardinals in 1879.

Keble continued his labors from the remove of Hampshire, where he was vicar of Hursley. In the late 1820s he had established himself as an authority on religious verse by publishing *The Christian Year,* an enormously popular book of poetry (it sold over 150 printings in less than 50 years). He continued to write verse all his life, and published a second book, *Lyra Innocentium,* in 1846. Most of his time, however, was consumed in parochial and controversial efforts. He died on March 29, 1866.

Sectarian differences aside, the Oxford Movement might be understood in broad terms as a reaction against both the rationalism of the Enlightenment and the enthusiasm of the Romantics. Its emphasis was upon *revealed* religion and the *authority* of the Church; and thus it ran directly counter to the prevailing currents of liberalism and latitudinarianism. Alone among intellectual movements in the nineteenth century, the Oxford movement asserted the possibility of human apprehension of the infinite—not directly, but only through the medium of an agent (the Church). This radically traditional point of view often degenerated into a stiflingly narrow clannishness, but when it was informed by a genuine intellectual sincerity—as in the case of both Keble and Newman—it was a potent thing, invigorating and palatable, which the cozy skepticism of the day could not dispose of.

# Sacred Poetry

There are many circumstances about this little volume [*The Star in the East; with other Poems* by Josiah Conder], which tend powerfully to disarm criticism. In the first place, it is, for the most part, of a *sacred* character: taken up with those subjects which least of all admit, with propriety, either in the author or critic, the exercise of intellectual subtlety. For the *practical* tendency, indeed, of such compositions, both are most deeply responsible; the author who publishes, and the critic who undertakes to recommend or to censure them. But if they appear to be written with any degree of sincerity and earnestness, we naturally shrink from treating them merely as literary efforts. To interrupt the current of a reader's sympathy in such a case, by critical objections, is not merely to deprive him of a little harmless pleasure, it is to disturb him almost in a devotional exercise. The most considerate reviewer, therefore, of a volume of sacred poetry, will think it a subject on which it is easier to say too much than too little.

In the present instance, this consideration is enforced by the unpretending tone of the volume, which bears internal evidence, for the most part, of not having been written to meet the eye of the world. It is in vain to say that this claim on the critic's favour is nullified by publication. The author may give it up, and yet the work may retain it. We may still feel that we have no right to judge severely of what was not, at first, intended to come before our judgement at all. This of course applies only to those compositions, which indicate, by something within themselves, this freedom from the pretension of authorship. And such are most of those to which we are now bespeaking our readers' attention.

*Most* of them, we say, because the first poem in the volume, *The Star in the East,* is of a more ambitious and less pleasing character. Although in blank verse, it is, in fact, a lyrical effusion; an ode on the rapid progress and final triumph of the Gospel. It looks like the composition of a young man: harsh and turgid in parts, but interspersed with some rather beautiful touches. The opening lines are a fair specimen.

O to have heard th' unearthly symphonies,
Which o'er the starlight peace of Syrian skies
Came floating like a dream, that blessed night
When angel songs were heard by sinful men,
Hymning Messiah's advent! O to have watch'd
The night with those poor shepherds, whom, when first
The glory of the Lord shed sudden day—
Day without dawn, starting from midnight, day
Brighter than morning—on those lonely hills
Strange fear surpris'd—fear lost in wondering joy,

When from th' angelic multitude swell'd forth
The many-voicèd consonance of praise:—
Glory in th' highest to God, and upon earth
Peace, towards men good will. But once before,
In such glad strains of joyous fellowship,
The silent earth was greeted by the heavens,
When at its first foundation they looked down
From their bright orbs, those heavenly ministries,
Hailing the new-born world with bursts of joy.

Notwithstanding beauties scattered here and there, there is an effort and constrained stateliness in the poem, very different from the rapidity and simplicity of many of the shorter lyrics, which follow under the titles of Sacred and Domestic Poems. Such, for instance, as the Poor Man's Hymn

As much have I of worldly good
  As e'er my master had:
I diet on as dainty food,
  And am as richly clad,
Tho' plain my garb, though scant my board,
As Mary's Son and Nature's Lord.

The manger was his infant bed,
  His home, the mountain-cave,
He had not where to lay his head,
  He borrow'd even his grave.
Earth yielded him no resting spot,—
Her Maker, but she knew him not.

As much the world's good will I bear,
  Its favours and applause,
As He, whose blessed name I bear,—
  Hated without a cause,
Despis'd, rejected, mock'd by pride,
Betray'd, forsaken, crucified.

Why should I court my Master's foe?
  Why should I fear its frown?
Why should I seek for rest below,
  Or sigh for brief renown?—
A pilgrim to a better land,
An heir of joys at God's right hand?

Or the following sweet lines on Home, which occur among the Domestic poems:

That is not home, where day by day
I wear the busy hours away.
That is not home, where lonely night

Prepares me for the toils of light—
'Tis hope, and joy, and memory, give
A home in which the heart can live—
These walls no lingering hopes endear,
No fond remembrance chains me here,
Cheerless I heave the lonely sigh—
Eliza, canst thou tell me why?
'Tis where thou art is home to me,
And home without thee cannot be.

There are who strangely love to roam,
And find in wildest haunts their home;
And some in halls of lordly state,
Who yet are homeless, desolate.
The sailor's home is on the main,
The warrior's, on the tented plain,
The maiden's, in her bower of rest,
The infant's, on his mother's breast—
But where thou art is home to me,
And home without thee cannot be.

There is no home in halls of pride,
They are too high, and cold, and wide.
No home is by the wanderer found:
'Tis not in place: it hath no bound.
It is a circling atmosphere
Investing all the heart holds dear;—
A law of strange attractive force,
That holds the feelings in their course;

It is a presence undefin'd,
O'er-shadowing the conscious mind,
Where love and duty sweetly blend
To consecrate the name of friend;—
Where'er thou art is home to me,
And home without thee cannot be.

My love, forgive the anxious sigh—
I hear the moments rushing by,
And think that life is fleeting fast,
That youth with us will soon be past.
Oh! when will time, consenting, give
The home in which my heart can live?
There shall the past and future meet,
And o'er our couch, in union sweet,
Extend their cherub wings, and shower
Bright influence on the present hour,

Oh! when shall Israel's mystic guide,
The pillar'd cloud, our steps decide,
Then, resting, spread its guardian shade,
To bless the home which love hath made?
Daily, my love, shall thence arise
Our hearts' united sacrifice;
And home indeed a home will be,
Thus consecrate and shar'd with thee.

We will add one more specimen of the same kind, which forms a natural and pleasing appendix to the preceding lines.

Louise! you wept, that morn of gladness
  Which made your Brother blest;
And tears of half-reproachful sadness
  Fell on the Bridegroom's vest:
Yet, pearly tears were those, to gem
A Sister's bridal diadem.

No words could half so well have spoken,
  What thus was deeply shown
By Nature's simplest, dearest token,
  How much was then my own;
Endearing her for whom they fell,
And Thee, for having loved so well.

But now no more—nor let a Brother,
  Louise, regretful see,
That still 'tis sorrow to another,
  That he should happy be.
Those were, I trust, the only tears
That day shall cost through coming years.

Smile with us. Happy and light-hearted,
  We three the time will while.
And, when sometimes a season parted,
  Still think of us, and smile.
But come to us in gloomy weather;
We'll weep, when we must weep, together.

Now, what is the reason of the great difference between these extracts and that from the *Star in the East*?—a difference which the earlier date of the latter, so far from accounting for, only makes the more extraordinary. In some instances, the interval of time is very short, but at all events more effort and turgidness might have been expected in the earlier poems, more simplicity and care and a more subdued tone in the later. We suspect a reason, which both poets and poetical readers are too apt to leave out of sight. There is a want of *truth* in the *Star in the East*—not that the author is otherwise than quite in earnest—but his earnestness seems rather an artificial glow, to which he has been worked up by reading and conversation of a particular cast, than the overflowing warmth of his own natural feelings, kindled by circumstances in which he was himself placed. In a word, when he writes of the success of the Bible Society, and the supposed amelioration of the world in consequence, he writes from report and fancy only; but when he speaks of a happy home, of kindly affections, of the comforts which piety can administer in disappointment and sorrow; either we are greatly mistaken, or he speaks from real and present experience. The poetical result is what the reader has seen:

*——mens onus reponit, et peregrino*
*Labore fessi venimus Larem ad nostrum—*

We turn gladly from our fairy voyage round the world to refresh ourselves with a picture, which we feel to be drawn from the life, of a happy and innocent fireside. Nor is it, in the slightest degree, derogatory to an author's talent to say that he has failed, comparatively, on that subject of which he must have known comparatively little.

Let us here pause a moment to explain what is meant when we speak of such prospects as are above alluded to, being shadowy and unreal in respect of what is matter of experience. It is not that we doubt the tenor of the Scripture, regarding the final conversion of the whole world, or that we close our eyes to the wonderful arrangements, if the expression may be used, which Divine Providence seems everywhere making, with a view to that great consummation. One circumstance, in particular, arrests our attention, as pervading the whole of modern history, but gradually standing out in a stronger light as the view draws nearer our own times: we mean the rapid increase of colonization *from Christian nations only*. So that the larger half of the globe, and what in the nature of things will soon become the more populous, is already, in profession, Christian. The event, therefore, is unquestionable: but experience, we fear, will hardly warrant the exulting anticipations, which our author, in common with many of whose sincerity there is no reason to doubt, has raised upon it. It is but too conceivable that the whole world may become nominally Christian, yet the face of things may be very little changed for the better. And any view of the progress of the gospel, whether in verse or in prose, which leaves out this possibility, is so far wanting in truth, and in that depth of thought which is as necessary to the higher kinds of poetical beauty as to philosophy or theology itself.

This, however, is too solemn and comprehensive a subject to be lightly or hastily spoken of. It is enough to have glanced at it, as accounting, in some measure, for the general failure of modern poets in their attempts to describe the predicted triumph of the gospel in the latter days.

To return to the sacred and domestic poems, thus advantageously distinguished from that which gives name to the volume. Affection, whether heavenly or earthly, is the simplest idea that can be; and in the graceful and harmonious expression of it lies the principal beauty of these poems. In the descriptive parts, and in the development of abstract sentiment, there is more of effort, and occasionally something very like affectation: approaching, in one instance (the *Nightingale,*) far nearer than we could wish, to the most vicious of all styles, the style of Mr. Leigh Hunt and his miserable followers.

Now, these are just the sort of merit and the sort of defect, which one might naturally expect to find united; the very simplicity of attachment, which qualifies the mind for sacred or domestic poetry, making its movements awkward and constrained, when scenes are to be described, or thoughts unravelled of more complication and less immediate interest. This is the rather to be observed, as many other sacred poets have become less generally pleasing and useful, than they otherwise would have been, from this very circumstance. The simple and touching devoutness of many of Bishop Ken's lyrical effusions has been unregarded, because of the ungraceful contrivances, and heavy movement of his narrative. The same may be said, in our own times, of some parts of Montgomery's writings. His bursts of sacred poetry, compared with his *Greenland,* remind us of a person singing enchantingly by ear, but becoming languid and powerless the moment he sits down to a note-book.

Such writers, it is obvious, do not sufficiently trust to the command which the simple expression of their feelings would obtain over their readers. They think it must be relieved with something of more variety and imagery, to which they work themselves up with laborious, and therefore necessarily unsuccessful, efforts. The model for correcting their error is to be found in the inspired volume. We can, in general, be but incompetent judges of this, because we have been used to it from our boyhood. But let us suppose a person, whose ideas of poetry were entirely gathered from modern compositions, taking up the Psalms for the first time. Among many other remarkable differences, he would surely be impressed with the sacred writer's total carelessness about originality, and what is technically called *effect.* He would say, 'This is something better than merely attractive poetry; it is absolute and divine truth.' The same remark ought to be suggested by all sacred hymns; and it is, indeed, greatly to be lamented, that such writers as we have just mentioned should have ever lost sight of it—should have had so little confidence in the power of simplicity, and have condescended so largely to the laborious refinements of the profane Muse.

To put the same truth in a light somewhat different; it is required, we apprehend, in all poets, but particularly in sacred poets, that they should seem to write with a view of unburthening their minds, and not for the sake of writing; for love of the subject, not of the employment. The distinction is very striking in descriptive poetry. Compare the landscapes of Cowper with those of Burns. There is, if we mistake not, the same sort of difference between them, as in the conversation of two persons on scenery, the one originally an enthusiast in his love of the works of nature, the other driven, by disappointment or weariness, to solace himself with them as he might. It is a contrast which every one must have observed, when such topics come under discussion in society; and those who think it worth while, may find abundant illustration of it in the writings of this unfortunate but illustrious pair. The one all overflowing with the love of nature, and indicating, at every turn, that whatever his lot in life, he could not have been happy without her. The other visibly and wisely soothing himself, but not without effort, by attending to rural objects, in default of some more congenial happiness, of which he had almost come to despair. The latter, in consequence, laboriously sketching every object that came in his way: the other, in one or two rapid lines, which operate, as it were, like a magician's spell, presenting to the fancy just that picture, which was wanted to put the reader's mind in unison with the writer's. We would quote, as an instance, the description of Evening in the Fourth Book of the *Task:*

Come Ev'ning, once again, season of peace;
Return, sweet Ev'ning, and continue long!
Methinks I see thee in the streaking west
With matron-step slow-moving, while the night
Treads on thy sweeping train; one hand employ'd
In letting fall the curtain of repose
On bird and beast, the other charg'd for man
With sweet oblivion of the cares of day:
Not sumptuously adorn'd, nor needing aid,
Like homely-featur'd night, of clust'ring gems;
A star or two, just twinkling on thy brow,
Suffices thee; save that the moon is thine
No less than her's, not worn indeed on high
With ostentatious pageantry, but set
With modest grandeur in thy purple zone,
Resplendent less, but of an ampler round.
Come then, and thou shalt find thy vot'ry calm,
Or make me so. Composure is thy gift.

And we would set over against it that purely pastoral chant:

Now rosy May comes in wi' flowers
To deck her gay, green spreading bowers;
And now comes in my happy hours,
To wander wi' my Davie.
Meet me on the warlock knowe,
Dainty Davie, dainty Davie.
There I'll spend the day wi' you.
My ain dear dainty Davie.

The crystal waters round us fa',
The merry birds are lovers a',
The scented breezes round us blaw,
A wandering wi' my Davie.
Meet me, &c.

When purple morning starts the hare
To steal upon her early fare,
Then thro' the dews I will repair,
   To meet my faithful Davie.
      Meet me, &c.

When day, expiring in the west,
The curtain draws o' nature's rest,
I flee to his arms I lo'e best,
   And that's my ain dear Davie.
      Meet me, &c.

There is surely no need to explain how this instinctive attachment to his subject is especially requisite in the sacred poet. If even the description of material objects is found to languish without it, much more will it be looked for when the best and highest of all affections is to be expressed and communicated to others. The nobler and worthier the object, the greater our disappointment to find it approached with anything like languor or constraint.

We must just mention one more quality, which may seem, upon consideration, essential to perfection in this kind: viz. that the feelings the writer expresses should appear to be specimens of his general tone of thought, not sudden bursts and mere flashes of goodness. Wordsworth's beautiful description of the Stock-dove might not unaptly be applied to him. He should sing

            of love with silence blending,
Slow to begin, yet never ending,
Of serious faith and inward glee.

Some may, perhaps, object to this, as a dull and languid strain of sentiment. But before we yield to their censures we would inquire of them what style they consider, themselves, as most appropriate to similar subjects in a kindred art. If grave, simple, sustained melodies—if tones of deep but subdued emotion are what our minds naturally suggest to us upon the mention of sacred *music*—why should there not be something analogous, a kind of plain chant, in sacred *poetry* also? fervent, yet sober; awful, but engaging; neither wild and passionate, nor light and airy; but such as we may with submission presume to be the most acceptable offering in its kind, as being indeed the truest expression of the best state of the affections. To many, perhaps to most, men, a tone of more violent emotion may sound at first more attractive. But before we *indulge* such a preference, we should do well to consider, whether it is quite agreeable to that spirit, which alone can make us worthy readers of sacred poetry. 'Ενθεον ή ποιήοις', it is true; there must be rapture and inspiration, but these will naturally differ in their character as the powers do from whom they proceed. The worshippers of Baal may be rude and frantic in their cries and gestures; but the true Prophet, speaking to or of the true God, is all dignity and calmness.

If then, in addition to the ordinary difficulties of poetry, all these things are essential to the success of the Christian lyrist—if what he sets before us must be true in substance, and in manner marked by a noble simplicity and confidence in that truth, by a sincere attachment to it, and entire familiarity with it—then we need not wonder that so few should have become eminent in this branch of their art, nor need we have recourse to the disheartening and unsatisfactory solutions which are sometimes given of that circumstance.

> 'Contemplative piety,' says Dr. Johnson, 'or the intercourse between God and the human soul, cannot be poetical. Man, admitted to implore the mercy of his Creator, and plead the merits of his Redeemer, is already in a higher state than poetry can confer.'
>
> —*Life of Waller*

The sentiment is not uncommon among serious, but somewhat fearful, believers; and though we believe it erroneous, we desire to treat it not only with tenderness, but with reverence. They start at the very mention of sacred poetry, as though poetry were in its essence a profane amusement. It is, unquestionably, by far the safer extreme to be too much afraid of venturing with the imagination upon sacred ground. Yet, if it be an error, and a practical error, it may be worth while cautiously to examine the grounds of it. In the generality, perhaps, it is not so much a deliberate opinion, as a prejudice against the use of the art, arising out of its abuse. But the great writer just referred to has endeavoured to establish it by direct reasoning. He argues the point, first, from the nature of poetry, and afterwards from that of devotion.

> The essence of poetry is invention; such invention as, by producing something unexpected, surprises and delights. The topics of devotion are few.

It is to be hoped that many men's experience will refute the latter part of this statement. How can the topics of devotion be few, when we are taught to make every part of life, every scene in nature, an occasion—in other words, a topic—of devotion? It might as well be said that connubial love is an unfit subject for poetry, as being incapable of novelty, because, after all, it is only ringing the changes upon one simple affection, which every one understands. The novelty there consists, not in the original topic, but in continually bringing ordinary things, by happy strokes of natural ingenuity, into new associations with the ruling passion.

> There's not a bonny flower that springs
> By fountain, shaw, or green;
> There's not a bonnie bird that sings
> But minds me of my Jean.

Why need we fear to extend this most beautiful and natural sentiment to 'the intercourse between the human soul and its Maker', possessing, as we do, the very highest warrant for the analogy which subsists between conjugal and divine love?

Novelty, therefore, sufficient for all the purposes of poetry, we may have on sacred subjects. Let us pass to the next objection.

> Poetry pleases by exhibiting an idea more grateful to the mind than things themselves afford. This effect proceeds from the display of those parts of nature which attract, and the concealment of those which repel, the imagination; but religion must be shown as it is, suppression and addition equally corrupt it; and, such as it is, it is known already.

A fallacy may be apprehended in both parts of this statement. There are, surely, real landscapes which delight the mind as sincerely and intensely as the most perfect description could; and there are family groups which give a more exquisite sensation of domestic happiness than anything in Milton, or even Shakespeare. It is partly by association with these, the treasures of the memory, and not altogether by mere excitement of the imagination, that Poetry does her work. By the same rule sacred pictures and sacred songs cannot fail to gratify the mind which is at all exercised in devotion; recalling, as they will, whatever of highest perfection in that way she can remember in herself, or has learned of others.

Then again, it is not the religious doctrine itself, so much as the effect of it upon the human mind and heart, which the sacred poet has to describe. What is said of suppression and addition may be true enough with regard to the former, but is evidently incorrect when applied to the latter: it being an acknowledged difficulty in all devotional writings, and not in devotional verse only, to keep clear of the extreme of languor on the one hand, and debasing rapture on the other. This requires a delicacy in the perception and enunciation of truth, of which the most earnest believer may be altogether destitute. And since, probably, no man's condition, in regard to eternal things, is exactly like that of any other man, and yet it is the business of the sacred poet to sympathize with all, his store of subjects is clearly inexhaustible, and his powers of discrimination—in other words, of suppression and addition—are kept in continual exercise.

Nor is he, by any means, so straitly limited in the other and more difficult branch of his art, the exhibition of religious doctrine itself, as is supposed in the following statement:

> Whatever is great, desirable, or tremendous, is comprised in the name of the Supreme Being. Omnipotence cannot be exalted; infinity cannot be amplified; perfection cannot be improved.

True: all perfection is implied in the name of God; and so all the beauties and luxuries of spring are comprised in that one word. But is it not the very office of poetry to develop and display the particulars of such complex ideas? in such a way, for example, as the idea of God's omnipresence is developed in the 139th Psalm? and thus detaining the mind for a while, to force or help her to think steadily on truths which she would hurry unprofitably over, how strictly soever they may be implied in the language which she uses. It is really surprising that this great and acute critic did not perceive that the objection applies as strongly against any kind of composition of which the Divine Nature is the subject, as against devotional poems.

We forbear to press the consideration that, even if the objection were allowed in respect of natural religion, it would not hold against the devotional composition of a Christian; the object of whose worship has condescended also to become the object of description, affection, and sympathy, in the literal sense of these words. But this is, perhaps, too solemn and awful an argument for this place; and therefore we pass on to the concluding statement of the passage under consideration, in which the writer turns his view downwards, and argues against sacred poetry from the nature of man, as he had before from the nature of God.

> The employments of pious meditation are faith, thanksgiving, repentance and supplication. Faith, invariably uniform, cannot be invested by fancy with decorations. Thanksgiving, the most joyful of all holy effusions, yet addressed to a Being without passions, is confined to a few modes, and is to be felt rather than expressed.

What we have said of the variation of the devout affections, as they exist in various persons, is sufficient, we apprehend, to answer this. But the rest of the paragraph requires some additional reflection:

> Repentance, trembling in the presence of the Judge, is not at leisure for cadences and epithets.

This is rather invidiously put, and looks as if the author had not entire confidence in the truth of what he was saying. Indeed, it may very well be questioned; since many of the more refined passions, it is certain, naturally express themselves in poetical language. But repentance is not merely a passion, nor is its only office to tremble in the presence of the Judge. So far from it, that one great business of sacred poetry, as of sacred music, is to quiet and sober the feelings of the penitent—to make his compunction as much of 'a reasonable service' as possible.

To proceed:

> Supplication of man to man may diffuse itself through many topics of persuasion: but supplication to God can only cry for mercy.

Certainly, this would be true, if the abstract nature of the Deity were alone considered. But if we turn to the sacred volume, which corrects so many of our erring anticipations, we there find that, whether in condescension to our infirmities, or for other wise purposes, we are furnished with inspired precedents for addressing ourselves to God in all the various tones, and by all the various topics, which we should use to a good and wise man standing in the highest and nearest relation to us. This is so palpably the case throughout the scriptures, that it is quite surprising how a person of so much serious thought as Dr. Johnson could have failed to recollect it when arguing on the subject of prayer. In fact, there is a simple test, by which, perhaps, the whole of his reasoning on Sacred Poetry might be fairly and decisively tried. Let the reader, as he goes over it, bear in mind the Psalms of David, and consider whether every one of his statements and arguments is not there practically refuted.

It is not, then, because sacred subjects are peculiarly unapt for poetry, that so few sacred poets are popular. We have already glanced at some of the causes to which we attribute it—we ought to add another, which strikes us as important. Let us consider how the case stands with regard to books of devotion in *prose*.

We may own it reluctantly, but must it not be owned? that if two new publications meet the eye at once, of which no more is known than that the one is what is familiarly called *a good book,* the other a work of mere literature, nine readers out of ten will take up the second rather than the first? If this be allowed, whatever accounts for it will contribute to account also for the comparative failure of devotional poetry. For this sort of coldness and languor in the reader must act upon the author in more ways than one. The large class who write for money or applause will of course be carried, by the tide of popularity, towards some other subject. Men of more sincere minds, either from true or false delicacy, will have little heart to expose their retired thoughts to the risk of mockery or neglect; and, if they do venture, will be checked every moment, like an eager but bashful musician before a strange audience, not knowing how far the reader's feelings will harmonize with their own. This leaves the field open, in a great measure, to harder or more enthusiastic spirits; who offending continually, in their several ways, against delicacy, the one by wildness, the other by coarseness, aggravate the evil which they wished to cure; till the sacred subject itself comes at last to bear the blame due to the indifference of the reader and the indiscretion of the writer.

Such, we apprehend, would be a probable account of the condition of sacred poetry, in a country where religion was coldly acknowledged, and literature earnestly pursued. How far the description may apply to England and English literature, in their various changes since the Reformation—how far it may hold true of our own times—is an inquiry which would lead us too far at present; but it is surely worth considering. It goes deeper than any question of mere literary curiosity. It is a sort of test of the genuineness of those pretensions, which many of us are, perhaps too forward to advance, to a higher state of morality and piety, as well as knowledge and refinement, than has been known elsewhere or in other times.

Those who, in spite of such difficulties, desire in earnest to do good by the poetical talent, which they may happen to possess, have only, as it should seem, the following alternative. Either they must veil, as it were, the sacredness of the subject—not necessarily by allegory, for it may be done in a thousand other ways—and so deceive the world of taste into devotional reading—

*Succhi amari intanto ei beve,*
*E dall' inganno sua vita riceve—*

or else, directly avowing that their subject as well as purpose is devotion, they must be content with a smaller number of readers; a disadvantage, however, compensated by the fairer chance of doing good to each.

It may be worth while to endeavour to trace this distinction, as exemplified in the most renowned of the sacred poets of England; and to glean from such a survey the best instruction we can, in the happy art of turning the most fascinating part of literature to the highest purposes of religion.

We must premise that we limit the title of 'sacred poet' by excluding those who only devoted a small portion of their time and talent now and then, to sacred subjects. In all ages of our literary history it seems to have been considered almost as an essential part of a poet's duty to give up some pages to scriptural story, or to the praise of his Maker, how remote so ever from anything like religion the general strain of his writings might be. Witness the Lamentation of Mary Magdalene in the works of Chaucer, and the beautiful legend of Hew of Lincoln, which he has inserted in his Canterbury Tales; witness also the hymns of Ben Jonson. But these fragments alone will not entitle their authors to be enrolled among sacred poets. They indicate the taste of their age, rather than their own; a fact which may be thought to stand rather in painful contrast with the literary history of later days.

There is another class likewise, of whom little need be said in this place; we mean those who composed, strictly and only, for the sake of unburthening their own minds, without any thought of publication. But as Chaucer's sacred effusions indicate chiefly the character of the times, so poems such as those we now allude to, mark only the turn of mind of the individual writers; and our present business is rather with that sort of poetry which combines both sorts of instruction; that, namely, which bears internal evidence of having been written by sincere men, with an intention of doing good, and with consideration of the taste of the age in which they lived.

Recurring then to the distinction above laid down, between the direct and indirect modes of sacred poetry; at the head of the two classes, as the reader may perhaps have anticipated, we set the glorious names of Spenser and of Milton. The claim of Spenser to be considered as a sacred poet does by no means rest upon his hymns alone: although even those would be enough alone to embalm and consecrate the whole volume which contains them; as a splinter of the true cross is supposed by Catholic sailors to ensure the safety of the vessel. But whoever will attentively consider the *Faerie Queene* itself, will find that it is, almost throughout, such as might have been expected from the author of those truly sacred hymns. It is a continual, deliberate endeavour to enlist the restless intellect and chivalrous feeling of an inquiring and romantic age, on the side of goodness and faith, of purity and justice.

This position is to be made good, not solely or perhaps chiefly, yet with no small force, from the allegorical structure of the poem. Most of us, perhaps, are rather disposed to undervalue this contrivance; and even among the genuine admirers of Spenser, there are not a few who on purpose leave it out of their thoughts; finding, as they say, that it only embarrasses their enjoyment of the poetry. This is certainly far from reasonable: it is a relic of childish feeling, and mere love of amusement, which ill becomes any one who is old enough to appreciate the real beauties of Spenser. Yet it is so natural, so obviously to be expected, that we must suppose a scholar and philosopher (for such Spenser was, as well as a poet) to have been aware of it, and to have made up his mind to it, with all its disadvantages, for some strong reason or other. And what reason so likely as the hope of being seriously useful, both to himself and his readers?

To *himself,* because the constant recurrence to his allegory would serve as a check upon a fancy otherwise too luxuriant, and would prevent him from indulging in such liberties as the Italian poets, in other respects his worthy masters, were too apt to take. The consequence is, that even in his freest passages, and those which one would most wish unwritten, Spenser is by no means a *seductive* poet. Vice in him, however truly described, is always made contemptible or odious. The same may be said of Milton and Shakespeare; but Milton was of a cast of mind originally austere and rigorous. He looked on vice as a judge; Shakespeare, as a satirist. Spenser was far more indulgent than either, and acted therefore the more wisely in setting himself a rule, which should make it essential to the plan of his poem to be always recommending some virtue; and remind him, like a voice from heaven, that the place on which he was standing was holy ground.

Then as to the benefit which the *readers* of the *Faerie Queene* may derive from its allegorical form; a good deal surely is to be gained from the mere habit of looking at things with a view to something beyond their qualities merely sensible; to their sacred and moral meaning, and to the high associations they were intended to create in us. Neither the works nor the word of God, neither poetry nor theology, can be duly comprehended without constant mental exercise of this kind. The comparison of the Old Testament with the New is nothing else from beginning to end. And without something of this sort, poetry, and all the other arts, would indeed be relaxing to the tone of the mind. The allegory obviates this ill effect, by serving as a frequent remembrancer of this higher application. Not that it is necessary to bend and strain everything into conformity with it; a little leaven, of the genuine kind, will go a good way towards leavening the whole lump. And so it is in the *Faerie Queene;* for one stanza of direct allegory there are perhaps fifty of poetical embellishment; and it is in these last, after all, that the chief moral excellency of the poem lies; as we are now about to show.

But to be understood rightly, we would premise, that there is a disposition,—the very reverse of that which leads to parody and caricature,—which is common indeed to all generous minds, but is perhaps unrivalled in Spenser. As parody and caricature debase what is truly noble, by connecting it with low and ludicrous associations; so a mind, such as we are now speaking of, ennobles what of itself might seem trivial; its thoughts and language, on all occasions, taking a uniform and almost involuntary direction towards the best and highest things.

This, however, is a subject which can be hardly comprehended without examples. The first which occurs to us is the passage which relates the origin of Belphœbe.

Her birth was of the womb of morning dew,
And her conception of the joyous prime,
And all her whole creation did her show
Pure and unspotted from all loathly crime
That is ingenerate in fleshly slime.
So was this Virgin born, so was she bred,
So was she trained up from time to time,
In all chaste virtue and true bounti-hed,
Till to her due perfection she was ripenèd.

It is evident how high and sacred a subject was present to the poet's mind in composing this stanza; and any person who is well read in the Bible, with a clue like this may satisfy himself that all Spenser's writings are replete with similar tacit allusions to the language and the doctrines of sacred writ; allusions breathed, if we may so speak, rather than uttered, and much fitter to be silently considered, than to be dragged forward for quotation or minute criticism. Of course, the more numerous and natural such allusions are, the more entirely are we justified in the denomination we have ventured to bestow on their author, of a truly 'sacred' poet.

It may be felt, as some derogation from this high character, what he has himself avowed—that much of his allegory has a turn designedly given it in honour of Queen Elizabeth; a turn which will be called courtly or adulatory according to the humour of the critic. But, in the first place, such was the custom of the times; it was adopted even in sermons by men whose sincerity it would be almost sacrilege to question. Then, the merits of Queen Elizabeth in respect of the Protestant cause were of that dazzling order, which might excuse a little poetical exuberance in her praise. And, what is very deserving of consideration, it is certain that the most gentle and generous spirits are commonly found laying themselves open tc this charge of excessive compliment in addressing princes and patrons. Witness the high style adopted by the venerable Hooker, in speaking of this very Queen Elizabeth: 'Whose sacred power, matched with incomparable goodness of nature, hath hitherto been God's most happy instrument, by him miraculously kept for works of so miraculous preservation and safety unto others,' &c. Another instance of the same kind may be seen in Jeremy Taylor's dedication of his *Worthy Communicant* to the Princess of Orange. Nor is it any wonder it should be so, since such men feel most ardently the blessing and benefit as well as the difficulty of whatever is right in persons of such exalted station; and are also most strongly tempted to bear their testimony against the illiberal and envious censures of the vulgar. All these things, duly weighed, may seem to leave little, if anything, in their panegyrical strains of this greatest of laureates, to be excused by the common infirmity of human nature little to detract from our deliberate conviction that he was seriously guided, in the exercise of his art, by a sense of duty, and zeal for what is durably important.

Spenser then was essentially a *sacred* poet; but the delicacy and insinuating gentleness of his disposition were better fitted to the veiled than the direct mode of instruction. His was a mind which would have shrunk more from the chance of debasing a sacred subject by unhandsome treatment, than of incurring ridicule by what would be called unseasonable attempts to hallow things merely secular. It was natural therefore for him to choose not a scriptural story, but a tale of chivalry and romance; and the popular literature, and, in no small measure, the pageantry and manners of his time, would join to attract his efforts that way. In this way too he was enabled, with more propriety and grace, to introduce allusions, political or courtly, to subjects with which his readers were familiar; thus agreeably diversifying his allegory, and gratifying his affection for his friends and patrons, without the coarseness of direct compliment.

In Milton, most evidently, a great difference was to be expected: both from his own character and from that of the times in which he lived. Religion was in those days the favourite topic of discussion; and it is indeed painful to reflect, how sadly it was polluted by intermixture with earthly passions: the most awful turns and most surprising miracles of the Jewish history being made to serve the base purposes of persons, of whom it is hard to say whether they were more successful in misleading others, or in deceiving themselves. It was an effort worthy of a manly and devout spirit to rescue religion from such degradation, by choosing a subject, which, being scriptural, would suit the habit of the times, yet, from its universal and eternal importance, would give least opportunity for debasing temporary application. Then it was the temper of the man always to speak out. He carried it to a faulty excess, as his prose works too amply demonstrate. The more unfashionable his moral was, the more he would have disdained to veil it: neither had he the shrinking delicacy of Spenser to keep him back, through fear of profaning things hallowed by an unworthy touch.

Thus the great epic poem of our language came to be, avowedly, a sacred poem. One hardly dares to wish any thing other than it is in such a composition; yet it may be useful to point out in what respects the moral infirmity of the times, or of the author, has affected the work; so that we are occasionally tempted to regret even Milton's choice. But as the leading error of his mind appears to have been *intellectual* pride, and as the leading fault of the generation with which he acted was unquestionably *spiritual* pride, so the main defects of his poetry may probably be attributed to the same causes.

There is a studious undervaluing of the female character, which may be most distinctly perceived by comparing the character of Eve with that of the Lady in Comus: the latter conceived, as we imagine, before the mind of the poet had become so deeply tainted with the fault here imputed to him. A remarkable instance of it is his describing Eve as unwilling, or unworthy, to discourse herself with the angel.

Such pleasure she reserved,
Adam relating, she sole auditress.

The sentiment may be natural enough, since the primaeval curse upon women: but does it not argue rather too strong a sense of her original inferiority, to put it into her mind before the fall?

What again can be said for the reproachful and insulting tone, in which, more than once, the good angels are made to address the bad ones? or of the too attractive colours, in which, perhaps unconsciously, the poet has clothed the Author of Evil himself? It is a well-known complaint among many of the readers of *Paradise Lost,* that they can hardly keep themselves from sympathizing, in some sort, with Satan, as the hero of the poem. The most probable account of which surely is, that the author himself partook largely of the haughty and vindictive republican spirit which he has assigned to the character, and consequently, though perhaps unconsciously, drew the portrait with a peculiar zest.

These blemishes are in part attributable to the times in which he lived: but there is another now to be mentioned, which cannot be so accounted for: we mean a want of purity and spirituality in his conceptions of Heaven and heavenly joys. His Paradise is a vision not to be surpassed; but his attempts to soar higher are embarrassed with too much of earth still clinging as it were to his wings. Remarks of this kind are in general best understood by comparison, and we invite our readers to compare Milton with Dante, in their descriptions of Heaven. The one as simple as possible in his imagery, producing intense effect by little more than various combinations of *three* leading ideas—light, motion, and music—as if he feared to introduce anything more gross and earthly, and would rather be censured, as doubtless he often is, for coldness and poverty of invention. Whereas Milton, with very little selection or refinement, transfers to the immediate neighbourhood of God's throne the imagery of Paradise and Earth. Indeed he seems himself to have been aware of something unsatisfactory in this, and has inserted into the mouth of an angel, a kind of apology for it:

Though what if earth
Be but the shadow of heav'n, and things therein
Each to other like, more than on earth is thought?

These are blemishes, and sometimes almost tempt us to wish that even Milton had taken some subject not so immediately and avowedly connected with religion. But they do not affect his claim to be considered as the very lodestar and pattern of that class of sacred poets in England. As such we have here considered him next to Spenser; not that there were wanting others of the same order before him. In fact, most of the distinguished names in the poetical annals of Elizabeth, James I, and Charles I, might be included in the list. It may be enough just to recollect Drayton and Cowley, Herbert, Crashaw and Quarles.

The mention of these latter names suggests the remark, how very desirable it is to encourage as indulgent and, if we may so term it, *catholic* a spirit as may be, in poetical criticism. From having been over-praised in their own days, they are come now to be as much undervalued; yet their quaintness of manner and constrained imagery, adopted perhaps in compliance with the taste of their age, should hardly suffice to overbalance their sterling merits. We speak especially of Crashaw and Quarles: for Herbert is a name too venerable to be more than mentioned in our present discussion.

After Milton, sacred poetry seems to have greatly declined, both in the number and merit of those who cultivated it. No other could be expected from the conflicting evils of those times: in which one party was used to brand everything sacred with the name of Puritanism, and the other to suspect every thing poetical of being contrary to morality and religion.

Yet most of the great names of that age, especially among the Romanists, as Dryden, Pope, and before them Habington, continued to dedicate some of their poetry to religion. By their faith they were remote from the controversies which agitated the established church, and their devotion might indulge itself without incurring the suspicion of a fanatical spirit. Then the solemnity of their worship is fitted to inspire splendid and gorgeous strains, such as Dryden's paraphrase of the Veni Creator; and their own fallen fortunes in England, no less naturally, would fill them with a sense of decay very favourable to the plaintive tenderness of Habington and Crashaw.

A feeling of this kind, joined to the effect of distressing languor and sickness, may be discerned, occasionally, in the writings of Bishop Ken; though he was far indeed from being a Romanist. We shall hardly find, in all ecclesiastical history, a greener spot than the later years of this courageous and affectionate pastor; persecuted alternately by both parties, and driven from his station in his declining age; yet singing on, with unabated cheerfulness, to the last. His poems are not popular, nor probably ever will be, for reasons already touched upon; but whoever in earnest loves his three well-known hymns, and knows how to value such unaffected strains of poetical devotion, will find his account, in turning over his four volumes, half narrative and half lyric, and all avowedly on sacred subjects; the narrative often cumbrous, and the lyric verse not seldom languid and redundant: yet all breathing such an angelic spirit, interspersed with such pure and bright touches of poetry, that such a reader as we have supposed will scarcely find it in his heart to criticize them.

Between that time and ours, the form of sacred poetry which has succeeded best in attracting public attention, is the didactic: of which Davies in Queen Elizabeth's reign, Sir Richard Blackmore in King William's, Young in the middle, and Cowper in the close, of the last century, may fairly be taken as specimens, differing from each other according to the differences of their respective literary eras. Davies, with his Lucretian majesty (although he wants the moral pathos of the Roman poet), representing aptly enough the age of Elizabeth; Blackmore, with his easy paragraphs, the careless style of King Charles's days; Young, with his pointed sentences, transferring to graver subjects a good deal of the manner of Pope; and Cowper, with his agreeable but too unsparing descriptions, coming nearer to the present day, which appears, both in manners and in scenery, to delight in Dutch painting, rather than in what is more delicately classical.

With regard to the indirect, and, perhaps, more effective, species of sacred poetry, we fear it must be acknowledged, to the shame of the last century, that there is hardly a single specimen of it (excepting, perhaps, Gray's Elegy, and possibly some of the most perfect of Collins's poems) which has obtained any celebrity. We except the writers of our own times, who do not fall within the scope of this inquiry.

To Spenser, therefore, upon the whole, the English reader must revert, as being, pre-eminently, the sacred poet of his country: as most likely, in every way, to answer the purposes of his art; especially in an age of excitation and refinement, in which the gentler and more homely beauties, both of character and of scenery, are too apt to be despised: with passion and interest enough to attract the most ardent, and grace enough to win the most polished; yet by a silent preference everywhere inculcating the love of better and more enduring things; and so most exactly fulfilling what he has himself declared to be 'the general end of all his book'—'to fashion a gentleman, or noble person, in virtuous and gentle discipline': and going the straight way to the accomplishment of his own high-minded prayer:

That with the glory of so goodly sight,
The hearts of men, which fondly here admire
Fair-seeming shows, and feed on vain delight,
Transported with celestial desire
Of those fair forms, may lift themselves up higher,
And learn to love, with zealous humble duty,
Th' eternal fountain of that heavenly beauty.

# POETRY

## *WITH REFERENCE TO ARISTOTLE'S "POETICS"*

This work [*The Theatre of the Greeks; or the History, Literature, and Criticism of the Grecian Drama*] is well adapted for the purpose it has in view—the illustration of the Greek drama. It has been usual for the young student to engage in a perusal of this difficult branch of classical literature, with none of that previous preparation or collateral assistance which it pre-eminently requires. Not to mention his ordinary want of information as regards the history of the drama, which, though necessary to the full understanding the nature of that kind of poetry, may still seem too remotely connected with the existing Greek plays to be an actual deficiency; nor, again, his ignorance of the dramatic dialect and metres, which, without external helps, may possibly be overcome by minds of superior talent while engaged upon them; at least without some clear ideas of the usages of the ancient stage, the Greek dramas are but partially intelligible. The circumstances under which the representation was conducted, the form and general arrangements of the theatre, the respective offices and disposition of the actors, the nature and duties of the chorus, the proprieties of the scene itself, are essential subjects of information, yet they are generally neglected. The publication before us is a compilation of the most useful works or parts of works on the criticism, history, and antiquities of the drama; among which will be found extracts from Bentley's *Dissertation on the Epistles of Phalaris* and from Schlegel's work on Dramatic Literature; the more important parts of Twining's Translation of Aristotle's *Poetics*, and critical remarks, by Dawes, Porson, Elmsley, Tate, and the writers in the *Museum Criticum*.

If we were disposed to find fault with a useful work, we should describe it as over-liberal of condensed critical information. Such ample assistance is given to the student, that little is left to exercise his own personal thought and judgement. This is a fault of not a few publications of the present day, written for our universities. From a false estimate of the advantages of accurate scholarship, the reader is provided with a multitude of minute facts, which are useful to his mind, not when barely remembered, but chiefly when he has acquired them for himself. It is of comparatively trifling importance, whether the scholar knows the force of οὐ μή or ἀλλὰ γάρ; but it may considerably improve his acumen or taste, to have gone through a process of observation, comparison, and induction, more or less original and independent of grammarians and critics. It is an officious aid which renders the acquisition of a language mechanical. Commentators are of service to stimulate the mind, and suggest thought; and though, when we view the wide field of criticism, it is impossible they should do more, yet, when that field is narrowed to the limit of academical success, there is a danger of their indulging indolence, or confirming the contracted views of dullness. These remarks are not so much directed against a valuable work like the present, the very perusal of which may be made an exercise for the mind, as against an especial fault of the age. The uses of knowledge in forming the intellectual and moral character, are too commonly overlooked; and the possession itself being viewed as a peculiar good, short ways are on all subjects excogitated for avoiding the labour of learning; whereas the very length and process of the journey is in many the chief, in all an important advantage.

But, dismissing a train of thought which would soon lead us very far from the range of subjects which the *Theatre of the Greeks* introduces to our notice, we propose to offer some speculations of our own on Greek tragedy and poetry in general, founded on the doctrine of Aristotle as contained in the publication before us. A compilation of standard works, (and such in its general character is the *Greek Theatre,*) scarcely affords the occasion of lengthened criticism on itself; whereas it may be of use to the classical student to add some further illustrations of the subject which is the common basis of the works compiled.

Aristotle considers the excellence of a tragedy to depend upon its *plot*—and, since a tragedy, as such, is obviously the exhibition of an *action,* no one can deny his statement to be abstractedly true. Accordingly he directs his principal attention to the economy of the fable; determines its range of subjects, delineates its proportions, traces its progress from a complication of incidents to their just and satisfactory arrangement, investigates the means of making a train of events striking or affecting, and shows how the exhibition of character may be made subservient to the purposes of the action. His treatise is throughout interesting and valuable. It is one thing, however, to form the beau idéal of a tragedy on scientific principles; another to point out the actual beauty of a particular school of dramatic composition. The Greek tragedians are not generally felicitous in the construction of their plots. Aristotle, then, rather tells us what tragedy should be, than what Greek tragedy really was. And this doubtless was the intention of the philosopher. Since, however, the Greek drama has obtained so extended and lasting a celebrity, and yet its excellence does not fall under the strict rules of the critical art, we should inquire in what it consists.

That the charm of Greek tragedy does not ordinarily arise from scientific correctness of plot, is certain as a matter of fact. Seldom does any great interest arise from the action; which, instead of being progressive and sustained, is commonly either a mere necessary condition of the drama, or a convenience for the introduction of matter more important than itself. It is often stationary—often irregular—sometimes either wants or outlives the catastrophe. In the plays of Aeschylus it is always simple and inartificial—in four out of the seven there is hardly any plot at all;—and, though it is of more prominent importance in those of Sophocles, yet even here the *Oedipus at Colonos* is a mere series of incidents, and the *Ajax* a union of two separate tales; while in the *Philoctetes,* which is apparently busy, the circumstances of the action are but slightly connected with the *dénouement.* The carelessness of Euripides in the construction of his plots is well known. The action then will be more justly viewed as the vehicle for introducing the personages of the drama, than as the principal object of the poet's art; it is not in the plot, but in the characters, sentiments, and diction, that the actual merit and poetry of the composition is placed. To show this to the satisfaction of the reader, would require a minuter investigation of details than our present purpose admits; yet a few instances in point may suggest others to the memory. E.g. in neither the *Oedipus Coloneus* nor the *Philoctetes,* the two most beautiful plays of Sophocles, is the plot striking; but how exquisite is the delineation of the characters of Antigone and Oedipus, in the former tragedy, particularly in their interview with Polynices, and the various descriptions of the scene itself which the Chorus furnishes! In the *Philoctetes,* again, it is the contrast between the worldly wisdom of Ulysses, the inexperienced frankness of Neoptolemus, and the simplicity of the afflicted Philoctetes, which constitutes the principal charm of the drama. Or we may instance the spirit and nature displayed in the grouping of the characters in the *Prometheus* which is almost without action;—the stubborn enemy of the new dynasty of gods; Oceanus trimming, as an accomplished politician, with the change of affairs; the single-hearted and generous Nereids; and Hermes the favourite and instrument of the usurping potentate. So again, the beauties of the *Thebae* are almost independent of the plot;—it is the Chorus which imparts grace and interest to the actionless scene; and the speech of Antigone at the end, one of the most simply striking in any play, has, scientifically speaking, no place in the tragedy, which should already have been brought to its conclusion. Amid the multitude of the beauties of the irregular Euripides, it is obvious to notice the characters of Alcestis and the Clytemnestra of the *Electra;* the soliloquies of *Medea;* the picturesque situation of Ion, the minister of the Pythian temple; the opening scene of the *Orestes;* and the dialogues between Phaedra and her attendant in the *Hippolytus,* and the old man and Antigone in the *Phoenissae;*—passages which are either unconnected with the development of the plot, or of an importance superior to it. Thus the Greek drama, as a fact, was modelled on no scientific principle. It was a pure recreation of the imagination, revelling without object or meaning beyond its own exhibition. Gods, heroes, kings, and dames, enter and retire: they may have a good reason for appearing—they may have a very poor one; whatever it is, still we have no right to ask for it;—the question is impertinent. Let us listen to their harmonious and majestic language—to the voices of sorrow, joy, compassion, or religious emotion—to the animated odes of the chorus. Why interrupt so divine a display of poetical genius by inquiries degrading it to the level of every-day events, and implying incompleteness in the action till a catastrophe arrives? The very spirit of beauty breathes through every part of the composition. We may liken the Greek drama to the music of the Italian school; in which the wonder is, how so much richness of invention in detail can be accommodated to a style so simple and uniform. Each is the development of grace, fancy, pathos, and taste, in the respective media of representation and sound.

However true then it may be, that one or two of the most celebrated dramas answer to the requisitions of Aristotle's doctrine, still, for the most part, Greek Tragedy has its own distinct and peculiar praise, which must not be lessened by a criticism conducted on principles, whether correct or not, still leading to excellence of another character. This being, as we hope, shown, we shall be still bolder, and proceed to question even the sufficiency of the rules of Aristotle for the production of dramas of the highest order. These rules, it would appear, require a plot not merely natural and unaffected, as a vehicle of more poetical matter, but one laboured and complicated as the sole legitimate channel of tragic effect; and thus tend to withdraw the mind of the poet from the spontaneous exhibition of pathos or imagination, to a minute diligence in the formation of a plan. To explain our views on the subject, we will institute a short comparison between three tragedies, the *Agamemnon,* the *Oedipus,* and the *Bacchae,* one of each of the tragic poets, where, by reference to Aristotle's principles, we think it will be found that the most perfect in plot is not the most poetical.

Of these the action of the *Oedipus Tyrannus* is frequently instanced by the critic as a specimen of judgement and skill in the selection and combination of the incidents; and in this point of view it is truly a masterly composition. The clearness, precision, certainty, and vigour, with which the line of the action moves on to its termination, is admirable. The character of Oedipus too is finely drawn, and identified with the development of the action.

The *Agamemnon* of Aeschylus presents us with the slow and difficult birth of a portentous secret—an event of old written in the resolves of destiny, a crime long meditated in the bosom of the human agents. The Chorus here has an importance altogether wanting in the Chorus of the *Oedipus*. They throw a pall of ancestral honour over the bier of the hereditary monarch, which would have been unbecoming in the case of the upstart king of Thebes. Till the arrival of Agamemnon, they occupy our attention, as the prophetic organ, not commissioned indeed but employed by heaven, to proclaim the impending horrors. Succeeding to the brief intimation of the watcher who opens the play, they seem oppressed with forebodings of woe and crime which they can neither justify nor analyse. The expression of their anxiety forms the stream in which the plot flows—every thing, even news of joy, takes a colouring from the depth of their gloom. On the arrival of the king, they retire before Cassandra, a more regularly commissioned prophetess; who, speaking first in figure, then in plain terms, only ceases that we may hear the voice of the betrayed monarch himself, informing us of the striking of the fatal blow. Here then the very simplicity of the fable constitutes its especial beauty. The death of Agamemnon is intimated at first—it is accomplished at last: throughout we find but the growing in volume and intensity of one and the same note—it is a working up of one musical ground, by fugue and imitation, into the richness of combined harmony. But we look in vain for the progressive and thickening incidents of the *Oedipus*.

The action of the *Bacchae* is also simple. It is the history of the reception of the worship of Bacchus in Thebes; who, first depriving Pentheus of his reason, and thereby drawing him on to his ruin, establishes his divinity. The interest of the scene arises from the gradual process by which the derangement of the Theban king is effected, which is powerfully and originally described. It would be comic, were it unconnected with religion. As it is, it exhibits the grave irony of a god triumphing over the impotent presumption of man, the sport and terrible mischievousness of an insulted deity. It is an exemplification of the adage, *quem deus vult perdere, prius dementat*. So delicately balanced is the action along the verge of the sublime and grotesque, that it is both solemn and humorous, without violence to the propriety of the composition: the mad and merry fire of the Chorus, the imbecile mirth of old Cadmus and Tiresias, and the infatuation of Pentheus, who is ultimately induced to dress himself in female garb to gain admittance among the Bacchae, are made to harmonize with the terrible catastrophe which concludes the life of the intruder. Perhaps the victim's first discovery of the disguised deity is the finest conception in this splendid drama. His madness enables him to discern the emblematic horns on the head of Bacchus, which were hid from him when in his sound mind; yet this discovery, instead of leading him to an acknowledgement of the divinity, provides him only with matter for a stupid and perplexed astonishment.

καὶ ταῦρος ἡμῖν πρόσθεν ἡγεῖσθαι δοκεῖς,
καὶ σῷ κέρατε κρατὶ προσπεφυκέναι.
ἀλλ' ἦ ποτ' ἦσθα θήρ; τεταύρωσαι γὰρ οὖν.

A Bull, thou seem'st to lead us; on thy head
Horns have grown forth: wast heretofore a beast?
For such thy semblance now.

This play is on the whole the most favourable specimen of the genius of Euripides—not breathing the sweet composure, the melodious fullness, the majesty and grace of Sophocles; nor rudely and overpoweringly tragic as Aeschylus; but brilliant, versatile, imaginative, as well as deeply pathetic.

Here then are two dramas of extreme poetical power, but deficient in skilfulness of plot. Are they on that account to be rated below the *Oedipus*, which, in spite of its many beauties, has not even a share of the richness and sublimity of either?

Aristotle, then, it must be allowed, treats dramatic composition more as an exhibition of ingenious workmanship, than as a free and unfettered effusion of genius. The inferior poem may, on his principle, be the better tragedy. He may indeed have intended solely to delineate the outward framework most suitable to the reception of the spirit of poetry, not to discuss the nature of poetry itself. If so, it cannot be denied that, the poetry being given equal in the two cases, the more perfect plot will merit the greater share of praise. And it may seem to agree with this view of his meaning, that he pronounces Euripides, in spite of the irregularity of his plots, to be, after all, the most tragic of the Greek dramatists, inasmuch (i.e.) as he excels in his appeal to those passions which the outward form of the drama merely subserves. Still there is surely too much stress laid by the philosopher upon the artificial part; which, after all, leads to negative, more than to positive excellence; and should rather be the natural and (so to say) unintentional result of the poet's feeling and imagination, than be separated from them as the direct object of his care. Perhaps it is hardly fair to judge of Aristotle's sentiments by the fragment of his work which has come down to us. Yet as his natural taste led him to delight in the explication of systems, and in those large and connected views which his vigorous talent for thinking through subjects supplied, we may be allowed to suspect him of entertaining too cold and formal conceptions of the nature of poetical composition, as if its beauties were less subtle and delicate than they really are. A word has power to convey a world of information to the imagination, and to act as a spell upon the feelings: there is no need of sustained fiction—often no room for it.[1] Some confirmation of the judgement we have ventured to pass on the greatest of analytical philosophers, is the account he gives of the source of poetical pleasure; which he almost identifies with a gratification of the reasoning faculty, placing it in the satisfaction derived from recognizing in fiction a resemblance to the realities of life—συμβαίνει θεωροῦντας μανθάνειν καὶ συλλογίζεσθαι, τί ἕκαστον.[2]

But as we have treated, rather unceremoniously, a deservedly high authority, we will try to compensate for our rudeness, by illustrating his general doctrine of the nature of poetry, which we hold to be most true and philosophical.

Poetry, according to Aristotle, is a representation of the ideal. Biography and history represent individual characters and actual facts; poetry, on the contrary, generalizing from the phenomena of nature and life, supplies us with pictures drawn not after an existing pattern, but after a creation of the mind. *Fidelity* is the primary merit of biography and history; the essence of poetry is *fiction. Poesis nihil aliud est* (says Bacon) *quam historiae imitatio ad placitum.* It delineates that perfection which the imagination suggests, and to which as a limit the present system of divine Providence actually tends. Moreover, by confining the attention to one series of events and scene of action, it bounds and finishes off the confused luxuriance of real nature; while, by a skilful adjustment of circumstances, it brings into sight the connexion of cause and effect, completes the dependence of the parts one on another, and harmonizes the proportions of the whole. It is then but the type and model of history or biography, if we may be allowed the comparison, bearing some resemblance to the abstract mathematical formula of physics, before it is modified by the contingencies of gravity and friction. Hence, while it recreates the imagination by the superhuman loveliness of its views, it provides a solace for the mind broken by the disappointments and sufferings of actual life; and becomes, moreover, the utterance of the inward emotions of a right moral feeling, seeking a purity and a truth which this world will not give.

It follows that the poetical mind is one full of the eternal forms of beauty and perfection; these are its material of thought, its instrument and medium of observation—these colour each object to which it directs its view. It is called imaginative or creative, from the originality and independence of its modes of thinking, compared with the common-place and matter-of-fact conceptions of ordinary minds, which are fettered down to the particular and individual. At the same time it feels a natural sympathy with everything great and splendid in the physical and moral world; and selecting such from the mass of common phenomena, incorporates them, as it were, into the substance of its own creations. From living thus in a world of its own, it speaks the language of dignity, emotion, and refinement. Figure is its necessary medium of communication with man; for in the feebleness of ordinary words to express its ideas, and in the absence of terms of abstract perfection, the adoption of metaphorical language is the only poor means allowed it for imparting to others its intense feelings. A metrical garb has, in all languages, been appropriated to poetry—it is but the outward development of the music and harmony within. The verse, far from being a restraint on the true poet, is the suitable index of his sense, and is adopted by his free and deliberate choice.

We shall presently show the applicability of our doctrine to the various departments of poetical composition; first, however, it will be right to volunteer an explanation which may save it from much misconception and objection. Let not our notion be thought arbitrarily to limit the number of poets, generally considered such. It will be found to lower particular works, or parts of works, rather than the writers themselves; sometimes to condemn only the vehicle in which the poetry is conveyed. There is an ambiguity in the word poetry, which is taken to signify both the talent itself, and the written composition which is the result of it. Thus there is an apparent, but no real contradiction, in saying a poem may be but partially poetical; in some passages more so than in others; and sometimes not poetical at all. We only maintain—not that writers forfeit the name of poet who fail at times to answer to our requisitions, but—that they are poets only so far forth and inasmuch as they do answer to them. We may grant, for instance, that the vulgarities of old Phoenix in the ninth *Iliad,* or of the nurse of Orestes in the *Choephoroe,* or perhaps of the grave-diggers in *Hamlet,* are in themselves unworthy of their respective authors, and refer them to the wantonness of exuberant genius; and yet maintain that the scenes in question contain much *incidental* poetry. Now and then the lustre of the true metal catches the eye, redeeming whatever is unseemly and worthless in the rude ore; still the ore is not the metal. Nay sometimes, and not unfrequently in Shakespeare, the introduction of unpoetical matter may be necessary for the sake of relief, or as a vivid expression of recondite conceptions, and (as it were) to make friends with the reader's imagination. This necessity, however, cannot make the additions in themselves beautiful and pleasing. Sometimes, on the other hand, while we do not deny the incidental beauty of a poem, we are ashamed and indignant on witnessing the unworthy substance in which that beauty is imbedded. This remark applies strongly to the immoral compositions to which Lord Byron devoted his last years. Now to proceed with our proposed investigation.

We will notice *descriptive poetry* first. Empedocles wrote his physics in verse, and Oppian his history of animals. Neither were poets—the one was an historian of nature, the other a sort of biographer of brutes. Yet a poet may make natural history or philosophy the material of his composition. But under his hands they are no longer a bare collection of facts or principles, but are painted with a meaning, beauty, and harmonious order not their own.

Thomson has sometimes been commended for the novelty and minuteness of his remarks upon nature. This is not the praise of a poet; whose office rather is to represent *known* phenomena in a new connexion or medium. In *L'Allegro* and *Il Penseroso* the poetical magician invests the commonest scenes of a country life with the hues, first of a mirthful, then of a pensive mind.[3] Pastoral poetry is a description of rustics, agriculture, and cattle, softened off and corrected from the rude health of nature. Virgil, and much more Pope and others, have run into the fault of colouring too highly;—instead of drawing generalized and ideal forms of *shepherds*, they have given us pictures of *gentlemen* and *beaux*. Their composition may be poetry, but it is not pastoral poetry.

The difference between poetical and historical *narrative* may be illustrated by the 'Tales Founded on Facts', generally of a religious character, so common in the present day, which we must not be thought to approve, because we use them for our purpose. The author finds in the circumstances of the case many particulars too trivial for public notice, or irrelevant to the main story, or partaking perhaps too much of the peculiarity of individual minds:—these he omits. He finds connected events separated from each other by time or place, or a course of action distributed among a multitude of agents; he limits the scene or duration of the tale, and dispenses with his host of characters by condensing the mass of incident and action in the history of a few. He compresses long controversies into a concise argument—and exhibits characters by dialogue—and (if such be his object) brings prominently forward the course of Divine Providence by a fit disposition of his materials. Thus he selects, combines, refines, colours—in fact, *poetizes*. His facts are no longer *actual* but *ideal*—a tale *founded on* facts is a tale *generalized from* facts. The authors of *Peveril of the Peak*, and of *Brambletye House*, have given us their respective descriptions of the profligate times of Charles II. Both accounts are interesting, but for different reasons. That of the latter writer has the fidelity of history; Walter Scott's picture is the hideous reality unintentionally softened and decorated by the poetry of his own mind. Miss Edgeworth sometimes apologizes for certain incidents in her tales, by stating they took place 'by one of those strange chances which occur in life, but seem incredible when found in writing'. Such an excuse evinces a misconception of the principle of fiction, which, being the *perfection* of the actual, prohibits the introduction of any such anomalies of experience. It is by a similar impropriety that painters sometimes introduce unusual sunsets, or other singular phenomena of lights and forms. Yet some of Miss Edgeworth's works contain much poetry of narrative. *Manœuvring* is perfect in its way—the plot and characters are natural, without being too real to be pleasing.

*Character* is made poetical by a like process. The writer draws indeed from experience; but unnatural peculiarities are laid aside, and harsh contrasts reconciled. If it be said, the fidelity of the imitation is often its greatest merit, we have only to reply, that in such cases the pleasure is not poetical, but consists in the mere recognition. All novels and tales which introduce real characters, are in the same degree unpoetical. Portrait-painting, to be poetical, should furnish an abstract representation of an individual; the abstraction being more rigid, inasmuch as the painting is confined to one point of time. The artist should draw independently of the accidents of attitude, dress, occasional feeling, and transient action. He should depict the general spirit of his subject—as if he were copying from memory, not from a few particular sittings. An ordinary painter will delineate with rigid fidelity, and will make a caricature. But the learned artist contrives so to temper his composition, as to sink all offensive peculiarities and hardnesses of individuality, without diminishing the striking effect of the likeness, or acquainting the casual spectator with the secret of his art. Miss Edgeworth's representations of the Irish character are actual, and not poetical—nor were they intended to be so. They are interesting, because they are faithful. If there is poetry about them, it exists in the personages themselves, not in her representation of them. She is only the accurate reporter in word of what was poetical in fact. Hence, moreover, when a deed or incident is striking in itself, a judicious writer is led to describe it in the most simple and colourless terms, his own being unnecessary; e.g. if the greatness of the action itself excites the imagination, or the depth of the suffering interests the feelings. In the usual phrase, the circumstances are left to 'speak for themselves'.

Let it not be said that our doctrine is adverse to that individuality in the delineation of character, which is a principal charm of fiction. It is not necessary for the ideality of a composition to avoid those minuter shades of difference between man and man, which give to poetry its plausibility and life; but merely such violation of general nature, such improbabilities, wanderings, or coarsenesses, as interfere with the refined and delicate enjoyment of the imagination; which would have the elements of beauty extracted out of the confused multitude of ordinary actions and habits, and combined with consistency and ease. Nor does it exclude the introduction of imperfect or odious characters. The original conception of a weak or guilty mind may have its intrinsic beauty. And much more so, when it is connected with a tale which finally adjusts whatever is reprehensible in the personages themselves. Richard and Iago are subservient to the plot. Moral excellence of character may sometimes be even a fault. The Clytemnestra of Euripides is so interesting, that the divine vengeance, which is the main subject of the drama, seems almost unjust. Lady Macbeth, on the contrary, is the conception of one deeply learned in the poetical art. She is polluted with the most heinous crimes, and meets the fate she deserves. Yet there is nothing in the picture to offend the taste, and much to feed the imagination. Romeo and Juliet are too good for the termination to which the plot leads—so are Ophelia and the bride of Lammermoor. In these cases there is something inconsistent with correct beauty, and therefore unpoetical. We do not say the fault could be avoided without sacrificing more than would be gained; still it is a fault. It is scarcely possible for a poet satisfactorily to connect innocence with ultimate unhappiness, when the notion of a future life is excluded. Honours paid to the memory of the dead are some alleviation of the harshness. In his use of the doctrine of a future life, Southey is admirable. Other writers are content to conduct their heroes to temporal happiness—Southey refuses present comfort to his Ladurlad, Thalaba, and Roderick, but carries them on through suffering to another world. The death of his hero is the termination of the action; yet so little in two of them, at least, does this catastrophe excite sorrowful feelings, that some readers may be startled to be reminded of the fact. If a melancholy is thrown over the conclusion of the *Roderick,* it is from the peculiarities of the hero's previous history.

Opinions, feelings, manners, and customs, are made poetical by the delicacy or splendour with which they are expressed. This is seen in the *ode, elegy, sonnet,* and *ballad;* in which a single idea perhaps, or familiar occurrence, is invested by the poet with pathos or dignity. The ballad of *Old Robin Gray* will serve, for an instance, out of a multitude; again, Lord Byron's *Hebrew Melody,* beginning 'Were my bosom as false', &c.; or Cowper's *Lines on his Mother's Picture;* or Milman's 'Funeral Hymn' in the *Martyr of Antioch;* or Milton's *Sonnet on his Blindness;* or Bernard Barton's *Dream.* As picturesque specimens, we may name Campbell's *Battle of the Baltic;* or Joanna Baillie's *Chough and Crow;* and for the more exalted and splendid style, Gray's *Bard;* or Milton's *Hymn on the Nativity;* in which facts, with which every one is familiar, are made new by the colouring of a poetical imagination. It must all along be observed, that we are not adducing instances for their own sake; but in order to illustrate our general doctrine, and to show its applicability to those compositions which are, by universal consent, acknowledged to be poetical.

The department of poetry we are now speaking of, is of much wider extent than might at first sight appear. It will include such moralizing and philosophical poems as Young's *Night Thoughts,* and Byron's *Childe Harold.*[4] There is much bad taste, at present, in the judgement passed on compositions of this kind. It is the fault of the day to mistake mere eloquence for poetry; whereas, in direct opposition to the conciseness and simplicity of the poet, the talent of the orator consists in making much of a single idea. *'Sic dicet ille ut verset saepe multis modis eandem et unam rem, ut haereat in eadem commoreturque sententia.'* This is the great art of Cicero himself, who, whether he is engaged in statement, argument, or raillery, never ceases till he has exhausted the subject; going round about it, and placing it in every different light, yet without repetition to offend or weary the reader. This faculty seems to consist in the power of throwing off harmonious sentences, which, while they have a respectable proportion of meaning, yet are especially intended to charm the ear. In popular poems, common ideas are unfolded with copiousness, and set off in polished verse—and this is called poetry. In the *Pleasures of Hope* we find this done with exquisite taste; but it is in his minor poems that the author's powerful and free poetical genius rises to its natural elevation. In *Childe Harold,* too, the writer is carried through his Spenserian stanza with the unweariness and equable fullness of accomplished eloquence; opening, illustrating, and heightening one idea, before he passes on to another. His composition is an extended funeral oration over buried joys and pleasures. His laments over Greece, Rome, and the fallen in various engagements, have quite the character of panegyrical orations; while by the very attempt to describe the celebrated buildings and sculptures of antiquity, he seems to confess that *they* are the poetical text, his the rhetorical comment. Still it is a work of splendid talent, though, as a whole, not of the highest poetical excellence. Juvenal is, perhaps, the only ancient author who habitually substitutes declamation for poetry.[5]

The *philosophy of mind* may equally be made subservient to poetry, as the philosophy of nature. It is a common fault to mistake a mere knowledge of the heart for poetical talent. Our greatest masters have known better;—they have subjected metaphysics to their art. In *Hamlet, Macbeth, Richard,* and *Othello,* the philosophy of mind is but the material of the poet. These personages are ideal; they are effects of the contact of a given internal character with given outward circumstances, the results of combined conditions determining (so to say) a moral curve of original and inimitable properties. Philosophy is exhibited in the same subserviency to poetry in many parts of Crabbe's *Tales of the Hall.* In the writings of this author there is much to offend a refined taste; but at least in the work in question there is much of a highly poetical cast. It is a representation of the action and re-action of two minds upon each other and upon the world around them. Two brothers of different characters and fortunes, and strangers to each other, meet. Their habits of mind, the formation of those habits by external circumstances, their respective media of judgement, their points of mutual attraction and repulsion, the mental position of each in relation to a variety of trifling phenomena of every-day nature and life, are beautifully developed in a series of tales moulded into a connected narrative. We are tempted to single out the fourth book, which gives an account of the childhood and education of the younger brother, and which for variety of thought as well as fidelity of description is in our judgement beyond praise. The Waverley novels would afford us specimens of a similar excellence. One striking peculiarity of these tales is the author's practice of describing a group of characters bearing the same general features of mind, and placed in the same general circumstances; yet so contrasted with each other in minute differences of mental constitution, that each diverges from the common starting-place into a path peculiar to himself. The brotherhood of villains in *Kenilworth,* of knights in *Ivanhoe,* and of enthusiasts in *Old Mortality* are instances of this. This bearing of character and plot on each other is not often found in Byron's poems. The Corsair is intended for a remarkable personage. We pass by the inconsistencies of his character, considered by itself. The grand fault is that, whether it be natural or not, we are obliged to accept the author's word for the fidelity of his portrait. We are told, not shown, what the hero was. There is nothing in the plot which results from his peculiar formation of mind. An every-day bravo might equally well have satisfied the requirements of the action. Childe Harold, again, if he is any thing, is a being professedly isolated from the world, and uninfluenced by it. One might as well draw Tityrus's stags grazing in the air, as a character of this kind; which yet, with more or less alteration passes through successive editions in his other poems. Byron had very little versatility or elasticity of genius; he did not know how to make poetry out of existing materials. He declaims in his own way, and has the upper hand as long as he is allowed to go on; but, if interrogated on principles of nature and good sense, he is at once put out and brought to a stand. Yet his conception of Sardanapalus and Myrrha is fine and ideal, and in the style of excellence which we have just been admiring in Shakespeare and Scott.

These illustrations of Aristotle's doctrine may suffice.

Now let us proceed to a fresh position; which, as before, shall first be broadly stated, then modified and explained. How does originality differ from the poetical talent? Without affecting the accuracy of a definition, we may call the latter the originality of right moral feeling.

Originality may perhaps be defined as the power of abstracting for oneself, and is in thought what strength of mind is in action. Our opinions are commonly derived from education and society. Common minds transmit as they receive, good and bad, true and false; minds of original talent feel a continual propensity to investigate subjects and strike out views for themselves;—so that even old and established truths do not escape modification and accidental change when subjected to this process of mental digestion. Even the style of original writers is stamped with the peculiarities of their minds. When originality is found apart from good sense, which more or less is frequently the case, it shows itself in paradox and rashness of sentiment, and eccentricity of outward conduct. Poetry, on the other hand, cannot be separated from its good sense, or taste, as it is called; which is one of its elements. It is originality energizing in the world of beauty; the originality of grace, purity, refinement, and feeling. We do not hesitate to say, that poetry is ultimately founded on correct moral perception;—that where there is no sound principle in exercise there will be no poetry, and that on the whole (originality being granted) in proportion to the standard of a writer's moral character, will his compositions vary in poetical excellence. This position, however, requires some explanation.[6]

Of course, then, we do not mean to imply that a poet must necessarily *display* virtuous and religious feeling;—we are not speaking of the actual *material* of poetry, but of its *sources*. A right moral state of heart is the formal and scientific condition of a poetical mind. Nor does it follow from our position that every poet must in fact be a man of consistent and practical principle; except so far as good feeling commonly produces or results from good practice. Burns was a man of inconsistent practice—still, it is known, of much really sound principle at bottom. Thus his acknowledged poetical talent is in no wise inconsistent with the truth of our doctrine, which will refer the beauty which exists in his compositions to the remains of a virtuous and diviner nature within him. Nay, further than this, our theory holds good even though it be shown that a bad man may write a poem. As motives short of the purest lead to actions intrinsically good, so frames of mind short of virtuous will produce a partial and limited poetry. But even where it is exhibited, the poetry of a vicious mind will be inconsistent and debased; i.e. so far only such, as the traces and shadows of holy truth still remain upon it. On the other hand, a right moral feeling places the mind in the very centre of that circle from which all the rays have their origin and range; whereas minds otherwise placed command but a portion of the whole circuit of poetry. Allowing for human infirmity and the varieties of opinion, Milton, Spenser, Cowper, Wordsworth, and Southey, may be considered, as far as their writings go, to approximate to this moral centre. The following are added as further illustrations of our meaning. Walter Scott's centre is chivalrous honour; Shakespeare exhibits the ἦθος, the physiognomy of an unlearned and undisciplined piety; Homer the religion of nature and the heart, at times debased by polytheism. All these poets are religious:—the occasional irreligion of Virgil's poetry is painful to the admirers of his general taste and delicacy. Dryden's *Alexander's Feast* is a magnificent composition, and has high poetical beauties; but to a delicate judgement there is something intrinsically unpoetical in the end to which it is devoted, the praises of revel and sensuality. It corresponds to a process of clever reasoning erected on an untrue foundation—the one is a fallacy, the other is out of taste. Lord Byron's *Manfred* is in parts intensely poetical; yet the refined mind naturally shrinks from the spirit which here and there reveals itself, and the basis on which the fable is built. From a perusal of it we should infer, according to the above theory, that there was right and fine feeling in the poet's mind, but that the central and consistent character was wanting. From the history of his life we know this to be the fact. The connexion between want of the religious principle and want of poetical feeling, is seen in the instances of Hume and Gibbon; who had radically unpoetical minds. Rousseau is not an exception to our doctrine, for his heart was naturally religious. Lucretius too had much poetical talent; but his work evinces that his miserable philosophy was rather the result of a bewildered judgement than a corrupt heart.

According to the above theory, revealed religion should be especially poetical—and it is so in fact. While its disclosures have an originality in them to engage the intellect, they have a beauty to satisfy the moral nature. It presents us with those ideal forms of excellence in which a poetical mind delights, and with which all grace and harmony are associated. It brings us into a new world—a world of overpowering interest, of the sublimest views, and the tenderest and purest feelings. The peculiar grace of mind of the New Testament writers is as striking as the actual effect produced upon the hearts of those who have imbibed their spirit. At present we are not concerned with the practical, but the poetical nature of revealed truth. With Christians a poetical view of things is a duty—we are bid to colour all things with hues of faith, to see a divine meaning in every event, and a superhuman tendency. Even our friends around are invested with unearthly brightness—no longer imperfect men, but beings taken into divine favour, stamped with his seal, and in training for future happiness. It may be added that the virtues peculiarly Christian are especially poetical;—meekness, gentleness, compassion, contentment, modesty, not to mention the devotional virtues: whereas the ruder and more ordinary feelings are the instruments of rhetoric more justly than of poetry—anger, indignation, emulation, martial spirit, and love of independence.

A few remarks on poetical composition, and we have done.—The art of composition is merely accessory to the poetical talent. But where that talent exists it necessarily gives its own character to the style, and renders it perfectly different from all others. As the poet's habits of mind lead to contemplation rather than communication with others, he is more or less obscure, according to the particular style of poetry he has adopted; less so, in epic or narrative and dramatic representation—more so, in odes and choruses. He will be obscure, moreover, from the depth of his feelings, which require a congenial reader to enter into them—and from their acuteness, which shrinks from any formal accuracy in the expression of them. And he will be obscure, not only from the carelessness of genius and from the originality of his conceptions, but (it may be) from natural deficiency in the power of clear and eloquent expression, which, we must repeat, is a talent distinct from poetry, though often mistaken for it.

Dexterity in composition, or *eloquence* as it may be called in a contracted sense of the word, is however manifestly more or less necessary in every branch of literature, though its elements may be different in each. *Poetical* eloquence consists, first in the power of illustration—which the poet uses, not as the orator, voluntarily, for the sake of clearness or ornament; but almost by constraint, as the sole outlet and expression of intense inward feeling. The spontaneous power of comparison is in some poetical minds entirely wanting; these of course cannot show to advantage as poets.—Another talent necessary to composition is the power of unfolding the meaning in an orderly manner. A poetical mind is often too impatient to explain itself justly; it is overpowered by a rush of emotions, which sometimes want of power, sometimes the indolence of inward enjoyment, prevents it from describing. Nothing is more difficult than to analyse the feelings of our own minds; and the power of doing so, whether natural or acquired, is clearly distinct from experiencing them. Yet, though distinct from the poetical talent, it is obviously necessary to its exhibition. Hence it is a common praise bestowed upon writers, that they express what we have often felt but could never describe. The power of arrangement, which is necessary for an extended poem, is a modification of the same talent;—being to poetry what method is to logic. Besides these qualifications, poetical composition requires that command of language which is the mere effect of practice. The poet is a compositor; words are his types; he must have them within reach, and in unlimited abundance. Hence the need of careful labour to the accomplished poet—not in order that his diction may attract, but that language may be subjected to him. He studies the art of composition as we might learn dancing or elocution; not that we may move or speak according to rule, but that by the very exercise our voice and carriage may become so unembarrassed as to allow of our doing what we will with them.

A talent for composition then is no essential part of poetry, though indispensable to its exhibition. Hence it would seem that attention to the language *for its own sake* evidences not the true poet but the mere artist. Pope is said to have tuned our tongue. We certainly owe much to him—his diction is rich, musical, and expressive. Still he is not on this account a poet; he elaborated his composition for its own sake. If we give him poetical praise on this account, we may as appropriately bestow it on a tasteful cabinetmaker. This does not forbid us to ascribe the grace of his verse to an inward principle of poetry, which supplied him with archetypes of the beautiful and splendid to work by. But a similar internal gift must direct the skill of every fancy-artist who subserves the luxuries and elegancies of life. On the other hand, though Virgil is celebrated as a master of composition, yet his style is so identified with his conceptions, as their outward development, as to preclude the possibility of our viewing the one apart from the other. In Milton, again, the harmony of the verse is but the echo of the inward music which the thoughts of the poet breathe. In Moore's style the ornament continually outstrips the sense. Cowper and Walter Scott, on the other hand, are slovenly in their versification. Sophocles writes, on the whole, without studied attention to the style; but Euripides frequently affects a simplicity and prettiness which exposed him to the ridicule of the comic poets. Lastly, the style of Homer's poems is perfect in their particular department. It is free, manly, simple, perspicuous, energetic, and varied. It is the style of one who rhapsodized without deference to hearer or judge, in an age prior to the temptations which more or less prevailed over succeeding writers—before the theatre had degraded poetry into an exhibition, and criticism narrowed it into an art.

## *NOTES*

1. The sudden inspiration, e.g. of the blind Oedipus, in the second play bearing his name, by which he is enabled, without a guide, to lead the way to his place of death, in our judgement, produces more poetical effect than all the skilful intricacy of the plot of the *Tyrannus*. The latter excites an interest which scarcely lasts beyond the first reading—the former *decies repetita placebit*.

2. In seeing the picture one is at the same time learning,—gathering the meaning of things.

3. It is the charm of the descriptive poetry of a religious mind, that nature is viewed in a moral connexion. Ordinary writers (e.g.) compare aged men to trees in autumn—a gifted poet will reverse the metaphor. Thus:

How quiet shows the woodland scene!
  Each flower and tree, its duty done,
Reposing in decay serene,
  *Like weary men when age is won . . .*

4. We would here mention Rogers's *Italy*, if such a cursory notice could convey our high opinion of its merit.

5. The difference between oratory and poetry is well illustrated by a passage in a recent tragedy.

*Col.* Joined! by what tie?
*Rien.* By hatred—
By danger—the two hands that tightest grasp
Each other—the two cords that soonest knit

A fast and stubborn tie; your true love knot
Is nothing to it. Faugh! the supple touch
Of pliant interest, or the dust of time,
Or the pin-point of temper, loose or rot
Or snap love's silken band. Fear and old hate,
They are sure weavers—they work for the storm,
The whirlwind, and the rocking surge; their knot
Endures till death.

The idea is good, and, if expressed in a line or two, might have been poetry—spread out into nine or ten lines, it yields but a languid and ostentatious declamation.

6. A living prelate, in his Academical Prelections, even suggests the converse of our position—'*Neque enim facile crediderim de eo qui semel hac imbutus fuerit disciplina, qui in id tota mentis acie assuefactus fuerit incumbere, ut quid sit in rebus decens, quid pulchrum, quid congruum, penitus intueretur, quin idem harum rerum perpetuum amorem foveat, et cum ab his studiis discesserit, etiam ad reliqua vitae officia earum imaginem quasi animo infixam transferat.*'

# *John Keats*

1795–1821

John Keats was born in Finsbury, North London, on October 31, 1795. His father managed a prosperous livery stable, but died in a riding accident in 1804, leaving John, two younger brothers, and one younger sister in dire financial straits. Keats's mother remarried soon after her husband's death, but left the children in the care of their elderly grandmother. Facing hardship, the children became fiercely devoted to each other, and grew even closer with the death of their mother from tuberculosis in 1810. This disease haunted Keats; it claimed both his brothers and eventually the poet himself at the age of 26.

Keats was not a precocious student. He attended John Clarke's school at Enfield from 1803 to 1811, but for most of his time there he seems to have been more interested in athletics than scholarship. Short of stature, Keats was stolid, scrappy, and even somewhat pugnacious. It was only in his last two or three years at school that Keats turned his energies to serious study. He began to read widely, even voluntarily attempting a translation of Vergil's *Aeneid*. He especially came to love the poetry of Edmund Spenser, and later emulated Spenser's imaginative abundance and metrical delicacy in his own verse.

After he left school in 1811, Keats was apprenticed to a surgeon for four years. In 1816, after some time as a student intern at Guy's Hospital in London, Keats passed his medical and apothecary examinations. But by now he had already begun seriously writing poetry: the sonnet "O Solitude" was published in May 1816. During this fruitful year he also wrote his magnificent "On First Looking into Chapman's Homer," and two long poems, *I Stood Tip-Toe* and *Sleep and Poetry*—uneven works that nonetheless showed great poetic promise. He soon gave up all thought of practicing medicine and devoted himself entirely to poetry.

Around this time Keats also became part of a literary and artistic circle that included the major Romantic figures of his time: Wordsworth, Coleridge, and Hazlitt among the "first generation," the leading younger Romantic Percy Shelley, the journalist and critic Leigh Hunt, and the painters Haydon and Severn, who became Keats's close friends. Hunt's anti-classicism was for a time the major influence on Keats's poetic style, and his first book of poems was dedicated to Hunt. Hazlitt later became a more important critical guide: his call for "gusto" in poetry found a willing student in the sensuous Keats. Not surprisingly, however, Keats had an ambivalent relationship to his poetic rivals Wordsworth and Shelley.

Socially, he found Wordsworth stiff and vain. But he came increasingly to admire Wordsworth's poetry, placing it above Milton's and second only to Shakespeare's in its explorations of "the dark passages" of the human heart. He found Shelley cold and aristocratic, and advised him in a famously presumptuous letter to be more poetical and less political. He would surely have been surprised by Shelley's elegaic effusions in *Adonais*—the poem that established Keats as a Romantic figure long before his poems were fully appreciated.

In 1818 Keats published *Endymion,* a 4,000-line mythological romance on which he had labored throughout the previous year. The poem was an ambitious and often sumptuous allegory of Keats's own growth as a poet, but it was flawed by immature diction and loose structure. The critics of the leading literary reviews savaged it. Legend has it that their abuse broke the fragile spirit of the young poet. In fact, Keats himself was the most severe critic of *Endymion,* but he obviously learned much from this splendid failure. In the next year-and-a-half Keats wrote some of the greatest lyrics in English poetry, including the five great odes; the two *Hyperion* fragments; *Lamia; The Eve of St. Agnes;* and several shorter poems.

Before this last great productive phase, Keats had taken an arduous walking tour of Scotland and the Lake District. It was during these travels that the usually-hearty poet first began to feel the effects of tuberculosis. He returned home in the fall of 1818 to find his brother Tom languishing in an advanced state of the disease. He nursed his brother devotedly until Tom's death on December 1st—finding relief from Tom's pained countenance, he said, in the "abstract images" of the first *Hyperion* fragment. At this time he also fell in love with Fanny Brawne, whom he described as a "beautiful and elegant, graceful, silly, fashionable and strange" girl of eighteen. She promised to marry him but did not reciprocate his ardent displays of affection. The experience of his brother's death, frustration in love, and perhaps also a foreboding of his own imminent death are all reflected in the greater psychological depth of Keats's later verse. He increasingly turned away from the desire for transcendence toward a tragic awareness of human mortality—an appreciation of the "agonies and the strifes of human hearts."

Keats's letters are invaluable not only for the rare insight they provide into the workings of a great imagination, but also for their more personal quality—a warm, courageous cheerfulness that Lionel Trilling has called nothing less than heroic. T. S. Eliot, usually a grudging critic of Romanticism, judged these letters to be "the most notable and the most important ever written by an English poet." The doctrine of "negative capability" that Keats here sets forth represents an original contribution to the poetic theory that has influenced modern poets of every school. And the Romantic faith in imagination finds in these letters one of its most eloquent and moving articulations.

# Selected Letters[1]

## *To BENJAMIN BAILEY*[2]

### *Saturday 22 Nov. 1817*

My dear Bailey,

I will get over the first part of this (*un*said)[3] Letter as soon as possible for it relates to the affair of poor Crips—To a Man of your nature such a Letter as Haydon's must have been extremely cutting—What occasions the greater part of the World's Quarrels? simply this, two Minds meet and do not understand each other time enough to prevent any shock or surprise at the conduct of either party—As soon as I had known Haydon three days I had got enough of his character not to have been surprised at such a Letter as he has hurt you with. Nor when I knew it was it a principle with me to drop his acquaintance although with you it would have been an imperious feeling. I wish you knew all that I think about Genius and the Heart—and yet I think you are thoroughly acquainted with my innermost breast in that respect, or you could not have known me even thus long and still hold me worthy to be your dear friend. In passing however I must say of one thing that has pressed upon me lately and encreased my Humility and capability of submission and that is this truth—Men of Genius are great as certain ethereal Chemicals operating on the Mass of neutral intellect—by ⟨*for* but⟩ they have not any individuality, any determined Character—I would call the top and head of those who have a proper self Men of Power—

But I am running my head into a Subject which I am certain I could not do justice to under five years S⟨t⟩udy and 3 vols octavo—and moreover long to be talking about the Imagination—so my dear Bailey do not think of this unpleasant affair if possible—do not—I defy any harm to come of it—I defy. I'll shall write to Crips this Week and request him to tell me all his goings on from time to time by Letter whererever I may be—it will all go on well so don't because you have suddenly discover'd a Coldness in Haydon suffer yourself to be teased. Do not my dear fellow. O I wish I was as certain of the end of all your troubles as that of your momentary start about the authenticity of the Imagination. I am certain of nothing but of the holiness of the Heart's affections and the truth of Imagination—What the imagination seizes as Beauty must be truth[4]—whether it existed before or not—for I have the same Idea of all our Passions as of Love they are all in their sublime, creative of essential Beauty. In a Word, you may know my favorite Speculation by my first Book and the little song I sent in my last—which is a representation from the fancy of the probable mode of operating in these Matters. The Imagination may be compared to Adam's dream[5]—he awoke and found it truth. I am the more zealous in this affair, because I have never yet been able to perceive how any thing can be known for truth by consequitive reasoning—and yet it must be. Can it be that even the greatest Philosopher ever arrived at his goal without putting aside numerous objections. However it may be, O for a Life of Sensations rather than of Thoughts! It is 'a Vision in the form of Youth' a Shadow of reality to come—and this consideration has further convinced me for it has come as auxiliary to another favorite Speculation of mine, that we shall enjoy ourselves here after by having what we called happiness on Earth repeated in a finer tone and so repeated. And yet such a fate can only befall those who delight in Sensation rather than hunger as you do after Truth. Adam's dream will do here and seems to be a conviction that Imagination and its empyreal reflection is the same as human Life and its Spiritual repetition. But as I was saying—the simple imaginative Mind may have its rewards in the repeti⟨ti⟩on of its own silent Working coming continually on the Spirit with a fine Suddenness—to compare great things with small—have you never by being Surprised with an old Melody—in a delicious place—by a delicious voice, fe⟨l⟩t over again your very Speculations and Surmises at the time it first operated on your Soul—do you not remember forming to yourself the singer's face more beautiful that ⟨*for* than⟩ it was possible and yet with the elevation of the Moment you did not think so—even then you were mounted on the Wings of Imagination so high—that the Protrotype must be here after—that delicious face you will see. What a time! I am continually running away from the subject—sure this cannot be exactly the case with a complex Mind—one that is imaginative and at the same time careful of its fruits—who would exist partly on Sensation partly on thought—to whom it is necessary that years should bring the philosophic Mind[6]—such an one I consider your's and therefore it is necessary to your eternal Happiness that you not only drink this old Wine of Heaven, which I shall call the redigestion of our most ethereal Musings on Earth; but also increase in knowledge and know all things. I am glad to hear you are in a fair way for Easter—you will soon get through your unpleasant reading and then!—but the world is full of troubles and I have not much reason to think myself pesterd with many—I think Jane or Marianne has a better opinion of me than I deserve—for really and truly I do not think my Brothers illness connected with mine—you know more of the real Cause than they do nor have I any chance of being rack'd as you have been—You perhaps at one time thought there was such a thing as Worldly Happiness to be arrived at, at certain periods of time marked out—you have of necessity from your disposition been thus led away—I scarcely remember counting upon any Happiness—I look not for it if it be not in the present hour—nothing startles me beyond the Moment. The setting Sun will always set me to rights—or if a Sparrow come before my Window I take part in its existince and pick about the Gravel. The first thing that strikes me on hearing a Misfortune having befalled another is this. 'Well it cannot be helped—he will have the pleasure of trying the resources of his spirit'—and I beg now my dear Bailey that hereafter should you observe any thing cold in me not to but ⟨*for* put⟩ it to the account of heartlessness but abstraction—for I assure you I sometimes feel not the influence of a Passion or affection during a whole week—and so long this sometimes continues I begin to suspect myself and the genui⟨ne⟩ness of my feelings at other times—thinking them a few barren Tragedy-tears—My Brother Tom is much improved—he is going to Devonshire—whither I shall follow him—at present I am just arrived at Dorking to change the Scene—change the Air and give me a spur to wind up my Poem, of which there are wanting 500 Lines. I should have been here a day sooner but the Reynoldses persuaded me to spop in Town to meet your friend Christie.[7] There were Rice and Martin—we talked about Ghosts. I will have some talk with Taylor and let you know—when please God I come down at Christmas. I will find that Examiner if possible. My best regards to Gleig. My Brothers to you and M[rs] Bentley's

Your affectionate friend
John Keats—

I want to say much more to you—a few hints will set me going.
Direct Burford Bridge near dorking

## *To GEORGE and THOMAS KEATS*

*Sunday 21 Dec. 1817*

Hampstead Sunday
22 December 1817

My dear Brothers,

I must crave your pardon for not having written ere this. * * * I saw Kean return to the public in Richard III.[8], and finely he did it, and at the request of Reynolds I went to criticise his Luke in Riches—the critique is in to-day's Champion, which I send you with the Examiner in which you will find very proper lamentation on the obsoletion of Christmas Gambols and pastimes:[9] but it was mixed up with so much egotism of that drivelling nature that pleasure is entirely lost. Hone the publisher's trial, you must find very amusing; and as Englishmen very encouraging—his *Not Guilty* is a thing, which not to have been, would have dulled still more Liberty's Emblazoning—Lord Ellenborough has been paid in his own coin—Wooler and Hone[10] have done us an essential service—I have had two very pleasant evenings with Dilke yesterday and to-day, and am at this moment just come from him and feel in the humour to go on with this, began in the morning, and from which he came to fetch me. I spent Friday evening with Wells[11] and went the next morning to see *Death on the Pale Horse*.[12] It is a wonderful picture, when West's age is considered; But there is nothing to be intense upon; no women one feels mad to kiss; no face swelling into reality—the excellence of every Art is its intensity, capable of making all disagreeables evaporate, from their being in close relationship with Beauty and Truth—Examine King Lear and you will find this exemplified throughout; but in this picture we have unpleasantness without any momentous depth of speculation excited, in which to bury its repulsiveness—The picture is larger than Christ rejected.[12] I dined with Haydon the Sunday after you left, and had a very pleasant day, I dined too (for I have been out too much lately) with Horace Smith and met his two Brothers with Hill[13] and Kingston and one Du Bois,[14] they only served to convince me, how superior humour is to wit in respect to enjoyment—These men say things which make one start, without making one feel, they are all alike; their manners are alike; they all know fashionables; they have a mannerism in their very eating and drinking, in their mere handling a Decanter—They talked of Kean and his low Company. Would I were with that Company—instead of yours said I to myself! I know such like acquaintance will never do for me and yet I am going to Reynolds, on Wednesday—Brown and Dilke walked with me and back from the Christmas pantomime. I had not a dispute but a disquisition with Dilke, on various subjects; several things dovetailed in my mind, and at once it struck me what quality went to form a Man of Achievement especially in Literature and which Shakespeare posessed so enormously—I mean *Negative Capability,* that is when man is capable of being in uncertainties, Mysteries, doubts, without any irritable reaching after fact and reason—Coleridge, for instance, would let go by a fine isolated verisimilitude[15] caught from the Penetralium of mystery, from being incapable of remaining Content with half knowledge. This pursued through Volumes would perhaps take us no further than this, that with a great poet the sense of Beauty overcomes every other consideration, or rather obliterates all consideration.

Shelley's poem[16] is out and there are words about its being objected too, as much as Queen Mab was. Poor Shelley I think he has his Quota of good qualities, in sooth la!! Write soon to your most sincere friend and affectionate Brother

John

## *To GEORGE AND THOMAS KEATS*

### *Friday 23 Jan. 1818*

Friday, 23 January 1818

My dear Brothers,

I was thinking what hindered me from writing so long, for I have many things to say to you and know not where to begin. It shall be upon a thing most interesting to you my Poem. Well! I have given the 1st Book to Taylor; he seemed more than satisfied with it, and to my surprise proposed publishing it in Quarto if Haydon would make a drawing of some event therein, for a Frontispiece. I called on Haydon, he said he would do anything I liked, but said he would rather paint a finished picture, from it, which he seems eager to do; this in a year or two will be a glorious thing for us; and it will be, for Haydon is struck with the 1st Book. I left Haydon and the next day received a letter from him, proposing to make, as he says with all his might, a finished Chalk sketch of my head, to be engraved in the first style and put at the head of my Poem, saying at the same time he had never done the thing for any human being, and that it must have considerable effect as he will put the name to it. I begin to day to copy my 2[nd] Book—"thus far into the bowels of the Land"[17]—You shall hear whether it will be Quarto or non Quarto, picture or non Picture. Leigh Hunt I showed my 1[st] Book to, he allows it not much merit as a whole; says it is unnatural and made ten objections to it in the mere skimming over. He says the conversation is unnatural and too high-flown for Brother and Sister. Says it should be simple forgetting do ye mind that they are both overshadowed by a Supernatural Power, and of force could not speak like Franchesca in the Rimini. He must first prove that Caliban's poetry is unnatural,—This with me completely overturns his objections—the fact is he and Shelley are hurt, and perhaps justly, at my not having showed them the affair officiously—and from several hints I have had they appear much disposed to dissect and anatomize, any trip or slip I may have made.—But who's afraid? Ay! Tom! demme if I am. I went last Tuesday, an hour too late, to Hazlitt's Lecture on poetry, got there just as they were coming out, when all these pounced upon me—Hazlitt, John Hunt and Son, Wells, Bewick, all the Landseers,[18] Bob Harris, Rox[18] of the Burrough aye and more; the Landseers enquired after you particularly—I know not whether Wordsworth has left town—But Sunday I dined with Hazlitt and Haydon, also that I took Haslam with me—I dined with Brown lately. Dilke having taken the Champion Theatricals[19] was obliged to be in town. Fanny has returned to Walthamstow—M[r] Abbey appeared very glum the last time I went to see her, and said in an indirect way that I had no business there—Rice has been ill, but has been mending much lately—

I think a little change has taken place in my intellect lately—I cannot bear to be uninterested or unemployed, I, who for so long a time have been addicted to passiveness. Nothing is finer for the purposes of great productions than a very gradual ripening of the intellectual powers. As an instance of this—observe—I sat down yesterday to read "King Lear" once again the thing appeared to demand the prologue of a Sonnet. I wrote it and began to read[20]—(I know you would like to see it.)

"On sitting down to ⟨read⟩ King Lear once again"

O golden tongued Romance with serene Lute!
  Fair-plumed Syren! Queen of[21] far-away!
  Leave melodizing on this wintry day,
Shut up thine olden volume and be mute.
Adieu! for once again the fierce dispute,
  Betwixt Hell torment and impassion'd Clay
  Must I burn through; once more assay
The bitter Sweet of this Shakespeareian fruit.
Chief Poet! and ye clouds of Albion,
  Begetters of our deep eternal theme,
When I am through the old oak forest gone
  Let me not wander in a barren dream

But when I am consumed with the Fire
Give me new Phœnix-wings[22] to fly at my desire

So you see I am getting at it, with a sort of determination and strength, though verily I do not feel it at this moment—this is my fourth letter this morning, and I feel rather tired, and my head rather swimming—so I will leave it open till to-morrow's post—

I am in the habit of taking my papers to Dilke's and copying there; so I chat and proceed at the same time. I have been there at my work this evening, and the walk over the Heath[23] takes off all sleep, so I will even proceed with you—I left off short in my last, just as I began an account of a private theatrical—Well it was of the lowest order, all greasy and oily, insomuch that if they had lived in olden times, when signs were hung over the doors; the only appropriate one for that oily place would have been—a guttered Candle—They played John Bull, The Review—and it was to conclude with Bombastes Furioso[24]—I saw from a Box the 1st Act of John Bull,[25] then I went to Drury and did not return till it was over—when by Wells's interest we got behind the scenes—there was not a yard wide all the way round for actors, scene-shifters and interlopers to move in; for 'Nota Bene' the Green Room was under the stage and there was I threatened over and over again to be turned out by the oily scene-shifters—There did I hear a little painted Trollop own, very candidly, that she had failed in Mary, with a "damned if she'd play a serious part again, as long as she lived", and at the same time she was habited as the Quaker in the Review—There was a quarrel, and a fat good-natured looking girl in soldiers' Clothes wished she had only been a man for Tom's sake—One fellow began a song but an unlucky finger-point from the Gallery sent him off like a shot, one chap was dressed to kill for the King in Bombastes, and he stood at the edge of the scene in the very sweat of anxiety to show himself, but Alas the thing was not played. The sweetest morsel of the night[26] moreover was, that the Musicians began pegging and fagging away at an overture—never did you see faces more in earnest, three times did they play it over, dropping all kinds of correctness and still did not the curtain draw up—Well then they went into a country-dance, then into a region they well knew, into their old boonsome Pothouse, and then to see how pompous o' the sudden they turned; how they looked about and chatted; how they did not care a damn; was a great treat—

I hope I have not tired you by this filling up of the dash in my last,—Constable, the bookseller, has offered Reynolds ten guineas a sheet to write for his Magazine—it is an Edinburgh one which Blackwood's started up in opposition to. Hunt said he was nearly sure that the 'Cockney School' was written by Scott[27] so you are right Tom!—There are no more little bits of news I can remember at present

I remain,
My dear Brothers, Your very affectionate Brother
John

## *To JOHN HAMILTON REYNOLDS*

### *Thursday 19 Feb. 1818*

My dear Reynolds,

I had an idea that a Man might pass a very pleasant life in this manner—let him on a certain day read a certain Page of full Poesy or distilled Prose, and let him wander with it, and muse upon it, and reflect upon it, and bring home to it, and prophesy upon it, and dream upon it, until it becomes stale—but when will it do so? Never. When Man has arrived at a certain ripeness in intellect any one grand and spiritual passage serves him as a starting-post towards all "the two-and-thirty Palaces".[28] How happy is such a voyage of conception, what delicious diligent Indolence! A doze upon a sofa does not hinder it, and a nap upon Clover engenders ethereal finger-pointings—the prattle of a child gives it wings, and the converse of middle-age a strength to beat them—a strain of music conducts to "an odd angle of the Isle",[29] and when the leaves whisper it puts a girdle round the earth.[30] Nor will this sparing touch of noble Books be any irreverence to their Writers—for perhaps the honors paid by Man to Man are trifles in comparison to the Benefit done by great Works to the Spirit and pulse of good[31] by their mere passive existence. Memory should not be called knowledge. Many have original minds who do not think it—they are led away by Custom. Now it appears to me that almost any Man may like the spider spin from his own inwards his own airy Citadel—the points of leaves and twigs on which the spider begins her work are few, and she fills the air with a beautiful circuiting. Man should be content with as few points to tip with the fine Web of his Soul, and weave a tapestry empyrean full of symbols for his spiritual eye, of softness for his spiritual touch, of space for his wandering, of distinctness for his luxury. But the Minds of Mortals are so different and bent on such diverse journeys that it may at first appear impossible for any common taste and fellowship to exist between two or three under these suppositions. It is however quite the contrary. Minds would leave each other in contrary directions, traverse each other in numberless points, and at last greet each other at the journey's end. An old Man and a child would talk together and the old Man be led on his path and the child left thinking. Man should not dispute or assert but whisper results to his neighbour and thus by every germ of spirit sucking the sap from mould ethereal every human[32] might become great, and Humanity instead of being a wide heath of Furze[33] and Briars with here and there a remote Oak or Pine, would become a grand democracy of Forest Trees! It has been an old comparison for our urging on—the Beehive; however, it seems to me that we should rather be the flower than the Bee—for it is a false notion that more is gained by receiving than giving—no, the receiver and the giver are equal in their benefits. The flower, I doubt not, receives a fair guerdon from the Bee—its leaves blush deeper in the next spring—and who shall say between Man and Woman which is the most delighted? Now it is more noble to sit like Jove than to fly like Mercury—let us not therefore go hurrying about and collecting honey, bee-like buzzing here and there impatiently from a knowledge of what is to be aimed at; but let us open our leaves like a flower and be passive and receptive—budding patiently under the eye of Apollo and taking hints from every noble insect that favours us with a visit—sap will be given us for meat and dew for drink. I was led into these thoughts, my dear Reynolds, by the beauty of the morning operating on a sense of Idleness—I have not read any Books—the Morning said I was right—I had no idea but of the morning, and the thrush said I was right—seeming to say,

> O thou whose face hath felt the Winter's wind,[34]
> Whose eye has seen the snow-clouds hung in mist,
> And the black elm-tops 'mong the freezing stars,
> To thee the Spring will be a harvest-time.
> O thou, whose only book has been the light
> Of supreme darkness which thou feddest on
> Night after night when Phœbus was away,
> To thee the Spring shall be a triple morn.
> O fret not after knowledge—I have none,
> And yet my song comes native with the warmth.
> O fret not after knowledge—I have none,
> And yet the Evening listens. He who saddens
> At thought of idleness cannot be idle,
> And he's awake who thinks himself asleep.

Now I am sensible all this is a mere sophistication (however it may neighbour to any truths), to excuse my own indolence—so I will not deceive myself that Man should be equal with Jove—but think himself very well off as a sort of scullion-Mercury, or even a humble Bee. It is no matter whether I am right or wrong, either one way or another, if there is sufficient to lift a little time from your shoulders.

Your affectionate friend
John Keats—

## *To GEORGE AND THOMAS KEATS*

### *Saturday 21 Feb. 1818*

Hampstead, Saturday.
February 21st. 1818—

My dear Brothers

I am extremely sorry to have given you so much uneasiness by not writing, however you know good news is no news or vice versâ. I do not like to write a short letter to you, or you would have had one long before. The weather although boisterous to-day has been very much milder; and I think Devonshire is not the last place to receive a temperate Change. I have been abominably idle since you left, but have just turned over a new leaf, and used as a marker a letter of excuse to an invitation from Horace Smith. The occasion of my writing to-day is the enclosed letter, by Postmark from Miss W⟨ylie⟩. Does she expect you in town George? I received a letter the other day from Haydon, in which he says, his Essays on the Elgin Marbles are being translated into Italian, the which he superintends. I did not mention that I had seen the British Gallery, there are some nice things by Stark,[35] and Bathsheba by Wilkie, which is condemned.[36] I could not bear Alston's[37] Uriel.

Reynolds has been very ill for some time, confined to the house, and had leeches applied to the chest; when I saw him on Wednesday he was much the same, and he is in the worst place in the world for amendment, among the strife of women's tongues, in a hot and parch'd room: I wish he would move to Butler's[38] for a short time. The Thrushes and Blackbirds have ben singing me into an idea that it was Spring, and almost that leaves were on the trees. So that black clouds and boisterous winds seem to have mustered and collected to full Divan, for the purpose of convincing me to the contrary. Taylor says my poem shall be out in a month, I think he will be out before it.— — —

The thrushes are singing now as if they would speak to the winds, because their big brother Jack, the Spring, was not far off. I am reading Voltaire and Gibbon, although I wrote to Reynolds the other day to prove reading of no use; I have not seen Hunt since, I am a good deal with Dilke and Brown, we are very thick; they are very kind to me, they are well. I don't think I could stop in Hampstead but for their neighbourhood. I hear Hazlitt's lectures regularly, his last was on Gray, Collins, Young, &c., and he gave a very fine piece of discriminating Criticism on Swift, Voltaire, and Rabelais. I was very disappointed at his treatment of Chatterton. I generally meet with many I know there. Lord Byron's 4th Canto is expected out, and I heard somewhere, that Walter Scott has a new Poem in readiness. I am sorry that Wordsworth has left a bad impression where-ever he visited in town by his egotism, Vanity, and bigotry. Yet he is a great poet if not a philosopher. I have not yet read Shelly's Poem,[39] I don't suppose you have it yet, at the Teignmouth libraries. These double letters must come rather heavy, I hope you have a moderate portion of cash, but don't fret at all, if you have not—Lord! I intend to play at Cut and run as well as Falstaff, that is to say, before he got so lusty.

I remain praying for your health my dear Brothers
Your Affectionate Brother.
John—

## *To JOHN TAYLOR*

### *Friday 27 Feb. 1818*

Hampstead 27 Feby—

My dear Taylor,

Your alteration strikes me as being a great improvement—the page looks much better. And now I will attend to the Punctuations you speak of—the comma should be at *soberly*,[40] and in the other passage the comma should follow *quiet*,[41]. I am extremely indebted to you for this attention and also for your after admonitions—It is a sorry thing for me that any one should have to overcome Prejudices in reading my Verses—that affects me more than any hypercriticism on any particular Passage. In *Endymion* I have most likely but moved into the Go-cart from the leading strings. In Poetry I have a few Axioms, and you will see how far I am from their Centre. I$^{st}$. I think Poetry should surprise by a fine excess and not by Singularity—it should strike the Reader as a wording of his own highest thoughts, and appear almost a Remembrance—2$^{nd}$. Its touches of Beauty should never be half way ther⟨e⟩ by making the reader breathless instead of content: the rise, the progress, the setting of imagery should like the Sun come natural too him—shine over him and set soberly although in magnificence leaving him in the Luxury of twilight—but it is easier to think what Poetry should be than to write it—and this leads me on to another axiom. That if Poetry comes not as naturally as the Leaves to a tree it had better not come at all. However it may be with me I cannot help looking into new courses with 'O for a Muse of fire to ascend!'[42] If Endymion serves me as a Pioneer perhaps I ought to be content. I have great reason to be content, for thank God I can read and perhaps understand Shakspeare to his depths, and I have I am sure many friends, who, if I fail, will attribute any change in my Life and Temper to Humbleness rather than to Pride—to a cowering under the Wings of great Poets rather than to a Bitterness that I am not appreciated.[43] I am anxious to get *Endymion* printed that I may forget it and proceed. I have coppied the 3$^{rd}$ Book and have begun the 4$^{th}$. On running my Eye over the Proofs—I saw one Mistake I will notice it presently and also any others if there be any. There should be no comma in 'the raft branch down sweeping from a tall ash top'.[44] I have besides made one or two alterations and also altered the 13 Line Page 32 to make sense of it as you will see. I will take care the Printer shall not trip up my Heels. There should be no dash after Dryope in this Line 'Dryope's lone lulling of her Child.[45] Remember me to Percy Street.

Your sincere and oblig$^{d}$ friend
John Keats—

P.S. You shall have a sho⟨r⟩t *Preface* in good time—

## *To JOHN TAYLOR*

### *Friday 24 April 1818*

Teignmouth Friday

My dear Taylor,

I think I did very wrong to leave you to all the trouble of Endymion—but I could not help it then—another time I shall be more bent to all sort of troubles and disagreeables—Young Men for some time have an idea that such a thing as happiness is to be had and therefore are extremely impatient under any unpleasant restraining—in time however, of such stuff is the world about them, they know better and instead of striving from Uneasiness greet it as an habitual sensation, a pannier which is to weigh upon them through life.

And in proportion to my disgust at the task is my sense of your kindness & anxiety—the book pleased me much—it is very free from faults; and although there are one or two words I should wish replaced, I see in many places an improvement greatly to the purpose—

I think those speeches which are related—those parts where the speaker repeats a speech—such as Glaucus' repetition of Circe's words, should have inverted commas to every line—In this there is a little confusion. If we divide the speeches into *identical* and *related:* and to the former put merely one inverted comma at the beginning and another at the end; and to the latter inverted commas before every line, the book will be better understood at the first glance. Look at pages 126 and 127 you will find in the 3 line the beginning of a *related* speech marked thus "Ah! art awake—while at the same time in the next page the continuation of the *identical speech* is mark'd in the same manner "Young Man of Latmos—You will find on the other side all the parts which should have inverted commas to every line.

I was purposing to travel over the north this Summer—there is but one thing to prevent me—I know nothing I have read nothing and I mean to follow Solomon's directions of 'get Wisdom—get understanding'[46]—I find cavalier days are gone by. I find that I can have no enjoyment in the World but continual drinking of Knowledge—I find there is no worthy pursuit but the idea of doing some good for the world—some do it with their society—some with their wit—some with their benevolence—some with a sort of power of conferring pleasure and good humour on all they meet and in a thousand ways all equally dutiful to the command of Great Nature—there is but one way for me—the road lies th⟨r⟩ough application study and thought. I will pursue it and to that end purpose retiring for some years. I have been hovering for some time between an exquisite sense of the luxurious and a love for Philosophy—were I calculated for the former I should be glad—but as I am not I shall turn all my soul to the latter.

My Brother Tom is getting better and I hope I shall see both him and Reynolds well before I retire from the World. I shall see you soon and have some talk about what Books I shall take with me—

Your very sincere friend
John Keats

Remember me to Hessey—Woodhouse and Percy Street

## *To JOHN HAMILTON REYNOLDS*

*Sunday 3 May 1818*

Teignmouth, May 3$^{d}$.

My dear Reynolds.

What I complain of is that I have been in so an uneasy a state of Mind as not to be fit to write to an invalid. I cannot write to any length under a disguised feeling. I should have loaded you with an addition of gloom, which I am sure you do not want. I am now thank God in a humour to give you a good groats worth—for Tom, after a Night without a Wink of sleep, and overburdened with fever, has got up after a refreshing day sleep and is better than he has been for a long time; and you I trust have been again round the Common without any effect but refreshment.—As to the Matter I hope I can say with Sir Andrew[47] "I have matter enough in my head" in your favor And now, in the second place, for I reckon that I have finished my Imprimis, I am glad you blow up the weather all through your letter there is a leaning towards a climate-curse, and you know what a delicate satisfaction there is in having a vexation anathematized: one would think there has been growing up for these last four thousand years, a grandchild Scion of the old forbidden tree, and that some modern Eve had just violated it; and that there was come with double charge

Notus and Afer, black with thunderous clouds
From Sierraleona.[48]

I shall breathe worsted stockings[49] sooner than I thought for—Tom wants to be in town—we will have some such days upon the heath like that of last summer—and why not with the same book: or what say you to a black-Letter Chaucer[50] printed in 1596: aye I've got one huzza! I shall have it bounden gothique—a nice sombre binding—it will go a little way to unmodernize. And also I see no reason, because I have been away this last month, why I should not have a peep at your Spencerian[51]—notwithstanding you speak of your office, in my thought a little too early, for I do not see why a Mind like yours is not capable of harbouring and digesting the whole Mystery of Law as easily as Parson Hugh does Pepins[52]—which did not hinder him from his poetic Canary—Were I to study physic or rather Medicine again, I feel it would not make the least difference in my Poetry; when the Mind is in its infancy a Bias is in reality a Bias, but when we have acquired more strength, a Bias becomes no Bias. Every department of Knowledge we see excellent and calculated towards a great whole. I am so convinced of this, that I am glad at not having given away my medical Books, which I shall again look over to keep alive the little I know thitherwards; and moreover intend through you and Rice to become a sort of pip-civilian. An extensive knowledge is needful to thinking people—it takes away the heat and fever; and helps, by widening speculation, to ease the Burden of the Mystery:[53] a thing I begin to understand a little, and which weighed upon you in the most gloomy and true sentence in your Letter. The difference of high Sensations with and without knowledge appears to me this—in the latter case we are falling continually ten thousand fathoms deep[54] and being blown up again without wings and with all ⟨the⟩ horror of a bare shouldered creature[55]—in the former case, our shoulders are fledge,[54] and we go thro' the same air and space without fear. This is running one's rigs on the score of abstracted benefit—when we come to human Life and the affections it is impossible ⟨to know⟩ how a parallel of breast and head can be drawn—(you will forgive me for thus privately treading out ⟨of⟩ my depth, and take it for treading as schoolboys tread the water)—It is impossible to know how far Knowledge will console us for the death of a friend and the ill "that flesh is heir to"[56]—With respect to the affections and Poetry you must know by a sympathy my thoughts that way; and I dare say these few lines will be but a ratification: I wrote them on May-day—and intend to finish the ode all in good time.—

> Mother of Hermes! and still youthful Maia!
> May I sing to thee
> As thou wast hymned on the shores of Baiæ?
> Or may I woo thee
> In earlier Sicilian? or thy smiles
> Seek as they once were sought, in Grecian isles,
> By Bards who died content on pleasant sward,
> Leaving great verse unto a little clan?
> O give me their old vigour, and unheard,
> Save of the quiet Primrose, and the span
> Of Heaven and few ears
> Rounded by thee My song should die away
> Content as theirs
> Rich in the simple worship of a day.—

You may be anxious to know for fact to what sentence in your Letter I allude. You say "I fear there is little chance of any thing else in this life". you seem by that to have been going through with a more painful and acute zest the same labyrinth that I have—I have come to the same conclusion thus far. My Branchings out therefrom have been numerous: one of them is the consideration of Wordsworth's genius and as a help, in the manner of gold being the meridian Line of worldly wealth,—how he differs from Milton.—And here I have nothing but surmises, from an uncertainty whether Miltons apparently less anxiety for Humanity proceeds from his seeing further or no than Wordsworth: And whether Wordsworth has in truth epic passion, and martyrs himself to the human heart, the main region of his song[57]—In regard to his genius alone—we find what he says true as far as we have experienced and we can judge no further but by larger experience—for axioms in philosophy are not axioms until they are proved upon our pulses: We read fine things but never feel them to the full until we have gone[58] the same steps as the Author.—I know this is not plain; you will know exactly my meaning when I say, that now I shall relish Hamlet more than I ever have done—Or, better—You are sensible no Man can set down Venery as a bestial or joyless thing until he is sick of it and therefore all philosophizing on it would be mere wording. Until we are sick, we understand not;—in fine, as Byron says, "Knowledge is Sorrow";[59] and I go on to say that "Sorrow is Wisdom"—and further for aught we can know for certainty "Wisdom is folly"!—So you see how I have run away from Wordsworth, and Milton, and shall still run away from what was in my head, to observe, that some kind of letters are good squares others handsome ovals, and other some orbicular, others spheroid—

and why should there not be another species with two rough edges like a Rat-trap? I hope you will find all my long letters of that species, and all will be well; for by merely touching the spring delicately and etherially, the rough edged will fly immediately into a proper compactness; and thus you may make a good wholesome loaf, with your own leaven in it, of my fragments—If you cannot find this said Rat-trap sufficiently tractable—alas for me, it being an impossibility in grain for my ink to stain otherwise: If I scribble long letters I must play my vagaries. I must be too heavy, or too light, for whole pages—I must be quaint and free of Tropes and figures—I must play my draughts as I please, and for my advantage and your erudition, crown a white with a black, or a black with a white, and move into black or white, far and near as I please—I must go from Hazlitt to Patmore,[60] and make Wordsworth and Coleman[61] play at leap-frog—or keep one of them down a whole half-holiday at fly the garter—"from Gray to Gay, from Little to Shakespeare"[62]—Also, as a long cause requires two or more sittings of the Court, so a long letter will require two or more sittings of the Breech wherefore I shall resume after dinner.—

Have you not seen a Gull, an orc, a Sea Mew[63], or any thing to bring this Line to a proper length, and also fill up this clear part; that like the Gull I may *dip*[64]—I hope, not out of sight—and also, like a Gull, I hope to be lucky in a good sized fish—This crossing a letter is not without its association—for chequer work leads us naturally to a Milkmaid, a Milkmaid to Hogarth Hogarth to Shakespeare Shakespear to Hazlitt—Hazlitt to Shakespeare and thus by merely pulling an apron string we set a pretty peal of Chimes at work—Let them chime on while, with your patience, I will return to Wordsworth—whether or no he has an extended vision or a circumscribed grandeur—whether he is an eagle in his nest, or on the wing—And to be more explicit and to show you how tall I stand by the giant, I will put down a simile of human life as far as I now perceive it; that is, to the point to which I say we both have arrived at—Well—I compare human life to a large Mansion of Many Apartments, two of which I can only describe, the doors of the rest being as yet shut upon me. The first we step into we call the infant or thoughtless Chamber, in which we remain as long as we do not think—We remain there a long while, and notwithstanding the doors of the second Chamber remain wide open, showing a bright appearance, we care not to hasten to it; but are at length imperceptibly impelled by the awakening of this thinking principle within us—we no sooner get into the second Chamber, which I shall call the Chamber of Maiden-Thought, than we become intoxicated with the light and the atmosphere, we see nothing but pleasant wonders, and think of delaying there for ever in delight: However among the effects this breathing is father of is that tremendous one of sharpening one's vision into the heart and nature of Man—of convincing one's nerves that the world is full of Misery and Heartbreak, Pain, Sickness and oppression[65]—whereby this Chamber of Maiden Thought becomes gradually darken'd and at the same time on all sides of it many doors are set open—but all dark—all leading to dark passages—We see not the ballance of good and evil. We are in a Mist. *We* are now in that state—We feel the "burden of the Mystery", To this Point was Wordsworth come, as far as I can conceive when he wrote 'Tintern Abbey' and it seems to me that his Genius is explorative of those dark Passages. Now if we live, and go on thinking, we too shall explore them—he is a Genius and superior ⟨to⟩ us, in so far as he can, more than we, make discoveries, and shed a light in them—Here I must think Wordsworth is deeper than Milton—though I think it has depended more upon the general and gregarious advance of intellect, than individual greatness of Mind—From the Paradise Lost and the other Works of Milton, I hope it is not too presuming, even between ourselves to say, that his Philosophy, human and divine, may be tolerably understood by one not much advanced in years, In his time englishmen were just emancipated from a great superstition—and Men had got hold of certain points and resting places in reasoning which were too newly born to be doubted, and too much opposed by the Mass of Europe not to be thought etherial and authentically divine—who could gainsay his ideas on virtue, vice, and Chastity in Comus, just at the time of the dismissal of Cod-pieces and a hundred other disgraces? who would not rest satisfied with his hintings at good and evil in the Paradise Lost, when just free from the inquisition and burning in Smithfield? The Reformation produced such immediate and great benefits, that Protestantism was considered under the immediate eye of heaven, and its own remaining Dogmas and superstitions, then, as it were, regenerated, constituted those resting places and seeming sure points of Reasoning—from that I have mentioned, Milton, whatever he may have thought in the sequel, appears to have been content with these by his writings—He did not think into the human heart, as Wordsworth has done—Yet Milton as a Philosopher, had sure as great powers as Wordsworth—What is then to be inferr'd? O many things—It proves there is really a grand march of intellect—, It proves that a mighty providence subdues the mightiest Minds to the service of the time being, whether it be in human Knowledge or Religion—I have often pitied a Tutor who has to hear "Nom: Musa"—so often dinn'd into his ears—I hope you may not have the same pain in this scribbling—I may have read these things before, but I never had even a thus dim perception of them; and moreover I like to say my lesson to one who will endure my tediousness for my own sake—After all there is certainly something real in the World—Moore's present to Hazlitt[66] is real—I like that Moore, and am glad I saw him at the Theatre just before I left Town. Tom has spit a leetle blood this afternoon, and that is rather a damper—but I know—the truth is there is something real in the World. Your third Chamber of Life shall be a lucky and a gentle one—stored with the wine of love—and the Bread of Friendship. When you see George if he should not have received a letter from me tell him he will find one at home most likely—tell Bailey I hope soon to see him—Remember me to all. The leaves have been out here, for mony a day—I have written to George for the first stanzas of my Isabel—I shall have them soon and will copy the whole out for you.

Your affectionate friend
John Keats.

## *To RICHARD WOODHOUSE*

### *Tuesday 27 Oct. 1818*

My dear Woodhouse,

Your Letter gave me a great satisfaction; more on account of its friendliness, than any relish of that matter in it which is accounted so acceptable in the 'genus irritabile'.[67] The best answer I can give you is in a clerk-like manner to make some observations on two principle points, which seem to point like indices into the midst of the whole pro and con, about genius, and views and atchievements and ambition and cœtera. I$^{st}$. As to the poetical Character itself (I mean that sort of which, if I am any thing, I am a Member; that sort distinguished from the wordsworthian or egotistical sublime; which is a thing per se and stands alone) it is not itself—it has no self—it is every thing and nothing—It has no character—it enjoys light and shade; it lives in gusto, be it foul or fair, high or low, rich or poor, mean or elevated—It has as much delight in conceiving an Iago as an Imogen. What shocks the virtuous philosopher, delights the camelion Poet. It does no harm from its relish of the dark side of things any more than from its taste for the bright one; because they both end in speculation. A Poet is the most unpoetical of any thing in existence; because he has no Identity—he is continually in for—[68] and filling some other Body—The Sun, the Moon, the Sea and Men and Women who are creatures of impulse are poetical and have about them an unchangeable attribute—the poet has none; no identity—he is certainly the most unpoetical of all God's Creatures. If then he has no self, and if I am a Poet, where is the Wonder that I should say I would write no more? Might I not at that very instant have been cogitating on the Characters of Saturn and Ops?[69] It is a wretched thing to confess; but is a very fact that not one word I ever utter can be taken for granted as an opinion growing out of my identical nature—how can it, when I have no nature? When I am in a room with People if I ever am free from speculating on creations of my own brain, then not myself goes home to myself: but the identity of every one in the room begins to ⟨*for* so⟩ to press upon me that I am in a very little time an⟨ni⟩hilated—not only among Men; it would be the same in a Nursery of children: I know not whether I make myself wholly understood: I hope enough so to let you see that no dependence is to be placed on what I said that day.

In the second place I will speak of my views, and of the life I purpose to myself. I am ambitious of doing the world some good: if I should be spared that may be the work of maturer years—in the interval I will assay to reach to as high a summit in Poetry as the nerve bestowed upon me will suffer. The faint conceptions I have of Poems to come brings the blood frequently into my forehead. All I hope is that I may not lose all interest in human affairs—that the solitary indifference I feel for applause even from the finest Spirits, will not blunt any acuteness of vision I may have. I do not think it will—I feel assured I should write from the mere yearning and fondness I have for the Beautiful even if my night's labours should be burnt every morning, and no eye ever shine upon them. But even now I am perhaps not speaking from myself: but from some character in whose soul I now live. I am sure however that this next sentence is from myself. I feel your anxiety, good opinion and friendliness in the highest degree, and am

Your's most sincerely
John Keats

## *To GEORGE AND GEORGIANA KEATS*

### *Friday 17-Monday 27 Sept. 1819*

Winchester Sept$^{r}$ Friday.

My dear George,

I was closely employed in reading and composition, in this place, whither I had come from Shanklin, for the convenience of a library, when I received your last, dated July 24$^{th}$. You will have seen by the short Letter I wrote from Shanklin how matters stand between us and M$^{rs}$ Jennings. They had not at all mov'd and I knew no way of overcoming the inveterate obstinacy of our affairs. On receiving your last I immediately took a place in the same night's coach for London.[70] M$^{r}$ Abbey behaved extremely well to me, appointed Monday evening at 7 to meet me and observed that he should drink tea at that hour. I gave him the inclosed note[71] and showed him the last leaf of yours to me. He really appeared anxious about it; promised he would forward your money as quickly as possible. I think I mention'd that Walton[72] was dead—He will apply to M$^{r}$ Gliddon the partner; endeavour to get rid of M$^{rs}$ Jennings's claim and be expeditious. He has received an answer from my Letter to Fry[79]—that is something. We are certainly in a very low estate: I say we, for I am in such a situation that were it not for the assistance of Brown & Taylor I must be as badly off as a Man can be. I could not raise any sum by the promise of any Poem—no, not by the mortgage of my intellect. We must wait a little while. I really have hopes of success. I have finish'd a Tragedy[74] which if it succeeds will enable me to sell what I may have in manuscript to a good a⟨d⟩vantage. I have pass'd my time in reading, writing and fretting—the last I intend to give up and stick to the other two. They are the only chances of benefit to us. Your wants will be a fresh spur to me. I assure you you shall more than share what I can get, whilst I am still young—the time may come when age will make me more selfish. I have not been well treated by the world—and yet I have capitally well. I do not know a Person to whom so many purse strings would fly open as to me—if I could possibly take advantage of them—which I cannot do for none of the owners of these purses are rich. Your present situation I will not suffer myself to dwell upon—when misfortunes are so real we are glad enough to escape them, and the thought of them. I cannot help thinking M$^{r}$ Audubon[75] a dishonest man. Why did he make you believe that he was a Man of Property? How is it his circumstances have altered so suddenly? In truth I do not believe you fit to deal with the world, or at least the american mould.[76] But good God—

who can avoid these chances—You have done your best—Take matters as coolly as you can, and confidently expecting help from England, act as if no help was nigh. Mine I am sure is a tolerable tragedy—it would have been a bank to me, if just as I had finish'd it I had not heard of Kean's resolution to go to America. That was the worst news I could have had. There is no actor can do the principal character[77] besides Kean. At Covent Garden there is a great chance of its being damn'd. Were it to succeed even there it would lift me out of the mire. I mean the mire of a bad reputation which is continually rising against me. My name with the literary fashionables is vulgar—I am a weaver boy[78] to them—a Tragedy would lift me out of this mess. And mess it is as far as it regards our Pockets. But be not cast down any more than I am; I feel I can bear real ills better than imaginary ones. Whenever I find myself growing vapourish, I rouse myself, wash and put on a clean shirt brush my hair and clothes, tie my shoestrings neatly and in fact adonize as I were going out—then all clean and comfortable I sit down to write.[79] This I find the greatest relief—Besides I am becoming accustom'd to the privations of the pleasures of sense. In the midst of the world I live like a Hermit. I have forgot how to lay plans for enjoyment of any Pleasure. I feel I can bear any thing,—any misery, even imprisonment—so long as I have neither wife nor child. Perhaps you will say yours are your only comfort—they must be. I return'd to Winchester the day before yesterday and am now here alone, for Brown some days before I left, went to Bedhampton and there he will be for the next fortnight. The term of his house[80] will be up in the middle of next month when we shall return to Hampstead. On Sunday I dined with your Mother and Hen and Charles in Henrietta Street—M^rs^ and Miss Millar were in the Country. Charles had been but a few days returned from Paris. I dare say you will have letters expressing the motives of his Journey. M^rs^ Wylie and Miss Waldegrave seem as quiet as two Mice there alone. I did not show your last—I thought it better not. For better times will certainly come and why should they be unhappy in the meantime. On Monday Morning I went to Walthamstow. Fanny look'd better than I had seen her for some time. She complains of not hearing from you appealing to me as if it was half my fault. I had been so long in retirement that London appeared a very odd place. I could not make out I had so many acquaintance, and it was a whole day before I could feel among Men. I had another strange sensation there was not one house I felt any pleasure to call at. Reynolds was in the Country and saving himself I am p⟨r⟩ejudiced against all that family. Dilke and his wife and child were in the Country. Taylor was at Nottingham. I was out and every body was out. I walk'd about the Streets as in a strange land. Rice was the only one at home. I pass'd some time with him. I know him better since we have liv'd a month together in the isle of Wight. He is the most sensible, and even wise Man I know—he has a few John Bull prejudices; but they improve him. His illness is at times alarming. We are great friends, and there is no one I like to pass a day with better. Martin call'd in to bid him good bye before he set out for Dublin. If you would like to hear one of his jokes here is one which at the time we laugh'd at a good deal. A Miss—— with three young Ladies, one of them Martin's sister had come a gadding in the

Isle of wight and took for a few days a Cottage opposite ours—we dined with them one day, and as I was saying they had fish. Miss——said she thought *they tasted of the boat*. No says Martin very seriously they haven't been kept long enough. I saw Haslam he is very much occupied with love and business being one of M^r^ Saunders executors and Lover to a young woman. He show'd me her Picture by Severn. I think she is, though not very cunning, too cunning for him. Nothing strikes me so forcibly with a sense of the rediculous as love. A Man in love I do think cuts the sorryest figure in the world. Even when I know a poor fool to be really in pain about it, I could burst out laughing in his face. His pathetic visage becomes irrisistable. Not that I take Haslam as a pattern for Lovers—he is a very worthy man and a good friend. His love is very amusing. Somewhere in the Spectator is related an account of a Man inviting a party of stutter⟨e⟩rs and squinters to his table. 't would please me more to scrape together a party of Lovers, not to dinner—no to tea. The⟨re⟩ would be no fighting as among Knights of old.

Pensive they sit, and roll their languid eyes.
Nibble their to⟨a⟩sts, and cool their tea with sighs,
Or else forget the purpose of the night
Forget their tea—forget their appetite.
See with cross'd arms they sit—ah hapless crew
The fire is going out, and no one rings
For coals, and therefore no coals betty brings.
A Fly is in the milk pot—must he die
Circled by a humane Society?
No no there m^r^ Werter[81] takes his spoon
Inverts it—dips the handle and lo, soon
The little struggler sav'd from perils dark
Across the teaboard draws a long wet mark.
Romeo! Arise! take Snuffers by the handle
There's a large Cauliflower in each candle.
A winding-sheet—Ah me! I must away
To no 7 just beyond the Circus gay.
'Alas! my friend! your Coat sits very well:
Where may your Taylor live?' 'I may not tell—
'O pardon me—I'm absent: now and then."
Where *might* my Taylor live?—I say again
I cannot tell—let me no more be teas'd—
He lives in wapping *might* live where he pleasd.

You see I cannot get on without writing as boys do at school a few nonsense verses. I begin them and before I have written six the whim has pass'd—if there is any thing deserving so respectable a name in them. I shall put in a bit of information any where just as it strikes me. M^r^ Abbey is to write to me as soon as he can bring matters to bear and then I am to go to Town to tell him the means of forwarding to you through Capper and Hazlewood. I wonder I did not put this before. I shall go on to-morrow—it is so fine now I must take a bit of a walk.

Saturday ⟨18 September⟩—

With my inconstant disposition it is no wonder that this morning, amid all our bad times and misfortunes, I should feel so alert and well spirited. At this moment you are perhaps in a very different state of Mind. It is because my hopes are very paramount to my despair. I have been reading over a part of a short poem I have composed lately call'd 'Lamia'—and I am certain there is that sort of fire in it which must take hold of people in some way—give them either pleasant or unpleasant sensation. What they want is a sensation of some sort. I wish I could pitch the Key of your spirits as high as mine is—but your organ loft is beyond the reach of my voice. I admire the exact admeasurement of my niece in your Mother's letter—O the little span long elf.[82] I am not in the least ⟨a⟩ judge of the proper weight and size of an infant. Never trouble yourselves about that: she is sure to be a fine woman. Let her have only delicate nails both on hands and feet and teeth as small as a May-fly's—who will live you his life on a square inch of oak-leaf. And nails she must have quite different from the market women here who plough into the butter and make a quarter pound taste of it. I intend to w⟨r⟩ite a letter to you⟨r⟩ Wifie and there I may say more on this little plump subject—I hope she's plump. 'Still harping on my daughter'[83] This Winchester is a place tolerably well suited to me; there is a fine Cathedral, a College, a Roman-Catholic Chapel, a Methodist do, an independent do,—and there is not one loom or any thing like manufacturing beyond bread & butter in the whole City. There are a number of rich Catholic⟨s⟩ in the place. It is a respectable, ancient aristocratical place—and moreover it contains a nunnery. Our set are by no means so hail fellow, well met, on literary subjects as we were wont to be. Reynolds has turn'd to the law. By the bye, he brought out a little piece at the Lyceum call'd *one, two, three, four, by advertisement*.[84] It met with complete success. The meaning of this odd title is explained when I tell you the principal actor is a mimic who takes off four of our best performers in the course of the farce. Our Stage is loaded with mimics. I did not see the Piece being out of Town the whole time it was in progress. Dilke is entirely swallowed up in his boy: 'tis really lamentable to what a pitch he carries a sort of parental mania. I had a Letter from him at Shanklin. He went on a word or two about the isle of Wight which is a bit of ⟨a⟩ hobby horse of his; but he soon deviated to his boy. 'I am sitting' says he "at the window expecting my Boy from School." I suppose I told you somewhere that he lives in Westminster, and his boy goes to the School there, where he gets beaten, and every bruise he has and I dare say deserves is very bitter to Dilke. The Place I am speaking of, puts me in mind of a circumsta⟨n⟩ce ⟨which⟩ occur⟨r⟩ed lately at Dilkes. I think it very rich and dramatic and quite illustrative of the little quiet fun that he will enjoy sometimes. First I must tell you their house is at the corner of Great Smith Street, so that some of the windows look into one Street, and the back windows into another round the corner. Dilke had some old people to dinner, I know not who—but there were two old ladies among them—Brown was there—they had know him from a Child. Brown is very pleasant with old women, and on that day, it seems, behaved himself so winningly they ⟨*for* that⟩ they became hand and glove together and a little complimentary. Brown was obliged to depart early. He bid them good bye and pass'd into the passage—no sooner was his back turn'd than the old women began lauding him. When Brown had reach'd the Street door and was just going, Dilke threw up the Window and call'd: 'Brown! Brown! They say you look younger than ever you did!' Brown went on and had just turn'd the corner into the other street when Dilke appeared at the back window crying "Brown! Brown! By God, they say you're handsome!" You see what a many words it requires to give any identity to a thing I could have told you in half a minute. I have been reading lately Burton's Anatomy of Melancholy; and I think you will be very much amused with a page I here coppy for you. I call it a Feu de joie round the batteries of Fort S$^{t.}$ Hyphen-de-Phrase on the birthday of the Digamma. The whole alphabet was drawn up in a Phalanx on the cover of an old Dictionary. Band playing "Amo, Amas, &c."

"Every Lover admires his Mistress, though she be very deformed of herself, ill-favored, wrinkled, pimpled, pale, red, yellow, tann'd, tallow-fac'd, have a swoln juglers platter face, or a thin, lean, chitty face, have clouds in her face, be crooked, dry, bald, goggle-eyed, blear-eyed or with staring eyes, she looks like a squis'd cat, hold her head still awry, heavy, dull, hollow-eyed, black or yellow about the eyes, or squint-eyed, sparrow-mouth'd, Persean hooknosed, have a sharp fox nose, a red nose, China flat, great nose, nare simo patuloque, a nose like a promontory, gubber-tush'd, rotten teeth, black, uneven, brown teeth, beetle-brow'd, a witches beard, her breath stink all over the room, her nose drop winter and summer, with a Bavarian poke under her chin, a sharp chin, lave-eared, with a long crane's neck, which stands awry too, pendulis mammis, her dugs like two double jugs, or else no dugs in the other extream, bloody falln fingers, she have filthy, long, unpaired, nails, scabbed hands or wrists, a tan'd skin, a rotton carcass, crooked back, she stoops, is lame, splea footed, as slender in the middle as a cow in the wast, gowty legs, her ankles hang over her shooes, her feet stink, she breed lice, a meer changeling, a very monster, an aufe imperfect, her whole complexion savors, an harsh voice, incondite gesture, vile gate, a vast virago, or an ugly tit, a slug, a fat fustilugs, a trusse, a long lean rawbone, a Skeleton, a Sneaker (si qua latent[85] meliora puta) and to thy Judgement looks like a mard in a Lanthorn, whom thou couldst not fancy for a world, but hatest, loathest, and wouldst have spit in her face, or blow thy nose in her bosom, remedium amoris to another man, a dowdy, a Slut, a scold, a nasty rank, rammy, filthy, beastly quean, dishonest peradventure, obscene, base, beggarly, rude, foolish, untaught—peevish, Irus' daughter, Thersite's sister, Grobian's Scholler; if he love her once, he admires her for all this, he takes no notice of any such errors or imperfections of boddy or mind." There's a dose for you—fine!! I would give my favourite leg to have written this as a speech in a Play: with what effect could Matthews pop-gun it at the pit! This I think will amuse you more than so much Poetry. Of that I do not like to copy any as I am affraid it is too mal apropo⟨s⟩ for you at present—and yet I will send you some—for by the time you receive it things in England may have taken a different turn. When I left M$^{r}$ Abbey on monday evening I walk'd up Cheapside but returned to put some letters in the Post and met him again in Bucklersbury: we walk'd together th⟨r⟩ough the Poultry as far as the hatter's shop he has some concern in. He spoke of it in such a way to me, I though⟨t⟩ he wanted me to make an offer to assist him in it. I do believe if I could be a hatter I might be one.[86] He seems anxious about me. He began blowing up Lord Byron while I was sitting with him, however says he the fellow says true things now & then; at which he took up a Magasine and read me some extracts from Don Juan, (Lord Byron's last flash poem) and particularly one against literary ambition. I do think I must be well spoken of among sets, for Hodgkinson is more than polite, and the coffee-german[87] endeavour'd to be very close to me the other night at covent garden where I went at half-price before I tumbled into bed. Every one however distant an acquaintance behaves in the most conciliating manner to me. You will see I speak of this as a matter of interest. On the next sheet I will give you a little politics. In every age there has been in England for some two or three centuries subjects of great popular interest on the carpet: so that however great the uproar one can scarcely prophesy any material change in the government, for as loud disturbances have agitated this country many times. All civil⟨iz⟩ed countries become gradually more enlighten'd and there should be a continual change for the better. Look at this Country at present and remember it when it was even though⟨t⟩ impious to doubt the justice of a trial by Combat. From that time there has been a gradual change. Three great changes have been in progress—First for the better, next for the worse, and a third time for the better once more. The first was the gradual annihilation of the tyranny of the nobles, when Kings found it their interest to conciliate the common people, elevate them and be just to them. Just when baronial Power ceased and before standing armies were so dangerous, Taxes were few, Kings were lifted by the people over the heads of their nobles, and those people held a rod over Kings. The change for the worse in Europe was again this. The obligation of Kings to the Multitude began to be forgotten. Custom had made noblemen the humble servants of Kings. Then Kings turned to the Nobles as the adorners of their power, the slaves of it, and from the people as creatures continually endeavouring to check them. Then in every Kingdom there was a long struggle of Kings to destroy all popular privileges. The english were the only people in europe who made a grand kick at this. They were slaves to Henry 8$^{th}$ but were freemen under william 3$^{rd}$ at the time the french were abject slaves under Lewis 14$^{th}$. The example of England, and the liberal writers of france and england sowed the seed of opposition to this Tyranny—and it was swelling in the ground till it burst out in the french revolution. That has had an unlucky termination. It put a stop to the rapid progress of free sentiments in England; and gave our Court hopes of turning back to the despotism of the 16 century. They have made a handle of this event in every way to undermine our freedom. They spread a horrid superstition against all in⟨n⟩ovation and improvement.

The present struggle in England of the people is to destroy this superstition. What has rous'd them to do it is their distresses—Perhaps on this account the present distresses of this nation are a fortunate thing—tho so horrid in their experience. You will see I mean that the french Revolution but ⟨*for* put⟩ a tempor⟨a⟩ry stop to this third change, the change for the better. Now it is in progress again and I thing in ⟨*for* think it⟩ an effectual one. This is no contest between whig and tory—but between right and wrong. There is scarcely a grain of party spirit now in England. Right and Wrong considered by each man abstractedly is the fashion. I know very little of these things. I am convinced however that apparently small causes make great alterations. There are little signs where⟨e⟩by we many ⟨*for* may⟩ know how matters are going on. This makes the business about Carlisle the Bookseller of great moment in my mind. He has been selling deistical pamphlets, republished Tom Payne[88] and many other works held in superstitious horror. He even has been selling for some time immense numbers of a work call⟨ed⟩ 'The Deist' which comes out in weekly numbers. For this Conduct he I think has had above a dozen inditements issued against him; for which he has found Bail to the amount of many thousand Pounds. After all they are affraid to prosecute: they are affraid of his defence: it would be published in all the papers all over the Empire: they shudder at this: the Trials would light a flame they could not extinguish. Do you not think this of great import? You will hear by the papers of the proceedings at Manchester and Hunt's triumphal entry into London.[89] I⟨t⟩ would take me a whole day and a quire of paper to give you any thing like detail. I will merely mention that it is calculated that 30,000 people were in the streets waiting for him—The whole distance from the Angel Islington to the Crown and anchor was lined with Multitudes. As I pass'd Colnaghi's window I saw a profil Portrait of Sands[4] the destroyer of Kotzebue. His very look must interest every one in his favour. I suppose they have represented him in his college dress. He seems to me like a young Abelard—A fine Mouth, cheek bones (and this is no joke) full of sentiment; a fine unvulgar nose and plump temples. On looking over some Letters I found the one I wrote intended for you from the foot of Helvellyn to Liverpool—but you had sail'd and therefore It was returned to me. It contained among other nonsense an Acrostic of my Sister's name—and a pretty long name it is. I wrote it in a great hurry which you will see. Indeed I would not copy it if I thought it would ever be seen by any but yourselves—

Give me your patience Sister while I frame
Exact in Capitals your golden name:
Or sue the fair apollo and he will
Rouse from his heavy slumber and instill
Great love in me for thee and Poesy.
Imagine not that greatest mastery
And Kingdom over all the Realms of verse
Nears more to Heaven in aught than when we nurse
And surety give to love and Brotherhood.

Anthropop⟨h⟩agi in Othel⟨l⟩o's mood;
Ulysses stormed, and his enchanted belt
Glow with the Muse, but they are never felt
Unbosom'd so and so eternal made,
Such tender insence in their Laurel shade,
To all the regent sisters of the Nine,
As this poor offering to you sister mine.

Kind Sister! aye, this third name says you are;
Enchanted has it been the Lord knows where.
And may it taste to you like good old wine
Take you to real happiness and give
Sons daughters and a home like honied hive.

Foot of Helvellyn June 27

I sent you in my first Packet some of my scotch Letters. I find I have one kept back which was written in the most interesting part of our Tour, and will copy parts of it in the hope you will not find it unamusing. I would give now any thing for Richardson's power of making mountains of mole hills. *Incipit Epistola Caledoniensa,* Dunancullen—I did not know the day of the month for I find I have not dated it—Brown must have been asleep. "Just after my last had gone to the post (before I go any further I must premise that I would send the identical Letter inste⟨a⟩d of taking the trouble to copy it: I do not do so for it would spoil my notion of the neat manner in which I intend to fold these thin genteel sheets. The original is written on course paper—and the soft ones would ride in the Postbag very uneasy; perhaps there might be a quarrel—) Just after my last had gone to the post, in came one of the Men with whom we endeavoured to agree about going to Staffa: He said what a pity it was we should turn aside and not see the curiosities. So we had a little talk and finally agreed that he should be our guide across the isle of Mull. We set out, cross'd two ferries, one to the isle of Kerrara of a short distance; the other from Kerrara to Mull 9 miles across. We did it in forty minutes with a fine breeze. The road, or rather the track through the Island is the most dreary you can think of; between dreary mountains; over bog and rock and river with our trowsers[90] tuck'd up and our stockings in hand. About eight o'Clock we arrived at a Shepherds Hut, into which we could scarcely get for the smoke through a door lower than my shoulders. We found our way into a little compartment, with the rafters and turf thatch blackened with Smoke—the earth floor full of hills and dales. We had some white bread with us, made a good supper and slept in our Clothes in some Blankets: our guide snored on another little bed about an arms length off. This next morning we have come about six[91] Miles to breakfast by rather a better path, and are now, by comparison, in a Mansion. Our Guide is a very obligind fellow. In our way this morning he sang us two gaelic songs—one made by a M^rs^ Brown on her husbands being drown'd; the other a jacobin one on Charles Stuart. For some days brown has been enquiring out his genealogy here. He thinks his Grandfather came from long island. He got a parcel of People at a Cottage door about him last evening: chatted with one[92] who had been a miss brown and who I think by the family likeness must have been a Relation. He talk'd[93] with the old woman pretty briskly, flattered a young one, kiss'd a child who was afraid of his Spectacles 'Scar'd at the silver rim and "oval glass"[94]—, and finally drank a pint of Milk. They handled his spectacles as we do a sensitive leaf. July 26. ⟨1818⟩ We had a most wretched walk across the island of Mull and then we cross'd to Iona, or Icolmkil: from Icolmkil we took a boat at a Bargain to take us to Staffa, and after land us at the head of Loch Nakgal ⟨na Keal⟩, whence we should only have to walk half the distance to Oban again and by a better road. All this is well pass'd and done with this singular piece of Luck, that there took place an intermission in the bad Weather just as we came in sight on Staffa, on which it is impossible to land but in a tolerably calm sea. But I will first mention Icolmkil. I know not whether you have heard much about this island; I never did before I was close to it. It is rich in the most interesting Antiquities. Who would expect to find the ruins of a fine Cathedral church; of Cloisters Colleges—Monastaries and nunneries in so remote an island? The beginning of these things was in the sixth Century under the Chaperonage[95] of a[96] Bishop-saint who landed from Ireland choosing this spot for its beauty; for at that time the now treeless place was covered with magnificent woods. His name was St. Columba—Now this saint Columba became the Dominic of the barbarian Christians of the North, and was fam'd also far South; but more especially was reverenced by the Scots, the Picts, the Norwegians and the Irish. In a course of years the island became to be considered the most holy ground of the North, and the ancient Kings of the forementioned nations chose it for their burial Place. We were show⟨n⟩ a spot in the churchyard where they say 61 Kings are buried. 48 Scotch from Fergus 2$^{nd}$ to Mackbeth, 8 irish, 2$^{5}$ Norwegian, and 1 french. They lie in rows compact. Then we were shown other matters of later date but still very ancient. Many tombs of Highland Chieftains, there effigies in complete armour face upwards—b⟨l⟩ack marble half covered with moss. There is in the ruins of the Church a Bishop on his monument as you see them in our cathedrals—as fine as any one I remember[97]—Abbots and Bishops of the islands always from one of the chief clans. There were plenty of Macleans and Macdonnels, among these latter the famous Macdonnel Lord of the Isles. There have been 300 crosses in the island: the Presbyterians destroyed all but two, one of which is a very fine one and entirely covered with a very deep coarse moss. The old Schoolmaster an ignorant little man, but reckoned very clever, showed us these things. He is a Maclean and is as much above 4 foot as he is under 4 foot, three—He stops at one glass of Wiskey unless you press a second, and at the second unless you press a third. I am puzzled how to give you an Idea of Staffa. It can only be represented by a first rate drawing. One may compare the Surface of the island to a roof—the roof is supported by grand pillars of Basalt standing together as thick as honey combs. The finest thing is Fingal's cave: it is entirely a breaking away of basalt pillars. Suppose now the Giants, who came down to the daughters of Men,[98] had taken a whole mass of these Columns and bound them together like Bunches of Matches; and then with immense axes had made a Cavern in the body of these Columns. Such is fingal's cave except that the Sea has done this work of excavation and is continually dashing there. So that we walk along the sides of the Cave on the heads of the shortest pillars which are left as for convenient stairs. The roof is arch'd somewhat gothic wise, and the length of some of the entire pillars is 50 feet. About the island you might seat an army of men one man on the extremity of each pillar snapped off at different heights. The length of the Cave is 120 feet, and from its extremity the View of the Sea through the large Arch at the Entrance is very grand. The colour of the columns is a sort of black with a lurking gloom of purple therein. For solemnity and grandeur it far surpasses the finest Cathedral. As we approached in the Boat there was such a fine swell of the sea that the columns seem'd rising immediat⟨e⟩ly out of the waves—it is impossible to describe it (I find I must keep memorandums of the verses I send you for I do not remember whether I have sent the following lines upon Staffa). I hope not 't would be a horrid balk to you, especially after reading this dull specimen of description. For myself I hate descriptions. I would not send if ⟨*for* it⟩ were it not mine.

*Incipit Poema Lyrica de Staffa tractans.*

Not Aladin magian
Ever such a work began;
Not the wizard of the Dee
Ever such a dream could see;
Not s[t.] John in Patmos isle,
In the Passion of his toil
Gaz'd on such a rugged wonder!
  As I stood its roofing under
Lo! I saw one sleeping there
On the marble cold and bare,
While the surges washed his feet
And his garments white did beat,
Drench'd, about the sombre rocks.
On his neck his well-grown locks,
Lifted dry above the main
Were upon the curl again.
  'What is this? And who art thou?'
Whisper'd I and to⟨u⟩ch'd his brow.
'What art thou and what is this?'
Whisper'd I and strove to kiss
The spirit's hand to wake his eyes.
Up he started in a thrice.
'I am Lycidas' said he
'Fam'd in funeral Minstrelsey
This was architected thus
By the great Oceanus:
He⟨re⟩ his mighty waters play
Hollow organs all the day;

Here by turns his Dolphins all
Finny Palmers, great and small
Come to pay devotion due,—
Each a Mouth of pearls must strew.
Many Mortals of these days
Dare to pass our sacred ways,
Dare to see audaciously
This Cathedral of the Sea.
I have been the Pontif Priest
Where the waters never rest,
Where a fledgy sea-bird quire
Soars for ever; holy fire
Have I hid from mortal Man;
Proteus is my Sacristan—

I ought to make a large Q[99] here: but I had better take the opportunity of telling you I have got rid of my haunting sore throat—and conduct myself in a manner not to catch another.

You speak of Lord Byron and me—There is this great difference between us. He describes what he sees—I describe what I imagine. Mine is the hardest task. You see the immense difference. The Edinburgh review are affraid to touch upon my Poem. They do not know what to make of it—they do not like to condemn it and they will not praise it for fear—They are as shy of it as I should be of wearing a Quaker's hat. The fact is they have no real taste—they dare not compromise their Judgements on so puzzling a Question. If on my next Publication they should praise me and so lug in Endymion[100]—I will address ⟨them⟩ in a manner they will not at all relish. The Cowardliness of the Edinburgh is worse than the abuse of the Quarterly. Monday ⟨20 September⟩—This day is a grand day for winchester—they elect the Mayor. It was indeed high time the place should have some sort of excitement. There was nothing going on—all asleep—Not an old Maids Sedan returning from a card party—and if any old women have got tipsy at christenings they have not exposed themselves in the Street. The first night tho' of our arrival here there was a slight uproar took place at about ten of the clock. We heard distinctly a noise patting down the high street as of a walking cane of the good old dowager breed; and a little minute after we heard a less voice observe 'What a noise the ferril made'—it must be loose." Brown wanted to call the Constables, but I observed 't was only a little breeze and would soon pass over. The side-Streets here are excessively maiden lady like. The door steps always fresh from the flannel. The Knockers have a very staid, ser⟨i⟩ous, nay almost awful qui⟨e⟩tness about them. I never saw so quiet a collection of Lions and rams heads—The doors ⟨are⟩ most part black with a little brass handle just above the Key hole—so that you may easily shut yourself out of your own house—he! he! There is none of your Lady Bellaston[101] rapping and ringing here—no thundering-Jupiter footmen, no opera-trebble-tattoos—but a modest lifting up of the knocker by a set of little wee old fingers that peep through the grey mittens, and a dying fall[102] thereof. The great beauty of Poetry is, that it makes every thing every place interesting—The palatine venice and the abbotine Winchester are equally interesting. Some time since I began a Poem call'd 'The Eve of $S^t$ Mark quite in the spirit of Town quietude. I think it will give you the Sensation of walking about an old county Town in a coolish evening. I know not yet whether I shall ever finish it—I will give it ⟨as⟩ far as I have gone. *Ut tibi placent!*

Upon a Sabbath day it fell;
Thrice holy was the sabbath bell
That call'd the folk to evening prayer.
The City Streets were clean and fair
From wholesome drench of April rains,
And on the western window pains
The chilly sunset faintly told
Of immaturd, green vallies cold,
Of the green, thorny, bloomless hedge,
Of Rivers new with spring tide sedge,
Of Primroses by shelterd rills,
And Da⟨i⟩sies on the aguish hills.
Thrice holy was the sabbath bell:
The silent streets were crowded well
With staid and pious companies
Warm from their fireside oratries,
And moving with demurest air
To even song and vesper prayer.
Each arched porch and entry low
Was fill'd with patient crowd and slow,
With whispers hush, and shuffling feet
While play'd the organs loud and sweet.

  The Bells had ceas'd, the Prayers begun,
And Bertha had not yet half done
A curious volume, patch'd and torn,
That all day long, from earliest morn,
Had taken captive her fair eyes,
Among its golden broideries:—
Perplex'd her with a thousand things—
The Stars of heaven, and Angels wings
Martyrs in a fiery blaze;
Azure Saints 'mid silver rays;
A⟨a⟩ron's[103] breastplate, and the seven
Candlesticks John saw in heaven;[104]
The winged Lion of Saint Mark,
And the Covenantal Arck
With its many Misteries
Cherubim and golden Mice.

Bertha was a Maiden fair,
Dwelling in the old Minster square;
From her fireside she could see
Sidelong its rich antiquity,
Far as the Bishop's garden wall,
Where Sycamores and elm trees tall
Full leav'd the forest had outstript,
By no sharp north wind ever nipt,
So sheltered by the mighty pile.

Bertha arose, and read awhile
With forehead 'gainst the window pane,—
Again she tried, and then again,
Until the dusk eve left her dark
Upon the Legend of St. Mark.

From pleated lawn-frill fine and thin
She lifted up her soft warm chin
With aching neck and swimming eyes,
All daz'd with saintly imageries.

All was gloom, and silent all,
Save now and then the still footfall
Of one returning homewards late
Past the echoing minster gate.
The clamourous daws that all the day
Above tree tops and towers play,
Pair by Pair had gone to rest,
Each in their ancient belfry nest
Where alseep they fall betimes
To music of the drowsy chimes.

All was silent, all was gloom
Abroad and in the homely room;—
Down she sat, poor cheated soul,
And struck a swart Lamp from the coal,
Leaned forward with bright drooping hair
And slant book full against the glare.
Her shadow, in uneasy guise,
Hover'd about, a giant size,
On ceiling, beam, and old oak chair,
The Parrot's cage and pannel square,
And the warm-angled winter screne,
On which were many monsters seen,
Call'd, Doves of Siam, Lima Mice,
And legless birds of Paradise,
Macaw, and tender Av'davat,
And silken-furr'd Angora Cat.

  Untir'd she read—her shadow still
Glowerd about as it would fill
The room with gastly forms and shades—
As though some ghostly Queen of Spades
Had come to mock behind her back,
And dance, and ruffle her garments black.

  Untir'd she read the Legend page
Of holy Mark from youth to age,
On Land, on Sea, in pagan-chains,
Rejoicing for his many pains.
Sometimes the learned Eremite
With golden star, or daggar bright,
Refer'd to pious poesies
Written in smallest crow quill size
Beneath the text and thus the rhyme
Was parcell'd out from time to time:

What follows is an imitation of the Authors in Chaucer's time—'tis more ancient than Chaucer himself and perhaps between him and Gower.

——Als writeth he of swevenis
Men han beforne they waken in blis,
When that hir friendes thinke hem bounde
In crimpide shroude farre under grounde:
And how a litling childe mote be
A Scainte er its natavitie,
Gif that the modre (Gode her blesse)
Kepen in Solitarinesse,
And kissen devoute the holy croce.
Of Goddis love and Sathan's force
He writithe; and things many moe,
Of swiche thinges I may not show,
Bot I must tellen verilie
Somedele of Saintè Cicilie,
And chieflie what he auctoreth
Of Saintè Markis life and dethe.

I hope you will like this for all its Carelessness. I must take an opportunity here to observe that though I am writing *to* you I am all the while writing *at* your Wife. This explanation will account for my speaking sometimes *hoitytoityishly*. Whereas if you were alone I should sport a little more sober sadness. I am like a squint⟨i⟩ng gentleman who saying soft things to one Lady ogles another—or what is as bad in arguing with a person on his left hand appeals with his eyes to one one ⟨*for* on⟩ the right. His Vision is elastic he bends it to a certain object but having a patent sp⟨r⟩ing it flies off. Writing has this disadvan⟨ta⟩ge of speaking—one cannot write a wink, or a nod, or a grin, or a purse of the Lips, or a *smile—O law!* One can-⟨not⟩ put ones finger to one's nose, or yerk ye in the ribs,[105] or lay hold of your button in writing—but in all the most lively and titterly parts of my Letter you must not fail to imaginc mc as the epic poets say—now here, now there, now with one foot pointed at the ceiling, now with another—now with my pen on my ear, now with my elbow in my mouth. O my friends you loose the action—and attitude is every thing as Fusili[106] said when he took up his leg like a Musket to shoot a Swallow just darting behind his shoulder. And yet does not the word mum! go for ones finger beside the nose. I hope it does. I have to make use of the word Mum! before I tell you that Severn has got a little Baby—all his own let us hope. He told Brown he had given up painting and had turn'd modeller. I hope sincerely tis not a party concern: that no Mʳ——or * * * * is the real *Pinxit* and Severn the poor *Sculpsit* to this work of art. You know he has long studied in the Life-Academy. Haydon—yes your wife will say, 'here is a sum total account of Haydon again I wonder your Brother don't put a monthly bulleteen in the Philadelphia Papers about him—I wont hear—no—skip down to the bottom—aye and there are some more of his verses, skip (lullaby-by) them too" "No, lets go regularly through" "I wont hear a word about Haydon—bless the child, how rioty she is!—there go on there" Now pray go on here for I have a few words to say about Haydon. Before this Chancery threat had cut of⟨f⟩ every legitimate supp⟨l⟩y of Cash from me I had a little at my disposal: Haydon being very much in want I lent him 30£ of it. Now in this se⟨e⟩-saw game of Life I got nearest to the ground and this chancery business rivetted me there so that I was sitting in that uneasy position where the seat slants so abominably. I applied to him for payment—he could not—that was no wonder; but goodman Delver,[107] where was the wonder then, why marry, in this, he did not seem to care much about it—and let me go without my money with almost non-chalance when he ought to have sold his drawings to supply me.[108] I shall perhaps still be acquainted with him, but for friendship that is at an end. Brown has been my friend in this he got him to sign a Bond payable at three Months. Haslam has assisted me with the return of part of the money you lent him. Hunt—'there,' says your wife, 'there's another of those dull folkes—not a syllable about my friends—well—Hunt—what about Hunt pray—you little thing see how she bites my finger—my! is not this a tooth". Well, when you have done with the tooth read on. Not a syllable about your friends! Here are some syllables. As far as I could smoke things on the Sunday before last, thus matters stood in Henrietta street. Henry was a greater blade than ever I remember to have seen him. He had on a very nice coat, a becoming waistcoat and buff trowsers. I think his face has lost a little of the spanish-brown, but no flesh. He carv'd some beef exactly to suit my appetite, as if I had been measured for it. As I stood looking out of the window with Charles after dinner, quizzing the Passengers, at which, I am sorry to say he is too apt, I observed that his young, son of a gun's whiskers had begun to curl and curl—little twists and twists, all down the sides of his face getting properly thickish on the angles of the visage. He certainly will have a notable pair of Whiskers. "How shiny your gown is in front" says Charles "Why, dont you see 'tis an apron says Henry" Whereat I scrutiniz'd and behold your mother had a purple stuff gown on, and over it an apron of the same colour, being the same cloth that was used for the lining—and furthermore to account for the shining it was the first day of wearing. I guess'd as much of the Gown—but that is entre-nous. Charles likes england better than france. They've got a fat, smiling, fair Cook as ever you saw—she is a little lame, but that improves her—it makes her go more swimmingly. When I ask'd 'Is M^rs^ Wylie within' she gave such a large, five-and-thirty-year-old smile, it made me look round upon the fo⟨u⟩rth stair—it might have been the fifth—but that's a puzzle. I shall never be able if I were to set myself a recollecting for a year, to recollect that. I think I remember two or three specks in her teeth but I really cant say exactly. Your mother said something about Miss Keasle—what that was is quite a riddle to me now. Whether she had got fatter or thinner, or broader or longer—straiter, or had taken to the zigzags—Whether she had taken to, or left off, asses Milk—that by the by she ought never to touch—how much better it would be to put her out to nurse with the Wise woman of Brentford.[109] I can say no more on so spare a subject. Miss Millar now is a different morsell if one knew how to divide and subdivide, theme her out into sections and subsections. Say a little on every part of her body as it is divided in common with all her fellow creatures, in Moor's Almanac. But Alas! I have not heard a word about her—no cue to begin upon. There was indeed a buzz about her and her mother's being at old M^rs^ So and So's *who was like to die*—as the jews say—but I dare say, keeping up their dialect, *she was not like to die*. I must tell you a good thing Reynolds *did:* 'twas the best thing he ever *said*. You know at taking leave of a party at a doorway, sometimes a Man dallies and foolishes and gets awkward, and does not know how to make off to advantage—Good bye—well—good-bye—and yet he does not go—good bye and so on—well—good bless you. You know what I mean. Now Reynolds was in this predicament and got out of it in a very witty way. He was leaving us at Hampstead. He delay'd, and we were joking at him and even said, 'be off'—at which he put the tails of his coat between his legs, and sneak'd off as nigh like a spanial as could be. He went with flying colours: this is very clever. I must, being upon the subject, tell you another good thing of him. He began, for the service it might be of to him in the law, to learn french. He had Lessons at the cheap rate of 2.6 per fag, and observed to Brown, 'Gad says he, the man sells his Lessons so cheap he must have stolen 'em.; You have heard of Hook[110] the farce writer. Horace Smith said to one who ask'd him if he knew Hook "Oh yes! Hook and I are very intimate." Theres a page of Wit for you, to put John Bunyan's emblems[111] out of countenance.

Tuesday ⟨21 September⟩. You see I keep adding a sheet daily till I send the packet off—which I shall not do for a few days as I am inclined to write a good deal: for there can be nothing so remembrancing and enchaining as a good long letter be it composed of what it may. From the time you left me, our friends say I have altered completely—am not the same person—perhaps in this letter I am for in a letter one takes up one's existence from the time we last met—I dare say you have altered also—every man does—our bodies every seven years are completely fresh-materiald—seven years ago it was not this hand that clench'd itself against Hammond.[112] We are like the relict garments of a Saint; the same and not the same: for the careful Monks patch it and patch it: till there's not a thread of the original garment left, and still they show it for S^t Anthony's shirt. This is the reason why men who had been bosom friends, on being separated for any number of years, afterwards meet coldly, neither of them knowing why. The fact is they are both altered—Men who live together have a silent moulding, and influencing power over each other. They interassimulate. 'Tis an uneasy thought that in seven years the same hands cannot greet each other again. All this may be obviated by a willful and dramatic exercise of our Minds towards each other. Some think I have lost that poetic ardour and fire 'tis said I once had—the fact is perhaps I have: but instead of that I hope I shall substitute a more thoughtful and quiet power. I am more frequently, now, contented to read and think—but now & then, haunted with ambitious thoughts. Qui⟨e⟩ter in my pulse, improved in my digestion; exerting myself against vexing speculations—scarcely content to write the best verses for the fever they leave behind. I want to compose without this fever. I hope I one day shall. You would scarcely imagine I could live alone so comfortably "Kepen in solitarinesse".[113] I told Anne, the Servant here, the other day, to say I was not at home if any one should call. I am not certain how I should endure loneliness and bad weather together. Now the time is beautiful. I take a walk every day for an hour before dinner and this is generally my walk. I go out at the back gate across one street, into the Cathedral yard, which is always interesting; then I pass under the trees along a paved path, pass the beautiful front of the Cathedral, turn to the left under a stone door way,—then I am on the other side of the building—which leaving behind me I pass on through two college-like squares seemingly built for the dwelling place of Deans and Prebendaries—garnished with grass and shaded with trees. Then I pass through one of the old city gates and then you are in one College Street through which I pass and at the end thereof crossing some meadows and at last a country alley of gardens I arrive, that is, my worship arrives at the foundation of Saint Cross, which is a very interesting old place, both for its gothic tower and alms-square, and for the appropriation of its rich rents to a relation of the Bishop of Winchester. Then I pass across St. Cross meadows till you come to the most beautifully clear river—now this is only one mile of my walk I will spare you the other two till after supper when they would do you more good. You must avoid going the first mile just after dinner. I could almost advise you to put by all this nonsense until you are lifted out of your difficulties—but when you come to this part feel with confidence what I now feel that though there can be no stop put to troubles we are inheritors of there can be and must be and ⟨*for* an⟩ end to immediate difficulties. Rest in the confidence that I will not omit any exertion to benefit you by some means or other. If I cannot remit you hundreds, I will tens and if not that ones. Let the next year be managed by you as well as possible—the next month I mean for I trust you will soon receive Abbey's remittance. What he can send you will not be a sufficient capital to ensure you any command in America. What he has of mine I nearly have anticipated by debts. So I would advise you not to sink it, but to live upon it in hopes of my being able to encrease it. To this end I will devote whatever I may gain for a few years to come—at which period I must begin to think of a security of my own comforts when quiet will become more pleasant to me than the World.[114] Still I would have you doubt my success. 'Tis at present the cast of a die with me. You say 'these things will be a great torment to me.' I shall not suffer them to be so. I shall only exert myself the more—while the seriousness of their nature will prevent me from nursing up imaginary griefs. I have not had the blue devils once since I received your last. I am advised not to publish till it is seen whether the Tragedy will or not succeed. Should it, a few mo⟨n⟩ths may see me in the way of acquiring property; should it not it will be a drawback and I shall have to perform a longer literary Pilgrimage. You will perceive that it is quite out of my interest to come to America. What could I do there? How could I employ myself? out of the reach of Libraries. You do not mention the name of the gentleman who assists you. 'Tis an extraordinary thing. How could you do without that assistance? I will not trust myself with brooding over this. The following is an extract from a Letter of Reynolds to me. "I am glad to hear you are getting on so well with your writings. I hope you are not neglecting the revision of your Poems for the press: from which I expect more than you do."

The first thought that struck me on reading your last, was to mo⟨r⟩tgage a Poem to Murray: but on more consideration I made up my mind not to do so: my reputation is very low: he would perhaps not have negociated my bill of intellect or given me a very small sum. I should have bound myself down for some time. 'Tis best to meet present misfortunes; not for a momentary good to sacrifice great benefits which one's own untram⟨m⟩ell'd and free industry may bring one in the end. In all this do never think of me as in any way unhappy: I shall not be so. I have a great pleasure in thinking of my responsibility to you and shall do myself the greatest luxury if I can succeed in any way so as to be of assistance to you. We shall look back upon these times—even before our eyes are at all dim—I am convinced of it. But be careful of those Americans—I could almost advise you to come whenever you have the sum of 500£ to England—Those Americans will I am affraid still fleece you. If ever you should think of such a thing you must bear in mind the very different state of society here—The immense difficulties of the times—The great sum required per annum to maintain yourself in any decency. In fact the whole is with Providence. I know now ⟨*for* not⟩ how to advise you but by advising you to advise with yourself. In your next tell me at large your thoughts about america; what chance there is of succeeding there: for it appears to me you have as yet been somehow deceived. I cannot help thinking M$^{r}$ Audubon has deceived you. I shall not like the sight of him. I shall endeavour to avoid seeing him. You see how puzzled I am. I have no meridian to fix you to—being the Slave of what is to happen. I think I may bid you finally remain in good hopes; and not tease yourself with my changes and variations of Mind. If I say nothing decisive in any one particular part of my Letter, you may glean the truth from the whole pretty correctly. You may wonder why I had not put your affairs with Abbey in train on receiving your Letter before last, to which there will reach you a short answer dated from Shanklin. I did write and speak to Abbey but to no purpose. Your last, with the enclosed note has appealed home to him. He will not see the necessity of a thing till hc is hit in thc mouth. 'Twill bc effectual. I am sorry to mix up foolish and serious things together—but in writing so much I am obliged to do so—and I hope sincerely the tenor of your mind will maintain itself better. In the course of a few months I shall be as good an Italian Scholar as I am a french one. I am reading Ariosto at present: not managing more than six or eight stanzas at a time. When I have done this language so as to be able to read it tolerably well—I shall set myself to get complete in latin, and there my learning must stop. I do not think of venturing upon Greek. I would not go even so far if I were not persuaded of the power the knowle⟨d⟩ge of any language gives one—the fact is I like to be acquainted with foreign languages. It is besides a nice way of filling up intervals &c Also the reading of Dante in ⟨*for* is⟩ well worth the while. And in latin there is a fund of curious literature of the middle ages. The Works of many great Men—Aretine and Sanazarius and Machievell.[115]—I shall never become attach'd to a foreign idiom so as to put it into my writings. The Paradise lost though so fine in itself is a curruption of our Language—it should be kept as it is unique—a curiosity—a beautiful and grand Curiosity. The most remarkable Production of the world. A northern dialect accommodating itself to greek and latin inversions and intonations. The purest english I think—or what ought to be the purest—is Chatterton's. The Language had existed long enough to be entirely uncorrupted of Chaucer's gallicisms, and still the old words are used. Chatterton's language is entirely northern. I prefer the native music of it to Milton's cut by feet. I have but lately stood on my guard against Milton. Life to him would be death to me. Miltonic verse cannot be written but it ⟨*for* in⟩ the vein of art—I wish to devote myself to another sensation—

⟨Friday, 24 September.⟩ I have been obliged to intermiten your Letter for two days (this being Friday morn) from having had to attend to other correspondence. Brown who was at Bedhampton, went thence to Chichester, and I still directing my letters Bedhampton—there arose a misunderstand⟨ing⟩ about them. I began to suspect my Letters had been stopped from curiosity. However yesterday Brown had four Letters from me all in a Lump—and the matter is clear'd up—Brown complained very much in his Letter to me of yesterday of the great alteration the Disposition of Dilke has undergone. He thinks of nothing but 'Political Justice'[116] and his Boy. Now the first political duty a Man ought to have a Mind to is the happiness of his friends. I wrote Brown a comment[117] on the subject, wherein I explained what I thought of Dilke's Character. Which resolved itself into this conclusion. That Dilke was a Man who cannot feel he has a personal identity unless he has made up his Mind about every thing. The only means of strengthening one's intellect is to make up ones mind about nothing—to let the mind be a thoroughfare for all thoughts. Not a select party. The genus is not scarce in population. All the stubborn arguers you meet with are of the same brood. They never begin upon a subject they have not preresolved on. They want to hammer their nail into you and if you turn the point, still they think you wrong. Dilke will never come at a truth as long as he lives; because he is always trying at it. He is a

Godwin-methodist. I must not forget to mention that your mother show'd me the lock of hair—'tis of a very dark colour for so young a creature. When it is two feet in length I shall not stand a barley corn higher. That's not fair—one ought to go on growing as well as others. At the end of this sheet I shall stop for the present—and send it off. You may expect another Letter immediately after it. As I never know the day of the mo⟨n⟩th but by chance I put here that this is *the 24th September*. I would wish you here to stop your ears, for I have a word or two to say to your Wife. My dear sister. In the first place I must quarrel with you for sending me such a shabby sheet of paper—though that is in some degree made up for by the beautiful impression of the seal. You should like to know what I was doing the first of May—let me see—I cannot recollect. I have all the Examiners ready to send. They will be a great treat to you when they reach you. I shall pack them up when my Business with Abbey[118] has come to a good conclusion and the remittance is on the road to you. I have dealt round your best wishes to our friends like a pack of cards, but being always given to cheat, myself, I have turned up ace. You see I am making game of you. I see you are not at all happy in that America. England however would not be over happy for us if you were here. Perhaps 'twould be better to be teased here than there. I must preach patience to you both. No step hasty or injurious to you must be taken. Your observation on the moschetos gives me great pleasure. 'Tis excessively poetical and humane. You say let one large sheet be all to me. You will find more than that in different parts of this packet for you. Certainly, I have been caught in rains. A Catch in the rain occasioned my last sore throat—but as for red-hair'd girls upon my word I do not recollect ever having seen one. Are you quizzing me or Miss Waldegrave when you talk of promenading. As for Pun-making, I wish it was as good a trade as pinmaking. There is very little business of that sort going on now. We struck for wages like the Manchester we⟨a⟩vers—but to no purpose—so we are all out of employ. I am more lucky than some you see by having an op⟨p⟩ortunity of exporting a few—getting into a little foreign trade—which is a comfortable thing. I wish one could get change for a pun in silver currency. I would give three and a half any night to get into Drury-pit. But they wont ring at all. No more will notes you will say—but notes are differing things—though they make together a Pun-note—as the term goes. If I were your Son I should't mind you, though you rapt me with the Scissors. But lord! I should be out of favor sin the little un be comm'd. You have made an Uncle of me, you have, and I don't know what to make of myself. I suppose next there'll be a Nevey. You say—in may last—write directly. I have not received your Letter above 10 days. The though⟨t⟩ of you⟨r⟩ little girl puts me in mind of a thing I heard a Mr Lamb say. A child in arms was passing by his chair toward the mother, in the nurses arms. Lamb took hold of the long clothes saying "Where, god bless me, where does it leave off?" *Saturday* ⟨25 September⟩. If you would prefer a joke or two to any thing else I have two for you fresh hatchd, just ris as the Baker's wives say by the rolls. The first I play'd off at Brown—the second I play'd *on* on myself. Brown when he left me "Keats" says he "my good fellow (staggering upon his left heel, and fetching an irregular pirouette with his right) Keats says he (depressing his left eyebrow and elevating his right one ((tho by the way, at the moment, I did not know which was the right one)) Keats says he (still in the same posture but furthermore both his hands in his waistcoat pockets and jutting out his stomach) "Keats—my—go-o-ood fell-o-o-o-ooh! says he (interlarding his exclamation with certain ventriloquial parentheses)—no this is all a lie—He was as sober as a Judge when a judge happens to be sober; and said "Keat⟨s⟩, if any Letters come for me—Do not forward them, but open them and give me the marrow of them in few words. At the time when I wrote my first to him no Letters had arrived. I thought I would invent one, and as I had not time to manufacture a long one I dabbed off as ⟨*for* a⟩ short one—and that was the reason of the joke succeeding beyond my expectations. Brown let his house to a M^r Benjamin a Jew. Now the water which furnishes the house is in a tank sided with a composition of lime and the lime imp⟨r⟩egnates the water unpleasantly. Taking advantage of this circumstance I pretended that M^r Benjamin had written the following short note—"Sir. By drinking your damn'd tank water I have got the gravel—what reparation can you make to me and my family? Nathan Benjamin" By a fortunate hit, I hit upon his right he⟨a⟩then name—his right Pronomen. Brown in consequence it appears wrote to the surprised M^r Benjamin the following "Sir, I cannot offer you any remuneration until your gravel shall have formed itself into a Stone when I will cut you with Pleasure. C. Brown" This of Browns M^r Benjamin has answered insisting on an explatinon of this singular circumstance. B. says "when I read your Letter and his following I roared, and in came M^r Snook who on reading them seem'd likely to burst the hoops of his fat sides—so the Joke has told well. Now for the one I played on myself—I must first give you the Scene and the dramatis Personæ. There are an old Major and his youngish wife live in the next apartments to me. His bed room door opens at an angle with my sitting room door. Yesterday I was reading as demurely as a Parish Clerk when I heard a rap at the door. I got up and opened it—no one was to be seen. I listened and heard some one in the Major's room. Not content with this I went up stairs and down look'd in the cubboards—and watch'd. At last I set myself to read again not quite so demurely—when there came a louder rap. I arose determin'd to find out who it was. I look⟨ed⟩ out the Stair cases were all silent. "This must be the Major's wife said I—at all events I will see the truth" so I rapt me at the Major's door and went in to the utter surprise and confusion of the Lady who was in reality there—after a little explanation, which I can no more describe than fly, I made my retreat from her convinced of my mistake. She is to all appearance a silly body and is really surprised about it. She must have been, for I have discovered that a little girl in the house was the Rappee—I assure you she has nearly make me Sneeze.[119] If the Lady tells tits I shall put a very grave and moral face on the matter with the old Gentleman, and make his little Boy a present of a humming top. My Dear George—This Monday morning the 27^th I have received your last dated July 12^th[120] You say you have not heard from Englan⟨——[121]⟩ nths—Then my Letter from Shanklin written I think at the en⟨——[121]⟩ have reach'd you. You shall not have cause to think I neglect you. I have kept this back a little time in expectation of hearing from M^r Abbey—

You will say I might have remained in Town to be Abbey's messenger in these affairs. That I offer'd him—but he in his answer convinced me he was anxious to bring the Business to an issue—He observed that by being himself the agent in the whole, people might be more expeditious. You say you have not heard for three mo⟨n⟩ths and yet you⟨r⟩ letters have the tone of knowing how our affairs are situated by which I conjecture I acquainted you with them in a Letter previous to the Shanklin one. That I may not have done. To be certain I will here state that it is in consequence of M^rs Jennings threat⟨e⟩ning a Chancery suit that you have been kept from the receipt of monies and myself deprived of any help from Abbey. I am glad you say you keep up your Spirits—I hope you make a true statement on that score. Still keep them up—for we are all young. I can only repeat here that you shall hear from me again immediately. Notwithstanding their bad intelligence I have experienced some pleasure in receiving so correctly two Letters from you, as it give⟨s⟩ me if I may so say a distant Idea of Proximity. This last improves upon my litt⟨l⟩e niece. Kiss her for me. Do not fret yourself about the delay of money on account of any immediate opportunity being lost: for in a new country whoever has money must have opportunity of employing it in many ways. The report runs now more in favor of Kean stopping in England. If he should I have confident hopes of our Tragedy—If he smokes the hotblooded character of Ludolph—and he is the only actor that can do it—He will add to his own fame, and improve my fortune. I will give you a half dozen lines of it before I part as a specimen—

> "Not as a Swordsman would I pardon crave,
> But as a Son: the bronz'd Centurion
> Long-toil'd in forreign wars, *and whose high deeds*
> *Are shaded in a forest of tall spears,*[122]
> *Known only to his troop,* hath greater plea
> Of favour with my Sire than I can have—"[123]

Believe me my dear brother and Sister—
Your affectionate and anxious Brother

⟨*Signature cut out.*⟩[124]

## *To PERCY BYSSHE SHELLEY*

### *Wednesday 16 Aug. 1820*

Hampstead August 16^th

My dear Shelley,

I am very much gratified that you, in a foreign country, and with a mind almost overoccupied, should write to me in the strain of the Letter beside me. If I do not take advantage of your invitation it will be prevented by a circumstance I have very much at heart to prophesy. There is no doubt that an english winter would put an end to me, and do so in a lingering hateful manner, therefore I must either voyage or journey to Italy as a soldier marches up to a battery. My nerves at present are the worst part of me, yet they feel soothed when I think that come what extreme may, I shall not be destined to remain in one spot long enough to take a hatred of any four particular bedposts. I am glad you take any pleasure in my poor Poem[125];—which I would willingly take the trouble to unwrite, if possible, did I care so much as I have done about Reputation. I received a copy of the Cenci, as from yourself from Hunt. There is only one part of it I am judge of; the Poetry, and dramatic effect, which by many spirits now a days is considered the mammon. A modern work it is said must have a purpose, which may be the God—*an artist* must serve Mammon—he must have "self concentration" selfishness perhaps. You I am sure will forgive me for sincerely remarking that you might curb your magnanimity and be more of an artist, and 'load every rift' of your subject with ore.[126] The thought of such discipline must fall like cold chains upon you, who perhaps never sat with your wings furl'd for six Months together. And is not this extraordinary talk for the writer of Endymion! whose mind was like a pack of scattered cards—I am pick'd up and sorted to a pip. My Imagination is a Monastry and I am its Monk—you must explain my metap$^{es}$ to yourself. I am in expectation of Prometheus every day. Could I have my own wish for its interest effected you would have it still in manuscript—or be but now putting an end to the second act. I remember you advising me not to publish my first-blights, on Hampstead heath—I am returning advice upon your hands. Most of the Poems in the volume I send you[127] have been written above two years, and would never have been publish'd but from a hope of gain; so you see I am inclined enough to take your advice now. I must express once more my deep sense of your Kindness, adding my sincere thanks and respects for M$^{rs}$ Shelley. In the hope of soon seeing you I remain

most sincerely yours,
John Keats—

## *To CHARLES BROWN*

### *Thursday 30 Nov. 1820*

Rome. 30 November 1820.

My dear Brown,

'Tis the most difficult thing in the world to me to write a letter. My stomach continues so bad, that I feel it worse on opening any book,—yet I am much better than I was in Quarantine. Then I am afraid to encounter the proing and conning of any thing interesting to me in England. I have an habitual feeling of my real life having past, and that I am leading a posthumous existence. God knows how it would have been—but it appears to me—however, I will not speak of that subject. I must have been at Bedhampton nearly at the time you were writing to me from Chichester—how unfortunate—and to pass on the river too! There was my star predominant![128] I cannot answer any thing in your letter, which followed me from Naples to Rome, because I am afraid to look it over again. I am so weak (in mind) that I cannot bear the sight of any hand writing of a friend I love so much as I do you. Yet I ride the little horse,—and, at my worst, even in Quarantine, summoned up more puns, in a sort of desperation, in one week than in any year of my life. There is one thought enough to kill me—I have been well, healthy, alert &c, walking with her—and now—the knowledge of contrast, feeling for light and shade, all that information (primitive sense) necessary for a poem are great enemies to the recovery of the stomach. There, you rogue, I put you to the torture,—but you must bring your philosophy to bear—as I do mine, really—or how should I be able to live? Dr. Clarke is very attentive to me; he says, there is very little the matter with my lungs, but my stomach, he says, is very bad. I am well disappointed in hearing good news from George,—for it runs in my head we shall all die young. I have not written to x x x x x yet, which he must think very neglectful; being anxious to send him a good account of my health, I have delayed it from week to week. If I recover, I will do all in my power to correct the mistakes made during sickness; and if I should not, all my faults will be forgiven. I shall write to x x x tomorrow, or next day. I will write to x x x x x in the middle of next week. Severn is very well, though he leads so dull a life with me. Remember me to all friends, and tell x x x x I should not have left London without taking leave of him, but from being so low in body and mind. Write to George as soon as you receive this, and tell him how I am, as far as you can guess;—and also a note to my sister—who walks about my imagination like a ghost—she is so like Tom. I can scarcely bid you good bye even in a letter. I always made an awkward bow.

God bless you!

John Keats.

## *NOTES*

1. Editorial insertions are contained in French brackets.

2. Address: Mr. B. Bailey / Magdalen Hall / Oxford.

3. A mild play upon the lawyerly phrase 'this said letter' which would be Haydon's to Bailey: 'this *un*said letter' Keats's to Bailey.

4. Compare this with the close of the 'Ode on a Grecian Urn'.

5. See 'Paradise Lost', viii. 460–90.

6. 'Mr. Bailey well remembered', says Lord Houghton, 'the exceeding delight that Keats took in Wordsworth's "Ode to Immortality". He was never weary of repeating it.'

7. C. W. Dilke notes—'This Christie was I think Lockhart's friend ⟨J. H. Christie⟩—who was unhappily drawn into Lockhart's quarrel with John Scott and killed him. Strange that this quarrel and the consequent loss of life of Scott, the Editor of the "London Magazine", is not once alluded to [in the "Life, Letters", &c], although the

quarrel originated in the attack on Lockhart as the writer of the articles on the Cockney School, or as Editor of "Blackwood". Christie I had met before and have since the duel: and he appeared to be a mild amiable man.'

8. Kean played the Duke of Gloucester in Shakespeare's 'King Richard the Third' on December 15, and Luke (Jeffrey has *Duke*) in 'Riches' on December 18. Keats's critique appeared in 'The Champion' of December 21, and was reprinted in Forman's edition of Keats's works in 1883.

9. 'Christmas and other old National Merry-makings considered, with reference to the Nature of the Age, and to the Desirableness of their Revival'. Leigh Hunt in 'The Examiner', December 21 and 28, 1817.

10. Popular publishers. The three trials of William Hone (1780–1842) for publishing 'impious, profane, and scandalous libels' took place on the 18th, 19th, and 20th of December 1817 respectively.

11. Charles Wells (1800–79), the author of 'Stories after Nature' and 'Joseph and his Brethren'. Keats wrote a sonnet to him, 'To a friend who sent me some Roses'.

12. Benjamin West, P.R.A. (1738–1820). There is a reference to this picture in Keats's paper on Kean in 'Richard Duke of York', which appeared in 'The Champion' for Sunday, the 28th of December 1817. 'Christ rejected' was also by West.

13. Thomas Hill (1760–1840), book collector, part proprietor of 'The Monthly Mirror' and 'discoverer' of Kirke White.

14. Edward du Bois (1774–1850), wit and man of letters and judge in the Court of Requests; contributed regularly to the 'Morning Chronicle': edited 'The Monthly Mirror'; wrote a skit on Godwin's 'St. Leon' (1800), &c.

15. Jeffrey has 'insolated verisimilature'.

16. Keats can hardly have known what intolerable vexation and disappointment Shelley was undergoing in his relations with the Olliers, whose doings with Keats's own first volume of poems had been so little to his satisfaction. 'Laon and Cythna', the book here referred to, had occupied months of Shelley's thought and labour, and was actually printed off and ready for issue when Charles Ollier found himself afraid to publish it. The book was withdrawn till it could be toned down by means of numerous cancel-leaves which made the hero and heroine, originally brother and sister, strangers in blood, and did away with some antitheistic passages. 'Laon and Cythna' was ready before the end of November; and a few copies were distributed. By the middle of December the struggle between publisher and poet was raging. On the 27th of that month Shelley was clamouring for the last proofs of the cancel-leaves. Up to the 15th of January he had not received completed copies of the book as converted into 'The Revolt of Islam'; but a week later he was giving instructions about advertising without relaxation: hence the book was no doubt finally out by then. Keats's reference must be to the volume in its original form, which was at that moment undergoing revision after a somewhat active attempt to recover all copies sent out to the booksellers.

17. 'Richard III', v. ii. 3.

18. 'All the Landseers' would include John (1769–1852) and his sons, Thomas (1795–1880), Charles (1799–1879), and Edwin (1802–73). George and Richard Rokes were undertakers in the Borough. Thomas Landseer published 'The Life and Letters of William Bewick' in 1871.

19. Thus there would seem to have been no fewer than three dramatic critics for the 'Champion' newspaper within a few weeks.

20. It is boldly written in a large blank space in the 1808 Shakespeare folio now in the Dilke Collection at Hampstead.

21. Jeffrey wrote *of* and altered it to *if*.

22. Jeffrey wrote 'Pheonix-wings'.

23. Presumably the walk from Wentworth Place to Well Walk.

24. Burlesque by William Barnes Rhodes (1772–1826).

25. By George Colman the younger (1762–1836).

26. '2 Henry IV', II. iv. 401.

27. C. W. Dilke notes that it was written by Lockhart, 'which is so close akin that it is by no means impossible that Scott encouraged the thing. That Lockhart was the writer was admitted to an American who published it on his return.' There is, however, no evidence to justify the association of Scott's name with the objectionable tirades.

28. The thirty-two 'places of delight' of the Buddhist doctrine.

29. 'Tempest', I. ii. 223.

30. 'Midsummer-Night's Dream', II. i. 175.

31. Cf. 'The Old Cumberland Beggar', l. 77.

32. Keats may have used this adjective as a noun; or he may have left out the word *being* accidentally.

33. Cf. 'Tempest', I. i. 71–2.

34. Cf. 'As You Like It', II. i. 7.

35. The exhibition was opened on Monday the 2nd of February. James Stark (1794–1859): the pictures Keats saw were 'Penning the Flock' and 'Lambeth, looking towards Westminster Bridge' for which the Directors of the British Institution awarded Stark a premium of £50; Sir David Wilkie (1785–1841); Washington Allston (1779–1843), resident in London 1811–18; 'Uriel' was exhibited with another painting and Allston was awarded £150 by the Directors of the British Institution; it was bought by the Marquess of Stafford for 150 guineas, and is reproduced in 'The Life and Letters of Washington Allston', by J. B. Flagg (Bentley, 1893).

36. In 'The Champion', 15th of February 1818, p. 109.

37. Jeffrey reads *Leslies* corrected to *Alston's* in the margin.

38. As he did later. Charles Butler had been a Surgeon's Pupil at Guy's, having entered on the 30th of September 1815, a day before Keats. He passed the Apothecaries' Society's examination at the same time as the poet, i.e. on the 25th of July 1816. Mrs. Butler was related to Eliza Powell Drewe who married John Hamilton Reynolds on the 31st of August 1822.

39. 'The Revolt of Islam.'

40. 'Endymion', i. 149.

41. Ibid. 247.

42. 'Henry V', Prologue 1.

43. Bailey informed Lord Houghton 'that one of Keats's favourite topics of conversation was the principle of melody in verse, which he believed to consist in the adroit management of open and close vowels. He had a theory that vowels could be as skillfully combined and interchanged as differing notes of music, and that all sense of monotony was to be avoided, except when expressive of a special purpose. Uniformity of metre is so much the rule of English poetry, that, undoubtedly, the carefully varied harmonies of Keats's verse were disagreeable, even to cultivated readers, often producing exactly the contrary impression from what was intended, and, combined as they were with rare and curious rhymes, diverted the attention from the beauty of the thoughts and the force of the imagery. In "Endymion", indeed, there was much which not only seemed, but was, experimental: and it is impossible not to observe the superior mastery of melody, and sure-footedness of the poetic paces, in "Hyperion".'

44. 'Endymion', i. 334–5.

45. Ibid. 495.

46. Proverbs iv. 5.
47. Cf. Slender, 'Merry Wives of Windsor', I. i. 128.
48. 'Paradise Lost', x. 702–3.
49. Under the same roof with the children of the Postman Bentley, at whose house the Keatses lodged.
50. Probably that of 1598; a 1596 Chaucer is unknown.
51. 'The Romance of Youth', in 104 Spenserian stanzas, published in 'The Garden of Florence and Other Poems', 1821.
52. Cf. 'Merry Wives of Windsor', I. ii. 13.
53. Wordsworth, 'Tintern Abbey', l. 38.
54. 'Paradise Lost', ii. 934 and iii. 627.
55. Cf. 'King Lear', III. iv. 111.
56. 'Hamlet', III. i. 63.
57. Wordsworth, fragment of 'The Recluse', l. 41.
58. Woodhouse queries 'overgone'.
59. 'Manfred', I. i. 10: 'Sorrow is knowledge.'
60. Peter George Patmore (1786–1855), the intimate of Hazlitt in the matter of 'Liber Amoris', was the author of 'The Mirror of the Months', 'Letters on England', 1823, and many later works, including 'My Friends and Acquaintance' (3 volumes, 1854). He was the father of Coventry Patmore.
61. George Colman the younger (1762–1836).
62. Cf. Pope, 'Essay on Man', iv. 380. Thomas Little was the pseudonym under which Moore issued his 'Poetical Works', 1801.
63. Cf. 'Paradise Lost', xi. 831.
64. Woodhouse has recorded that the first page of the letter was crossed, and that the first two lines, being written in the margin, stood out clearly, while the word 'dip' was the first word that dipped into the obscurity of the writing which at that point Keats began to cross.
65. Cf. 'The Fall of Hyperion', i. 147–9.
66. Mr. P. P. Howe in 'The Life of William Hazlitt' (1922) says: 'We do not know what Moore's present to Hazlitt can have been, unless it was a copy of "The Fudge Family in Paris" which Moore sent at this time, and which as a tribute of respect from a fashionable poet to the leading spirit of "The Yellow Dwarf" was not unacceptable'. A copy of the third edition of 'The Fudge Family in Paris' (1818) inscribed 'To William Hazlitt Esq$^{r}$, as a small mark of respect for his literary talents & political principles from the Author. April 27th, 1818'—came into Mr. Howe's possession in October 1934.
67. Horace, *Epistles,* II. ii. 102.
68. Mr. G. Beaumont in 'The Times Literary Supplement', February 27 and May 1, 1930, suggests that Keats intended to write 'informing'. The facts are that the words 'in' and 'for', the last words on the page, are written closer together than other words on the same page, that they are followed by a dash which might very well be read as a hyphen, and that 'informing' is in every way an improvement to an otherwise clumsy parenthesis.
69. In 'Hyperion'.
70. On the 10th of September.
71. Presumably from George Keats to Abbey, enclosed to John.
72. Possibly William Walton, attorney, of Girdlers' Hall, 39 Basinghall Street.
73. Not extant. Possibly Thomas Fry, stock-broker, of 4 Angel Court, Throgmorton Street.
74. 'Otho the Great.'

75. Mr. Speed says, 'Audubon, the naturalist, sold to George Keats a boat loaded with merchandise, which at the time of the sale Audubon knew to be at the bottom of the Mississippi River.'

76. Previously printed as world, but Keats wrote mould.

77. The part of Ludolph.

78. See the reference to the cotton-spinners' strike in this letter under date the 24th of September.

79. Cf. 'Tristram Shandy', Book ix, Chap. xiii.

80. Brown was in the habit of letting his house in Wentworth Place, where he and Keats domesticated together, and he generally arranged to go off on country trips during those terms for which the house was thus profitably employed.

81. Goethe's 'Sorrows of Werther' (1774).

82. Ben Jonson, 'The Sad Shepherd', II. viii.

83. 'Hamlet', II. ii. 190.

84. The title of the piece in question is 'One, Two, Three, Four, Five: By Advertisement, a Musical Entertainment in one Act'. It was published in 1819 in a demy 8vo pamphlet with a portrait of John Reeve by Wageman, and it held the stage firmly enough to be included later in Cumberland's 'British Theatre', where it is stated that the play was written for John Reeve, and brought out at the English Opera, with him in the principal part, on the 17th of July 1819. The following abstract of the fable is added:—'Mr Coupleton wishing to retire from the bustle and turmoil of a city life, and enjoy the country and spring-tide, "*solus cum sola* with his lovely May," advertises for a husband for his daughter; a young lady of a *thousand* in point of *mental* accomplishments, and of *ten thousand* in a *pecuniary* sense. Miss Sophy, however, anticipating her papa, has secured to herself a lover, in the person of Harry Alias, a theatrical amateur. To punish the match-maker for his indecorous mode of proceeding in an affair of so much delicacy, and promote his own views, Mr Alias resolves to answer the advertisement, by waiting upon Old Coupleton in a variety of characters; and Sir Peter Teazle, Dr Endall, Sam Dabbs, and Buskin, appear successively before him, in the persons of "Farren", "Harley", "Munden", and "Mathews", all of whom were aped with wonderful fidelity. In Buskin, Mr Reeve also introduced imitations of "John Kemble", "Kean", and "Liston".'

85. Keats wrote *patent* instead of *latent*.

86. A reference to Lansdowne.

87. Perhaps some one in the employ of Abbey, tea and coffee dealer.

88. Thomas Paine (1737–1809).

89. The entry alluded to by Keats was made between the Manchester Massacre and Henry Hunt's trial. The procession started at Islington and proceeded to the crown and Anchor Tavern in the Strand. 'The Gentleman's Magazine' for September 1819. p. 269, states that the crowds through which Hunt passed and those by whom he was accompanied numbered not less than 200,000.

90. 'Breeches' to Tom Keats, 'trowsers' to Georgiana!

91. 'Sax' to Tom, but the joke has worn off.

92. 'ane' to Tom.

93. 'jawed' to Tom.

94. The quotation, the source of which I have failed to trace, was not in the letter to Tom. Perhaps Keats had in mind 'Scared by the fife, and rumbling drum's alarms'; Wordsworth, 'Descriptive Sketches', l. 752.

95. 'superstition' to Tom.

96. 'would-be' to Tom.

97. This monument is not mentioned in the letter to Tom.

98. Genesis vi. 2–4.

99. i.e. Query, suggesting some doubts as to the riddance of his sore throat.

100. Actually Jeffrey did write of Endymion and the Lamia volume in the 'Edinburgh Review', August 1820.

101. A profligate character in 'Tom Jones'.

102. 'Twelfth Night', I. i. 4.

103. Hitherto 'Moses' in all editions but 'Aron's' in this letter and in the holograph in the Keats Manuscript Book in the British Museum.

104. 'The two lines omitted near the beginning of the Staffa poem were:

When he saw the churches seven
Golden aisled built up in heaven.

Perhaps Keats thought he was overworking these rhymes in connexion with St. John in Patmos.

105. Cf. 'Othello', I. ii. 5.

106. Henry Fuseli (1741–1825), but here Keats is merely punning on the painter's name.

107. 'Hamlet', V. i. 14.

108. Subsequent letters confirm this.

109. Cf. 'The Merry Wives of Windsor', IV. v. 27.

110. Theodore Edward Hook (1788–1841).

111. 'Book for Boys and Girls', 1686; in later editions called 'Divine Emblems'.

112. This phrase taken literally points to an early stage in the rupture that led to his quitting his apprenticeship to Hammond.

113. These words from 'The Eve of St. Mark' seem to have pleased their author specially: he quotes them in his letter to Reynolds of the 21st of September 1819.

114. Cf. the beginning of this letter: 'The time may come when age will make me more selfish.'

115. Pietro Aretino (1492–1557); Jacopo Sannazaro (1458–1530): Niccolo Machiavelli (1469–1527).

116. Godwin's 'Political Justice' (1793).

117. Letter not extant.

118. Opposite Lord Houghton's version of this passage Dilke notes: 'The business for George mentioned P 19 and this with Abbey related I have no doubt to a settlement of Tom's property. To settle with Abbey was a difficult thing—and must have been particularly so while George was abroad. John I think got money for himself, as I have before mentioned, though only in part.'

119. Rappee, a coarse kind of snuff.

120. This would seem to be a slip of Keats's, unless by 'last' he means 'last to arrive', because at the beginning of this letter he mentions one from George dated the 24th of July, previously received. Probably the later letter was sent from the Settlement by speedier means than the earlier one.

121. The signature to this letter is neatly cut away, probably for an autograph collector, and with it the words written on the back belonging to these spaces. The missing words supplied by Speed in his 1883 edition of the letters are 'for three months' and 'end of June, has not'; but as they would not fill the empty spaces in the holograph and the second phrase does not fit in with the passage following, they are unacceptable, though they no doubt convey the sense of what Keats wrote.

122. Cf. 'Paradise Lost', i. 547: 'A forest huge of spears'.

123. 'Otho the Great', I. iii. 24–9.

124. Possibly that given by George to Lewis J. Cist of Cincinnatti on June 18, 1837. See 'Keats' Reputation in America to 1848', by H. E. Rollins, Cambridge, Mass., 1846, p. 46.

125. 'Endymion'.

126. Cf. Spenser, 'Faerie Queene', II. vii. 28, l. 5.

127. 'Lamia, Isabella, &c.', a copy of which, belonging to Hunt, was found doubled back in the drowned Shelley's pocket, and was cast by Hunt upon the burning relics of his friend.

128. Cf. 'All's Well that Ends Well', I. i. 213–14, and 'The Winter's Tale', I. ii. 201–2.

# *Thomas Carlyle*

1795–1881

Thomas Carlyle was born in Ecclefechan, in Scotland on December 4, 1795. His family was Calvinist, in the harsh Scots tradition, but was nevertheless a source of great emotional support to the young scholar. At school, the precocious boy got on badly with his peers, and was often involved in brawls. His attraction to learning, however, soon curbed his belligerance, or, at least, channeled it into more wholesome outlets, such as debating and argumentation.

In 1809 Carlyle was admitted to the University of Edinburgh. In this thriving intellectual capital, which just one generation before had seen the heyday of Adam Smith, David Hume, Robert Adam, and other luminaries of the "Scottish Enlightenment," Carlyle soon rose to a position of prominence. At first he studied mathematics and then divinity, but upon meeting Edward Irving, and availing himself of his fine library, he began to devote himself to historiography (Gibbon especially), French literature, German idealism, and, above all, Goethe.

In 1816 Carlyle accepted a position as schoolmaster in Kirkcaldy, a post which he held for less than two years. He was an irascible, highly eccentric teacher, with a reputation not only for learning, but also for excesses of speech and habit that led many to believe him insane. Like Dr. Johnson, Carlyle suffered from a variety of—real and imaginary—physical ailments; unlike Johnson, he showed none of the humanity and compassion that could temper hypocondria. Friends of Carlyle (such as Irving) had as their cohort not only the greatest complainer in Scotland but also the man most sensitive to the various intellectual currents emanating from Germany: a scholar of broad learning, stupendous imagination, and wild philosophic zeal.

By the middle of the 1820s, Carlyle had declared himself to be the sole interpreter of German thought to the English mind. With characteristic arrogance, he regarded Coleridge, who also aspired to occupy this position, as an intellectual nullity. He wrote a biography of Schiller and worked on a translation of *Wilhelm Meister*. He was ecstatic when he received favorable acknowledgement from Goethe himself. Along with Wordsworth, Scott, and other English friends of German thought, he sent the great man a commemorative seal on his birthday in 1831.

Carlyle was wedded to Jane Walsh on October 17, 1826. As a married man, he had to find a way to make a livelihood which would allow him the time to participate in the intellectual life of the Scottish capital. Through the good offices of Francis Jeffrey, editor of the *Edinburgh Review,* he found opportunities to write extensive essays that gave him a reputation as the head of a "mystic" school of thought. He combined his passion for German thought, natural irony, and outrageous sense of satire to produce the work known as *Sartor Resartus*. After failing to meet with the approval of London editors, it was finally published in *Fraser's Magazine* in 1833. Carlyle's portrait of Treufelsdroenckh, his Philosophy of Clothing, and the whole creaky, murky machinery of his prose could not fail to make an impression, although the initial reviews were unfavorable. His fame was spreading, and he was honored to have as his guest Emerson, who had worshipped him from America even as Carlyle had worshipped Goethe from Edinburgh.

The heavy Germanic tone that characterizes *Sartor Resartus,* its bizarre humor, and its unusual brand of Platonism all combined to put off many readers. Yet Carlyle's next project, *The French Revolution,* marked the turning-point of his career. Here was historiography writ large: a work of novelistic dimensions, possessing vivid characterizations, and written—in spite of some serious lapses in accuracy—in a truly masterful narrative. Its political stance marked him as one of the leading "radicals" of his generation, along with his friend (and later philosophical opponent) John Stuart Mill. His book *Chartism,* with its attack on Adam Smith and *laissez-faire* economic theory placed him far to the left of most English thinkers and showed him to be a precursor of later socialist thought. Yet his position contained an inordinate respect for power and heroism; his lecture "On Hero Worship" has been used as moral support by thinkers on the right as well.

In his later years Carlyle experienced afresh the torments and derangements of his youth. He complained of "demon-fowls" crowing in the vicinity of his house, became extremely ill-tempered and surly, and, according to Edith Sitwell, was a "terror" to his guests. He absorbed himself in writing dreary, interminable historical studies of heroic figures such as Cromwell and Frederick the Great. Shortly after he was appointed Rector of the University of Edinburgh in 1865, his wife died—a calamity from which he never truly recovered. He now had disciples, fame, status, and financial security—but all this meant nothing to him. He occasionally voiced suicidal thoughts. When he died on February 4, 1881, he was, according to his express desire, laid to rest in the village of Ecclefechan, preferring Scottish soil to what he would have deemed the empty and English splendor of Westminster Abbey.

# Signs of the Times

It is no very good symptom either of nations or individuals, that they deal much in vaticination. Happy men are full of the present, for its bounty suffices them; and wise men also, for its duties engage them. Our grand business undoubtedly is, not to *see* what lies dimly at a distance, but to *do* what lies clearly at hand.

> Know'st thou *Yesterday,* its aim and reason;
> Work'st thou well *To-day,* for worthy things?
> Calmly wait the *Morrow's* hidden season,
> Need'st not fear what hap soe'er it brings.

But man's "large discourse of reason" *will* look "before and after;" and, impatient of the "ignorant present time," will indulge in anticipation far more than profits him. Seldom can the unhappy be persuaded that the evil of the day is sufficient for it; and the ambitious will not be content with present splendor, but paints yet more glorious triumphs, on the cloud-curtain of the future.

The case, however, is still worse with nations. For here the prophets are not one, but many; and each incites and confirms the other; so that the fatidical fury spreads wider and wider, till at last even Saul must join in it. For there is still a real magic in the action and reaction of minds on one another. The casual deliration of a few becomes, by this mysterious reverberation, the frenzy of many; men lose the use, not only of their understandings, but of their bodily senses; while the most obdurate unbelieving hearts melt, like the rest, in the furnace where all are cast as victims and as fuel. It is grievous to think, that this noble omnipotence of Sympathy has been so rarely the Aaron's-rod of Truth and Virtue, and so often the Enchanter's-rod of Wickedness and Folly! No solitary miscreant, scarcely any solitary maniac, would venture on such actions and imaginations, as large communities of sane men have, in such circumstances, entertained as sound wisdom. Witness long scenes of the French Revolution, in these late times! Levity is no protection against such visitations, nor the utmost earnestness of character. The New-England Puritan burns witches, wrestles for months with the horrors of Satan's invisible world, and all ghastly phantasms, the daily and hourly precursors of the Last Day; then suddenly bethinks him that he is frantic, weeps bitterly, prays contritely, and the history of that gloomy season lies behind him like a frightful dream.

Old England too has had her share of such frenzies and panics; though happily, like other old maladies, they have grown milder of late: and since the days of Titus Oates have mostly passed without loss of men's lives; or indeed without much other loss than that of reason, for the time, in the sufferers. In this mitigated form, however, the distemper is of pretty regular recurrence; and may be reckoned on at intervals, like other natural visitations; so that reasonable men deal with it, as the Londoners do with their fogs,—go cautiously out into the groping crowd, and patiently carry lanterns at noon; knowing, by a well-grounded faith, that the sun is still in existence, and will one day reappear. How often have we heard, for the last fifty years, that the country was wrecked, and fast sinking; whereas, up to this date, the country is entire and afloat! The "State in Danger" is a condition of things, which we have witnessed a hundred times; and as for the Church, it has seldom been out of "danger" since we can remember it.

All men are aware that the present is a crisis of this sort; and why it has become so. The repeal of the Test Acts, and then of the Catholic disabilities, has struck many of their admirers with an indescribable astonishment. Those things seemed fixed and immovable; deep as the foundations of the world; and lo, in a moment they have vanished, and their place knows them no more! Our worthy friends mistook the slumbering Leviathan for an island; often as they had been assured, that Intolerance was, and could be nothing but a Monster; and so, mooring under the lee, they had anchored comfortably in his scaly rind, thinking to take good cheer; as for some space they did. But now their Leviathan has suddenly dived under; and they can no longer be fastened in the stream of time; but must drift forward on it, even like the rest of the world: no very appalling fate, we think, could they but understand it; which, however, they will not yet, for a season. Their little island is gone; sunk deep amid confused eddies; and what is left worth caring for in the universe? What is it to them that the great continents of the earth are still standing; and the polestar and all our loadstars, in the heavens, still shining and eternal? Their cherished little haven is gone, and they will not be comforted! And therefore, day after day, in all manner of periodical or perennial publications, the most lugubrious predictions are sent forth. The King has virtually abdicated; the Church is a widow, without jointure; public principle is gone; private honesty is going; society, in short, is fast falling in pieces; and a time of unmixed evil is come on us.

At such a period, it was to be expected that the rage of prophecy should be more than usually excited. Accordingly, the Millennarians have come forth on the right hand, and the Millites on the left. The Fifth-monarchy men prophesy from the Bible, and the Utilitarians from Bentham. The one announces that the last of the seals is to be opened, positively, in the year 1860; and the other assures us that "the greatest-happiness principle" is to make a heaven of earth, in a still shorter time. We know these symptoms too well, to think it necessary or safe to interfere with them. Time and the hours will bring relief to all parties. The grand encourager of Delphic or other noises is—the Echo. Left to themselves, they will the sooner dissipate, and die away in space.

Meanwhile, we too admit that the present is an important time; as all present time necessarily is. The poorest Day that passes over us is the conflux of two Eternities; it is made up of currents that issue from the remotest Past, and flow onwards into the remotest Future. We were wise indeed, could we discern truly the signs of our own time; and by knowledge of its wants and advantages, wisely adjust our own position in it. Let us, instead of gazing idly into the obscure distance, look calmly around us, for a little, on the perplexed scene where we stand. Perhaps, on a more serious inspection, something of its perplexity will disappear, some of its distinctive characters and deeper tendencies more clearly reveal themselves; whereby our own relations to it, our own true aims and endeavors in it, may also become clearer.

Were we required to characterize this age of ours by any single epithet, we should be tempted to call it, not an Heroical, Devotional, Philosophical, or Moral Age, but, above all others, the Mechanical Age. It is the Age of Machinery, in every outward and inward sense of that word; the age which, with its whole undivided might, forwards, teaches and practises the great art of adapting means to ends. Nothing is now done directly, or by hand; all is by rule and calculated contrivance. For the simplest operation, some helps and accompaniments, some cunning abbreviating process is in readiness. Our old modes of exertion are all discredited, and thrown aside. On every hand, the living artisan is driven from his workshop, to make room for a speedier, inanimate one. The shuttle drops from the fingers of the weaver, and falls into iron fingers that ply it faster. The sailor furls his sail, and lays down his oar; and bids a strong, unwearied servant, on vaporous wings, bear him through the waters. Men have crossed oceans by steam; the Birmingham Fire-king has visited the fabulous East; and the genius of the Cape, were there any Camoens now to sing it, has again been alarmed, and with far stranger thunders than Gama's. There is no end to machinery. Even the horse is stripped of his harness, and finds a fleet fire-horse yoked in his stead. Nay, we have an artist that hatches chickens by steam; the very brood-hen is to be superseded! For all earthly, and for some unearthly purposes, we have machines and mechanic furtherances; for mincing our cabbages; for casting us into magnetic sleep. We remove mountains, and make seas our smooth highway; nothing can resist us. We war with rude Nature; and, by our resistless engines, come off always victorious, and loaded with spoils.

What wonderful accessions have thus been made, and are still making, to the physical power of mankind; how much better fed, clothed, lodged and, in all outward respects, accommodated men now are, or might be, by a given quantity of labor, is a grateful reflection which forces itself on every one. What changes, too, this addition of power is introducing into the Social System; how wealth has more and more increased, and at the same time gathered itself more and more into masses, strangely altering the old relations, and increasing the distance between the rich and the poor, will be a question for Political Economists, and a much more complex and important one than any they have yet engaged with.

But leaving these matters for the present, let us observe how the mechanical genius of our time has diffused itself into quite other provinces. Not the external and physical alone is now managed by machinery, but the internal and spiritual also. Here too nothing follows its spontaneous course, nothing is left to be accomplished by old natural methods. Everything has its cunningly devised implements, its pre-established apparatus; it is not done by hand, but by machinery. Thus we have machines for Education: Lancastrian machines; Hamiltonian machines; monitors, maps and emblems. Instruction, that mysterious communing of Wisdom with Ignorance, is no longer an indefinable tentative process, requiring a study of individual aptitudes, and a perpetual variation of means and methods, to attain the same end; but a secure, universal, straightforward business, to be conducted in the gross, by proper mechanism, with such intellect as comes to hand. Then, we have Religious machines, of all imaginable varieties; the Bible-Society, professing a far higher and heavenly structure, is found, on inquiry, to be altogether an earthly contrivance; supported by collection of moneys, by fomenting of vanities, by puffing, intrigue and chicane; a machine for converting the Heathen. It is the same in all other departments. Has any man, or any society of men, a truth to speak, a piece of spiritual work to do; they can nowise proceed at once and with the mere natural organs, but must first call a public meeting, appoint committees, issue prospectuses, eat a public dinner; in a word, construct or borrow machinery, wherewith to speak it and do it. Without machinery they were hopeless, helpless; a colony of Hindoo weavers squatting in the heart of Lancashire. Mark, too, how every machine must have its moving power, in some of the great currents of society; every little sect among us, Unitarians, Utilitarians, Anabaptists, Phrenologists, must have its Periodical, its monthly or quarterly Magazine;—hanging out, like its windmill, into the *popularis aura*, to grind meal for the society.

With individuals, in like manner, natural strength avails little. No individual now hopes to accomplish the poorest enterprise single-handed and without mechanical aids; he must make interest with some existing corporation, and till his field with their oxen. In these days, more emphatically than ever, "to live, signifies to unite with a party, or to make one." Philosophy, Science, Art, Literature, all depend on machinery. No Newton, by silent meditation, now discovers the system of the world from the falling of an apple; but some quite other than Newton stands in his Museum, his Scientific Institution, and behind whole batteries of retorts, digesters and galvanic piles imperatively "interrogates Nature,"—who, however, shows no haste to answer. In defect of Raphaels, and Angelos, and Mozarts, we have Royal Academies of Painting, Sculpture, Music; whereby the languishing spirit of Art may be strengthened, as by the more generous diet of a Public Kitchen. Literature, too, has its Paternoster-row mechanism, its Trade-dinners, its Editorial conclaves, and huge subterranean, puffing bellows; so that books are not only printed, but, in a great measure, written and sold, by machinery.

National culture, spiritual benefit of all sorts, is under the same management. No Queen Christina, in these times, needs to send for her Descartes; no King Frederick for his Voltaire, and painfully nourish him with pensions and flattery: any sovereign of taste, who wishes to enlighten his people, has only to impose a new tax, and with the proceeds establish Philosophic Institutes. Hence the Royal and Imperial Societies, the Bibliothèques, Glyptothèques, Technothèques, which front us in all capital cities; like so many well-finished hives, to which it is expected the stray agencies of Wisdom will swarm of their own accord, and hive and make honey. In like manner, among ourselves, when it is thought that religion is declining, we have only to vote half-a-million's worth of bricks and mortar, and build new churches. In Ireland it seems they have gone still farther, having actually established a "Penny-a-week Purgatory-Society"! Thus does the Genius of Mechanism stand by to help us in all difficulties and emergencies, and with his iron back bears all our burdens.

These things, which we state lightly enough here, are yet of deep import, and indicate a mighty change in our whole manner of existence. For the same habit regulates not our modes of action alone, but our modes of thought and feeling. Men are grown mechanical in head and in heart, as well as in hand. They have lost faith in individual endeavor, and in natural force, of any kind. Not for internal perfection, but for external combinations and arrangements, for institutions, constitutions,—for Mechanism of one sort or other, do they hope and struggle. Their whole efforts, attachments, opinions, turn on mechanism, and are of a mechanical character.

We may trace this tendency in all the great manifestations of our time; in its intellectual aspect, the studies it most favors and its manner of conducting them; in its practical aspects, its politics, arts, religion, morals; in the whole sources, and throughout the whole currents, of its spiritual, no less than its material activity.

Consider, for example, the state of Science generally, in Europe, at this period. It is admitted, on all sides, that the Metaphysical and Moral Sciences are falling into decay, while the Physical are engrossing, every day, more respect and attention. In most of the European nations there is now no such thing as a Science of Mind; only more or less advancement in the general science, or the special sciences, of matter. The French were the first to desert Metaphysics; and though they have lately affected to revive their school, it has yet no signs of vitality. The land of Malebranche, Pascal, Descartes and Fénelon, has now only its Cousins and Villemains; while, in the department of Physics, it reckons far other names. Among ourselves, the Philosophy of Mind, after a rickety infancy, which never reached the vigor of manhood, fell suddenly into decay, languished and finally died out, with its last amiable cultivator, Professor Stewart. In no nation but Germany has any decisive effort been made in psychological science; not to speak of any decisive result. The science of the age, in short, is physical, chemical, physiological; in all shapes mechanical. Our favorite Mathematics, the highly prized exponent of all these other sciences, has also become more and more mechanical. Excellence in what is called its higher departments depends less on natural genius than on acquired expertness in wielding its machinery. Without undervaluing the wonderful results which a Lagrange or Laplace educes by means of it, we may remark, that their calculus, differential and integral, is little else than a more cunningly constructed arithmetical mill; where the factors being put in, are, as it were, ground into the true product, under cover, and without other effort on our part than steady turning of the handle. We have more Mathematics than ever; but less Mathesis. Archimedes and Plato could not have read the

*Mécanique Céleste;* but neither would the whole French Institute see aught in that saying, "God geometrizes!" but a sentimental rhodomontade.

Nay, our whole Metaphysics itself, from Locke's time downwards, has been physical; not a spiritual philosophy, but a material one. The singular estimation in which his Essay was so long held as a scientific work (an estimation grounded, indeed, on the estimable character of the man) will one day be thought a curious indication of the spirit of these times. His whole doctrine is mechanical, in its aim and origin, in its method and its results. It is not a philosophy of the mind: it is a mere discussion concerning the origin of our consciousness, or ideas, or whatever else they are called; a genetic history of what we see *in* the mind. The grand secrets of Necessity and Free-will, of the Mind's vital or non-vital dependence on Matter, of our mysterious relations to Time and Space, to God, to the Universe, are not, in the faintest degree, touched on in these inquiries; and seem not to have the smallest connection with them.

The last class of our Scotch Metaphysicians had a dim notion that much of this was wrong; but they knew not how to right it. The school of Reid had also from the first taken a mechanical course, not seeing any other. The singular conclusions at which Hume, setting out from their admitted premises, was arriving, brought this school into being; they let loose Instinct, as an undiscriminating bandog, to guard them against these conclusions;—they tugged lustily at the logical chain by which Hume was so coldly towing them and the world into bottomless abysses of Atheism and Fatalism. But the chain somehow snapped between them; and the issue has been that nobody now cares about either,—any more than about Hartley's, Darwin's or Priestley's contemporaneous doings in England. Hartley's vibrations and vibratiuncles, one would think, were material and mechanical enough; but our Continental neighbors have gone still farther. One of their philosophers has lately discovered, that "as the liver secretes bile, so does the brain secrete thought;" which astonishing discovery Dr. Cabanis, more lately still, in his *Rapports du physique et du morale de l'homme,* has pushed into its minutest developments.

The metaphysical philosophy of this last inquirer is certainly no shadowy or unsubstantial one. He fairly lays open our moral structure with his dissecting-knives and real metal probes; and exhibits it to the inspection of mankind, by Leuwenhoek microscopes, and inflation with the anatomical blowpipe. Thought, he is inclined to hold, is still secreted by the brain; but then Poetry and Religion (and it is really worth knowing) are "a product of the smaller intestines"! We have the greatest admiration for this learned doctor: with what scientific stoicism he walks through the land of wonders, unwondering; like a wise man through some huge, gaudy, imposing Vauxhall, whose fire-works, cascades and symphonies, the vulgar may enjoy and believe in,—but where he finds nothing real but the saltpetre, pasteboard and catgut. His book may be regarded as the ultimatum of mechanical metaphysics in our time; a remarkable realization of what in Martinus Scriblerus was still only an idea, that "as the jack had a meat-roasting quality, so had the body a thinking quality,"—upon the strength of which the Nurembergers were to build a wood-and-leather man, "who should reason as well as most country parsons." Vaucanson did indeed make a wooden duck, that seemed to eat and digest; but that bold scheme of the Nurembergers remained for a more modern virtuoso.

This condition of the two great departments of knowledge,—the outward, cultivated exclusively on mechanical principles; the inward, finally abandoned, because, cultivated on such principles, it is found to yield no result,—sufficiently indicates the intellectual bias of our time, its all-pervading disposition towards that line of inquiry. In fact, an inward persuasion has long been diffusing itself, and now and then even comes to utterance, That, except the external, there are no true sciences; that to the inward world (if there be any) our only conceivable road is through the outward; that, in short, what cannot be investigated and understood mechanically, cannot be investigated and understood at all. We advert the more particularly to these intellectual propensities, as to prominent symptoms of our age, because Opinion is at all times doubly related to Action, first as cause, then as effect, and the speculative tendency of any age will therefore give us, on the whole, the best indications of its practical tendency.

Nowhere, for example, is the deep, almost exclusive faith we have in Mechanism more visible than in the Politics of this time. Civil government does by its nature include much that is mechanical, and must be treated accordingly. We term it indeed, in ordinary language, the Machine of Society, and talk of it as the grand working wheel from which all private machines must derive, or to which they must adapt, their movements. Considered merely as a metaphor, all this is well enough; but here, as in so many other cases, the "foam hardens itself into a shell," and the shadow we have wantonly evoked stands terrible before us and will not depart at our bidding. Government includes much also that is not mechanical, and cannot be treated mechanically; of which latter truth, as appears to us, the political speculations and exertions of our time are taking less and less cognizance.

Nay, in the very outset, we might note the mighty interest taken in *mere political arrangements,* as itself the sign of a mechanical age. The whole discontent of Europe takes this direction. The deep, strong cry of all civilized nations,—a cry which, every one now sees, must and will be answered, is: Give us a reform of Government! A good structure of legislation, a proper check upon the executive, a wise arrangement of the judiciary, is *all* that is wanting for human happiness. The Philosopher of this age is not a Socrates, a Plato, a Hooker, or Taylor, who inculcates on men the necessity and infinite worth of moral goodness, the great truth that our happiness depends on the mind which is within us, and not on the circumstances which are without us; but a Smith, a De Lolme, a Bentham, who chiefly inculcates the reverse of this,—that our happiness depends entirely on external circumstances; nay, that the strength and dignity of the mind within us is itself the creature and consequence of these. Were the laws, the government, in good order, all were well with us; the rest would care for itself! Dissentients from this opinion, expressed or implied, are now rarely to be met with; widely and angrily as men differ in its application, the principle is admitted by all.

Equally mechanical, and of equal simplicity, are the methods proposed by both parties for completing or securing this all-sufficient perfection of arrangement. It is no longer the moral, religious, spiritual condition of the people that is our concern, but their physical, practical, economical condition, as regulated by public laws. Thus is the Body-politic more than ever worshipped and tendered; but the Soul-politic less than ever. Love of country, in any high or generous sense, in any other than an almost animal sense, or mere habit, has little importance attached to it in such reforms, or in the opposition shown them. Men are to be guided only by their self-interests. Good government is a good balancing of these; and, except a keen eye and appetite for self-interest, requires no virtue in any quarter. To both parties it is emphatically a machine: to the discontented, a "taxing-machine;" to the contented, a "machine for securing property." Its duties and its faults are not those of a father, but of an active parish constable.

Thus it is by the mere condition of the machine, by preserving it untouched, or else by reconstructing it, and oiling it anew, that man's salvation as a social being is to be insured and indefinitely promoted. Contrive the fabric of law aright, and without farther effort on your part, that divine spirit of Freedom, which all hearts venerate and long for, will of herself come to inhabit it; and under her healing wings every noxious influence will wither, every good and salutary one more and more expand. Nay, so devoted are we to this principle, and at the same time so curiously mechanical, that a new trade, specially grounded on it, has arisen among us, under the name of "Codification," or code-making in the abstract; whereby any people, for a reasonable consideration, may be accommodated with a patent code;—more easily than curious individuals with patent breeches, for the people does *not* need to be measured first.

To us who live in the midst of all this, and see continually the faith, hope and practice of every one founded on Mechanism of one kind or other, it is apt to seem quite natural, and as if it could never have been otherwise. Nevertheless, if we recollect or reflect a little, we shall find both that it has been, and might again be otherwise. The domain of Mechanism—meaning thereby political, ecclesiastical or other outward establishments—was once considered as embracing, and we are persuaded can at any time embrace, but a limited portion of man's interests, and by no means the highest portion.

To speak a little pedantically, there is a science of *Dynamics* in man's fortunes and nature, as well as of *Mechanics*. There is a science which treats of, and practically addresses, the primary, unmodified forces and energies of man, the mysterious springs of Love, and Fear, and Wonder, of Enthusiasm, Poetry, Religion, all which have a truly vital and *infinite* character; as well as a science which practically addresses the finite, modified development of these, when they take the shape of immediate "motives," as hope of reward, or as fear of punishment.

Now it is certain, that in former times the wise men, the enlightened lovers of their kind, who appeared generally as Moralists, Poets or Priests, did, without neglecting the Mechanical province, deal chiefly with the Dynamical, applying themselves chiefly to regulate, increase and purify the inward primary powers of man; and fancying that herein lay the main difficulty, and the best service they could undertake. But a wide difference is manifest in our age. For the wise men, who now appear as Political Philosophers, deal exclusively with the Mechanical province; and occupying themselves in counting up and estimating men's motives, strive by curious checking and balancing, and other adjustments of Profit and Loss, to guide them to their true advantage: while, unfortunately, those same "motives" are so innumerable, and so variable in every individual, that no really useful conclusion can ever be drawn from their enumeration. But though Mechanism, wisely contrived, has done much for man in a social and moral point of view, we cannot be persuaded that it has ever been the chief source of his worth or happiness. Consider the great elements of human enjoyment, the attainments and possessions that exalt man's life to its present height, and see what part of these he owes to institutions, to Mechanism of any kind; and what to the instinctive, unbounded force, which Nature herself lent him, and still continues to him. Shall we say, for example, that Science and Art are indebted principally to the founders of Schools and Universities? Did not Science originate rather, and gain advancement, in the obscure closets of the Roger Bacons, Keplers, Newtons; in the workshops of the Fausts and the Watts; wherever, and in what guise soever Nature, from the first times downwards, had sent a gifted spirit upon the earth? Again, were Homer and Shakspeare members of any beneficed guild, or made Poets by means of it? Were Painting and Sculpture created by forethought, brought into the world by institutions for that end? No; Science and Art have, from first to last, been the free gift of Nature; an unsolicited, unexpected gift; often even a fatal one. These things rose up, as it were, by spontaneous growth, in the free soil and sunshine of Nature. They were not planted or grafted, nor even greatly multiplied or improved by the culture or manuring of institutions. Generally speaking, they have derived only partial help from these; often enough have suffered damage. They made constitutions for themselves. They originated in the Dynamical nature of man, not in his Mechanical nature.

Or, to take an infinitely higher instance, that of the Christian Religion, which, under every theory of it, in the believing or unbelieving mind, must ever be regarded as the crowning glory, or rather the life and soul, of our whole modern culture: How did Christianity arise and spread abroad among men? Was it by institutions, and establishments and well-arranged systems of mechanism? Not so; on the contrary, in all past and existing institutions for those ends, its divine spirit has invariably been found to languish and decay. It arose in the mystic deeps of man's soul; and was spread abroad by the "preaching of the word," by simple, altogether natural and individual efforts; and flew, like hallowed fire, from heart to heart, till all were purified and illuminated by it; and its heavenly light shone, as it still shines, and (as sun or star) will ever shine, through the whole dark destinies of man. Here again was no Mechanism; man's highest attainment was accomplished Dynamically, not Mechanically.

Nay, we will venture to say, that no high attainment, not even any far-extending movement among men, was ever accomplished otherwise. Strange as it may seem, if we read History with any degree of thoughtfulness, we shall find that the checks and balances of Profit and Loss have never been the grand agents with men; that they have never been roused into deep, thorough, all-pervading efforts by any computable prospect of Profit and Loss, for any visible, finite object; but always for some invisible and infinite one. The Crusades took their rise in Religion; their visible object was, commercially speaking, worth nothing. It was the boundless Invisible world that was laid bare in the imaginations of those men; and in its burning light, the visible shrunk as a scroll. Not mechanical, nor produced by mechanical means, was this vast movement. No dining at Freemasons' Tavern, with the other long train of modern machinery; no cunning reconciliation of "vested interests," was required here: only the passionate voice of one man, the rapt soul looking through the eyes of one man; and rugged, steel-clad Europe trembled beneath his words, and followed him whither he listed. In later ages it was still the same. The Reformation had an invisible, mystic and ideal aim; the result was indeed to be embodied in external things; but its spirit, its worth, was internal, invisible, infinite. Our English Revolution too originated in Religion. Men did battle, in those old days, not for Purse-sake, but for Conscience-sake. Nay, in our own days it is no way different. The French Revolution itself had something higher in it than cheap bread and a Habeas-corpus act. Here too was an Idea; a Dynamic, not a Mechanic force. It was a struggle, though a blind and at last an insane one, for the infinite, divine nature of Right, of Freedom, of Country.

Thus does man, in every age, vindicate, consciously or unconsciously, his celestial birthright. Thus does Nature hold on her wondrous, unquestionable course; and all our systems and theories are but so many froth-eddies or sand-banks, which from time to time she casts up, and washes away. When we can drain the Ocean into mill-ponds, and bottle up the Force of Gravity, to be sold by retail, in gas-jars; then may we hope to comprehend the infinitudes of man's soul under formulas of Profit and Loss; and rule over this too, as over a patent engine, by checks, and valves, and balances.

Nay, even with regard to Government itself, can it be necessary to remind any one that Freedom, without which indeed all spiritual life is impossible, depends on infinitely more complex influences than either the extension or the curtailment of the "democratic interest"? Who is there that, "taking the high *priori* road," shall point out what these influences are; what deep, subtle, inextricably entangled influences they have been and may be? For man is not the creature and product of Mechanism; but, in a far truer sense, its creator and producer: it is the noble People that makes the noble Government; rather than conversely. On the whole, Institutions are much; but they are not all. The freest and highest spirits of the world have often been found under strange outward circumstances: Saint Paul and his brother

Apostles were politically slaves; Epictetus was personally one. Again, forget the influences of Chivalry and Religion, and ask: What countries produced Columbus and Las Casas? Or, descending from virtue and heroism to mere energy and spiritual talent: Cortes, Pizarro, Alba, Ximenes? The Spaniards of the sixteenth century were indisputably the noblest nation of Europe; yet they had the Inquisition and Philip II. They have the same government at this day; and are the lowest nation. The Dutch too have retained their old constitution; but no Siege of Leyden, no William the Silent, not even an Egmont or De Witt any longer appears among them. With ourselves also, where much has changed, effect has nowise followed cause as it should have done: two centuries ago, the Commons Speaker addressed Queen Elizabeth on bended knees, happy that the virago's foot did not even smite him; yet the people were then governed, not by a Castlereagh, but by a Burghley; they had their Shakspeare and Philip Sidney, where we have our Sheridan Knowles and Beau Brummel.

These and the like facts are so familiar, the truths which they preach so obvious, and have in all past times been so universally believed and acted on, that we should almost feel ashamed for repeating them; were it not that, on every hand, the memory of them seems to have passed away, or at best died into a faint tradition, of no value as a practical principle. To judge by the loud clamor of our Constitution-builders, Statists, Economists, directors, creators, reformers of Public Societies; in a word, all manner of Mechanists, from the Cartwright up to the Code-maker; and by the nearly total silence of all Preachers and Teachers who should give a voice to Poetry, Religion and Morality, we might fancy either that man's Dynamical nature was, to all spiritual intents, extinct, or else so perfected that nothing more was to be made of it by the old means; and henceforth only in his Mechanical contrivances did any hope exist for him.

To define the limits of these two departments of man's activity, which work into one another, and by means of one another, so intricately and inseparably, were by its nature an impossible attempt. Their relative importance, even to the wisest mind, will vary in different times, according to the special wants and dispositions of those times. Meanwhile, it seems clear enough that only in the right co-ordination of the two, and the vigorous forwarding of *both,* does our true line of action lie. Undue cultivation of the inward or Dynamical province leads to idle, visionary, impracticable courses, and, especially in rude eras, to Superstition and Fanaticism, with their long train of baleful and well-known evils. Undue cultivation of the outward, again, though less immediately prejudicial, and even for the time productive of many palpable benefits, must, in the long-run, by destroying Moral Force, which is the parent of all other Force, prove not less certainly, and perhaps still more hopelessly, pernicious. This, we take it, is the grand characteristic of our age. By our skill in Mechanism, it has come to pass, that in the management of external things we excel all other ages; while in whatever respects the pure moral nature, in true dignity of soul and character, we are perhaps inferior to most civilized ages.

In fact, if we look deeper, we shall find that this faith in Mechanism has now struck its roots down into man's most intimate, primary sources of conviction; and is thence sending up, over his whole life and activity, innumerable stems,—fruit-bearing and poison-bearing. The truth is, men have lost their belief in the Invisible, and believe, and hope, and work only in the Visible; or, to speak it in other words: This is not a Religious age. Only the material, the immediately practical, not the divine and spiritual, is important to us. The infinite, absolute character of Virtue has passed into a finite, conditional one; it is no longer a worship of the Beautiful and Good; but a calculation of the Profitable. Worship, indeed, in any sense, is not recognized among us, or is mechanically explained into Fear of pain, or Hope of pleasure. Our true Deity is Mechanism. It has subdued external Nature for us, and we think it will do all other things. We are Giants in physical power: in a deeper than metaphorical sense, we are Titans, that strive, by heaping mountain on mountain, to conquer Heaven also.

The strong Mechanical character, so visible in the spiritual pursuits and methods of this age, may be traced much farther into the condition and prevailing disposition of our spiritual nature itself. Consider, for example, the general fashion of Intellect in this era. Intellect, the power man has of knowing and believing, is now nearly synonymous with Logic, or the mere power of arranging and communicating. Its implement is not Meditation, but Argument. "Cause and effect" is almost the only category under which we look at, and work with, all Nature. Our first question with regard to any object is not, What is it? but, How is it? We are no longer instinctively driven to apprehend, and lay to heart, what is Good and Lovely, but rather to inquire, as on-lookers, how it is produced, whence it comes, whither it goes. Our favorite Philosophers have no love and no hatred; they stand among us not to do, nor to create anything, but as a sort of Logic-mills to grind out the true causes and effects of all that is done and created. To the eye of a Smith, a Hume or a Constant, all is well that works quietly. An Order of Ignatius Loyola, a Prebyterianism of John Knox, a Wickliffe or a Henry the Eighth, are simply so many mechanical phenomena, caused or causing.

The *Euphuist* of our day differs much from his pleasant predecessors. An intellectual dapperling of these times boasts chiefly of his irresistible perspicacity, his "dwelling in the daylight of truth," and so forth; which, on examination, turns out to be a dwelling in the *rush*-light of "closet-logic," and a deep unconsciousness that there is any other light to dwell in or any other objects to survey with it. Wonder, indeed, is, on all hands, dying out: it is the sign of uncultivation to wonder. Speak to any small man of a high, majestic Reformation, of a high, majestic Luther, and forthwith he sets about "accounting" for it; how the "circumstances of the time" called for such a character, and found him, we suppose, standing girt and road-ready, to do its errand; how the "circumstances of the time" created, fashioned, floated him quietly along into the result; how, in short, this small man, had he been there, could have performed the like himself! For it is the "force of circumstances" that does everything; the force of one man can do nothing. Now all this is grounded on little more than a metaphor. We figure Society as a "Machine," and that mind is opposed to mind, as body is to body; whereby two, or at most ten, little minds must be stronger than one great mind. Notable absurdity! For the plain truth, very plain, we think, is, that minds are opposed to minds in quite a different way; and *one* man that has a higher Wisdom, a hitherto unknown spiritual Truth in him, is stronger, not than ten men that have it not, or than ten thousand, but than *all* men that have it not; and stands among them with a quite ethereal, angelic power, as with a sword out of Heaven's own armory, sky-tempered, which no buckler, and no tower of brass, will finally withstand.

But to us, in these times, such considerations rarely occur. We enjoy, we see nothing by direct vision; but only by reflection, and in anatomical dismemberment. Like Sir Hudibras, for every Why we must have a Wherefore. We have our little *theory* on all human and divine things. Poetry, the workings of genius itself, which in all times, with one or another meaning, has been called Inspiration, and held to be mysterious and inscrutable, is no longer without its scientific exposition. The building of the lofty rhyme is like any other masonry or bricklaying: we have theories of its rise, height, decline and fall,—which latter, it would seem, is now near, among all people. Of our "Theories of Taste," as they are called, wherein the deep, infinite, unspeakable Love of Wisdom and Beauty, which dwells in all men, is "explained," made mechanically visible, from "Association" and the like, why should we say anything? Hume has written us a "Natural History of Religion;" in which one Natural History all the rest are included. Strangely too does the general feeling coincide with Hume's in this wonderful problem; for whether his "Natural History" be the right one or not, that Religion must have a Natural History, all of us, cleric and laic, seem to be agreed. He indeed regards it as a Disease, we again as Health; so far there is a difference; but in our first principle we are at one.

To what extent theological Unbelief, we mean intellectual dissent from the Church, in its view of Holy Writ, prevails at this day, would be a highly important, were it not, under any circumstances, an almost impossible inquiry. But the Unbelief, which is of a still more fundamental character, every man may see prevailing, with scarcely any but the faintest contradiction, all around him; even in the Pulpit itself. Religion in most countries, more or less in every country, is no longer what it was, and should be,—a thousand-voiced psalm from the heart of Man to his invisible Father, the fountain of all Goodness, Beauty, Truth, and revealed in every revelation of these; but for the most part, a wise prudential feeling grounded on mere calculation; a matter, as all others now are, of Expediency and Utility; whereby some smaller quantum of earthly enjoyment may be exchanged for a far larger quantum of celestial enjoyment. Thus Religion too is Profit, a working for wages; not Reverence, but vulgar Hope or Fear. Many, we know, very many we hope, are still religious in a far different sense; were it not so, our case were too desperate: but to witness that such is the temper of the times, we take any calm observant man, who agrees or disagrees in our feeling on the matter, and ask him whether our *view* of it is not in general well-founded.

Literature, too, if we consider it, gives similar testimony. At no former era has Literature, the printed communication of Thought, been of such importance as it is now. We often hear that the Church is in danger; and truly so it is,—in a danger it seems not to know of: for, with its tithes in the most perfect safety, its functions are becoming more and more superseded. The true Church of England, at this moment, lies in the Editors of its Newspapers. These preach to the people daily, weekly; admonishing kings themselves; advising peace or war, with an authority which only the first Reformers, and a long past class of Popes, were possessed of; inflicting moral censure; imparting moral encouragement, consolation, edification; in all ways diligently "administering the Discipline of the Church." It may be said too, that in private disposition the new Preachers somewhat resemble the Mendicant Friars of old times: outwardly full of holy zeal; inwardly not without stratagem, and hunger for terrestrial things. But omitting this class, and the boundless host of watery personages who pipe, as they are able, on so many scrannel straws, let us look at the higher regions of Literature, where, if anywhere, the pure melodies of Poesy and Wisdom should be heard. Of natural talent there is no deficiency: one or two richly endowed individuals even give us a superiority in this respect. But what is the song they sing? Is it a tone of the Memnon Statue, breathing music as the *light* first touches it? A "liquid wisdom," disclosing to our sense the deep, infinite harmonies of Nature and man's soul? Alas, no! It is not a matin or vesper hymn to the Spirit of Beauty, but a fierce clashing of cymbals, and shouting of multitudes, as children pass through the fire to Moloch! Poetry itself has no eye for the Invisible. Beauty is no longer the god it worships, but some brute image of Strength; which we may well call an idol, for true Strength is one and the same with Beauty, and its worship also is a hymn. The meek, silent Light can mould, create and purify all Nature; but the loud Whirlwind, the sign and product of Disunion, of Weakness, passes on, and is forgotten. How widely this veneration for the physically Strongest has spread itself through Literature, any one may judge who reads either criticism or poem. We praise a work, not as "true," but as "strong;" our highest praise is that it has "affected" us, has "terrified" us. All this, it has been well observed, is the "maximum of the Barbarous," the symptom, not of vigorous refinement, but of luxurious corruption. It speaks much, too, for men's indestructible love of truth, that nothing of this kind will abide with them; that even the talent of a Byron cannot permanently seduce us into idol worship; that he too, with all his wild siren charming, already begins to be disregarded and forgotten.

Again, with respect to our Moral condition: here also, he who runs may read that the same physical, mechanical influences are everywhere busy. For the "superior morality," of which we hear so much, we too would desire to be thankful: at the same time, it were but blindness to deny that this "superior morality" is properly rather an "inferior criminality," produced not by greater love of Virtue, but by greater perfection of Police; and of that far subtler and stronger Police, called Public Opinion. This last watches over us with its Argus eyes more keenly than ever; but the "inward eye" seems heavy with sleep. Of any belief in invisible, divine things, we find as few traces in our Morality as elsewhere. It is by tangible, material considerations that we are guided, not by inward and spiritual. Self-denial, the parent of all virtue, in any true sense of that word, has perhaps seldom been rarer: so rare is it, that the most, even in their abstract speculations, regard its existence as a chimera. Virtue is Pleasure, is Profit; no celestial, but an earthly thing. Virtuous men, Philanthropists, Martyrs are happy accidents; their "taste" lies the right way! In all senses, we worship and follow after Power; which may be called a physical pursuit. No man now loves Truth, as Truth must be loved, with an infinite love; but only with a finite love, and as it were *par amours*. Nay, properly speaking, he does not *believe* and know it, but only "*thinks*" it, and that "there is every probability"! He preaches it aloud, and rushes courageously forth with it,—if there is a multitude huzzaing at his back; yet ever keeps looking over his shoulder, and the instant the huzzaing languishes, he too stops short.

In fact, what morality we have takes the shape of Ambition, of "Honor:" beyond money and money's worth, our only rational blessedness is Popularity. It were but a fool's trick to die for conscience. Only for "character," by duel, or, in case of extremity, by suicide, is the wise man bound to die. By arguing on the "force of circumstances," we have argued away all force from ourselves; and stand leashed together, uniform in dress and movement, like the rowers of some boundless galley. This and that may be right and true; *but* we must not do it. Wonderful "Force of Public Opinion"! We must act and walk in all points as it prescribes; follow the traffic it bids us, realize the sum of money, the degree of "influence" it expects of us, *or* we shall be lightly esteemed; certain mouthfuls of articulate wind will be blown at us, and this what mortal courage can front? Thus, while civil liberty is more and more secured to us, our moral liberty is all but lost. Practically considered, our creed is Fatalism; and, free in hand and foot, we are shackled in heart and soul with far straiter than feudal chains. Truly may we say, with the Philosopher, "the deep meaning of the Laws of Mechanism lies heavy on us;" and in the closet, in the market-place, in the temple, by the social hearth, encumbers the whole movements of our mind, and over our noblest faculties is spreading a nightmare sleep.

These dark features, we are aware, belong more or less to other ages, as well as to ours. This faith in Mechanism, in the all-importance of physical things, is in every age the common refuge of Weakness and blind Discontent; of all who believe, as many will ever do, that man's true good lies without him, not within. We are aware also, that, as applied to ourselves in all their aggravation, they form but half a picture; that in the whole picture there are bright lights as well as gloomy shadows. If we here dwell chiefly on the latter, let us not be blamed: it is in general more profitable to reckon up our defects than to boast of our attainments.

Neither, with all these evils more or less clearly before us, have we at any time despaired of the fortunes of society. Despair, or even despondency, in that respect, appears to us, in all cases, a groundless feeling. We have a faith in the imperishable dignity of man; in the high vocation to which, throughout this his earthly history, he has been appointed. However it may be with individual nations, whatever melancholic speculators may assert, it seems a well-ascertained fact, that in all times, reckoning even from those of the Heraclides and Pelasgi, the happiness and greatness of mankind at large have been continually progressive. Doubtless this age also is advancing. Its very unrest, its ceaseless activity, its discontent contains matter of promise. Knowledge, education are opening the eyes of the humblest; are increasing the number of thinking minds without limit. This is as it should be; for not in turning back, not in resisting, but only in resolutely struggling forward, does our life consist.

Nay, after all, our spiritual maladies are but of Opinion; we are but fettered by chains of our own forging, and which ourselves also can rend asunder. This deep, paralyzed subjection to physical objects comes not from Nature, but from our own unwise mode of *viewing* Nature. Neither can we understand that man wants, at this hour, any faculty of heart, soul or body, that ever belonged to him. "He, who has been born, has been a First Man;" has had lying before his young eyes, and as yet unhardened into scientific shapes, a world as plastic, infinite, divine, as lay before the eyes of Adam himself. If Mechanism, like some glass bell, encircles and imprisons us; if the soul looks forth on a fair heavenly country which it cannot reach, and pines, and in its scanty atmosphere is ready to perish,—yet the bell is but of glass; "one bold stroke to break the bell in pieces, and thou art delivered!" Not the invisible world is wanting, for it dwells in man's soul, and this last is still here. Are the solemn temples, in which the Divinity was once visibly revealed among us, crumbling away? We can repair them, we can rebuild them. The wisdom, the heroic worth of our forefathers, which we have lost, we can recover. That admiration of old nobleness, which now so often shows itself as a faint *dilettantism,* will one day become a generous emulation, and man may again be all that he has been, and more than he has been. Nor are these the mere day-dreams of fancy; they are clear possibilities; nay, in this time they are even assuming the character of hopes. Indications we do see in other countries and in our own, signs infinitely cheering to us, that Mechanism is not always to be our hard taskmaster, but one day to be our pliant, all-ministering servant; that a new and brighter spiritual era is slowly evolving itself for all men. But on these things our present course forbids us to enter.

Meanwhile, that great outward changes are in progress can be doubtful to no one. The time is sick and out of joint. Many things have reached their height; and it is a wise adage that tells us, "the darkest hour is nearest the dawn." Wherever we can gather indication of the public thought, whether from printed books, as in France or Germany, or from Carbonari rebellions and other political tumults, as in Spain, Portugal, Italy and Greece, the voice it utters is the same. The thinking minds of all nations call for change. There is a deep-lying struggle in the whole fabric of society; a boundless grinding collision of the New with the Old. The French Revolution, as is now visible enough, was not the parent of this mighty movement, but its offspring. Those two hostile influences, which always exist in human things, and on the constant intercommunion of which depends their health and safety, had lain in separate masses, accumulating through generations, and France was the scene of their fiercest explosion; but the final issue was not unfolded in that country: nay it is not yet anywhere unfolded. Political freedom is hitherto the object of these efforts; but they will not and cannot stop there. It is towards a higher freedom than mere freedom from oppression by his fellow-mortal, that man dimly aims. Of this higher, heavenly freedom, which is "man's reasonable service," all his noble institutions, his faithful endeavors and loftiest attainments, are but the body, and more and more approximated emblem.

On the whole, as this wondrous planet, Earth, is journeying with its fellows through infinite Space, so are the wondrous destinies embarked on it journeying through infinite Time, under a higher guidance than ours. For the present, as our astronomy informs us, its path lies towards *Hercules*, the constellation of *Physical Power:* but that is not our most pressing concern. Go where it will, the deep HEAVEN will be around it. Therein let us have hope and sure faith. To reform a world, to reform a nation, no wise man will undertake; and all but foolish men know, that the only solid, though a far slower reformation, is what each begins and perfects on *himself*.

FROM

# SARTOR RESARTUS

## *Chapter VIII*

### *Natural Supernaturalism*

It is in his stupendous Section, headed *Natural Supernaturalism,* that the Professor first becomes a Seer; and, after long effort, such as we have witnessed, finally subdues under his feet this refractory Clothes-Philosophy, and takes victorious possession thereof. Phantasms enough he has had to struggle with; "Cloth-webs and Cob-webs," of Imperial Mantles, Superannuated Symbols, and what not: yet still did he courageously pierce through. Nay, worst of all, two quite mysterious, world-embracing Phantasms, TIME and SPACE, have ever hovered round him, perplexing and bewildering: but with these also he now resolutely grapples, these also he victoriously rends asunder. In a word, he has looked fixedly on Existence, till, one after the other, its earthly hulls and garnitures have all melted away; and now, to his rapt vision, the interior celestial Holy-of-Holies lies disclosed.

Here, therefore, properly it is that the Philosophy of Clothes attains to Transcendentalism; this last leap, can we but clear it, takes us safe into the promised land, where *Palingenesia,* in all senses, may be considered as beginning. "Courage, then!" may our Diogenes exclaim, with better right than Diogenes the First once did. This stupendous Section we, after long painful meditation, have found not to be unintelligible; but, on the contrary, to grow clear, nay radiant, and all-illuminating. Let the reader, turning on it what utmost force of speculative intellect is in him, do his part; as we, by judicious selection and adjustment, shall study to do ours:—

"Deep has been, and is, the significance of Miracles," thus quietly begins the Professor; "far deeper perhaps than we imagine. Meanwhile, the question of questions were: What specially is a Miracle? To that Dutch King of Siam, an icicle had been a miracle; whoso had carried with him an air-pump, and vial of vitriolic ether, might have worked a miracle. To my Horse, again, who unhappily is still more unscientific, do not I work a miracle, and magical *'Open sesame!'* every time I please to pay twopence, and open for him an impassable *Schlagbaum,* or shut Turnpike?

"'But is not a real Miracle simply a violation of the Laws of Nature?' ask several. Whom I answer by this new question: What are the Laws of Nature? To me perhaps the rising of one from the dead were no violation of these Laws, but a confirmation; were some far deeper Law, now first penetrated into, and by Spiritual Force, even as the rest have all been, brought to bear on us with its Material Force.

"Here too may some inquire, not without astonishment: On what ground shall one, that can make Iron swim, come and declare that therefore he can teach Religion? To us, truly, of the Nineteenth Century, such declaration were inept enough; which nevertheless to our fathers, of the First Century, was full of meaning.

"'But is it not the deepest Law of Nature that she be constant?' cries an illuminated class: 'Is not the Machine of the Universe fixed to move by unalterable rules?' Probable enough, good friends; nay I, too, must believe that the God whom ancient inspired men assert to be 'without variableness or shadow of turning,' does indeed never change; that Nature, that the Universe, which no one whom it so pleases can be prevented from calling a Machine, does move by the most unalterable rules. And now of you, too, I make the old inquiry: What those same unalterable rules, forming the complete Statute-Book of Nature, may possibly be?

"They stand written in our Works of Science, say you; in the accumulated records of Man's Experience?—Was Man with his Experience present at the Creation, then, to see how it all went on? Have any deepest scientific individuals yet dived down to the foundations of the Universe, and gauged everything there? Did the Maker take them into His counsel; that they read His ground-plan of the incomprehensible All; and can say, This stands marked therein, and no more than this? Alas, not in anywise! These scientific individuals have been nowhere but where we also are; have seen some hand-breadths deeper than we see into the Deep that is infinite, without bottom as without shore.

"Laplace's Book on the Stars, wherein he exhibits that certain Planets, with their Satellites, gyrate round our worthy Sun, at a rate and in a course, which, by greatest good fortune, he and the like of him have succeeded in detecting,—is to me as precious as to another. But is this what thou namest 'Mechanism of the Heavens,' and 'System of the World;' this, wherein Sirius and the Pleiades, and all Herschel's Fifteen thousand Suns per minute, being left out, some paltry handful of Moons, and inert Balls, had been—looked at, nicknamed, and marked in the Zodiacal Way-bill; so that we can now prate of their Whereabout; their How, their Why, their What, being hid from us, as in the signless Inane?

"System of Nature! To the wisest man, wide as is his vision, Nature remains of quite *infinite* depth, of quite infinite expansion; and all Experience thereof limits itself to some few computed centuries and measured square-miles. The course of Nature's phases, on this our little fraction of a Planet, is partially known to us: but who knows what deeper courses these depend on; what infinitely larger Cycle (of causes) our little Epicycle revolves on? To the Minnow every cranny and pebble, and quality and accident, of its little native Creek may have become familiar: but does the Minnow understand the Ocean Tides and periodic Currents, the Trade-winds, and Monsoons, and Moon's Eclipses; by all which the condition of its little Creek is regulated, and may, from time to time (*un*miraculously enough), be quite overset and reversed? Such a minnow is Man; his Creek this Planet Earth; his Ocean the immeasurable All; his Monsoons and periodic Currents the mysterious Course of Providence through Æons of Æons.

"We speak of the Volume of Nature: and truly a Volume it is,—whose Author and Writer is God. To read it! Dost thou, does man, so much as well know the Alphabet thereof? With its Words, Sentences, and grand descriptive Pages, poetical and philosophical, spread out through Solar Systems, and Thousands of Years, we shall not try thee. It is a Volume written in celestial hieroglyphs, in the true Sacred-writing; of which even Prophets are happy that they can read here a line and there a line. As for your Institutes, and Academies of Science, they strive bravely; and, from amid the thick-crowded, inextricably intertwisted hieroglyphic writing, pick out, by dexterous combination, some Letters in the vulgar Character, and therefrom put together this and the other economic Recipe, of high avail in Practice. That Nature is more than some boundless Volume of such Recipes, or huge, well-nigh inexhaustible Domestic-Cookery Book, of which the whole secret will in this manner one day evolve itself, the fewest dream.

"Custom," continues the Professor, "doth make dotards of us all. Consider well, thou wilt find that Custom is the greatest of Weavers; and weaves air-raiment for all the Spirits of the Universe; whereby indeed these dwell with us visibly, as ministering servants, in our houses and workshops; but their spiritual nature becomes, to the most, forever hidden. Philosophy complains that Custom has hoodwinked us, from the first; that we do everything by Custom, even Believe by it; that our very Axioms, let us boast of Free-thinking as we may, are oftenest simply such Beliefs as we have never heard questioned. Nay, what is Philosophy throughout but a continual battle against Custom; an ever-renewed effort to *transcend* the sphere of blind Custom, and so become Transcendental?

"Innumerable are the illusions and legerdemain-tricks of Custom: but of all these, perhaps the cleverest is her knack of persuading us that the Miraculous, by simple repetition, ceases to be Miraculous. True, it is by this means we live; for man must work as well as wonder: and herein is Custom so far a kind nurse, guiding him to his true benefit. But she is a fond foolish nurse, or rather we are false foolish nurslings, when, in our resting and reflecting hours, we prolong the same deception. Am I to view the Stupendous with stupid indifference, because I have seen it twice, or two hundred, or two million times? There is no reason in Nature or in Art why I should: unless, indeed, I am a mere Work-Machine, for whom the divine gift of Thought were no other than the terrestrial gift of Steam is to the Steam-engine; a power whereby cotton might be spun, and money and money's worth realized.

"Notable enough too, here as elsewhere, wilt thou find the potency of Names; which indeed are but one kind of such custom-woven, wonder-hiding Garments. Witchcraft, and all manner of Spectre-work, and Demonology, we have now named Madness, and Diseases of the Nerves. Seldom reflecting that still the new question comes upon us: What is Madness, what are Nerves? Ever, as before, does Madness remain a mysterious-terrific, altogether *infernal* boiling-up of the Nether Chaotic Deep, through this fair-painted Vision of Creation, which swims thereon, which we name the Real. Was Luther's

Picture of the Devil less a Reality, whether it were formed within the bodily eye, or without it? In every the wisest Soul lies a whole world of internal Madness, an authentic Demon-Empire; out of which, indeed, his world of Wisdom has been creatively built together, and now rests there, as on its dark foundations does a habitable flowery Earth-rind.

"But deepest of all illusory Appearances, for hiding Wonder, as for many other ends, are your two grand fundamental world-enveloping Appearances, SPACE and TIME. These, as spun and woven for us from before Birth itself, to clothe our celestial ME for dwelling here, and yet to blind it,—lie all-embracing, as the universal canvas, or warp and woof, whereby all minor Illusions, in this Phantasm Existence, weave and paint themselves. In vain, while here on Earth, shall you endeavor to strip them off; you can, at best, but rend them asunder for moments, and look through.

"Fortunatus had a wishing Hat, which when he put on, and wished himself Anywhere, behold he was There. By this means had Fortunatus triumphed over Space, he had annihilated Space; for him there was no Where, but all was Here. Were a Hatter to establish himself, in the Wahngasse of Weissnichtwo, and make felts of this sort for all mankind, what a world we should have of it! Still stranger, should, on the opposite side of the street, another Hatter establish himself; and, as his fellow-craftsman made Space-annihilating Hats, make Time-annihilating! Of both would I purchase, were it with my last groschen; but chiefly of this latter. To clap on your felt, and, simply by wishing that you were Any*where*, straightway to be *There!* Next to clap on your other felt, and, simply by wishing that you were Any*when*, straightway to be *Then!* This were indeed the grander: shooting at will from the Fire-Creation of the World to its Fire-Consummation; here historically present in the First Century, conversing face to face with Paul and Seneca; there prophetically in the Thirty-first, conversing also face to face with other Pauls and Senecas, who as yet stand hidden in the depth of that late Time!

"Or thinkest thou it were impossible, unimaginable? Is the Past annihilated, then, or only past; is the Future nonextant, or only future? Those mystic faculties of thine, Memory and Hope, already answer: already through those mystic avenues, thou the Earth-blinded summonest both Past and Future, and communest with them, though as yet darkly, and with mute beckonings. The curtains of Yesterday drop down, the curtains of To-morrow roll up; but Yesterday and To-morrow both *are*. Pierce through the Time-element, glance into the Eternal. Believe what thou findest written in the sanctuaries of Man's Soul, even as all Thinkers, in all ages, have devoutly read it there: that Time and Space are not God, but creations of God; that with God as it is a universal HERE, so is it an everlasting NOW.

"And seest thou therein any glimpse of IMMORTALITY?—O Heaven! Is the white Tomb of our Loved One, who died from our arms, and had to be left behind us there, which rises in the distance, like a pale, mournfully receding Milestone, to tell how many toilsome uncheered miles we have journeyed on alone,—but a pale spectral Illusion! Is the lost Friend still mysteriously Here, even as we are Here mysteriously, with God!—Know of a truth that only the

Time-shadows have perished, or are perishable; that the real Being of whatever was, and whatever is, and whatever will be, *is* even now and forever. This, should it unhappily seem new, thou mayest ponder at thy leisure; for the next twenty years, or the next twenty centuries: believe it thou must; understand it thou canst not.

"That the Thought-forms, Space and Time, wherein, once for all, we are sent into this Earth to live, should condition and determine our whole Practical reasonings, conceptions, and imagings or imaginings, seems altogether fit, just, and unavoidable. But that they should, furthermore, usurp such sway over pure spiritual Meditation, and blind us to the wonder everywhere lying close on us, seems nowise so. Admit Space and Time to their due rank as Forms of Thought; nay even, if thou wilt, to their quite undue rank of Realities: and consider, then, with thyself how their thin disguises hide from us the brightest God-effulgences! Thus, were it not miraculous, could I stretch forth my hand and clutch the Sun? Yet thou seest me daily stretch forth my hand and therewith clutch many a thing, and swing it hither and thither. Art thou a grown baby, then, to fancy that the Miracle lies in miles of distance, or in pounds avoirdupois of weight; and not to see that the true inexplicable God-revealing Miracle lies in this, that I can stretch forth my hand at all; that I have free Force to clutch aught therewith? Innumerable other of this sort are the deceptions, and wonder-hiding stupefactions, which Space practises on us.

"Still worse is it with regard to Time. Your grand antimagician, and universal wonder-hider, is this same lying Time. Had we but the Time-annihilating Hat, to put on for once only, we should see ourselves in a World of Miracles, wherein all fabled or authentic Thaumaturgy, and feats of Magic, were outdone. But unhappily we have not such a Hat; and man, poor fool that he is, can seldom and scantily help himself without one.

"Were it not wonderful, for instance, had Orpheus, or Amphion, built the walls of Thebes by the mere sound of his Lyre? Yet tell me, Who built these walls of Weissnichtwo; summoning out all the sandstone rocks, to dance along from the *Steinbruch* (now a huge Troglodyte Chasm, with frightful green-mantled pools); and shape themselves into Doric and Ionic pillars, squared ashlar houses and noble streets? Was is not the still higher Orpheus, or Orpheuses, who, in past centuries, by the divine Music of Wisdom, succeeded in civilizing Man? Our highest Orpheus walked in Judea, eighteen hundred years ago: his sphere-melody, flowing in wild native tones, took captive the ravished souls of men; and, being of a truth sphere-melody, still flows and sounds, though now with thousand-fold accompaniments, and rich symphonies, through all our hearts; and modulates, and divinely leads them. Is that a wonder, which happens in two hours; and does it cease to be wonderful if happening in two million? Not only was Thebes built by the music of an Orpheus; but without the music of some inspired Orpheus was no city ever built, no work that man glories in ever done.

"Sweep away the Illusion of Time; glance, if thou have eyes, from the near moving-cause to its far distant Mover: The stroke that came transmitted through a whole galaxy of elastic balls, was it less a stroke than if the last ball only had been struck, and sent flying? Oh, could I (with the Time-annihilating Hat) transport thee direct from the Beginnings to the Endings, how were thy eyesight unsealed, and thy heart set flaming in the Light-sea of celestial wonder! Then sawest thou that this fair Universe, were it in the meanest province thereof, is in very deed the star-domed City of God; that through every star, through every grass-blade, and most through every Living Soul, the glory of a present God still beams. But Nature, which is the Time-vesture of God, and reveals Him to the wise, hides Him from the foolish.

"Again, could anything be more miraculous than an actual authentic Ghost? The English Johnson longed, all his life, to see one; but could not, though he went to Cock Lane, and thence to the church-vaults, and tapped on coffins. Foolish Doctor! Did he never, with the mind's eye as well as with the body's, look round him into that full tide of human Life he so loved; did he never so much as look into Himself? The good Doctor was a Ghost, as actual and authentic as heart could wish; well-nigh a million of Ghosts were travelling the streets by his side. Once more I say, sweep away the illusion of Time; compress the threescore years into three minutes: what else was he, what else are we? Are we not Spirits, that are shaped into a body, into an Appearance; and that fade away again into air and Invisibility? This is no metaphor, it is a simple scientific *fact:* we start out of Nothingness, take figure, and are Apparitions; round us, as round the veriest spectre, is Eternity; and to Eternity minutes are as years and æons. Come there not tones of Love and Faith, as from celestial harp-strings, like the Song of beatified Souls? And again, do not we squeak and gibber (in our discordant, screech-owlish debatings and recriminatings); and glide bodeful, and feeble, and fearful; or uproar *(poltern),* and revel in our mad Dance of the Dead,—till the scent of the morning air summons us to our still Home; and dreamy Night becomes awake and Day? Where now is Alexander of Macedon: does the steel Host, that yelled in fierce battle-shouts at Issus and Arbela, remain behind him; or have they all vanished utterly, even as perturbed Goblins must? Napoleon too, and his Moscow Retreats and Austerlitz Campaigns! Was it all other than the veriest Spectre-hunt; which has now, with its howling tumult that made Night hideous, flitted away?—Ghosts! There are nigh a thousand million walking the Earth openly at noontide; some half-hundred have vanished from it, some half-hundred have arisen in it, ere thy watch ticks once.

"O Heaven, it is mysterious, it is awful to consider that we not only carry each a future Ghost within him; but are, in very deed, Ghosts! These Limbs, whence had we them; this stormy Force; this life-blood with its burning Passion? They are dust and shadow; a Shadow-system gathered round our ME: wherein, through some moments or years, the Divine Essence is to be revealed in the Flesh. That warrior on his strong war-horse, fire flashes through his eyes; force dwells in his arm and heart: but warrior and war-horse are a vision; a revealed Force, nothing more. Stately they tread the Earth, as if it were a firm substance: fool! the Earth is but a film; it cracks in twain, and warrior and war-horse sink beyond plummet's sounding. Plummet's? Fantasy herself will not follow them. A little while ago, they were not; a little while, and they are not, their very ashes are not.

"So has it been from the beginning, so will it be to the end. Generation after generation takes to itself the Form of a Body; and forth issuing from Cimmerian Night, on Heaven's mission APPEARS. What Force and Fire is in each he expends: one grinding in the mill of Industry; one hunter-like climbing the giddy Alpine heights of Science; one madly dashed in pieces on the rocks of Strife, in war with his fellow:—and then the Heaven-sent is recalled; his earthly Vesture falls away, and soon even to Sense becomes a vanished Shadow. Thus, like some wild-flaming, wild-thundering train of Heaven's Artillery, does this mysterious MANKIND thunder and flame, in long-drawn, quick-succeeding grandeur, through the unknown Deep. Thus, like a God-created, fire-breathing Spirit-host, we emerge from the Inane; haste stormfully across the astonished Earth; then plunge again into the Inane. Earth's mountains are levelled, and her seas filled up, in our passage: can the Earth, which is but dead and a vision, resist Spirits which have reality and are alive? On the hardest adamant some footprint of us is stamped in; the last Rear of the host will read traces of the earliest Van. But whence?—O Heaven, whither? Sense knows not; Faith knows not; only that it is through Mystery to Mystery, from God and to God.

'We *are such stuff*
As Dreams are made of, and our little Life
Is rounded with a sleep!'"

# THE HERO AS POET

## *DANTE: SHAKSPEARE*

The Hero as Divinity, the Hero as Prophet, are productions of old ages; not to be repeated in the new. They presuppose a certain rudeness of conception, which the progress of mere scientific knowledge puts an end to. There needs to be, as it were, a world vacant, or almost vacant of scientific forms, if men in their loving wonder are to fancy their fellow-man either a god or one speaking with the voice of a god. Divinity and Prophet are past. We are now to see our Hero in the less ambitious, but also less questionable, character of Poet; a character which does not pass. The Poet is a heroic figure belonging to all ages; whom all ages possess, when once he is produced, whom the newest age as the oldest may produce;—and will produce, always when Nature pleases. Let Nature send a Hero-soul; in no age is it other than possible that he may be shaped into a Poet.

Hero, Prophet, Poet,—many different names, in different times, and places, do we give to Great Men; according to varieties we note in them, according to the sphere in which they have displayed themselves! We might give many more names, on this same principle. I will remark again, however, as a fact not unimportant to be understood, that the different *sphere* constitutes the grand origin of such distinction; that the Hero can be Poet, Prophet, King, Priest or what you will, according to the kind of world he finds himself born into. I confess, I have no notion of a truly great man that could not be *all* sorts of men. The Poet who could merely sit on a chair, and compose stanzas, would never make a stanza worth much. He could not sing the Heroic warrior, unless he himself were at least a Heroic warrior too. I fancy there is in him the Politician, the Thinker, Legislator, Philosopher;—in one or the other degree, he could have been, he is all these. So too I cannot understand how a Mirabeau, with that great glowing heart, with the fire that was in it, with the bursting tears that were in it, could not have written verses, tragedies, poems, and touched all hearts in that way, had his course of life and education led him thitherward. The grand fundamental character is that of Great Man; that the man be great. Napoleon has words in him which are like Austerlitz Battles. Louis Fourteenth's Marshals are a kind of poetical men withal; the things Turenne says are full of sagacity and geniality, like sayings of Samuel Johnson. The great heart, the clear deep-seeing eye: there it lies; no man whatever, in what province soever, can prosper at all without these. Petrarch and Boccaccio did diplomatic messages, it seems, quite well: one can easily believe it; they had done things a little harder than these! Burns, a gifted song-writer, might have made a still better Mirabeau. Shakspeare,—one knows not what *he* could not have made, in the supreme degree.

True, there are aptitudes of Nature too. Nature does not make all great men, more than all other men, in the self-same mould. Varieties of aptitude doubtless; but infinitely more of circumstance; and far oftenest it is the *latter* only that are looked to. But it is as with common men in the learning of trades. You take any man, as yet a vague capability of a man, who could be any kind of craftsman; and make him into a smith, a carpenter, a mason: he is then and thenceforth that and nothing else. And if, as Addison complains, you sometimes see a street-porter, staggering under his load on spindle-shanks, and near at hand a tailor with the frame of a Samson handling a bit of cloth and small Whitechapel needle,—it cannot be considered that aptitude of Nature alone has been consulted here either!—The Great Man also, to what shall he be bound apprentice? Given your Hero, is he to become Conqueror, King, Philosopher, Poet? It is an inexplicably complex controversial-calculation between the world and him! He will read the world and its laws; the world with its laws will be there to be read. What the world, on *this* matter, shall permit and bid is, as we said, the most important fact about the world.

Poet and Prophet differ greatly in our loose modern notions of them. In some old languages, again, the titles are synonymous; *Vates* means both Prophet and Poet: and indeed at all times, Prophet and Poet, well understood, have much kindred of meaning. Fundamentally indeed they are still the same; in this most important respect especially, That they have penetrated both of them into the sacred mystery of the Universe; what Goethe calls "the open secret." "Which is the great secret?" asks one.—"The *open* secret,"—open to all, seen by almost none! That divine mystery, which lies everywhere in all Beings, "the Divine Idea of the World, that which lies at the bottom of Appearance," as Fichte styles it; of which all Appearance, from the starry sky to the grass of the field, but especially the Appearance of Man and his work, is but the *vesture,* the embodiment that renders it visible. This divine mystery *is* in all times and in all places; veritably is. In most times and places it is greatly overlooked; and the Universe, definable always in one or the other dialect, as the realized Thought of God, is considered a trivial, inert, commonplace matter,—as if, says the Satirist, it were a dead thing, which some upholsterer had put together! It could do no good, at present, to *speak* much about this; but it is a pity for every one of us if we do not know it, live ever in the knowledge of it. Really a most mournful pity;—a failure to live at all, if we live otherwise!

But now, I say, whoever may forget this divine mystery, the *Vates,* whether Prophet or Poet, has penetrated into it; is a man sent hither to make it more impressively known to us. That always is his message; he is to reveal that to us,—that sacred mystery which he more than others lives ever present with. While others forget it, he knows it;—I might say, he has been driven to know it; without consent asked of *him,* he finds himself living in it, bound to live in it. Once more, here is no Hearsay, but a direct Insight and Belief; this man too could not help being a sincere man! Whosoever may live in the shows of things, it is for him a necessity of nature to live in the very fact of things. A man once more, in earnest with the Universe, though all others were but toying with it. He is a *Vates,* first of all, in virtue of being sincere. So far Poet and Prophet, participators in the "open secret," are one.

With respect to their distinction again: The *Vates* Prophet, we might say, has seized that sacred mystery rather on the moral side, as Good and Evil, Duty and Prohibition; the *Vates* Poet on what the Germans call the æsthetic side, as Beautiful, and the like. The one we may call a revealer of what we are to do, the other of what we are to love. But indeed these two provinces run into one another, and cannot be disjoined. The Prophet too has his eye on what we are to love: how else shall he know what it is we are to do? The highest Voice ever heard on this earth said withal, "Consider the lilies of the field; they toil not, neither do they spin: yet Solomon in all his glory was not arrayed like one of these." A glance, that, into the deepest deep of Beauty. "The lilies of the field,"—dressed finer than earthly princes, springing up there in the humble furrow-field; a beautiful *eye* looking out on you, from the great inner Sea of Beauty! How could the rude Earth make these, if her Essence, rugged as she looks and is, were not inwardly Beauty? In this point of view, too, a saying of Goethe's, which has staggered several, may have meaning: "The Beautiful," he intimates, "is higher than the Good; the Beautiful includes in it the Good." The *true* Beautiful; which however, I have said somewhere, "differs from the *false* as Heaven does from Vauxhall!" So much for the distinction and identity of Poet and Prophet.—

In ancient and also in modern periods we find a few Poets who are accounted perfect; whom it were a kind of treason to find fault with. This is noteworthy; this is right: yet in strictness it is only an illusion. At bottom, clearly enough, there is no perfect Poet! A vein of Poetry exists in the hearts of all men; no man is made altogether of Poetry. We are all poets when we *read* a poem well. The "imagination that shudders at the Hell of Dante," is not that the same faculty, weaker in degree, as Dante's own? No one but Shakspeare can embody, out of *Saxo Grammaticus,* the story of *Hamlet* as Shakspeare did: but every one models some kind of story out of it; every one embodies it better or worse. We need not spend time in defining. Where there is no specific difference, as between round and square, all definition must be more or less arbitrary. A man that has *so* much more of the poetic element developed in him as to have become noticeable, will be called Poet by his neighbors. World-Poets too, those whom we are to take for perfect Poets, are settled by critics in the same way. One who rises *so* far above the general level of Poets will, to such and such critics, seem a Universal Poet; as he ought to do. And yet it is, and must be, an arbitrary distinction. All Poets, all men, have some touches of the Universal; no man is wholly made of that. Most Poets are very soon forgotten: but not the noblest Shakspeare or Homer of them can be remembered *forever;*—a day comes when he too is not!

Nevertheless, you will say, there must be a difference between true Poetry and true Speech not poetical: what is the difference? On this point many things have been written, especially by late German Critics, some of which are not very intelligible at first. They say, for example, that the Poet has an *infinitude* in him; communicates an *Unendlichkeit,* a certain character of "infinitude," to whatsoever he delineates. This, though not very precise, yet on so vague a matter is worth remembering: if well meditated, some meaning will gradually be found in it. For my own part, I find considerable meaning in the old vulgar distinction of Poetry being *metrical,* having music in it, being a Song. Truly, if pressed to give a definition, one might say this as soon as anything else: If your delineation be authentically *musical,* musical not in word only, but in heart and substance, in all the thoughts and utterances of it, in the whole conception of it, then it will be poetical; if not, not.—Musical: how much lies in that! A *musical* thought is one spoken by a mind that has penetrated into the inmost heart of the thing; detected the inmost mystery of it, namely the *melody* that lies hidden in it; the inward harmony of coherence which is its soul, whereby it exists, and has a right to be, here in this world. All inmost things, we may say, are melodious; naturally utter themselves in Song. The meaning of Song goes deep. Who is there that, in logical words, can express the effect music has on us? A kind of inarticulate unfathomable speech, which leads us to the edge of the Infinite, and lets us for moments gaze into that!

Nay all speech, even the commonest speech, has something of song in it: not a parish in the world but has its parish-accent;—the rhythm or *tune* to which the people there *sing* what they have to say! Accent is a kind of chanting; all men have accent of their own,—though they only *notice* that of others. Observe too how all passionate language does of itself become musical,—with a finer music than the mere accent; the speech of a man even in zealous anger becomes a chant, a song. All deep things are Song. It seems somehow the very central essence of us, Song; as if all the rest were but wrappages and hulls! The primal element of us; of us, and of all things. The Greeks fabled of Sphere-Harmonies: it was the feeling they had of the inner structure of Nature; that the soul of all her voices and utterances was perfect music. Poetry, therefore, we will call *musical Thought.* The Poet is he who *thinks* in that manner. At bottom, it turns still on power of intellect; it is a man's sincerity and depth of vision that makes him a Poet. See deep enough, and you see musically; the heart of Nature *being* everywhere music, if you can only reach it.

The *Vates* Poet, with his melodious Apocalypse of Nature, seems to hold a poor rank among us, in comparison with the *Vates* Prophet; his function, and our esteem of him for his function, alike slight. The Hero taken as Divinity; the Hero taken as Prophet; then next the Hero taken only as Poet: does it not look as if our estimate of the Great Man, epoch after epoch, were continually diminishing? We take him first for a god, then for one god-inspired; and now in the next stage of it, his most miraculous word gains from us only the recognition that he is a Poet, beautiful verse-maker, man of genius, or such like!—It looks so; but I persuade myself that intrinsically it is not so. If we consider well, it will perhaps appear that in man still there is the *same* altogether peculiar admiration for the Heroic Gift, by what name soever called, that there at any time was.

I should say, if we do not now reckon a Great Man literally divine, it is that our notions of God, of the supreme unattainable Fountain of Splendor, Wisdom and Heroism, are ever rising *higher;* not altogether that our reverence for these qualities, as manifested in our like, is getting lower. This is worth taking thought of. Sceptical Dilettantism, the curse of these ages, a curse which will not last forever, does indeed in this the highest province of human things, as in all provinces, make sad work; and our reverence for great men, all crippled, blinded, paralytic as it is, comes out in poor plight, hardly recognizable. Men worship the shows of great men; the most disbelieve that there is any reality of great men to worship. The dreariest, fatalest faith; believing which, one would literally despair of human things. Nevertheless look, for example, at Napoleon! A Corsican lieutenant of artillery; that is the show of *him:* yet is he not obeyed, *worshipped* after his sort, as all the Tiaraed and Diademed of the world put together could not be? High Duchesses, and ostlers of inns, gather round the Scottish rustic, Burns;—a strange feeling dwelling in each that they never heard a man like this; that, on the whole, this is the man! In the secret heart of these people it still dimly reveals itself, though there is no accredited way of uttering it at present, that this rustic, with his black brows and flashing sun-eyes, and strange words moving laughter and tears, is of a dignity far beyond all others, incommensurable with all others. Do not we feel it so? But now, were Dilettantism, Scepticism, Triviality, and all that sorrowful brood, cast out of us,—as, by God's blessing, they shall one day be; were faith in the shows of things entirely swept out, replaced by clear faith in the *things,* so that a man acted on the impulse of that only, and counted the other non-extant; what a new livelier feeling towards this Burns were it!

Nay here in these ages, such as they are, have we not two mere Poets, if not deified, yet we may say beatified? Shakspeare and Dante are Saints of Poetry; really, if we will think of it, *canonized,* so that it is impiety to meddle with them. The unguided instinct of the world, working across all these perverse impediments, has arrived at such result. Dante and Shakspeare are a peculiar Two. They dwell apart, in a kind of royal solitude; none equal, none second to them: in the general feeling of the world, a certain transcendentalism, a glory as of complete perfection, invests these two. They *are* canonized, though no Pope or Cardinals took hand in doing it! Such, in spite of every perverting influence, in the most unheroic times, is still our indestructible reverence for heroism.—We will look a little at these Two, the Poet Dante and the Poet Shakspeare: what little it is permitted us to say here of the Hero as Poet will most fitly arrange itself in that fashion.

Many volumes have been written by way of commentary on Dante and his Book; yet, on the whole, with no great result. His Biography is, as it were, irrecoverably lost for us. An unimportant, wandering, sorrow-stricken man, not much note was taken of him while he lived; and the most of that has vanished, in the long space that now intervenes. It is five centuries since he ceased writing and living here. After all commentaries, the Book itself is mainly what we know of him. The Book;—and one might add that Portrait commonly attributed to Giotto, which, looking on it, you cannot help inclining to think genuine, whoever did it. To me it is a most touching face; perhaps of all faces that I know, the most so. Lonely there, painted as on vacancy, with the simple laurel wound round it; the deathless sorrow and pain, the known victory which is also deathless;—significant of the whole history of Dante! I think it is the mournfulest face that ever was painted from reality; an altogether tragic, heart-affecting face. There is in it, as foundation of it, the softness, tenderness, gentle affection as of a child; but all this is as if congealed into sharp contradiction, into abnegation, isolation, proud hopeless pain. A soft ethereal soul looking out so stern, implacable, grim-trenchant, as from imprisonment of thick-ribbed ice! Withal it is a silent pain too, a silent scornful one: the lip is curled in a kind of godlike disdain of the thing that is eating out his heart,—as if it were withal a mean insignificant thing, as if he whom it had power to torture and strangle were greater than it. The face of one wholly in protest, and lifelong unsurrendering battle, against the world. Affection all converted into indignation: an implacable indignation; slow, equable, silent, like that of a god! The eye too, it looks out as in a kind of *surprise*, a kind of inquiry, Why the world was of such a sort? This is Dante, so he looks, this "voice of ten silent centuries," and sings us "his mystic unfathomable song."

The little that we know of Dante's Life corresponds well enough with this Portrait and this Book. He was born at Florence, in the upper class of society, in the year 1265. His education was the best then going; much school-divinity, Aristotelean logic, some Latin classics,—no inconsiderable insight into certain provinces of things: and Dante, with his earnest intelligent nature, we need not doubt, learned better than most all that was learnable. He has a clear cultivated understanding, and of great subtlety; this best fruit of education he had contrived to realize from these scholastics. He knows accurately and well what lies close to him; but, in such a time, without printed books or free intercourse, he could not know well what was distant: the small clear light, most luminous for what is near, breaks itself into singular *chiaroscuro* striking on what is far off. This was Dante's learning from the schools. In life, he had gone through the usual destinies; been twice out campaigning as a soldier for the Florentine State, been on embassy; had in his thirty-fifth year, by natural gradation of talent and service, become one of the Chief Magistrates of Florence. He had met in boyhood a certain Beatrice Portinari, a beautiful little girl of his own age and rank, and grown up thenceforth in partial sight of her, in some distant intercourse with her. All readers know his graceful affecting account of this; and then of their being parted; of her being wedded to another, and of her death soon after. She makes a great figure in Dante's Poem; seems to have made a great figure in his life. Of all beings it might seem as if she, held apart from him, far apart at last in the dim Eternity, were the only one he had ever with his whole strength of affection loved. She died: Dante himself was wedded; but it seems not happily, far from happily. I fancy, the rigorous earnest man, with his keen excitabilities, was not altogether easy to make happy.

We will not complain of Dante's miseries: had all gone right with him as he wished it, he might have been Prior, Podestà, or whatsoever they call it, of Florence, well accepted among neighbors,—and the world had wanted one of the most notable words ever spoken or sung. Florence would have had another prosperous Lord Mayor; and the ten dumb centuries continued voiceless, and the ten other listening centuries (for there will be ten of them and more) had no *Divina Commedia* to hear! We will complain of nothing. A nobler destiny was appointed for this Dante; and he, struggling like a man led towards death and crucifixion, could not help fulfilling it. Give *him* the choice of his happiness! He knew not, more than we do, what was really happy, what was really miserable.

In Dante's Priorship, the Guelf-Ghibelline, Bianchi-Neri, or some other confused disturbances rose to such a height, that Dante, whose party had seemed the stronger, was with his friends cast unexpectedly forth into banishment; doomed thenceforth to a life of woe and wandering. His property was all confiscated and more; he had the fiercest feeling that it was entirely unjust, nefarious in the sight of God and man. He tried what was in him to get reinstated; tried even by warlike surprisal, with arms in his hand: but it would not do; bad only had become worse. There is a record, I believe, still extant in the Florence Archives, dooming this Dante, wheresoever caught, to be burnt alive. Burnt alive; so it stands, they say: a very curious civic document. Another curious document, some considerable number of years later, is a Letter of Dante's to the Florentine Magistrates, written in answer to a milder proposal of theirs, that he should return on condition of apologizing and paying a fine. He answers, with fixed stern pride: "If I cannot return without calling myself guilty, I will never return, *nunquam revertar.*"

For Dante there was now no home in this world. He wandered from patron to patron, from place to place; proving, in his own bitter words, "How hard is the path, *Come è duro calle.*" The wretched are not cheerful company. Dante, poor and banished, with his proud earnest nature, with his moody humors, was not a man to conciliate men. Petrarch reports of him that being at Can della Scala's court, and blamed one day for his gloom and taciturnity, he answered in no courtier-like way. Della Scala stood among his courtiers, with mimes and buffoons *(nebulones ac histriones)* making him heartily merry; when turning to Dante, he said: "Is it not strange, now, that this poor fool should make himself so entertaining; while you, a wise man, sit there day after day, and have nothing to amuse us with at all?" Dante answered bitterly: "No, not strange; your Highness is to recollect the Proverb, *Like to Like;*"—given the amuser, the amusee must also be given! Such a man, with his proud silent ways, with his sarcasms and sorrows, was not made to succeed at court. By degrees, it came to be evident to him that he had no longer any resting-place, or hope of benefit, in this earth. The earthly world had cast him forth, to wander, wander; no living heart to love him now; for his sore miseries there was no solace here.

The deeper naturally would the Eternal World impress itself on him; that awful reality over which, after all, this Time-world, with its Florences and banishments, only flutters as an unreal shadow. Florence thou shalt never see: but Hell and Purgatory and Heaven thou shalt surely see! What is Florence, Can della Scala, and the World and Life altogether? ETERNITY: thither, of a truth, not elsewhither, art thou and all things bound! The great soul of Dante, homeless on earth, made its home more and more in that awful other world. Naturally his thoughts brooded on that, as on the one fact important for him. Bodied or bodiless, it is the one fact important for all men:—but to Dante, in that age, it was bodied in fixed certainty of scientific shape; he no more doubted of that *Malebolge* Pool, that it all lay there with its gloomy circles, with its *alti guai,* and that he himself should see it, than we doubt that we should see Constantinople if we went thither. Dante's heart, long filled with this, brooding over it in speechless thought and awe, bursts forth at length into "mystic unfathomable song;" and this his *Divine Comedy,* the most remarkable of all modern Books, is the result.

It must have been a great solacement to Dante, and was, as we can see, a proud thought for him at times, That he, here in exile, could do this work; that no Florence, nor no man or men, could hinder him from doing it, or even much help him in doing it. He knew too, partly, that it was great; the greatest a man could do. "If thou follow thy star, *Se tu segui tua stella,*"—so could the Hero, in his forsakenness, in his extreme need, still say to himself: "Follow thou thy star, thou shalt not fail of a glorious haven!" The labor of writing, we find, and indeed could know otherwise, was great and painful for him; he says, This Book, "which has made me lean for many years." Ah yes, it was won, all of it, with pain and sore toil,—not in sport, but in grim earnest. His Book, as indeed most good Books are, has been written, in many senses, with his heart's blood. It is his whole history, this Book. He died after finishing it; not yet very old, at the age of fifty-six;—broken-hearted rather, as is said. He lies buried in his death-city Ravenna: *Hic claudor Dantes patriis extorris ab oris.* The Florentines begged back his body, in a century after; the Ravenna people would not give it. "Here am I Dante laid, shut out from my native shores."

I said, Dante's Poem was a Song: it is Tieck who calls it "a mystic unfathomable Song;" and such is literally the character of it. Coleridge remarks very pertinently somewhere, that wherever you find a sentence musically worded, of true rhythm and melody in the words, there is something deep and good in the meaning too. For body and soul, word and idea, go strangely together here as everywhere. Song: we said before, it was the Heroic of Speech! All *old* Poems, Homer's and the rest, are authentically Songs. I would say, in strictness, that all right Poems are; that whatsoever is not *sung* is properly no Poem, but a piece of Prose cramped into jingling lines,—to the great injury of the grammar, to the great grief of the reader, for most part! What we want to get at is the *thought* the man had, if he had any: why should he twist it into jingle, if he *could* speak it out plainly? It is only when the heart of him is rapt into true passion of melody, and the very tones of him, according to Coleridge's remark, become musical by the greatness, depth and music of his thoughts, that we can give him right to rhyme and sing; that we call him a Poet, and listen to him as the Heroic of Speakers,—whose speech *is* Song. Pretenders to this are many; and to an earnest reader, I doubt, it is for most part a very melancholy, not to say an insupportable business, that of reading rhyme! Rhyme that had no inward necessity to be rhymed;—it ought to have told us plainly, without any jingle, what it was aiming at. I would advise all men who *can* speak their thought, not to sing it; to understand that, in a serious time, among serious men, there is no vocation in them for singing it. Precisely as we love the true song, and are charmed by it as by something divine, so shall we hate the false song, and account it a mere wooden noise, a thing hollow, superfluous, altogether an insincere and offensive thing.

I give Dante my highest praise when I say of his *Divine Comedy* that it is, in all senses, genuinely a Song. In the very sound of it there is a *canto fermo;* it proceeds as by a chant. The language, his simple *terza rima,* doubtless helped him in this. One reads along naturally with a sort of *lilt*. But I add, that it could not be otherwise; for the essence and material of the work are themselves rhythmic. Its depth, and rapt passion and sincerity, makes it musical;—go *deep* enough, there is music everywhere. A true inward symmetry, what one calls an architectural harmony, reigns in it, proportionates it all: architectural; which also partakes of the character of music. The three kingdoms, *Inferno, Purgatorio, Paradiso,* look out on one another like compartments of a great edifice; a great supernatural world-cathedral, piled up there, stern, solemn, awful; Dante's World of Souls! It is, at bottom, the *sincerest* of all Poems; sincerity, here too, we find to be the measure of worth. It came deep out of the author's heart of hearts; and it goes deep, and through long generations, into ours. The people of Verona, when they saw him on the streets, used to say, "*Eccovi l' uom ch' è stato all' Inferno,* See, there is the man that was in Hell!" Ah yes, he had been in Hell;—in Hell enough, in long severe sorrow and struggle; as the like of him is pretty sure to have been. Commedias that come out *divine* are not accomplished otherwise. Thought, true labor of any kind, highest virtue itself, is it not the daughter of Pain? Born as out of the black whirlwind;—true *effort,* in fact, as of a captive struggling to free himself: that is Thought. In all ways we are "to become perfect through *suffering*."— But, as I say, no work known to me is so elaborated as this of Dante's. It has all been as if molten, in the hottest furnace of his soul. It had made him "lean" for many years. Not the general whole only; every compartment of it is worked out, with intense earnestness, into truth, into clear visuality. Each answers to the other; each fits in its place, like a marble stone accurately hewn and polished. It is the soul of Dante, and in this the soul of the middle ages, rendered forever rhythmically visible there. No light task; a right intense one: but a task which is *done*.

Perhaps one would say, *intensity,* with the much that depends on it, is the prevailing character of Dante's genius. Dante does not come before us as a large catholic mind; rather as a narrow, and even sectarian mind: it is partly the fruit of his age and position, but partly too of his own nature. His greatness has, in all senses, concentred itself into fiery emphasis and depth. He is world-great not because he is world-wide, but because he is world-deep. Through all objects he pierces as it were down into the heart of Being. I know nothing so intense as Dante. Consider, for example, to begin with the outermost development of his intensity, consider how he paints. He has a great power of vision; seizes the very type of a thing; presents that and nothing more. You remember that first view he gets of the Hall of Dite: *red* pinnacle, red-hot cone of iron glowing through the dim immensity of gloom;—so vivid, so distinct, visible at once and forever! It is as an emblem of the whole genius of Dante. There is a brevity, an abrupt precision in him: Tacitus is not briefer, more condensed; and then in Dante it seems a natural condensation, spontaneous to the man. One smiting word; and then there is silence, nothing more said. His silence is more eloquent than words. It is strange with what a sharp decisive grace he snatches the true likeness of a matter: cuts into the matter as with a pen of fire. Plutus, the blustering giant, collapses at Virgil's rebuke; it is "as the sails sink, the mast being suddenly broken." Or that poor Brunetto Latini, with the *cotto aspetto,* "face *baked,*" parched brown and lean; and the "fiery snow" that falls on them there, a "fiery snow without wind," slow, deliberate, never-ending! Or the lids of those Tombs; square sarcophaguses, in that silent dim-burning Hall, each with its Soul in torment; the lids laid open there; they are to be shut at the Day of Judgment, through Eternity. And how Farinata rises; and how Cavalcante falls—at hearing of his Son, and the past tense *"fue"!* The very movements in Dante have something brief; swift, decisive, almost military. It is of the inmost essence of his genius this sort of painting. The fiery, swift Italian nature of the man, so silent, passionate, with its quick abrupt movements, its silent "pale rages," speaks itself in these things.

For though this of painting is one of the outermost developments of a man, it comes like all else from the essential faculty of him; it is physiognomical of the whole man. Find a man whose words paint you a likeness, you have found a man worth something; mark his manner of doing it, as very characteristic of him. In the first place, he could not have discerned the object at all, or seen the vital type of it, unless he had, what we may call, *sympathized* with it,—had sympathy in him to bestow on objects. He must have been *sincere* about it too; sincere and sympathetic: a man without worth cannot give you the likeness of any object; he dwells in vague outwardness, fallacy and trivial hearsay, about all objects. And indeed may we not say that intellect altogether expresses itself in this power of discerning what an object is? Whatsoever of faculty a man's mind may have will come out here. Is it even of business, a matter to be done? The gifted man is he who *sees* the essential point, and leaves all the rest aside as surplusage: it is his faculty too, the man of business's faculty, that he discern the true *likeness,* not the false superficial one, of the thing he has got to work in. And how much of *morality* is in the kind of insight we get of anything; "the eye seeing in all things what it brought with it the faculty of seeing"! To the mean eye all things are trivial, as certainly as to the jaundiced they are yellow. Raphael, the Painters tell us, is the best of all Portrait-painters withal. No most gifted eye can exhaust the significance of any object. In the commonest human face there lies more than Raphael will take away with him.

Dante's painting is not graphic only, brief, true, and of a vividness as of fire in dark night; taken on the wider scale, it is every way noble, and the outcome of a great soul. Francesca and her Lover, what qualities in that! A thing woven as out of rainbows, on a ground of eternal black. A small flute-voice of infinite wail speaks there, into our very heart of hearts. A touch of womanhood in it too:

*della bella persona, che mi fu tolta;* and how, even in the Pit of woe, it is a solace that *he* will never part from her! Saddest tragedy in these *alti guai*. And the racking winds, in that *aer bruno,* whirl them away again, to wail forever!—Strange to think: Dante was the friend of this poor Francesca's father; Francesca herself may have sat upon the Poet's knee, as a bright innocent little child. Infinite pity, yet also infinite rigor of law: it is so Nature is made; it is so Dante discerned that she was made. What a paltry notion is that of his *Divine Comedy's* being a poor splenetic impotent terrestrial libel; putting those into Hell whom he could not be avenged upon on earth! I suppose if every pity, tender as a mother's, was in the heart of any man, it was in Dante's. But a man who does not know rigor cannot pity either. His very pity will be cowardly, egoistic,—sentimentality, or little better. I know not in the world an affection equal to that of Dante. It is a tenderness, a trembling, longing, pitying love: like the wail of Æolian harps, soft, soft; like a child's young heart;—and then that stern, sore-saddened heart! These longings of his towards his Beatrice; their meeting together in the *Paradiso;* his gazing in her pure transfigured eyes, her that had been purified by death so long, separated from him so far:—one likens it to the song of angels; it is among the purest utterances of affection, perhaps the very purest, that ever came out of a human soul.

For the *intense* Dante is intense in all things; he has got into the essence of all. His intellectual insight as painter, on occasion too as reasoner, is but the result of all other sorts of intensity. Morally great, above all, we must call him; it is the beginning of all. His scorn, his grief are as transcendent as his love;—as indeed, what are they but the *inverse* or *converse* of his love? "*A Dio spiacenti ed a' nemici sui,* Hateful to God and to the enemies of God:" lofty scorn, unappeasable silent reprobation and aversion; "*Non ragionam di lor,* We will not speak of *them,* look only and pass." Or think of this; "They have not the *hope* to die, *Non han speranza di morte*." One day, it had risen sternly benign on the scathed heart of Dante, that he, wretched, never-resting, worn as he was, would full surely *die;* "that Destiny itself could not doom him not to die." Such words are in this man. For rigor, earnestness and depth, he is not to be paralleled in the modern world; to seek his parallel we must go into the Hebrew Bible, and live with the antique Prophets there.

I do not agree with much modern criticism, in greatly preferring the *Inferno* to the two other parts of the Divine *Commedia*. Such preference belongs, I imagine, to our general Byronism of taste, and is like to be a transient feeling. The *Purgatorio* and *Paradiso,* especially the former, one would almost say, is even more excellent than it. It is a noble thing that *Purgatorio,* "Mountain of Purification;" an emblem of the noblest conception of that age. If sin is so fatal, and Hell is and must be so rigorous, awful, yet in Repentance too is man purified; Repentance is the grand Christian act. It is beautiful how Dante works it out. The *tremolar dell' onde,* that "trembling" of the ocean-waves, under the first pure gleam of morning, dawning afar on the wandering Two, is as the type of an altered mood. Hope has now dawned; never-dying Hope, if in company still with heavy sorrow. The obscure sojourn of demons and reprobate is underfoot; a soft breathing of penitence mounts higher and higher, to the Throne of Mercy itself. "Pray for me," the denizens of that Mount of Pain all say to him. "Tell my Giovanna to pray for me," my daughter Giovanna; "I think her mother loves me no more!" They toil painfully up by that winding steep, "bent down like corbels of a building," some of them,—crushed together so "for the sin of pride;" yet nevertheless in years, in ages and æons, they shall have reached the top, which is heaven's gate, and by Mercy shall have been admitted in. The joy too of all, when one has prevailed; the whole Mountain shakes with joy, and a psalm of praise rises, when one soul has perfected repentance and got its sin and misery left behind! I call all this a noble embodiment of a true noble thought.

But indeed the Three compartments mutually support one another, are indispensable to one another. The *Paradiso,* a kind of inarticulate music to me, is the redeeming side of the *Inferno;* the *Inferno* without it were untrue. All three make up the true Unseen World, as figured in the Christianity of the Middle Ages; a thing forever memorable, forever true in the essence of it, to all men. It was perhaps delineated in no human soul with such depth of veracity as in this of Dante's; a man *sent* to sing it, to keep it long memorable. Very notable with what brief simplicity he passes out of the every-day reality, into the Invisible one; and in the second or third stanza, we find ourselves in the World of Spirits; and dwell there, as among things palpable, indubitable! To Dante they *were* so; the real world, as it is called, and its facts, was but the threshold to an infinitely higher Fact of a World. At bottom, the one was as *preter*natural as the other. Has not each man a soul? He will not only be a spirit, but is one. To the earnest Dante it is all one visible Fact; he believes it, sees it; is the Poet of it in virtue of that. Sincerity, I say again, is the saving merit, now as always.

Dante's Hell, Purgatory, Paradise, are a symbol withal, an emblematic representation of his Belief about this Universe:—some Critic in a future age, like those Scandinavian ones the other day, who has ceased altogether to think as Dante did, may find this too all an "Allegory," perhaps an idle Allegory! It is a sublime embodiment, or sublimest, of the soul of Christianity. It expresses, as in huge world-wide architectural emblems, how the Christian Dante felt Good and Evil to be the two polar elements of this Creation, on which it all turns; that these two differ not by *preferability* of one to the other, but by incompatibility absolute and infinite; that the one is excellent and high as light and Heaven, the other hideous, black as Gehenna and the Pit of Hell! Everlasting Justice, yet with Penitence, with everlasting Pity,—all Christianism, as Dante and the Middle Ages had it, is emblemed here. Emblemed: and yet, as I urged the other day, with what entire truth of purpose; how unconscious of any embleming! Hell, Purgatory, Paradise: these things were not fashioned as emblems; was there, in our Modern European Mind, any thought at all of their being emblems! Were they not indubitable awful facts; the whole heart of man taking them for practically true, all Nature everywhere confirming them? So is it always in these things. Men do not believe an Allegory. The future Critic, whatever his new thought may be, who considers this of Dante to have been all got up as an Allegory, will commit one sore mistake!—Paganism we recognized as a veracious expression of the earnest awe-struck feeling of man towards the Universe; veracious, true once, and still not without worth for us. But mark here the difference of Paganism and Christianism; one great difference. Paganism emblemed chiefly the Operations of Nature; the destinies, efforts, combinations, vicissitudes of things and men in this world; Christianism emblemed the Law of Human Duty, the Moral Law of Man. One was for the sensuous nature: a rude helpless utterance of the *first* Thought of men,—the chief recognized virtue, Courage, Superiority to Fear. The other was not for the sensuous nature, but for the moral. What a progress is here, if in that one respect only!—

And so in this Dante, as we said, had ten silent centuries, in a very strange way, found a voice. The *Divina Commedia* is of Dante's writing; yet in truth *it* belongs to ten Christian centuries, only the finishing of it is Dante's. So always. The craftsman there, the smith with that metal of his, with these tools, with these cunning methods,—how little of all he does is properly *his* work! All past inventive men work there with him;—as indeed with all of us, in all things. Dante is the spokesman of the Middle Ages; the Thought they lived by stands here, in everlasting music. These sublime ideas of his, terrible and beautiful, are the fruit of the Christian Meditation of all the good men who had gone before him. Precious they; but also is not he precious? Much, had not he spoken, would have been dumb; not dead, yet living voiceless.

On the whole, is it not an utterance, this mystic Song, at once of one of the greatest human souls, and of the highest thing that Europe had hitherto realized for itself? Christianism, as Dante sings it, is another than Paganism in the rude Norse mind; another than "Bastard Christianism" half-articulately spoken in the Arab Desert, seven hundred years before!—The noblest *idea* made *real* hitherto among men, is sung, and emblemed forth abidingly, by one of the noblest men. In the one sense and in the other, are we not right glad to possess it? As I calculate, it may last yet for long thousands of years. For the thing that is uttered from the inmost parts of a man's soul, differs altogether from what is uttered by the outer part. The outer is of the day, under the empire of mode; the outer passes away, in swift endless changes; the inmost is the same yesterday, to-day and forever. True souls, in all generations of the world, who look on this Dante, will find a brotherhood in him; the deep sincerity of his thoughts, his woes and hopes, will speak likewise to their sincerity; they will feel that this Dante too was a brother. Napoleon in Saint Helena is charmed with the genial veracity of old Homer. The oldest Hebrew Prophet, under a vesture the most diverse from ours, does yet, because he speaks from the heart of man, speak to all men's hearts. It is the one sole secret of continuing long memorable. Dante, for depth of sincerity, is like an antique Prophet too; his words, like theirs, come from his very heart. One need not wonder if it were predicted that his Poem might be the most enduring thing our Europe has yet made; for nothing so endures as a truly spoken word. All cathedrals, pontificalities, brass and stone, and outer arrangement never so lasting, are brief in comparison to an unfathomable heart-song like this: one feels as if it might survive, still of importance to men, when these had all sunk into new irrecognizable combinations, and had ceased individually to be. Europe has made much; great cities, great empires, encyclopædias, creeds, bodies of opinion and practice: but it has made little of the class of Dante's Thought. Homer yet *is,* veritably present face to face with every open soul of us; and Greece, where is *it*? Desolate for thousands of years; away, vanished; a bewildered heap of stones and rubbish, the life and existence of it all gone. Like a dream; like the dust of King Agamemnon! Greece was; Greece, except in the *words* it spoke, is not.

The uses of this Dante? We will not say much about his "uses." A human soul who has once got into that primal element of *Song,* and sung forth fitly somewhat therefrom, has worked in the *depths* of our existence; feeding through long times the life-*roots* of all excellent human things whatsoever,—in a way that "utilities" will not succeed well in calculating! We will not estimate the Sun by the quantity of gaslight it saves us; Dante shall be invaluable, or of no value. One remark I may make: the contrast in this respect between the Hero-Poet and the Hero-Prophet. In a hundred years, Mahomet, as we saw, had his Arabians at Grenada and at Delhi; Dante's Italians seem to be yet very much where they were. Shall we say, then, Dante's effect on the world was small in comparison? Not so: his arena is far more restricted; but also it is far nobler, clearer;—perhaps not less but more important. Mahomet speaks to great masses of men, in the coarse dialect adapted to such; a dialect filled with inconsistencies, crudities, follies: on the great masses alone can he act, and there with good and with evil strangely blended. Dante speaks to the noble, the pure and great, in all times and places. Neither does he grow obsolete, as the other does. Dante burns as a pure star, fixed there in the firmament, at which the great and the high of all ages kindle themselves: he is the possession of all the chosen of the world for uncounted time. Dante, one calculates, may long survive Mahomet. In this way the balance may be made straight again.

But, at any rate, it is not by what is called their effect on the world, by what *we* can judge of their effect there, that a man and his work are measured. Effect? Influence? Utility? Let a man *do* his work; the fruit of it is the care of Another than he. It will grow its own fruit; and whether embodied in Caliph Thrones and Arabian Conquests, so that it "fills all Morning and Evening Newspapers," and all Histories, which are a kind of distilled Newspapers; or not embodied so at all;—what matters that? That is not the real fruit of it! The Arabian Caliph, in so far only as he did something, was something. If the great Cause of Man, and Man's work in God's Earth, got no furtherance from the Arabian Caliph, then no matter how many scimetars he drew, how many gold piasters pocketed, and what uproar and blaring he made in this world,—*he* was but a loud-sounding inanity and futility; at bottom, he *was* not at all. Let us honor the great empire of *Silence,* once more! The boundless treasury which we do *not* jingle in our pockets, or count up and present before men! It is perhaps, of all things, the usefulest for each of us to do, in these loud times.—

As Dante, the Italian man, was sent into our world to embody musically the Religion of the Middle Ages, the Religion of our Modern Europe, its Inner Life; so Shakspeare, we may say, embodies for us the Outer Life of our Europe as developed then, its chivalries, courtesies, humors, ambitions, what practical way of thinking, acting, looking at the world, men then had. As in Homer we may still construe Old Greece; so in Shakspeare and Dante, after thousands of years, what our modern Europe was, in Faith and in Practice, will still be legible. Dante has given us the Faith or soul; Shakspeare, in a not less noble way, has given us the Practice or body. This latter also we were to have; a man was sent for it, the man Shakspeare. Just when that chivalry way of life had reached its last finish, and was on the point of breaking down into slow or swift dissolution, as we now see it everywhere, this other sovereign Poet, with his seeing eye, with his perennial singing voice, was sent to take note of it, to give long-enduring record of it. Two fit men: Dante, deep, fierce as the central fire of the world; Shakspeare, wide, placid, far-seeing, as the Sun, the upper light of the world. Italy produced the one world-voice; we English had the honor of producing the other.

Curious enough how, as it were by mere accident, this man came to us. I think always, so great, quiet, complete and self-sufficing is this Shakspeare, had the Warwickshire Squire not prosecuted him for deer-stealing, we had perhaps never heard of him as a Poet! The woods and skies, the rustic Life of Man in Stratford there, had been enough for this man! But indeed that strange outbudding of our whole English Existence, which we call the Elizabethan Era, did not it too come as of its own accord? The "Tree Igdrasil" buds and withers by its own laws,—too deep for our scanning. Yet it does bud and wither, and every bough and leaf of it is there, by fixed eternal laws; not a Sir Thomas Lucy but comes at the hour fit for him. Curious, I say, and not sufficiently considered: how everything does co-operate with all; not a leaf rotting on the highway but is indissoluble portion of solar and stellar systems; no thought, word or act of man but has sprung withal out of all men, and works sooner or later, recognizably or irrecognizably, on all men! It is all a Tree: circulation of sap and influences, mutual communication of every minutest leaf with the lowest talon of a root, with every other greatest and minutest portion of the whole. The Tree Igdrasil, that has its roots down in the Kingdoms of Hela and Death, and whose boughs overspread the highest Heaven!—

In some sense it may be said that this glorious Elizabethan Era with its Shakspeare, as the outcome and flowerage of all which had preceded it, is itself attributable to the Catholicism of the Middle Ages. The Christian Faith, which was the theme of Dante's Song, had produced this Practical Life which Shakspeare was to sing. For Religion then, as it now and always is, was the soul of Practice; the primary vital fact in men's life. And remark here, as rather curious, that Middle-Age Catholicism was abolished, so far as Acts of Parliament could abolish it, before Shakspeare, the noblest product of it, made his appearance. He did make his appearance nevertheless. Nature at her own time, with Catholicism or what else might be necessary, sent him forth; taking small thought of Acts of Parliament. King Henrys, Queen Elizabeths go their way; and Nature too goes hers. Acts of Parliament, on the whole, are small, notwithstanding the noise they make. What Act of Parliament, debate at St. Stephen's, on the hustings or elsewhere, was it that brought this Shakspeare into being? No dining at Freemason's Tavern, opening subscription-lists, selling of shares, and infinite other jangling and true or false endeavoring! This Elizabethan Era, and all its nobleness and blessedness, came without proclamation, preparation of ours. Priceless Shakspeare was the free gift of Nature; given altogether silently;—received altogether silently, as if it had been a thing of little account. And yet, very literally, it is a priceless thing. One should look at that side of matters too.

Of this Shakspeare of ours, perhaps the opinion one sometimes hears a little idolatrously expressed is, in fact, the right one; I think the best judgment not of this country only, but of Europe at large, is slowly pointing to the conclusion, that Shakspeare is the chief of all Poets hitherto; the greatest intellect who, in our recorded world, has left record of himself in the way of Literature. On the whole, I know not such a power of vision, such a faculty of thought, if we take all the characters of it, in any other man. Such a calmness of depth; placid joyous strength; all things imaged in that great soul of his so true and clear, as in a tranquil unfathomable sea! It has been said, that in the constructing of Shakspeare's Dramas there is, apart from all other "faculties" as they are called, an understanding manifested, equal to that in Bacon's *Novum Organum*. That is true; and it is not a truth that strikes every one. It would become more apparent if we tried, any of us for himself, how, out of Shakspeare's dramatic materials, *we* could fashion such a result! The built house seems all so fit,—every way as it should be, as if it came there by its own law and the nature of things,—we forget the rude disorderly quarry it was shaped from. The very perfection of the house, as if Nature herself had made it, hides the builder's merit. Perfect, more perfect than any other man, we may call Shakspeare in this: he discerns, knows as by instinct, what condition he works under, what his materials are, what his own force and its relation to them is. It is not a transitory glance of insight that will suffice; it is deliberate illumination of the whole matter; it is a calmly *seeing* eye; a great intellect, in short. How a man, of some wide thing that he has witnessed, will construct a narrative, what kind of picture and delineation he will give of it,—is the best measure you could get of what intellect is in the man. Which circumstance is vital and shall stand prominent; which unessential, fit to be suppressed; where is the true *beginning*, the true sequence and ending? To find out this, you task the whole force of insight that is in the man. He must *understand* the thing; according to the depth of his understanding, will the fitness of his answer be. You will try him so. Does like join itself to like; does the spirit of method stir in that confusion, so that its embroilment becomes order? Can the man say, *Fiat lux,* Let there be light; and out of chaos make a world? Precisely as there is *light* in himself, will he accomplish this.

Or indeed we may say again, it is in what I called Portrait-painting, delineating of men and things, especially of men, that Shakspeare is great. All the greatness of the man comes out decisively here. It is unexampled, I think, that calm creative perspicacity of Shakspeare. The thing he looks at reveals not this or that face of it, but its inmost heart, and generic secret: it dissolves itself as in light before him, so that he discerns the perfect structure of it. Creative, we said: poetic creation, what is this too but *seeing* the thing sufficiently? The *word* that will describe the thing, follows of itself from such clear intense sight of the thing. And is not Shakspeare's *morality,* his valor, candor, tolerance, truthfulness; his whole victorious strength and greatness, which can triumph over such obstructions, visible there too? Great as the world. No *twisted,* poor convex-concave mirror, reflecting all objects with its own convexities and concavities; a perfectly *level* mirror;—that is to say withal, if we will understand it, a man justly related to all things and men, a good man. It is truly a lordly spectacle how this great soul takes in all kinds of men and objects, a Falstaff, an Othello, a Juliet, a Coriolanus; sets them all forth to us in their round completeness; loving, just, the equal brother of all. *Novum Organum,* and all the intellect you will find in Bacon, is of a quite secondary order; earthy, material, poor in comparison with this. Among modern men, one finds, in strictness, almost nothing of the same rank. Goethe alone, since the days of Shakspeare, reminds me of it. Of him too you say that he *saw* the object; you may say what he himself says of Shakspeare: "His characters are like watches with dial-plates of transparent crystal; they show you the hour like others, and the inward mechanism also is all visible."

The seeing eye! It is this that discloses the inner harmony of things; what Nature meant, what musical idea Nature has wrapped up in these often rough embodiments. Something she did mean. To the seeing eye that something were discernible. Are they base, miserable things? You can laugh over them, you can weep over them; you can in some way or other genially relate yourself to them;—you can, at lowest, hold your peace about them, turn away your own and others' face from them, till the hour come for practically exterminating and extinguishing them! At bottom, it is the Poet's first gift, as it is all men's, that he have intellect enough. He will be a Poet if he have: a Poet in word; or failing that, perhaps still better, a Poet in act. Whether he write at all; and if so, whether in prose or in verse, will depend on accidents: who knows on what extremely trivial accidents,—perhaps on his having had a singing-master, on his being taught to sing in his boyhood! But the faculty which enables him to discern the inner heart of things, and the harmony that dwells there (for whatsoever exists has a harmony in the heart of it, or it would not hold together and exist), is not the result of habits or accidents, but the gift of Nature herself; the primary outfit for a Heroic Man in what sort soever. To the Poet, as to every other, we say first of all, *See.* If you cannot do that, it is of no use to keep stringing rhymes together, jingling sensibilities against each other, and *name* yourself a Poet; there is no hope for you. If you can, there is, in prose or verse, in action or speculation, all manner of hope. The crabbed old Schoolmaster used to ask, when they brought him a new pupil, "But are ye sure he's *not a dunce*?" Why, really one might ask the same thing, in regard to every man proposed for whatsoever function; and consider it as the one inquiry needful: Are ye sure he's not a dunce? There is, in this world, no other entirely fatal person.

For, in fact, I say the degree of vision that dwells in a man is a correct measure of the man. If called to define Shakspeare's faculty, I should say superiority of Intellect, and think I had included all under that. What indeed are faculties? We talk of faculties as if they were distinct, things separable; as if a man had intellect, imagination, fancy, &c., as he has hands, feet and arms. That is a capital error. Then again, we hear of a man's "intellectual nature," and of his "moral nature," as if these again were divisible, and existed apart. Necessities of language do perhaps prescribe such forms of utterance; we must speak, I am aware, in that way, if we are to speak at all. But words ought not to harden into things for us. It seems to me, our apprehension of this matter is, for most part, radically falsified thereby. We ought to know withal, and to keep forever in mind, that these divisions are at bottom but *names;* that man's spiritual nature, the vital Force which dwells in him, is essentially one and indivisible; that what we call imagination, fancy, understanding, and so forth, are but different figures of the same Power of Insight, all indissolubly connected with each other, physiognomically related; that if we knew one of them, we might know all of them. Morality itself, what we call the moral quality of a man, what is this but another *side* of the one vital Force whereby he is and works? All that a man does is physiognomical of him. You may see how a man would fight, by the way in which he sings; his courage, or want of courage, is visible in the word he utters, in the opinion he has formed, no less than in the stroke he strikes. He is *one;* and preaches the same Self abroad in all these ways.

Without hands a man might have feet, and could still walk: but, consider it,—without morality, intellect were impossible for him; a thoroughly immoral *man* could not know anything at all! To know a thing, what we can call knowing, a man must first *love* the thing, sympathize with it: that is, be *virtuously* related to it. If he have not the justice to put down his own selfishness at every turn, the courage to stand by the dangerous-true at every turn, how shall he know? His virtues, all of them, will lie recorded in his knowledge. Nature, with her truth, remains to the bad, to the selfish and the pusillanimous forever a sealed book: what such can know of Nature is mean, superficial, small; for the uses of the day merely.—But does not the very Fox know something of Nature? Exactly so: it knows where the geese lodge! The human Reynard, very frequent everywhere in the world, what more does he know but this and the like of this? Nay, it should be considered too, that if the Fox had not a certain vulpine *morality,* he could not even know where the geese were, or get at the geese! If he spent his time in splenetic atrabiliar reflections on his own misery, his ill usage by Nature, Fortune and other Foxes, and so forth; and had not courage, promptitude, practicality, and other suitable vulpine gifts and graces, he would catch no geese. We may say of the Fox too, that his morality and insight are of the same dimensions; different faces of the same internal unity of vulpine life!—These things are worth stating; for the contrary of them acts with manifold very baleful perversion, in this time: what limitations, modifications they require, your own candor will supply.

If I say, therefore, that Shakspeare is the greatest of Intellects, I have said all concerning him. But there is more in Shakspeare's intellect than we have yet seen. It is what I call an unconscious intellect; there is more virtue in it than he himself is aware of. Novalis beautifully remarks of him, that those Dramas of his are Products of Nature too, deep as Nature herself. I find a great truth in this saying. Shakspeare's Art is not Artifice; the noblest worth of it is not there by plan or precontrivance. It grows up from the deeps of Nature, through this noble sincere soul, who is a voice of Nature. The latest generations of men will find new meanings in Shakspeare, new elucidations of their own human being; "new harmonies with the infinite structure of the Universe; concurrences with later ideas, affinities with the higher powers and senses of man." This well deserves meditating. It is Nature's highest reward to a true simple great soul, that he get thus to be *a part of herself*. Such a man's works, whatsoever he with utmost conscious exertion and forethought shall accomplish, grow up withal *un*consciously, from the unknown deeps in him;—as the oak-tree grows from the Earth's bosom, as the mountains and waters shape themselves; with a symmetry grounded on Nature's own laws, conformable to all Truth whatsoever. How much in Shakspeare lies hid; his sorrows, his silent struggles known to himself; much that was not known at all, not speakable at all: like *roots*, like sap and forces working underground! Speech is great; but Silence is greater.

Withal the joyful tranquillity of this man is notable. I will not blame Dante for his misery: it is as battle without victory; but true battle,—the first, indispensable thing. Yet I call Shakspeare greater than Dante, in that he fought truly, and did conquer. Doubt it not, he had his own sorrows: those *Sonnets* of his will even testify expressly in what deep waters he had waded, and swum struggling for his life;—as what man like him ever failed to have to do? It seems to me a heedless notion, our common one, that he sat like a bird on the bough; and sang forth, free and off-hand, never knowing the troubles of other men. Not so; with no man is it so. How could a man travel forward from rustic deer-poaching to such tragedy-writing, and not fall in with sorrows by the way? Or, still better, how could a man delineate a Hamlet, a Coriolanus, a Macbeth, so many suffering heroic hearts, if his own heroic heart had never suffered?—And now, in contrast with all this, observe his mirthfulness, his genuine overflowing love of laughter! You would say, in no point does he *exaggerate* but only in laughter. Fiery objurgations, words that pierce and burn, are to be found in Shakspeare; yet he is always in measure here; never what Johnson would remark as a specially "good hater." But his laughter seems to pour from him in floods; he heaps all manner of ridiculous nicknames on the butt he is bantering, tumbles and tosses him in all sorts of horse-play; you would say, with his whole heart laughs. And then, if not always the finest, it is always a genial laughter. Not at mere weakness, at misery or poverty; never. No man who *can* laugh, what we call laughing, will laugh at these things. It is some poor character only *desiring* to laugh, and have the credit of wit, that does so. Laughter means sympathy; good laughter is not "the crackling of thorns under the pot." Even at stupidity and pretension this

Shakspeare does not laugh otherwise than genially. Dogberry and Verges tickle our very hearts; and we dismiss them covered with explosions of laughter: but we like the poor fellows only the better for our laughing; and hope they will get on well there, and continue Presidents of the City-watch. Such laughter, like sunshine on the deep sea, is very beautiful to me.

We have no room to speak of Shakspeare's individual works; though perhaps there is much still waiting to be said on that head. Had we, for instance, all his plays reviewed as *Hamlet,* in *Wilhelm Meister,* is! A thing which might, one day, be done. August Wilhelm Schlegel has a remark on his Historical Plays, *Henry Fifth* and the others, which is worth remembering. He calls them a kind of National Epic. Marlborough, you recollect, said, he knew no English History but what he had learned from Shakspeare. There are really, if we look to it, few as memorable Histories. The great salient points are admirably seized; all rounds itself off, into a kind of rhythmic coherence; it is, as Schlegel says, *epic;*—as indeed all delineation by a great thinker will be. There are right beautiful things in those Pieces, which indeed together form one beautiful thing. That battle of Agincourt strikes me as one of the most perfect things, in its sort, we anywhere have of Shakspeare's. The description of the two hosts: the worn-out, jaded English; the dread hour, big with destiny, when the battle shall begin; and then that deathless valor: "Ye good yeomen, whose limbs were made in England!" There is a noble Patriotism in it,—far other than the "indifference" you sometimes hear ascribed to Shakspeare. A true English heart breathes, calm and strong, through the whole business; not boisterous, protrusive, all the better for that. There is a sound in it like the ring of steel. This man too had a right stroke in him, had it come to that!

But I will say, of Shakspeare's works generally, that we have no full impress of him there; even as full as we have of many men. His works are so many windows, through which we see a glimpse of the world that was in him. All his works seem, comparatively speaking, cursory, imperfect, written under cramping circumstances; giving only here and there a note of the full utterance of the man. Passages there are that come upon you like splendor out of Heaven; bursts of radiance, illuminating the very heart of the thing: you say, "That is *true,* spoken once and forever; wheresoever and whensoever there is an open human soul, that will be recognized as true!" Such bursts, however, make us feel that the surrounding matter is not radiant; that it is, in part, temporary, conventional. Alas, Shakspeare had to write for the Globe Playhouse: his great soul had to crush itself, as it could, into that and no other mould. It was with him, then, as it is with us all. No man works save under conditions. The sculptor cannot set his own free Thought before us; but his Thought as he could translate it into the stone that was given, with the tools that were given. *Disjecta membra* are all that we find of any Poet, or of any man.

Whoever looks intelligently at this Shakspeare may recognize that he too was a *Prophet,* in his way; of an insight analogous to the Prophetic, though he took it up in another strain. Nature seemed to this man also divine; *un*speakable, deep as Tophet, high as Heaven: "We are such stuff as Dreams are made of!" That scroll in Westminster Abbey, which few read with understanding, is of the depth of any seer. But the man sang; did not preach, except musically. We called Dante the melodious Priest of Middle-Age Catholicism. May we not call Shakspeare the still more melodious Priest of a *true* Catholicism, the "Universal Church" of the Future and of all times? No narrow superstition, harsh asceticism, intolerance, fanatical fierceness or perversion: a Revelation, so far as it goes, that such a thousand-fold hidden beauty and divineness dwells in all Nature; which let all men worship as they can! We may say without offence, that there rises a kind of universal Psalm out of this Shakspeare too; not unfit to make itself heard among the still more sacred Psalms. Not in disharmony with these, if we understood them, but in harmony!—I cannot call this Shakspeare a "Sceptic," as some do; his indifference to the creeds and theological quarrels of his time misleading them. No; neither unpatriotic, though he says little about his Patriotism; nor sceptic, though he says little about his Faith. Such "indifference" was the fruit of his greatness withal: his whole heart was in his own grand sphere of worship (we may call it such); these other controversies, vitally important to other men, were not vital to him.

But call it worship, call it what you will, is it not a right glorious thing, and set of things, this that Shakspeare has brought us? For myself, I feel that there is actually a kind of sacredness in the fact of such a man being sent into this Earth. Is he not an eye to us all; a blessed heaven-sent Bringer of Light?—And, at bottom, was it not perhaps far better that this Shakspeare, every way an unconscious man, was *conscious* of no Heavenly message? He did not feel, like Mahomet, because he saw into those internal Splendors, that he specially was the "Prophet of God:" and was he not greater than Mahomet in that? Greater; and also, if we compute strictly, as we did in Dante's case, more successful. It was intrinsically an error that notion of Mahomet's, of his supreme Prophethood; and has come down to us inextricably involved in error to this day; dragging along with it such a coil of fables, impurities, intolerances, as makes it a questionable step for me here and now to say, as I have done, that Mahomet was a true Speaker at all, and not rather an ambitious charlatan, perversity and simulacrum; no Speaker, but a Babbler! Even in Arabia, as I compute, Mahomet will have exhausted himself and become obsolete, while this Shakspeare, this Dante may still be young;—while this Shakspeare may still pretend to be a Priest of Mankind, of Arabia as of other places, for unlimited periods to come!

Compared with any speaker or singer one knows, even with Æschylus or Homer, why should he not, for veracity and universality, last like them? He is *sincere* as they; reaches deep down like them, to the universal and perennial. But as for Mahomet, I think it had been better for him *not* to be so conscious! Alas, poor Mahomet; all that he was *conscious* of was a mere error; a futility and triviality,—as indeed such ever is. The truly great in him too was the unconscious: that he was a wild Arab lion of the desert, and did speak out with that great thunder-voice of his, not by words which he *thought* to be great, but by actions, by feelings, by a history which *were* great! His Koran has become a stupid piece of prolix absurdity; we do not believe, like him, that God wrote that! The Great Man here too, as always, is a Force of Nature: whatsoever is truly great in him springs up from the *in*articulate deeps.

Well: this is our poor Warwickshire Peasant, who rose to be Manager of a Playhouse, so that he could live without begging; whom the Earl of Southampton cast some kind glances on; whom Sir Thomas Lucy, many thanks to him, was for sending to the Treadmill! We did not account him a god, like Odin, while he dwelt with us;—on which point there were much to be said. But I will say rather, or repeat: In spite of the sad state Hero-worship now lies in, consider what this Shakspeare has actually become among us. Which Englishman we ever made, in this land of ours, which million of Englishmen, would we not give up rather than the Stratford Peasant? There is no regiment of highest Dignitaries that we would sell him for. He is the grandest thing we have yet done. For our honor among foreign nations, as an ornament to our English Household, what item is there that we would not surrender rather than him? Consider now, if they asked us, Will you give up your Indian Empire or your Shakspeare, you English; never have had any Indian Empire, or never have had any Shakspeare? Really it were a grave question. Official persons would answer doubtless in official language; but we, for our part too, should not we be forced to answer: Indian Empire, or no Indian Empire; we cannot do without Shakspeare! Indian Empire will go, at any rate, some day; but this Shakspeare does not go, he lasts forever with us; we cannot give up our Shakspeare!

Nay, apart from spiritualities; and considering him merely as a real, marketable, tangibly useful possession. England, before long, this Island of ours, will hold but a small fraction of the English: in America, in New Holland, east and west to the very Antipodes, there will be a Saxondom covering great spaces of the Globe. And now, what is it that can keep all these together into virtually one Nation, so that they do not fall out and fight, but live at peace, in brotherlike intercourse, helping one another? This is justly regarded as the greatest practical problem, the thing all manner of sovereignties and governments are here to accomplish: what is it that will accomplish this? Acts of Parliament, administrative prime-ministers cannot. America is parted from us, so far as Parliament could part it. Call it not fantastic, for there is much reality in it: Here, I say, is an English King, whom no time or chance, Parliament or combination of Parliaments, can dethrone! This King Shakspeare, does not he shine, in crowned sovereignty, over us all, as the noblest, gentlest, yet strongest of rallying-signs; *in*destructible; really more valuable in that point of view than any other means or appliance whatsoever? We can fancy him as radiant aloft over all the Nations of Englishmen, a thousand years hence. From Paramatta, from New York, wheresoever, under what sort of Parish-Constable soever, English men and women are, they will say to one another: "Yes, this Shakspeare is ours; we produced him, we speak and think by him; we are of one blood and kind with him." The most common-sense politician, too, if he pleases, may think of that.

Yes, truly, it is a great thing for a Nation that it get an articulate voice; that it produce a man who will speak forth melodiously what the heart of it means! Italy, for example, poor Italy lies dismembered, scattered asunder, not appearing in any protocol or treaty as a unity at all; yet the noble Italy is actually *one:* Italy produced its Dante; Italy can speak! The Czar of all the Russias, he is strong with so many bayonets, Cossacks and cannons; and does a great feat in keeping such a tract of Earth politically together; but he cannot yet speak. Something great in him, but it is a dumb greatness. He has had no voice of genius, to be heard of all men and times. He must learn to speak. He is a great dumb monster hitherto. His cannons and Cossacks will all have rusted into nonentity, while that Dante's voice is still audible. The Nation that has a Dante is bound together as no dumb Russia can be.—We must here end what we had to say of the *Hero-Poet.*

# *Heinrich Heine*

1797–1856

Heinrich Heine was born on December 13, 1797—eight years after the start of the French Revolution—the son of a wealthy Jewish merchant in Düsseldorf. After a childhood in a liberal milieu (Düsseldorf had no Jewish ghetto and Heine's family had many contacts with their predominantly Catholic neighbors), a primary education in a Jesuit school and a brief failed business apprenticeship, Heine enrolled in the University of Bonn in 1819. Like many other writers (and even composers, such as Schumann), he was ostensibly to study jurisprudence, although his chief interests were history and literature. Despite an acquaintanceship with August Wilhelm Schlegel, one of the founders of German Romanticism (who was later to come under sharp attack from Heine's pen), he transferred after two semesters to Göttingen and thence to Berlin, where he was to hear and meet Hegel. The effect of Hegel on Heine was too great to be easily pinpointed: what probably impressed Heine most was Hegel's idea of history as inevitable progress from religion toward reason, a view that supported his own strong anti-clerical and Enlightenment opinions.

Upon graduating in 1825—and receiving, for purely opportunistic reasons, baptism from a Lutheran pastor—Heine wandered for several years through Germany and Italy, writing intermittently his *Reisebilder (Travel Pictures)*. The outbreak of the July Revolution of 1830 in Paris, however, terminated this period of wandering and decided him in favor of what was to be a permanent exile in the French capital; this was not entirely a matter of choice, since Heine had early on achieved notoriety for his revolutionary sentiments and was *persona non grata* in many parts of Germany—especially Prussia, which he made no secret of despising for its rigid military autocracy. The move to Paris took place in May 1831; Heine's arrival was heralded by announcements in the Saint-Simonian newspaper *The Globe,* and he was eventually to be in contact with Balzac, Hugo, Gautier, Gérard de Nerval, Musset, Chopin, Berlioz, and Liszt, among others. The cosmopolitan environment in which Heine was to live could not have been more unlike the cozy, provincial, small-town world in which most German Romantics produced their work, and this difference was to set his writing sharply apart from the childlike and inward fantasies, usually set in an idealized and mythic medieval past, that had been the stock in trade of his compatriots. There were few German artists in the 19th century who managed to escape the narrowness of the small-town idyll as completely as did Heine; his closest parallel here may be Richard Wagner, who also lived in Paris for some time.

Heine's first book of poetry, and the one which was to remain his most famous, had already been published in Hamburg in 1827 under the simple title of *Buch der Lieder (Book of Songs).* The book is, together with Baudelaire's *Les Fleurs du mal,* probably the single most important volume of poetry to be published in the 19th century, and it was so popular that it kept the rest of the poet's considerable output in its shadow. At first glance the *Book of Songs* seems to offer little new: the entire book consists of endless variations on the theme of unrequited love, all written in short, homely four-line stanzas, in a language so disarmingly simple and close to everyday speech that one hardly notices the versification. It is, however, just this apparent naturalness that was the result of much hard work, as becomes clear upon rereading. Most of the poems depend for their effect on slight, deft touches of irony or doubt that abruptly deepen a seemingly innocuous idyllic scene, painfully disrupting the harmony of lyrical subject and surrounding nature: this disharmony Heine called *Zerrissenheit* (literally, "tornness" within oneself), and it has become so much a part of Romanticism's legacy to modernity that we are hardly aware of it any more; not many people know that Heine invented the term *Weltschmerz,* nor that the phrase "religion is the opiate of the people" was taken by Marx from Heine. The inner disharmony of the poetic subject was not Heine's invention—one can trace it back to E. T. A. Hoffmann and even to Goethe's Faust, who complained of having "two souls" within himself; but Heine gave the idea a new nervous edge and bitterness that make him in many ways a predecessor of Baudelaire. It is thus not surprising that despite his popularity in France, where he was known as "l'adorable Henri Heine," his biting sarcasm made him unpopular in Germany even into the 20th century (as Adorno's essay, *Die Wunde Heine* [*The Wound Heine*] attests). The deceptive simplicity and surface clarity of the poems have in any case given Heine an international reputation second only to Goethe—and, more recently, Rilke—despite the fact that the subtle assonances and inflections of his poetry are not easily brought over into translation.

Heine himself regarded the *Book of Songs* as of secondary importance; his own real interest lay in his prose works, which are, particularly to non-German readers, less well-known. Among them are the *Travel Pictures* (including the famous *Journey through the Harz*), describing regions of Germany, England and Italy, and mixing autobiographical reflection, historical criticism, humorous anecdotes and portraits, sometimes most unflattering, of local noteworthies. This deliberately disquieting mixing of genre has been the chief obstacle to the *Travel Pictures'* popularity, but the reader who can forget normal genre distinctions will find here some of the most lively writing in the German language. Other prose works include two little-known plays; several novellas and ballet scenarios; a biography of the poet's onetime friend, the political thinker Ludwig Börne; the famous critical review of his German literary contemporaries, *Die Romantische Schule (The Romantic School);* and two long narrative poems, *Atta Troll* and *Deutschland: Ein Wintermärchen (Germany: A Winter's Fairy Tale).* These latter two might be called "mock epics"; like the *Travel Pictures,* they mix historical references with contemporary caricatures, often openly polemical or political in nature, and are written in a style approaching deliberate doggerel. It might be said that with these poems Heine managed to write a German equivalent of Byron's *Don Juan,* the chatty, informal tone of which Goethe had said could never be reproduced in German!

Evident in all these works is Heine's own intense involvement with the political life of his time; he was occupied for much of his time in Paris as a journalist and observer of Parisian life, even a "mediator" between France and Germany. His earlier revolutionary views were only strengthened by his friendship with Karl Marx during 1843—although he nonetheless retained a deeper belief in the Hegelian supremacy of ideas than did the younger Marx, and often voiced fears that there would be no place for the freedom of the poet under a socialist or communist regime. Most remarkable is that Heine's own "program" included not only political but also moral (including sexual) freedom; this separated him from the puritanical bent of many revolutionaries such as Robespierre or Börne—whom Heine designated generically as "Nazarenes," denoting thereby their zealotry in contrast to his own "Hellenic" desire to enjoy life for its own sake. Another belief that separated him from other socially engaged writers of his time was his persistent belief in the independence of art from any political doctrine; thus, the same Heine who severely criticized Goethe (whom he had met earlier in 1824; the meeting was a distinct disappointment) for not using his immense prestige to further the cause of social progress, found himself later falling back on the example of Goethe in defense against those who saw art only as a servant of revolution. The paradox is typical of Heine's stubborn, almost perverse isolation, and makes his struggle a foreshadowing of that faced by the Surrealists in our own century who agonized over the relation between art and politics.

Heine himself, exhausted by his journalistic efforts and a battle over a family inheritance, failed drastically in health around his fifty-first year; in May 1848 he left his house for the last time—to view the Venus de Milo in the Louvre, before which he broke down in tears. This was the year of the March revolution which spelled the end of monarchy in France; but Heine, who had expected a liberation of a more dignified and intellectual sort, was sorely disappointed by the crude vulgarity of the popular uprising, and even more by the accession of Louis Napoleon in 1852. Thus, upon this disillusionment and failing health was to follow the poet's reconciliation with the idea of God—not the God of the official Church and clergy, but an heroic and personal Old Testament God, who could be the poet's sure defense against the constant misunderstanding and stupidity he perceived around him. In one of the poems written in a last burst of deathbed productivity—published in a collection titled *Romanzero*—Heine writes: "Only to God does he [the poet] answer, / Not to the people. In art / As in life, the people can only / Kill us, never judge us." Throughout these last years until his death, Heine retained the most extraordinary humor and clarity, never allowing self-pity to overcome him, although he was completely confined to his bed for his last eight years. He died on February 17, 1856 and was buried in Montmartre.

# I Meet August Wilhelm Schlegel

How delighted and astonished I was, when as a very young man, in the year 1819, I studied at the University of Bonn, and there had the honor of seeing that poetic genius, August Wilhelm Schlegel, face to face. He was, with the exception of Napoleon, the first great man it had been my fortune to behold, and I shall never forget that sublime sight. To this very day I feel the sacred tremor which shook my soul when I stood before his desk and heard him speak. In those days I wore the coarse white student coat, the scarlet cap, long blond hair, but no gloves. But Herr A. W. Schlegel wore kid gloves, and was dressed in the latest Paris fashion. He exhaled the scent of fashionable society and *eau de mille fleurs*—he was neatness and elegance personified, and when he spoke of the Lord Chancellor of England, he always added "my friend." At his side stood his valet, dressed in the most complete baronial livery of the House of Schlegel, and trimmed the tapers in the silver candelabra which stood alongside a glass of sugar-water on the lectern in front of this wondrous man. Footmen in livery! Wax tapers! Silver candelabra! "My friend," the Lord Chancellor of England! Kid gloves! Sugar-water! What unheard-of things in the lecture room of a German professor! This magnificence dazzled all of us young people not a little—and especially me—and I composed three odes in honor of Herr Schlegel, all beginning,

"Oh, thou—who—," etc.

But only in verse would I have presumed to address the distinguished man in so familiar a style. His external appearance was not unimposing. A few silver hairs shone on his small head, and his figure was so slender, wasted, and transparent, that he seemed to be all spirit—and almost a symbol of spiritualism.

# The Romantic School

What was the Romantic School in Germany?

It was nothing else than the reawakening of the poetry of the Middle Ages as it manifested itself in the poems, paintings, and sculptures, in the art and life of those times. This poetry, however, had been developed out of Christianity; it was a passion-flower which had blossomed from the blood of Christ. I know not if the melancholy flower which in Germany we call the passion-flower is known by the same name in France, and if the popular tradition has ascribed to it the same mystical origin. It is that motley-hued, melancholic flower in whose calyx one may behold a counterfeit presentment of the tools used at the crucifixion of Christ—namely, hammer, pincers, and nails. This flower is by no means unsightly, but only spectral: its aspect fills our souls with a dread pleasure, like those convulsive, sweet emotions that arise from grief. In this respect the passion-flower would be the fittest symbol of Christianity itself, whose most awe-inspiring charm consists in the voluptuousness of pain.

Although in France Christianity and Roman Catholicism are synonymous terms, yet I desire to emphasize the fact, that I here refer to the latter only. I refer to that religion whose earliest dogmas contained a condemnation of all flesh, and not only admitted the supremacy of the spirit over the flesh, but sought to mortify the latter in order thereby to glorify the former. I refer to that religion through whose unnatural mission vice and hypocrisy came into the world, for through the odium which it cast on the flesh the most innocent gratifications of the senses were accounted sins; and, as it was impossible to be entirely spiritual, the growth of hypocrisy was inevitable. I refer to that religion which, by teaching the renunciation of all earthly pleasures, and by inculcating abject humility and angelic patience, became the most efficacious support of despotism. Men now recognize the nature of that religion, and will no longer be put off with promises of a heaven hereafter; they know that the material world has also its good, and is not wholly given over to Satan, and now they vindicate the pleasures of the world, this beautiful garden of the gods, our inalienable heritage. Just because we now comprehend so fully all the consequences of that absolute spirituality, we are warranted in believing that the Christian-Catholic theories of the universe are at an end; for every epoch is a sphinx which plunges into the abyss as soon as its problem is solved.

We by no means deny the benefits which the Christian-Catholic theories effected in Europe. They were needed as a wholesome reaction against the terrible colossal materialism which was developed in the Roman Empire, and threatened the annihilation of all the intellectual grandeur of mankind. Just as the licentious memoirs of the last century form the *pièces justificatives* of the French Revolution; just as the reign of terror seems a necessary medicine when one is familiar with the confessions of the French nobility since the Regency; so the wholesomeness of ascetic spirituality becomes manifest when we read Petronius or Apuleius, books which may be considered as *pièces justificatives* of Christianity. The flesh had become so insolent in this Roman world that Christian discipline was needed to chasten it. After the banquet of a Trimalchio, a hunger-cure, such as Christianity, was required.

Or did, perhaps, the hoary sensualists seek by scourgings to stimulate the cloyed flesh to renewed capacity for enjoyment? Did ageing Rome submit to monkish flagellations in order to discover exquisite pleasure in torture itself, voluptuous bliss in pain?

Unfortunate excess! it robbed the Roman body-politic of its last energies. Rome was not destroyed by the division into two empires. On the Bosporus as on the Tiber, Rome was eaten up by the same Judaic spiritualism, and in both Roman history became the record of a slow dying-away, a death agony that lasted for centuries. Did perhaps murdered Judea, by bequeathing its spiritualism to the Romans, seek to avenge itself on the victorious foe, as did the dying centaur, who so cunningly wheedled the son of Jupiter into wearing the deadly vestment poisoned with his own blood? In truth, Rome, the Hercules among nations, was so effectually consumed by the Judaic poison that helm and armour fell from its decaying limbs, and its imperious battle tones degenerated into the prayers of snivelling priests and the trilling of eunuchs.

But that which enfeebles the aged strengthens the young. That spiritualism had a wholesome effect on the over-robust races of the north; the ruddy barbarians became spiritualized through Christianity; European civilization began. This is a praiseworthy and sacred phase of Christianity. The Catholic Church earned in this regard the highest title to our respect and admiration. Through grand, genial institutions it controlled the bestiality of the barbarian hordes of the north, and tamed their brutal materialism.

The works of art in the Middle Ages give evidence of this mastery of matter by the spirit; and that is often their whole purpose. The epic poems of that time may be easily classified according to the degree in which they show that mastery. Of lyric and dramatic poems nothing is here to be said; for the latter do not exist, and the former are as much alike in all ages as are the songs of the nightingales in each succeeding spring.

Although the epic poetry of the Middle Ages was divided into sacred and secular, yet both classes were purely Christian in their nature; for if the sacred poetry related exclusively to the Jewish people and its history, which alone was considered sacred; if its themes were the heroes of the Old and the New Testaments, and their legends—in brief, the Church—still all the Christian views and aims of that period were mirrored in the secular poetry. The flower of the German sacred poetry of the Middle Ages is, perhaps, *Barlaam and Josaphat,* a poem in which the dogma of self-denial, of continence, of renunciation, of the scorn of all worldly pleasures, is most consistently expressed. Next in order of merit I would rank *Lobgesang auf den Heiligen Anno,* but the latter poem already evinces a marked tendency towards secular themes. It differs in general from the former somewhat as an old German representation of a saint differs from a Byzantine image. Just as in those Byzantine pictures, so also do we find in *Barlaam and Josaphat* the greatest simplicity; there is no perspective, and the long, lean, statue-like forms, and the grave, ideal countenances, stand severely outlined, as though in bold relief against a background of pale gold. In the *Lobgesang auf den Heiligen Anno,* as in the old German pictures, the accessories seem almost more prominent than the subject; and, notwithstanding the bold outlines, every detail is most minutely executed, and one knows not which to admire most, the giantlike conception or the dwarflike patience of execution. Ottfried's *Evangeliengedicht,* which is generally praised as the masterpiece of this sacred poetry, is far inferior to both of these poems.

In the secular poetry we find, as intimated above, first, the cycle of legends called the *Nibelungenlied,* and the *Book of Heroes.* In these poems all the ante-Christian modes of thought and feelings are dominant; brute force is not yet moderated into chivalry; the sturdy warriors of the North stand like statues of stone, and the soft light and moral atmosphere of Christianity have not yet penetrated their iron armour. But dawn is gradually breaking over the old German forests, the ancient Druid oaks are being felled, and in the open arena Christianity and Paganism are battling: all this is portrayed in the cycle of traditions of Charlemagne; even the Crusades with their religious tendencies are mirrored therein. But now from this Christianized, spiritualized brute force is developed the peculiar feature of the Middle Ages, chivalry, which finally becomes exalted into a religious knighthood. The earlier knighthood is most felicitously portrayed in the legends of King Arthur, which are full of the most charming gallantry, the most finished courtesy, and the most daring bravery. From the midst of the pleasing, though bizarre, arabesques, and the fantastic, flowery mazes of these tales, we are greeted by the gentle Gawain, by the worthy Lancelot of the Lake, by the valiant, gallant, and honest, but somewhat tedious, Wigalois. By the side of this cycle of legends we find the kindred and connected legends of the Holy Grail, in which the religious knighthood is glorified, and in which are to be found the three grandest poems of the Middle Ages, *Titurel, Parcival,* and *Lohengrin.* In these poems we stand face to face, as it were, with the Muse of romantic poetry; we look deep into her large, sad eyes, and ere we are aware she has ensnared us in her network of scholasticism, and drawn us down into the weird depths of medieval mysticism. But farther on in this period we find poems which do not unconditionally bow down to Christian spirituality; poems in which it is even attacked, and in which the poet, breaking loose from the fetters of an abstract Christian morality, complacently plunges into the delightful realm of glorious sensuousness. Nor is it an inferior poet who has left us *Tristan and Isolde,* the masterpiece of this class. Verily, I must confess that Gottfried von Strassburg, the author of this, the most exquisite poem of the Middle Ages, is perhaps also the loftiest poet of that period. He surpasses even the grandeur of Wolfram von Eschenbach, whose *Parcival,* and fragments of *Titurel,* are so much admired. At present, it is perhaps permissible to praise Meister Gottfried without stint, but in his own time his book and similar poems, to which even *Lancelot* belonged, were considered godless and dangerous. Francesca da Polenta and her handsome friend paid dearly for reading together such a book—the greater danger, it is true, lay in the fact that they suddenly stopped reading.

All the poetry of the Middle Ages has a certain definite character, through which it differs from the poetry of the Greeks and Romans. In reference to this difference the former is called Romantic, the latter Classic. These names, however, are misleading, and have hitherto caused the most vexatious confusion, which is even increased when we call the antique poetry plastic as well as classic. In this, particularly, lies the germ of misunderstandings; for artists ought always to treat their subject-matter plastically. Whether it be Christian or pagan, the subject ought to be portrayed in clear contours. In short, plastic configuration should be the main requisite in the modern romantic as well as in antique art. And, in fact, are not the figures in Dante's *Divine Comedy* or in the paintings of Raphael just as plastic as those in Virgil or on the walls of Herculaneum?

The difference consists in this—that the plastic figures in antique art are identical with the thing represented, with the idea which the artist seeks to communicate. Thus, for example, the wanderings of the Odyssey mean nothing else than the wanderings of the man who was a son of Laertes and the husband of Penelope, and was called Ulysses. Thus, again, the Bacchus which is to be seen in the Louvre is nothing more than the charming son of Semele, with a daring melancholy look in his eyes, and an inspired voluptuousness on the soft arched lips. It is otherwise in romantic art: here the wanderings of a knight have an esoteric signification; they typify, perhaps, the mazes of life in general. The dragon that is vanquished is sin; the almond-tree, that from afar so encouragingly wafts its fragrance to the hero, is the Trinity, the God-Father, God-Son, and God-Holy-Ghost, who together constitute one, just as shell, fibre, and kernel together constitute the almond. When Homer describes the armour of a hero, it is naught else than good armour, which is worth so many oxen; but when a monk of the Middle Ages describes in his poem the garments of the Mother of God, you may depend upon it, that by each fold of those garments he typifies some special virtue, and that a peculiar meaning lies hidden in the sacred robes of the immaculate Virgin Mary; as her Son is the kernel of the almond, she is quite appropriately described in the poem as an almond-blossom. Such is the character of that poesy of the Middle Ages which we designate *romantic*.

Classic art had to portray only the finite, and its forms could be identical with the artist's idea. Romantic art had to represent, or rather to typify, the infinite and the spiritual, and therefore was compelled to have recourse to a system of traditional, or rather parabolic, symbols, just as Christ Himself had endeavoured to explain and make clear His spiritual meaning through beautiful parables. Hence the mystic, enigmatical, miraculous, and transcendental character of the art-productions of the Middle Ages. Fancy strives frantically to portray through concrete images that which is purely spiritual, and in the vain endeavour invents the most colossal absurdities; it piles Ossa on Pelion, Parcival on Titurel, to reach heaven.

Similar monstrous abortions of imagination have been produced by the

Scandinavians, the Hindus, and the other races which likewise strive through poetry to represent the infinite; among them also do we find poems which may be regarded as romantic.

But human genius can transfigure deformity itself, and many painters succeeded in accomplishing the unnatural task beautifully and sublimely. The Italians, in particular, glorified beauty—it is true, somewhat at the expense of spirituality—and raised themselves aloft to an ideality which reached its perfection in the many representations of the Madonna. Where it concerned the Madonna, the Catholic clergy always made some concessions to sensuality. This image of an immaculate beauty, transfigured by motherly love and sorrow, was privileged to receive the homage of poet and painter, and to be decked with all the charms that could allure the senses. For this image was a magnet, which was to draw the great masses into the pale of Christianity. Madonna Maria was the pretty *dame du comptoir* of the Catholic Church, whose customers, especially the barbarians of the north, she attracted and held fast by her celestial smiles.

During the Middle Ages architecture was of the same character as the other arts; for, indeed, at that period all manifestations of life harmonized most wonderfully. In architecture, as in poetry, this parabolizing tendency was evident. Now, when we enter an old cathedral, we have scarcely a hint of the esoteric meaning of its stony symbolism. Only the general impression forces itself on our mind. We feel the exaltation of the spirit and the abasement of the flesh. The interior of the cathedral is a hollow cross, and we walk here amid the instruments of martyrdom itself. The variegated windows cast on us their red and green lights, like drops of blood and ichor; requiems for the dead resound through the aisles; under our feet are gravestones and decay; in harmony with the colossal pillars, the soul soars aloft, painfully tearing itself away from the body, which sinks to the ground like a cast-off garment. When one views from without these Gothic cathedrals, these immense structures, that are built so airily, so delicately, so daintily, as transparent as if carved, like Brabant laces made of marble, then only does one realize the might of that art which could achieve a mastery over stone, so that even this stubborn substance should appear spectrally etherealized, and be an exponent of Christian spiritualism.

But the arts are only the mirror of life; and when Catholicism disappeared from daily life, so also it faded and vanished out of the arts. At the time of the Reformation Catholic poetry was gradually dying out in Europe, and in its place we behold the long-buried Grecian style of poetry again reviving. It was, in sooth, only an artificial spring, the work of the gardener and not of the sun; the trees and flowers were stuck in narrow pots, and a glass sky protected them from the wind and cold weather.

In the world's history every event is not the direct consequence of another, but all events mutually act and react on one another. It was not alone through the Greek scholars who, after the conquest of Constantinople, immigrated over to us, that the love for Grecian art, and the striving to imitate it, became universal among us; but in art as in life, there was stirring a contemporary Protestantism. Leo X, the magnificent Medici, was just as zealous a Protestant as Luther; and as in Wittenberg protest was offered in Latin prose, so in Rome the protest was made in stone, colours, and *ottave rime*. For do not the vigorous marble statues of Michael Angelo, Giulio Romano's laughing nymph-faces, and the life-intoxicated merriment in the verses of Messer Ludovico, offer a protesting contrast to the old, gloomy, withered Catholicism? The painters of Italy combated priestdom more effectively, perhaps, than did the Saxon theologians. The glowing flesh in the paintings of Titian—all that is simple Protestantism. The limbs of his Venus are much more fundamental theses than those which the German monk nailed to the church door of Wittenberg. Mankind felt itself suddenly liberated, as it were, from the thraldom of a thousand years; the artists, in particular, breathed freely again when the Alp-like burden of Christianity was rolled from off their breasts; they plunged enthusiastically into the sea of Grecian mirthfulness, from whose foam the goddess of beauty again rose to meet them; again did the painters depict the ambrosial joys of Olympus; again did the sculptors, with the olden love, chisel the heroes of antiquity from out the marble blocks; again did the poets sing of the house of Atreus and of Laius; a new era of classic poetry arose.

In France, under Louis XIV, this neo-classic poetry exhibited a polished perfection, and, to a certain extent, even originality. Through the political influence of the *grand monarque* this new classic poetry spread over the rest of Europe. In Italy, where it was already at home, it received a French colouring; the Anjous brought with them to Spain the heroes of French tragedy; it accompanied Princess Henrietta to England; and, as a matter of course, we Germans modelled our clumsy temple of art after the bepowdered Olympus of Versailles. The most famous high priest of this temple was Gottsched, that old periwigged pate, whom our dear Goethe has so felicitously described in his memoirs.

Lessing was the literary Arminius who emancipated our theatre from that foreign rule. He showed us the vapidness, the ridiculousness, the tastelessness, of those apings of the French stage, which itself was but an imitation of the Greek. But not only by his criticism, but also through his own works of art, did he become the founder of modern German original literature. All the paths of the intellect, all the phases of life, did this man pursue with disinterested enthusiasm. Art, theology, antiquarianism, poetry, dramatic criticism, history—he studied all these with the same zeal and with the same aim. In all his works breathes the same grand social idea, the same progressive humanity, the same religion of reason, whose John he was, and whose Messiah we still await. This religion he preached always, but alas! often quite alone and in the desert. Moreover, he lacked the skill to transmute stones into bread. The greater portion of his life was spent in poverty and misery—a curse which rests on almost all the great minds of Germany, and which probably will only be overcome by political emancipation. Lessing was more deeply interested in political questions than was imagined—a characteristic which we entirely miss in his contemporaries. Only now do we comprehend what he had in view by his description of the petty despotisms in *Emilia Galotti*. At that time he was considered merely a champion of intellectual liberty and an opponent of clerical intolerance; his theological writings were better understood. The fragments 'Concerning the Education of the Human Race,' which have been translated into French by Eugène Rodrigue, will perhaps suffice to give the French an idea of the wide scope of Lessing's genius. His two critical works which have had the most influence on art are his *Hamburger Dramaturgie* and his *Laocoön, or Concerning the Limits of Painting and Poetry*. His best dramatic works are *Emilia Galotti, Minna von Barnhelm,* and *Nathan the Wise*.

Gotthold Ephraim Lessing was born 22nd January 1729, at Kamenz, in Upper Lusatia, and died 15th February 1781, at Brunswick. He was a whole man, who, while with his polemics waging destructive battle against the old, at the same time created something newer and better. 'He resembled,' says a German author, 'those pious Jews, who, at the second building of the temple, were often disturbed by the attacks of their enemies, and with one hand would fight against the foe, while with the other hand they continued to work at the house of God.' This is not the place to discuss Lessing more fully, but I cannot refrain from saying that, in the whole range of literary history, he is the author whom I most love.

I desire here to call attention to another author, who worked in the same spirit and with the same aim, and who may be regarded as Lessing's most legitimate successor. It is true, a criticism of this author would be out of place here, for he occupies a peculiarly isolated place in the history of literature, and his relation to his epoch and contemporaries cannot even now be definitely pronounced. I refer to Johann Gottfried Herder, born in 1744, at Mohrungen, in East Prussia; died in 1803, at Weimar, in Saxony.

The history of literature is a great morgue, wherein each seeks the dead who are near or dear to him. And when, among the corpses of so many petty men, I behold the noble features of a Lessing or a Herder, my heart throbs with emotion. How could I pass you without pressing a hasty kiss on your pale lips?

But if Lessing effectually put an end to the servile apings of Franco-Grecian art, yet, by directing attention to the true artworks of Grecian antiquity, to a certain extent he gave an impetus to a new and equally silly species of imitation. Through his warfare against religious superstitution he even advanced a certain narrow-minded jejune enlightenment, which at that time vaunted itself in Berlin; the sainted Nicolai was its principal mouthpiece, and the *German Encyclopaedia* its arsenal. The most wretched mediocrity began to raise its head, more disgustingly than ever. Imbecility, vapidity, and the commonplace distended themselves like the frog in the fable.

It is an error to believe that Goethe, who at that time had already appeared upon the scene, had met with general recognition. His *Goetz von Berlichingen* and his *Werther* were received with enthusiasm, but the works of the most ordinary bungler not less so, and Goethe occupied but a small niche in the temple of literature. It is true, as said before, that the public welcomed *Goetz* and *Werther* with delight, but more on account of their subject-matter than their artistic merits, which few were able to appreciate. Of these masterpieces, *Goetz von Berlichingen* was a dramatized romance of chivalry, which was the popular style at that time. In *Werther* the public saw only an embellished account of an episode in real life—namely, the story of young Jerusalem, a youth who shot himself from disappointed love, thereby creating quite a commotion in that dead-calm period. Tears were shed over his pathetic letters, and it was shrewdly observed that the manner in which Werther had been ostracized from the society of the nobility must have increased his weariness of life. The discussion concerning suicide brought the book still more into notice; a few fools hit upon the idea of shooting themselves in imitation of Werther, and thus the book made a marked sensation. But the romances of August Lafontaine were in equal demand, and as the latter was a voluminous writer, it followed that he was more famous than Wolfgang Goethe. Wieland was the great poet of that period, and his only rival was Herr Ramler of Berlin. Wieland was worshipped idolatrously, more than Goethe ever was. Iffland, with his lachrymose domestic dramas, and Kotzebue's farces, with their stale witticisms, ruled the stage.

It was against this literature that, in the closing years of the last century, there arose in Germany a new school, which we have designated the Romantic School. At the head of this school stand the brothers August Wilhelm and Friedrich Schlegel. Jena, where these two brothers, together with many kindred spirits, were wont to come and go, was the central point from which the new aesthetic dogma radiated. I advisedly say dogma, for this school began with a criticism of the art productions of the past, and with recipes for the art works of the future. In both of these fields the Schlegelian school has rendered good service to aesthetic criticism. In criticizing the art works of the past, either their defects and imperfections were set forth, or their merits and beauties illustrated. In their polemics, in their exposure of artistic shortcomings and imperfections, the Schlegels were entirely imitators of Lessing; they seized upon his great battle-sword, but the arm of August Wilhelm Schlegel was far too feeble, and the sight of his brother Friedrich too much obscured by mystic clouds; the former could not strike so strong, nor the latter so sure and telling a blow as Lessing. In reproductive criticism, however, where the beauties of a work of art were to be brought out clearly; where a delicate perception of the individualities was required; and where these were to be made intelligible, the Schlegels are far superior to Lessing. But what shall I say concerning their recipes for producing masterpieces? Here the Schlegels reveal the same impotency that we seem to discover in Lessing. The latter also, strong as he is in negation, is weak in affirmation; seldom can he lay down any fundamental principle, and even more rarely a correct one. He lacks the firm foundation of a philosophy, or a synthetic system. In this respect the Schlegels are still more woefully lacking. Many fables are rife concerning the influence of Fichtean idealism and Schelling's philosophy of nature upon the romantic school, and it is even asserted that the latter is entirely the result of the former. I can, however, at the most discover the traces of only a few stray thoughts of Fichte and Schelling, but by no means the impress of a system of philosophy. It is true that Schelling, who at that time was delivering lectures at Jena, had personally a great influence upon the romantic school. Schelling is also somewhat of a poet, a fact not generally known in France, and it is said that he is still in doubt whether he shall not publish his entire philosophical works in poetical, yes, even in metrical form. This doubt is characteristic of the man.

But if the Schlegels could give no definite, reliable theory for the masterpieces which they bespoke of the poets of their school, they atoned for these shortcomings by commending as models the best works of art of the past, and by making them accessible to their disciples. These were chiefly the Christian-Catholic productions of the Middle Ages. The translation of Shakespeare, who stands at the frontier of this art and with Protestant clearness smiles over into our modern era, was solely intended for polemical purposes, the present discussion of which space forbids. It was undertaken by A. W. Schlegel at a time when the enthusiasm for the Middle Ages had not yet reached its most extravagant height. Later, when this did occur, Calderon was translated and ranked far above Shakespeare. For the works of Calderon bear most distinctly the impress of the poetry of the Middle Ages—particularly of the two principal epochs of knight-errantry and monasticism. The pious comedies of the Castilian priest-poet, whose poetical flowers had been besprinkled with holy water and canonical perfumes, with all their pious *grandezza,* with all their sacerdotal splendour, with all their sanctimonious balderdash, were now set up as models, and Germany swarmed with fantastically-pious, insanely-profound poems, over which it was the fashion to work oneself into a mystic ecstasy of admiration, as in *The Devotion to the Cross,* or to fight in honour of the Madonna, as in *The Constant Prince.* Zacharias Werner carried the nonsense as far as it might be safely done without being imprisoned by the authorities in a lunatic asylum.

# *Giacomo Leopardi*

1798–1837

Giacomo Leopardi was Italy's foremost 19th-century poet and her most profound moral and aesthetic philosopher. In him are united vast erudition, penetrating introspection, and a peerless lyric sensibility. The great 19th-century critic Francesco De Sanctis describes Leopardi as the writer who exemplifies the loss of faith in progress, the return of mystery to philosophy, and the consciousness of solitude and pain attendant upon the death of theology that marks the transition from the 18th to the 19th century in intellectual Italy. With Leopardi Italian literature, and above all the Italian language itself, underwent a transformation more profound than that it had experienced at the hands of any single author since Petrarch or Dante.

Under the influence of a centuries-old lyric and pastoral tradition derived from antiquity and Italian literature, Leopardi transmutes his earliest apprehension of landscape and nature into a meditation on the constitution of the cosmos. Nature itself, which at first seems to offer an image of paradise, of Arcadia, becomes, under the pressure of solitude, an image of strife and horror—the justification of a stoicism so pure that it breaks free of heroism, and moves beyond the egoism and self-assertion of the heroic impulse. It would be wrong to compare Leopardi with Wordsworth or German nature mysticism. His is a poetic sensibility that transcends Romantic and Classical categories, not merely in the polemicist or aestheticist sense, but most powerfully from within. Nothing endures under Leopardi's abysmal gaze, save the utterance that can restore some meaning to a broken world.

Born in 1798 into a noble family in the town of Recanati, Leopardi was the son of Adelaide Antici, a repressive, imperious, and unforgiving woman, and Monaldo Leopardi, a provincial *litterateur*, book collector, and poet. Recanati, within the domain of the Papal States, shared the papacy's distrust of all liberalizing currents, and the Leopardi family was among the most traditionalist in the entire region. The cruelty of restraint is not without its benefits: such an atmosphere can, in the earliest years of a poet's education, impose fundamental principles against which he can later struggle and define himself. The ideological conservatism of Leopardi's parents, with the attendant emphasis on classical education, was of enormous value to the boy. Words and learning were as much a part of his infancy as toys were to most children. At the age of eleven, he translated the entire first book of Horace's *Odes;* two years later he mastered Greek, immediately set to translating the pseudo-Homeric poems, and began to study Hebrew—all the while writing tragedies, epigrams, and fables.

His first scholarly works, the *Storia dell'Astronomia* and the *Saggio sugli Errori Popolari degli Antichi,* are a strange amalgamation of Enlightenment skepticism with a fascination for the fantastic, the imaginary, the exquisitely speculative. This period, coinciding with that stage of adolescence which provides the first new perspective on one's early years, was the happiest time of his life. The *Zibaldone,* written for the most part in the 1820s, captures the fugitive images of this happiness of late childhood, which almost seem like intimations from some other world. "I myself remember," he writes in a famous passage, "possessing in my childhood . . . the sensation of a sound so sweet that such is not heard in this world; I recall having figured to myself in fantasy, while gazing up at some images of shepherds and little lambs painted on the heaven of my bedroom ceiling, such beauty of idyllic life, that if a similar life were granted to us, we would not be in earth but rather in paradise."

In 1819 he composed the ultimate expression of his poetic genius, the idyll *L'Infinito (The Infinite)*. Contemplation of the infinite in spatial and temporal terms here provides for the possibility of a kind of nostalgia that transcends nostalgia, of a pure or objective nostalgia. Historical pain (i.e., the contemplation of the dead in nature and in history) gives the poet a recognition of distance from that pain, which is then expressed in terms of a meditation upon the natural imagery of hills and plants outside his window at Recanati. At the end of the poem he is ready to plunge again into this pain, having introjected distance into himself, so that the re-plunge and return is a source of pleasure. The sound of the wind at the heart of the poem is the image around which all other thoughts and sensations gather; far from lapsing into a kind of self-indulgent sentimentalism, this poem speaks with a wise and tranquil voice, a voice that has known despair and meaninglessness, the voice of the wind.

From historical pessimism (i.e., the disparaging of the present at the expense of the past), Leopardi moved into a "final" phase, cosmic pessimism. The satirical impulse that characterizes his later works is the comic expression of this pessimism. His models are Lucian and Plautus. The *Operette Morali,* written in the period from 1824–27, contains wild, unimaginable dialogues—between gnomes and elves, Nature and an Icelander, Torquato Tasso and the Genius of his madness, Death and Fashion—revealing the gaiety at the core of loneliness, the profound sprightliness of Leopardi's thought, which always saves it from contemptuous disdain and mere solemnity. His is a Stoic vision tempered by the apparent absurdity of all facets of human existence: love, the striving for success, heroism.

In 1830 Leopardi moved to Naples in an attempt to shore up his health, accompanied by his constant friend Ranieri. In the last years of his life his fascination with art never ceased, despite almost constant physical suffering; about this time, he conceived a Byronic poem that cast the great men of Europe, in pseudo-Homeric fashion, as mice, frogs, rats, etc. This was no mere frivolity: it expressed his conviction in the redemptive power of comedy. He completed no large projects in his last years, but the subtlety of his scattered writings reflects the monumentality and profundity of his mind. His most erudite researches into the subterranean enclaves of philology and literary history form part of an uninterrupted continuum with his reflections on suffering and beauty. As a poet, and a sober and great one, he was devoted to and respectful of beauty, but never for its own sake. In this he displayed that impersonality which De Sanctis accorded to him: he never permitted, in his writing or his life, the ability to create beauty from despair to be his own personal possession. Thus, in more than one sense he will always yield his poetry up to history.

FROM

# The Zibaldone

## *Various Thoughts about Philosophy and Belles-Lettres*

I have just finished reading, in No. 91 of *Lo Spettatore,* Ludovico di Breme's[1] *Observations* on modern or (if we prefer to call it so) Romantic poetry, and since I have found in them a series of arguments that might be confusing or disturbing, and since I am myself, by nature, always prone to doubt, even with regard to things considered indisputable, but yet have in my mind the answers that can and should be given to these observations, I will set them down, for my own peace of mind. The writer (like all the Romantics) wishes modern poetry to be based on an ideal, which he calls poetic and which is more commonly called sentimental, and he rightly makes a distinction between pathos and melancholy, since pathos, he says, is the depth of feeling experienced by sensitive hearts, through the impression made on their senses by any natural thing, for instance—he says—the bell of their native city, or—I would add—the sight of a landscape or a ruined tower, etc. That is, in short, to his mind, the difference between modern and classical poetry, for the ancients did not feel these emotions, or much less than we do; so that, according to him, we are superior *in this* to the ancients, and since, to his mind, it is *in this* that poetry truly consists, therefore we are infinitely more poetic than the ancients. . . . So this pathos, this depth of feeling, must be stirred up in our hearts, and it is in this, naturally, that the poet's most sublime art will consist.

It is here that Breme and all the Romantics and Chateaubriandists, etc., etc., are taking a wrong turn. What is it that excites these feelings in men? Nature, pure nature, as it is, as the ancients saw it. Now what did the ancients do? They described nature, and the objects and circumstances that must perforce awaken these feelings, very simply, and they knew how to depict and imitate them in such a manner that we see those very objects in their verses, that is, we feel as if we were seeing them, in so far as possible, as they are in nature. . . .

And behold, thus the ancients achieved the great effect that the Romantics require, and did so in such a way as to transport us and raise us up and plunge us into a gentle world of delight, and every age and century and all the great men and poets who have come after them, can bear witness to this. But are we to believe that when these poets imitated nature like this and prepared this wealth of sentiment for their readers, they did not feel it themselves, or did not say that they did so, but very simply, like shepherd boys, described what they saw, and added nothing to it of their own; and that therein lies the great defect of ancient poetry, owing to which it is not poetry any more, and the moderns are a hundred times superior to the ancients, etc.? The Romantics do not realize that if these feelings are awakened by *naked* nature, it is necessary, in order to reawaken them, to imitate nature's *nakedness,* and to transpose into poetry those simple and innocent objects which *by their own strength alone,* and *unawares,* produce that effect upon our spirit, just as they are, and neither more nor less; and that, if they are so well and divinely imitated, adding the wonder and attention aroused by each minute part of them, which we did not observe in reality but do see in the imitation, they cannot fail to awaken in us those very sentiments that the Romantics are seeking, and which they are very far from knowing how to awaken in us. For the more a poet speaks in his own person and the more he adds of his own, the less well does he imitate (an observation already made by Aristotle, to whom, whether one wishes to or not, one always inadvertently returns), and sentiment is not produced by sentiment, but by nature, *as it really is,* and it is this nature, *as it is,* that one must imitate and that the ancients did imitate. That is why a simple simile of Homer's, without convulsions or swoonings, or an ode of Anacreon's, arouses in us a multitude of fancies, and fills our mind and heart incomparably more than a thousand sentimental verses; for there it was nature speaking, and here, a poet. And they [the Romantics] do not realize that it is precisely this great ideal of our time, an intimate knowledge of our own heart, and the analyzing, foretelling, and distinguishing of every most minute emotion, in short the art of psychology, that destroys the very illusion without which poetry will be no more. . . . (I, 21–23)

Were I to express the indefinable effect that Anacreon's odes have upon me, I could find no more fitting image than that of a summer breeze, scented and refreshing, which somehow suddenly gives you new life and opens your lungs and heart to delight, but which—before you have fully savored that pleasure or analyzed its quality, or discerned why it has refreshed you so much—has already fled. Precisely as it does in Anacreon, in whom that indefinable sensation is almost instantaneous and escapes you if you try to analyze it: you do not hear it any more, you read it over again, but only the bare, dry words are left, while the melody, so to speak, is gone, and you can scarcely remember in your heart the sensations which, a moment before, had been aroused in you by the very words that lie before your eyes. (I, 46)

Our true Theocritan idylls are not the *Eclogues* of Sannazzaro, etc., but rustic poems like "La Nencia," "Cecco di Varlunga," etc.—most lovely and similar to Theocritus in their beautiful roughness and admirable truth. (I, 86)

Everything has been perfected since Homer's time: not poetry. (I, 87)

The illusion of anniversaries is truly a beautiful one, by means of which, even though that particular day has nothing more to do with the past than any other, we say: "Such and such a thing happened today, I felt this or that delight, or I was so cast down," and it truly seems to us that those things, which are dead forever and never can come back, have yet come to life again and are present in the shade. (I, 90)

*La speme che nasce in un col giorno.*
[The hope that is renewed with every dawn.] (I, 108)

It seems absurd, yet is precisely true, that since all reality is nought, illusions are, in this world, the only true and substantial things. (I, 126)

Melancholy and sentimental poetry is a breath of the soul. An oppression of the heart, whether caused by passion, by discouragement with life, or by a deep sense of the nothingness of things, constrains it and gives it no room to breathe. . . . I believe that Tasso's continual misfortunes are the reason why, in originality and invention, he remained inferior to the other three greatest Italian poets, while certainly his soul was equal if not superior to theirs in sentiment, affection, grandeur, tenderness, etc., as is shown by his letters and his other writings in prose. But although a man who has not suffered some misfortune knows nothing at all, it is indisputable that both imagination and a melancholy sensibility lose some of their power without a certain aura of well-being, a certain vigor of spirit, which cannot exist without a gleam, a ray, a glimmer of joy. (June 24, 1820) (I, 156)

Once, when I was feeling very much disgusted with life and entirely hopeless and so anxious for death that I was in despair at not being able to die, a letter came from a friend of mine, who had always encouraged me to hope and implored me to go on living, assuring me (he being a man of great intelligence and renown) that I would become great and would make Italy proud of me. In this letter he said that he now had become so conscious of the extent of my afflictions that if God should send me death, I should accept it as a blessing, and that for both my sake and his own, he hoped it would be soon. Will you believe that this letter, far from detaching me more completely from life, caused me to feel some affection again for everything I had already given up? Thinking of my hopes in the past and of the consolations and forecasts that this same friend had offered me, and that he now no longer seemed to care to see confirmed, nor to see my promised greatness realized, and looking back at my writings and my studies and remembering my childhood with its thoughts and desires and the fine prospects and occupations of youth, my heart was so oppressed that I no longer knew how to give up hope, and death terrified me—not indeed in itself, but as bringing to an end all those great expectations of the past. . . .

I had taken pleasure in the thought of death, but as something imaginary. I had thought it certain that my friends—few in number indeed, but at least those few, and especially that one—would prefer me to be alive, would not abandon me to my despair, and that, if I died, they would be astonished and cast down, saying, "So it is all over? Oh, God, so many hopes, such greatness of soul, such gifts, and all without fruit! No glory, no pleasure, all is passed as if it had never been." But to think that they would say instead: "Praise God, his sufferings are ended, I rejoice for him, for nothing else was left to him, may he rest in peace," that seemed to me like sealing down the tomb over my head, and this sudden and complete acceptance of my death, however reasonable, stifled me with a sense of my complete annihilation. . . .

From this one may learn how to behave in comforting a friend in trouble. Do not deny his suffering, if it is real. You would not convince him and would cast him down still deeper, by depriving him of compassion. He knows his afflictions well, and you, in admitting them, will agree with him. But remember that in the last recesses of his heart a drop of illusion still lingers. . . . Beware of drying it up, and err rather in minimizing his sufferings and showing yourself too unpitying than in making him feel certain of those things as to which his imagination is still contradicting his reason. If even he exaggerates his calamities to you, be assured that within his own heart he is doing just the opposite. I say within, that is, at a level hidden even from himself. Agree not with his words but with his heart. (I, 157–59)

Speech is an art acquired by men, as is proved by the variety of tongues. Gesture is a natural thing and taught by nature. . . . Therefore in great gusts of passion, even as the force of nature is greater than usual, words do not suffice to express it, and men are so occupied that the practice of an art, however familiar, is impossible to them, while gestures come naturally. . . . Silence is the language of every strong passion, of love (even in the sweetest moments), of anger, wonder, fear. (June 27, 1820) (I, 160)

In my poetic career my spirit has followed the same course as the human spirit in general. At first my imagination was my strong point, and my verses were full of images, and when I read poetry I always sought what would feed my fancy. I was most sensitive to emotion, too, but did not know how to express it in verse. I had not yet meditated on these things and had only a glimmering of philosophy, and that a very vague one, with the common illusion that the world and life would always make an exception on my behalf. I have always been unfortunate, but then my misfortunes were vital ones, and only aroused despair in me because I thought (unreasonably, but owing to my strong imagination) that they held me back from happiness, a thing I believed other men enjoyed. In short my condition was in every way that of the ancients. . . .

This complete change in me, and the passage from the old condition to the new, occurred within about a year, that is in 1819, when—being deprived of the use of my sight and of the constant diversion of reading—my unhappiness seemed much darker, and I began to give up hope, to reflect deeply about such things . . . to become a professional philosopher instead of the poet that I had been before, to feel the world's certain unhappiness instead of only knowing about it—and this also owing to a certain physical lassitude, which made me less like the ancients and more like the men of our own time. Then my imagination became much less vivid, and although my faculty of invention greatly increased, indeed almost began to take shape, it chiefly took the form of prose or sentimental poetry. And if I tried to set my verses down, the images came with the greatest effort. Indeed my imagination was almost dried up (even apart from poetry, that is in contemplating beautiful natural scenes, etc.), as it is now, when I am as cold as a stone. (I, 161–63)

Often it has happened to me to fall asleep with some verses or words on my lips, which I had often repeated to myself during the day, or in the hours before sleep, or else with the recollection of the air of some melody; and, having thought or dreamed during my sleep about quite other things, I would wake up repeating to myself the same verses or words, or the same air. It would seem that the soul, in falling asleep, lays down the thoughts and images it holds, as we lay down our clothes, in some place very near at hand, so as to find them at once again on waking. (I, 198)

Illusions, however weakened and unmasked by reason, still remain in this world and form the chief part of our life. Even if we have learned to know all and to realize that they are vain, this is not enough to make us lose them. Nor, once lost, are they lost in such a way that they do not retain a very vigorous root; and, in continuing to live, they flower again, in spite of all the experience and certainty we had acquired. . . . And to me, too, the same thing has happened a hundred times: to fall into despair because I could not die, and then to return to my old plans and castles in the air about my future life, and even to a little passing cheerfulness. (I, 221–22)

Reading is, in relation to the art of writing, what experience is to the art of living in the world and of discovering the nature of men and things. (I, 227)

Lord Byron, in his notes to *The Corsair,* quotes historical examples of the effects of the passions and of the characters he had described. That is bad. The reader should feel and not learn the relation between your description and truth and nature . . . otherwise the poetic delight fades away . . . and the poem is transformed into a treatise and acts upon the intellect, no longer upon the imagination or the heart. (I, 229)

A house suspended in the air, held by ropes to a star. (I, 251)

What is peculiar to works of genius is that, even when they vividly show the nothingness of things and plainly represent and convey to us the inevitable unhappiness of life, even when they express the most terrible despair, yet to a man of a noble soul, even if he finds himself in a state of extreme despair, disillusionment, blankness, and discouragement with life, or suffering from the most bitter and deadly misfortunes . . . they always bring consolation, reawaken enthusiasm, and, though they do not describe or represent anything but death, they yet give back to him, at least for a while, the life that he had lost. (I, 252–53)

Generally fame, especially in literature, is sweet when a man nourishes it in the silence of his own study and uses it as a spur toward other successful

enterprises and as a foundation for new hopes. For then fame still holds the power of an illusion, its only real power. But when it is enjoyed in the world and in society, it usually turns out to be either nothing at all or a very little thing, incapable in short of filling your soul or of satisfying it. So, too, all pleasures seem great from far off, and from near by seem small, arid, void, and null.
(I, 260)

An old man who has no present or future is not consequently devoid of life. If he has never been a man, he needs nothing more than the trifles that suffice to distract him, and anything is enough to keep him alive. If he has been a man, he has had a past, and lives in that. . . .

A young man has no past. The little of it that he has only serves to sadden and oppress his heart. The memories of his childhood and early youth, the pleasures of those years, irreparably lost, the flowery hopes, the radiant ideas, the airy plans for future prosperity, for action, life, glory, pleasure—all have vanished. His desires and passions are most ardent and exacting. A little is not enough: he needs the most. The more intense his inner life has been, the greater the intensity and extent of his need of the outer life that he desires. And if this is lacking, his sense of death, of nothingness, of *noia,* is proportionate to his inner life. . . . The young man suffers mortal despair, reflecting that he will only pass through this world once, and that during this one time he will not enjoy life, will not live, and will have lost, without finding any use for it, his only existence: every moment of his youth that passes in this manner will seem to him the irreparable loss of a time that never can return. (October 16, 1820)
(I, 264)

His pleasure was in walking, counting the stars. (I, 265)

It is not enough to know that a statement is true, one must also *feel* its truth. There is a feeling of truth, as of passion, emotion, beauty. . . . (I, 307)

Just as among the peoples who do not know or value gold or silver, the richest among us, scattering money, would not be held in esteem . . . so where intelligence or wit is not valued, the most able and wittiest and greatest man, if he has no other gifts, will be despised and given the last place. . . . In every place and every time, one must use the common currency. The man who is not provided with that is poor. (December 23, 1820) (I, 371–72)

On the few occasions on which I have met with some little piece of good fortune, or a reason for joy, instead of showing it outwardly, I have yielded to an external melancholy, though inwardly I was happy. But I feared to trouble this peaceful and hidden content, to alter, spoil, or lose it by scattering it to the winds. And so I handed over my content into the care of melancholy. (December 27, 1820) (I, 375)

Not only the faculty of the mind or the heart, but even that of the imagination, cannot attain infinity, nor even conceive it, but can only recall or conceive the idea of what is indefinite, unbounded. And this delights it; because the soul, not perceiving any boundaries, receives an impression of a sort of infinity, and confuses the indefinite with the infinite, but does not either comprehend or conceive infinity at all. For indeed it is especially in its most vague and indefinite fancies, which are therefore the most sublime and delightful, that the soul feels a certain constraint, a certain struggle, a certain insufficiency of desire, an impotence that is yet determined to seize to the full its fancy or conception or idea. So that, although these may fill and delight and satisfy it more than any other thing obtainable upon this earth, they yet do not entirely fulfill or satisfy it, and when they fade away, they leave it discontented, for the soul feels and knows (or thinks it does) that it has not conceived or seen these fancies or delighted in them in their entirety, and persuades itself that it could have done so, and therefore feels a certain remorse, which in truth is wrong, for this was not the soul's fault. (January 4, 1821) (I, 382–83)

It is said as a joke, but not without some truth, that one must satisfy a child's desires, if one does not wish to find him dead behind a door. (I, 454)

*"La solitude est l'infirmerie des âmes."*
[Madame de Lambert, quoted by Leopardi.] (I, 467)

*"Nous ne vivons que pour perdre et pour nous détacher."* (I, 467)

That is so. Every day we lose something; one of the illusions, which are our only riches, perishes or diminishes. Experience or truth divests us every day of part of our possessions. We do not live, except in losing. (I, 467)

I do not usually believe in allegories or look for them in mythology, or in the inventions of the poets, or in popular beliefs. But the fable of Psyche, that is of the Soul, who was very contented without knowledge and happy just to enjoy, and whose unhappiness came from her desire for knowledge, seems to me so apt and precise and at the same time so profound a symbol of the nature of men and things and of our true destiny upon this earth . . . that I can hardly believe that this myth is not a fruit of the deepest wisdom and knowledge of the nature of man and of the world. (I, 468)

I praise the Italians for turning away from a blind love and imitation of foreign things, and still more for beginning again to use and to value their own; I praise the men who try to reawaken a national spirit, without which there has never been any greatness in this world—not only national greatness, but even individual greatness; but I cannot find it admirable that our present condition, and, in the field of study, our contemporary literature, and the greater part of our writers should be exalted and celebrated every day as if they were almost superior to the greatest men abroad, when they are inferior to the least of them; that they should be offered us as models, and that finally we should be advised to go on following the path we already tread. If we are to wake up at last and recover a national spirit, our first emotion should be, not pride or satisfaction in things as they are with us now, but shame. And it is this that should spur us on to take a new road altogether and to renew everything. (I, 579)

England . . . has one of the freest languages in Europe in its nature and in practice the freest of all, and similarly perhaps the most free literature and literary taste in Europe. I am referring to her own literature, both modern and Shakespeare's in the past, not to the second-hand one she has borrowed from France. (I, 703)

When a language, generally speaking (that is, not in one or more sentences, or in this or that particular subtlety, but in general), is not sufficient to render in a translation the refinements of another language, that is a certain proof that the nation into whose language one is translating has a less deep culture than the first. (I, 731)

Some other reasons for the richness and variety of the Italian language are the following:

> (1) That we have never given up any of our riches, however old. . . .
> (2) The great liveliness, imagination, fecundity, and variety of the gifts of our writers, qualities that appertain to a nation that has adapted itself to all sorts of circumstances, enterprises, characters, and purposes.
> (3) The large extent to which our written language (for it is of this that we are speaking, and comparing with foreign languages) is indebted to the spoken speech of the people. . . .

A nation, especially as lively a one as the Italian, and in particular the Tuscan, and very civilized besides (as the Tuscans and Italians were before any other people in Europe), and constantly in touch with other peoples (as indeed Tuscany has been, both owing to her reputation for culture, her political circumstances, her freedom, and especially her trade), naturally invents or adopts a very large number of words and idioms and many forms of both. These, however, unless the use and form of them is spread by the written word (which varies all over the country), to establish their form and meaning and ensure their permanence, will not spread very far nor become very precise, but will remain uncertain, fluctuating, and arbitrary, and will soon be lost, with new ones taking their place. But Italian literature has done precisely what I have specified. It has adopted with a greater care than any other literature, and with great goodwill and delight, many popular expressions, idioms, and forms, especially the Tuscan, and has itself been formed by them. . . .

The pseudo-philosophers may say what they please. A richness that consists of variety, beauty, expression, efficacy, force, brio, grace, ease, softness, and naturalness, will never belong and never has belonged to any language that has not been drawn from the popular tongue, not only originally but constantly, and not by writing as the people speak, but by turning what has been adopted from the people into the universal forms and rules of literature and of the national language. (I, 838–41)

Rapidity and concision of style are pleasing because they present to the mind a multitude of simultaneous ideas, or rather ideas that succeed each other so rapidly that they seem simultaneous, and flutter the soul with such an abundance of thoughts, images, and spiritual sensations that it is incapable of embracing all of them, or each one fully, and has no time left in which to remain idle and feelingless. . . .

The beauty and charm of Horace's style, and of other vigorous, swift styles, especially in poetry—since the qualities I am about to describe belong chiefly to poetry, and especially to lyric verse—also derive chiefly from this, that it keeps the mind in constant and lively movement and action, transporting it suddenly, and often abruptly, from one thought, image, idea, or object to another, and often to one very remote and different; so that the mind must work hard to overtake them all, and, as it is flung about here and there, feels invigorated, as one does in walking quickly or in being carried along by swift horses, in taking part in some energetic action or in being in some center of activity. It is overwhelmed by the multiplicity and variety of things (see my theory of pleasure), etc., etc. And even if those things are neither great, vast, or new, nevertheless this single quality in a style is enough to please the soul, which needs action, because it loves life above all things, and therefore enjoys, both in life and literature, a certain but not excessive effort, which compels it to behave in a lively manner. And this is the case with Horace, who after all is a lyric poet only in his style. That is how style, even considered separately from its subject, can yet be a thing in itself, and an important one: so that a man can be a poet who has nothing poetic about him but his style, and a very true and universal poet, for reasons that are inward; and very deep and elemental qualities, and therefore universal in the human soul.

Horace constantly produces the effects I have described, with a boldness of phrase with which, in a single digression, he transports and flings you about several times, leaping from one idea to another very remote and different one. (As he also does with his very figurative use of words, and with the effort and consequent activity that he produces in his readers.) Courageous metaphors, singular and farfetched epithets, inversions, placement of words, suppressions, all within the limits of what is not excessive *(it might seem excessive to the Germans, and insufficiently so to Orientals),* all these produce these effects anywhere you please in his poems.

*Pone me pigris ubi nulla campis*
*Arbor aestiva recreatur aura,*
*Quod latus mundi nebulae malusque*
*Juppiter urget.*[2]

Here first you have *sluggishness*, then this is applied to the *plains*, and here at once are the *trees* and the *summer breeze* and then a *side of the world*, the *mists*, and then *Jove* instead of the *sky*, and *hostile* instead of *contrary, jostling* or *pushing* or *harassing* that part of the world. . . .

It is in the nature of such styles (proper to all great and true poets, more or less, and especially to those who are also distinctive in their style) that many of their images—often contained in a very brief phrase or a single word—etc., should be only suggested, and that there should also be no more than a suggestion of their connection and relation with their subject and with the other images, ideas, or maxims, which they resemble, or to which they belong or refer, etc. And this, too, is pleasing, for it compels the mind to a constant activity, to supply what the poet does not say, to finish what he has only begun, to color what he has outlined, to discover those distant relationships that he has scarcely pointed out, etc.

*et aridus altis*
*Montibus audiri fragor.*[3]

What has that *cracking* to do with *dry*? Our thoughts must realize that it is justified in so far as it is cracking among the dry branches of a wood. That is how the mind must supply the connection of ideas (barely suggested, indeed almost neglected by the poet), within one very short sentence. And it must then complete the image that is only suggested by that *aridus fragor*. (I do not know whether the interpretation I have given to this passage is true. See the commentators. It is enough for me that this example explains my thoughts to myself.) That is how the very suppression of words, phrases, conceptions, is turned into beauty, because it pleasantly compels the mind to action and does not leave it idle. Such qualities in style may sometimes be excessive, as in the seventeenth century. Then the mind does not delight in them, at least not in all periods or people, etc. For an excess, like a defect, in this and in everything else, is relative. (I, 1269–73)

People always prefer to call a man who has a physical or moral defect, or else to hear him called, by nothing but the name of this defect: the deaf man, the cripple, the hunchback, the madman. . . . In using such names or in hearing them, these people feel superior to those others, enjoy the image of their defect, feel and remind themselves, in a way, of their own superiority, and their self-love is flattered and satisfied. It has happened to me to see a common man with such a defect, talking and playing with some people of his own class, who never called him by any other name than that of his defect, so that I never succeeded in hearing his real name. (May 13, 1822) (I, 1466–67)

So long as a young man keeps some *tenderness* toward himself, this means that he continues to love himself with that most lively, sensitive, and vulnerable love, which is natural; and until he has cast himself adrift into the world, and has learned to think of himself almost as he would of anyone else, he will never be able to avoid suffering nor enjoy a single moment of comfort and pleasure in the habits and incidents of social life. To enjoy life, a state of despair is necessary. (July 6, 1822)[4] (I, 1524)

Ideas are enclosed and almost bound in words, like jewels in a ring, indeed they become embodied in them, as the soul is in the body, so as to form one entity. Thus ideas are inseparable from words, and if parted from them, are no longer the same; they escape our intellect and our powers of conception, and become unrecognizable, as would happen to our soul, if it were separated from our body. (July 27, 1822) (I, 1536)

The Italians have no customs: they only have habits. And so it is with all civilized peoples that have not become nations. (July 9, 1823) (II, 172)

A Frenchman, an Englishman, or a German, who has cultivated his talents and is capable of thought, has nothing to do but to set them down. Each one of them finds a modern national language, which is already formed, established, and perfected, and of which he only has to make use, once he has learned it. . . .

It is more than a hundred and fifty years since Italy has either created or cultivated any kind of literature, for she has not produced any original writers during this time in any field, and those whom she has produced, having never done anything but copy their predecessors, do not deserve the title of cultivators of literature, since a man does not cultivate his field who only walks about it carefully observing it, but leaving everything as it was before.[5] Neither has any branch of our literature been advanced or improved by any of these writers, nor any new branch introduced. So that Italian literature has come to a standstill. . . .

An ancient language cannot serve to say modern things, and to say them as they should be said, in a modern fashion; nor was our language in particular fit to express new kinds of knowledge, and to provide what is needed for so many and such vast novelties. As we gradually heard what was happening in the literatures and disciplines of other countries, the few Italians who were excited by the new sciences and who possessed the necessary mental equipment to add to these something of their own . . . having found that the old Italian language did not suffice them, gave it up altogether and went to study with foreigners, not only for their new ideas and thoughts, but for their language; and having taken their ideas from those men (sometimes merely repeating and sometimes increasing and improving them), they also took from them their idioms, and their ways and forms of speech and writing. And the true scientists—with regard to whom our country has never at any time been second to any other—since they always cared little for questions of language, followed this barbarous new habit, using the language that was at hand. . . .

Now we have a language of our own; very old indeed, but very rich, beautiful, powerful, in every sort of way; for we have a literature, which is also ancient, but vast, varied, most beautiful, most rich in splendid classical authors and in styles, and which lasted for three centuries or more. . . . So what is necessary, evident, and certain is that in the wish to give a modern literature to modern Italy, we should not change her ancient tongue or dissolve it, or renew it, but preserve its fundamental character and attributes and modernize them in such a way that the fine living Italian language should be a true derivation of the old, indeed a continuation of it. Just as the French language of the second half of the past century and of the present one is nothing but that of the time of Louis XIV, passed on from hand to hand.

Now this was easy for the French, since their literature has never been interrupted since the time of Louis XIV, so that their language has a natural and effortless continuity, and, having gradually adapted itself to the times, has been modern in each period, but also a single whole, when all its periods are considered as one. But we must force the matter, and almost erase or conceal what has happened to us in the past, that is, we must behave in such a manner that what did happen should seem not to have occurred, and that our language should seem never to have interrupted its course. . . . How can this be done? It would seem less difficult to create it anew. If Italy only had a very imperfect language, very poor and childish, it would be less difficult for a great mind to perfect, enrich, and broaden it, and lead it to maturity. But Italy has a language as perfect as it is vast, although put aside a long time ago and now unsuited to her needs, for which it has not yet been adapted or used. So it is indispensable that the man of talent whom we are imagining, before beginning to write, should master this vast language of his perfectly, embrace it wholly, turn it into sap and blood. . . . And this language being old, he cannot learn it from his nurse, but only through study . . . with great sweat and deep research into its properties, and a constant practice in reading and writing and a most assiduous and attentive study of its numerous classics. . . . It is certain that a true knowledge and mastery of the Italian language require, without exaggeration, almost half a lifetime. . . . But do not a man's learning, knowledge, and study require a whole lifetime? (II, 384–90)

All primitive nations and peoples, like savage ones today, used to regard a man who was unhappy or unfortunate as an enemy of the gods, either because of some vice or crime of which he was guilty, or because of envy or some other caprice that had caused the divinities to hate either him in particular or his whole family. . . . A man who was often unsuccessful in his enterprises was undoubtedly hated by the gods. An illness, a shipwreck, or other such misfortunes whose origins were more directly natural were even more certain tokens of divine wrath. So the unhappy man was shunned, like a criminal; he was denied succor and compassion, for men feared thus to become accomplices in his crime and so to have to share his penalty. . . . Signs still remain in classical languages of these opinions: κακοδαίμων ἄθλιος, and similar names referred to a man who was both unhappy and a scoundrel. (II, 397)

What is life? The journey of a sick cripple who, with a heavy burden on his back, climbs over steep mountains and through desolate, exhausting, and arduous lands, in the snow, the frost, the rain, the wind, under the blazing sun,

for many days, without ever resting by day or night, in order to reach a certain precipice or ditch into which inevitably he must fall. (January 17, 1826)
(II, 990)

It is natural to man—weak, wretched, and exposed to so many dangers—to suppose, imagine, and even gratuitously pretend that a wisdom, sagacity, and prudence, a purpose and discernment, a perspicacity and experience superior to his own, exist in some other person, whom he watches during any time of hard trial, finding comfort or fear according to whether he sees him looking cheerful or sad, alarmed or courageous, and thus resting on his authority, without any reason. . . . So children often feel, especially those of tender years, with regard to their parents. And so did I, even at a ripe and stable age, with regard to my father; for in any difficulty or danger it was my habit, before determining the degree of my own trouble or dread, to examine or conjecture his, and also his opinion or judgment, just as if I had been incapable of judging for myself. . . . And this human characteristic is one of the reasons why a belief is so gladly embraced and still held in an all-provident God, that is, in a being superior to us in sense and wisdom, who watches over our fate. . . . (II, 1057)

Of our great poets, two have met with much misfortune, Dante and Tasso. We possess and visit both their tombs, which are both far away from their own home. But I, who wept by Tasso's tomb, had no feeling of tenderness by Dante's: and I think this is generally so. And yet neither I nor anyone else fails to have the highest esteem and indeed admiration for Dante: perhaps more so (and rightly) than for the other poet. Besides, the misfortunes of the first were undoubtedly real and great, while as to those of the other, we are uncertain whether they were not, at last partly, imaginary. . . . But we see in Dante a man with a strong soul, brave enough to bear ill-fortune, and also to fight against it, and against necessity and fate. All the more admirable, assuredly, but also the less lovable and pitiable. In Tasso we see a man defeated by his wretchedness, laid low in the dust, who had given way to adversity, who was constantly suffering and enduring. Even if his calamities were imaginary and untrue, his unhappiness was certainly real. If less unfortunate than Dante, he was assuredly more miserable. (March 14, 1827) (II, 1087)

To eat alone, μονοφαγία, was considered infamous by the Greeks and Latins and considered *inhuman,* and the title of μονοφάγος, the man who eats alone, was given to a man as an insult, like that of τοιχωρύχος, thief. I would have deserved that insult. But the ancients were right, for they did not converse with each other at table, but after eating, or during the actual symposium, that is while drinking together, as was their custom after the meal (and as is done today by the English); at most nibbling some little dry piece of food to make them wish to drink. That is the time when one can be most cheerful and good-humored and most inclined to talk and chatter. But during the meal they were silent, or spoke very little. We have lost the very natural and gay custom of drinking at table, but talk when we are eating. Now I cannot get into my head that the only hour of the day in which our mouth is occupied . . . should be precisely the one in which one ought to talk. (II,1012–13)

Another reason why I like μονοφαγία [eating alone] is in order to avoid having persons serving my meal and standing round my table, as I necessarily must if I eat in company—*"d'importuns laquais, épiant nos discours, critiquant tout bas nos maintiens . . ."* [Rousseau, *Émile*]. Unfortunately I have never become accustomed to enjoying myself in the presence of people who, to my certain knowledge, are condemning or mocking my enjoyment, or who are bored by it; I have never been able to understand how others could bear, and indeed be proud of, such witnesses, whose occupations and thoughts everyone knows to be precisely those I have described. The ancients, too, were served at table, but by slaves, that is by people whom they considered to be less than men, or certainly less fully men than they. . . . But our servants are our equals. . . . (II, 1109)

Having often changed my abode and lived in some places for either months or years, I discovered that I was never contented, never at home, never naturalized in any place, however excellent, until I had some memories to attach to it, to the rooms in which I lived, and to the streets and houses I visited. These memories did not consist in anything more than being able to say: "This is where I was so long ago, this is what I did, saw, heard here, so many months ago"; a thing that would not otherwise have had any importance, but the memory of it, the fact that I could remember it, made it important and sweet. Therefore I was always sad in any place during the first few months, and as time went on I became contented and attached to it. Through remembrance, it almost became my home. (Florence, July 23, 1827)(II, 1121)

It has been observed that great grief, like great passion, has no external language. I must add that it has also not got an inner one. I mean that in great grief a man is incapable of circumscribing and defining to himself any idea or emotion concerning the subject of his passion, which he can express even to himself, thus directing and exercising, so to speak, his thoughts and his grief. He feels a thousand emotions, sees a thousand confused ideas, or rather does not see or feel anything but one very vast emotion or idea, which absorbs his whole capacity for thinking or feeling, without being able either to embrace it as a whole or to define its parts. . . . If he weeps (and I have noticed this in myself) he weeps as if by chance, without even being able to say to himself, *for what.* (II, 1231)

In my solitary walks in the city, very pleasant sensations and beautiful images are aroused in me by a glimpse of the interior of the rooms that I see from the street below, through their open windows. These same rooms would not awaken any feeling in me if I saw them from within. Is not this an image of human life? . . . (Recanati, December 1, 1828) (II, 1233)

After reading a passage of true poetry of our own time, whether in verse or prose (but the most powerful impressions come from verse), one can say, even in these prosaic times, what Sterne said about a smile: that it adds a thread to the short canvas of our life. . . . (February 1, 1829) (II, 1259)

Certain ideas, certain images, of supremely vague, fantastic, fanciful, impossible things, cause us great delight, whether in poetry or in our own fancy, because they call back to us our most remote memories, those of our childhood, in which such ideas and images and beliefs were familiar and usual. And the poets who have the greatest number of ideas of this kind (which are supremely poetical) are dearest to us. If you will analyze your most poetic sensations and fancies, those which raise you up most, and draw you out of yourselves and out of the real world, you will discover that they, and the pleasure they give you (at least after childhood), consist wholly or principally in memories. (May 21, 1829) (II, 1321)

## *Notes*

1. Ludovico Arborio Gattinara di Breme (1780–1820), an ardent follower of Napoleon in his youth, became well known in Milan as a man of letters and a Liberal, and one of the leading figures of the Romantic movement. He was a friend of both Byron and Hobhouse, and also of Stendhal.

2. Horace, *Carmen Seculare,* I, XXII, 17–20. "Set me in sluggish plains where no tree is restored to life by the summer breeze, the side of the world harassed by mists and hostile Jove."

3. Virgil, *Georgics,* I, 357. ". . . and a dry cracking [begins] to be heard in the high mountains."

4. In a letter from Rome, written on April 19, 1823, Leopardi gave almost similar advice to his sister Paolina, who was grieving over a disappointment of her own: "I assure you, my Paolina, that if we do not acquire a little indifference toward ourselves, it is not possible, I do not say to be happy, but even to remain alive."

5. Elsewhere Leopardi said that Alfieri was the only exception, "for he had a free spirit and rebelled against his time and the notions of the government under which he lived."

# *Ralph Waldo Emerson*

1803–1882

Ralph Waldo Emerson came from a family of preachers. An unbroken line of Puritan divines stretched back in his family to the late 1600s. His father was the Reverend William Emerson, a Unitarian minister who was a great patron of the arts. His mother, on the other hand, was a staunch Episcopalian, a fact that biographers have connected to Emerson's first-hand acquaintance with such exponents of Anglican intellectuality as Cudworth or Coleridge. As a boy Emerson studied at the elite Boston Latin School, a stepping-stone to Harvard, which accepted him in 1817. There he began the journals which provided so much material for his later essays. His studies were interrupted by an extended sojourn in the South—undertaken on account of ill-health—but he was still able to receive his degree in 1821. In 1829 he was ordained as a Unitarian minister and assigned to a parish in Boston. His congregation must have perceived that a new force was at work in their pulpit; the freethinking preacher with the fiery, lyrical style gave Boston—even Unitarian Boston—something of a shock.

In the 1830s Emerson went through a period of intense spiritual crisis as a result of the death of his young wife, Ellen Tucker. He questioned received morality and searched for answers in Boehme, Swedenborg, Fox, and Wesley. After his breakthrough to perception of what he called the "over-soul," conventional Unitarianism had little to offer him. He resigned his ministry and traveled to Europe in search of guidance. He met with such figures as Coleridge, Wordsworth, and Carlyle. He also visited the *Musée Nationale d'Histoire Naturelle* in Paris; a number of specimens preserved there led him to some important meditations on the correspondence between himself and the natural world.

In 1834 Emerson returned to America and began to write poetry. His philosophy began to form itself in the idealism of the essay "Nature," while his poetry contained an orphic power within an eccentric and gnomic style. As was later to be the case with Yeats, Romanticism and the occult became a potent mixture in Emerson. But while the spiritual content of Emerson's message had changed, it retained a rhetorical debt to the Unitarian tradition of preaching. Emerson's great early essays were like philosophical sermons; in this sense he always remained a preacher.

The 1840s were years of practical consolidation of career and home life. In 1840 Emerson helped to establish the *Dial,* which was to become the leading literary magazine in the country. In 1844 he collected his greatest essays, including "History," "Self-Reliance," "The Poet," and "Compensation" into one volume. In these essays he perfected a style of philosophical meditation that is perhaps the strongest instance of American aphorism. Emerson's love of paradox and close observation of psychology endeared him to Nietzsche, who also found in this peculiar mixture of neo-Platonism and optimism hints of his own philosophy of "joy before death."

The remainder of Emerson's life was spent not so much in practical struggle as in an attempt to describe the ideal. He became especially interested in the idea of "great men," an obsession he shared with his long-time friend Thomas Carlyle. But between *Representative Men* (1849) and *Conduct of Life* (1860) there also lies evidence of a darkening trend in Emerson's thought, a mature aspect that in some ways anticipates the Nietzschean idea of *Untergang*—decline seen as a necessary part of spiritual regeneration. Even as he allowed for the apprehension of a fallen world, Emerson continued to uphold the ideal of self-perfection. The sage of Concord was able to draw circles around life's contradictions, hoping, by encompassing them, to integrate, ennoble, and—above all—liberate the individual mind. Arguably, his own biography followed this spiraling path; even when he swerved from his ideals, Emerson's never-resting mind contained and drew strength from the deviation.

# Poetry and Imagination

The perception of matter is made the common sense, and for cause. This was the cradle, this the go-cart, of the human child. We must learn the homely laws of fire and water; we must feed, wash, plant, build. These are ends of necessity, and first in the order of nature. Poverty, frost, famine, disease, debt, are the beadles and guardsmen that hold us to common-sense. The intellect, yielded up to itself, cannot supersede this tyrannic necessity. The restraining grace of common-sense is the mark of all the valid minds,—of Æsop, Aristotle, Alfred, Luther, Shakspeare, Cervantes, Franklin, Napoleon. The common-sense which does not meddle with the absolute, but takes things at their word,—things as they appear,—believes in the existence of matter, not because we can touch it or conceive of it, but because it agrees with ourselves, and the universe does not jest with us, but is in earnest, is the house of health and life. In spite of all the joys of poets and the joys of saints, the most imaginative and abstracted person never makes with impunity the least mistake in this particular,—never tries to kindle his oven with water, nor carries a torch into a powder-mill, nor seizes his wild charger by the tail. We should not pardon the blunder in another, nor endure it in ourselves.

But whilst we deal with this as finality, early hints are given that we are not to stay here; that we must be making ready to go;—a warning that this magnificent hotel and conveniency we call Nature is not final. First innuendoes, then broad hints, then smart taps are given, suggesting that nothing stands still in nature but death; that the creation is on wheels, in transit, always passing into something else, streaming into something higher; that matter is not what it appears;—that chemistry can blow it all into gas. Faraday, the most exact of natural philosophers, taught that when we should arrive at the monads, or primordial elements (the supposed little cubes or prisms of which all matter was built up), we should not find cubes, or prisms, or atoms, at all, but spherules of force. It was whispered that the globes of the universe were precipitates of something more subtle; nay, somewhat was murmured in our ear that dwindled astronomy into a toy;—that too was no finality; only provisional, a makeshift; that under chemistry was power and purpose: power and purpose ride on matter to the last atom. It was steeped in thought, did everywhere express thought; that, as great conquerors have burned their ships when once they were landed on the wished-for shore, so the noble house of Nature we inhabit has temporary uses, and we can afford to leave it one day. The ends of all are moral, and therefore the beginnings are such. Thin or solid, everything is in flight. I believe this conviction makes the charm of chemistry,—that we have the same avoirdupois matter in an alembic, without a vestige of the old form; and in animal transformation not less, as in grub and fly, in egg and bird, in embryo and man; everything undressing and stealing away from its old into new form, and nothing fast but those invisible cords which we call laws, on which all is strung. Then we see that things wear different names and faces, but belong to one family; that the secret cords or laws show their well-known virtue through every variety, be it animal, or plant, or planet, and the interest is gradually transferred from the forms to the lurking method.

This hint, however conveyed, upsets our politics, trade, customs, marriages, nay, the common-sense side of religion and literature, which are all founded on low nature,—on the clearest and most economical mode of administering the material world, considered as final. The admission, never so covertly, that this is a makeshift, sets the dullest brain in ferment: our little sir, from his first tottering steps, as soon as he can crow, does not like to be practised upon, suspects that some one is "doing" him, and at this alarm everything is compromised; gunpowder is laid under every man's breakfast-table.

But whilst the man is startled by this closer inspection of the laws of matter, his attention is called to the independent action of the mind; its strange suggestions and laws; a certain tyranny which springs up in his own thoughts, which have an order, method, and beliefs of their own, very different from the order which this common-sense uses.

Suppose there were in the ocean certain strong currents which drove a ship, caught in them, with a force that no skill of sailing with the best wind, and no strength of oars, or sails, or steam, could make any head against, any more than against the current of Niagara. Such currents, so tyrannical, exist in thoughts, those finest and subtilest of all waters, that as soon as once thought begins, it refuses to remember whose brain it belongs to; what country, tradition, or religion; and goes whirling off—swim we merrily—in a direction self-chosen, by law of thought and not by law of kitchen clock or county committee. It has its own polarity. One of these vortices or self-directions of thought is the impulse to search resemblance, affinity, identity, in all its objects, and hence our science, from its rudest to its most refined theories.

The electric word pronounced by John Hunter a hundred years ago, *arrested and progressive development,* indicating the way upward from the invisible protoplasm to the highest organisms, gave the poetic key to Natural Science, of which the theories of Geoffrey St. Hilaire, of Oken, of Goethe, of Agassiz and Owen and Darwin in zoölogy and botany, are the fruits,—a hint whose power is not yet exhausted, showing unity and perfect order in physics.

The hardest chemist, the severest analyzer, scornful of all but dryest fact, is forced to keep the poetic curve of nature, and his result is like a myth of Theocritus. All multiplicity rushes to be resolved into unity. Anatomy, osteology, exhibit arrested or progressive ascent in each kind; the lower pointing to the higher forms, the higher to the highest, from the fluid in an elastic sack, from radiate, mollusk, articulate, vertebrate, up to man; as if the whole animal world were only a Hunterian museum to exhibit the genesis of mankind.

Identity of law, perfect order in physics, perfect parallelism between the laws of Nature and the laws of thought exist. In botany we have the like, the poetic perception of metamorphosis,—that the same vegetable point or eye which is the unit of the plant can be transformed at pleasure into every part, as bract, leaf, petal, stamen, pistil, or seed.

In geology, what a useful hint was given to the early inquirers on seeing in the possession of Professor Playfair a bough of a fossil tree which was perfect wood at one end and perfect mineral coal at the other. Natural objects, if individually described and out of connection, are not yet known, since they are really parts of a symmetrical universe, like words of a sentence; and if their true order is found, the poet can read their divine significance orderly as in a Bible. Each animal or vegetable form remembers the next inferior and predicts the next higher.

There is one animal, one plant, one matter, and one force. The laws of light and of heat translate each other;—so do the laws of sound and of color; and so galvanism, electricity, and magnetism are varied forms of the selfsame energy. While the student ponders this immense unity, he observes that all things in Nature, the animals, the mountain, the river, the seasons, wood, iron, stone, vapor, have a mysterious relation to his thoughts and his life; their growths, decays, quality and use so curiously resemble himself, in parts and in wholes, that he is compelled to speak by means of them. His words and his thoughts are framed by their help. Every noun is an image. Nature gives him, sometimes in a flattered likeness, sometimes in caricature, a copy of every humor and shade in his character and mind. The world is an immense picture-book of every passage in human life. Every object he beholds is the mask of a man.

The privates of man's heart
They speken and sound in his ear
As tho' they loud winds were;

for the universe is full of their echoes.

Every correspondence we observe in mind and matter suggests a substance older and deeper than either of these old nobilities. We see the law gleaming through, like the sense of a half-translated ode of Hafiz. The poet who plays with it with most boldness best justifies himself; is most profound and most devout. Passion adds eyes; is a magnifying-glass. Sonnets of lovers are mad enough, but are valuable to the philosopher, as are prayers of saints, for their potent symbolism.

Science was false by being unpoetical. It assumed to explain a reptile or mollusk, and isolated it,—which is hunting for life in graveyards. Reptile or mollusk or man or angel only exists in system, in relation. The metaphysician, the poet, only sees each animal form as an inevitable step in the path of the creating mind. The Indian, the hunter, the boy with his pets, have sweeter knowledge of these than the savant. We use semblances of logic until experience puts us in possession of real logic. The poet knows the missing link by the joy it gives. The poet gives us the eminent experiences only,—a god stepping from peak to peak, nor planting his foot but on a mountain.

Science does not know its debt to imagination. Goethe did not believe that a great naturalist could exist without this faculty. He was himself conscious of its help, which made him a prophet among the doctors. From this vision he gave brave hints to the zoölogist, the botanist, and the optician.

*Poetry.*—The primary use of a fact is low; the secondary use, as it is a figure or illustration of my thought, is the real worth. First the fact; second its impression, or what I think of it. Hence Nature was called "a kind of adulterated reason." Seas, forests, metals, diamonds and fossils interest the eye, but 't is only with some preparatory or predicting charm. Their value to the intellect appears only when I hear their meaning made plain in the spiritual truth they cover. The mind, penetrated with its sentiment or its thought, projects it outward on whatever it beholds. The lover sees reminders of his mistress in every beautiful object; the saint, an argument for devotion in every natural process; and the facility with which Nature lends itself to the thoughts of man, the aptness with which a river, a flower, a bird, fire, day or night, can express his fortunes, is as if the world were only a disguised man, and, with a change of form, rendered to him all his experience. We cannot utter a sentence in sprightly conversation without a similitude. Note our incessant use of the word *like,*—like fire, like a rock, like thunder, like a bee, "like a year without a spring." Conversation is not permitted without tropes; nothing but great weight in things can afford a quite literal speech. It is ever enlivened by inversion and trope. God himself does not speak prose, but communicates with us by hints, omens, inference, and dark resemblances in objects lying all around us.

Nothing so marks a man as imaginative expressions. A figurative statement arrests attention, and is remembered and repeated. How often has a phrase of this kind made a reputation. Pythagoras's Golden Sayings were such, and Socrates's, and Mirabeau's, and Burke's, and Bonaparte's. Genius thus makes the transfer from one part of Nature to a remote part, and betrays the rhymes and echoes that pole makes with pole. Imaginative minds cling to their images, and do not wish them rashly rendered into prose reality, as children resent your showing them that their doll Cinderella is nothing but pine wood and rags; and my young scholar does not wish to know what the leopard, the wolf, or Lucia, signify in Dante's Inferno, but prefers to keep their veils on. Mark the delight of an audience in an image. When some familiar truth or fact appears in a new dress, mounted as on a fine horse, equipped with a grand pair of ballooning wings, we cannot enough testify our surprise and pleasure. It is like the new virtue shown in some unprized old property, as when a boy finds that his pocket-knife will attract steel filings and take up a needle; or when the old horseblock in the yard is found to be a Torso Hercules of the Phidian age. Vivacity of expression may indicate this high gift, even when the thought is of no great scope, as when Michel Angelo, praising the *terra cottas,* said, "If this earth were to become marble, woe to the antiques!" A happy symbol is a sort of evidence that your thought is just. I had rather have a good symbol of my thought, or a good analogy, than the suffrage of Kant or Plato. If you agree with me, or if Locke or Montesquieu agree, I may yet be wrong; but if the elm-tree thinks the same thing, if running water, if burning coal, if crystals, if alkalies, in their several fashions say what I say, it must be true. Thus a good symbol is the best argument, and is a missionary to persuade thousands. The Vedas, the Edda, the Koran, are each remembered by their happiest figure. There is no more welcome gift to men than a new symbol. That satiates, transports, converts them. They assimilate themselves to it, deal with it in all ways, and it will last a hundred years. Then comes a new genius, and brings another. Thus the Greek mythology called the sea "the tear of Saturn." The return of the soul to God was described as "a flask of water broken in the sea." Saint John gave us the Christian figure of "souls washed in the blood of Christ." The aged Michel Angelo indicates his perpetual study as in boyhood,—"I carry my satchel still." Machiavel described the papacy as "a stone inserted in the body of Italy to keep the wound open." To the Parliament debating how to tax America, Burke exclaimed, "Shear the wolf." Our Kentuckian orator said of his dissent from his companion, "I showed him the back of my hand." And our proverb of the courteous soldier reads: "An iron hand in a velvet glove."

This belief that the higher use of the material world is to furnish us types or pictures to express the thoughts of the mind, is carried to its logical extreme by the Hindoos, who, following Buddha, have made it the central doctrine of their religion that what we call Nature, the external world, has no real existence,—is only phenomenal. Youth, age, property, condition, events, persons,—self, even,—are successive *maias* (deceptions) through which Vishnu mocks and instructs the soul. I think Hindoo books the best gymnastics for the mind, as showing treatment. All European libraries might almost be read without the swing of this gigantic arm being suspected. But these Orientals deal with worlds and pebbles freely.

For the value of a trope is that the hearer is one: and indeed Nature itself is a vast trope, and all particular natures are tropes. As the bird alights on the bough, then plunges into the air again, so the thoughts of God pause but for a moment in any form. All thinking is analogizing, and it is the use of life to learn metonymy. The endless passing of one element into new forms, the incessant metamorphosis, explains the rank which the imagination holds in our catalogue of mental powers. The imagination is the reader of these forms. The poet accounts all productions and changes of Nature as the nouns of language, uses them representatively, too well pleased with their ulterior to value much their primary meaning. Every new object so seen gives a shock of agreeable surprise. The impressions on the imagination make the great days of life: the book, the landscape, or the personality which did not stay on the surface of the eye or ear but penetrated to the inward sense, agitates us, and is not forgotten. Walking, working, or talking, the sole question is how many strokes vibrate on this mystic string,—how many diameters are drawn quite through from matter to spirit; for whenever you enunciate a natural law you discover that you have enunciated a law of the mind. Chemistry, geology, hydraulics, are secondary science. The atomic theory is only an interior process *produced,* as geometers say, or the effect of a foregone metaphysical theory. Swedenborg saw gravity to be only an external of the irresistible attractions of affection and faith. Mountains and oceans we think we understand;—yes, so long as they are contented to be such, and are safe with the geologist,—but when they are melted in Promethean alembics and come out men, and then, melted again, come out words, without any abatement, but with an exaltation of power!

In poetry we say we require the miracle. The bee flies among the flowers, and gets mint and marjoram, and generates a new product, which is not mint and marjoram, but honey; the chemist mixes hydrogen and oxygen to yield a new product, which is not these, but water; and the poet listens to conversation and beholds all objects in nature, to give back, not them, but a new and transcendent whole.

Poetry is the perpetual endeavor to express the spirit of the thing, to pass the brute body and search the life and reason which causes it to exist;—to see that the object is always flowing away, whilst the spirit or necessity which causes it subsists. Its essential mark is that it betrays in every word instant activity of mind, shown in new uses of every fact and image, in preternatural quickness or perception of relations. All its words are poems. It is a presence of mind that gives a miraculous command of all means of uttering the thought and feeling of the moment. The poet squanders on the hour an amount of life that would more than furnish the seventy years of the man that stands next him.

The term "genius," when used with emphasis, implies imagination; use of symbols, figurative speech. A deep insight will always, like Nature, ultimate its thought in a thing. As soon as a man masters a principle and sees his facts in relation to it, fields, waters, skies, offer to clothe his thoughts in images. Then all men understand him; Parthian, Mede, Chinese, Spaniard, and Indian hear their own tongue. For he can now find symbols of universal significance, which are readily rendered into any dialect; as a painter, a sculptor, a musician, can in their several ways express the same sentiment of anger, or love, or religion.

The thoughts are few, the forms many; the large vocabulary or many-colored coat of the indigent unity. The *savans* are chatty and vain, but hold them hard to principle and definition, and they become mute and near-sighted. What is motion? what is beauty? what is matter? what is life? what is force? Push them hard and they will not be loquacious. They will come to Plato, Proclus, and Swedenborg. The invisible and imponderable is the sole fact. "Why changes not the violet earth into musk?" What is the term of the ever-flowing metamorphosis? I do not know what are the stoppages, but I see that a devouring unity changes all into that which changes not.

The act of imagination is ever attended by pure delight. It infuses a certain volatility and intoxication into all nature. It has a flute which sets the atoms of our frame in a dance. Our indeterminate size is a delicious secret which it reveals to us. The mountains begin to dislimn, and float in the air. In the presence and conversation of a true poet, teeming with images to express his enlarging thought, his person, his form, grows larger to our fascinated eyes. And thus begins that deification which all nations have made of their heroes in every kind,—saints, poets, lawgivers, and warriors.

*Imagination*.—Whilst common-sense looks at things or visible nature as real and final facts, poetry, or the imagination which dictates it, is a second sight, looking through these, and using them as types or words for thoughts which they signify. Or is this belief a metaphysical whim of modern times, and quite too refined? On the contrary, it is as old as the human mind. Our best definition of poetry is one of the oldest sentences, and claims to come down to us from the Chaldæan Zoroaster, who wrote it thus: "Poets are standing transporters, whose employment consists in speaking to the Father and to matter; in producing apparent imitations of unapparent natures, and inscribing things unapparent in the apparent fabrication of the world;" in other words, the world exists for thought: it is to make appear things which hide: mountains, crystals, plants, animals, are seen; that which makes them is not seen: these, then, are "apparent copies of unapparent natures." Bacon expressed the same sense in his definition, "Poetry accommodates the shows of things to the desires of the mind;" and Swedenborg, when he said, "There is nothing existing in human thought, even though relating to the most mysterious tenet of faith, but has combined with it a natural and sensuous image." And again: "Names, countries, nations, and the like are not at all known to those who are in heaven; they have no idea of such things, but of the realities signified thereby." A symbol always stimulates the intellect; therefore is poetry ever the best reading. The very design of imagination is to domesticate us in another, in a celestial nature.

This power is in the image because this power is in nature. It so affects, because it so is. All that is wondrous in Swedenborg is not his invention, but his extraordinary perception;—that he was necessitated so to see. The world realizes the mind. Better than images is seen through them. The selection of the image is no more arbitrary than the power and significance of the image. The selection must follow fate. Poetry, if perfected, is the only verity; is the speech of man after the real, and not after the apparent.

Or shall we say that the imagination exists by sharing the ethereal currents? The poet contemplates the central identity, sees it undulate and roll this way and that, with divine flowings, through remotest things; and, following it, can detect essential resemblances in natures never before compared. He can class them so audaciously because he is sensible of the sweep of the celestial stream, from which nothing is exempt. His own body is a fleeing apparition,—his personality as fugitive as the trope he employs. In certain hours we can almost pass our hand through our own body. I think the use or value of poetry to be the suggestion it affords of the flux or fugaciousness of the poet. The mind delights in measuring itself thus with matter, with history, and flouting both. A thought, any thought, pressed, followed, opened, dwarfs matter, custom, and all but itself. But this second sight does not necessarily impair the primary or common sense. Pindar, and Dante, yes, and the gray and timeworn sentences of Zoroaster, may all be parsed, though we do not parse them. The poet has a logic, though it be subtile. He observes higher laws than he transgresses. "Poetry must first be good sense, though it is something better."

This union of first and second sight reads nature to the end of delight and of moral use. Men are imaginative, but not overpowered by it to the extent of confounding its suggestions with external facts. We live in both spheres, and must not mix them. Genius certifies its entire possession of its thought, by translating it into a fact which perfectly represents it, and is hereby education. Charles James Fox thought "Poetry the great refreshment of the human mind,—the only thing, after all; that men first found out they had minds, by making and tasting poetry."

Man runs about restless and in pain when his condition or the objects about him do not fully match his thought. He wishes to be rich, to be old, to be young, that things may obey him. In the ocean, in fire, in the sky, in the forest, he finds facts adequate and as large as he. As his thoughts are deeper than he can fathom, so also are these. It is easier to read Sanscrit, to decipher the arrowhead character, than to interpret these familiar sights. It is even much to name them. Thus Thomson's "Seasons" and the best parts of many old and many new poets are simply enumerations by a person who felt the beauty of the common sights and sounds, without any attempt to draw a moral or affix a meaning.

The poet discovers that what men value as substances have a higher value as symbols; that Nature is the immense shadow of man. A man's action is only a picture-book of his creed. He does after what he believes. Your condition, your employment, is the fable of *you*. The world is thoroughly anthropomorphized, as if it had passed through the body and mind of man, and taken his mould and form. Indeed, good poetry is always personification, and heightens every species of force in nature by giving it a human volition. We are advertised that there is nothing to which man is not related; that everything is convertible into every other. The staff in his hand is the *radius vector* of the sun. The chemistry of this is the chemistry of that. Whatever one act we do, whatever one thing we learn, we are doing and learning all things,—marching in the direction of universal power. Every healthy mind is a true Alexander or Sesostris, building a universal monarchy.

The senses imprison us, and we help them with metres as limitary,—with a pair of scales and a foot-rule and a clock. How long it took to find out what a day was, or what this sun, that makes days! It cost thousands of years only to make the motion of the earth suspected. Slowly, by comparing thousands of observations, there dawned on some mind a theory of the sun,—and we found the astronomical fact. But the astronomy is in the mind: the senses affirm that the earth stands still and the sun moves. The senses collect the surface facts of matter. The intellect acts on these brute reports, and obtains from them results which are the essence or intellectual form of the experiences. It compares, distributes, generalizes and uplifts them into its own sphere. It knows that these transfigured results are not the brute experiences, just as souls in heaven are not the red bodies they once animated. Many transfigurations have befallen them. The atoms of the body were once nebulæ, then rock, then loam, then corn, then chyme, then chyle, then blood; and now the beholding and co-energizing mind sees the same refining and ascent to the third, the seventh, or the tenth power of the daily accidents which the senses report, and which make the raw material of knowledge. It was sensation; when memory came, it was experience; when mind acted, it was knowledge; when mind acted on it as knowledge, it was thought.

This metonymy, or seeing the same sense in things so diverse, gives a pure pleasure. Every one of a million times we find a charm in the metamorphosis. It makes us dance and sing. All men are so far poets. When people tell me they do not relish poetry, and bring me Shelley, or Aikin's Poets, or I know not what volumes of rhymed English, to show that it has no charm, I am quite of their mind. But this dislike of the books only proves their liking of poetry. For they relish Æsop,—cannot forget him, or not use him; bring them Homer's Iliad, and they like that; or the Cid, and that rings well; read to them from Chaucer, and they reckon him an honest fellow. Lear and Macbeth and Richard III. they know pretty well without guide. Give them Robin Hood's ballads or Griselda, or Sir Andrew Barton, or Sir Patrick Spense, or Chevy Chase, or Tam O'Shanter, and they like these well enough. They like to see statues; they like to name the stars; they like to talk and hear of Jove, Apollo, Minerva, Venus, and the Nine. See how tenacious we are of the old names. They like poetry without knowing it as such. They like to go to the theatre and be made to weep; to Faneuil Hall, and be taught by Otis, Webster, or Kossuth, or Phillips, what great hearts they have, what tears, what new possible enlargements to their narrow horizons. They like to see sunsets on the hills or on a lake shore. Now a cow does not gaze at the rainbow, or show or affect any interest in the landscape, or a peacock, or the song of thrushes.

Nature is the true idealist. When she serves us best, when, on rare days, she speaks to the imagination, we feel that the huge heaven and earth are but a web drawn around us, that the light, skies, and mountains are but the painted vicissitudes of the soul. Who has heard our hymn in the churches without accepting the truth,

> As o'er our heads the seasons roll,
> And soothe with *change of bliss* the soul?

Of course, when we describe man as poet, and credit him with the triumphs of the art, we speak of the potential or ideal man,—not found now in any one person. You must go through a city or a nation, and find one faculty here, one there, to build the true poet withal. Yet all men know the portrait when it is drawn, and it is part of religion to believe its possible incarnation.

He is the healthy, the wise, the fundamental, the manly man, seer of the secret; against all the appearance he sees and reports the truth, namely that the soul generates matter. And poetry is the only verity,—the expression of a sound mind speaking after the ideal, and not after the apparent. As a power it is the perception of the symbolic character of things, and the treating them as representative: as a talent it is a magnetic tenaciousness of an image, and by the treatment demonstrating that this pigment of thought is as palpable and objective to the poet as is the ground on which he stands, or the walls of houses about him. And this power appears in Dante and Shakspeare. In some individuals this insight or second sight has an extraordinary reach which compels our wonder, as in Behmen, Swedenborg, and William Blake the painter.

William Blake, whose abnormal genius, Wordsworth said, interested him more than the conversation of Scott or of Byron, writes thus: "He who does not imagine in stronger and better lineaments and in stronger and better light than his perishing mortal eye can see, does not imagine at all. The painter of this work asserts that all his imaginations appear to him infinitely more perfect and more minutely organized than anything seen by his mortal eye. . . . I assert for myself that I do not behold the outward creation, and that to me it would be a hindrance, and not action. I question not my corporeal eye any more than I would question a window concerning a sight. I look through it, and not with it."

It is a problem of metaphysics to define the province of Fancy and Imagination. The words are often used, and the things confounded. Imagination respects the cause. It is the vision of an inspired soul reading arguments and affirmations in all nature of that which it is driven to say. But as soon as this soul is released a little from its passion, and at leisure plays with the resemblances and types, for amusement, and not for its moral end, we call its action Fancy. Lear, mad with his affliction, thinks every man who suffers must have the like cause with his own. "What, have his daughters brought him to this pass?" But when, his attention being diverted, his mind rests from this thought, he becomes fanciful with Tom, playing with the superficial resemblances of objects. Bunyan, in pain for his soul, wrote "Pilgrim's Progress;" Quarles, after he was quite cool, wrote "Emblems."

Imagination is central; fancy, superficial. Fancy relates to surface, in which a great part of life lies. The lover is rightly said to fancy the hair, eyes, complexion of the maid. Fancy is a wilful, imagination a spontaneous act; fancy, a play as with dolls and puppets which we choose to call men and women; imagination, a perception and affirming of a real relation between a thought and some material fact. Fancy amuses; imagination expands and exalts us. Imagination uses an organic classification. Fancy joins by accidental resemblance, surprises and amuses the idle, but is silent in the presence of great passion and action. Fancy aggregates; imagination animates. Fancy is related to color; imagination, to form. Fancy paints; imagination sculptures.

*Veracity.*—I do not wish, therefore, to find that my poet is not partaker of the feast he spreads, or that he would kindle or amuse me with that which does not kindle or amuse him. He must believe in his poetry. Homer, Milton, Hafiz, Herbert, Swedenborg, Wordsworth, are heartily enamored of their sweet thoughts. Moreover, they know that this correspondence of things to thoughts is far deeper than they can penetrate,—defying adequate expression; that it is elemental, or in the core of things. Veracity therefore is that which we require in poets,—that they shall say how it was with them, and not what might be said. And the fault of our popular poetry is that it is not sincere.

"What news?" asks man of man everywhere. The only teller of news is the poet. When he sings, the world listens with the assurance that now a secret of God is to be spoken. The right poetic mood is or makes a more complete sensibility, piercing the outward fact to the meaning of the fact; shows a sharper insight: and the perception creates the strong expression of it, as the man who sees his way walks in it.

It is a rule in eloquence, that the moment the orator loses command of his audience, the audience commands him. So in poetry, the master rushes to deliver his thought, and the words and images fly to him to express it; whilst colder moods are forced to respect the ways of saying it, and insinuate, or, as it were, muffle the fact to suit the poverty or caprice of their expression, so that they only hint the matter, or allude to it, being unable to fuse and mould their words and images to fluid obedience. See how Shakspeare grapples at once with the main problem of the tragedy, as in Lear and Macbeth, and the opening of the Merchant of Venice.

All writings must be in a degree exoteric, written to a human *should* or *would,* instead of to the fatal *is:* this holds even of the bravest and sincerest writers. Every writer is a skater, and must go partly where he would, and partly where the skates carry him; or a sailor, who can only land where sails can be blown. And yet it is to be added that high poetry exceeds the fact, or nature itself, just as skates allow the good skater far more grace than his best walking would show, or sails more than riding. The poet writes from a real experience, the amateur feigns one. Of course one draws the bow with his fingers and the other with the strength of his body; one speaks with his lips and the other with a chest voice. Talent amuses, but if your verse has not a necessary and autobiographic basis, though under whatever gay poetic veils, it shall not waste my time.

For poetry is faith. To the poet the world is virgin soil; all is practicable; the men are ready for virtue; it is always time to do right. He is a true re-commencer, or Adam in the garden again. He affirms the applicability of the ideal law to this moment and the present knot of affairs. Parties, lawyers and men of the world will invariably dispute such an application, as romantic and dangerous: they admit the general truth, but they and their affair always constitute a case in bar of the statute. Free-trade, they concede, is very well as a principle, but it is never quite the time for its adoption without prejudicing actual interests. Chastity, they admit, is very well,—but then think of Mirabeau's passion and temperament! Eternal laws are very well, which admit no violation,—but so extreme were the times and manners of mankind, that you must admit miracles, for the times constituted a case. Of course, we know what you say, that legends are found in all tribes,—but this legend is different. And so throughout; the poet affirms the laws, prose busies itself with exceptions,—with the local and individual.

I require that the poem should impress me so that after I have shut the book it shall recall me to itself, or that passages should. And inestimable is the criticism of memory as a corrective to first impressions. We are dazzled at first by new words and brilliancy of color, which occupy the fancy and deceive the judgment. But all this is easily forgotten. Later, the thought, the happy image which expressed it and which was a true experience of the poet, recurs to mind, and sends me back in search of the book. And I wish that the poet should foresee this habit of readers, and omit all but the important passages. Shakspeare is made up of important passages, like Damascus steel made up of old nails. Homer has his own,

> One omen is best, to fight for one's country;

and again,

> They heal their griefs, for curable are the hearts of the noble.

Write, that I may know you. Style betrays you, as your eyes do. We detect at once by it whether the writer has a firm grasp on his fact or thought,—exists at the moment for that alone, or whether he has one eye apologizing, deprecatory, turned on his reader. In proportion always to his possession of his thought is his defiance of his readers. There is no choice of words for him who clearly sees the truth. That provides him with the best word.

Great design belongs to a poem, and is better than any skill of execution,—but how rare! I find it in the poems of Wordsworth,—Laodamia, and the Ode to Dion, and the plan of The Recluse. We want design, and do not forgive the bards if they have only the art of enamelling. We want an architect, and they bring us an upholsterer.

If your subject do not appear to you the flower of the world at this moment, you have not rightly chosen it. No matter what it is, grand or gay, national or private, if it has a natural prominence to you, work away until you come to the heart of it: then it will, though it were a sparrow or a spider-web, as fully represent the central law and draw all tragic or joyful illustration, as if it were the book of Genesis or the book of Doom. The subject—we must so often say it—is indifferent. Any word, every word in language, every circumstance, becomes poetic in the hands of a higher thought.

The test or measure of poetic genius is the power to read the poetry of affairs,—to fuse the circumstance of to-day; not to use Scott's antique superstitions, or Shakspeare's, but to convert those of the nineteenth century and of the existing nations into universal symbols. 'T is easy to repaint the mythology of the Greeks, or of the Catholic Church, the feudal castle, the crusade, the martyrdoms of mediæval Europe; but to point out where the same creative force is now working in our own houses and public assemblies; to convert the vivid energies acting at this hour in New York and Chicago and San Francisco, into universal symbols, requires a subtile and commanding thought. 'T is boyish in Swedenborg to cumber himself with the dead scurf of Hebrew antiquity, as if the Divine creative energy had fainted in his own century. American life storms about us daily, and is slow to find a tongue. This contemporary insight is transubstantiation, the conversion of daily bread into the holiest symbols; and every man would be a poet if his intellectual digestion were perfect. The test of the poet is the power to take the passing day, with its news, its cares, its fears, as he shares them, and hold it up to a divine reason, till he sees it to have a purpose and beauty, and to be related to astronomy and history and the eternal order of the world. Then the dry twig blossoms in his hand. He is calmed and elevated.

The use of "occasional poems" is to give leave to originality. Every one delights in the felicity frequently shown in our drawing-rooms. In a game-party or picnic poem each writer is released from the solemn rhythmic traditions which alarm and suffocate his fancy, and the result is that one of the partners offers a poem in a new style that hints at a new literature. Yet the writer holds it cheap, and could do the like all day. On the stage, the farce is commonly far better given than the tragedy, as the stock actors understand the farce, and do not understand the tragedy. The writer in the parlor has more presence of mind, more wit and fancy, more play of thought, on the incidents that occur at table or about the house, than in the politics of Germany or Rome. Many of the fine poems of Herrick, Jonson, and their contemporaries had this casual origin.

I know there is entertainment and room for talent in the artist's selection of ancient or remote subjects; as when the poet goes to India, or to Rome, or Persia, for his fable. But I believe nobody knows better than he that herein he consults his ease rather than his strength or his desire. He is very well convinced that the great moments of life are those in which his own house, his own body, the tritest and nearest ways and words and things have been illuminated into prophets and teachers. What else is it to be a poet? What are his garland and singing-robes? What but a sensibility so keen that the scent of an elder-blow, or the timber-yard and corporation-works of a nest of pismires is event enough for him,—all emblems and personal appeals to him. His wreath and robe is to do what he enjoys; emancipation from other men's questions, and glad study of his own; escape from the gossip and routine of society, and the allowed right and practice of making better. He does not give his hand, but in sign of giving his heart; he is not affable with all, but silent, uncommitted, or in love, as his heart leads him. There is no subject that does not belong to him,—politics, economy, manufactures and stock-brokerage, as much as sunsets and souls; only, these things, placed in their true order, are poetry; displaced, or put in kitchen order, they are unpoetic. Malthus is the right organ of the English proprietors; but we shall never understand political economy until Burns or Béranger or some poet shall teach it in songs, and he will not teach Malthusianism.

Poetry is the *gai science*. The trait and test of the poet is that he builds, adds, and affirms. The critic destroys: the poet says nothing but what helps somebody; let others be distracted with cares, he is exempt. All their pleasures are tinged with pain. All his pains are edged with pleasure. The gladness he imparts he shares. As one of the old Minnesingers sung,

> Oft have I heard, and now believe it true,
> Whom man delights in, God delights in too.

Poetry is the consolation of mortal men. They live cabined, cribbed, confined in a narrow and trivial lot,—in wants, pains, anxieties and superstitions, in profligate politics, in personal animosities, in mean employments,—and victims of these; and the nobler powers untried, unknown. A poet comes who lifts the veil; gives them glimpses of the laws of the universe; shows them the circumstance as illusion; shows that nature is only a language to express the laws, which are grand and beautiful;—and lets them, by his songs, into some of the realities. Socrates, the Indian teachers of the Maia, the Bibles of the nations, Shakspeare, Milton, Hafiz, Ossian, the Welsh Bards;—these all deal with nature and history as means and symbols, and not as ends. With such guides they begin to see that what they had called pictures are realities, and the mean life is pictures. And this is achieved by words; for it is a few oracles spoken by perceiving men that are the texts on which religions and states are founded. And this perception has at once its moral sequence. Ben Jonson said, "The principal end of poetry is to inform men in the just reason of living."

*Creation.*—But there is a third step which poetry takes, and which seems higher than the others, namely, creation, or ideas taking forms of their own,—when the poet invents the fable, and invents the language which his heroes speak. He reads in the word or action of the man its yet untold results. His inspiration is power to carry out and complete the metamorphosis, which, in the imperfect kinds arrested for ages, in the perfecter proceeds rapidly in the same individual. For poetry is science, and the poet a truer logician. Men in the courts or in the street think themselves logical and the poet whimsical. Do they think there is chance or wilfulness in what he sees and tells? To be sure, we demand of him what he demands of himself,—veracity, first of all. But with that, he is the lawgiver, as being an exact reporter of the essential law. He knows that he did not make his thought,—no, his thought made him, and made the sun and the stars. Is the solar system good art and architecture? the same wise achievement is in the human brain also, can you only wile it from interference and marring. We cannot look at works of art but they teach us how near man is to creating. Michel Angelo is largely filled with the Creator that made and makes men. How much of the original craft remains in him, and he a mortal man! In him and the like perfecter brains the instinct is resistless, knows the right way, is melodious, and at all points divine. The reason we set so high a value on any poetry,—as often on a line or a phrase as on a poem,—is that it is a new work of Nature, as a man is. It must be as new as foam and as old as the rock. But a new verse comes once in a hundred years; therefore Pindar, Hafiz, Dante, speak so proudly of what seems to the clown a jingle.

The writer, like the priest, must be exempted from secular labor. His work needs a frolic health; he must be at the top of his condition. In that prosperity he is sometimes caught up into a perception of means and materials, of feats and fine arts, of fairy machineries and funds of power hitherto utterly unknown to him, whereby he can transfer his visions to mortal canvas, or reduce them into iambic or trochaic, into lyric or heroic rhyme. These successes are not less admirable and astonishing to the poet than they are to his audience. He has seen something which all the mathematics and the best industry could never bring him unto. Now at this rare elevation above his usual sphere, he has come into new circulations, the marrow of the world is in his bones, the opulence of forms begins to pour into his intellect, and he is permitted to dip his brush into the old paint-pot with which birds, flowers, the human check, the living rock, the broad landscape, the ocean and the eternal sky were painted.

These fine fruits of judgment, poesy, and sentiment, when once their hour is struck, and the world is ripe for them, know as well as coarser how to feed and replenish themselves, and maintain their stock alive, and multiply; for roses and violets renew their race like oaks, and flights of painted moths are as old as the Alleghanies. The balance of the world is kept, and dewdrop and haze and the pencil of light are as long-lived as chaos and darkness.

Our science is always abreast of our self-knowledge. Poetry begins, or all becomes poetry, when we look from the centre outward, and are using all as if the mind made it. That only can we see which we are, and which we make. The weaver sees gingham; the broker sees the stock-list; the politician, the ward and county votes; the poet sees the horizon, and the shores of matter lying on the sky, the interaction of the elements,—the large effect of laws which correspond to the inward laws which he knows, and so are but a kind of extension of himself. "The attractions are proportional to the destinies." Events or things are only the fulfilment of the prediction of the faculties. Better men saw heavens and earths; saw noble instruments of noble souls. We see railroads, mills, and banks, and we pity the poverty of these dreaming Buddhists. There was as much creative force then as now, but it made globes and astronomic heavens, instead of broadcloth and wine-glasses.

The poet is enamored of thoughts and laws. These know their way, and, guided by them, he is ascending from an interest in visible things to an interest in that which they signify, and from the part of a spectator to the part of a maker. And as everything streams and advances, as every faculty and every desire is procreant, and every perception is a destiny, there is no limit to his hope. "Anything, child, that the mind covets, from the milk of a cocoa to the throne of the three worlds, thou mayest obtain, by keeping the law of thy members and the law of thy mind." It suggests that there is higher poetry than we write or read.

Rightly, poetry is organic. We cannot know things by words and writing, but only by taking a central position in the universe and living in its forms. We sink to rise:

> None any work can frame,
> Unless himself become the same.

All parts and forms of nature are the expression or production of divine faculties, and the same are in us. And the fascination of genius for us is this awful nearness to Nature's creations.

I have heard that the Germans think the creator of Trim and Uncle Toby, though he never wrote a verse, a greater poet than Cowper, and that Goldsmith's title to the name is not from his Deserted Village, but derived from the Vicar of Wakefield. Better examples are Shakspeare's Ariel, his Caliban, and his fairies in the Midsummer Night's Dream. Barthold Niebuhr said well, "There is little merit in inventing a happy idea or attractive situation, so long as it is only the author's voice which we hear. As a being whom we have called into life by magic arts, as soon as it has received existence acts independently of the master's impulse, so the poet creates his persons, and then watches and relates what they do and say. Such creation is poetry, in the literal sense of the term, and its possibility is an unfathomable enigma. The gushing fulness of speech belongs to the poet, and it flows from the lips of each of his magic beings in the thoughts and words peculiar to its nature."

This force of representation so plants his figures before him that he treats them as real; talks to them as if they were bodily there; puts words in their mouth such as they should have spoken, and is affected by them as by persons. Vast is the difference between writing clean verses for magazines, and creating these new persons and situations,—new language with emphasis and reality. The humor of Falstaff, the terror of Macbeth, have each their swarm of fit thoughts and images, as if Shakspeare had known and reported the men, instead of inventing them at his desk. This power appears not only in the outline or portrait of his actors, but also in the bearing and behavior and style of each individual. Ben Jonson told Drummond that "Sidney did not keep a decorum in making every one speak as well as himself."

We all have one key to this miracle of the poet, and the dunce has experiences that may explain Shakspeare to him,—one key, namely, dreams. In dreams we are true poets; we create the persons of the drama; we give them appropriate figures, faces, costume; they are perfect in their organs, attitude, manners: moreover they speak after their own characters, not ours;—they speak to us, and we listen with surprise to what they say. Indeed, I doubt if the best poet has yet written any five-act play that can compare in thoroughness of invention with this unwritten play in fifty acts, composed by the dullest snorer on the floor of the watch-house.

*Melody, Rhyme, Form.*—Music and rhyme are among the earliest pleasures of the child, and, in the history of literature, poetry precedes prose. Every one may see, as he rides on the highway through an uninteresting landscape, how a little water instantly relieves the monotony: no matter what objects are near it,—a gray rock, a grasspatch, an alder-bush, or a stake,—they become beautiful by being reflected. It is rhyme to the eye, and explains the charm of rhyme to the ear. Shadows please us as still finer rhymes. Architecture gives the like pleasure by the repetition of equal parts in a colonnade, in a row of windows, or in wings; gardens by the symmetric contrasts of the beds and walks. In society you have this figure in a bridal company, where a choir of white-robed maidens give the charm of living statues; in a funeral procession, where all wear black; in a regiment of soldiers in uniform.

The universality of this taste is proved by our habit of casting our facts into rhyme to remember them better, as so many proverbs may show. Who would hold the order of the almanac so fast but for the ding-dong,

> Thirty days hath September, . . .

or of the Zodiac, but for

> The Ram, the Bull, the heavenly Twins, . . . ?

We are lovers of rhyme and return, period and musical reflection. The babe is lulled to sleep by the nurse's song. Sailors can work better for their *yo-heave-o.* Soldiers can march better and fight better for the drum and trumpet. Metre begins with pulse-beat, and the length of lines in songs and poems is determined by the inhalation and exhalation of the lungs. If you hum or whistle the rhythm of the common English metres,—of the decasyllabic quatrain, or the octosyllabic with alternate sexisyllabic, or other rhythms,—you can easily believe these metres to be organic, derived from the human pulse, and to be therefore not proper to one nation, but to mankind. I think you will also find a charm heroic, plaintive, pathetic, in these cadences, and be at once set on searching for the words that can rightly fill these vacant beats. Young people like rhyme, drum-beat, tune, things in pairs and alternatives; and, in higher degrees, we know the instant power of music upon our temperaments to change our mood, and give us its own; and human passion, seizing these constitutional tunes, aims to fill them with appropriate words, or marry music to thought, believing, as we believe of all marriage, that matches are made in heaven, and that for every thought its proper melody or rhyme exists, though the odds are immense against our finding it, and only genius can rightly say the banns.

Another form of rhyme is iterations of phrase, as the record of the death of Sisera:

> At her feet he bowed, he fell, he lay down: at her feet he bowed, he fell: where he bowed, there he fell down dead.

The fact is made conspicuous, nay, colossal, by this simple rhetoric:

> They shall perish, but thou shalt endure: yea, all of them shall wax old like a garment; as a vesture shalt thou change them, and they shall be changed: but thou art the same, and thy years shall have no end.

Milton delights in these iterations:

> Though fallen on evil days,
> On evil days though fallen, and evil tongues.

> Was I deceived, or did a sable cloud
> Turn forth its silver lining on the night?

I did not err, there does a sable cloud
Turn forth its silver lining on the night.
*Comus*

A little onward lend thy guiding hand,
To these dark steps a little farther on.
*Samson*

So in our songs and ballads the refrain skilfully used, and deriving some novelty or better sense in each of many verses:

Busk thee, busk thee, my bonny bonny bride,
Busk thee, busk thee, my winsome marrow.
HAMILTON

Of course rhyme soars and refines with the growth of the mind. The boy liked the drum, the people liked an overpowering jewsharp tune. Later they like to transfer that rhyme to life, and to detect a melody as prompt and perfect in their daily affairs. Omen and coincidence show the rhythmical structure of man; hence the taste for signs, sortilege, prophecy and fulfilment, anniversaries, etc. By and by, when they apprehend real rhymes, namely, the correspondence of parts in nature,—acid and alkali, body and mind, man and maid, character and history, action and reaction,—they do not longer value rattles and ding-dongs, or barbaric word-jingle. Astronomy, Botany, Chemistry, Hydraulics and the elemental forces have their own periods and returns, their own grand strains of harmony not less exact, up to the primeval apothegm that "there is nothing on earth which is not in the heavens in a heavenly form, and nothing in the heavens which is not on the earth in an earthly form." They furnish the poet with grander pairs and alternations, and will require an equal expansion in his metres.

There is under the seeming poverty of metres an infinite variety, as every artist knows. A right ode (however nearly it may adopt conventional metre, as the Spenserian, or the heroic blank-verse, or one of the fixed lyric metres) will by any sprightliness be at once lifted out of conventionality, and will modify the metre. Every good poem that I know I recall by its rhythm also. Rhyme is a pretty good measure of the latitude and opulence of a writer. If unskilful, he is at once detected by the poverty of his chimes. A small, well-worn, sprucely brushed vocabulary serves him. Now try Spenser, Marlow, Chapman, and see how wide they fly for weapons, and how rich and lavish their profusion. In their rhythm is no manufacture, but a vortex, or musical tornado, which falling on words and the experience of a learned mind, whirls these materials into the same grand order as planets and moons obey, and seasons, and monsoons.

There are also prose poets. Thomas Taylor, the Platonist, for instance, is really a better man of imagination, a better poet, or perhaps I should say a better feeder to a poet, than any man between Milton and Wordsworth. Thomas Moore had the magnanimity to say, "If Burke and Bacon were not poets (measured lines not being necessary to constitute one), he did not know what poetry meant." And every good reader will easily recall expressions or passages in works of pure science which have given him the same pleasure which he seeks in professed poets. Richard Owen, the eminent paleontologist, said:

> All hitherto observed causes of extirpation point either to continuous slowly operating geologic changes, or to no greater sudden cause than the, so to speak, spectral appearance of mankind on a limited tract of land not before inhabited.

St. Augustine complains to God of his friends offering him the books of the philosophers:

> And these were the dishes in which they brought to me, being hungry, the Sun and the Moon instead of Thee.

It would not be easy to refuse to Sir Thomas Browne's "Fragments on Mummies" the claim of poetry:

> Of their living habitations they made little account, conceiving them but as *hospitia*, or inns, while they adorned the sepulchres of the dead, and, planting thereon lasting bases, defied the crumbling touches of time, and the misty vaporousness of oblivion. Yet all were but Babel vanities. Time sadly overcometh all things, and is now dominant and sitteth upon a Sphinx, and looketh unto Memphis and old Thebes, while his sister Oblivion reclineth semi-somnous on a pyramid, gloriously triumphing, making puzzles of Titanian erections, and turning old glories into dreams. History sinketh beneath her cloud. The traveller as he paceth through those deserts asketh of her, Who builded them? and she mumbleth something, but what it is he heareth not.

Rhyme, being a kind of music, shares this advantage with music, that it has a privilege of speaking truth which all Philistia is unable to challenge. Music is the poor man's Parnassus. With the first note of the flute or horn, or the first strain of a song, we quit the world of common-sense and launch on the sea of ideas and emotions: we pour contempt on the prose you so magnify; yet the sturdiest Philistine is silent. The like allowance is the prescriptive right of poetry. You shall not speak ideal truth in prose uncontradicted: you may in verse. The best thoughts run into the best words; imaginative and affectionate thoughts into music and metre. We ask for food and fire, we talk of our work, our tools and material necessities, in prose; that is, without any elevation or aim at beauty; but when we rise into the world of thought, and think of these things only for what they signify, speech refines into order and harmony. I know what you say of mediæval barbarism and sleighbell-rhyme, but we have not done with music, no, nor with rhyme, nor must console ourselves with prose poets so long as boys whistle and girls sing.

Let Poetry then pass, if it will, into music and rhyme. That is the form which itself puts on. We do not enclose watches in wooden, but in crystal cases, and rhyme is the transparent frame that allows almost the pure architecture of thought to become visible to the mental eye. Substance is much, but so are mode and form much. The poet, like a delighted boy, brings you heaps of rainbow bubbles, opaline, air-born, spherical as the world, instead of a few drops of soap and water. Victor Hugo says well, "An idea steeped in verse becomes suddenly more incisive and more brilliant: the iron becomes steel." Lord Bacon, we are told, "loved not to see poesy go on other feet than poetical dactyls and spondees;" and Ben Jonson said that "Donne, for not keeping of accent, deserved hanging."

Poetry being an attempt to express, not the common-sense,—as the avoirdupois of the hero, or his structure in feet and inches,—but the beauty and soul in his aspect as it shines to fancy and feeling; and so of all other objects in nature; runs into fable, personifies every fact:—"the clouds clapped their hands,"—"the hills skipped,"—"the sky spoke." This is the substance, and this treatment always attempts a metrical grace. Outside of the nursery the beginning of literature is the prayers of a people, and they are always hymns, poetic,—the mind allowing itself range, and therewith is ever a corresponding freedom in the style, which becomes lyrical. The prayers of nations are rhythmic, have iterations and alliterations like the marriage-service and burial-service in our liturgies.

Poetry will never be a simple means, as when history or philosophy is rhymed, or laureate odes on state occasions are written. Itself must be its own end, or it is nothing. The difference between poetry and stock poetry is this, that in the latter the rhythm is given and the sense adapted to it; while in the former the sense dictates the rhythm, I might even say that the rhyme is there in the theme, thought, and image themselves. Ask the fact for the form. For a verse is not a vehicle to carry a sentence as a jewel is carried in a case: the verse must be alive, and inseparable from its contents, as the soul of man inspires and directs the body, and we measure the inspiration by the music. In reading prose, I am sensitive as soon as a sentence drags; but in poetry, as soon as one word drags. Ever as the thought mounts, the expression mounts. 'T is cumulative also; the poem is made up of lines each of which fill the ear of the poet in its turn, so that mere synthesis produces a work quite superhuman.

Indeed, the masters sometimes rise above themselves to strains which charm their readers, and which neither any competitor could outdo, nor the bard himself again equal. Try this strain of Beaumont and Fletcher:

Hence, all ye vain delights,
As short as are the nights
In which you spend your folly!
There 's naught in this life sweet,
If men were wise to see 't,
But only melancholy.
Oh! sweetest melancholy!
Welcome, folded arms and fixed eyes,

A sigh that piercing mortifies,
A look that 's fastened on the ground,
A tongue chained up without a sound;
Fountain-heads and pathless groves,
Places which pale Passion loves,
Midnight walks, when all the fowls
Are warmly housed, save bats and owls;
A midnight bell, a passing groan,
These are the sounds we feed upon,
Then stretch our bones in a still, gloomy valley.
Nothing 's so dainty sweet as lovely melancholy.

Keats disclosed by certain lines in his "Hyperion" this inward skill; and Coleridge showed at least his love and appetency for it. It appears in Ben Jonson's songs, including certainly "The faery beam upon you," etc., Waller's "Go, lovely rose!" Herbert's "Virtue" and "Easter," and Lovelace's lines "To Althea" and "To Lucasta," and Collins's "Ode to Evening," all but the last verse, which is academical. Perhaps this dainty style of poetry is not producible to-day, any more than a right Gothic cathedral. It belonged to a time and taste which is not in the world.

As the imagination is not a talent of some men but is the health of every man, so also is this joy of musical expression. I know the pride of mathematicians and materialists, but they cannot conceal from me their capital want. The critic, the philosopher, is a failed poet. Gray avows that "he thinks even a bad verse as good a thing or better than the best observation that was ever made on it." I honor the naturalist; I honor the geometer, but he has before him higher power and happiness than he knows. Yet we will leave to the masters their own forms. Newton may be permitted to call Terence a play-book, and to wonder at the frivolous taste for rhymers; he only predicts, one would say, a grander poetry: he only shows that he is not yet reached; that the poetry which satisfies more youthful souls is not such to a mind like his, accustomed to grander harmonies;—this being a child's whistle to his ear; that the music must rise to a loftier strain, up to Handel, up to Beethoven, up to the thorough-base of the sea-shore, up to the largeness of astronomy: at last that great heart will hear in the music beats like its own; the waves of melody will wash and float him also, and set him into concert and harmony.

*Bards and Trouveurs.*—The metallic force of primitive words makes the superiority of the remains of the rude ages. It costs the early bard little talent to chant more impressively than the later, more cultivated poets. His advantage is that his words are things, each the lucky sound which described the fact, and we listen to him as we do to the Indian, or the hunter, or miner, each of whom represents his facts as accurately as the cry of the wolf or the eagle tells of the forest or the air they inhabit. The original force, the direct smell of the earth or the sea, is in these ancient poems, the Sagas of the North, the Nibelungen Lied, the songs and ballads of the English and Scotch.

I find or fancy more true poetry, the love of the vast and the ideal, in the Welsh and bardic fragments of Taliessin and his successors, than in many volumes of British Classics. An intrepid magniloquence appears in all the bards, as:

> The whole ocean flamed as one wound.
> *King Regnar Lodbrok*

> God himself cannot procure good for the wicked.
> *Welsh Triad*

A favorable specimen is Taliessin's "Invocation of the Wind" at the door of Castle Teganwy:

> Discover thou what it is,—
> The strong creature from before the flood,
> Without flesh, without bone, without head, without feet,
> It will neither be younger nor older than at the beginning;
> It has no fear, nor the rude wants of created things.
> Great God! how the sea whitens when it comes!
> It is in the field, it is in the wood,
> Without hand, without foot,
> Without age, without season,
> It is always of the same age with the ages of ages,
> And of equal breadth with the surface of the earth.
> It was not born, it sees not,
> And is not seen; it does not come when desired;
> It has no form, it bears no burden,
> For it is void of sin.
> It makes no perturbation in the place where God wills it,
> On the sea, on the land.

In one of his poems he asks:

> Is there but one course to the wind?
> But one to the water of the sea?
> Is there but one spark in the fire of boundless energy?

He says of his hero, Cunedda,

> He will assimilate, he will agree with the deep and the shallow.

To another,

> When I lapse to a sinful word,
> May neither you, nor others hear.

Of an enemy,

> The cauldron of the sea was bordered round by his land, but it would not boil the food of a coward.

To an exile on an island he says,

> The heavy blue chain of the sea didst thou, O just man, endure.

Another bard in like tone says,

> I am possessed of songs such as no son of man can repeat; one of them is called the 'Helper;' it will help thee at thy need in sickness, grief, and all adversities. I know a song which I need only to sing when men have loaded me with bonds: when I sing it, my chains fall in pieces and I walk forth at liberty.

The Norsemen have no less faith in poetry and its power, when they describe it thus:

> Odin spoke everything in rhyme. He and his temple-gods were called song-smiths. He could make his enemies in battle blind or deaf, and their weapons so blunt that they could no more cut than a willow-twig. Odin taught these arts in runes or songs, which are called incantations.

The Crusades brought out the genius of France, in the twelfth century, when Pierre d'Auvergne said,

> I will sing a new song which resounds in my breast: never was a song good or beautiful which resembled any other.

And Pons de Capdeuil declares,

> Since the air renews itself and softens, so must my heart renew itself, and what buds in it buds and grows outside of it.

There is in every poem a height which attracts more than other parts, and is best remembered. Thus, in "Morte d'Arthur," I remember nothing so well as Sir Gawain's parley with Merlin in his wonderful prison:

> After the disappearance of Merlin from King Arthur's court he was seriously missed, and many knights set out in search of him. Among others was Sir Gawain, who pursued his search till it was time to return to the court. He came into the forest of Broceliande, lamenting as he went along. Presently he heard the voice of one groaning on his right hand; looking that way, he could see nothing save a kind of smoke which seemed like air, and through which he could not pass; and this impediment made him so wrathful that it deprived him of speech. Presently he heard a voice which said, 'Gawain, Gawain, be not out of heart, for everything which must happen will come to pass.' And when he heard the voice which thus called him by his right name, he replied, 'Who can this be who hath spoken to me?' 'How,' said the voice, 'Sir Gawain, know you me not? You were wont to know me well, but thus things are interwoven and thus the proverb says true, "Leave the court and the court will leave you." So is it with me. Whilst I served

> King Arthur, I was well known by you and by other barons, but because I have left the court, I am known no longer, and put in forgetfulness, which I ought not to be if faith reigned in the world.' When Sir Gawain heard the voice which spoke to him thus, he thought it was Merlin, and he answered, 'Sir, certes I ought to know you well, for many times I have heard your words. I pray you appear before me so that I may be able to recognize you.' 'Ah, sir,' said Merlin, 'you will never see me more, and that grieves me, but I cannot remedy it, and when you shall have departed from this place, I shall nevermore speak to you nor to any other person, save only my mistress; for never other person will be able to discover this place for anything which may befall; neither shall I ever go out from hence, for in the world there is no such strong tower as this wherein I am confined; and it is neither of wood, nor of iron, nor of stone, but of air, without anything else; and made by enchantment so strong that it can never be demolished while the world lasts; neither can I go out, nor can any one come in, save she who hath enclosed me here and who keeps me company when it pleaseth her: she cometh when she listeth, for her will is here.' 'How, Merlin, my good friend,' said Sir Gawain, 'are you restrained so strongly that you cannot deliver yourself nor make yourself visible unto me; how can this happen, seeing that you are the wisest man in the world?' 'Rather,' said Merlin, 'the greatest fool; for I well knew that all this would befall me, and I have been fool enough to love another more than myself, for I taught my mistress that whereby she hath imprisoned me in such a manner that none can set me free.' 'Certes, Merlin,' replied Sir Gawain, 'of that I am right sorrowful, and so will King Arthur, my uncle, be, when he shall know it, as one who is making search after you throughout all countries.' 'Well,' said Merlin, 'it must be borne, for never will he see me, nor I him; neither will any one speak with me again after you, it would be vain to attempt it; for you yourself, when you have turned away, will never be able to find the place: but salute for me the king and the queen and all the barons, and tell them of my condition. You will find the king at Carduel in Wales; and when you arrive there you will find there all the companions who departed with you, and who at this day will return. Now then go in the name of God, who will protect and save the King Arthur, and the realm of Logres, and you also, as the best knights who are in the world.' With that Sir Gawain departed joyful and sorrowful; joyful because of what Merlin had assured him should happen to him, and sorrowful that Merlin had thus been lost.

*Morals.*—We are sometimes apprised that there is a mental power and creation more excellent than anything which is commonly called philosophy and literature; that the high poets, that Homer, Milton, Shakspeare, do not fully content us. How rarely they offer us the heavenly bread! The most they have done is to intoxicate us once and again with its taste. They have touched this heaven and retain afterwards some sparkle of it: they betray their belief that such discourse is possible. There is something—our brothers on this or that side of the sea do not know it or own it; the eminent scholars of England, historians and reviewers, romancers and poets included, might deny and blaspheme it,—which is setting us and them aside and the whole world also, and planting itself. To true poetry we shall sit down as the result and justification of the age in which it appears, and think lightly of histories and statutes. None of your parlor or piano verse, none of your carpet poets, who are content to amuse, will satisfy us. Power, new power, is the good which the soul seeks. The poetic gift we want, as the health and supremacy of man,—not rhymes and sonneteering, not bookmaking and bookselling; surely not cold spying and authorship.

Is not poetry the little chamber in the brain where is generated the explosive force which, by gentle shocks, sets in action the intellectual world? Bring us the bards who shall sing all our old ideas out of our heads, and new ones in; men-making poets; poetry which, like the verses inscribed on Balder's columns in Breidablik, is capable of restoring the dead to life;—poetry like that verse of Saadi, which the angels testified "met the approbation of Allah in Heaven;"—poetry which finds its rhymes and cadences in the rhymes and iterations of nature, and is the gift to men of new images and symbols, each the ensign and oracle of an age; that shall assimilate men to it, mould itself into religions and mythologies, and impart its quality to centuries;—poetry which tastes the world and reports of it, upbuilding the world again in the thought;

> Not with tickling rhymes,
> But high and noble matter, such as flies
> From brains entranced, and filled with ecstasies.

Poetry must be affirmative. It is the piety of the intellect. "Thus saith the Lord," should begin the song. The poet who shall use nature as his hieroglyphic must have an adequate message to convey thereby. Therefore when we speak of the Poet in a high sense, we are driven to such examples as Zoroaster and Plato, St. John and Menu, with their moral burdens. The Muse shall be the counterpart of Nature, and equally rich. I find her not often in books. We know Nature and figure her exuberant, tranquil, magnificent in her fertility, coherent; so that every creation is omen of every other. She is not proud of the sea, of the stars, of space or time, or man or woman. All her kinds share the attributes of the selectest extremes. But in current literature I do not find her. Literature warps away from life, though at first it seems to bind it. In the world of letters how few commanding oracles! Homer did what he could; Pindar, Æschylus, and the Greek Gnomic poets and the tragedians. Dante was faithful when not carried away by his fierce hatreds. But in so many alcoves of English poetry I can count only nine or ten authors who are still inspirers and lawgivers to their race.

The supreme value of poetry is to educate us to a height beyond itself, or which it rarely reaches;—the subduing mankind to order and virtue. He is the true Orpheus who writes his ode, not with syllables, but men. "In poetry," said Goethe, "only the really great and pure advances us, and this exists as a second nature, either elevating us to itself, or rejecting us." The poet must let Humanity sit with the Muse in his head, as the charioteer sits with the hero in the Iliad. "Show me," said Sarona in the novel, "one wicked man who has written poetry, and I will show you where his poetry is not poetry; or rather, I will show you in his poetry no poetry at all."

I have heard that there is a hope which precedes and must precede all science of the visible or the invisible world; and that science is the realization of that hope in either region. I count the genius of Swedenborg and Wordsworth as the agents of a reform in philosophy, the bringing poetry back to nature,—to the marrying of nature and mind, undoing the old divorce in which poetry had been famished and false, and nature had been suspected and pagan. The philosophy which a nation receives, rules its religion, poetry, politics, arts, trades, and whole history. A good poem—say Shakspeare's Macbeth, or Hamlet, or the Tempest—goes about the world offering itself to reasonable men, who read it with joy and carry it to their reasonable neighbors. Thus it draws to it the wise and generous souls, confirming their secret thoughts, and, through their sympathy, really publishing itself. It affects the characters of its readers by formulating their opinions and feelings, and inevitably prompting their daily action. If they build ships, they write "Ariel" or "Prospero" or "Ophelia" on the ship's stern, and impart a tenderness and mystery to matters of fact. The ballad and romance work on the hearts of boys, who recite the rhymes to their hoops or their skates if alone, and these heroic songs or lines are remembered and determine many practical choices which they make later. Do you think Burns has had no influence on the life of men and women in Scotland,—has opened no eyes and ears to the face of nature and the dignity of man and the charm and excellence of woman?

We are a little civil, it must be owned, to Homer and Æschylus, to Dante and Shakspeare, and give them the benefit of the largest interpretation. We must be a little strict also, and ask whether, if we sit down at home, and do not go to Hamlet, Hamlet will come to us? whether we shall find our tragedy written in his,—our hopes, wants, pains, disgraces, described to the life,—and the way opened to the paradise which ever in the best hour beckons us? But our overpraise and idealization of famous masters is not in its origin a poor Boswellism, but an impatience of mediocrity. The praise we now give to our heroes we shall unsay when we make larger demands. How fast we outgrow the books of the nursery,—then those that satisfied our youth. What we once admired as poetry has long since come to be a sound of tin pans; and many of our later books we have outgrown. Perhaps Homer and Milton will be tin pans yet. Better not to be easily pleased. The poet should rejoice if he has taught us to despise his song; if he has so moved us as to lift us,—to open the eye of the intellect to see farther and better.

In proportion as a man's life comes into union with truth, his thoughts approach to a parallelism with the currents of natural laws, so that he easily expresses his meaning by natural symbols, or uses the ecstatic or poetic speech. By successive states of mind all the facts of nature are for the first time interpreted. In proportion as his life departs from this simplicity, he uses circumlocution,—by many words hoping to suggest what he cannot say. Vexatious to find poets, who are by excellence the thinking and feeling of the world, deficient in truth of intellect and of affection. Then is conscience unfaithful, and thought unwise. To know the merit of Shakspeare, read Faust. I find Faust a little too modern and intelligible. We can find such a fabric at several mills, though a little inferior. Faust abounds in the disagreeable. The vice is prurient, learned, Parisian. In the presence of Jove, Priapus may be allowed as an offset, but here he is an equal hero. The egotism, the wit, is calculated. The book is undeniably written by a master, and stands unhappily related to the whole modern world; but it is a very disagreeable chapter of literature, and accuses the author as well as the times. Shakspeare could no doubt have been disagreeable, had he less genius, and if ugliness had attracted him. In short, our English nature and genius has made us the worst critics of Goethe,

> We, who speak the tongue
> That Shakspeare spake, the faith and manners hold
> Which Milton held.

It is not style or rhymes, or a new image more or less that imports, but sanity; that life should not be mean; that life should be an image in every part beautiful; that the old forgotten splendors of the universe should glow again for us;—that we should lose our wit, but gain our reason. And when life is true to the poles of nature, the streams of truth will roll through us in song.

*Transcendency.*—In a cotillion some persons dance and others await their turn when the music and the figure come to them. In the dance of God there is not one of the chorus but can and will begin to spin, monumental as he now looks, whenever the music and figure reach his place and duty. O celestial Bacchus! drive them mad,—this multitude of vagabonds, hungry for eloquence, hungry for poetry, starving for symbols, perishing for want of electricity to vitalize this too much pasture, and in the long delay indemnifying themselves with the false wine of alcohol, of politics, or of money.

Every man may be, and at some time a man is, lifted to a platform whence he looks beyond sense to moral and spiritual truth, and in that mood deals sovereignly with matter, and strings worlds like beads upon his thought. The success with which this is done can alone determine how genuine is the inspiration. The poet is rare because he must be exquisitely vital and sympathetic, and, at the same time, immovably centred. In good society, nay, among the angels in heaven, is not everything spoken in fine parable, and not so servilely as it befell to the sense? All is symbolized. Facts are not foreign, as they seem, but related. Wait a little and we see the return of the remote hyperbolic curve. The solid men complain that the idealist leaves out the fundamental facts; the poet complains that the solid men leave out the sky. To every plant there are two powers; one shoots down as rootlet, and one upward as tree. You must have eyes of science to see in the seed its nodes; you must have the vivacity of the poet to perceive in the thought its futurities. The poet is representative,—whole man, diamond-merchant, symbolizer, emancipator; in him the world projects a scribe's hand and writes the adequate genesis. The nature of things is flowing, a metamorphosis. The free spirit sympathizes not only with the actual form, but with the power or possible forms; but for obvious municipal or parietal uses God has given us a bias or a rest on to-day's forms. Hence the shudder of joy with which in each clear moment we recognize the metamorphosis, because it is always a conquest, a surprise from the heart of things. One would say of the force in the works of nature, all depends on the battery. If it give one shock, we shall get to the fish form, and stop; if two shocks, to the bird; if three, to the quadruped; if four, to the man. Power of generalizing differences men. The number of successive saltations the nimble thought can make, measures the difference between the highest and lowest of mankind. The habit of saliency, of not pausing but going on, is a sort of importation or domestication of the Divine effort in a man. After the largest circle has been drawn, a larger can be drawn around it. The problem of the poet is to unite freedom with precision; to give the pleasure of color, and be not less the most powerful of sculptors. Music seems to you sufficient, or the subtle and delicate scent of lavender; but Dante was free imagination,—all wings,—yet he wrote like Euclid. And mark the equality of Shakspeare to the comic, the tender and sweet, and to the grand and terrible. A little more or less skill in whistling is of no account. See those weary pentameter tales of Dryden and others. Turnpike is one thing and blue sky another. Let the poet, of all men, stop with his inspiration. The inexorable rule in the muses' court, *either inspiration or silence,* compels the bard to report only his supreme moments. It teaches the enormous force of a few words, and in proportion to the inspiration checks loquacity. Much that we call poetry is but polite verse. The high poetry which shall thrill and agitate mankind, restore youth and health, dissipate the dreams under which men reel and stagger, and bring in the new thoughts, the sanity and heroic aims of nations, is deeper hid and longer postponed than was America or Australia, or the finding of steam or of the galvanic battery. We must not conclude against poetry from the defects of poets. They are, in our experience, men of every degree of skill,—some of them only once or twice receivers of an inspiration, and presently falling back on a low life. The drop of *ichor* that tingles in their veins has not yet refined their blood and cannot lift the whole man to the digestion and function of ichor,—that is, to godlike nature. Time will be when ichor shall be their blood, when what are now glimpses and aspirations shall be the routine of the day. Yet even partial ascents to poetry and ideas are forerunners, and announce the dawn. In the mire of the sensual life, their religion, their poets, their admiration of heroes and benefactors, even their novel and newspaper, nay, their superstitions also, are hosts of ideals,—a cordage of ropes that hold them up out of the slough. Poetry is inestimable as a lonely faith, a lonely protest in the uproar of atheism.

But so many men are ill-born or ill-bred,—the brains are so marred, so imperfectly formed, unheroically, brains of the sons of fallen men, that the doctrine is imperfectly received. One man sees a spark or shimmer of the truth and reports it, and his saying becomes a legend or golden proverb for ages, and other men report as much, but none wholly and well. Poems!—we have no poem. Whenever that angel shall be organized and appear on earth, the Iliad will be reckoned a poor ballad-grinding. I doubt never the riches of nature, the gifts of the future, the immense wealth of the mind. O yes, poets we shall have, mythology, symbols, religion, of our own. We too shall know how to take up all this industry and empire, this Western civilization, into thought, as easily as men did when arts were few; but not by holding it high, but by holding it low. The intellect uses and is not used,—uses London and Paris and Berlin, East and West, to its end. The only heart that can help us is one that draws, not from our society, but from itself, a counterpoise to society. What if we find partiality and meanness in us? The grandeur of our life exists in spite of us,—all over and under and within us, in what of us is inevitable and above our control. Men are facts as well as persons, and the involuntary part of their life is so much as to fill the mind and leave them no countenance to say aught of what is so trivial as their selfish thinking and doing. Sooner or later that which is now life shall be poetry, and every fair and manly trait shall add a richer strain to the song.

# Quotation and Originality

Whoever looks at the insect world, at flies, aphides, gnats and innumerable parasites, and even at the infant mammals, must have remarked the extreme content they take in suction, which constitutes the main business of their life. If we go into a library or newsroom, we see the same function on a higher plane, performed with like ardor, with equal impatience of interruption, indicating the sweetness of the act. In the highest civilization the book is still the highest delight. He who has once known its satisfactions is provided with a resource against calamity. Like Plato's disciple who has perceived a truth, "he is preserved from harm until another period." In every man's memory, with the hours when life culminated are usually associated certain books which met his views. Of a large and powerful class we might ask with confidence, What is the event they most desire? what gift? What but the book that shall come, which they have sought through all libraries, through all languages, that shall be to their mature eyes what many a tinsel-covered toy pamphlet was to their childhood, and shall speak to the imagination? Our high respect for a well-read man is praise enough of literature. If we encountered a man of rare intellect, we should ask him what books he read. We expect a great man to be a good reader; or in proportion to the spontaneous power should be the assimilating power. And though such are a more difficult and exacting class, they are not less eager. "He that borrows the aid of an equal understanding," said Burke, "doubles his own; he that uses that of a superior elevates his own to the stature of that he contemplates."

We prize books, and they prize them most who are themselves wise. Our debt to tradition through reading and conversation is so massive, our protest or private addition so rare and insignificant,—and this commonly on the ground of other reading or hearing,—that, in a large sense, one would say there is no pure originality. All minds quote. Old and new make the warp and woof of every moment. There is no thread that is not a twist of these two strands. By necessity, by proclivity and by delight, we all quote. We quote not only books and proverbs, but arts, sciences, religion, customs and laws; nay, we quote temples and houses, tables and chairs by imitation. The Patent-Office Commissioner knows that all machines in use have been invented and re-invented over and over; that the mariner's compass, the boat, the pendulum, glass, movable types, the kaleidoscope, the railway, the power-loom, etc., have been many times found and lost, from Egypt, China and Pompeii down; and if we have arts which Rome wanted, so also Rome had arts which we have lost; that the invention of yesterday of making wood indestructible by means of vapor of coal-oil or paraffine was suggested by the Egyptian method which has preserved its mummy-cases four thousand years.

The highest statement of new philosophy complacently caps itself with some prophetic maxim from the oldest learning. There is something mortifying in this perpetual circle. This extreme economy argues a very small capital of invention. The stream of affection flows broad and strong; the practical activity is a river of supply; but the dearth of design accuses the penury of intellect. How few thoughts! In a hundred years, millions of men and not a hundred lines of poetry, not a theory of philosophy that offers a solution of the great problems, not an art of education that fulfils the conditions. In this delay and vacancy of thought we must make the best amends we can by seeking the wisdom of others to fill the time.

If we confine ourselves to literature, 't is easy to see that the debt is immense to past thought. None escapes it. The originals are not original. There is imitation, model and suggestion, to the very archangels, if we knew their history. The first book tyrannizes over the second. Read Tasso, and you think of Virgil; read Virgil, and you think of Homer; and Milton forces you to reflect how narrow are the limits of human invention. The Paradise Lost had never existed but for these precursors; and if we find in India or Arabia a book out of our horizon of thought and tradition, we are soon taught by new researches in its native country to discover its foregoers, and its latent, but real connection with our own Bibles.

Read in Plato and you shall find Christian dogmas, and not only so, but stumble on our evangelical phrases. Hegel preëxists in Proclus, and, long before, in Heraclitus and Parmenides. Whoso knows Plutarch, Lucian, Rabelais, Montaigne and Bayle will have a key to many supposed originalities. Rabelais is the source of many a proverb, story and jest, derived from him into all modern languages; and if we knew Rabelais's reading we should see the rill of the Rabelais river. Swedenborg, Behmen, Spinoza, will appear original to uninstructed and to thoughtless persons: their originality will disappear to such as are either well read or thoughtful; for scholars will recognize their dogmas as reappearing in men of a similar intellectual elevation throughout history. Albert, the "wonderful doctor," St. Buonaventura, the "seraphic doctor," Thomas Aquinas, the "angelic doctor" of the thirteenth century, whose books made the sufficient culture of these ages, Dante absorbed, and he survives for us. Renard the Fox, a German poem of the thirteenth century, was long supposed to be the original work, until Grimm found fragments of another original a century older. M. Le Grand showed that in the old Fabliaux were the originals of the tales of Molière, La Fontaine, Boccaccio, and of Voltaire.

Mythology is no man's work; but, what we daily observe in regard to the *bon-mots* that circulate in society,—that every talker helps a story in repeating it, until, at last, from the slenderest filament of fact a good fable is constructed,—the same growth befalls mythology: the legend is tossed from believer to poet, from poet to believer, everybody adding a grace or dropping a fault or rounding the form, until it gets an ideal truth.

Religious literature, the psalms and liturgies of churches, are of course of this slow growth,—a fagot of selections gathered through ages, leaving the worse and saving the better, until it is at last the work of the whole communion of worshippers. The Bible itself is like an old Cremona; it has been played upon by the devotion of thousands of years until every word and particle is public and tunable. And whatever undue reverence may have been claimed for it by the prestige of philonic inspiration, the stronger tendency we are describing is likely to undo. What divines had assumed as the distinctive revelations of Christianity, theologic criticism has matched by exact parallelisms from the Stoics and poets of Greece and Rome. Later, when Confucius and the Indian scriptures were made known, no claim to monopoly of ethical wisdom could be thought of; and the surprising results of the new researches into the history of Egypt have opened to us the deep debt of the churches of Rome and England to the Egyptian hierology.

The borrowing is often honest enough, and comes of magnanimity and stoutness. A great man quotes bravely, and will not draw on his invention when his memory serves him with a word as good. What he quotes, he fills with his own voice and humor, and the whole cyclopædia of his table-talk is presently believed to be his own. Thirty years ago, when Mr. Webster at the bar or in the Senate filled the eyes and minds of young men, you might often hear cited as Mr. Webster's three rules: first, never to do to-day what he could defer till to-morrow; secondly, never to do himself what he could make another do for him; and, thirdly, never to pay any debt to-day. Well, they are none the worse for being already told, in the last generation, of Sheridan; and we find in Grimm's Mémoires that Sheridan got them from the witty D'Argenson; who, no doubt, if we could consult him, could tell of whom he first heard them told. In our own college days we remember hearing other pieces of Mr. Webster's advice to students,—among others, this: that, when he opened a new book, he turned to the table of contents, took a pen, and sketched a sheet of matters and topics, what he knew and what he thought, before he read the book. But we find in Southey's Commonplace Book this said of the Earl of Strafford: "I learned one rule of him," says Sir G. Radcliffe, "which I think worthy to be remembered. When he met with a well-penned oration or tract upon any subject, he framed a speech upon the same argument, inventing and disposing what seemed fit to be said upon that subject, before he read the book; then, reading, compared his own with the author's, and noted his own defects and the author's art and fulness; whereby he drew all that ran in the author more strictly, and might better judge of his own wants to supply them." I remember to have heard Mr. Samuel Rogers, in London, relate, among other anecdotes of the Duke of Wellington, that a lady having expressed in his presence a passionate wish to witness a great victory, he replied: "Madam, there is nothing so dreadful as a great victory,—excepting a great defeat." But this speech is also D'Argenson's, and is reported by Grimm. So the sarcasm attributed to Baron Alderson upon Brougham, "What a wonderful versatile mind has Brougham! he knows politics, Greek, history, science; if he only knew a little of law, he would know a little of everything." You may find the original of this gibe in Grimm, who says that Louis XVI., going out of chapel after hearing a sermon from the Abbé Maury, said, "*Si l' Abbé nous avait parlé un peu de religion, il nous aurait parlé de tout.*" A pleasantry which ran through all the newspapers a few years since, taxing the eccentricities of a gifted family connection in New England, was only a theft of Lady Mary

Wortley Montagu's *mot* of a hundred years ago, that "the world was made up of men and women and Hcrvcys."

Many of the historical proverbs have a doubtful paternity. Columbus's egg is claimed for Brunelleschi. Rabelais's dying words, "I am going to see the great Perhaps" *(le grand Peutêtre),* only repeats the "IF" inscribed on the portal of the temple at Delphi. Goethe's favorite phrase, "the open secret," translates Aristotle's answer to Alexander, "These books are published and not published." Madame de Staël's "Architecture is frozen music" is borrowed from Goethe's "dumb music," which is Vitruvius's rule, that "the architect must not only understand drawing, but music." Wordsworth's hero acting "on the plan which pleased his childish thought," is Schiller's "Tell him to reverence the dreams of his youth," and earlier, Bacon's *"Consilia juventutis plus divinitatis habent."*

In romantic literature examples of this vamping abound. The fine verse in the old Scotch ballad of The Drowned Lovers—

> Thou art roaring ower loud, Clyde water,
>   Thy streams are ower strang;
> Make me thy wrack when I come back,
>   But spare me when I gang—

is a translation of Martial's epigram on Hero and Leander, where the prayer of Leander is the same:

> Parcite dum propero, mergite dum redeo.

Hafiz furnished Burns with the song of John Barleycorn, and furnished Moore with the original of the piece,

> When in death I shall calm recline,
> Oh, bear my heart to my mistress dear,

There are many fables which, as they are found in every language, and betray no sign of being borrowed, are said to be agreeable to the human mind. Such are The Seven Sleepers, Gyges's Ring, The Travelling Cloak, The Wandering Jew, The Pied Piper, Jack and his Beanstalk, the Lady Diving in the Lake and Rising in the Cave,—whose omnipresence only indicates how easily a good story crosses all frontiers. The popular incident of Baron Munchausen, who hung his bugle up by the kitchen fire and the frozen tune thawed out, is found in Greece in Plato's time. Antiphanes, one of Plato's friends, laughingly compared his writings to a city where the words froze in the air as soon as they were pronounced, and the next summer, when they were warmed and melted by the sun, the people heard what had been spoken in the winter. It is only within this century that England and America discovered that their nursery-tales were old German and Scandinavian stories; and now it appears that they came from India, and are the property of all the nations descended from the Aryan race, and have been warbled and babbled between nurses and children for unknown thousands of years.

If we observe the tenacity with which nations cling to their first types of costume, of architecture, of tools and methods in tillage, and of decoration,—if we learn how old are the patterns of our shawls, the capitals of our columns, the fret, the beads, and other ornaments on our walls, the alternate lotus-bud and leaf-stem of our iron fences,—we shall think very well of the first men, or ill of the latest.

Now shall we say that only the first men were well alive, and the existing generation is invalided and degenerate? Is all literature eaves-dropping, and all art Chinese imitation? our life a custom, and our body borrowed, like a beggar's dinner, from a hundred charities? A more subtle and severe criticism might suggest that some dislocation has befallen the race; that men are off their centre; that multitudes of men do not live with Nature, but behold it as exiles. People go out to look at sunrises and sunsets who do not recognize their own, quietly and happily, but know that it is foreign to them. As they do by books, so they *quote* the sunset and the star, and do not make them theirs. Worse yet, they live as foreigners in the world of truth, and quote thoughts, and thus disown them. Quotation confesses inferiority. In opening a new book we often discover, from the unguarded devotion with which the writer gives his motto or text, all we have to expect from him. If Lord Bacon appears already in the preface, I go and read the Instauration instead of the new book.

The mischief is quickly punished in general and in particular. Admirable mimics have nothing of their own. In every kind of parasite, when Nature has finished an aphis, a teredo or a vampire bat,—an excellent sucking-pipe to tap another animal, or a mistletoe or dodder among plants,—the self-supplying organs wither and dwindle, as being superfluous. In common prudence there is an early limit to this leaning on an original. In literature, quotation is good only when the writer whom I follow goes my way, and, being better mounted than I, gives me a cast, as we say; but if I like the gay equipage so well as to go out of my road, I had better have gone afoot.

But it is necessary to remember there are certain considerations which go far to qualify a reproach too grave. This vast mental indebtedness has every variety that pecuniary debt has,—every variety of merit. The capitalist of either kind is as hungry to lend as the consumer to borrow; and the transaction no more indicates intellectual turpitude in the borrower than the simple fact of debt involves bankruptcy. On the contrary, in far the greater number of cases the transaction is honorable to both. Can we not help ourselves as discreetly by the force of two in literature? Certainly it only needs two well placed and well tempered for coöperation, to get somewhat far transcending any private enterprise! Shall we converse as spies? Our very abstaining to repeat and credit the fine remark of our friend is thievish. Each man of thought is surrounded by wiser men than he, if they cannot write as well. Cannot he and they combine? Cannot they sink their jealousies in God's love, and call their poem Beaumont and Fletcher, or the Theban Phalanx's? The city will for nine days or nine years make differences and sinister comparisons: there is a new and more excellent public that will bless the friends. Nay, it is an inevitable fruit of our social nature. The child quotes his father, and the man quotes his friend.

Each man is a hero and an oracle to somebody, and to that person whatever he says has an enhanced value. Whatever we think and say is wonderfully better for our spirits and trust, in another mouth. There is none so eminent and wise but he knows minds whose opinion confirms or qualifies his own, and men of extraordinary genius acquire an almost absolute ascendant over their nearest companions. The Comte de Crillon said one day to M. d'Allonville, with French vivacity, "If the universe and I professed one opinion and M. Necker expressed a contrary one, I should be at once convinced that the universe and I were mistaken."

Original power is usually accompanied with assimilating power, and we value in Coleridge his excellent knowledge and quotations perhaps as much, possibly more, than his original suggestions. If an author give us just distinctions, inspiring lessons, or imaginative poetry, it is not so important to us whose they are. If we are fired and guided by these, we know him as a benefactor, and shall return to him as long as he serves us so well. We may like well to know what is Plato's and what is Montesquieu's or Goethe's part, and what thought was always dear to the writer himself; but the worth of the sentences consists in their radiancy and equal aptitude to all intelligence. They fit all our facts like a charm. We respect ourselves the more that we know them.

Next to the originator of a good sentence is the first quoter of it. Many will read the book before one thinks of quoting a passage. As soon as he has done this, that line will be quoted east and west. Then there are great ways of borrowing. Genius borrows nobly. When Shakspeare is charged with debts to his authors, Landor replies: "Yet he was more original than his originals. He breathed upon dead bodies and brought them into life." And we must thank Karl Ottfried Müller for the just remark, "Poesy, drawing within its circle all that is glorious and inspiring, gave itself but little concern as to where its flowers originally grew." So Voltaire usually imitated, but with such superiority that Dubuc said: "He is like the false Amphitryon; although the stranger, it is always he who has the air of being master of the house." Wordsworth, as soon as he heard a good thing, caught it up, meditated upon it, and very soon reproduced it in his conversation and writing. If De Quincey said, "That is what I told you," he replied, "No: that is mine,—mine, and not yours." On the whole we like the valor of it. 'T is on Marmontel's principle, "I pounce on what is mine, wherever I find it;" and on Bacon's broader rule, "I take all knowledge to be my province." It betrays the consciousness that truth is the property of no individual, but is the treasure of all men. And inasmuch as any writer has ascended to a just view of man's condition, he has adopted this tone. In so far as the receiver's aim is on life, and not on literature, will be his indifference to the source. The nobler the truth or sentiment, the less imports the question of authorship. It never troubles the simple seeker from whom he derived such or such a sentiment. Whoever expresses to us a just thought makes ridiculous the pains of the critic who should tell him where such a word had been said before. "It is no more according to Plato than according to me." Truth is always present: it only needs to lift the iron lids of the mind's eye to read its oracles.

But the moment there is the purpose of display, the fraud is exposed. In fact, it is as difficult to appropriate the thoughts of others, as it is to invent. Always some steep transition, some sudden alteration of temperature, or of point of view, betrays the foreign interpolation.

There is, besides, a new charm in such intellectual works as, passing through long time, have had a multitude of authors and improvers. We admire that poetry which no man wrote,—no poet less than the genius of humanity itself,—which is to be read in a mythology, in the effect of a fixed or national style of pictures, of sculptures, or drama, or cities, or sciences, on us. Such a poem also is language. Every word in the language has once been used happily. The ear, caught by that felicity, retains it, and it is used again and again, as if the charm belonged to the word and not to the life of thought which so enforced it. These profane uses, of course, kill it, and it is avoided. But a quick wit can at any time reinforce it, and it comes into vogue again. Then people quote so differently: one finding only what is gaudy and popular; another, the heart of the author, the report of his select and happiest hour; and the reader sometimes giving more to the citation than he owes to it. Most of the classical citations you shall hear or read in the current journals or speeches were not drawn from the originals, but from previous quotations in English books; and you can easily pronounce, from the use and relevancy of the sentence, whether it had not done duty many times before,—whether your jewel was got from the mine or from an auctioneer. We are as much informed of a writer's genius by what he selects as by what he originates. We read the quotation with his eyes, and find a new and fervent sense; as a passage from one of the poets, well recited, borrows new interest from the rendering. As the journals say, "the italics are ours." The profit of books is according to the sensibility of the reader. The profoundest thought or passion sleeps as in a mine until an equal mind and heart finds and publishes it. The passages of Shakspeare that we most prize were never quoted until within this century; and Milton's prose, and Burke, even, have their best fame within it. Every one, too, remembers his friends by their favorite poetry or other reading.

Observe also that a writer appears to more advantage in the pages of another book than in his own. In his own he waits as a candidate for your approbation; in another's he is a lawgiver.

Then another's thoughts have a certain advantage with us simply because they are another's. There is an illusion in a new phrase. A man hears a fine sentence out of Swedenborg, and wonders at the wisdom, and is very merry at heart that he has now got so fine a thing. Translate it out of the new words into his own usual phrase, and he will wonder again at his own simplicity, such tricks do fine words play with us.

It is curious what new interest an old author acquires by official canonization in Tiraboschi, or Dr. Johnson, or Von Hammer-Purgstall, or Hallam, or other historian of literature. Their registration of his book, or citation of a passage, carries the sentimental value of a college diploma. Hallam, though never profound, is a fair mind, able to appreciate poetry unless it becomes deep, being always blind and deaf to imaginative and analogy-loving souls, like the Platonists, like Giordano Bruno, like Donne, Herbert, Crashaw and Vaughan; and Hallam cites a sentence from Bacon or Sidney, and distinguishes a lyric of Edwards or Vaux, and straightway it commends itself to us as if it had received the Isthmian crown.

It is a familiar expedient of brilliant writers, and not less of witty talkers, the device of ascribing their own sentence to an imaginary person, in order to give it weight,—as Cicero, Cowley, Swift, Landor and Carlyle have done. And Cardinal de Retz, at a critical moment in the Parliament of Paris, described himself in an extemporary Latin sentence, which he pretended to quote from a classic author, and which told admirably well. It is a curious reflex effect of this enhancement of our thought by citing it from another, that many men can write better under a mask than for themselves; as Chatterton in archaic ballad, Le Sage in Spanish costume, Macpherson as "Ossian"; and, I doubt not, many a young barrister in chambers in London, who forges good thunder for the Times, but never works as well under his own name. This is a sort of dramatizing talent; it is not rare to find great powers of recitation, without the least original eloquence,—or people who copy drawings with admirable skill, but are incapable of any design.

In hours of high mental activity we sometimes do the book too much honor, reading out of it better things than the author wrote,—reading, as we say, between the lines. You have had the like experience in conversation: the wit was in what you heard, not in what the speakers said. Our best thought came from others. We heard in their words a deeper sense than the speakers put into them, and could express ourselves in other people's phrases to finer purpose than they knew. In Moore's Diary, Mr. Hallam is reported as mentioning at dinner one of his friends who had said, "I don't know how it is, a thing that falls flat from me seems quite an excellent joke when given at second hand by Sheridan. I never like my own *bon-mots* until he adopts them." Dumas was exalted by being used by Mirabeau, by Bingham and by Sir Philip Francis, who, again, was less than his own "Junius"; and James Hogg (except in his poems Kilmeny and The Witch of Fife) is but a third-rate author, owing his fame to his effigy colossalized through the lens of John Wilson,—who, again, writes better under the domino of "Christopher North" than in his proper clothes. The bold theory of Delia Bacon, that Shakspeare's plays were written by a society of wits,—by Sir Walter Raleigh, Lord Bacon and others around the Earl of Southampton,—had plainly for her the charm of the superior meaning they would acquire when read under this light; this idea of the authorship controlling our appreciation of the works themselves. We once knew a man overjoyed at the notice of his pamphlet in a leading newspaper. What range he gave his imagination! Who could have written it? Was it not Colonel Carbine, or Senator Tonitrus, or, at the least, Professor Maximilian? Yes, he could detect in the style that fine Roman hand. How it seemed the very voice of the refined and discerning public, inviting merit at last to consent to fame, and come up and take place in the reserved and authentic chairs! He carried the journal with haste to the sympathizing Cousin Matilda, who is so proud of all we do. But what dismay when the good Matilda, pleased with his pleasure, confessed she had written the criticism, and carried it with her own hands to the post-office! "Mr. Wordsworth," said Charles Lamb, "allow me to introduce to you my only admirer."

Swedenborg threw a formidable theory into the world, that every soul existed in a society of souls, from which all its thoughts passed into it, as the blood of the mother circulates in her unborn child; and he noticed that, when in his bed, alternately sleeping and waking,—sleeping, he was surrounded by persons disputing and offering opinions on the one side and on the other side of a proposition; waking, the like suggestions occurred for and against the proposition as his own thoughts; sleeping again, he saw and heard the speakers as before: and this as often as he slept or waked. And if we expand the image, does it not look as if we men were thinking and talking out of an enormous antiquity, as if we stood, not in a coterie of prompters that filled a sitting-room, but in a circle of intelligences that reached through all thinkers, poets, inventors and wits, men and women, English, German, Celt, Aryan, Ninevite, Copt,—back to the first geometer, bard, mason, carpenter, planter, shepherd,—back to the first negro, who, with more health or better perception, gave a shriller sound or name for the thing he saw and dealt with? Our benefactors are as many as the children who invented speech, word by word. Language is a city to the building of which every human being brought a stone; yet he is no more to be credited with the grand result than the acaleph which adds a cell to the coral reef which is the basis of the continent.

Πάντα ῥεῖ: all things are in flux. It is inevitable that you are indebted to the past. You are fed and formed by it. The old forest is decomposed for the composition of the new forest. The old animals have given their bodies to the earth to furnish through chemistry the forming race, and every individual is only a momentary fixation of what was yesterday another's, is to-day his and will belong to a third to-morrow. So it is in thought. Our knowledge is the amassed thought and experience of innumerable minds: our language, our science, our religion, our opinions, our fancies we inherited. Our country, customs, laws, our ambitions, and our notions of fit and fair,—all these we never made, we found them ready-made; we but quote them. Goethe frankly said, "What would remain to me if this art of appropriation were derogatory to genius? Every one of my writings has been furnished to me by a thousand different persons, a thousand things: wise and foolish have brought me, without suspecting it, the offering of their thoughts, faculties and experience. My work is an aggregation of beings taken from the whole of Nature; it bears the name of Goethe."

But there remains the indefeasible persistency of the individual to be himself. One leaf, one blade of grass, one meridian, does not resemble another. Every mind is different; and the more it is unfolded, the more pronounced is that difference. He must draw the elements into him for food, and, if they be granite and silex, will prefer them cooked by sun and rain, by time and art, to his hand. But, however received, these elements pass into the substance of his constitution, will be assimilated, and tend always to form, not a partisan, but a possessor of truth. To all that can be said of the preponderance of the Past, the single word Genius is a sufficient reply. The divine resides in the new. The divine never quotes, but is, and creates. The profound apprehension of the Present is Genius, which makes the Past forgotten. Genius believes its faintest presentiment against the testimony of all history; for it knows that facts are not ultimates, but that a state of mind is the ancestor of everything. And what is Originality? It is being, being one's self, and reporting accurately what we see and are. Genius is in the first instance, sensibility, the capacity of receiving just impressions from the external world, and the power of coördinating these after the laws of thought. It implies Will, or original force, for their right distribution and expression. If to this the sentiment of piety be added, if the thinker feels that the thought most strictly his own is not his own, and recognizes the perpetual suggestion of the Supreme Intellect, the oldest thoughts become new and fertile whilst he speaks them.

Originals never lose their value. There is always in them a style and weight of speech which the immanence of the oracle bestowed, and which cannot be counterfeited. Hence the permanence of the high poets. Plato, Cicero and Plutarch cite the poets in the manner in which Scripture is quoted in our churches. A phrase or a single word is adduced, with honoring emphasis, from Pindar, Hesiod or Euripides, as precluding all argument, because thus had they said: importing that the bard spoke not his own, but the words of some god. True poets have always ascended to this lofty platform, and met this expectation. Shakspeare, Milton, Wordsworth, were very conscious of their responsibilities. When a man thinks happily, he finds no foot-track in the field he traverses. All spontaneous thought is irrespective of all else. Pindar uses this haughty defiance, as if it were impossible to find his sources: "There are many swift darts within my quiver, which have a voice for those with understanding; but to the crowd they need interpreters. He is gifted with genius who knoweth much by natural talent."

Our pleasure in seeing each mind take the subject to which it has a proper right is seen in mere fitness in time. He that comes second must needs quote him that comes first. The earliest describers of savage life, as Captain Cook's account of the Society Islands, or Alexander Henry's travels among our Indian tribes, have a charm of truth and just point of view. Landsmen and sailors freshly come from the most civilized countries, and with no false expectation, no sentimentality yet about wild life, healthily receive and report what they saw,—seeing what they must, and using no choice; and no man suspects the superior merit of the description, until Châteaubriand, or Moore, or Campbell, or Byron, or the artists, arrive, and mix so much art with their picture that the incomparable advantage of the first narrative appears. For the same reason we dislike that the poet should choose an antique or far-fetched subject for his muse, as if he avowed want of insight. The great deal always with the nearest. Only as braveries of too prodigal power can we pardon it, when the life of genius is so redundant that out of petulance it flings its fire into some old mummy, and, lo! it walks and blushes again here in the street.

We cannot overstate our debt to the Past, but the moment has the supreme claim. The Past is for us; but the sole terms on which it can become ours are its subordination to the Present. Only an inventor knows how to borrow, and every man is or should be an inventor. We must not tamper with the organic motion of the soul. 'Tis certain that thought has its own proper motion, and the hints which flash from it, the words overheard at unawares by the free mind, are trustworthy and fertile when obeyed and not perverted to low and selfish account. This vast memory is only raw material. The divine gift is ever the instant life, which receives and uses and creates, and can well bury the old in the omnipotency with which Nature decomposes all her harvest for recomposition.

# The Poet

A moody child and wildly wise
Pursued the game with joyful eyes,
Which chose, like meteors, their way,
And rived the dark with private ray:
They overleapt the horizon's edge,
Searched with Apollo's privilege;
Through man, and woman, and sea, and star
Saw the dance of nature forward far;
Through worlds, and races, and terms, and times
Saw musical order, and pairing rhymes.

Olympian bards who sung
  Divine ideas below,
Which always find us young,
  And always keep us so.

Those who are esteemed umpires of taste are often persons who have acquired some knowledge of admired pictures or sculptures, and have an inclination for whatever is elegant; but if you inquire whether they are beautiful souls, and whether their own acts are like fair pictures, you learn that they are selfish and sensual. Their cultivation is local, as if you should rub a log of dry wood in one spot to produce fire, all the rest remaining cold. Their knowledge of the fine arts is some study of rules and particulars, or some limited judgment of color or form, which is exercised for amusement or for show. It is a proof of the shallowness of the doctrine of beauty as it lies in the minds of our amateurs, that men seem to have lost the perception of the instant dependence of form upon soul. There is no doctrine of forms in our philosophy. We were put into our bodies, as fire is put into a pan to be carried about; but there is no accurate adjustment between the spirit and the organ, much less is the latter the germination of the former. So in regard to other forms, the intellectual men do not believe in any essential dependence of the material world on thought and volition. Theologians think it a pretty air-castle to talk of the spiritual meaning of a ship or a cloud, of a city or a contract, but they prefer to come again to the solid ground of historical evidence; and even the poets are contented with a civil and conformed manner of living, and to write poems from the fancy, at a safe distance from their own experience. But the highest minds of the world have never ceased to explore the double meaning, or shall I say the quadruple or the centuple or much more manifold meaning, of every sensuous fact; Orpheus, Empedocles, Heraclitus, Plato, Plutarch, Dante, Swedenborg, and the masters of sculpture, picture and poetry. For we are not pans and barrows, nor even porters of the fire and torch-bearers, but children of the fire, made of it, and only the same divinity transmuted and at two or three removes, when we know least about it. And this hidden truth, that the fountains whence all this river of Time and its creatures floweth are intrinsically ideal and beautiful, draws us to the consideration of the nature and functions of the Poet, or the man of Beauty; to the means and materials he uses, and to the general aspect of the art in the present time.

The breadth of the problem is great, for the poet is representative. He stands among partial men for the complete man, and apprises us not of his wealth, but of the common wealth. The young man reveres men of genius, because, to speak truly, they are more himself than he is. They receive of the soul as he also receives, but they more. Nature enhances her beauty, to the eye of loving men, from their belief that the poet is beholding her shows at the same time. He is isolated among his contemporaries by truth and by his art, but with this consolation in his pursuits, that they will draw all men sooner or later. For all men live by truth and stand in need of expression. In love, in art, in avarice, in politics, in labor, in games, we study to utter our painful secret. The man is only half himself, the other half is his expression.

Notwithstanding this necessity to be published, adequate expression is rare. I know not how it is that we need an interpreter, but the great majority of men seem to be minors, who have not yet come into possession of their own, or mutes, who cannot report the conversation they have had with nature. There is no man who does not anticipate a supersensual utility in the sun and stars, earth and water. These stand and wait to render him a peculiar service. But there is some obstruction or some excess of phlegm in our constitution, which does not suffer them to yield the due effect. Too feeble fall the impressions of nature on us to make us artists. Every touch should thrill. Every man should be so much an artist that he could report in conversation what had befallen him. Yet, in our experience, the rays or appulses have sufficient force to arrive at the senses, but not enough to reach the quick and compel the reproduction of themselves in speech. The poet is the person in whom these powers are in balance, the man without impediment, who sees and handles that which others dream of, traverses the whole scale of experience, and is representative of man, in virtue of being the largest power to receive and to impart.

For the Universe has three children, born at one time, which reappear under different names in every system of thought, whether they be called cause, operation and effect; or, more poetically, Jove, Pluto, Neptune; or, theologically, the Father, the Spirit and the Son; but which we will call here the Knower, the Doer and the Sayer. These stand respectively for the love of truth, for the love of good, and for the love of beauty. These three are equal. Each is that which he is, essentially, so that he cannot be surmounted or analyzed, and each of these three has the power of the others latent in him and his own, patent.

The poet is the sayer, the namer, and represents beauty. He is a sovereign, and stands on the center. For the world is not painted or adorned, but is from the beginning beautiful; and God has not made some beautiful things, but Beauty is the creator of the universe. Therefore the poet is not any permissive potentate, but is emperor in his own right. Criticism is infested with a cant of materialism, which assumes that manual skill and activity is the first merit of all men, and disparages such as say and do not, overlooking the fact that some men, namely poets, are natural sayers, sent into the world to the end of expression, and confounds them with those whose province is action but who quit it to imitate the sayers. But Homer's words are as costly and admirable to Homer as Agamemnon's victories are to Agamemnon. The poet does not wait for the hero or the sage, but, as they act and think primarily, so he writes primarily what will and must be spoken, reckoning the others, though primaries also, yet, in respect to him, secondaries and servants; as sitters or models in the studio of a painter, or as assistants who bring building-materials to an architect.

For poetry was all written before time was, and whenever we are so finely organized that we can penetrate into that region where the air is music, we hear those primal warblings and attempt to write them down, but we lose ever and anon a word or a verse and substitute something of our own, and thus miswrite the poem. The men of more delicate ear write down these cadences more faithfully, and these transcripts, though imperfect, become the songs of the nations. For nature is as truly beautiful as it is good, or as it is reasonable, and must as much appear as it must be done, or be known. Words and deeds are quite indifferent modes of the divine energy. Words are also actions, and actions are a kind of words.

The sign and credentials of the poet are that he announces that which no man foretold. He is the true and only doctor;[1] he knows and tells; he is the only teller of news, for he was present and privy to the appearance which he describes. He is a beholder of ideas and an utterer of the necessary and causal. For we do not speak now of men of poetical talents, or of industry and skill in meter, but of the true poet. I took part in a conversation the other day concerning a recent writer of lyrics, a man of subtle mind, whose head appeared to be a music-box of delicate tunes and rhythms, and whose skill and command of language we could not sufficiently praise. But when the question arose whether he was not only a lyrist but a poet, we were obliged to confess that he is plainly a contemporary, not an eternal man. He does not stand out of our low limitations, like a Chimborazo under the line, running up from a torrid base through all the climates of the globe, with belts of the herbage of every latitude on its high and mottled sides; but this genius is the landscape-garden of a modern house, adorned with fountains and statues, with well-bred men and women standing and sitting in the walks and terraces. We hear, through all the varied music, the ground-tone of conventional life. Our poets are men of talents who sing, and not the children of music. The argument is secondary, the finish of the verses is primary.

For it is not meters, but a meter-making argument that makes a poem,—a thought so passionate and alive that like the spirit of a plant or an animal it has an architecture of its own, and adorns nature with a new thing. The thought and the form are equal in the order of time, but in the order of genesis the thought is prior to the form. The poet has a new thought; he has a whole new experience to unfold; he will tell us how it was with him, and all men will be the richer in his fortune. For the experience of each new age requires a new confession, and the world seems always waiting for its poet. I remember when I was young how much I was moved one morning by tidings that genius had appeared in a youth who sat near me at table. He had left his work and gone rambling none knew whither, and had written hundreds of lines, but could not tell whether that which was in him was therein told; he could tell nothing but that all was changed,—man, beast, heaven, earth and sea. How gladly we listened! how credulous! Society seemed to be compromised. We sat in the aurora of a sunrise which was to put out all the stars. Boston seemed to be at twice the distance it had the night before, or was much farther than that. Rome,—what was Rome? Plutarch and Shakespeare were in the yellow leaf, and Homer no more should be heard of. It is much to know that poetry has been written this very day, under this very roof, by your side. What! that wonderful spirit has not expired! These stony moments are still sparkling and animated! I had fancied that the oracles were all silent, and nature had spent her fires; and behold! all night, from every pore, these fine auroras have been streaming. Every one has some interest in the advent of the poet, and no one knows how much it may concern him. We know that the secret of the world is profound, but who or what shall be our interpreter, we know not. A mountain ramble, a new style of face, a new person, may put the key into our hands. Of course the value of genius to us is in the veracity of its report. Talent may frolic and juggle; genius realizes and adds. Mankind in good earnest have availed so far in understanding themselves and their work, that the foremost watchman on the peak announces his news. It is the truest word ever spoken, and the phrase will be the fittest, most musical, and the unerring voice of the world for that time.

All that we call sacred history attests that the birth of a poet is the principal event in chronology. Man, never so often deceived, still watches for the arrival of a brother who can hold him steady to a truth until he has made it his own. With what joy I begin to read a poem which I confide in as an inspiration! And now my chains are to be broken; I shall mount above these clouds and opaque airs in which I live,—opaque, though they seem transparent,—and from the heaven of truth I shall see and comprehend my relations. That will reconcile me to life and renovate nature, to see trifles animated by a tendency, and to know what I am doing. Life will no more be a noise; now I shall see men and women, and know the signs by which they may be discerned from fools and satans. This day shall be better than my birthday: then I became an animal; now I am invited into the science of the real. Such is the hope, but the fruition is postponed. Oftener it falls that this winged man, who will carry me into the heaven, whirls me into mists, then leaps and frisks about with me as it were from cloud to cloud, still affirming that he is bound heavenward; and I, being myself a novice, am slow in perceiving that he does not know the way into the heavens, and is merely bent that I should admire his skill to rise like a fowl or a flying fish, a little way from the ground or the water; but the all-piercing, all-feeding and ocular air of heaven that man shall never inhabit. I tumble down again soon into my old nooks, and lead the life of exaggerations as before, and have lost my faith in the possibility of any guide who can lead me thither where I would be.

But, leaving these victims of vanity, let us, with new hope, observe how nature, by worthier impulses, has insured the poet's fidelity to his office of announcement and affirming, namely by the beauty of things, which becomes a new and higher beauty when expressed. Nature offers all her creatures to him as a picture-language. Being used as a type, a second wonderful value appears in the object, far better than its old value; as the carpenter's stretched cord, if you hold your ear close enough, is musical in the breeze. "Things more excellent than every image," says Jamblichus, "are expressed through images." Things admit of being used as symbols because nature is a symbol, in the whole, and in every part. Every line we can draw in the sand has expression; and there is no body without its spirit or genius. All form is an effect of character; all condition, of the quality of the life; all harmony, of health; and for this reason a perception of beauty should be sympathetic, or proper only to the good. The beautiful rests on the foundations of the necessary. The soul makes the body, as the wise Spenser teaches:

> So every spirit, as it is more pure,
> And hath in it the more of heavenly light,
> So it the fairer body doth procure
> To habit in, and it more fairly dight,
> With cheerful grace and amiable sight.
> For, of the soul, the body form doth take,
> For soul is form, and doth the body make.

Here we find ourselves suddenly not in a critical speculation but in a holy place, and should go very warily and reverently. We stand before the secret of the world, there where Being passes into Appearance and Unity into Variety.

The Universe is the externization of the soul. Wherever the life is, that bursts into appearance around it. Our science is sensual, and therefore superficial. The earth and the heavenly bodies, physics and chemistry, we sensually treat, as if they were self-existent; but these are the retinue of that Being we have. "The mighty heaven," said Proclus, "exhibits, in its transfigurations, clear images of the splendor of intellectual perceptions; being moved in conjunction with the unapparent periods of intellectual natures." Therefore science always goes abreast with the just elevation of the man, keeping step with religion and metaphysics; or the state of science is an index of our self-knowledge. Since every thing in nature answers to a moral power, if any phenomenon remains brute and dark it is because the corresponding faculty in the observer is not yet active.

No wonder then, if these waters be so deep, that we hover over them with a religious regard. The beauty of the fable proves the importance of the sense; to the poet, and to all others; or, if you please, every man is so far a poet as to be susceptible of these enchantments of nature; for all men have the thoughts whereof the universe is the celebration. I find that the fascination resides in the symbol. Who loves nature? Who does not? Is it only poets, and men of leisure and cultivation, who live with her? No; but also hunters, farmers, grooms and butchers, though they express their affection in their choice of life and not in their choice of words. The writer wonders what the coachman or the hunter values in riding, in horses and dogs. It is not superficial qualities. When you talk with him he holds these at as slight a rate as you. His worship is sympathetic; he has no definitions, but he is commanded in nature by the living power which he feels to be there present. No imitation or playing of these things would content him; he loves the earnest of the north wind, of rain, of stone and wood and iron. A beauty not explicable is dearer than a beauty which we can see to the end of. It is nature the symbol, nature certifying the supernatural, body overflowed by life which he worships with coarse but sincere rites.

The inwardness and mystery of this attachment drive men of every class to the use of emblems. The schools of poets and philosophers are not more intoxicated with their symbols than the populace with theirs. In our political parties, compute the power of badges and emblems. See the great ball which they roll from Baltimore to Bunker Hill! In the political processions, Lowell goes in a loom, and Lynn in a shoe, and Salem in a ship. Witness the cider-barrel, the log-cabin, the hickory-stick, the palmetto, and all the cognizances of party. See the power of national emblems. Some stars, lilies, leopards, a crescent, a lion, an eagle, or other figure which came into credit God knows how, on an old rag of bunting, blowing in the wind on a fort at the ends of the earth, shall make the blood tingle under the rudest or the most conventional exterior. The people fancy they hate poetry, and they are all poets and mystics!

Beyond this universality of the symbolic language, we are apprised of the divineness of this superior use of things, whereby the world is a temple whose walls are covered with emblems, pictures and commandments of the Deity,—in this, that there is no fact in nature which does not carry the whole sense of nature; and the distinctions which we make in events and in affairs, of low and high, honest and base, disappear when nature is used as a symbol. Thought makes everything fit for use. The vocabulary of an omniscient man would embrace words and images excluded from polite conversation. What would be base, or even obscene, to the obscene, becomes illustrious, spoken in a new connection of thought. The piety of the Hebrew prophets purges their grossness. The circumcision is an example of the power of poetry to raise the low and offensive. Small and mean things serve as well as great symbols. The meaner the type by which a law is expressed, the more pungent it is, and the more lasting in the memories of men; just as we choose the smallest box or case in which any needful utensil can be carried. Bare lists of words are found suggestive to an imaginative and excited mind, as it is related of Lord Chatham that he was accustomed to read in Bailey's Dictionary when he was preparing to speak in Parliament. The poorest experience is rich enough for all the purposes of expressing thought. Why covet a knowledge of new facts? Day and night, house and garden, a few books, a few actions, serve us as well as would all trades and all spectacles. We are far from having exhausted the significance of the few symbols we use. We can come to use them yet with a terrible simplicity. It does not need that a poem should be long. Every word was once a poem. Every new relation is a new word. Also we use defects and deformities to a sacred purpose, so expressing our sense that the evils of the world are such only to the evil eye. In the old mythology, mythologists observe, defects are ascribed to divine natures, as lameness to Vulcan, blindness to Cupid, and the like,—to signify exuberances.

For as it is dislocation and detachment from the life of God that makes things ugly, the poet, who re-attaches things to nature and the Whole,—re-attaching even artificial things and violation of nature, to nature, by a deeper insight,—disposes very easily of the most disagreeable facts. Readers of poetry see the factory-village and the railway, and fancy that the poetry of the landscape is broken up by these; for these works of art are not yet consecrated in their reading; but the poet sees them fall within the great Order not less than the beehive or the spider's geometrical web. Nature adopts them very fast into her vital circles, and the gliding train of cars she loves like her own. Besides, in a centered mind, it signifies nothing how many mechanical inventions you exhibit. Though you add millions, and never so surprising, the fact of mechanics has not gained a grain's weight. The spiritual fact remains unalterable, by many or by few particulars; as no mountain is of any appreciable height to break the curve of the sphere. A shrewd country-boy goes to the city for the first time, and the complacent citizen is not satisfied with his little wonder. It is not that he does not see all the fine houses and know that he never saw such before, but he disposes of them as easily as the poet finds place for the railway. The chief value of the new fact is to enhance the great and constant fact of Life, which can dwarf any and every circumstance, and to which the belt of wampum and the commerce of America are alike.

The world being thus put under the mind for verb and noun, the poet is he who can articulate it. For though life is great, and fascinates and absorbs; and though all men are intelligent of the symbols through which it is named; yet they cannot originally use them. We are symbols and inhabit symbols; workmen, work, and tools, words and things, birth and death, all are emblems; but we sympathize with the symbols, and being infatuated with the economical uses of things, we do not know that they are thoughts. The poet, by an ulterior intellectual perception, gives them a power which makes their old use forgotten, and puts eyes and a tongue into every dumb and inanimate object. He perceives the independence of the thought on the symbol, the stability of the thought, the accidency and fugacity of the symbol. As the eyes of Lyncaeus were said to see through the earth, so the poet turns the world to glass, and shows us all things in their right series and procession. For through that better perception he stands one step nearer to things, and sees the flowing or metamorphosis; perceives that thought is multiform; that within the form of every creature is a force impelling it to ascend into a higher form; and following with his eyes the life, uses the forms which express that life, and so his speech flows with the flowing of nature. All the facts of the animal economy, sex, nutriment, gestation, birth, growth, are symbols of the passage of the world into the soul of man, to suffer there a change and reappear a new and higher fact. He uses forms according to the life, and not according to the form. This is true science. The poet alone knows astronomy, chemistry, vegetation and animation, for he does not stop at these facts, but employs them as signs. He knows why the plain or meadow of space was strown with these flowers we call suns and moons and stars; why the great deep is adorned with animals, with men, and gods; for in every word he speaks he rides on them as the horses of thought.

By virtue of this science the poet is the Namer or Language-maker, naming things sometimes after their appearance, sometimes after their essence, and giving to every one its own name and not another's, thereby rejoicing the intellect, which delights in detachment or boundary. The poets made all the words, and therefore language is the archives of history, and, if we must say it, a sort of tomb of the muses. For though the origin of most of our words is forgotten, each word was at first a stroke of genius, and obtained currency because for the moment it symbolized the world to the first speaker and to the hearer. The etymologist finds the deadest word to have been once a brilliant picture. Language is fossil poetry. As the limestone of the continent consists of infinite masses of the shells of animalcules, so language is made up of images or tropes, which now, in their secondary use, have long ceased to remind us of their poetic origin. But the poet names the thing because he sees it, or comes one step nearer to it than any other. This expression or naming is not art, but a second nature, grown out of the first, as a leaf out of a tree. What we call nature is a certain self-regulated motion or change; and nature does all things by her own hands, and does not leave another to baptize her but baptizes herself; and this through the metamorphosis again. I remember that a certain poet described it to me thus:

> Genius is the activity which repairs the decays of things, whether wholly or partly of a material and finite kind. Nature, through all her kingdoms, insures herself. Nobody cares for planting the poor fungus; so she shakes down from the gills of one agaric countless spores, any one of which, being preserved, transmits new billions of spores tomorrow or next day. The new agaric of this hour has a chance which the old one had not. This atom of seed is thrown into a new place, not subject to the accidents which destroyed its parent two rods off. She makes a man; and having brought him to ripe age, she will no longer run the risk of losing this wonder at a blow, but she detaches from him a new self, that the kind may be safe from accidents to which the individual is exposed. So when the soul of the poet has come to ripeness of thought, she detaches and sends away from it its poems or songs,—a fearless, sleepless, deathless progeny, which is not exposed to the accidents of the weary kingdom of time; a fearless, vivacious offspring, clad with wings (such was the virtue of the soul out of which they came) which carry them fast and far, and infix them irrecoverably

> into the hearts of men. These wings are the beauty of the poet's soul. The songs, thus flying immortal from their mortal parent, are pursued by clamorous flights of censures, which swarm in far greater numbers and threaten to devour them; but these last are not winged. At the end of a very short leap they fall plump down and rot, having received from the souls out of which they came no beautiful wings. But the melodies of the poet ascend and leap and pierce into the deeps of infinite time.

So far the bard taught me, using his freer speech. But nature has a higher end, in the production of new individuals, than security, namely *ascension,* or the passage of the soul into higher forms. I knew in my younger days the sculptor who made the statue of the youth which stands in the public garden. He was, as I remember, unable to tell directly what made him happy or unhappy, but by wonderful indirections he could tell. He rose one day, according to his habit, before the dawn, and saw the morning break, grand as the eternity out of which it came, and for many days after, he strove to express this tranquillity, and lo! his chisel had fashioned out of marble the form of a beautiful youth, Phosphorus, whose aspect is such that it is said all persons who look on it become silent. The poet also resigns himself to his mood, and that thought which agitated him is expressed, but *alter idem,*[2] in a manner totally new. The expression is organic, or the new type which things themselves take when liberated. As, in the sun, objects paint their images on the retina of the eye, so they, sharing the aspiration of the whole universe, tend to paint a far more delicate copy of their essence in his mind. Like the metamorphosis of things into higher organic forms is their change into melodies. Over everything stands its daemon or soul, and, as the form of the thing is reflected by the eye, so the soul of the thing is reflected by a melody. The sea, the mountain-ridge, Niagara, and every flower-bed, pre-exist, or super-exist, in pre-cantations, which sail like odors in the air, and when any man goes by with an ear sufficiently fine, he overhears them and endeavors to write down the notes without diluting or depraving them. And herein is the legitimation of criticism, in the mind's faith that the poems are a corrupt version of some text in nature with which they ought to be made to tally. A rhyme in one of our sonnets should not be less pleasing than the iterated nodes of a seashell, or the resembling difference of a group of flowers. The pairing of the birds is an idyl, not tedious as our idyls are; a tempest is a rough ode, without falsehood or rant; a summer, with its harvest sown, reaped and stored, is an epic song, subordinating how many admirably executed parts. Why should not the symmetry and truth that modulate these, glide into our spirits, and we participate in the invention of nature?

This insight, which expresses itself by what is called Imagination, is a very high sort of seeing, which does not come by study, but by the intellect being where and what it sees; by sharing the path or circuit of things through forms, and so making them translucid to others. The path of things is silent. Will they suffer a speaker to go with them? A spy they will not suffer; a lover, a poet, is the transcendency of their own nature,—him they will suffer. The condition of true naming, on the poet's part, is his resigning himself to the divine *aura* which breathes through forms, and accompanying that.

It is a secret which every intellectual man quickly learns, that beyond the energy of his possessed and conscious intellect he is capable of a new energy (as of an intellect doubled on itself), by abandonment to the nature of things; that beside his privacy of power as an individual man, there is a great public power on which he can draw, by unlocking, at all risks, his human doors, and suffering the ethereal tides to roll and circulate through him; then he is caught up into the life of the Universe, his speech is thunder, his thought is law, and his words are universally intelligible as the plants and animals. The poet knows that he speaks adequately then only when he speaks somewhat wildly, or "with the flower of the mind"; not with the intellect used as an organ, but with the intellect released from all service and suffered to take its direction from its celestial life; or as the ancients were wont to express themselves, not with intellect alone but with the intellect inebriated by nectar. As the traveler who has lost his way throws his reins on his horse's neck and trusts to the instinct of the animal to find his road, so must we do with the divine animal who carries us through this world. For if in any manner we can stimulate this instinct, new passages are opened for us into nature; the mind flows into and through things hardest and highest, and the metamorphosis is possible.

This is the reason why bards love wine, mead, narcotics, coffee, tea, opium, the fumes of sandalwood and tobacco, or whatever other procurers of animal exhilaration. All men avail themselves of such means as they can, to add this extraordinary power to their normal powers; and to this end they prize conversation, music, pictures, sculpture, dancing, theaters, traveling, war, mobs, fires, gaming, politics, or love, or science, or animal intoxication,—which are several coarser or finer *quasi*-mechanical stubstitutes for the true nectar, which is the ravishment of the intellect by coming nearer to the fact. These are auxiliaries to the centrifugal tendency of a man, to his passage out into free space, and they help him to escape the custody of that body in which he is pent up, and of that jail-yard of individual relations in which he is enclosed. Hence a great number of such as were professionally expressers of Beauty, as painters, poets, musicians and actors, have been more than others wont to lead a life of pleasure and indulgence; all but the few who received the true nectar; and, as it was a spurious mode of attaining freedom, as it was an emancipation not into the heavens but into the freedom of baser places, they were punished for that advantage they won, by a dissipation and deterioration. But never can any advantage be taken of nature by a trick. The spirit of the world, the great calm presence of the Creator, comes not forth to the sorceries of opium or of wine. The sublime vision comes to the pure and simple soul in a clean and chaste body. That is not an inspiration, which we owe to narcotics, but some counterfeit excitement and fury. Milton says that the lyric poet may drink wine and live generously, but the epic poet, he who shall sing of the gods and their descent unto men, must drink water out of a wooden bowl. For poetry is not "Devil's wine," but God's wine. It is with this as it is with toys. We fill the hands and nurseries of our children with all manner of dolls, drums and horses; withdrawing their eyes from the plain face and sufficing objects of nature, the sun and moon, the animals, the water and stones, which should be their toys. So the poet's habit of living should be set on a key so low that the common influences should delight him. His cheerfulness should be the gift of the sunlight; the air should suffice for his inspiration, and he should be tipsy with water. That spirit which suffices quiet hearts, which seems to come forth to such from every dry knoll of sere grass, from every pine stump and half-imbedded stone on which the dull March sun shines, comes forth to the poor and hungry, and such as are of simple taste. If thou fill thy brain with Boston and New York, with fashion and covetousness, and wilt stimulate thy jaded senses with wine and French coffee, thou shalt find no radiance of wisdom in the lonely waste of the pine woods.

If the imagination intoxicates the poet, it is not inactive in other men. The metamorphosis excites in the beholder an emotion of joy. The use of symbols has a certain power of emancipation and exhilaration for all men. We seem to be touched by a wand which makes us dance and run about happily, like children. We are like persons who come out of a cave or cellar into the open air. This is the effect on us of tropes, fables, oracles and all poetic forms. Poets are thus liberating gods. Men have really got a new sense, and found within their world another world, or nest of worlds; for, the metamorphosis once seen, we divine that it does not stop. I will not now consider how much this makes the charm of algebra and the mathematics, which also have their tropes, but it is felt in every definition; as when Aristotle defines *space* to be an immovable vessel in which things are contained;—or when Plato defines a *line* to be a flowing point; or *figure* to be a bound of solid; and many the like. What a joyful sense of freedom we have when Vitruvius announces the old opinion of artists that no architect can build any house well who does not know something of anatomy. When Socrates, in Charmides, tells us that the soul is cured of its maladies by certain incantations, and that these incantations are beautiful reasons, from which temperance is generated in souls; when Plato calls the world an animal, and Timaeus affirms that the plants also are animals; or affirms a man to be a heavenly tree, growing with his root, which is his head, upward; and, as George Chapman, following him, writes,

> So in our tree of man, whose nervie root
> Springs in his top;

when Orpheus speaks of hoariness as "that white flower which marks extreme old age"; when Proclus calls the universe the statue of the intellect; when Chaucer, in his praise of "Gentilesse," compares good blood in mean condition to fire, which, though carried to the darkest house betwixt this and the mount of Caucasus, will yet hold its natural office and burn as bright as if twenty thousand men did it behold; when John saw, in the Apocalypse, the ruin of the world through evil, and the stars fall from heaven as the fig tree casteth her untimely fruit; when Aesop reports the whole catalogue of common daily relations through the masquerade of birds and beasts;—we take the cheerful hint of the immortality of our essence and its versatile habit and escapes, as when the gypsies say of themselves "it is in vain to hang them, they cannot die."

The poets are thus liberating gods. The ancient British bards had for the title of their order, "Those who are free throughout the world." They are free, and they make free. An imaginative book renders as much more service at first, by stimulating us through its tropes, than afterward when we arrive at the precise sense of the author. I think nothing is of any value in books excepting the transcendental and extraordinary. If a man is inflamed and carried away by his thought, to that degree that he forgets the authors and the public and heeds only this one dream which holds him like an insanity, let me read his paper, and you may have all the arguments and histories and criticism. All the value which attaches to Pythagoras, Paracelsus, Cornelius Agrippa, Cardan, Kepler, Swedenborg, Schelling, Oken, or any other who introduces questionable facts into his cosmogony, as angels, devils, magic, astrology, palmistry, mesmerism, and so on, is the certificate we have of departure from routine, and that here is a new witness. That also is the best success in conversation, the magic of liberty, which puts the world like a ball in our hands. How cheap even the liberty then seems; how mean to study, when an emotion communicates to the intellect the power to sap and upheave nature; how great the perspective! nations, times, systems, enter and disappear like threads in tapestry of large figure and many colors; dream delivers us to dream, and while the drunkenness lasts we will sell our bed, our philosophy, our religion, in our opulence.

There is good reason why we should prize this liberation. The fate of the poor shepherd, who, blinded and lost in the snowstorm, perishes in a drift within a few feet of his cottage door, is an emblem of the state of man. On the brink of the waters of life and truth, we are miserably dying. The inaccessibleness of every thought but that we are in, is wonderful. What if you come neat to it; you are as remote when you are nearest as when you are farthest. Every thought is also a prison; every heaven is also a prison. Therefore we love the poet, the inventor, who in any form, whether in an ode or in an action or in looks and behavior, has yielded us a new thought. He unlocks our chains and admits us to a new scene.

This emancipation is dear to all men, and the power to impart it, as it must come from greater depth and scope of thought, is a measure of intellect. Therefore all books of the imagination endure, all which ascend to that truth that the writer sees nature beneath him, and uses it as his exponent. Every verse or sentence possessing this virtue will take care of its own immortality. The religions of the world are the ejaculations of a few imaginative men.

But the quality of the imagination is to flow, and not to freeze. The poet did not stop at the color or the form, but read their meaning; neither may he rest in this meaning, but he makes the same objects exponents of his new thought. Here is the difference betwixt the poet and the mystic, that the last nails a symbol to one sense, which was a true sense for a moment, but soon becomes old and false. For all symbols are fluxional; all language is vehicular and transitive, and is good, as ferries and horses are, for conveyance, not as farms and houses are, for homestead. Mysticism consists in the mistake of an accidental and individual symbol for an universal one. The morning-redness happens to be the favorite meteor to the eyes of Jacob Behmen, and comes to stand to him for truth and faith; and, he believes, should stand for the same realities to every reader. But the first reader prefers as naturally the symbol of a mother and child, or a gardener and his bulb, or a jeweler polishing a gem. Either of these, or of a myriad more, are equally good to the person to whom they are significant. Only they must be held lightly, and be very willingly translated into the equivalent terms which others use. And the mystic must be steadily told,—All that you say is just as true without the tedious use of that symbol as with it. Let us have a little algebra, instead of this trite rhetoric,—universal signs, instead of these village symbols,—and we shall both be gainers. The history of hierarchies seems to show that all religious error consisted in making the symbol too stark and solid, and was at last nothing but an excess of the organ of language.

Swedenborg, of all men in the recent ages, stands eminently for the translator of nature into thought. I do not know the man in history to whom things stood so uniformly for words. Before him the metamorphosis continually plays. Everything on which his eye rests, obeys the impulses of moral nature. The figs become grapes whilst he eats them. When some of his angels affirmed a truth, the laurel twig which they held blossomed in their hands. The noise which at a distance appeared like gnashing and thumping, on coming nearer was found to be the voice of disputants. The men in one of his visions, seen in heavenly light, appeared like dragons, and seemed in darkness; but to each other they appeared as men, and when the light from heaven shone into their cabin, they complained of the darkness, and were compelled to shut the window that they might see.

There was this perception in him which makes the poet or seer an object of awe and terror, namely that the same man or society of men may wear one aspect to themselves and their companions, and a different aspect to higher intelligences. Certain priests, whom he describes as conversing very learnedly together, appeared to the children who were at some distance, like dead horses; and many the like misappearances. And instantly the mind inquires whether these fishes under the bridge, yonder oxen in the pasture, those dogs in the yard, are immutably fishes, oxen and dogs, or only so appear to me, and perchance to themselves appear upright men; and whether I appear as a man to all eyes. The Brahmins and Pythagoras propounded the same question, and if any poet has witnessed the transformation he doubtless found it in harmony with various experiences. We have all seen changes as considerable in wheat and caterpillars. He is the poet and shall draw us with love and terror, who sees through the flowing vest the firm nature, and can declare it.

I look in vain for the poet whom I describe. We do not with sufficient plainness or sufficient profoundness address ourselves to life, nor dare we chaunt our own times and social circumstance. If we filled the day with bravery, we should not shrink from celebrating it. Time and nature yield us many gifts, but not yet the timely man, the new religion, the reconciler, whom all things await. Dante's praise is that he dared to write his autobiography in colossal cipher, or into universality. We have yet had no genius in America, with tyrannous eye, which knew the value of our incomparable materials, and saw, in the barbarism and materialism of the times, another carnival of the same gods whose picture he so much admires in Homer; then in the Middle Age; then in Calvinism. Banks and tariffs, the newspaper and caucus, Methodism and Unitarianism, are flat and dull to dull people, but rest on the same foundations of wonder as the town of Troy and the temple of Delphi, and are as swiftly passing away. Our log-rolling, our stumps and their politics, our fisheries, our Negroes and Indians, our boats and our repudiations, the wrath of rogues and the pusillanimity of honest men, the northern trade, the southern planting, the western clearing, Oregon and Texas, are yet unsung. Yet America is a poem in our eyes; its ample geography dazzles the imagination, and it will not wait long for meters. If I have not found that excellent combination of gifts in my countrymen which I seek, neither could I aid myself to fix the idea of the poet by reading now and then in Chalmers's collection of five centuries of English poets. These are wits more than poets, though there have been poets among them. But when we adhere to the ideal of the poet, we have our difficulties even with Milton and Homer. Milton is too literary, and Homer too literal and historical.

But I am not wise enough for a national criticism, and must use the old largeness a little longer, to discharge my errand from the muse to the poet concerning his art.

Art is the path of the creator to his work. The paths or methods are ideal and eternal, though few men ever see them; not the artist himself for years, or for a lifetime, unless he come into the conditions. The painter, the sculptor, the composer, the epic rhapsodist, the orator, all partake one desire, namely to express themselves symmetrically and abundantly, not dwarfishly and fragmentarily. They found or put themselves in certain conditions, as, the painter and sculptor before some impressive human figures; the orator into the assembly of the people; and the others in such scenes as each has found exciting to his intellect; and each presently feels the new desire. He hears a voice, he sees a beckoning. Then he is apprised, with wonder, what herds of daemons hem him in. He can no more rest; he says, with the old painter, "By God it is in me and must go forth of me." He pursues a beauty, half seen, which flies before him. The poet pours out verses in every solitude. Most of the things he says are conventional, no doubt; but by and by he says something which is original and beautiful. That charms him. He would say nothing else but such things. In our way of talking we say "That is yours, this is mine"; but the poet knows well that it is not his; that it is as strange and beautiful to him as to you; he would fain hear the like eloquence at length. Once having tasted this immortal ichor,[3] he cannot have enough of it, and as an admirable creative power exists in these intellections, it is of the last importance that these things get spoken. What a little of all we know is said! What drops of all the sea of our science are baled up! and by what accident it is that these are exposed, when so many secrets sleep in nature! Hence the necessity of speech and song;

hence these throbs and heart-beatings in the orator, at the door of the assembly, to the end namely that thought may be ejaculated as Logos, or Word.

Doubt not, O poet, but persist. Say "It is in me, and shall out." Stand there, balked and dumb, stuttering and stammering, hissed and hooted, stand and strive, until at last rage draw out of thee that *dream*-power which every night shows thee is thine own; a power transcending all limit and privacy, and by virtue of which a man is the conductor of the whole river of electricity. Nothing walks, or creeps, or grows, or exists, which must not in turn arise and walk before him as exponent of his meaning. Comes he to that power, his genius is no longer exhaustible. All the creatures by pairs and by tribes pour into his mind as into a Noah's ark, to come forth again to people a new world. This is like the stock of air for our respiration or for the combustion of our fireplace; not a measure of gallons, but the entire atmosphere if wanted. And therefore the rich poets, as Homer, Chaucer, Shakespeare, and Raphael, have obviously no limits to their works except the limits of their lifetime, and resemble a mirror carried through the street, ready to render an image of every created thing.

O poet! a new nobility is conferred in groves and pastures, and not in castles or by the sword-blade any longer. The conditions are hard, but equal. Thou shalt leave the world, and know the muse only. Thou shalt not know any longer the times, customs, graces, politics, or opinions of men, but shalt take all from the muse. For the time of towns is tolled from the world by funereal chimes, but in nature the universal hours are counted by succeeding tribes of animals and plants, and by growth of joy on joy. God wills also that thou abdicate a manifold and duplex life, and that thou be content that others speak for thee. Others shall be thy gentlemen and shall represent all courtesy and worldly life for thee; others shall do the great and resounding actions also. Thou shalt lie close hid with nature, and canst not be afforded to the Capitol or the Exchange. The world is full of renunciations and apprenticeships, and this is thine; thou must pass for a fool and a churl for a long season. This is the screen and sheath in which Pan has protected his well-beloved flower, and thou shalt be known only to thine own, and they shall console thee with tenderest love. And thou shalt not be able to rehearse the names of thy friends in thy verse, for an old shame before the holy ideal. And this is the reward; that the ideal shall be real to thee, and the impressions of the actual world shall fall like summer rain, copious, but not troublesome to thy invulnerable essence. Thou shalt have the whole land for thy park and manor, the sea for thy bath and navigation, without tax and without envy; the woods and the rivers thou shalt own, and thou shalt possess that wherein others are only tenants and boarders. Thou true land-lord! sea-lord! air-lord! Wherever snow falls or water flows or birds fly, wherever day and night meet in twilight, wherever the blue heaven is hung by clouds or sown with stars, wherever are forms with transparent boundaries, wherever are outlets into celestial space, wherever is danger, and awe, and love,—there is Beauty, plenteous as rain, shed for thee, and though thou shouldst walk the world over, thou shalt not be able to find a condition inopportune or ignoble.

## *NOTES*

1. Teacher.
2. The same yet different.
3. Blood of the gods (Greek). The shades in Hades had to drink blood before they could speak.

# Montaigne; Or, The Skeptic

Every fact is related on one side to sensation, and on the other to morals. The game of thought is, on the appearance of one of these two sides, to find the other: given the upper, to find the under side. Nothing so thin but has these two faces, and when the observer has seen the obverse, he turns it over to see the reverse. Life is a pitching of this penny,—heads or tails. We never tire of this game, because there is still a slight shudder of astonishment at the exhibition of the other face, at the contrast of the two faces. A man is flushed with success, and bethinks himself what this good luck signifies. He drives his bargain in the street; but it occurs that he also is bought and sold. He sees the beauty of a human face, and searches the cause of that beauty, which must be more beautiful. He builds his fortunes, maintains the laws, cherishes his children; but he asks himself, Why? and whereto? This head and this tail are called, in the language of philosophy, Infinite and Finite; Relative and Absolute; Apparent and Real; and many fine names beside.

Each man is born with a predisposition to one or the other of these sides of nature; and it will easily happen that men will be found devoted to one or the other. One class has the perception of difference, and is conversant with facts and surfaces, cities and persons, and the bringing certain things to pass;—the men of talent and action. Another class have the perception of identity, and are men of faith and philosophy, men of genius.

Each of these riders drives too fast. Plotinus believes only in philosophers; Fenelon,[1] in saints; Pindar and Byron, in poets. Read the haughty language in which Plato and the Platonists speak of all men who are not devoted to their own shining abstractions: other men are rats and mice. The literary class is usually proud and exclusive. The correspondence of Pope and Swift describes mankind around them as monsters; and that of Goethe and Schiller, in our own time, is scarcely more kind.

It is easy to see how this arrogance comes. The genius is a genius by the first look he casts on any object. Is his eye creative? Does he not rest in angles and colors, but beholds the design?—he will presently undervalue the actual object. In powerful moments, his thought has dissolved the works of art and nature into their causes, so that the works appear heavy and faulty. He has a conception of beauty which the sculptor cannot embody. Picture, statue, temple, railroad, steam-engine, existed first in an artist's mind, without flaw, mistake, or friction, which impair the executed models. So did the Church, the State, college, court, social circle, and all the institutions. It is not strange that these men, remembering what they have seen and hoped of ideas, should affirm disdainfully the superiority of ideas. Having at some time seen that the happy soul will carry all the arts in power, they say, Why cumber ourselves with superfluous realizations? and like dreaming beggars they assume to speak and act as if these values were already substantiated.

On the other part, the men of toil and trade and luxury,—the animal world, including the animal in the philosopher and poet also, and the practical world, including the painful drudgeries which are never excused to philosopher or poet any more than to the rest,—weigh heavily on the other side. The trade in our streets believes in no metaphysical causes, thinks nothing of the force which necessitated traders and a trading planet to exist: no, but sticks to cotton, sugar, wool and salt. The ward meetings, on election days, are not softened by any misgiving of the value of these ballotings. Hot life is streaming in a single direction. To the men of this world, to the animal strength and spirits, to the men of practical power, whilst immersed in it, the man of ideas appears out of his reason. They alone have reason.

Things always bring their own philosophy with them, that is, prudence. No man acquires property without acquiring with it a little arithmetic also. In England, the richest country that ever existed, property stands for more, compared with personal ability, than in any other. After dinner, a man believes less, denies more: verities have lost some charm. After dinner, arithmetic is the only science: ideas are disturbing, incendiary, follies of young men, repudiated by the solid portion of society: and a man comes to be valued by his athletic and animal qualities. Spence relates that Mr. Pope was with Sir Godfrey Kneller one day, when his nephew, a Guinea trader, came in. "Nephew," said Sir Godfrey, "you have the honor of seeing the two greatest men in the world." "I don't know how great men you may be," said the Guinea man, "but I don't like your looks. I have often bought a man much better than both of you, all muscles and bones, for ten guineas." Thus the men of the senses revenge themselves on the professors and repay scorn for scorn. The first had leaped to conclusions not yet ripe, and say more than is true; the others make themselves merry with the philosopher, and weigh man by the pound. They believe that mustard bites the tongue, that pepper is hot, friction-matches incendiary, revolvers are to be avoided, and suspenders hold up pantaloons; that there is much sentiment in a chest of tea; and a man will be eloquent, if you give him good wine. Are you tender and scrupulous,—you must eat more mince-pie. They hold that Luther had milk in him when he said,—

Wer nicht liebt Wein, Weiber, Gesang,
Der bleibt ein Narr sein Leben lang;[2]

and when he advised a young scholar, perplexed with fore-ordination and free-will, to get well drunk. "The nerves," says Cabanis, "they are the man." My neighbor, a jolly farmer, in the tavern bar-room, thinks that the use of money is sure and speedy spending. For his part, he says, he puts his down his neck and gets the good of it.

The inconvenience of this way of thinking is that it runs into indifferentism and then into disgust. Life is eating us up. We shall be fables presently. Keep cool: it will be all one a hundred years hence. Life's well enough, but we shall be glad to get out of it, and they will all be glad to have us. Why should we fret and drudge? Our meat will taste tomorrow as it did yesterday, and we may at last have had enough of it. "Ah," said my languid gentleman at Oxford, "there's nothing new or true,—and no matter."

With a little more bitterness, the cynic moans; our life is like an ass led to market by a bundle of hay being carried before him; he sees nothing but the bundle of hay. "There is so much trouble in coming into the world," said Lord Bolingbroke, "and so much more, as well as meanness, in going out of it, that 'tis hardly worth while to be here at all." I knew a philosopher of this kidney who was accustomed briefly to sum up his experience of human nature in saying, "Mankind is a damned rascal": and the natural corollary is pretty sure to follow,—"The world lives by humbug, and so will I."

The abstractionist and the materialist thus mutually exasperating each other, and the scoffer expressing the worst of materialism, there arises a third party to occupy the middle ground between these two, the skeptic, namely. He finds both wrong by being in extremes. He labors to plant his feet, to be the beam of the balance. He will not go beyond his card. He sees the onesidedness of these men of the street; he will not be a Gibeonite; he stands for the intellectual faculties, a cool head and whatever serves to keep it cool; no unadvised industry, no unrewarded selfdevotion, no loss of the brains in toil. Am I an ox, or a dray?—You are both in extremes, he says. You that will have all solid, and a world of pig-lead, deceive yourselves grossly. You believe yourselves rooted and grounded on adamant; and yet, if we uncover the last facts of our knowledge, you are spinning like bubbles in a river, you know not whither or whence, and you are bottomed and capped and wrapped in delusions. Neither will he be betrayed to a book and wrapped in a gown. The studious class are their own victims; they are thin and pale, their feet are cold, their heads are hot, the night is without sleep, the day a fear of interruption,—pallor, squalor, hunger and egotism. If you come near them and see what conceits they entertain,—they are abstractionists, and spend their days and nights in dreaming some dream; in expecting the homage of society to some precious scheme, built on a truth, but destitute of proportion in its presentment, of justness in its application, and of all energy of will in the schemer to embody and vitalize it.

But I see plainly, he says, that I cannot see. I know that human strength is not in extremes, but in avoiding extremes. I, at least, will shun the weakness of philosophizing beyond my depth. What is the use of pretending to powers we have not? What is the use of pretending to assurances we have not, respecting the other life? Why exaggerate the power of virtue? Why be an angel before your time? These strings, wound up too high, will snap. If there is a wish for immortality, and no evidence, why not say just that? If there are conflicting evidences, why not state them? If there is not ground for a candid thinker to make up his mind, yea or nay,—why not suspend the judgment? I weary of these dogmatizers. I tire of these hacks of routine, who deny the dogmas. I neither affirm nor deny. I stand here to try the case. I am here to consider, σκοπεῖν[3] to consider how it is. I will try to keep the balance true. Of what use to take the chair and glibly rattle off theories of society, religion and nature, when I know that practical objections lie in the way, insurmountable by me and by my mates? Why so talkative in public, when each of my neighbors can pin me to my seat by arguments I cannot refute? Why pretend that life is so simple a game, when we know how subtle and elusive the Proteus is? Why think to shut up all things in your narrow coop, when we know there are not one or two only, but ten, twenty, a thousand things, and unlike? Why fancy that you have all the truth in your keeping? There is much to say on all sides.

Who shall forbid a wise skepticism, seeing that there is no practical question on which any thing more than an approximate solution can be had? Is not marriage an open question, when it is alleged, from the beginning of the world, that such as are in the institution wish to get out, and such as are out wish to get in? And the reply of Socrates, to him who asked whether he should choose a wife, still remains reasonable, that "whether he should choose one or not, he would repent it." Is not the State a question? All society is divided in opinion on the subject of the State. Nobody loves it; great numbers dislike it and suffer conscientious scruples to allegiance; and the only defense set up, is the fear of doing worse in disorganizing. Is it otherwise with the Church? Or, to put any of the questions which touch mankind nearest,—shall the young man aim at a leading part in law, in politics, in trade? It will not be pretended that a success in either of these kinds is quite coincident with what is best and inmost in his mind. Shall he then, cutting the stays that hold him fast to the social state, put out to sea with no guidance but his genius? There is much to say on both sides. Remember the open question between the present order of "competition" and the friends of "attractive and associated labor." The generous minds embrace the proposition of labor shared by all; it is the only honesty; nothing else is safe. It is from the poor man's hut alone that strength and virtue come: and yet, on the other side, it is alleged that labor impairs the form and breaks the spirit of man, and the laborers cry unanimously, "We have no thoughts." Culture, how indispensable! I cannot forgive you the want of accomplishments; and yet culture will instantly impair that chiefest beauty of spontaneousness. Excellent is culture for a savage; but once let him read in the book, and he is no longer able not to think of Plutarch's heroes. In short, since true fortitude of understanding consists "in not letting what we know be embarrassed by what we do not know," we ought to secure those advantages which we can command, and not risk them by clutching after the airy and unattainable. Come, no chimeras! Let us go abroad; let us mix in affairs; let us learn and get and have and climb. "Men are a sort of moving plants, and, like trees, receive a great part of their nourishment from the air. If they keep too much at home, they pine." Let us have a robust, manly life; let us know what we know, for certain; what we have, let it be solid and seasonable and our own. A world in the hand is worth two in the bush. Let us have to do with real men and women, and not with skipping ghosts.

This then is the right ground of the skeptic,—this of consideration, of self-containing; not at all of unbelief; not at all of universal denying, nor of universal doubting,—doubting even that he doubts; least of all of scoffing and profligate jeering at all that is stable and good. These are no more his moods than are those of religion and philosophy. He is the considerer, the prudent, taking in sail, counting stock, husbanding his means, believing that a man has too many enemies than that he can afford to be his own foe; that we cannot give ourselves too many advantages in this unequal conflict, with powers so vast and unweariable ranged on one side, and this little conceited vulnerable popinjay that a man is, bobbing up and down into every danger, on the other. It is a position taken up for better defense, as of more safety, and one that can be maintained; and it is one of more opportunity and range: as, when we build a house, the rule is to set it not too high nor too low, under the wind, but out of the dirt.

The philosophy we want is one of fluxions and mobility. The Spartan and Stoic schemes are too stark and stiff for our occasion. A theory of Saint John,[4] and of non-resistance, seems, on the other hand, too thin and aerial. We want some coat woven of elastic steel, stout as the first and limber as the second. We want a ship in these billows we inhabit. An angular, dogmatic house would be rent to chips and splinters in this storm of many elements. No, it must be tight, and fit to the form of man, to live at all; as a shell must dictate the architecture of a house founded on the sea. The soul of man must be the type of our scheme, just as the body of man is the type after which a dwelling-house is built. Adaptiveness is the peculiarity of human nature. We are golden averages, volitant stabilities, compensated or periodic errors, houses founded on the sea. The wise skeptic wishes to have a near view of the best game and the chief players; what is best in the planet; art and nature, places and events; but mainly men. Every thing that is excellent in mankind,—a form of grace, an arm of iron, lips of persuasion, a brain of resources, every one skilful to play and win,—he will see and judge.

The terms of admission to this spectacle are, that he have a certain solid and intelligible way of living of his own; some method of answering the inevitable needs of human life; proof that he has played with skill and success; that he has evinced the temper, stoutness and the range of qualities which, among his contemporaries and countrymen, entitle him to fellowship and trust. For the secrets of life are not shown except to sympathy and likeness. Men do not confide themselves to boys, or coxcombs, or pedants, but to their peers. Some wise limitation, as the modern phrase is; some condition between the extremes, and having, itself, a positive quality; some stark and sufficient man, who is not salt or sugar, but sufficiently related to the world to do justice to Paris or London, and, at the same time, a vigorous and original thinker, whom cities can not overawe, but who uses them,—is the fit person to occupy this ground of speculation.

These qualities meet in the character of Montaigne. And yet, since the personal regard which I entertain for Montaigne may be unduly great, I will, under the shield of this prince of egotists, offer, as an apology for electing him as the representative of skepticism, a word or two to explain how my love began and grew for this admirable gossip.

A single odd volume of Cotton's translation of the Essays remained to me from my father's library, when a boy. It lay long neglected, until, after many years, when I was newly escaped from college, I read the book, and procured the remaining volumes. I remember the delight and wonder in which I lived with it. It seemed to me as if I had myself written the book, in some former life, so sincerely it spoke to my thought and experience. It happened, when in Paris, in 1833, that, in the cemetery of Père Lachaise, I came to a tomb of Auguste Collignon, who died in 1830, aged sixty-eight years, and who, said the monument, "lived to do right, and had formed himself to virtue on the Essays of Montaigne." Some years later, I became acquainted with an accomplished English poet, John Sterling; and, in prosecuting my correspondence, I found that, from a love of Montaigne, he had made a pilgrimage to his chateau, still standing near Castellan, in Périgord, and, after two hundred and fifty years, had copied from the walls of his library the inscriptions which Montaigne had written there. That Journal of Mr. Sterling's, published in the Westminster Review, Mr. Hazlitt has reprinted in the *Prolegomena* to his edition of the Essays. I heard with pleasure that one of the newly-discovered autographs of William Shakespeare was in a copy of Florio's translation of Montaigne. It is the only book which we certainly know to have been in the poet's library. And, oddly enough, the duplicate copy of Florio, which the British Museum purchased with a view of protecting the Shakespeare autograph (as I was informed in the Museum), turned out to have the autograph of Ben Jonson in the fly-leaf. Leigh Hunt relates of Lord Byron, that Montaigne was the only great writer of past times whom he read with avowed satisfaction. Other coincidences, not needful to be mentioned here, concurred to make this old Gascon still new and immortal for me.

In 1571, on the death of his father, Montaigne, then thirty-eight years old, retired from the practice of law at Bordeaux, and settled himself on his estate. Though he had been a man of pleasure and sometimes a courtier, his studious habits now grew on him, and he loved the compass,[5] staidness and independence of the country gentleman's life. He took up his economy in good earnest, and made his farms yield the most. Downright and plain-dealing, and abhorring to be deceived or to deceive, he was esteemed in the country for his sense and probity. In the civil wars of the League,[6] which converted every house into a fort, Montaigne kept his gates open and his house without defense. All parties freely came and went, his courage and honor being universally esteemed. The neighboring lords and gentry brought jewels and papers to him for safe-keeping. Gibbon reckons, in these bigoted times, but two men of liberality in France,—Henry IV and Montaigne.

Montaigne is the frankest and honestest of all writers. His French freedom runs into grossness; but he has anticipated all censure by the bounty of his own confessions. In his times, books were written to one sex only, and almost all were written in Latin; so that in a humorist a certain nakedness of statement was permitted, which our manners, of a literature addressed equally to both sexes, do not allow. But though a biblical plainness coupled with a most uncanonical levity may shut his pages to many sensitive readers, yet the offence is superficial. He parades it: he makes the most of it: nobody can think or say worse of him than he does. He pretends to most of the vices; and, if there be any virtue in him, he says, it got in by stealth. There is no man, in his opinion, who has not deserved hanging five or six times; and he pretends no exception in his own behalf. "Five or six as ridiculous stories," too, he says, "can be told of me, as of any man living." But, with all this really superfluous frankness, the opinion of an invincible probity grows into every reader's mind. "When I the most strictly and religiously confess myself, I find that the best virtue I have has in it some tincture of vice; and I, who am as sincere and perfect a lover of virtue of that stamp as any other whatever, am afraid that Plato, in his purest virtue, if he had listened and laid his ear close to himself, would have heard some jarring sound of human mixture; but faint and remote and only to be perceived by himself."

Here is an impatience and fastidiousness at color or pretence of any kind. He has been in courts so long as to have conceived a furious disgust at appearances; he will indulge himself with a little cursing and swearing; he will talk with sailors and gipsies, use flash and street ballads; he has stayed in-doors till he is deadly sick; he will to the open air, though it rain bullets. He has seen too much of gentlemen of the long robe, until he wishes for cannibals; and is so nervous, by factitious life, that he thinks the more barbarous man is, the better he is. He likes his saddle. You may read theology, and grammar, and metaphysics elsewhere. Whatever you get here shall smack of the earth and of real life, sweet, or smart, or stinging. He makes no hesitation to entertain you with the records of his disease, and his journey to Italy is quite full of that matter. He took and kept this position of equilibrium. Over his name he drew an emblematic pair of scales, and wrote *Que sçais je?*[7] under it. As I look at his effigy opposite the title-page, I seem to hear him say, "You may play old Poz,[8] if you will; you may rail and exaggerate,—I stand here for truth, and will not, for all the states and churches and revenues and personal reputations of Europe, overstate the dry fact, as I see it; I will rather mumble and prose about what I certainly know,—my house and barns; my father, my wife and my tenants; my old lean bald pate; my knives and forks; what meats I eat and what drinks I prefer, and a hundred straws just as ridiculous,—than I will write, with a fine crowquill, a fine romance. I like gray days, and autumn and winter weather. I am gray and autumnal myself, and think an undress and old shoes that do not pinch my feet, and old friends who do not constrain me, and plain topics where I do not need to strain myself and pump my brains, the most suitable. Our condition as men is risky and ticklish enough. One cannot be sure of himself and his fortune an hour, but he may be whisked off into some pitiable or ridiculous plight. Why should I vapor and play the philosopher, instead of ballasting, the best I can, this dancing balloon? So, at least, I live within compass, keep myself ready for action, and can shoot the gulf at last with decency. If there be anything farcical in such a life, the blame is not mine: let it lie at fate's and nature's door."

The Essays, therefore, are an entertaining solilquy on every random topic that comes into his head; treating every thing without ceremony, yet with masculine sense. There have been men with deeper insight; but, one would say, never a man with such abundance of thoughts: he is never dull, never insincere, and has the genius to make the reader care for all that he cares for.

The sincerity and marrow of the man reaches to his sentences. I know not anywhere the book that seems less written. It is the language of conversation transferred to a book. Cut these words, and they would bleed; they are vascular and alive. One has the same pleasure in it that he feels in listening to the necessary speech of men about their work, when any unusual circumstance gives momentary importance to the dialogue. For blacksmiths and teamsters do not trip in their speech; it is a shower of bullets. It is Cambridge men who correct themselves and begin again at every half sentence, and, moreover, will pun, and refine too much, and swerve from the matter to the expression. Montaigne talks with shrewdness, knows the world and books and himself, and uses the positive degree; never shrieks, or protests, or prays: no weakness, no convulsion, no superlative: does not wish to jump out of his skin, or play any antics, or annihilate space or time, but is stout and solid; tastes every moment of the day; likes pain because it makes him feel himself and realize things; as we pinch ourselves to know that we are awake. He keeps the plain; he rarely mounts or sinks; likes to feel solid ground and the stones underneath. His writing has no enthusiasms, no aspiration; contented, self-respecting and keeping the middle of the road. There is but one exception,—in his love for Socrates. In speaking of him, for once his cheek flushes and his style rises to passion.

Montaigne died of a quinsy, at the age of sixty, in 1592. When he came to die he caused the mass to be celebrated in his chamber. At the age of thirty-three, he had been married. "But," he says, "might I have had my own will, I would not have married Wisdom herself, if she would have had me: but 'tis to much purpose to evade it, the common custom and use of life will have it so. Most of my actions are guided by example, not choice." In the hour of death, he gave the same weight to custom. *Que sçais je?* What do I know?

This book of Montaigne the world has endorsed by translating it into all tongues and printing seventy-five editions of it in Europe; and that, too, a circulation somewhat chosen, namely among courtiers, soldiers, princes, men of the world and men of wit and generosity.

Shall we say that Montaigne has spoken wisely, and given the right and permanent expression of the human mind, on the conduct of life?

We are natural believers. Truth, or the connection between cause and effect, alone interests us. We are persuaded that a thread runs through all things: all worlds are strung on it, as beads; and men, and events, and life, come to us only because of that thread: they pass and repass only that we may know the direction and continuity of that line. A book or statement which goes to show that there is no line, but random and chaos, a calamity out of nothing, a prosperity and no account of it, a hero born from a fool, a fool from a hero,—dispirits us. Seen or unseen, we believe the tie exists. Talent makes counterfeit ties; genius finds the real ones. We hearken to the man of science, because we anticipate the sequence in natural phenomena which he uncovers. We love whatever affirms, connects, preserves; and dislike what scatters or pulls down.

One man appears whose nature is to all men's eyes conserving and constructive; his presence supposes a well-ordered society, agriculture, trade, large institutions and empire. If these did not exist, they would begin to exist through his endeavors. Therefore he cheers and comforts men, who feel all this in him very readily. The noncomformist and the rebel say all manner of unanswerable things against the existing republic, but discover to our sense no plan of house or state of their own. Therefore, though the town and state and way of living, which our counsellor contemplated, might be a very modest or musty prosperity, yet men rightly go for him, and reject the reformer so long as he comes only with axe and crowbar.

But though we are natural conservers and causationists, and reject a sour, dumpish unbelief, the skeptical class, which Montaigne represents, have reason, and every man, at some time, belongs to it. Every superior mind will pass through this domain of equilibration,—I should rather say, will know how to avail himself of the checks and balances in nature, as a natural weapon against the exaggeration and formalism of bigots and blockheads.

Skepticism is the attitude assumed by the student in relation to the particulars which society adores, but which he sees to be reverend only in their tendency and spirit. The ground occupied by the skeptic is the vestibule of the temple. Society does not like to have any breath of question blown on the existing order. But the interrogation of custom at all points is an inevitable stage in the growth of every superior mind, and is the evidence of its perception of the flowing power which remains itself in all changes.

The superior mind will find itself equally at odds with the evils of society and with the projects that are offered to relieve them. The wise skeptic is a bad citizen; no conservative, he sees the selfishness of property and the drowsiness of institutions. But neither is he fit to work with any democratic party that ever was constituted; for parties wish every one committed, and he penetrates the popular patriotism. His politics are those of the "Soul's Errand" of Sir Walter Raleigh; or of Krishna, in the Bhagavat,[9] "There is none who is worthy of my love or hatred"; whilst he sentences law, physic, divinity, commerce and custom. He is a reformer; yet he is no better member of the philanthropic association. It turns out that he is not the champion of the operative, the pauper, the prisoner, the slave. It stands in his mind that our life in this world is not of quite so easy interpretation as churches and schoolbooks say. He does not wish to take ground against these benevolences, to play the part of devil's attorney, and blazon every doubt and sneer that darkens the sun for him. But he says, There are doubts.

I mean to use the occasion, and celebrate the calendar-day of our Saint Michel de Montaigne, by counting and describing these doubts or negations. I wish to ferret them out of their holes and sun them a little. We must do with them as the police do with old rogues, who are shown up to the public at the marshal's office. They will never be so formidable when once they have been identified and registered. But I mean honestly by them,—that justice shall be done to their terrors. I shall not take Sunday objections, made up on purpose to be put down. I shall take the worst I can find, whether I can dispose of them or they of me.

I do not press the skepticism of the materialist. I know the quadruped opinion will not prevail. 'Tis of no importance what bats and oxen think. The first dangerous symptom I report is, the levity of intellect; as if it were fatal to earnestness to know much. Knowledge is the knowing that we can not know. The dull pray; the geniuses are light mockers. How respectable is earnestness on every platform! but intellect kills it. Nay, San Carlo,[10] my subtle and admirable friend, one of the most penetrating of men, finds that all direct ascension, even of lofty piety, leads to this ghastly insight and sends back the votary orphaned. My astonishing San Carlo thought the lawgivers and saints infected. They found the ark empty; saw, and would not tell; and tried to choke off their approaching followers, by saying, "Action, action, my dear fellows, is for you!" Bad as was to me this detection by San Carlo, this frost in July, this blow from a bride, there was still a worse, namely the cloy or satiety of the saints. In the mount of vision, ere they have yet risen from their knees, they say, "We discover that this our homage and beatitude is partial and deformed: we must fly for relief to the suspected and reviled Intellect, to the Understanding, the Mephistopheles, to the gymnastics of talent."

This is hobgoblin the first; and though it has been the subject of much elegy in our nineteenth century, from Byron, Goethe and other poets of less fame, not to mention many distinguished private observers,—I confess it is not very affecting to my imagination; for it seems to concern the shattering of baby-houses and crockery-shops. What flutters the Church of Rome, or of England, or of Geneva, or of Boston, may yet be very far from touching any principle of faith. I think that the intellect and moral sentiment are unanimous; and that though philosophy extirpates bugbears, yet it supplies the natural checks of vice, and polarity to the soul. I think that the wiser a man is, the more stupendous he finds the natural and moral economy, and lifts himself to a more absolute reliance.

There is the power of moods, each setting at nought all but its own tissue of facts and beliefs. There is the power of complexions, obviously modifying the dispositions and sentiments. The beliefs and unbeliefs appear to be structural; and as soon as each man attains the poise and vivacity which allow the whole machinery to play, he will not need extreme examples, but will rapidly alternate all opinions in his own life. Our life is March weather, savage and serene in one hour. We go forth austere, dedicated, believing in the iron links of Destiny, and will not turn on our heel to save our life: but a book, or a bust, or only the sound of a name, shoots a spark through the nerves, and we suddenly believe in will: my finger-ring shall be the seal of Solomon; fate is for imbeciles; all is possible to the resolved mind. Presently a new experience gives a new turn to our thoughts: common sense resumes its tyranny; we say, "Well, the army, after all, is the gate to fame, manners and poetry: and, look you,—on the whole, selfishness plants best, prunes best, makes the best commerce and the best citizen." Are the opinions of a man on right and wrong, on fate and causation, at the mercy of a broken sleep or an indigestion? Is his belief in God and Duty no deeper than a stomach evidence? And what guaranty for the permanence of his opinions? I like not the French celerity,—a new Church and State once a week. This is the second negation; and I shall let it pass for what it will. As far as it asserts rotation of states of mind, I suppose it suggests its own remedy, namely in the record of larger periods. What is the mean of many states; of all the states? Does the general voice of ages affirm any principle, or is no community of sentiment discoverable in distant times and places? And when it shows the power of self-interest, I accept that as part of the divine law and must reconcile it with aspiration the best I can.

The word Fate, or Destiny, expresses the sense of mankind, in all ages, that the laws of the world do not always befriend, but often hurt and crush us. Fate, in the shape of *Kinde* or nature, grows over us like grass. We paint Time with a scythe; Love and Fortune, blind; and Destiny, deaf. We have too little power of resistance against this ferocity which champs us up. What front can we make against these unavoidable, victorious, maleficent forces? What can I do against the influence of Race, in my history? What can I do against hereditary and constitutional habits; against scrofula, lymph, impotence? against climate, against barbarism, in my country? I can reason down or deny every thing, except this perpetual Belly: feed he must and will, and I cannot make him respectable.

But the main resistance which the affirmative impulse finds, and one including all others, is in the doctrine of the Illusionists. There is a painful rumor in circulation that we have been practiced upon in all the principal performances of life, and free agency is the emptiest name. We have been sopped and drugged with the air, with food, with woman, with children, with sciences, with events, which leave us exactly where they found us. The mathematics, 'tis complained, leave the mind where they find it: so do all sciences; and so do all events and actions. I find a man who has passed through all the sciences, the churl he was; and, through all the offices, learned, civil and social, can detect the child. We are not the less necessitated to dedicate life to them. In fact we may come to accept it as the fixed rule and theory of our state of education, that God is a substance, and his method is illusion. The Eastern sages owned the goddess Yoganidra, the great illusory energy of Vishnu, by whom, as utter ignorance, the whole world is beguiled.

Or shall I state it thus?—The astonishment of life is the absence of any appearance of reconciliation between the theory and practice of life. Reason, the prized reality, the Law, is apprehended, now and then, for a serene and profound moment amidst the hubbub of cares and works which have no direct bearing on it;—is then lost for months or years, and again found for an interval, to be lost again. If we compute it in time, we may, in fifty years, have half a dozen reasonable hours. But what are these cares and works the better? A method in the world we do not see, but this parallelism of great and little, which never react on each other, nor discover the smallest tendency to converge. Experiences, fortunes, governings, readings, writings, are nothing to the purpose; as when a man comes into the room it does not appear whether he has been fed on yams or buffalo,—he has contrived to get so much bone and fiber as he wants, out of rice or out of snow. So vast is the disproportion between the sky of law and the pismire of performance under it, that whether he is a man of worth or a sot is not so great a matter as we say. Shall I add, as one juggle of this enchantment, the stunning non-intercourse law which makes cooperation impossible? The young spirit pants to enter society. But all the ways of culture and greatness lead to solitary imprisonment. He has been often balked. He did not expect a sympathy with his thought from the village, but he went with it to the chosen and intelligent, and found no entertainment for it, but mere misapprehension, distaste and scoffing. Men are strangely mistimed and misapplied; and the excellence of each is an inflamed individualism which separates him more.

There are these, and more than these diseases of thought, which our ordinary teachers do not attempt to remove. Now shall we, because a good nature inclines us to virtue's side, say, There are no doubts,—and lie for the right? Is life to be led in a brave or in a cowardly manner? and is not the satisfaction of the doubts essential to all manliness? Is the name of virtue to be a barrier to that which is virtue? Can you not believe that a man of earnest and burly habit may find small good in tea, essays and catechism, and want a rougher instruction, want men, labor, trade, farming, war, hunger, plenty, love, hatred, doubt and terror to make things plain to him; and has he not a right to insist on being convinced in his own way? When he is convinced, he will be worth the pains.

Belief consists in accepting the affirmations of the soul; unbelief, in denying them. Some minds are incapable of skepticism. The doubts they profess to entertain are rather a civility or accommodation to the common discourse of their company. They may well give themselves leave to speculate, for they are secure of a return. Once admitted to the heaven of thought, they see no relapse into night, but infinite invitation on the other side. Heaven is within heaven, and sky over sky, and they are encompassed with divinities. Others there are to whom the heaven is brass, and it shuts down to the surface of the earth. It is a question of temperament, or of more or less immersion in nature. The last class must needs have a reflex or parasite faith; not a sight of realities, but an instinctive reliance on the seers and believers of realities. The manners and thoughts of believers astonish them and convince them that these have seen something which is hid from themselves. But their sensual habit would fix the believer to his last position, whilst he as inevitably advances; and presently the unbeliever, for love of belief, burns the believer.

Great believers are always reckoned infidels, impracticable, fantastic, atheistic, and really men of no account. The spiritualist finds himself driven to express his faith by a series of skepticisms. Charitable souls come with their projects and ask his coöperation. How can he hesitate? It is the rule of mere comity and courtesy to agree where you can, and to turn your sentence with something auspicious, and not freezing and sinister. But he is forced to say, "O, these things will be as they must be: what can you do? These particular griefs and crimes are the foliage and fruit of such trees as we see growing. It is vain to complain of the leaf or the berry; cut it off, it will bear another just as bad. You must begin your cure lower down." The generosities of the day prove an intractable element for him. The people's questions are not his; their methods are not his; and against all the dictates of good nature he is driven to say he has no pleasure in them.

Even the doctrines dear to the hope of man, of the divine Providence and of the immortality of the soul, his neighbors can not put the statement so that he shall affirm it. But he denies out of more faith, and not less. He denies out of honesty. He had rather stand charged with the imbecility of skepticism, than with untruth. I believe, he says, in the moral design of the universe; it exists hospitably for the weal of souls; but your dogmas seem to me caricatures: why should I make believe them? Will any say, This is cold and infidel? The wise and magnanimous will not say so. They will exult in his far-sighted good-will that can abandon to the adversary all the ground of tradition and common belief, without losing a jot of strength. It sees to the end of all transgression. George Fox saw that there was "an ocean of darkness and death; but withal an infinite ocean of light and love which flowed over that of darkness."

The final solution in which skepticism is lost, is in the moral sentiment, which never forfeits its supremacy. All moods may be safely tried, and their weight allowed to all objections: the moral sentiment as easily outweighs them all, as any one. This is the drop which balances the sea. I play with the miscellany of facts, and take those superficial views which we call skepticism; but I know that they will presently appear to me in that order which makes skepticism impossible. A man of thought must feel the thought that is parent of the universe; that the masses of nature do undulate and flow.

This faith avails to the whole emergency of life and objects. The world is saturated with deity and with law. He is content with just and unjust, with sots and fools, with the triumph of folly and fraud. He can behold with serenity the yawning gulf between the ambition of man and his power of performance, between the demand and supply of power, which makes the tragedy of all souls.

Charles Fourier announced that "the attractions of man are proportioned to his destinies"; in other words, that every desire predicts its own satisfaction. Yet all experience exhibits the reverse of this; the incompetency of power is the universal grief of young and ardent minds. They accuse the divine Providence of a certain parsimony. It has shown the heaven and earth to every child and filled him with a desire for the whole; a desire raging, infinite; a hunger, as of space to be filled with planets; a cry of famine, as of devils for souls. Then for the satisfaction,—to each man is administered a single drop, a bead of dew of vital power, *per day,*—a cup as large as space, and one drop of the water of life in it. Each man woke in the morning with an appetite that could eat the solar system like a cake; a spirit for action and passion without bounds; he could lay his hand on the morning star; he could try conclusions with gravitation or chemistry; but, on the first motion to prove his strength,—hands, feet, senses, gave way and would not serve him. He was an emperor deserted by his states, and left to whistle by himself, or thrust into a mob of emperors, all whistling: and still the sirens sang, "The attractions are proportioned to the destinies." In every house, in the heart of each maiden and of each boy, in the soul of the soaring saint, this chasm is found,—between the largest promise of ideal power, and the shabby experience.

The expansive nature of truth comes to our succor, elastic, not to be surrounded. Man helps himself by larger generalizations. The lesson of life is practically to generalize; to believe what the years and the centuries say, against the hours; to resist the usurpation of particulars; to penetrate to their catholic sense. Things seem to say one thing, and say the reverse. The appearance is immoral; the result is moral. Things seem to tend downward, to justify despondency, to promote rogues, to defeat the just; and by knaves as by martyrs the just cause is carried forward. Although knaves win in every political struggle, although society seems to be delivered over from the hands of one set of criminals into the hands of another set of criminals, as fast as the government is changed, and the march of civilization is a train of felonies,—yet, general ends are somehow answered. We see, now, events forced on which seem to retard or retrograde the civility of ages. But the world-spirit is a good swimmer, and storms and waves cannot drown him. He snaps his finger at laws: and so, throughout history, heaven seems to affect low and poor means. Through the years and the centuries, through evil agents, through toys and atoms, a great and beneficent tendency irresistibly streams.

Let a man learn to look for the permanent in the mutable and fleeting; let him learn to bear the disappearance of things he was wont to reverence without losing his reverence; let him learn that he is here, not to work but to be worked upon; and that, though abyss open under abyss, and opinion displace opinion, all are at last contained in the Eternal Cause:—

If my bark sink, 'tis to another sea.

## *NOTES*

1. Seventeenth-century French theologian, defender of Quietism.
2. Who does not love wine, women, song,
   Remains a fool his whole life long.
3. Skopein, to look out.
4. Teacher of Love.
5. Moderate bounds.
6. Against Protestants; then turned against Henry IV.
7. What do I know?
8. One sure of all his opinions.
9. *Bhagavad-Gita*, a Hindu scripture. Cf. "Brahma."
10. "St. Charles": Charles K. Newcomb.

# Shakespeare; Or, The Poet

Great men are more distinguished by range and extent than by originality. If we require the originality which consists in weaving, like a spider, their web from their own bowels; in finding clay, and making bricks, and building the house; no great men are original. Nor does valuable originality consist in unlikeness to other men. The hero is in the press of knights, and the thick of events; and, seeing what men want, and sharing their desire, he adds the needful length of sight and of arm, to come at the desired point. The greatest genius is the most indebted man. A poet is no rattlebrain, saying what comes uppermost, and, because he says everything, saying, at last, something good; but a heart in unison with his time and country. There is nothing whimsical and fantastic in his production, but sweet and sad earnest, freighted with the weightiest convictions, and pointed with the most determined aim which any man or class knows of in his times.

The Genius of our life is jealous of individuals, and will not have any individual great, except through the general. There is no choice to genius. A great man does not wake up on some fine morning, and say, 'I am full of life, I will go to sea, and find an Antarctic continent: to-day I will square the circle: I will ransack botany, and find a new food for man: I have a new architecture in my mind: I foresee a new mechanic power:' no, but he finds himself in the river of the thoughts and events, forced onward by the ideas and necessities of his contemporaries. He stands where all the eyes of men look one way, and their hands all point in the direction in which he should go. The church has reared him amidst rites and pomps, and he carries out the advice which her music gave him, and builds a cathedral needed by her chants and processions. He finds a war raging: it educates him, by trumpet, in barracks, and he betters the instruction. He finds two counties groping to bring coal, or flour, or fish, from the place of production to the place of consumption, and he hits on a railroad. Every master has found his material collected, and his power lay in his sympathy with his people, and in his love of the materials he wrought in. What an economy of power! and what a compensation for the shortness of life! All is done to his hand. The world has brought him thus far on his way. The human race has gone out before him, sunk the hills, filled the hollows, and bridged the rivers. Men, nations, poets, artisans, women, all have worked for him, and he enters into their labours. Choose any other thing, out of the line of tendency, out of the national feeling and history, and he would have all to do for himself; his powers would be expended in the first preparations. Great genial power, one would almost say, consists in not being original at all; in being altogether receptive; in letting the world do all, and suffering the spirit of the hour to pass unobstructed through the mind.

Shakespeare's youth fell in a time when the English people were importunate for dramatic entertainments. The court took offence easily at political allusions, and attempted to suppress them. The Puritans, a growing and energetic party, and the religious among the Anglican church, would suppress them. But the people wanted them. Inn-yards, houses without roofs, and extemporaneous enclosures at country fairs, were the ready theatres of strolling players. The people had tasted this new joy; and, as we could not hope to suppress newspapers now,—no, not by the strongest party,—neither then could king, prelate, or puritan, alone or united, suppress an organ, which was ballad, epic, newspaper, caucus, lecture, punch, and library, at the same time. Probably king, prelate, and puritan, all found their own account in it. It had become, by all causes, a national interest,—by no means conspicuous, so that some great scholar would have thought of treating it in an English history,—but not a whit less considerable, because it was cheap, and of no account, like a baker's shop. The best proof of its vitality is the crowd of writers which suddenly broke into this field: Kyd, Marlowe, Greene, Jonson, Chapman, Dekker, Webster, Heywood, Middleton, Peele, Ford, Massinger, Beaumont, and Fletcher.

The secure possession, by the stage, of the public mind, is of the first importance to the poet who works for it. He loses no time in idle experiments. Here is audience and expectation prepared. In the case of Shakespeare, there is much more. At the time when he left Stratford, and went up to London, a great body of stage-plays, of all dates and writers, existed in manuscript, and were in turn produced on the boards. Here is the Tale of Troy, which the audience will bear hearing some part of every week; the Death of Julius Cæsar, and other stories out of Plutarch, which they never tire of; a shelf full of English history, from the chronicles of Brut and Arthur, down to the royal Henries, which men hear eagerly; and a string of doleful tragedies, merry Italian tales, and Spanish voyages, which all the London prentices know. All the mass has been treated, with more or less skill, by every playwright, and the prompter has the soiled and tattered manuscripts. It is now no longer possible to say who wrote them first. They have been the property of the Theatre so long, and so many rising geniuses have enlarged or altered them, inserting a speech, or a whole scene, or adding a song, that no man can any longer claim copyright in this work of numbers. Happily, no man wishes to. They are not yet desired in that way. We have few readers, many spectators and hearers. They had best lie where they are.

Shakespeare, in common with his comrades, esteemed the mass of old plays, waste stock, in which any experiment could be freely tried. Had the *prestige* which hedges about a modern tragedy existed, nothing could have been done. The rude warm blood of the living England circulated in the play, as in street-ballads, and gave body which he wanted to his airy and majestic fancy. The poet needs a ground in popular tradition on which he may work, and which, again, may restrain his art within the due temperance. It holds him to the people, supplies a foundation for his edifice; and, in furnishing so much work done to his hand, leaves him at leisure, and in full strength for the audacities of his imagination. In short, the poet owes to his legend what sculpture owed to the temple. Sculpture in Egypt, and in Greece, grew up in subordination to architecture. It was the ornament of the temple wall: at first, a rude relief carved on pediments, then the relief became bolder, and a head or arm was projected from the wall, the groups being still arranged with reference to the building, which serves also as a frame to hold the figures; and when, at last, the greatest freedom of style and treatment was reached, the prevailing genius of architecture still enforced a certain calmness and continence in the statue. As soon as the statue was begun for itself, and with no reference to the temple or palace, the art began to decline; freak, extravagance, and exhibition, took the place of the old temperance. This balance-wheel, which the sculptor found in architecture, the perilous irritability of poetic talent found in the accumulated dramatic materials to which the people were already wonted, and which had a certain excellence which no single genius, however extraordinary, could hope to create.

In point of fact, it appears that Shakespeare did owe debts in all directions, and was able to use whatever he found; and the amount of indebtedness may be inferred from Malone's laborious computations in regard to the First, Second, and Third parts of *Henry VI,* in which, 'out of 6043 lines, 1771 were written by some author preceding Shakespeare; 2373 by him, on the foundation laid by his predecessors; and 1899 were entirely his own.' And the proceeding investigation hardly leaves a single drama of his absolute invention. Malone's sentence is an important piece of external history. In *Henry VIII,* I think I see plainly the cropping out of the original rock on which his own finer stratum was laid. The first play was written by a superior, thoughtful man, with a vicious ear. I can mark his lines, and know well their cadence. See Wolsey's soliloquy, and the following scene with Cromwell, where,—instead of the metre of Shakespeare, whose secret is, that the thought constructs the tune, so that reading for the sense will best bring out the rhythm,—here the lines are constructed on a given tune, and the verse has even a trace of pulpit eloquence. But the play contains, through all its length, unmistakable traits of Shakespeare's hand, and some passages, as the account of the coronation, are like autographs. What is odd, the compliment to Queen Elizabeth is in the bad rhythm.

Shakespeare knew that tradition supplies a better fable than any invention can. If he lost any credit of design, he augmented his resources; and, at that day, our petulant demand for originality was not so much pressed. There was no literature for the million. The universal reading, the cheap press, were unknown. A great poet, who appears in illiterate times, absorbs into his sphere all the light which is anywhere radiating. Every intellectual jewel, every flower of sentiment, it is his fine office to bring to his people; and he comes to value his memory equally with his invention. He is therefore little solicitous whence his thoughts have been derived; whether through translation, whether through tradition, whether by travel in distant countries, whether by inspiration; from whatever source, they are equally welcome to his uncritical audience. Nay, he borrows very near home. Other men say wise things as well as he; only they say a good many foolish things, and do not know when they have spoken wisely. He knows the sparkle of the true stone, and puts it in high place, wherever he finds it. Such is the happy position of Homer, perhaps; of Chaucer, of Saadi. They felt that all wit was their wit. And they are librarians and historiographers, as well as poets. Each romancer was heir and dispenser of all the hundred tales of the world,

> Presenting Thebes' and Pelops' line,
> And the tale of Troy divine.

The influence of Chaucer is conspicuous in all our early literature; and, more recently, not only Pope and Dryden have been beholden to him, but, in the whole society of English writers, a large unacknowledged debt is easily traced. One is charmed with the opulence which feeds so many pensioners. But Chaucer is a huge borrower. Chaucer, it seems, drew continually, through Lydgate and Caxton, from Guido di Colonna, whose Latin romance of the Trojan war was in turn a compilation from Dares Phrygius, Ovid, and Statius. Then Petrarch, Boccaccio, and the Provençal poets are his benefactors: the *Romaunt of the Rose* is only judicious translation from William of Lorris and John of Meun: *Troilus and Creseide,* from Lollius of Urbino: *The Cock and the Fox,* from the *Lais* of Marie: *The House of Fame,* from the French or Italian: and poor Gower he uses as if he were only a brick-kiln or stone-quarry, out of which to build his house. He steals by this apology; that what he takes has no worth where he finds it, and the greatest where he leaves it. It has come to be practically a sort of rule in literature, that a man, having once shown himself capable of original writing, is entitled thenceforth to steal from the writings of others at discretion. Thought is the property of him who can entertain it; and of him who can adequately place it. A certain awkwardness marks the use of borrowed thoughts; but, as soon as we have learned what to do with them, they become our own.

Thus, all originality is relative. Every thinker is retrospective. The learned member of the legislature at Westminster or at Washington, speaks and votes for thousands. Show us the constituency, and the now invisible channels by which the senator is made aware of their wishes, the crowd of practical and knowing men, who, by correspondence or conversation, are feeding him with evidence, anecdotes, and estimates, and it will bereave his fine attitude and resistance of something of their impressiveness. As Sir Robert Peel and Mr. Webster vote, so Locke and Rousseau think for thousands; and so there were fountains all around Homer, Menu, Saadi, or Milton, from which they drew; friends, lovers, books, traditions, proverbs,—all perished,—which, if seen, would go to reduce the wonder. Did the bard speak with authority? Did he feel himself overmatched by any companion? The appeal is to the consciousness of the writer. Is there at last in his breast a Delphi whereof to ask concerning any thought or thing, whether it be verily so, yea or nay? and to have answer, and to rely on that? All the debts which such a man could contract to other wit, would never disturb his consciousness of originality: for the ministrations of books, and of other minds, are a whiff of smoke to that most private reality with which he has conversed.

It is easy to see that what is best written or done by genius, in the world, was no man's work, but came by wide social labour, when a thousand wrought like one, sharing the same impulse. Our English Bible is a wonderful specimen of the strength and music of the English language. But it was not made by one man, or at one time; but centuries and churches brought it to perfection. There never was a time when there was not some translation existing. The Liturgy, admired for its energy and pathos, is an anthology of the piety of ages and nations, a translation of the prayers and forms of the Catholic church,—these collected, too, in long periods, from the prayers and meditations of every saint and sacred writer, all over the world. Grotius makes the like remark in respect to the Lord's Prayer, that the single clauses of which it is composed, were already in use, in the time of Christ, in the rabbinical forms. He picked out the grains of gold. The nervous language of the Common Law, the impressive forms of our courts, and the precision and substantial truth of the legal distinctions, are the contribution of all the sharp-sighted, strong-minded men who have lived in the countries where these laws govern. The translation of Plutarch gets its excellence by being translation on translation. There never was a time when there was none. All the truly idiomatic and national phrases are kept, and all others successively picked out, and thrown away. Something like the same process had gone on, long before, with the originals of these books. The world takes liberties with world-books. Vedas, Æsop's Fables, Pilpay, Arabian Nights, Cid, Iliad, Robin Hood, Scottish Minstrelsy, are not the work of single men. In the composition of such works, the time thinks, the market thinks, the mason, the carpenter, the merchant, the farmer, the fop, all think for us. Every book supplies its time with one good word; every municipal law, every trade, every folly of the day, and the generic catholic genius who is not afraid or ashamed to owe his originality to the originality of all, stands with the next age as the recorder and embodiment of his own.

We have to thank the researches of antiquaries, and the Shakespeare Society, for ascertaining the steps of the English drama, from the Mysteries celebrated in churches and by churchmen, and the final detachment from the church, and the completion of secular plays, from *Ferrex and Porrex,* and *Gammer Gurton's Needle,* down to the possession of the stage by the very pieces which Shakespeare altered, remodelled, and finally made his own. Elated with success, and piqued by the growing interest of the problem, they have left no bookstall unsearched, no chest in a garret unopened, no file of old yellow accounts to decompose in damp and worms, so keen was the hope to discover whether the boy Shakespeare poached or not, whether he held horses at the theatre door, whether he kept school, and why he left in his will only his second-best bed to Ann Hathaway, his wife.

There is something touching in the madness with which the passing age mischooses the object on which all candles shine, and all eyes are turned; the care with which it registers every trifle touching Queen Elizabeth, and King James, and the Essexes, Leicesters, Burleighs, and Buckinghams; and lets pass without a single valuable note the founder of another dynasty, which alone will cause the Tudor dynasty to be remembered,—the man who carries the Saxon race in him by the inspiration which feeds him, and on whose thoughts the foremost people of the world are now for some ages to be nourished, and minds to receive this and not another bias. A popular player,—nobody suspected he was the poet of the human race; and the secret was kept as faithfully from poets and intellectual men, as from courtiers and frivolous people. Bacon, who took the inventory of the human understanding for his times, never mentioned his name. Ben Jonson, though we have strained his few words of regard and panegyric, had no suspicion of the elastic fame whose first vibrations he was attempting. He no doubt thought the praise he has conceded to him generous, and esteemed himself, out of all question, the better poet of the two.

If it need wit to know wit, according to the proverb, Shakespeare's time should be capable of recognizing it. Sir Henry Wotton was born four years after Shakespeare, and died twenty-three years after him; and I find, among his correspondents and acquaintances, the following persons: Theodore Beza, Isaac Casaubon, Sir Philip Sidney, Earl of Essex, Lord Bacon, Sir Walter Raleigh, John Milton, Sir Henry Vane, Izaac Walton, Dr. Donne, Abraham Cowley, Bellarmine, Charles Cotton, John Pym, John Hales, Kepler, Vieta, Albericus Gentilis, Paul Sarpi, Arminius; with all of whom exists some token of his having communicated, without enumerating many others, whom doubtless he saw,—Shakespeare, Spenser, Jonson, Beaumont, Massinger, two Herberts, Marlowe, Chapman, and the rest. Since the constellation of great men who appeared in Greece in the time of Pericles, there was never any such society; yet their genius failed them to find out the best head in the universe. Our poet's mask was impenetrable. You cannot see the mountain near. It took a century to make it suspected; and not until two centuries had passed, after his death, did any criticism which we think adequate begin to appear. It was not possible to write the history of Shakespeare till now; for he is the father of German literature: it was on the introduction of Shakespeare into German, by Lessing, and the translation of his works by Wieland and Schlegel, that the rapid burst of German literature was most intimately connected. It was not until the nineteenth century, whose speculative genius is a sort of living Hamlet, that the tragedy of Hamlet could find such wondering readers. Now, literature, philosophy, and thought are Shakespearized. His mind is the horizon beyond which, at present, we do not see. Our ears are educated to music by his rhythm. Coleridge and Goethe are the only critics who have expressed our convictions with any adequate fidelity; but there is in all cultivated minds a silent appreciation of his superlative power and beauty, which, like Christianity, qualifies the period.

The Shakespeare Society have inquired in all directions, advertised the missing facts, offered money for any information that will lead to proof; and with what result? Beside some important illustration of the history of the English stage, to which I have adverted, they have gleaned a few facts touching the property, and dealings in regard to property, of the poet. It appears that, from year to year, he owned a larger share in the Blackfriars Theatre: its wardrobe and other appurtenances were his; that he bought an estate in his native village, with his earnings as writer and shareholder; that he lived in the best house in Stratford; was intrusted by his neighbours with their commissions in London, as of borrowing money, and the like; that he was a veritable farmer. About the time when he was writing *Macbeth,* he sues Philip Rogers, in the borough-court of Stratford, for thirty-five shillings, ten pence, for corn delivered to him at different times; and, in all respects, appears as a good husband, with no reputation for eccentricity or excess. He was a good-natured sort of man, an actor and shareholder in the theatre, not in any striking manner distinguished from other actors and managers. I admit the importance of this information. It was well worth the pains that have been taken to procure it.

But whatever scraps of information concerning his condition these researches may have rescued, they can shed no light upon that infinite invention which is the concealed magnet of his attraction for us. We are very clumsy writers of history. We tell the chronicle of parentage, birth, birth-place, schooling, schoolmates, earning of money, marriage, publication of books, celebrity, death; and when we have come to an end of this gossip, no ray of relation appears between it and the goddess-born; and it seems as if, had we dipped at random into the *Modern Plutarch* and read any other life there, it would have fitted the poems as well. It is the essence of poetry to spring, like the rainbow daughter of Wonder, from the invisible, to abolish the past, and refuse all history. Malone, Warburton, Dyce, and Collier have wasted their oil. The famed theatres, Covent Garden, Drury Lane, the Park, and Tremont, have vainly assisted. Betterton, Garrick, Kemble, Kean and Macready dedicate their lives to this genius, him they crown, elucidate, obey, and express. The genius knows them not. The recitation begins; one golden word leaps out immortal from all this painted pedantry, and sweetly torments us with invitations to its own inaccessible homes. I remember, I went once to see the Hamlet of a famed performer, the pride of the English stage; and all I then heard, and all I now remember, of the tragedian, was that in which the tragedian had no part; simply, Hamlet's question to the ghost:

> What may this mean,
> That thou, dead corse, again in complete steel
> Revisit'st thus the glimpses of the moon?

That imagination which dilates the closet he writes in to the world's dimension, crowds it with agents in rank and order, as quickly reduces the big reality to be the glimpses of the moon. These tricks of his magic spoil for us the illusions of the green-room. Can any biography shed light on the localities into which the *Midsummer Night's Dream* admits me? Did Shakespeare confide to any notary or parish recorder, sacristan, or surrogate, in Stratford, the genesis of that delicate creation? The forest of Arden, the nimble air of Scone Castle, the moonlight of Portia's villa, 'the antres vast and desarts idle' of Othello's captivity,—where is the third cousin, or grand-nephew, the chancellor's file of accounts, or private letter, that has kept one word of those transcendent secrets? In fine, in this drama, as in all great works of art,—in the Cyclopean architecture of Egypt and India; in the Phidian sculpture; the Gothic minsters; the Italian painting; the Ballads of Spain and Scotland;—the Genius draws up the ladder after him, when the creative age goes up to heaven, and gives way to a new age, which sees the works, and asks in vain for a history.

Shakespeare is the only biographer of Shakespeare; and even he can tell nothing, except to the Shakespeare in us; that is, to our most apprehensive and sympathetic hour. He cannot step from off his tripod, and give us anecdotes of his inspirations. Read the antique documents extricated, analysed, and compared by the assiduous Dyce and Collier; and now read one of those skyey sentences,—aerolites,—which seem to have fallen out of heaven, and which, not your experience, but the man within the breast, has accepted as words of fate; and tell me if they match; if the former account in any manner for the latter; or which gives the most historical insight into the man.

Hence, though our external history is so meagre, yet with Shakespeare for biographer, instead of Aubrey and Rowe, we have really the information which is material, that which describes character and fortune, that which, if we were about to meet the man and deal with him, would most import us to know. We have his recorded convictions on those questions which knock for answer at every heart,—on life and death, on love, on wealth and poverty, on the prizes of life, and the ways whereby we come at them; on the characters of men, and the influences, occult and open, which affect their fortunes; and on those mysterious and demoniacal powers which defy our science, and which yet interweave their malice and their gift in our brightest hours. Who ever read the volume of the Sonnets, without finding that the poet had there revealed, under masks that are no masks to the intelligent, the lore of friendship and of love; the confusion of sentiments in the most susceptible, and, at the same time, the most intellectual of men? What trait of his private mind has he hidden in his dramas? One can discern, in his ample pictures of the gentleman and the king, what forms and humanities pleased him; his delight in troops of friends, in large hospitality, in cheerful giving. Let Timon, let Warwick, let Antonio the merchant, answer for his great heart. So far from Shakespeare's being the least known, he is the one person, in all modern history, known to us. What point of morals, of manners, of economy, of philosophy, of religion, of taste, of the conduct of life, has he not settled? What mystery has he not signified his knowledge of? What office, or function, or district of man's work, has he not remembered? What king has he not taught state, as Talma taught Napoleon? What maiden has not found him finer than her delicacy? What lover has he not outloved? What sage has he not outseen? What gentleman has he not instructed in the rudeness of his behaviour?

Some able and appreciating critics think no criticism on Shakespeare valuable, that does not rest purely on the dramatic merit; that he is falsely judged as poet and philosopher. I think as highly as these critics of his dramatic merit, but still think it secondary. He was a full man, who liked to talk; a brain exhaling thoughts and images, which, seeking vent, found the drama next at hand. Had he been less we should have had to consider how well he filled his place, how good a dramatist he was, and he is the best in the world. But it turns out, that what he has to say is of that weight as to withdraw some attention from the vehicle; and he is like some saint whose history is to be rendered into all languages, into verse and prose, into songs and pictures, and cut up into proverbs; so that the occasion which gave the saint's meaning the form of a conversation, or of a prayer, or of a code of laws, is immaterial, compared with the universality of its application. So it fares with the wise Shakespeare and his book of life. He wrote the airs for all our modern music: he wrote the text of modern life; the text of manners: he drew the man of England and Europe; the father of the man in America: he drew the man, and described the day, and what is done in it; he read the hearts of men and women, their probity, and their second thought, and wiles; the wiles of innocence, and the transitions by which virtues and vices slide into their contraries: he could divide the mother's part from the father's part in the face of the child, or draw the fine demarcations of freedom and of fate: he knew the laws of repression which make the police of nature: and all the sweets and all the terrors of human lot lay in his mind as truly but as softly as the landscape lies on the eye. And the importance of this wisdom of life sinks the form, as of Drama or Epic, out of notice. 'Tis like making a question concerning the paper on which a king's message is written.

Shakespeare is as much out of the category of eminent authors, as he is out of the crowd. He is inconceivably wise; the others, conceivably. A good reader can, in a sort, nestle into Plato's brain, and think from thence; but not into Shakespeare's. We are still out of doors. For executive faculty, for creation, Shakespeare is unique. No man can imagine it better. He was the farthest reach of subtlety compatible with an individual self,—the subtilest of authors, and only just within the possibility of authorship. With this wisdom of life, is the equal endowment of imaginative and of lyric power. He clothed the creatures of his legend with form and sentiments, as if they were people who had lived under his roof; and few real men have left such distinct characters as these fictions. And they spoke in language as sweet as it was fit. Yet his talents never seduced him into an ostentation, nor did he harp on one string. An omnipresent humanity co-ordinates all his faculties. Give a man of talents a story to tell, and his partiality will presently appear. He has certain observations, opinions, topics, which have some accidental prominence, and which he disposes all to exhibit. He crams this part, and starves that other part, consulting not the fitness of the thing, but his fitness and strength. But Shakespeare has no peculiarity, no importunate topic; but all is duly given; no veins, no curiosities: no cow-painter, no bird-fancier, no mannerist is he: he has no discoverable egotism: the great he tells greatly; the small, subordinately. He is wise without emphasis or assertion; he is strong, as nature is strong, who lifts the land into mountain slopes without effort, and by the same rule as she floats a bubble in the air, and likes as well to do the one as the other. This makes that equality of power in farce, tragedy, narrative, and love-songs;

a merit so incessant, that each reader is incredulous of the perception of other readers.

This power of expression, or of transferring the inmost truth of things into music and verse, makes him the type of the poet, and has added a new problem to metaphysics. This is that which throws him into natural history, as a main production of the globe, and as announcing new eras and ameliorations. Things were mirrored in his poetry without loss or blur; he could paint the fine with precision, the great with compass; the tragic and the comic indifferently, and without any distortion or favour. He carried his powerful execution into minute details, to a hair point; finishes an eyelash or a dimple as firmly as he draws a mountain; and yet these, like nature's, will bear the scrutiny of the solar microscope.

In short, he is the chief example to prove that more or less of production, more or fewer pictures, is a thing indifferent. He had the power to make one picture. Daguerre learned how to let one flower etch its image on his plate of iodine; and then proceeds at leisure to etch a million. There are always objects; but there was never representation. Here is perfect representation, at last; and now let the world of figures sit for their portraits. No recipe can be given for the making of a Shakespeare; but the possibility of the translation of things into song is demonstrated.

His lyric power lies in the genius of the piece. The sonnets, though their excellence is lost in the splendour of the dramas, are as inimitable as they; and it is not a merit of lines, but a total merit of the piece; like the tone of voice of some incomparable person, so is this a speech of poetic beings, and any clause as unproducible now as a whole poem.

Though the speeches in the plays, and single lines, have a beauty which tempts the ear to pause on them for their euphuism, yet the sentence is so loaded with meaning, and so linked with its foregoers and followers, that the logician is satisfied. His means are as admirable as his ends; every subordinate invention, by which he helps himself to connect some irreconcilable opposites, is a poem too. He is not reduced to dismount and walk, because his horses are running off with him in some distant direction: he always rides.

The finest poetry was first experience: but the thought has suffered a transformation since it was an experience. Cultivated men often attain a good degree of skill in writing verses; but it is easy to read, through their poems, their personal history: any one acquainted with parties can name every figure: this is Andrew, and that is Rachel. The sense thus remains prosaic. It is a caterpillar with wings, and not yet a butterfly. In the poet's mind, the fact has gone quite over into the new element of thought, and has lost all that is exuvial. This generosity abides with Shakespeare. We say, from the truth and closeness of his pictures, that he knows the lesson by heart. Yet there is not a trace of egotism.

One more royal trait properly belongs to the poet. I mean his cheerfulness, without which no man can be a poet,—for beauty is his aim. He loves virtue, not for its obligation, but for its grace: he delights in the world, in man, in woman, for the lovely light that sparkles from them. Beauty, the spirit of joy and hilarity, he sheds over the universe. Epicurus relates that poetry hath such charms that a lover might forsake his mistress to partake of them. And the true bards have been noted for their firm and cheerful temper. Homer lies in sunshine; Chaucer is glad and erect; and Saadi says, 'It was rumoured abroad that I was penitent; but what had I to do with repentance?' Not less sovereign and cheerful,—much more sovereign and cheerful, is the tone of Shakespeare. His name suggests joy and emancipation to the heart of men. If he should appear in any company of human souls, who would not march in his troop? He touches nothing that does not borrow health and longevity from his festal style.

And now, how stands the account of man with this bard and benefactor, when in solitude, shutting our ears to the reverberations of his fame, we seek to strike the balance? Solitude has austere lessons; it can teach us to spare both heroes and poets; and it weighs Shakespeare also, and finds him to share the halfness and imperfection of humanity.

Shakespeare, Homer, Dante, Chaucer, saw the splendour of meaning that plays over the visible world; knew that a tree had another use than for apples, and corn another than for meal, and the ball of the earth, than for tillage and roads: that these things bore a second and finer harvest to the mind, being emblems of its thoughts, and conveying in all their natural history a certain mute commentary on human life. Shakespeare employed them as colours to compose his picture. He rested in their beauty; and never took the step which seemed inevitable to such genius, namely, to explore the virtue which resides in these symbols, and imparts this power,—What is that which they themselves say? He converted the elements, which waited on his command, into entertainments. He was master of the revels to mankind. Is it not as if one should have, through majestic powers of science, the comets given into his hand, or the planets and their moons, and should draw them from their orbits to glare with the municipal fireworks on a holiday night, and advertise in all towns, 'very superior pyrotechny this evening!' Are the agents of nature, and the power to understand them, worth no more than a street serenade, or the breath of a cigar? One remembers again the trumpet-text in the Koran,—'The heavens and the earth, and all that is between them, think ye we have created them in jest?' As long as the question is of talent and mental power, the world of men has not his equal to show. But when the question is to life, and its materials, and its auxiliaries, how does he profit me? What does it signify? It is but a Twelfth Night, or Midsummer Night's Dream, or a Winter Evening's Tale: what signifies another picture more or less? The Egyptian verdict of the Shakespeare Societies comes to mind, that he was a jovial actor and manager. I cannot marry this fact to his verse. Other admirable men have led lives in some sort of keeping with their thought; but this man, in wide contrast. Had he been less, had he reached only the common measure of great authors, of Bacon, Milton, Tasso, Cervantes, we might leave the fact in the twilight of human fate: but, that this man of men, he who gave to the science of mind a new and larger subject than had ever existed, and planted the standard of humanity some furlongs forward into Chaos,—that he should not be wise for himself,—it must even go into the world's history, that the best poet led an obscure and profane life, using his genius for the public amusement.

Well, other men, priest and prophet, Israelite, German, and Swede, beheld the same objects: they also saw through them that which was contained. And to what purpose? The beauty straightway vanished; they read commandments, all-excluding mountainous duty; an obligation, a sadness, as of piled mountains, fell on them, and life became ghastly, joyless, a pilgrim's progress, a probation, beleaguered round with doleful histories of Adam's fall and curse, behind us; with doomsdays and purgatorial and penal fires before us; and the heart of the seer and the heart of the listener sank in them.

It must be conceded that these are half-views of half-men. The world still wants its poet-priest, a reconciler, who shall not trifle with Shakespeare the player, nor shall grope in graves with Swedenborg the mourner; but who shall see, speak, and act, with equal inspiration. For knowledge will brighten the sunshine; right is more beautiful than private affection; and love is compatible with universal wisdom.

# *Charles-Augustin Sainte-Beuve*

1804–1869

Born in 1804 at Boulogne-sur-Mer, Sainte-Beuve was the child of a controller of town dues. His father died before Charles was born and his mother, of English descent, raised her fatherless son with the help of her sister. At the age of fourteen, Sainte-Beuve went to Paris, and attended classes at the Collège Bourbon and the Collège Charlemagne. Despite literary inclinations, he began to study medicine in 1823, but quickly gave it up when one of his old teachers founded a Liberal newspaper, the *Globe,* and called his former pupil to his aid.

Sainte-Beuve contributed historical and literary articles to the *Globe,* among them a number of studies on Pierre de Ronsard and the Plèiade poets, later collected and published in 1828 as the *Tableau historique et critique de la poésie et du théâtre français au 16ème siècle*. He made his real literary debut when his reviews of Victor Hugo's "Odes et Ballades" attracted the notice of Goethe, and introduced Sainte-Beuve to the Romantic school. He met Lamartine and Merimée and was admitted into Hugo's literary circle, though Sainte-Beuve's alleged affair with the poet's wife, Adele Hugo, soon caused an irreparable rift between the two men.

Sainte-Beuve made his first venture as a poet in 1829 with "Vie, poésie et pensées de Joseph Delormé." But his poetic efforts remained misunderstood, as were his other attempts as a creative writer. Although he produced two other books of poetry and one novel, *Volupté,* it seems clear that Sainte-Beuve's true calling was in interpreting literature rather than creating it. The writer in him gradually gave way to the critic. In 1831 he began to write his famous sketches of literary figures, the "Portraits," for the *Revue des Deux Mondes*.

Six years later, Sainte-Beuve accepted an invitation from the Academy of Lausanne to present in a series of lectures the first outline of his major work on the Jansenist movement of the seventeenth century, *Port Royal*. It was in this work that he first set forth the principles of his "literary science," attempting to build a "moral natural history" of intellectuals.

In 1840 Sainte-Beuve declared his independence from the Romantic movement and started in 1849 the celebrated *Causeries du lundi,* which brought him fame and established his influence over the literary world of nineteenth-century France. Louis-Napoleon was then in power and Sainte-

Beuve, contrary to most French literary figures of his time, did not show any hostility to the Empire. After the Revolution of 1848 which forced him to flee France, he accepted with satisfaction the twenty-year political stability inaugurated by the Imperial regime. Nevertheless, Sainte-Beuve had become by the early 1860s the most powerful voice on the French literary scene and remained so until his death in Paris in 1869.

Pledging that the study of literature led him "naturally to the study of human nature," Sainte-Beuve paid close and insightful attention to the "character" of the writers he discussed, often making connections between a writer's personal and moral traits and his style of writing. In this he was a precursor of modern Freudians and other biographical critics. But Sainte-Beuve's moralistic prejudice eventually prompted him to underrate such great individual geniuses as Stendhal, Flaubert, and even Baudelaire. Sainte-Beuve thus failed to recognize the future fruit of the Modernist revolution. Proust attacked Sainte-Beuve on the grounds that he failed to "see the gulf that separates the writer from the man of the world," failed "to understand that the writer's true self is manifested in his books alone." Nevertheless Sainte-Beuve remains the foremost literary critic of pre-Modernist writing, and the recent revival of interest in the relation of the writer to society may give a new *raison d'être* to Sainte-Beuve's literary achievements.

# What Is a Classic?

A difficult question! One that could be answered in many different ways, depending on the time and the place. Today I shall try, if not to answer it, at least to examine it and discuss it, if only to encourage my readers to answer it for themselves, and to clarify, if possible, my own ideas and theirs on this matter. Why, after all, should not the critic venture now and then to treat a subject that is not personal, to discuss not a given man, but a given thing? Why should he not write something of the sort that our neighbors, the English, modestly call an "essay" and have developed into a genre? Of course, in order to treat such subjects, which are always somewhat abstract and moral, one must speak in an atmosphere of calm, one must be sure of one's own and the reader's interest: one must, in short, take advantage of one of those brief moments of silence, moderation, and leisure which are rarely the lot of lovely France—which, indeed, her brilliant genius bears with impatience, even during periods when she is trying to behave herself and is not engaged in making revolutions.

According to the usual definition, a classic is a universally admired old author, an authority in his field. The term "classic" taken in this sense appeared first in ancient Rome. There the name of *classici* was given, not to all citizens of various classes, but only to those of the first class, those who enjoyed an income above a certain figure. Those whose income was inferior were referred to as *infra classem,* i.e., as being below class as such. The word was used in a figurative sense by Aulus Gellius. *Classicus assiduusque scriptor* was his term for a prominent writer of quality, a writer who counts, who has achievements to his credit, who is not swallowed up in the proletarian crowd. The expression presupposes a sufficiently advanced stage of development, a conscious differentiation within existing literature.

At first, the only true classics for the moderns were, of course, the ancients. The Greeks, by a singular good fortune, which greatly simplified matters for them, had only Greek classics, and they were the only classics for some time thereafter, in the eyes of the Romans who sought to imitate them. When the golden age of their own literature was reached, with Cicero and Virgil, the Romans in turn had their own classics, most of whom remained classics throughout the following centuries. The medieval epoch was less ignorant of Roman antiquity than might be supposed, but it lacked taste and moderation, as well as a sense of value. It preferred Ovid to Homer and ranked Boethius as a classic at least the equal of Plato. The revival of letters in the fifteenth and sixteenth centuries did away with this long confusion, and only then did admiration begin to acquire perspective. The genuinely classical Greek and Roman authors now stood out against a luminous background, and were harmoniously grouped in their two camps.

Meanwhile the modern literatures had come into being, and some of the most precocious among them, such as the Italian, had their own ancient period. There was Dante, soon hailed by his posterity as a "classic." Italian poetry since Dante has sometimes been less great, but it has often recovered greatness and has always preserved some of the impetus and resonance of its high origins. It is not without importance for a poetry to find its point of departure, its classical source, at such an altitude—to descend from Dante rather than to develop laboriously from a Malherbe.

Modern Italy had her classics, and Spain had every right to think that she too had hers, at a time when France was still trying to discover herself. A few talented writers, endowed with originality and exceptional verve—scattered brilliant efforts, not followed up—are not enough to put a nation's literary fortunes on a solid foundation. The idea of the classical implies continuity and consistency, a tradition that forms a whole, is handed down, and endures. Not until after the golden age of Louis XIV did the French feel with a thrill of pride that such good fortune had finally come to them. The multitude of voices who kept proclaiming this advent to Louis XIV may have flattered the king and exaggerated the glory, yet at the same time they believed much of what they said, and rightly so. Now arose a curious, interesting difference of opinion. The very men who were most carried away by the marvels of the *grand siècle* and who went so far as to be willing to sacrifice the Ancients to the Moderns—the party, that is, whose leader was Perrault—tended paradoxically to exalt and to consecrate the very authors who most passionately contradicted and fought them. Boileau angrily took up the cudgels for the Ancients, defending them against Perrault, who was championing Corneille, Molière, Pascal, and other eminent men of the century, especially Boileau himself! The good-natured La Fontaine was on the side of the learned Huet in this quarrel, scarcely realizing that before long he himself would be a classic.

The best definition is by example. Once France had had her *grand siècle* and was able to look at it in perspective, she knew what the term "classic" meant better than by any theories. The eighteenth century, by its very variety, enriched this idea through the fine works we owe to its four great men. Read Voltaire's *Siècle de Louis XIV*, Montesquieu's *La Grandeur et la décadence des romains*, Buffon's *Les Epoques de la nature*, and Jean-Jacques Rousseau's *Le Vicaire savoyard* and his beautiful descriptions and meditations on nature, and tell me whether the eighteenth century did not, at its most memorable, reconcile tradition with freedom of development and independence.

At the beginning of the nineteenth century and during the Empire, when the first attempts at a decidedly new, rather adventurous literature were being made, certain peevish—rather than purist—opponents of the new style took it upon themselves to place severe restrictions on the term "classical." The first Dictionary of the Academy (1694) had defined a classical author merely as "an old author strongly approved, who is an authority in the matter he treats." The Dictionary of the Academy of 1835 goes much further: the originally rather vague definition has become narrower, much more exclusive. Classical authors are those "who have become *models* in a given language," and in the articles which follow, the term "models" is linked with "rules" set down for composition and style. There are repeated references to the "strict rules" which a writer must observe. Clearly, this definition of the classical was drawn up by worthy academicians in reaction to what was called at the time "the romantic." Theirs was a defense against a present enemy. It seems to me that the time has come to renounce such limiting, timorous definitions, and to suggest others, broader in spirit.

A true classic, as I should like the term to be defined, is an author who has enriched the human mind, who has actually added to its treasures and carried it a step forward, one who has discovered some unmistakable moral truth or recaptured some eternal passion in a human heart where everything seemed known and explored; who may have expressed his thought, observation, or discovery in any number of genres, but in a form at once great and sweeping, subtle and yet sensible, sound and beautiful in itself; who speaks to all in a style of his own, which happens also to be that of common speech, a style new but without neologisms, new and old at the same time, easily acceptable to any epoch.

A classic author such as this might well be revolutionary for a time, or at least seem so. But in truth, if he was violent at first and overthrew what stood in his way, he did so only in order quickly to right the scales in favor of order and beauty.

I should like to make this definition grandiose, broad, generous. If I were asked to illustrate it with names, I should mention first of all the Corneille of *Polyeucte, Cinna,* and *Horace*. I should name Molière, the most complete and comprehensive French genius.

"Molière is so great," said Goethe (that king of critics), "that he surprises us every time we read him. He stands apart; his plays come close to the tragic, and no one dares imitate them. His *Avare,* where the vice depicted destroys all affection between father and son, is one of the sublimest of all works, and dramatic to the highest degree. . . . In a play, every action must be important in itself and point to one still greater. In this respect, *Le Tartufe* is a model. What an exposition, the first scene! From the beginning everything is significant and foreshadows something more important. There are beautiful expositions in several plays by Lessing, but that in *Le Tartufe* is unique, the greatest of its kind. . . . Every year I read a play by Molière, just as from time to time I pore over some engraving done from one of the great Italian masters."

[Goethe also said:] "I call the classic healthy, and the romantic sick. For me the poem of the Nibelungen is as classical as Homer; both are healthy and vigorous. The works of today are romantic not because they are new, but because they are weak, sickly or sick. The old works are classical not because they are old, but because they are energetic, hale and hearty. If we considered the classical and the romantic from these two points of view, we should all soon be in agreement."

Indeed, I should like every free mind, before he reaches a final decision in this matter, to make a tour of the world and to survey the various literatures in their primitive vigor and infinite diversity. What would he see? First of all Homer, the father of the classical world—who is certainly, however, less a simple and distinct individual than a vast living expression of a whole age of semibarbarian civilization. To make him a classic in the proper sense of the term, it was necessary to ascribe to him, after the fact, a design, a plan, literary intentions, and qualities of Atticism and urbanity which he certainly never dreamed of—his natural inspiration abundantly sufficed. Next to him, we see great and venerable figures like Aeschylus and Sophocles, of whose works we possess only a small portion; they stand there as though to remind us of others, who deserved no doubt to survive as much as they, but who succumbed to the ravages of time. This alone should teach us not to oversimplify our view of literature, even of classical literature. We should recognize that the order which has prevailed for so long, which is so exact and well-proportioned, is a highly artificial creation, based on our limited knowledge of the past.

This, of course, applies with even greater force to the modern world. The greatest names we find at the beginnings of the various literatures are such as to upset our most traditional concepts of what is beautiful and proper in poetry. For instance, is Shakespeare a classic? Yes, today he is one for England and for the world, but in the period of Pope he was not. Pope and his friends were the only "classics" par excellence; they seemed definitively so the day they died. Today they are still classics, and they deserve the title, but they are classics of the second rank, and they are forever dominated and put back in their place by the one who has finally come into his own.

I am certainly not one to speak against Pope and his excellent disciples, particularly when they are as gentle and natural as Goldsmith; next to the greatest, they are perhaps the most pleasant among the writers and poets, those most apt to add charm to life. One day Pope added a postscript to a letter Bolingbroke wrote to Swift saying in effect: "I fancy that if we three were to spend only three years together, some profit might result for our century." No, we must never speak lightly about those who had the right to say such things about themselves without bragging. We should rather envy the fortunate, favored ages when talented men could propose to form such associations, which at the time had nothing chimerical about them. Whether named after Louis XIV or Queen Anne, such ages are the only truly classical ones in the broader sense of the word, the only ones which provided superior talents with a propitious climate and shelter. We know this only too well, living as we do in an age without inner unity, when talents, possibly equal to those of other ages, have been lost or frittered away because of the uncertainties and inclemencies of the times. Still, we must recognize that there are many kinds of greatness or superiority. The authentic sovereign geniuses surmount difficulties where others fail. Dante, Shakespeare, and Milton succeeded in rising to their full height and produced their imperishable works despite obstacles, oppression, and storms.

There has been a great deal of discussion on the subject of Byron's opinions about Pope, and attempts have been made to account for the apparent contradiction in the spectacle of the author of *Don Juan* and *Childe Harold* exalting the purely classical school and declaring it to be the only good one, while taking himself an entirely different tack. Once again, Goethe hit the nail on the head when he said that Byron, whose poetic inspiration was so great and noble, feared Shakespeare, who was so much more powerful in the creation and management of characters in action: "He would have been glad to ignore him; he was embarrassed by his sublimity completely devoid of egotism; he felt that he could never take wing beside him. He never wished to ignore Pope, because he did not fear him; he knew very well that Pope was a sheltering wall." If the school of Pope had retained, as Byron wished, its supremacy and a kind of honorary sway over the past, Byron would have been unique and uncontested in his genre; the erection of Pope's "wall" would mask our view of the great figure of Shakespeare, beside whom Byron is but second best.

In France we had no great classic author before the seventeenth century, no Dante or Shakespeare capable of giving guidance to every subsequent period of literary renewal. We had some potentially great poets, such as Mathurin Régnier and Rabelais, but they lacked ideas; they did not possess the required passion and gravity. Montaigne was a kind of premature classic in the Horatian tradition, but he was as capricious as an undisciplined child; he gave in to every passing libertine mood and fancy. Our ancestors provided us with scantier foundations to build upon than is the case with any other nation. When the day came to recover our literary freedoms and rights, it was more difficult for us to remain classical while emancipating ourselves. However, with Molière and La Fontaine among our seventeenth-century classics, we have models great enough to inspire daring and talented writers.

What seems to me the important thing today is to preserve and cherish the idea of classicism, while at the same time broadening it. There is no formula for producing a classic: this much must be recognized as self-evident.

The best and greatest classics are the most unexpected, as witness those virile geniuses who are truly born immortal and flourish forever. The seemingly least classical of the four great poets of the *grand siècle* was Molière; his contemporaries applauded him more than they respected him, enjoyed him without realizing his worth. Next to him the least classical seemed to be La Fontaine: and you see what happened to both of them two centuries later! Far above Boileau, even above Racine, are they not today unanimously recognized as the most fertile, the richest contributors to our knowledge of human nature?

This is not to say that we have to discard the rest or think less of them. I believe the Temple of Taste needs to be remodeled, but in rebuilding it our task is merely to enlarge it, to make it the Pantheon of all noble men, of all who have notably and durably increased the sum total of the human spirit, the enjoyments and conquests of the mind. For my part—and it is only too obvious that I could not in any degree lay claim to being the architect or designer of such a temple—I shall confine myself to expressing a few wishes, contributing to the blueprint, as it were. Above all, I should not exclude anyone among the worthy: I want everyone so entitled to have his place there, from that freest of creative geniuses, that greatest and least self-conscious of all the classics—Shakespeare—to the very least of the classics in miniature, to Andrieux. "My Father's house has many mansions"—let this be true of the Kingdom of the Beautiful no less than the Kingdom of Heaven. Homer, as always and everywhere, would be the first in such a realm, the most resembling a god; but behind him, like the procession of the Magi, would stand those three magnificent poets, those three Homers so long unknown to us, who composed immense revered epics for the ancient nations of Asia: Valmiki and Vyasa the Hindus, and Firdusi the Persian. In the domain of taste it is a good thing to know at least that such men have existed, so that the human race is seen as a whole. Having paid our respects, however, we should not linger in these distant climes. Closer to home, we could find myriad attractions, both pleasant and sublime, and we could enjoy a rich variety of changing scenes, often enough startling, but in whose seeming disorder we would never find disharmony. The most ancient poets and sages who expressed human morality in simply stated maxims would converse among themselves in words "rare and suave" and would not be surprised at understanding one another at once. Men like Solon, Hesiod, Theognis, Job, Solomon—and why not Confucius, too?—would welcome to their company such ingenious moderns as La Rochefoucauld and La Bruyère. Listening to the others, these latecomers would say, "They already knew all we know; all we did was to give new life to their wisdom." At the most prominent elevation, standing above broad and gently rising slopes, Virgil, surrounded by Menander, Tibullus, Terence, and Fénelon, would engage them in conversation of great charm and dignity. His radiant features ringed with modesty would recall the distant day when he entered the theater in Rome just after his verses had been recited, and the whole audience rose as one man—giving him the same tribute as it was accustomed to give Augustus. Not far away, unwilling to be separated from so dear a friend, Horace would in turn preside—in so far as a poet and so subtle a sage can preside—over the group of witty worldly poets who speak as other men sing: Pope become less irritable; Boileau grown less of a scold; Montaigne, whose appearance here in this charming corner would remove the last possibility of any resemblance to a literary school. La Fontaine would feel at ease here and, having lost much of his restlessness, would never depart. Voltaire would stop by, but though he would be fond of the place, he would not have the patience to stay. On the same elevation as Virgil, a little below him, one would see Xenophon, wearing an air of simplicity that suggests nothing of the captain but rather a priest of the Muses. Around him we would find the Atticists of all languages and countries—men like Addison, Pellisson, Vauvenargues, all those who know the value of easy persuasiveness, exquisite simplicity, and graceful casualness. At the center three great men would at last be reunited in front of the main temple (for there would be several temples in the precincts), and when they were together, no fourth man, however great, would dream of drawing near to share either their words or their silence. Such beauty would emanate from them, such unmistakable grandeur, that no one would dare. Theirs is the perfection of harmony which appears but for a day when the world is young. Their names have become the ideal of art: Plato, Sophocles, Demosthenes. And yet, when all due honor has been paid these demigods, we may yet observe a familiar throng of excellent minds who prefer to cluster around Cervantes, Molière, and others of that class: the depicters of ordinary life, friendly, indulgent benefactors of mankind who see us steadily and whole, who teach us to laugh and to be wise, and who do not find it beneath them to appeal to our warmer feelings and love of pleasure.

I shall not prolong this description: to be complete, it would require a book in itself. The Middle Ages, you may well believe, would with Dante occupy hallowed heights; at the feet of the poet of the Paradiso, most of Italy would spread out like a garden. Boccaccio and Ariosto would disport themselves there, and Tasso would rediscover the orange groves of Sorrento. More generally, every nation would have a corner of its own, but no one would feel constrained to remain within it; I see the authors strolling about in search of teachers and brothers and finding them in the least likely places. Lucretius, for example, would want to discuss with Milton the origin of the world and the ordering of the primeval chaos; and while each of them would argue in favor of his own theory, they would agree at least on the divine nature of poetry.

Such are our classics; the imagination of each reader may complete the drawing and pick out the group he prefers. For one must choose, and the first condition of taste—once one has understood the whole—is not to flit from group to group, but to settle permanently in one. Nothing blunts or extinguishes taste more than continual flitting about: the poetic spirit is no Wandering Jew. However, when I speak of choosing a place to settle down, I do not mean that we should imitate even those who are most congenial to us among the masters of old. Let us content ourselves with understanding them, admiring them, and let us, who have come along so much later, try at least to be ourselves. Let us make a choice on the basis of our own instincts. Let us keep the sincerity and the naturalness of our own thoughts and feelings, as surely as we can; let us add something more difficult, which is elevation, if this is possible, and orientation toward some high goal. Speaking our own language and governed by the conditions of the age in which we find ourselves, from which we derive our strengths as well as our shortcomings, let us ask ourselves from time to time, our heads lifted up to the peaks, our eyes on the group of mortals we most revere: "What would they say of us?"

But why always speak about being an author, about writing? Perhaps you have reached an age when you will write no more. Happy those who read and reread, who follow their own inclinations in perfect freedom! There comes a time in life when, having been everywhere and done everything, there is no intenser pleasure than to study the things we already know, going ever deeper into them, relishing the feelings we have already had, as we see over and over again the persons we most care for: these are the pure delights of maturity. It is then that the term "classic" takes on its true meaning—when every man of taste makes his choice on a basis of irresistible predilection. Then taste is formed and becomes definitive; then we achieve good sense, if we ever do. We have no more time to experiment, no more desire to set out on journeys of discovery. We confine ourselves to our friends, to those who have stood the test of time. Old wine, old books, old friends. Then we say to ourselves what Voltaire put into these delightful lines:

*Jouissons, écrivons, vivons, mon cher Horace! . . .*
*J'ai vécu plus que toi: mes vers dureront moins;*
*Mais au bord du tombeau, je mettrai tous mes soins*
*A suivre les leçons de ta philosophie,*
*A mépriser la mort en savourant la vie,*
*A lire tes écrits pleins de grâce et de sens,*
*Comme on boit d'un vin vieux qui rajeunit les sens.*

[Let us enjoy life, let us write, my dear Horace! . . .
Though I have lived longer than you, my verses will not live so long;
But on edge of the grave, I shall do all I can
To follow the lessons of your philosophy,
To despise death while enjoying life,
To read your writings full of grace and meaning,
Just as we drink old wine to rejuvenate our senses.]

In short, whether it be Horace or another, whichever old author best renders our thought when we are ripe with years, he it is with whom we shall find ourselves in steady conversation, as with an old friend. His friendship will never fail or deceive us, and the cloudless serenity he brings to our lives will reconcile us with our fellow men and with ourselves.

# Rousseau's "Confessions"

The writer who brought about the greatest single change in the French language since Pascal, and who ushered in, linguistically speaking, the nineteenth century, is Rousseau. Before him, from Fénelon on, there had been a number of writers who attempted to go beyond the pure seventeenth-century manner. Fontenelle had a manner all his own, if any writer ever had, and Montesquieu had also—a stronger, firmer, more striking manner, but a manner nonetheless. Voltaire alone was free of mannerism, and his lively, incisive, swift language ripples as though but a stone's throw from the spring. "You say that I express myself quite clearly," he writes somewhere. "I am like a little brook that is transparent because it is not too deep." He says this jokingly, expressing a half-truth as we all do on such occasions. But the eighteenth century was not content with this; it wanted to be stirred, enthused, rejuvenated by ideas and feelings as yet not clearly formulated, for the expression of which it was still groping. Buffon's prose, in the first volumes of the *Histoire naturelle,* provided something of what the century was searching for, but it was a prose more majestic than spontaneous, a little beyond the ordinary grasp, and too closely associated with scientific subjects. Then came Rousseau: the day he bared himself wholly to himself, the century recognized in him the writer most capable of giving expression to the unformed ideas which had been agitating it, the writer best able to state them with originality, vigor, and impassioned logic. In his efforts to master the language and make it docile to his purposes, he forced it a bit and left his indelible mark upon it. However, he more than made up for whatever it lost as a result of his influence, and in many respects he regenerated it and gave it new vigor. The mold of language he created and gave currency to has stamped all the greatest writers who came after him, whatever their innovations and attempts to outdo him. In them, the pure seventeenth-century form of French, as we like to recall it, became little more than a lovely relic, to the great regret of many cultivated persons.

Although the *Confessions* did not appear until after Rousseau's death, at a time when his influence was already enormous, this is the work that enables us most conveniently to examine the manifold merits, brilliancies, and defects of his talent. In what follows we will confine ourselves to consideration of the writer, but will feel free to make observations on the man and his ideas. The present moment is not too well-disposed toward Rousseau. His is condemned as the author or originator of the many evils from which we currently suffer. "There is no writer," it has been rightly said, "more apt to infuse the poor with arrogance." But for all that may be said on this score, in this study we shall try not to be too influenced by quasi-personal feelings, such as induce otherwise well-intentioned persons to hold a grudge against him in our present painful circumstances. Men who have influenced posterity as powerfully as Rousseau are not to be judged solely by emotional reactions which are, after all, ephemeral.

It seems so natural to us that Rousseau should have written his "confessions," so consonant with his disposition and his talent, that it comes as a surprise to learn that the idea was not his own. The fact is, however, that it was first suggested to him by his publisher, Rey of Amsterdam, and then also by Duclos. Having completed *La Nouvelle Héloïse* and the *Emile,* Rousseau began to compose the *Confessions* in 1764, at the age of fifty-four. This was after he had left Montmorency and was staying at Motiers in Switzerland. The latest issue of the *Revue suisse* (October 1850) contains an early version of the opening pages of the *Confessions,* from a manuscript in the library of Neuchâtel. It was Rousseau's first draft. The original version is far less rhetorical and less elaborate than the final one. Here we do not hear "the trumpet of the day of judgment," nor is there any apostrophe to "the Eternal Being." In the older text, Rousseau develops at greater length, in a more philosophical spirit, his plan to set down a description of himself and to make public confession, whatever the consequences. He shows very clearly that he understands the originality, the singularity of his intentions:

"The story of a man's life can be written only by himself. His inner being, his true life, is known to no one else. However, when he tries to describe his life, he is false to it; what he calls his life becomes an apology for it; he shows himself as he wants to be seen, not as he is. The most sincere [autobiographers] are at best truthful in what they say; where they lie is in what they leave out, and their reticences alter the value of their frank statements to such a degree that when they give us only part of the truth, they give us nothing. I put Montaigne at the head of these 'pseudo-sincere' persons who, while speaking the truth, aim to deceive. He shows himself to us with his failings, but only with likable ones; now, no man but has some hateful ones. Montaigne draws a good likeness of himself, but only in profile. Who can tell whether a saber cut on the other cheek—perhaps with the loss of an eye—did not make him look very different, seen in full face?"

It is clear that Rousseau is embarked on something no one before him had ever undertaken, ever dared to attempt. As for the style, he tells us that he must invent a style as new as the task he has set himself, one adapted to the diversity and disproportionateness of the many things he proposes to describe:

"Were I trying to produce a work as carefully composed as my other works, I should not be depicting myself but playing a part. What I have in mind is a portrait, not a book. I shall work in camera oscura, so to speak; the only art I shall need is the ability to trace exactly the features as outlined. Therefore I have no choice with respect to style, any more than with respect to subject. I shall not try to make it uniform; I shall use whatever style seems best to fit the given episode, and I will change it according to my mood, without a qualm. I shall say what I have to say in the way I feel about it, as I see it, without effort or embarrassment, not worrying about being consistent. As I recollect my original impressions and set down my present feelings about them, I shall depict my state of mind at the moment the given event occurred as well as at the moment I describe it. The style, uneven but natural, now rapid and now diffuse, now sensible and now extravagant, now grave and now gay, will itself be part of my story. Apart from the manner of its writing, this book will by its subject prove valuable to philosophers; I repeat, it is a work destined for the comparative study of the human heart, the only existing work of its kind."

Rousseau's mistake lay not in his belief that public confession, in a spirit very different from that of Christian humility, was something unique, indeed, of a very great interest as a study of the human heart. His mistake was to think that it would be useful. He did not realize that he was like the doctor who might set out to describe to ignorant laymen, in an intelligible, attractive way, some specific mental infirmity or illness; such a doctor would be partly to blame for the maniacs and madmen his book would produce by imitation or contagion.

The opening pages of the *Confessions* (as finally published) are too rhetorical and rather labored. They contain a number of awkward expressions and clichés. And yet, alongside touches of crudity, there is something else—a new, familiar, and penetrating simplicity:

"I felt before I thought; it is the common fate of humanity. I have proved it more than anyone. I am ignorant of what passed until I was five or six years old. I know not how I learned to read; I remember my first studies only, and their effect on me. . . . My mother left some romances; my father and I read them after supper. At that time the point was merely to use these entertaining books to give me practice in reading; but very soon the interest in them became so strong, that we read them by turns without ceasing, and passed whole nights at this employment. We could never leave off but at the end of the volume. Sometimes my father, on hearing the swallows in the morning, would say, quite ashamed: 'Come, let us go to bed; I am more a child than you.'"

Take good note of those swallows; they are the harbingers of a new springtime in our language; they did not appear before Rousseau. The feeling for nature in eighteenth-century France begins with him.

The same is true of his feeling for domestic life, the everyday life of the family in all its homeliness, its poverty, and its intimacy, its virtues and its satisfactions. There are a number of details in bad taste, as when he speaks of "volerie" and "mangeaille"—"swiping vittles," but they are more than made up for by that old childhood song of which he remembers only the tune and a few random words, but of which he has always been trying to remember the rest—and even now that he is old he still cannot remember it without being moved to tears.

"It is a caprice I don't understand," he says, "but I cannot sing it to the end without being choked by tears. I have a hundred times intended to write to Paris, to get the remaining words, in the hope that someone may still know them. But I am almost sure the pleasure I take in recalling them would be spoiled if I had proof that any other than my poor Aunt Suzon sang them."

This is what is new in the author of the *Confessions*, what enchants us and opens up to us unexpectedly the whole range of intimate, domestic sensibility. The other day I spoke to you of Mme. de Caylus' *Souvenirs*. What do her recollections of childhood amount to? What did she care about? What were her regrets at leaving the home where she had been born and brought up? It never even occurred to her to tell us. These refined, aristocratic breeds, endowed with such exquisite tact and so keen a sense of *raillerie,* either did not care for such simple things or did not dare to show that they did. We recognize and enjoy their wit, but where is their heart? One has to be of the people and to have been born in the provinces—in short to be a "new man" like Rousseau—to be able to display one's own natural feelings.

When we note with a certain regret how Rousseau wrestled with the language, plowing it and harrowing it, so to speak, we are nonetheless obliged to recognize how at the same time he reclaimed it, fertilized it, and made it give forth new growths.

M. de Chateaubriand, descendant of a proud, aristocratic family, but who sat at Rousseau's feet as a writer and had nearly as little fear of making a fool of himself as his master, employed the same more or less direct manner of personal confession in *René* and his *Mémoires,* and he achieved surprising, magical effects with it. But there are differences between them. Rousseau lacks innate nobility; he was not quite—far from it!—what is called a "wellborn" child; he had a penchant for vice—and for the baser vices besides. He had shameful secret desires which are remote from our notions of gentlemanliness. After long periods of timidity he suddenly bursts out violently with all the impudence of a *polisson* and a *vaurien,* as he puts it. In short, he lacked that inner check, a sense of honor, which Chateaubriand possessed from childhood, and which served as a rein on his failings. However, for all his shortcomings—shortcomings we no longer fear to call by their right names, because he taught us to do so—Rousseau is superior to Chateaubriand in that he is more human and manly, with deeper feelings. He lacks Chateaubriand's incredible hardness of heart (a truly medieval trait), as evidenced in the emotional unawareness with which the latter speaks of his father and mother, for instance. When Rousseau discusses his father's shortcomings—describing him as a decent man who was given to pleasure, a bit frivolous, and who abandoned him when he married again—with what delicacy Rousseau treats this sore point, with what sensitivity he puts himself in the other's position! There is nothing chivalric about this delicacy—but it is genuine, a true inner delicacy, specifically moral and human.

It is inconceivable that this inner moral sense with which he was endowed, and which made him so alive to other people's feelings, should not have warned Rousseau to what extent he derogated from it in his behavior and in many of the locutions he affected. His style, like his life, never quite rose above what had been vicious in his early life and surroundings. After a normal childhood spent in the bosom of his family, he went to work as an apprentice and was subjected to hardships which spoiled his taste and depraved his delicacy. He never thinks twice about using such words as *polisson, vaurien, gueux, fripon;* indeed, there seems to be a certain complaisance in the way they come again and again to his pen. His language always kept something of the commonness of his early years. I distinguish two kinds of impurity in his language. One is traceable merely to his provincial background, to the fact that he speaks French like someone born outside France. He articulates strongly and harshly; at moments it is as though he speaks with a goiter. But this defect is readily forgiven, so completely did he overcome it in his most felicitous passages. By dint of hard work and deep feeling he made his organ more supple and succeeded in giving his intricate, difficult style the semblance of ease and spontaneity. The other kind of impurity or corruption that can be noted in him is more serious, in that it is of a moral nature: he never seems to have suspected that there are certain things which should never be given expression: certain ignoble, disgusting, cynical phrases that decent men dispense with or are ignorant of. Rousseau had actually been employed as a lackey at one time, and this is sometimes reflected in his style. He detests neither the term nor the thing the term denotes. "If Fénelon were still alive, you would be a Catholic," Bernardin de Saint-Pierre said to him one day when he saw him deeply moved by some religious ceremony. "Oh, if Fénelon were still alive," Rousseau exclaimed in tears, "I would try to be his lackey in the hope of one day being worthy of becoming his valet." We see that he lacked taste even in matters of feeling. Rousseau is not only a craftsman of language, who had to be an apprentice before he could become a master, and whose works occasionally show traces of the labor involved; more than that, he is, morally speaking, a man who in youth had an extremely rude experience of life, and he is not disgusted himself when he writes of certain ugly and sordid things. I shall say no more about this essential vice, this blemish which it is so painful to have to come upon and to denounce in so great a writer, so great a painter, such a man.

Slow to think, prompt to feel, burning with suppressed desires, continually suffering at being held back, Rousseau portrays himself as follows on reaching the age of sixteen:

"Thus I reached sixteen, uneasy, discontented with everything including myself, without love for my trade, deprived of the pleasures of youth, tormented by desires whose object I was ignorant of, weeping without reason, sighing without knowing for what; in short, cherishing my illusions for want of seeing anything around me that could match them. On Sunday, my companions came to fetch me after sermon to join them in their games. I would have gladly refused them if I could; but once I began to play, I was more eager and went further than the others; it was as difficult to stop me as it had been to get me started."

Always extreme! We recognize here in their original form the thoughts of René—and in very nearly the same words:

"My disposition was impetuous, my character uneven. By turns noisy and joyous, silent and sad, I gathered my young companions around me and then, suddenly deserting them, I would go off by myself and lie staring at some stray cloud or listen to the raindrops pattering among the leaves. . . ."

And:

"When I was young, I cultivated the Muses; there is nothing more poetic, in the freshness of its passions, than a heart of sixteen. The morning of life is like the morning of time, all purity, the sights and sounds alike."

Indeed, René is simply that other young man of sixteen transposed, set in another natural environment and another social condition; no longer an apprentice engraver, son of a humble burgher of Geneva, but a noble knight embarking on distant journeys, in love with the Muses. From the very first everything in Chateaubriand takes on greater lushness, more poetic color; the unexpected landscape and background enhance the character and define a new manner, but the prototype of the sensitive young man is where we found him first. It was Rousseau who discovered him, looking into himself.

René makes a more flattering model for us, because in him all the more sordid aspects of humanity are veiled; there is a tinge of Greece, of chivalry, of Christendom about him which makes for a different play of light over his features. In this masterpiece of art words have taken on new magic, they are luminous and harmonious. The horizon now stretches out in every direction, touched with gleams from Olympus. At first glimpse, there is nothing of this in Rousseau, but at bottom his is the truer work, more real, more alive. This tradesman's child who runs off to find his playmates "after sermon" or goes off by himself when he can to wander and dream his dreams—this slim, graceful youth with the bright eyes and fine features who always bears down a bit more heavily on life than we should prefer him to do, is a real person; he is in touch with the world around him. Besides feelings, he has physical presence. Both René and Rousseau have their morbid side; in them excessive passion co-exists with passivity and a disposition to idleness; their imaginations and sensibilities turn inward and feed on themselves. But of the two, Rousseau is the more genuinely sensitive, the more original and sincere in his chimerical impulses and vain regrets, in his idealizations of a bliss he might have known but turned his back upon. At the close of Book One of the *Confessions*, when he is about to leave his native land, he evokes a simple and touching picture of the modest happiness he might have known had he stayed. He tells us: "I should have passed, in the bosom of my religion, of my native country, of my family and my friends, a calm and peaceable life, such as my character wanted, in the uniformity of a labor suited to my taste and in a society according to my heart; I should have been a good Christian, a good citizen, a good father, a kind friend, a good artist, a good man. I should have liked my condition, perhaps been an honor to it, and after having passed an obscure and simple life, but even and calm, I should have died peaceably on the breast of my own family. Soon forgot, doubtless, I had been regretted at least whenever I was remembered." When he tells us this, we believe that he is sincere: that he did desire such a life and that he is sorry things turned out otherwise. His words exhale a profound feeling for the gentle, untroubled joys of a modest life lived far from the madding crowd.

We of this century, all more or less sick from the sickness of introspection, often tend to behave like newly created nobles who are ashamed of their ancestors; we forget that before we became the unworthy sons of the noble René, we were much more unmistakably the grandsons of the obscure citizen Rousseau.

Book One of the *Confessions* is not the most remarkable, but Rousseau is already fully present, in all his conceit, his budding vices, his bizarre and grotesque moods, his meannesses and salaciousness; but we have him also in his pride and independence, the firmness of purpose that will raise him above himself. Already in the account of his happy, healthy childhood and his tormented adolescence, we anticipate the apostrophes to society and the vengeful reprisals which he will later be inspired to make. His wistful evocation of the joys of life in the bosom of his family (which he did not long enjoy), like his intimations of sensitivity to nature and the seasons, will both come to flower in the literature of the following century. Today we risk being insufficiently sensitive to these first picturesque pages of Rousseau; we have been so spoiled by more colorful treatments of these motifs that we forget how fresh and new they seemed at the time, how extraordinary an irruption they represented in the midst of a very witty and highly refined, but extremely arid society, which was as devoid of imagination as of true sensibility—a society that lacked utterly that inner sap which by its circulation brings forth new flowers in every season. It was Rousseau who first brought back this potent vegetal sap and infused it into the fragile, dessicated tree. The French public, accustomed to the factitious climate of the salons—"urbane" readers, as he called them—were enchanted by the fresh mountain air he brought with him from the Alps, breathing new life into a literature which had been sterile for all its distinction.

It was high time, and this is why Rousseau was no corrupter of the language, but, all in all, a regenerator.

Before him, in France only La Fontaine had known and felt the life of nature, the pleasures of idle revery in the open countryside, to any such degree. His example, however, had scarcely been followed. The gentle old man with his fables was allowed to come and go, but the public stayed in the salons. Rousseau was the first to get fashionable people out of them, to persuade them to leave their stately formal gardens and take a real walk in the country.

The beginning of Book Two of the *Confessions* is delightfully fresh: Mme. de Warens appears for the first time. In portraying her, Rousseau's style softens and becomes more graceful; at the same time we are made acquainted with one more of his basic traits of character, namely, his sensuality. "Rousseau had a voluptuous mind," one good critic has noted. Women played a great role in his life; absent or present, their persons occupied him, inspired him, and moved him, and in everything he writes we find something feminine. "How, in approaching for the first time an amiable, polite, and dazzling woman," he says of Mme. de Warens, "a lady in a superior situation to mine, and such as I never had access to before . . . how did I at once find myself as free, as easy, as if perfectly sure of pleasing her?" Though he usually was far from feeling so easy in the presence of women, his style always exhibits ease and freedom when he writes of them. The most adorable pages of the *Confessions* are those devoted to his first meeting with Mme. de Warens, as well as those in which he describes how he was received by Mme. Basile, the pretty tradeswoman in Turin: "She was brilliant and dressy, and despite her charming manner all this luster intimidated me. But she received me with such kindness, she spoke to me so gently, compassionately, and even caressingly, that I was soon brought to myself. I saw I was succeeding, and that made me succeed the more." What a touch of Italian sunshine that passage conveys! And he goes on to relate the lively wordless scene that no reader ever forgets, a scene all gestures, just stopped in time, full of blushes and youthful desire. One might add to this the walk with Mlle. Galley and Mlle. de Graffenried just outside Annecy, every detail of which is ravishing. In the history of French literature, pages like these mark the discovery of a whole new world, a world of sunshine and fresh air that had never been taken proper notice of before, though it had always been just at hand. This mixture of sensibility and naturalness, in which sensuality is kept within conventional bounds, was necessary to liberate us at last from a false metaphysics of the heart and conventional "spirituality." The sensualness of the artist's brush, when carried no farther than this, cannot displease; there is sobriety, and there is no more than meets the eye. Rousseau is thus a good deal more innocent than many painters who have come after him.

As a painter, Rousseau has in all things a sense of *reality*. He has it whenever he speaks of beauty. Even when it is an imaginary beauty, as in *Julie, ou la Nouvelle Héloïse,* it takes on very visible body and form; it is never an impalpable Iris suspended in midair. His sense of reality is such that every scene he recalls or invents, every character he introduces, is given a specific habitation in which to develop, the smallest details of which remain engraved in our memories. One of the criticisms leveled against the great novelist Richardson was that he never linked his characters with a recognizable locale. Rousseau, on the other hand, gave his Julie and his Saint-Preux their perfect setting in the Vaud country, on the shores of the lake to which he remained forever attached. His clear, firm mind serves always as a burin to his imagination, so that nothing essential is ever left out. And lastly, his sense of reality manifests itself in the care with which, in the midst of whatever circumstances or adventures he depicts—even the most romantic ones—he never forgets to mention that people had something to eat; he gives the details of their healthy, frugal fare, designed to rejoice the heart as well as the mind.

This feature is basic, rooted in Rousseau's nature as a burgher and man of the people, as I noted above. He had known hunger: in the *Confessions* he mentions, with an expression of gratitude to rescuing Providence, the last time he was literally too poor to buy food. This was why he never forgot, even in the idealized picture of his happiness that he later painted, to introduce elements of our common humanity, the simplest facts of life. Such details, combined with his eloquence, catch our sympathy and engage it.

Nature sincerely felt and loved for herself is the source of Rousseau's inspiration, whenever his inspiration is healthy, not morbid. When he comes back from Turin and seeks out Mme. de Warens again, he stays for some time in her house, and from his room he looks out over the garden and has a view of the countryside. "It was, since Bossey [a village where he had been put out to board as a child], the first time I had seen verdure from my window." Until then, it had been a matter of indifference to French readers whether or not there was greenery before their eyes; Rousseau made them notice it. He was, so to speak, the first to introduce greenery into our literature. Living in the house of a woman he loved, but to whom the nineteen-year-old Rousseau did not dare declare his passion, he was filled with a sadness "which had, however, nothing gloomy about it, and which was allayed by flattering hope." One day, a religious holiday, while everybody was at vespers, he went for a walk outside the town.

"The sound of the bells," he says, "which always singularly affected me, the singing of the birds, the clearness of the weather, the sweetness of the landscape, the houses scattered and rural, in which I placed in fancy our common abode; all this struck me with an impression so lively, so tender, so melancholy, and so touching, that I saw myself, as in a trance, transported to those happy times, and in those happy abodes, where my heart, possessing every felicity that could delight it, tasted them in raptures inexpressible, without ever thinking of sensual voluptuousness."

That is what the boy from Geneva felt at Annecy in the year 1731, when Paris was reading Montesquieu's *Le Temple de Gnide*. That very day he made the discovery of *rêverie,* the sort of inward reflection which had hitherto been recognized merely as a peculiarity of La Fontaine. Rousseau was to introduce it successfully into a literature whose only subjectivity was in the realm of eroticism. *Rêverie:* this was Rousseau's innovation, his personal discovery, his New World. The dream he dreamed that day came true a few years later, while he was staying at Les Charmettes. On St. Louis' Day he took another walk, and he describes it as no one had ever done before:

"Everything seemed to contribute to the happiness of the day. It had lately rained, there was no dust, and the brooks ran full. A gentle wind stirred the leaves, the air was pure, the horizon without a cloud; serenity reigned in the heavens as in our minds. Our dinner was served at a peasant's, and shared with his family, who heartily blessed us. What good people these poor Savoyards are!"

That moment at Les Charmettes, when a freshness of feeling as yet untried blossoms for the first time, is the most divine in all the *Confessions.* There is nothing like it again—not even when Rousseau has gone into seclusion at The Hermitage. His description of the Hermitage years and of the passion that comes to him there is doubtless deeply moving—and all the more so for all that has gone immediately before. Yet Rousseau was quite right to exclaim that, after all, "It was not the same as Les Charmettes!" The misanthropic suspiciousness he was already filled with plagued him even in his solitude. He kept thinking back to the people he had left behind in Paris, especially the Holbach clique; he enjoyed his retreat despite them, but thoughts of them poisoned his purest enjoyments. These were the years when he grew embittered and contracted the illness that proved incurable. To be sure, he still knew moments of delight right up to his death. On the Ile de Saint-Pierre, in the middle of the Lake of Bienne, he had a peaceful interval that inspired some of his finest pages. Indeed, the Fifth Promenade in the *Rêveries du promeneur solitaire,* together with the third letter to M. de

Malesherbes, must be grouped with the most divine passages of the *Confessions*. And yet nothing equals in lightness, freshness and cheerfulness the description of his life at Les Charmettes. Rousseau's true happiness, the happiness that no one—not even himself—could take away, lay in his ability to evoke and recapture in brilliant detail such images of his youth as these—an ability he still possessed in his most troubled, most harassed later years.

Rousseau's evocations of nature are firm, clear, and restrained, even at his most luxuriating; his colors are always laid on over a well-defined drawing; in this respect, the native of Geneva falls within the purest French tradition. Although at times he lacks the warmer, more brilliant light of Italy or Greece, and—as happens sometimes along the shores of the lovely Lake of Geneva—a wind from the north brings a sudden chill to the air, or a cloud suddenly casts a gray shadow over the mountains, there are hours and whole days of perfect serenity. Subsequent writers have attempted to improve on this style, have even believed they could surpass it, and certainly have been successful with some effects of color and sound. Nevertheless, so far as modern innovations are concerned, Rousseau's style remains the firmest and surest, his language is the most balanced. His successors have gone farther; they have not only transferred the seat of the empire to Byzantium, they have often carried it as far as Antioch, into the heart of Asia. In them, imagination degenerates into pretentiousness.

The portraits in the *Confessions* are sharply drawn, lively, and witty. His friend Bâcle, the musician Venture, the judge-magician Simon are shrewdly observed. Less boldly drawn than the portraits in *Gil Blas,* they seem more like engravings. In this connection, Rousseau went back to the trade he practiced first.

I have confined myself to brief mentions of Rousseau's major traits. A master of the French language, he created *rêverie,* taught us to feel the presence and moods of nature, and sired the literature of home and family life realistically portrayed. It is unfortunate, of course, that such achievements are tinged with overweening pride and misanthropy, and that a note of cynicism spoils many a passage of charm and beauty. But Rousseau's follies and vices do not outweigh his solid merits and originality, nor do they overshadow his continuing superiority to those who have come after him.

# *John Stuart Mill*

1806–1873

John Stuart Mill, the great British liberal philosopher and economist, was born in London on May 20, 1806. His father, James Mill, was an important economic and philosophical figure in his own right—a close friend of Jeremy Bentham, he was one of the most rigorous champions of Utilitarianism. As an empiricist, James Mill believed that the mind was a blank sheet, passive clay whose eventual shape depended entirely upon external forces. He tried this theory upon his son by means of a rigid control of his influences; as a youth, John was allowed no frivolity, no indulgence in childish emotions, no ordinary friendships—all his time was spent in the rigorous exercise and development of his extraordinary intellectual potential. By the time he was eight he was fluent in ancient Greek; he could read all of Herodotus in the original, and at least six dialogues of Plato; at twelve he read Latin as easily as he spoke English and was better versed in the particulars of English history than most of his elder compatriots; by thirteen, his studies had taken a turn towards economics in the works of David Ricardo and Adam Smith, a discipline he would soon not only master but entirely overhaul. By the time he went to Oxford he already had "an advantage of a quarter-century over my contemporaries." But the psychic toll of this almost inconceivable precocity was enormous.

Mill himself dates his breakdown to his twenty-first year. Although his father's experiment had been successful in producing a nearly perfect thinking instrument, the child had developed no imagination, no social graces, and, above all, no consciousness of emotions. But as his manhood crept upon him, this lopsided situation began to right itself with a vengeance. For two whole years Mill suffered a crisis of almost unbearable melancholia. Ruth Borchard makes the following comments concerning the origins and character of Mill's profound melancholia: "The longer this condition lasted the more hopeless it seemed to him. He strained his will to the utmost—but how can one will to *feel*? He tried to argue himself out of his state. The mature brain set restlessly to work—and succeeded only in finding more reasons to prove that his case was unredeemable; that the early analytical habits had forever killed in him the springs of feeling. Idealism as well as ambition had lost all power to stir."

It took nothing less than his father's death in 1836 to break this melancholy. For the first time in his life, at thirty years of age, the younger Mill felt he could cry; his father's rigor, his very presence, had always forbade him even this. Even before his father's death the discovery of Wordsworth's poetry had begun to reawaken Mill's slumbering emotions. Now as part of his newfound freedom he eagerly devoured the works of Coleridge and Carlyle, Goethe and the German idealists. He left behind the sterile confines of methodical rationalism, and broke ground in an ever-widening intellectual territory that he would enrich for years to come.

Second only to that of his father, the most important relationship in Mill's life was his long friendship with Harriet Henry Taylor—"the honor and chief blessing of my existence." Freethinking, intuitive, and passionate, she in many ways represented the opposite of his father's rigid rationalism. When Mill met her in the early 1830s she was married to a businessman but dissatisfied with what she felt was a stifling bond intellectually and emotionally. Mill fell hopelessly in love with her, but since voluntary restraint was part of their social ideal, the relationship remained platonic until the death of Harriet's husband twenty years later. Nevertheless they scandalized English society by their open affection. Mill grew increasingly devoted to and extremely dependent upon Taylor. When she died in 1858 he was utterly confounded; he bought a cottage within sight of the cemetery and stayed there for most of his remaining years. In 1861 he published *The Subjugation of Women;* a few years later he became the first English legislator to introduce the issue of women's right to vote.

Mill's mature genius combines the various opposed tendencies of his rationalist and Romantic education into a dialectical liberal synthesis. In his mature years he was no longer as stalwart in his controversial stands; always classed as a radical in the tradition of his father, his approach to political, economic, social, and aesthetic questions was more rounded, filled out, aware of itself. In the 1830s, after assuming the editorship of the *London Review,* he began systematically to map out and explore logic and political economy, utterly transforming these disciplines in the process. In 1844 he published *Essays on Some Unsettled Questions of Political Economy,* which display an astonishing lucidity in the exposition of the most bewildering technical problems of contemporary economic theory. But in topical matters he was becoming decidedly a liberal; in regard to the Irish Question he proposed, for instance, the creation of proprietary holdings to be given to peasants. In general, Mill advocated a re-thinking, in the most vigorous terms, of the bases of capitalism. He questioned the necessity of property for the ensurance of peace in primitive society, thereby throwing into doubt its justification in later stages of societal development. This alone was a daring intellectual challenge to the apologists of the Industrial Revolution. But Mill never proposed anything like the "scientific socialism" that Marx was formulating at the same time. He championed the cause of the lower classes from a decided intellectual remove, and he was anxious about the threat to the individual implicit in any "ideal" society. As Isaiah Berlin points out, Mill differed crucially from

Marx in his tragic awareness that "out of the crooked timber of humanity no straight thing was ever made."

Whereas his stern father would have agreed with Plato in banning all poets from the ideal commonwealth, the mature son understood the value of poetry in itself. Reading Wordsworth had literally changed Mill's life, and like Wordsworth he defended poetry as essential to the education of a well-balanced, humane individual. His essay *On Poetry and Its Varieties* is a thoroughly Romantic meditation on poetry as the voice of feeling. He distinguishes poetry from eloquence on the grounds that eloquence is intended to be heard, whereas poetry is always "overheard"—at its best poetry is always soliloquy, the melancholy or exuberant language of inwardness.

# Thoughts on Poetry and Its Varieties

## *I*

It has often been asked, What is Poetry? And many and various are the answers which have been returned. The vulgarest of all—one with which no person possessed of the faculties to which Poetry addresses itself can ever have been satisfied—is that which confounds poetry with metrical composition: yet to this wretched mockery of a definition, many have been led back, by the failure of all their attempts to find any other that would distinguish what they have been accustomed to call poetry, from much which they have known only under other names.

That, however, the word 'poetry' imports something quite peculiar in its nature, something which may exist in what is called prose as well as in verse, something which does not even require the instrument of words, but can speak through the other audible symbols called musical sounds, and even through the visible ones which are the language of sculpture, painting, and architecture; all this, we believe, is and must be felt, though perhaps indistinctly, by all upon whom poetry in any of its shapes produces any impression beyond that of tickling the ear. The distinction between poetry and what is not poetry, whether explained or not, is felt to be fundamental: and where every one feels a difference, a difference there must be. All other appearances may be fallacious, but the appearance of a difference is a real difference. Appearances too, like other things, must have a cause, and that which can cause anything, even an illusion, must be a reality. And hence, while a half-philosophy disdains the classifications and distinctions indicated by popular language, philosophy carried to its highest point frames new ones, but rarely sets aside the old, content with correcting and regularizing them. It cuts fresh channels for thought, but does not fill up such as it finds ready-made; it traces, on the contrary, more deeply, broadly, and distinctly, those into which the current has spontaneously flowed.

Let us then attempt, in the way of modest inquiry, not to coerce and confine nature within the bounds of an arbitrary definition, but rather to find the boundaries which she herself has set, and erect a barrier round them; not calling mankind to account for having misapplied the word 'poetry', but attempting to clear up the conception which they already attach to it, and to bring forward as a distinct principle that which, as a vague feeling, has really guided them in their employment of the term.

The object of poetry is confessedly to act upon the emotions; and therein is poetry sufficiently distinguished from what Wordsworth affirms to be its logical opposite, namely, not prose, but matter of fact or science. The one addresses itself to the belief, the other to the feelings. The one does its work by convincing or persuading, the other by moving. The one acts by presenting a proposition to the understanding, the other by offering interesting objects of contemplation to the sensibilities.

This, however, leaves us very far from a definition of poetry. This distinguishes it from one thing, but we are bound to distinguish it from everything. To bring thoughts or images before the mind for the purpose of acting upon the emotions, does not belong to poetry alone. It is equally the province (for example) of the novelist: and yet the faculty of the poet and that of the novelist are as distinct as any other two faculties; as the faculties of the novelist and of the orator, or of the poet and the metaphysician. The two characters may be united, as characters the most disparate may; but they have no natural connexion.

Many of the greatest poems are in the form of fictitious narratives, and in almost all good serious fictions there is true poetry. But there is a radical distinction between the interest felt in a story as such, and the interest excited by poetry; for the one is derived from incident, the other from the representation of feeling. In one, the source of the emotion excited is the exhibition of a state or states of human sensibility; in the other, of a series of states of mere outward circumstances. Now, all minds are capable of being affected more or less by representations of the latter kind, and all, or almost all, by those of the former; yet the two sources of interest correspond to two distinct, and (as respects their greatest development) mutually exclusive, characters of mind.

At what age is the passion for a story, for almost any kind of story, merely as a story, the most intense? In childhood. But that also is the age at which poetry, even of the simplest description, is least relished and least understood; because the feelings with which it is especially conversant are yet undeveloped, and not having been even in the slightest degree experienced, cannot be sympathized with. In what stage of the progress of society, again, is story-telling most valued, and the story-teller in greatest request and honour?—In a rude state like that of the Tartars and Arabs at this day, and of almost all nations in the earliest ages. But in this state of society there is little poetry except ballads, which are mostly narrative, that is, essentially stories, and derive their principal interest from the incidents. Considered as poetry, they are of the lowest and most elementary kind: the feelings depicted, or rather indicated, are the simplest our nature has; such joys and griefs as the immediate pressure of some outward event excites in rude minds, which live wholly immersed in outward things, and have never, either from choice or a force they could not resist, turned themselves to the contemplation of the world within. Passing now from childhood, and from the childhood of society, to the grown-up men and women of this most grown-up and unchildlike age—the minds and hearts of greatest depth and elevation are commonly those which take greatest delight in poetry; the shallowest and emptiest, on the contrary, are, at all events, not those least addicted to novel-reading. This accords, too, with all analogous experience of human nature. The sort of persons whom not merely in books but in their lives, we find perpetually engaged in hunting for excitement from without, are invariably those who do not possess, either in the vigour of their intellectual powers or in the depth of their sensibilities, that which would enable them to find ample excitement nearer home. The most idle and frivolous persons take a natural delight in fictitious narrative; the excitement it affords is of the kind which comes from without. Such persons are rarely lovers of poetry, though they may fancy themselves so, because they relish novels in verse. But poetry, which is the delineation of the deeper and more secret workings of human emotion, is interesting only to those to whom it recalls what they have felt, or whose imagination it stirs up to conceive what they could feel, or what they might have been able to feel, had their outward circumstances been different.

Poetry, when it is really such, is truth; and fiction also, if it is good for anything, is truth: but they are different truths. The truth of poetry is to paint the human soul truly: the truth of fiction is to give a true picture of life. The two kinds of knowledge are different, and come by different ways, come mostly to different persons. Great poets are often proverbially ignorant of life. What they know has come by observation of themselves; they have found within them one highly delicate and sensitive specimen of human nature, on which the laws of emotion are written in large characters, such as can be read off without much study. Other knowledge of mankind, such as comes to men of the world by outward experience, is not indispensable to them as poets: but to the novelist such knowledge is all in all; he has to describe outward things, not the inward man; actions and events, not feelings; and it will not do for him to be numbered among those who, as Madame Roland said of Brissot, know man but not *men*.

All this is no bar to the possibility of combining both elements, poetry and narrative or incident, in the same work, and calling it either a novel or a poem; but so may red and white combine on the same human features, or on the same canvas. There is one order of composition which requires the union of poetry and incident, each in its highest kind—the dramatic. Even there the two elements are perfectly distinguishable, and may exist of unequal quality, and in the most various proportion. The incidents of a dramatic poem may be scanty and ineffective, though the delineation of passion and character may be of the highest order; as in Goethe's admirable *Torquato Tasso;* or again, the story as a mere story may be well got up for effect, as is the case with some of the most trashy productions of the Minerva press: it may even be, what those are not, a coherent and probable series of events, though there be scarcely a feeling exhibited which is not represented falsely, or in a manner absolutely commonplace. The combination of the two excellences is what renders Shakespeare so generally acceptable, each sort of readers finding in him what is suitable to their faculties. To the many he is great as a story-teller, to the few as a poet.

In limiting poetry to the delineation of states of feeling, and denying the name where nothing is delineated but outward objects, we may be thought to have done what we promised to avoid—to have not found, but made a definition, in opposition to the usage of language, since it is established by common consent that there is a poetry called descriptive. We deny the charge. Description is not poetry because there is descriptive poetry, no more than science is poetry because there is such a thing as a didactic poem. But an object which admits of being described, or a truth which may fill a place in a scientific treatise, may also furnish an occasion for the generation of poetry, which we thereupon choose to call descriptive or didactic. The poetry is not in the object itself, nor in the scientific truth itself, but in the state of mind in which the one and the other may be contemplated. The mere delineation of the dimensions and colours of external objects is not poetry, no more than a geometrical ground-plan of St. Peter's or Westminster Abbey is painting. Descriptive poetry consists, no doubt, in description, but in description of things as they appear, not as they are; and it paints them not in their bare and natural lineaments, but seen through the medium and arrayed in the colours of the imagination set in action by the feelings. If a poet describes a lion, he does not describe him as a naturalist would, nor even as a traveller would, who was intent upon stating the truth, the whole truth, and nothing but the truth. He describes him by imagery, that is, by suggesting the most striking likenesses and contrasts which might occur to a mind contemplating the lion, in the state of awe, wonder, or terror, which the spectacle naturally excites, or is, on the occasion, supposed to excite. Now this is describing the lion professedly, but the state of excitement of the spectator really. The lion may be described falsely or with exaggeration, and the poetry be all the better; but if the human emotion be not painted with scrupulous truth, the poetry is bad poetry, i.e. is not poetry at all, but a failure.

Thus far our progress towards a clear view of the essentials of poetry has brought us very close to the last two attempts at a definition of poetry which we happen to have seen in print, both of them by poets and men of genius. The one is by Ebenezer Elliott, the author of *Corn-Law Rhymes*, and other poems of still greater merit. 'Poetry', says he, 'is impassioned truth.' The other is by a writer in *Blackwood's Magazine*, and comes, we think, still nearer the mark. He defines poetry, 'man's thoughts tinged by his feelings'. There is in either definition a near approximation to what we are in search of. Every truth which a human being can enunciate, every thought, even every outward impression, which can enter into his consciousness, may become poetry when shown through any impassioned medium, when invested with the colouring of joy, or grief, or pity, or affection, or admiration, or reverence, or awe, or even hatred or terror: and, unless so coloured, nothing, be it as interesting as it may, is poetry. But both these definitions fail to discriminate between poetry and eloquence. Eloquence, as well as poetry, is impassioned truth; eloquence, as well as poetry, is thoughts coloured by the feelings. Yet common apprehension and philosophic criticism alike recognize a distinction between the two: there is much that every one would call eloquence, which no one would think of classing as poetry. A question will sometimes arise, whether some particular author is a poet; and those who maintain the negative commonly allow that, though not a poet, he is a highly eloquent writer. The distinction between poetry and eloquence appears to us to be equally fundamental with the distinction between poetry and narrative, or between poetry and description, while it is still farther from having been satisfactorily cleared up than either of the others.

Poetry and eloquence are both alike the expression or utterance of feeling. But if we may be excused the antithesis, we should say that eloquence is *heard*, poetry is *over*heard. Eloquence supposes an audience; the peculiarity of poetry appears to us to lie in the poet's utter unconsciousness of a listener. Poetry is feeling confessing itself to itself, in moments of solitude, and embodying itself in symbols which are the nearest possible representations of the feeling in the exact shape in which it exists in the poet's mind. Eloquence is feeling pouring itself out to other minds, courting their sympathy, or endeavouring to influence their belief or move them to passion or to action.

All poetry is of the nature of soliloquy. It may be said that poetry which is printed on hot-pressed paper and sold at a bookseller's shop, is a soliloquy in full dress, and on the stage. It is so; but there is nothing absurd in the idea of such a mode of soliloquizing. What we have said to ourselves, we may tell to others afterwards; what we have said or done in solitude, we may voluntarily reproduce when we know that other eyes are upon us. But no trace of consciousness that any eyes are upon us must be visible in the work itself. The actor knows that there is an audience present; but if he acts as though he knew it, he acts ill. A poet may write poetry not only with the intention of printing it, but for the express purpose of being paid for it; that it should *be* poetry, being written under such influences, is less probable; not, however, impossible; but no otherwise possible than if he can succeed in excluding from his work every vestige of such lookings-forth into the outward and every-day world, and can express his emotions exactly as he has felt them in solitude, or as he is conscious that he should feel them though they were to remain for ever unuttered, or (at the lowest) as he knows that others feel them in similar circumstances of solitude. But when he turns round and addresses himself to another person; when the act of utterance is not itself the end, but a means to an end,—viz. by the feelings he himself expresses, to work upon the feelings, or upon the belief, or the will, of another,—when the expression of his emotions, or of his thoughts tinged by his emotions, is tinged also by that purpose, by that desire of making an impression upon another mind, then it ceases to be poetry, and becomes eloquence.

Poetry, accordingly, is the natural fruit of solitude and meditation; eloquence, of intercourse with the world. The persons who have most feeling of their own, if intellectual culture has given them a language in which to express it, have the highest faculty of poetry; those who best understand the feelings of others, are the most eloquent. The persons, and the nations, who commonly excel in poetry, are those whose character and tastes render them least dependent upon the applause, or sympathy, or concurrence of the world in general. Those to whom that applause, that sympathy, that concurrence are most necessary, generally excel most in eloquence. And hence, perhaps, the French, who are the least poetical of all great and intellectual nations, are among the most eloquent: the French, also, being the most sociable, the vainest, and the least self-dependent.

If the above be, as we believe, the true theory of the distinction commonly admitted between eloquence and poetry; or even though it be not so, yet if, as we cannot doubt, the distinction above stated be a real bona fide distinction, it will be found to hold, not merely in the language of words, but in all other language, and to intersect the whole domain of art.

Take, for example, music: we shall find in that art, so peculiarly the expression of passion, two perfectly distinct styles; one of which may be called the poetry, the other the oratory of music. This difference, being seized, would put an end to much musical sectarianism. There has been much contention whether the music of the modern Italian school, that of Rossini and his successors, be impassioned or not. Without doubt, the passion it expresses is not the musing, meditative tenderness, or pathos, or grief of Mozart or Beethoven. Yet it is passion, but garrulous passion—the passion which pours itself into other ears; and therein the better calculated for dramatic effect, having a natural adaptation for dialogue. Mozart also is great in musical oratory; but his most touching compositions are in the opposite style—that of soliloquy. Who can imagine 'Dove sono' *heard?* We imagine it *over*heard.

Purely pathetic music commonly partakes of soliloquy. The soul is absorbed in its distress, and though there may be bystanders, it is not thinking of them. When the mind is looking within, and not without, its state does not often or rapidly vary; and hence the even, uninterrupted flow, approaching almost to monotony, which a good reader, or a good singer, will give to words or music of a pensive or melancholy cast. But grief taking the form of a prayer, or of a complaint, becomes oratorical; no longer low, and even, and subdued, it assumes a more emphatic rhythm, a more rapidly returning accent; instead of a few slow equal notes, following one after another at regular intervals, it crowds note upon note, and often assumes a hurry and bustle like joy. Those who are familiar with some of the best of Rossini's serious compositions, such as the air 'Tu che i miseri conforti', in the opera of *Tancredi,* or the duet 'Ebben per mia memoria', in *La Gazza Ladra,* will at once understand and feel our meaning. Both are highly tragic and passionate; the passion of both is that of oratory, not poetry. The like may be said of that most moving invocation in Beethoven's *Fidelio*—

> Komm, Hoffnung, lass das letzte Stern
> Der Müde nicht erbleichen;

in which Madame Schröder Devrient exhibited such consummate powers of pathetic expression. How different from Winter's beautiful 'Paga fui', the very soul of melancholy exhaling itself in solitude; fuller of meaning, and, therefore, more profoundly poetical than the words for which it was composed—for it seems to express not simple melancholy, but the melancholy of remorse.

If, from vocal music, we now pass to instrumental, we may have a specimen of musical oratory in any fine military symphony or march: while the poetry of music seems to have attained its consummation in Beethoven's Overture to Egmont, so wonderful in its mixed expression of grandeur and melancholy.

In the arts which speak to the eye, the same distinctions will be found to hold, not only between poetry and oratory, but between poetry, oratory, narrative, and simple imitation or description.

Pure description is exemplified in a mere portrait or a mere landscape—productions of art, it is true, but of the mechanical rather than of the fine arts, being works of simple imitation, not creation. We say, a mere portrait, or a mere landscape, because it is possible for a portrait or a landscape, without ceasing to be such, to be also a picture; like Turner's landscapes, and the great portraits by Titian or Vandyke.

Whatever in painting or sculpture expresses human feeling—or character, which is only a certain state of feeling grown habitual—may be called, according to circumstances, the poetry, or the eloquence, of the painter's or the sculptor's art: the poetry, if the feeling declares itself by such signs as escape from us when we are unconscious of being seen; the oratory, if the signs are those we use for the purpose of voluntary communication.

The narrative style answers to what is called historical painting, which it is the fashion among connoisseurs to treat as the climax of the pictorial art. That it is the most difficult branch of the art we do not doubt, because, in its perfection, it includes the perfection of all the other branches: as in like manner an epic poem, though in so far as it is epic (i.e. narrative) it is not poetry at all, is yet esteemed the greatest effort of poetic genius, because there is no kind whatever of poetry which may not appropriately find a place in it. But an historical picture as such, that is, as the representation of an incident, must necessarily, as it seems to us, be poor and ineffective. The narrative powers of painting are extremely limited. Scarcely any picture, scarcely even any series of pictures, tells its own story without the aid of an interpreter. But it is the single figures which, to us, are the great charm even of an historical picture. It is in these that the power of the art is really seen. In the attempt to narrate, visible and permanent signs are too far behind the fugitive audible ones, which follow so fast one after another, while the faces and figures in a narrative picture, even though they be Titian's, stand still. Who would not prefer one Virgin and Child of Raphael, to all the pictures which Rubens, with his fat, frouzy Dutch Venuses, ever painted? Though Rubens, besides excelling almost every one in his mastery over the mechanical parts of his art, often shows real genius in *grouping* his figures, the peculiar problem of historical painting. But then, who, except a mere student of drawing and colouring, ever cared to look twice at any of the figures themselves? The power of painting lies in poetry, of which Rubens had not the slightest tincture—not in narrative, wherein he might have excelled.

The single figures, however, in an historical picture, are rather the eloquence of painting than the poetry: they mostly (unless they are quite out of place in the picture) express the feelings of one person as modified by the presence of others. Accordingly the minds whose bent leads them rather to eloquence than to poetry, rush to historical painting. The French painters, for instance, seldom attempt, because they could make nothing of, single heads, like those glorious ones of the Italian masters, with which they might feed themselves day after day in their own Louvre. They must all be historical; and they are, almost to a man, attitudinizers. If we wished to give any young artist the most impressive warning our imagination could devise against that kind of vice in the pictorial, which corresponds to rant in the histrionic art, we would advise him to walk once up and once down the gallery of the Luxembourg. Every figure in French painting or statuary seems to be showing itself off before spectators; they are not poetical, but in the worst style of corrupted eloquence.

## *II*

*Nascitur Poeta* is a maxim of classical antiquity, which has passed to these latter days with less questioning than most of the doctrines of that early age. When it originated, the human faculties were occupied, fortunately for posterity, less in examining how the works of genius are created, than in creating them: and the adage, probably, had no higher source than the tendency common among mankind to consider all power which is not visibly the effect of practice, all skill which is not capable of being reduced to mechanical rules, as the result of a peculiar gift. Yet this aphorism, born in the infancy of psychology, will perhaps be found, now when that science is in its adolescence, to be as true as an epigram ever is, that is, to contain some truth: truth, however, which has been so compressed and bent out of shape, in order to tie it up into so small a knot of only two words that it requires an almost infinite amount of unrolling and laying straight, before it will resume its just proportions.

We are not now intending to remark upon the grosser misapplications of this ancient maxim, which have engendered so many races of poetasters. The days are gone by when every raw youth whose borrowed phantasies have set themselves to a borrowed tune, mistaking, as Coleridge says, an ardent desire of poetic reputation for poetic genius, while unable to disguise from himself that he had taken no means whereby he might *become* a poet, could fancy himself a born one. Those who would reap without sowing, and gain the victory without fighting the battle, are ambitious now of another sort of distinction, and are born novelists, or public speakers, not poets. And the wiser thinkers understand and acknowledge that poetic excellence is subject to the same necessary conditions with any other mental endowment; and that to no one of the spiritual benefactors of mankind is a higher or a more assiduous intellectual culture needful than to the poet. It is true, he possesses this advantage over others who use the 'instrument of words', that, of the truths which he utters, a larger proportion are derived from personal consciousness, and a smaller from philosophic investigation. But the power itself of discriminating between what really is consciousness, and what is only a process of inference completed in a single instant—and the capacity of distinguishing whether that of which the mind is conscious be an eternal truth, or but a dream—are among the last results of the most matured and perfect intellect. Not to mention that the poet, no more than any other person who writes, confines himself altogether to intuitive truths, nor has any means of communicating even these but by words, every one of which derives all its power of conveying a meaning, from a whole host of acquired notions, and facts learnt by study and experience.

Nevertheless, it seems undeniable in point of fact, and consistent with the principles of a sound metaphysics, that there are poetic *natures*. There is a mental and physical constitution or temperament, peculiarly fitted for poetry. This temperament will not of itself make a poet, no more than the soil will the fruit; and as good fruit may be raised by culture from indifferent soils, so may good poetry from naturally unpoetical minds. But the poetry of one who is a poet by nature, will be clearly and broadly distinguishable from the poetry of mere culture. It may not be truer; it may not be more useful; but it will be different: fewer will appreciate it, even though many should affect to do so; but in those few it will find a keener sympathy, and will yield them a deeper enjoyment.

One may write genuine poetry, and not be a poet; for whosoever writes out truly any human feeling, writes poetry. All persons, even the most unimaginative, in moments of strong emotion, speak poetry; and hence the drama is poetry, which else were always prose, except when a poet is one of the characters. What *is* poetry, but the thoughts and words in which emotion spontaneously embodies itself? As there are few who are not, at least for some moments and in some situations, capable of some strong feeling, poetry is natural to most persons at some period of their lives. And any one whose feelings are genuine, though but of the average strength,—if he be not diverted by uncongenial thoughts or occupations from the indulgence of them, and if he acquire by culture, as all persons may, the faculty of delineating them correctly,—has it in his power to be a poet, so far as a life passed in writing unquestionable poetry may be considered to confer that title. But *ought* it to do so? Yes, perhaps, in a collection of 'British Poets'. But 'poet' is the name also of a variety of man, not solely of the author of a particular variety of book: now, to have written whole volumes of real poetry is possible to almost all kinds of characters, and implies no greater peculiarity of mental construction, than to be the author of a history, or a novel.

Whom, then, shall we call poets? Those who are so constituted, that emotions are the links of association by which their ideas, both sensuous and spiritual, are connected together. This constitution belongs (within certain limits) to all in whom poetry is a pervading principle. In all others, poetry is something extraneous and superinduced: something out of themselves, foreign to the habitual course of their everyday lives and characters; a world to which they may make occasional visits, but where they are sojourners, not dwellers, and which, when out of it, or even when in it, they think of, peradventure, but as a phantom-world, a place of *ignes fatui* and spectral illusions. Those only who have the peculiarity of association which we have mentioned, and which is a natural though not a universal consequence of intense sensibility, instead of seeming not themselves when they are uttering poetry, scarcely seem themselves when uttering anything to which poetry is foreign. Whatever be the thing which they are contemplating, if it be capable of connecting itself with their emotions, the aspect under which it first and most naturally paints itself to them, is its poetic aspect. The poet of culture sees his object in prose, and describes it in poetry; the poet of nature actually sees it in poetry.

This point is perhaps worth some little illustration; the rather, as metaphysicians (the ultimate arbiters of all philosophical criticism), while they have busied themselves for two thousand years, more or less, about the few *universal* laws of human nature, have strangely neglected the analysis of its *diversities*. Of these, none lie deeper or reach further than the varieties which difference of nature and of education makes in what may be termed the habitual bond of association. In a mind entirely uncultivated, which is also without any strong feelings, objects whether of sense or of intellect arrange themselves in the mere casual order in which they have been seen, heard, or otherwise perceived. Persons of this sort may be said to think chronologically. If they remember a fact, it is by reason of a fortuitous coincidence with some trifling incident or circumstance which took place at the very time. If they have a story to tell, or testimony to deliver in a witness-box, their narrative must follow the exact order in which the events took place: *dodge* them, and the thread of association is broken; they cannot go on. Their associations, to use the language of philosophers, are chiefly of the successive, not the synchronous kind, and whether successive or synchronous, are mostly casual.

To the man of science, again, or of business, objects group themselves according to the artificial classifications which the understanding has voluntarily made for the convenience of thought or of practice. But where any of the impressions are vivid and intense, the associations into which these enter are the ruling ones: it being a well-known law of association, that the stronger a feeling is, the more quickly and strongly it associates itself with any other object or feeling. Where, therefore, nature has given strong feelings, and education has not created factitious tendencies stronger than the natural ones, the prevailing associations will be those which connect objects and ideas with emotions, and with each other through the intervention of emotions. Thoughts and images will be linked together, according to the similarity of feelings which cling to them. A thought will introduce a thought by first introducing a feeling which is allied with it. At the centre of each group of thoughts or images will be found a feeling; and the thoughts or images will be there only because the feeling was there. The combinations which the mind puts together, the pictures which it paints, the wholes which Imagination constructs out of the materials supplied by Fancy, will be indebted to some dominant *feeling*, not as in other natures to a dominant *thought*, for their unity and consistency of character, for what distinguishes them from incoherencies.

The difference, then, between the poetry of a poet, and the poetry of a cultivated but not naturally poetic mind, is, that in the latter, with however bright a halo of feeling the thought may be surrounded and glorified, the thought itself is always the conspicuous object; while the poetry of a poet is Feeling itself, employing Thought only as the medium of its expression. In the one, feeling waits upon thought; in the other, thought upon feeling. The one writer has a distinct aim, common to him with any other didactic author; he desires to convey the thought, and he conveys it clothed in the feelings which it excites in himself, or which he deems most appropriate to it. The other merely pours forth the overflowing of his feelings; and all the thoughts which those feelings suggest are floated promiscuously along the stream.

It may assist in rendering our meaning intelligible, if we illustrate it by a parallel between the two English authors of our own day who have produced the greatest quantity of true and endearing poetry, Wordsworth and Shelley. Apter instances could not be wished for; the one might be cited as the type, the *exemplar*, of what the poetry of culture may accomplish: the other as perhaps the most striking example ever known of the poetic temperament. How different, accordingly, is the poetry of these two great writers! In Wordsworth, the poetry is almost always the mere setting of a thought. The thought may be more valuable than the setting, or it may be less valuable, but there can be no question as to which was first in his mind: what he is impressed with, and what he is anxious to impress, is some proposition, more or less distinctly conceived; some truth, or something which he deems such. He lets the thought dwell in his mind, till it excites, as is the nature of thought, other thoughts, and also such feelings as the measure of his sensibility is adequate to supply. Among these thoughts and feelings, had he chosen a different walk of authorship (and there are many in which he might equally have excelled), he would probably have made a different selection of media for enforcing the parent thought: his habits, however, being those of poetic composition, he selects in preference the strongest feelings, and the thoughts with which most of feeling is naturally or habitually connected. His poetry, therefore, may be defined to be, his thoughts, coloured by, and impressing themselves by means of, emotions. Such poetry, Wordsworth has occupied a long life in producing. And well and wisely has he so done. Criticisms, no doubt, may be made occasionally both upon the thoughts themselves, and upon the skill he has demonstrated in the choice of his media: for an affair of skill and study, in the most rigorous sense, it evidently was. But he has not laboured in vain; he has exercised, and continues to exercise, a powerful, and mostly a highly beneficial influence over the formation and growth of not a few of the most cultivated and vigorous of the youthful minds of our time, over whose heads poetry of the opposite description would have flown, for want of an original organization, physical or mental, in sympathy with it.

On the other hand, Wordsworth's poetry is never bounding, never ebullient; has little even of the appearance of spontaneousness: the well is never so full that it overflows. There is an air of calm deliberateness about all he writes, which is not characteristic of the poetic temperament: his poetry seems one thing, himself another; he seems to be poetical because he wills to be so, not because he cannot help it: did he will to dismiss poetry, he need never again, it might almost seem, have a poetical thought. He never seems *possessed* by any feeling; no emotion seems ever so strong as to have entire sway, for the time being, over the current of his thoughts. He never, even for the space of a few stanzas, appears entirely given up to exultation, or grief, or pity, or love, or admiration, or devotion, or even animal spirits. He now and then, though seldom, attempts to write as if he were: and never, we think, without leaving an impression of poverty: as the brook which on nearly level ground quite fills its banks, appears but a thread when running rapidly down a precipitous declivity. He has feeling enough to form a decent, graceful, even beautiful decoration to a thought which is in itself interesting and moving; but not so much as suffices to stir up the soul by mere sympathy with itself in its simplest manifestation, nor enough to summon up that array of 'thoughts of power' which in a richly stored mind always attends the call of really intense feeling. It is for this reason, doubtless, that the genius of Wordsworth is essentially unlyrical. Lyric poetry, as it was the earliest kind, is also, if the view we are now taking of poetry be correct, more eminently and peculiarly poetry than any other: it is the poetry most natural to a really poetic temperament, and least capable of being successfully imitated by one not so endowed by nature.

Shelley is the very reverse of all this. Where Wordsworth is strong, he is weak; where Wordsworth is weak, he is strong. Culture, that culture by which Wordsworth has reared from his own inward nature the richest harvest ever brought forth by a soil of so little depth, is precisely what was wanting to Shelley: or let us rather say, he had not, at the period of his deplorably early death, reached sufficiently far in that intellectual progression of which he was capable, and which, if it has done so much for greatly inferior natures, might have made of him the most perfect, as he was already the most gifted of our poets. For him, voluntary mental discipline had done little: the vividness of his emotions and of his sensations had done all. He seldom follows up an idea; it starts into life, summons from the fairy-land of his inexhaustible fancy some three or four bold images, then vanishes, and straight he is off on the wings of some casual association into quite another sphere. He had scarcely yet acquired the consecutiveness of thought necessary for a long poem; his more ambitious compositions too often resemble the scattered fragments of a mirror; colours brilliant as life, single images without end, but no picture. It is only when under the overruling influence of some one state of feeling, either actually experienced, or summoned up in the vividness of reality by a fervid imagination, that he writes as a great poet; unity of feeling being to him the harmonizing principle which a central idea is to minds of another class, and supplying the coherency and consistency which would else have been wanting. Thus it is in many of his smaller, and especially his lyrical poems. They are obviously written to exhale, perhaps to relieve, a state of feeling, or of conception of feeling, almost oppressive from its vividness. The thoughts and imagery are suggested by the feeling, and are such as it finds unsought. The state of feeling may be either of soul or of sense, or oftener (might we not say invariably?) of both: for the poetic temperament is usually, perhaps always, accompanied by exquisite senses. The exciting cause may be either an object or an idea. But whatever of sensation enters into the feeling, must not be local, or consciously organic; it is a condition of the whole frame, not of a part only. Like the state of sensation produced by a fine climate, or indeed like all strongly pleasurable or painful sensations in an impassioned nature, it pervades the entire nervous system. States of feeling, whether sensuous or spiritual, which thus possess the whole being, are the fountains of that which we have called the poetry of poets; and which is little else than a pouring forth of the thoughts and images that pass across the mind while some permanent state of feeling is occupying it.

To the same original fineness of organization, Shelley was doubtless indebted for another of his rarest gifts, that exuberance of imagery, which when unrepressed, as in many of his poems it is, amounts to a fault. The susceptibility of his nervous system, which made his emotions intense, made also the impressions of his external senses deep and clear; and agreeably to the law of association by which, as already remarked, the strongest impressions are those which associate themselves the most easily and strongly, these vivid sensations were readily recalled to mind by all objects or thoughts which had co-existed with them, and by all feelings which in any degree resembled them. Never did a fancy so teem with sensuous imagery as Shelley's. Wordsworth economizes an image, and detains it until he has distilled all the poetry out of it, and it will not yield a drop more: Shelley lavishes his with a profusion which is unconscious because it is inexhaustible.

If, then, the maxim *Nascitur poeta* mean, either that the power of producing poetical compositions is a peculiar faculty which the poet brings into the world with him, which grows with his growth like any of his bodily powers, and is as independent of culture as his height, and his complexion; or that any natural peculiarity whatever is implied in producing poetry, real poetry, and in any quantity—such poetry too, as, to the majority of educated and intelligent readers, shall appear quite as good as, or even better than, any other; in either sense the doctrine is false. And nevertheless, there *is* poetry which could not emanate but from a mental and physical constitution peculiar, not in the kind, but in the degree of its susceptibility: a constitution which makes its possessor capable of greater happiness than mankind in general, and also of greater unhappiness; and because greater, so also more various. And such poetry, to all who know enough of nature to own it as being in nature, is much more poetry, is poetry in a far higher sense, than any other; since the common element of all poetry, that which constitutes poetry, human feeling, enters far more largely into this than into the poetry of culture. Not only because the natures which we have called poetical, really feel more, and consequently have more feeling to express; but because, the capacity of feeling being so great, feeling, when excited and not voluntarily resisted, seizes the helm of their thoughts, and the succession of ideas and images becomes the mere utterance of an emotion; not, as in other natures, the emotion a mere ornamental colouring of the thought.

Ordinary education and the ordinary course of life are constantly at work counteracting this quality of mind, and substituting habits more suitable to their own ends: if instead of substituting they were content to superadd, there would be nothing to complain of. But when will education consist, not in repressing any mental faculty or power, from the uncontrolled action of which danger is apprehended, but in training up to its proper strength the corrective and antagonistic power?

In whomsoever the quality which we have described exists, and is not stifled, that person is a poet. Doubtless he is a greater poet in proportion as the fineness of his perceptions, whether of sense or of internal consciousness, furnishes him with an ampler supply of lovely images—the vigour and richness of his intellect, with a greater abundance of moving thoughts. For it is through these thoughts and images that the feeling speaks, and through their impressiveness that it impresses itself, and finds response in other hearts; and from these media of transmitting it (contrary to the laws of physical nature) increase of intensity is reflected back upon the feeling itself. But all these it is possible to have, and not be a poet; they are mere materials, which the poet shares in common with other people. What constitutes the poet is not the imagery nor the thoughts, nor even the feelings, but the law according to which they are called up. He is a poet, not because he has ideas of any particular kind, but because the succession of his ideas is subordinate to the course of his emotions.

Many who have never acknowledged this in theory, bear testimony to it in their particular judgements. In listening to an oration, or reading a written discourse not professedly poetical, when do we begin to feel that the speaker or author is putting off the character of the orator or the prose writer, and is passing into the poet? Not when he begins to show strong feeling; *then* we merely say, he is in earnest, he feels what he says; still less when he expresses himself in imagery; then, unless illustration be manifestly his sole object, we are apt to say, this is affectation. It is when the feeling (instead of passing away, or, if it continue, letting the train of thoughts run on exactly as they would have done if there were no influence at work but the mere intellect) becomes itself the originator of another train of association, which expels or blends with the former; when (for example) either his words, or the mode of their arrangement, are such as we spontaneously use only when in a state of excitement, proving that the mind is at least as much occupied by a passive state of its own feelings, as by the desire of attaining the premeditated end which the discourse has in view.[1]

Our judgements of authors who lay actual claim to the title of poets, follow the same principle. Whenever, after a writer's meaning is fully understood, it is still matter of reasoning and discussion whether he is a poet or not, he will be found to be wanting in the characteristic peculiarity of association so often adverted to. When, on the contrary, after reading or hearing one or two passages, we instinctively and without hesitation cry out, 'This is a poet', the probability is, that the passages are strongly marked with this peculiar quality. And we may add that in such case, a critic who, not having sufficient feeling to respond to the poetry, is also without sufficient philosophy to understand it though he feel it not, will be apt to pronounce, not 'this is prose', but 'this is exaggeration', 'this is mysticism', or, 'this is nonsense'.

Although a philosopher cannot, by culture, make himself, in the peculiar sense in which we now use the term, a poet, unless at least he have that peculiarity of nature which would probably have made poetry his earliest pursuit; a poet may always, by culture, make himself a philosopher. The poetic laws of association are by no means incompatible with the more ordinary laws; are by no means such as *must* have their course, even though a deliberate purpose require their suspension. If the peculiarities of the poetic temperament were uncontrollable in any poet, they might be supposed so in Shelley; yet how powerfully, in the *Cenci,* does he coerce and restrain all the characteristic qualities of his genius; what severe simplicity, in place of his usual barbaric splendour; how rigidly does he keep the feelings and the imagery in subordination to the thought.

The investigation of nature requires no habits or qualities of mind, but such as may always be acquired by industry and mental activity. Because at one time the mind may be so given up to a state of feeling, that the succession of its ideas is determined by the present enjoyment or suffering which pervades it, this is no reason but that in the calm retirement of study, when under no peculiar excitement either of the outward or of the inward sense, it may form any combinations, or pursue any train of ideas, which are most conducive to the purposes of philosophic inquiry; and may, while in that state, form deliberate convictions, from which no excitement will afterwards make it swerve. Might we not go even further than this? We shall not pause to ask whether it be not a misunderstanding of the nature of passionate feeling to imagine that it is inconsistent with calmness; whether they who so deem of it, do not mistake passion in the militant or antagonistic state, for the type of passion universally; do not confound passion struggling towards an outward object, with passion brooding over itself. But without entering into this deeper investigation; that capacity of strong feeling, which is supposed necessarily to disturb the judgement, is also the material out of which all *motives* are made; the motives, consequently, which lead human beings to the pursuit of truth. The greater the individual's capability of happiness and of misery, the stronger interest has that individual in arriving at truth; and when once that interest is felt, an impassioned nature is sure to pursue this, as to pursue any other object, with greater ardour; for energy of character is commonly the offspring of strong feeling. If, therefore, the most impassioned natures do not ripen into the most powerful intellects, it is always from defect of culture, or something wrong in the circumstances by which the being has originally or successively been surrounded. Undoubtedly strong feelings require a strong intellect to carry them, as more sail requires more ballast: and when, from neglect, or bad education, that strength is wanting, no wonder if the grandest and swiftest vessels make the most utter wreck.

Where, as in some of our older poets, a poetic nature has been united with logical and scientific culture, the peculiarity of association arising from the finer nature so perpetually alternates with the associations attainable by commoner natures trained to high perfection, that its own particular law is not so conspiciously characteristic of the result produced, as in a poet like Shelley, to whom systematic intellectual culture, in a measure proportioned to the intensity of his own nature, has been wanting. Whether the superiority will naturally be on the side of the philosopher-poet or of the mere poet—whether the writings of the one ought, as a whole, to be truer, and their influence more beneficent, than those of the other—is too obvious in principle to need statement: it would be absurd to doubt whether two endowments are better than one; whether truth is more certainly arrived at by two processes, verifying and correcting each other, than by one alone. Unfortunately, in practice the matter is not quite so simple; there the question often is, which is least prejudicial to the intellect, uncultivation or malcultivation. For, as long as education consists chiefly of the mere inculcation of traditional opinions, many of which, from the mere fact that the human intellect has not yet reached perfection, must necessarily be false; so long as even those who are best taught, are rather taught to know the thoughts of others than to think, it is not always clear that the poet of acquired ideas has the advantage over him whose feeling has been his sole teacher. For the depth and durability of wrong as well as of right impressions is proportional to the fineness of the material; and they who have the greatest capacity of natural feeling are generally those whose artificial feelings are the strongest. Hence, doubtless, among other reasons, it is, that in an age of revolutions in opinion, the contemporary poets, those at least who deserve the name, those who have any individuality of character, if they are not before their age, are almost sure to be behind it. An observation curiously verified all over Europe in the present century. Nor let it be thought disparaging. However urgent may be the necessity for a breaking up of old modes of belief, the most strongminded and discerning, next to those who head the movement, are generally those who bring up the rear of it.

## *NOTES*

1. And this, we may remark by the way, seems to point to the true theory of poetic diction; and to suggest the true answer to as much as is erroneous of Wordsworth's celebrated doctrine on that subject. For on the one hand, *all* language which is the natural expression of feeling, is really poetical, and will be felt as such, apart from conventional associations; but on the other, whenever intellectual culture has afforded a choice between several modes of expressing the same emotion, the stronger the feeling is, the more naturally and certainly will it prefer the language which is most peculiarly appropriated to itself, and kept sacred from the contact of more vulgar objects of contemplation.

# *Edgar Allan Poe*

1809–1849

Edgar Allan Poe was born in Boston on January 9, 1809. In 1811 both his father and mother died, leaving the two-year-old child with no means of support. He was adopted by John Allan, a merchant of Scottish descent who sent him to school in England and spared him no luxury. He grew up a spoiled child, although an extremely sensitive and nervous one. In 1825 he entered the University of Virginia, where he developed a taste for gambling and drink. Upon his expulsion in 1826 he entered the army, an institution which for a time he found much more to his liking. Poe made a good soldier and was raised to the rank of sergeant-major. He was nominated for West Point in 1830, but upon taking up residence there he became consumed in obscure studies and refused to let the duties of a soldier command his life. He was soon court-martialled.

Without a position, and having expended Mr. Allan's financial generosity, Poe had nowhere to turn. As early as 1827 he had published poetry anonymously, but now he had to make writing his livelihood. In 1833 he won a prize of $100 offered by a Baltimore paper in a short story competition. From this point until his death he was employed by various newspapers, writing literary criticism and poetry. His poem "The Raven" brought him fame, but he received only a small fraction of the money his publishers made on it.

Although he was now writing short stories which would ensure him immortality, Poe's financial situation became desperate. Because of his severe alcoholism, he could not hold a job for any length of time. A subdued and courtly man when sober, he became violent, capricious, and manic when drunk. And his amorous life was just as unstable. In 1835 he married Virginia Clemm, his cousin and "child-bride," then fourteen. She died soon afterwards, inspiring one of Poe's finest poems—the Gnostic, necrophilic *Annabel Lee*. Twice he tried to marry wealthy women, but both times he failed. Later in his career Poe started his own magazine, *The Stylus*, but it was discontinued due to his erratic behavior. Literary myth has it that he died in the gutters of Baltimore, but in fact the effects of poverty, exhaustion, and alcohol had put him into a hospital where he died after five days in the autumn of 1849.

Poe was a brilliant short story writer, a variable critic, and a poet of sometimes questionable merit. He gave form and impetus to two subgenres of the short story—the horror and detective story—and might be said to have been the bearer of a new sensibility in American literature.

Unlike other American writers of his generation Poe did not try to display or define his American qualities. Rather, his persona and his method consisted of the attempt to be more European—more *Gothic*—than the European fantastic writers; he was obsessed with the grotesque for its own sake, he had command of a peculiar diction, and he wrote in sinuous, Latinate sentences. In Poe style and genre were virtually undistinguishable, a fact which had the singular and paradoxical effect of giving his writing the power of conciseness and compression as well as an aura of the amorphous and the vague.

Poe's influence is perhaps more significant than his art. But his influence has been great. Without him there would have been a very different Baudelaire, or none at all, and Borges has named Poe his most important precursor. The great French poet and critic Paul Valéry was also indebted to Poe—particularly to the essays here reprinted—for his recommendation of deliberation and pre-meditation in the construction of verse.

# The Rationale of Verse

The word "Verse" is here used not in its strict or primitive sense, but as the term most convenient for expressing generally and without pedantry all that is involved in the consideration of rhythm, rhyme, metre, and versification.

There is, perhaps, no topic in polite literature which has been more pertinaciously discussed, and there is certainly not one about which so much inaccuracy, confusion, misconception, misrepresentation, mystification, and downright ignorance on all sides, can be fairly said to exist. Were the topic really difficult, or did it lie, even, in the cloud-land of metaphysics, where the doubt-vapors may be made to assume any and every shape at the will or at the fancy of the gazer, we should have less reason to wonder at all this contradiction and perplexity; but in fact the subject is exceedingly simple; one tenth of it, possibly, may be called ethical; nine tenths, however, appertain to mathematics; and the whole is included within the limits of the commonest common-sense.

"But, if this is the case, how," it will be asked, "can so much misunderstanding have arisen? It is conceivable that a thousand profound scholars, investigating so very simple a matter for centuries, have not been able to place it in the fullest light, at least, of which it is susceptible?" These queries, I confess, are not easily answered:—at all events, a satisfactory reply to them might cost more trouble, than would, if properly considered, the whole *vexata quæstio* to which they have reference. Nevertheless, there is little difficulty or danger in suggesting that the "thousand profound scholars" *may* have failed, first, because they were scholars, secondly, because they were profound, and thirdly, because they were a thousand—the impotency of the scholarship and profundity having been thus multiplied a thousand-fold. I am serious in these suggestions; for, first again, there is something in "scholarship" which seduces us into blind worship of Bacon's Idol of the Theatre—into irrational deference to antiquity; secondly, the proper "profundity" is rarely profound—it is the nature of truth in general, as of some ores in particular, to be richest when most superficial; thirdly, the clearest subject may be overclouded by mere superabundance of talk. In chemistry, the best way of separating two bodies is to add a third; in speculation, fact often agrees with fact and argument with argument, until an additional well-meaning fact or argument sets every thing by the ears. In one case out of a hundred a point is excessively discussed because it is obscure; in the ninety-nine remaining it is obscure because excessively discussed. When a topic is thus circumstanced, the readiest mode of investigating it is to forget that any previous investigation has been attempted.

But, in fact, while much has been written on the Greek and Latin rhythms, and even on the Hebrew, little effort has been made at examining that of any of the modern tongues. As regards the English, comparatively nothing has been done. It may be said, indeed, that we are without a treatise on our own verse. In our ordinary grammars and in our works on rhetoric or prosody in general, may be found occasional chapters, it is true, which have the heading "Versification," but these are, in all instances, exceedingly meagre. They pretend to no analysis; they propose nothing like system; they make no attempt at even rule; every thing depends upon "authority." They are confined, in fact, to mere exemplification of the supposed varieties of English feet and English lines;—although in no work with which I am acquainted are these feet correctly given or these lines detailed in any thing like their full extent. Yet what has been mentioned is all—if we except the occasional introduction of some pedagogue-ism, such as this, borrowed from the Greek Prosodies: "When a syllable is wanting, the verse is said to be catalectic; when the measure is exact, the line is acatalectic; when there is a redundant syllable it forms hypermeter." Now whether a line be termed catalectic or acatalectic is, perhaps, a point of no vital importance; it is even possible that the student may be able to decide, promptly, when the *a* should be employed and when omitted, yet be incognizant, at the same time, of *all* that is worth knowing in regard to the structure of verse.

A leading defect in each of our treatises (if treatises they can be called), is the confining the subject to mere *Versification,* while *Verse* in general, with the understanding given to the term in the heading of this paper, is the real question at issue. Nor am I aware of even one of our grammars which so much as properly defines the word versification itself. "Versification," says a work now before me, of which the accuracy is far more than usual—the "English Grammar" of Goold Brown,—"Versification is the art of arranging words into lines of correspondent length, so as to produce harmony by the regular alternation of syllables differing in quantity." The commencement of this definition might apply, indeed, to the *art* of versification, but not versification itself. Versification is not the art of arranging, etc., but the actual arranging—a distinction too obvious to need comment. The error here is identical with one which has been too long permitted to disgrace the initial page of every one of our school grammars. I allude to the definitions of English grammar itself. "English grammar," it is said, "is the art of speaking and writing the English language correctly." This phraseology, or something essentially similar, is employed, I believe, by Bacon, Miller, Fisk, Greenleaf, Ingersoll, Kirkland, Cooper, Flint, Pue, Comly, and many others. These gentlemen, it is presumed, adopted it without examination from Murray, who derived it from Lily (whose work was *"quam solam Regia Majestas in omnibus scholis docendam præcipit"*), and who appropriated it without acknowledgment, but with some unimportant modification, from the Latin Grammar of Leonicenus. It may be shown, however, that this definition, so complacently received, is not, and cannot be, a proper definition of English grammar. A definition is that which so describes its object as to distinguish it from all others; it is no definition of any one thing if its terms are applicable to any one other. But if it be asked: "What is the design—the end—the aim of English grammar?" our obvious answer is: "The art of speaking and writing the English language correctly,"—

that is to say, we must use the precise words employed as the definition of English grammar itself. But the object to be attained by any means is, assuredly, not the means. English grammar and the end contemplated by English grammar are two matters sufficiently distinct; nor can the one be more reasonably regarded as the other than a fishing-hook as a fish. The definition, therefore, which is applicable in the latter instance, *cannot,* in the former, be true. Grammar in general is the analysis of language; English grammar of the English.

But to return to Versification as defined in our extract above. "It is the art," says the extract, "of arranging words into lines *of correspondent length.*" Not so; a correspondence in the length of lines is by no means essential. Pindaric odes are, surely, instances of versification, yet these compositions are noted for extreme diversity in the length of their lines.

The arrangement is, moreover, said to be for the purpose of producing "*harmony* by the regular alternation," etc. But *harmony* is not the sole aim—not even the principal one. In the construction of verse, *melody* should never be left out of view; yet this is a point which all our prosodies have most unaccountably forborne to touch. Reasoned rules on this topic should form a portion of all systems of rhythm.

"So as to produce harmony," says the definition, "by the *regular alternation,*" etc. A *regular* alternation, as described, forms no part of any principle of versification. The arrangement of spondees and dactyls, for example, in the Greek hexameter, is an arrangement which may be termed *at random.* At least it is arbitrary. Without interference with the line as a whole, a dactyl may be substituted for a spondee, or the converse, at any point other than the ultimate and penultimate feet, of which the former is always a spondee, the latter nearly always a dactyl. Here, it is clear, we have no "*regular* alternation of syllables differing in quantity."

"So as to produce harmony," proceeds the definition, "by the regular alternation of *syllables differing in quantity,*"—in other words, by the alternation of long and short syllables; for in rhythm all syllables are necessarily either short or long. But not only do I deny the necessity of any *regularity* in the succession of feet and, by consequence, of syllables, but dispute the essentiality of any *alternation,* regular or irregular, of syllables long and short. Our author, observe, is now engaged in a definition of versification in general, not of English versification in particular. But the Greek and Latin metres abound in the spondee and pyrrhic—the former consisting of two long syllables, the latter of two short; and there are innumerable instances of the immediate succession of many spondees and many pyrrhics.

Here is a passage from Silius Italicus:

Fallis te mensas inter quod credis inermem
Tot bellis quæsita viro, tot cædibus armat
Majestas eterna ducem: si admoveris ora
Cannas et Trebium ante oculos Trasymenaque busta,
Et Pauli stare ingentem miraberis umbram.

Making the elisions demanded by the classic prosodies, we should scan these hexameters thus:

Fāllīs | tē mēn | sās īn | tēr qūod | crēdĭs ĭn | ērmēm |
Tōt bēl | līs qūæ | sītă vĭ | rō tōt | cædĭbŭs | ārmāt |
Mājēs | tās ē | tērnă dŭ | cēm s'ād | mōvĕrĭs | ōrā |
Cānnās | ēt Trĕbĭ | ānt'ŏcŭ | lōs Trăsy | mēnăqŭe | būstā |
Et Pāu | lī stā | r'īngēn | tēm mī | rābĕrĭs | ūmbrām |

It will be seen that, in the first and last of these lines, we have only two short syllables in thirteen, with an uninterrupted succession of no less than *nine* long syllables. But how are we to reconcile all this with a definition of versification which describes it as "the art of arranging words into lines of correspondent length so as to produce harmony by the *regular alternation of syllables differing in quantity*"?

It may be argued, however, that our prosodist's *intention* was to speak of the English metres alone, and that, by omitting all mention of the spondee and pyrrhic, he has virtually avowed their exclusion from our rhythms. A grammarian is never excusable on the ground of good intentions. We demand from him, if from any one, rigorous precision of style. But grant the design. Let us admit that our author, following the example of all authors on English Prosody, has, in defining versification at large, intended a definition merely of the English. All these prosodists, we will say, reject the spondee and pyrrhic. Still all admit the iambus, which consists of a short syllable followed by a long; the trochee, which is the converse of the iambus; the dactyl, formed of one long syllable followed by two short; and the anapæst—two short succeded by a long. The spondee is improperly rejected, as I shall presently show. The pyrrhic is rightfully dismissed. Its existence in either ancient or modern rhythm is purely chimerical, and the insisting on so perplexing a nonentity as a foot of *two short* syllables, affords, perhaps, the best evidence of the gross irrationality and subservience to authority whch characterize our Prosody. In the meantime the acknowledged dactyl and anapæst are enough to sustain my proposition about the "alternation," etc., without reference to feet which are assumed to exist in the Greek and Latin metres alone: for an anapæst and a dactyl may meet in the same line; when, of course, we shall have an uninterrupted succession of four short syllables. The meeting of these two feet, to be sure, is an accident not contemplated in the definition now discussed; for this definition, in demanding a "regular alternation of syllables differing in quantity," insists on a regular succession of similar *feet*. But here is an example:

Sīng tŏ mĕ | Isăbēlle.

This is the opening line of a little ballad now before me, which proceeds in the same rhythm—a peculiarly beautiful one. More than all this: English lines are often well composed, entirely, of a regular succession of syllables *all of the same quantity*—the first lines, for instance, of the following quatrain by Arthur C. Coxe:

*March! march! march!*
  Making sounds as they tread.
Ho! ho! how they step,
  Going down to the dead!

The line italicised is formed of three cæsuras. The cæsura, of which I have much to say hereafter, is rejected by the English Prosodies and grossly misrepresented in the classic. It is a perfect foot—the most important in all verse—and consists of a single *long* syllable; *but the length of this syllable varies.*

It has thus been made evident that there is *not one* point of the definition in question which does not involve an error. And for any thing more satisfactory or more intelligible we shall look in vain to any published treatise on the topic.

So general and so total a failure can be referred only to radical misconception. In fact the English Prosodists have blindly followed the pedants. These latter, like *les moutons de Panurge,* have been occupied in incessant tumbling into ditches, for the excellent reason that their leaders have so tumbled before. The Iliad, being taken as a starting-point, was made to stand in stead of Nature and common-sense. Upon this poem, in place of facts and deduction from fact, or from natural law, were built systems of feet, metres, rhythms, rules,—rules that contradict each other every five minutes, and for nearly all of which there may be found twice as many exceptions as examples. If any one has a fancy to be thoroughly confounded—to see how far the infatuation of what is termed "classical scholarship" can lead a book-worm in the manufacture of darkness out of sunshine, let him turn over, for a few moments, any of the German Greek prosodies. The only thing clearly made out in them is a very magnificent contempt for Leibnitz' principle of "a sufficient reason."

To divert attention from the real matter in hand by any farther reference to these works, is unnecessary, and would be weak. I cannot call to mind, at this moment, one essential particular of information that is to be gleaned from them; and I will drop them here with merely this one observation: that, employing from among the numerous "*ancient*" feet the spondee, the trochee, the iambus, the anapæst, the dactyl, and the cæsura alone, I will engage to scan *correctly* any of the Horatian rhythms, or any true rhythm that human ingenuity can conceive. And this excess of chimerical feet is, perhaps, the very least of the scholastic supererogations. *Ex uno disce omnia.* The fact is that *Quantity* is a point in whose investigation the lumber of mere learning may be dispensed with, if ever in any. Its appreciation is universal. It appertains to no region, nor race, nor era in especial. To melody and to harmony the Greeks hearkened with ears precisely similar to those which we employ for similar purposes at present; and I should not be condemned for heresy in asserting that a pendulum at Athens would have vibrated much after the same fashion as does a pendulum in the city of Penn.

*Verse* originates in the human enjoyment of equality, fitness. To this enjoyment, also, all the moods of verse—rhythm, metre, stanza, rhyme, alliteration, the *refrain,* and other analogous effects—are to be referred. As there are some readers who habitually confound rhythm and metre, it may be as well here to say that the former concerns the *character* of feet (that is, the arrangement of syllables) while the latter has to do with the *number* of these feet. Thus, by "a dactylic *rhythm*" we express a sequence of dactyls. By "a dactylic hexa*meter*" we imply a line or measure consisting of six of these dactyls.

To return to *equality*. Its idea embraces those of similarity, proportion, identity, repetition, and adaptation or fitness. It might not be very difficult to go even behind the idea of equality, and show both how and why it is that the human nature takes pleasure in it, but such an investigation would, for any purpose now in view, be supererogatory. It is sufficient that the *fact* is undeniable—the fact that man derives enjoyment from his perception of equality. Let us examine a crystal. We are at once interested by the equality between the sides and between the angles of one of its faces: the equality of the sides pleases us; that of the angles doubles the pleasure. On bringing to view a second face in all respects similar to the first, this pleasure seems to be squared; on bringing to view a third, it appears to be cubed, and so on. I have no doubt, indeed, that the delight experienced, if measurable, would be found to have exact mathematical relations such as I suggest; that is to say, as far as a certain point, beyond which there would be a decrease in similar relations.

The perception of pleasure in the equality of *sounds* is the principle of *Music*. Unpractised ears can appreciate only simple equalities, such as are found in ballad airs. While comparing one simple sound with another they are too much occupied to be capable of comparing the equality subsisting between these two simple sounds, taken conjointly, and two other similar simple sounds taken conjointly. Practised ears, on the other hand, appreciate both equalities at the same instant—although it is absurd to suppose that both are *heard* at the same instant. One is heard and appreciated from itself: the other is heard by the memory; and the instant glides into and is confounded with the secondary, appreciation. Highly cultivated musical taste in this manner enjoys not only these double equalities, all appreciated at once, but takes pleasurable cognizance, through memory, of equalities the members of which occur at intervals so great that the uncultivated taste loses them altogether. That this latter can properly estimate or decide on the merits of what is called scientific music, is of course impossible. But scientific music has no claim to intrinsic excellence—it is fit for scientific ears alone. In its excess it is the triumph of the *physique* over the *morale* of music. The sentiment is overwhelmed by the sense. On the whole, the advocates of a simpler melody and harmony have infinitely the best of the argument; although there has been very little of real argument on the subject.

In *verse,* which cannot be better designated than as an inferior or less capable Music, there is, happily, little chance for perplexity. Its rigidly simple character not even Science—not even Pedantry can greatly pervert.

The rudiment of verse may, possibly, be found in the *spondee*. The very germ of a thought seeking satisfaction in equality of sound, would result in the construction of words of two syllables, equally accented. In corroboration of this idea we find that spondees most abound in the most ancient tongues. The second step we can easily suppose to be the comparison, that is to say, the collocation, of two spondees—of two words composed each of a spondee. The third step would be the juxtaposition of three of these words. By this time the perception of monotone would induce farther consideration: and thus arises what Leigh Hunt so flounders in discussing under the title of "The *Principle* of Variety in Uniformity." Of course there is no principle in the case—nor in maintaining it. The "Uniformity" is the principle; the "Variety" is but the principle's natural safeguard from self-destruction by excess of self. "Uniformity," besides, is the very worst word that could have been chosen for the expression of the *general* idea at which it aims.

The perception of monotone having given rise to an attempt at its relief, the first thought in this new direction would be that of collating two or more words formed each of two syllables differently accented (that is to say, short and long) but having the same order in each word,—in other terms, of collating two or more iambuses, or two or more trochees. And here let me pause to assert that more pitiable nonsense has been written on the topic of *long* and *short* syllables than on any other subject under the sun. In general, a syllable is long or short, just as it is difficult or easy of enunciation. The *natural* long syllables are those encumbered—the *natural* short syllables are those *un*emcumbered, with consonants; all the rest is mere artificiality and jargon. The Latin prosodies have a rule that "a vowel before two consonants is long." This rule is deduced from "authority"—that is, from the observation that vowels so circumstanced, in the ancient poems, are always in syllables long by the laws of scansion. The philosophy of the rule is untouched, and lies simply in the physical difficulty of giving voice to such syllables—of performing the lingual evolutions necessary for their utterance. Of course, it is not the *vowel* that is long (although the rule says so), but the syllable of which the vowel is a part. It will be seen that the length of a syllable, depending on the facility or difficulty of its enunciation, must have great variation in various syllables; but for the purposes of verse we suppose a long syllable equal to two short ones:—and the natural deviation from this relativeness we correct in perusal. The more closely our long syllables approach this relation with our short ones, the better, *ceteris paribus*, will be our verse: but if the relation does not exist of itself, we force it by emphasis, which can, of course, make any syllable as long as desired;—or, by an effort we can pronounce with unnatural brevity a syllable that is naturally too long. *Accented* syllables are of course always long—but, where *un*encumbered with consonants, must be classed among the *unnaturally* long. Mere custom has declared that we shall accent them—that is to say, dwell upon them; but no inevitable lingual difficulty forces us to do so. In line, every long syllable must of its own accord occupy in its utterance, or must be *made* to occupy, precisely the time demanded for two short ones. The only exception to this rule is found in the cæsura—of which more anon.

The success of the experiment with the trochees or iambuses (the one would have suggested the other) must have led to a trial of dactyls or anapæsts—natural dactyls or anapæsts—dactylic or anapæstic *words*. And now some degree of complexity has been attained. There is an appreciation, first, of the equality between the several dactyls, or anapæsts, and, secondly, of that between the long syllable and the two short conjointly. But here it may be said that step after step would have been taken, in continuation of this routine, until all the feet of the Greek prosodies became exhausted. Not so; these remaining feet have no existence except in the brains of the scholiasts. It is needless to imagine men inventing these things, and folly to explain how and why they invented them, until it shall be first shown that they are actually invented. All other "feet" than those which I have specified, are, if not impossible at first view, merely combinations of the specified; and, although this assertion is rigidly true, I will, to avoid misunderstanding, put it in a somewhat different shape. I will say, then, that at present I am aware of no *rhythm*—nor do I believe that any one can be constructed—which, in its last analysis, will not be found to consist altogether of the feet I have mentioned, either existing in their individual and obvious condition, or interwoven with each other in accordance with simple natural laws which I will endeavor to point out hereafter.

We have now gone so far as to suppose men constructing indefinite sequences of spondaic, iambic, trochaic, dactylic, or anapæstic words. In *extending* the sequences, they would be again arrested by the sense of monotone. A succession of spondees would *immediately* have displeased; one of iambuses or of trochees, on account of the variety included within the foot itself, would have taken longer to displease; one of dactyls or anapæsts, still longer; but even the last, if extended very far, must have become wearisome. The idea, first, of curtailing, and, secondly, of defining the length of, a sequence, would thus at once have arisen. Here then is the *line,* or verse proper.[1] The principle of equality being constantly at the bottom of the whole process, lines would naturally be made, in the first instance, equal in the number of their feet; in the second instance, there would be variation in the mere number: one line would be twice as long as another; then one would be some less obvious multiple of another; then still less obvious proportions would be adopted;—nevertheless there would be *proportion,* that is to say, a phase of equality, still.

Lines being once introduced, the necessity of distinctly defining these lines *to the ear* (as yet written verse does not exist), would lead to a scrutiny of their capabilities *at their terminations:*—and now would spring up the idea of equality in sound between the final syllables—in other words, of *rhyme*. First, it would be used only in the iambic, anapæstic, and spondaic rhythms (granting that the latter had not been thrown aside, long since, on account of its tameness), because in these rhythms, the concluding syllable being long, could best sustain the necessary protraction of the voice. No great while could elapse, however, before the effect, found pleasant as well as useful, would be applied to the two remaining rhythms. But as the chief force of rhyme must lie in the accented syllable, the attempt to create rhyme at all in these two remaining rhythms, the trochaic and dactylic, would necessarily result in double and triple rhymes, such as *beauty* with *duty* (trochaic) and *beautiful* with *dutiful* (dactylic).

It must be observed, that in suggesting these processes, I assign them no date; nor do I even insist upon their order. Rhyme is supposed to be of modern origin, and were this proved, my positions remain untouched. I may say, however, in passing, that several instances of rhyme occur in the "Clouds" of Aristophanes, and that the Roman poets occasionally employ it. There is an effective species of ancient rhyming which has never descended to the moderns: that in which the ultimate and penultimate syllables rhyme with each other. For example:

> Parturiunt montes et nascitur ridic*ulus mus*.

And again:

> Litoreis ingens inventa sub ilici*bus sus*.

The terminations of Hebrew verse (as far as understood) show no signs of rhyme; but what thinking person can doubt that it did actually exist? That men have so obstinately and blindly insisted, *in general*, even up to the present day, in confining rhyme to the *ends* of lines, when its effect is even better applicable elsewhere, intimates, in my opinion, the sense of some *necessity* in the connection of the end with the rhyme,—hints that the origin of rhyme lay in a necessity which connected it with the end,—shows that neither mere accident nor mere fancy gave rise to the connection,—points, in a word, at the very necessity which I have suggested (that of some mode of defining lines *to the ear*) as the true origin of rhyme. Admit this, and we throw the origin far back in the night of Time—beyond the origin of written verse.

But, to resume. The amount of complexity I have now supposed to be attained is very considerable. Various systems of equalization are appreciated at once (or nearly so) in their respective values and in the value of each system with reference to all the others. As our present *ultimatum* of complexity, we have arrived at triple-rhymed, natural-dactylic lines, existing proportionally as well as equally with regard to other triple-rhymed, natural-dactylic lines. For example:

> Virginal Lilian, rigidly, humblily, dutiful;
> Saintlily, lowlily,
> Thrillingly, holily
> Beautiful!

Here we appreciate, first, the absolute equality between the long syllable of each dactyl and the two short conjointly; secondly, the absolute equality between each dactyl and any other dactyl—in other words, among all the dactyls; thirdly, the absolute equality between the two middle lines; fourthly, the absolute equality between the first line and the three others taken conjointly; fifthly, the absolute equality between the last two syllables of the respective words "dutiful" and "beautiful"; sixthly, the absolute equality between the last two syllables of the respective words "lowlily" and "holily"; seventhly, the proximate equality between the first syllable of "dutiful" and the first syllable of "beautiful"; eighthly, the proximate equality between the first syllable of "lowlily" and that of "holily"; ninthly, the proportional equality (that of five to one) between the first line and each of its members, the dactyls; tenthly, the proportional equality (that of two to one) between each of the middle lines and its members, the dactyls; eleventhly, the proportional equality between the first line and each of the two middle—that of five to two; twelfthly, the proportional equality between the first line and the last—that of five to one; thirteenthly, the proportional equality between each of the middle lines and the last—that of two to one; lastly, the proportional equality, as concerns number, between all the lines, taken collectively and any individual line—that of four to one.

The consideration of this last equality would give birth immediately to the idea of *stanza*[2]—that is to say, the insulation of lines into equal or obviously proportional masses. In its primitive (which was also its best) form, the stanza would most probably have had absolute unity. In other words, the removal of any one of its lines would have rendered it imperfect; as in the case above, where, if the last line, for example, be taken away, there is left no rhyme to the "dutiful" of the first. Modern stanza is excessively loose—and where so, ineffective, as a matter of course.

Now, although in the deliberate written statement which I have here given of these various systems of equalities, there seems to be an infinity of complexity—so much that it is hard to conceive the mind taking cognizance of them all in the brief period occupied by the perusal or recital of the stanza—yet the difficulty is in fact apparent only when we will it to become so. Any one fond of mental experiment may satisfy himself, by trial, that, in listening to the lines, he does actually (although with a seeming unconsciousness, on account of the rapid evolutions of sensation) recognize and instantaneously appreciate (more or less intensely as his ear is cultivated) each and all of the equalizations detailed. The pleasure received, or receivable, has very much such progressive increase, and in very nearly such mathematical relations, as those which I have suggested in the case of the crystal.

It will be observed that I speak of merely a proximate equality between the first syllable of "dutiful" and that of "beautiful"; and it may be asked why we cannot imagine the earliest rhymes to have had absolute instead of proximate equality of sound. But absolute equality would have involved the use of identical words; and it is the duplicate sameness or monotony—that of sense as well as that of sound—which would have caused these rhymes to be rejected in the very first instance.

The narrowness of the limits within which verse composed of natural feet alone must necessarily have been confined, would have led, after a *very* brief interval, to the trial and immediate adoption of artificial feet—that is to say, of feet *not* constituted each of a single word, but two or even three words; or of parts of words. These feet would be intermingled with natural ones. For example:

ă brēath | căn māke | thĕm ās | ă brēath | hăs māde.

This is an iambic line in which each iambus is formed of two words. Again:

Thĕ ūn | ĭmā | gĭnā | blĕ mīght | ŏf Jōve.

This is an iambic line in which the first foot is formed of a word and a part of a word; the second and third, of parts taken from the body or interior of a word; the fourth, of a part and a whole; the fifth, of two complete words. There are no *natural* feet in either lines. Again:

Cān ĭt bĕ | fānciĕd thăt | Dēĭty | ēvĕr vĭn | dīctĭvely<br>
Māde ĭn hĭs | īmăge ă | mānnĭkĭn | mērely tŏ | māddĕn ĭt?

These are two dactylic lines in which we find natural feet ("Deity," "mannikin"), feet composed of two words ("fancied that," "image a," "merely to," "madden it"), feet composed of three words ("can it be," "made in his"), a foot composed of a part of a word ("dictively"), and a foot composed of a word and a part of a word ("ever vin").

And now, in our supposititious progress, we have gone so far as to exhaust all the *essentialities* of verse. What follows may, strictly speaking, be regarded as embellishment merely—but even in this embellishment, the rudimental sense of *equality* would have been the never-ceasing impulse. It would, for example, be simply in seeking farther administration to this sense that men would come, in time, to think of the *refrain,* or burden, where, at the closes of the several stanzas of a poem, one word or phrase is *repeated;* and of alliteration, in whose simplest form a consonant is *repeated* in the commencements of various words. This effect would be extended so as to embrace repetitions both of vowels and of consonants, in the bodies as well as in the beginnings of words; and, at a later period would be made to infringe on the province of rhyme, by the introduction of general similarity of sound between whole feet occuring in the body of a line:—all of which modifications I have exemplified in the line above,

*M*ade in his *im*age a *mannikin m*erely to *madden it.*

Farther cultivation would improve also the *refrain* by relieving its monotone in slightly varying the phrase at each repetition, or (as I have attempted to do in "The Raven") in retaining the phrase and varying its application—although this latter point is not strictly a rhythmical effect *alone.* Finally, poets when fairly wearied with following precedent—following it the more closely the less they perceived it in company with Reason—would adventure so far as to indulge in positive rhyme at other points than the ends of lines. First, they would put it in the middle of the line; then at some point where the multiple would be less obvious; then, alarmed at their own audacity, they would undo all their work by cutting these lines in two. And here is the fruitful source of the infinity of "short metre," by which modern poetry, if not distinguished, is at least disgraced. It would require a high degree, indeed, both of cultivation and of courage, on the part of any versifier, to enable him to place his rhymes—and let them remain—at unquestionably their best position, that of unusual and *unanticipated* intervals.

On account of the stupidity of some people, or (if talent be a more respectable word), on account of their talent for misconception—I think it necessary to add here, first, that I believe the "processes" above detailed to be nearly if not accurately those which *did* occur in the gradual creation of what we now call verse; secondly, that, although I so believe, I yet urge neither the assumed fact nor my belief in it as a part of the true propositions of this paper; thirdly, that in regard to the aim of this paper, it is of no consequence whether these processes did occur either in the order I have assigned them, or at all; my design being simply, in presenting a general type of what such processes *might* have been and *must* have resembled, to help *them,* the "some people," to an easy understanding of what I have farther to say on the topic of Verse.

There is one point which, in my summary of the processes, I have purposely forborne to touch; because this point, being the most important of all, on account of the immensity of error usually involved in its consideration, would have led me into a series of detail inconsistent with the object of a summary.

Every reader of verse must have observed how seldom it happens that even any one line proceeds uniformly with a succession, such as I have supposed, of absolutely equal feet; that is to say, with a succession of iambuses only, or of trochees only, or of dactyls only, or of anapæsts only, or of spondees only. Even in the most musical lines we find the succession interrupted. The iambic pentameters of Pope, for example, will be found, on examination, frequently varied by trochees in the beginning, or by (what seem to be) anapæsts in the body, of the line.

Ŏh thoū whătē | vĕr tī | tlĕ plēase | thĭne ēar |
Dĕan Drā | pĭĕr Bīck | ĕrstāff | ŏr Gūl | ĭvēr |
Whēthĕr | thŏu choōse | Cĕrvān | tĕs' sē | rĭoŭs aīr |
Ŏr laūgh | ănd shāke | ĭn Rāb | ĕlăis' ēa | sy chāir. |

Were any one weak enough to refer to the prosodies for the solution of the difficulty here, he would find it *solved* as usual by a *rule,* stating the fact (or what it, the rule, supposes to be the fact), but without the slightest attempt at the *rationale.* "By a *synœresis* of the two short syllables," say the books, "an anapæst may sometimes be employed for an iambus, or a dactyl for a trochee. . . . In the beginning of a line a trochee is often used for an iambus."

*Blending* is the plain English for *synœresis*—but there should be *no* blending; neither is an anapæst *ever* employed for an iambus, or a dactyl for a trochee. These feet differ in time; and *no* feet so differing can ever be legitimately used in the same line. An anapæst is equal to four short syllables—an iambus only to three. Dactyls and trochees hold the same relation. The principle of *equality,* in verse, admits, it is true, of variation at certain points, for the relief of monotone, as I have already shown, but the point of *time* is that point which, being the rudimental one, must never be tampered with at all.

To explain:—In farther efforts for the relief of monotone than those to which I have alluded in the summary, men soon came to see that there was no absolute necessity for adhering to the precise number of syllables, provided the time required for the whole foot was preserved inviolate. They saw, for instance, that in such a line as

ŏr laūgh | ănd shāke | ĭn Rāb | ĕlăis' ēa | sy chāir, |

the equalization of the three syllables *elais' ea* with the two syllables composing any of the other feet, could be readily effected by pronouncing the two syllables *elais'* in double quick time. By pronouncing each of the syllables *e* and *lais'* twice as rapidly as the syllable *sy,* or the syllable *in,* or any other syllable, they could bring the two of them, taken together, to the length, that is to say, to the time, of any one short syllable. This consideration enabled them to effect the agreeable variation of three syllables in place of the uniform two. And variation was the object—variation to the ear. What sense is there, then, in supposing this object rendered null by the *blending* of the two syllables so as to render them, in absolute effect, one? Of course, there must be *no* blending. Each syllable must be pronounced as distinctly as possible (or the variation is lost), but with twice the rapidity in which the ordinary syllable is enunciated. That the syllables *elais' ea* do not compose an *anapæst* is evident, and the signs (ăăā) of their accentuation are erroneous. The foot might be written thus (āăă), the inverted crescents expressing double quick time; and might be called a bastard iambus.

Here is a trochaic line:

Sēe thĕ dēlĭcăte | fōotĕd | rēin-deĕr. |

The prosodies—that is to say, the most considerate of them—would here decide that "*delicate*" is a dactyl used in place of a trochee, and would refer to what they call their "rule," for justification. Others, varying the stupidity, would insist upon a Procrustean adjustment thus (del-cate)—an adjustment recommended to all such words as *silvery, murmuring,* etc., which, it is said, should be not only pronounced, but written *silv'ry, murm'ring,* and so on, whenever they find themselves in trochaic predicament. I have only to say that "delicate," when circumstanced as above, is neither a dactyl nor a dactyl's equivalent; that I would suggest for it this (āăă) accentuation; that I think it as well to call it a bastard trochee; and that all words, at all events, should be written and pronounced *in full,* and as nearly as possible as nature intended them.

About eleven years ago, there appeared in the *American Monthly Magazine* (then edited, I believe, by Messrs. Hoffman and Benjamin) a review of Mr. Willis' Poems; the critic putting forth his strength or his weakness, in an endeavor to show that the poet was either absurdly affected, or grossly ignorant of the laws of verse; the accusation being based altogether on the fact that Mr. W. made occasional use of this very word "delicate," and other similar words, in "the Heroic measure, which every one knew consisted of feet of two syllables." Mr. W. has often, for example, such lines as

> That binds him to a woman's *delicate* love—
> In the gay sunshine, *reverent* in the storm—
> With its *invisible* fingers my loose hair.

Here, of course, the feet *licate love, verent in,* and *sible fin,* are bastard iambuses; are *not* anapæsts; and are *not* improperly used. Their employment, on the contrary, by Mr. Willis, is but one of the innumerable instances he has given of keen sensibility in all those matters of taste which may be classed under the general head of *fanciful embellishment.*

It is also about eleven years ago, if I am not mistaken, since Mr. Horne (of England), the author of "Orion," one of the noblest epics in any language, thought it necessary to preface his "Chaucer Modernized" by a very long and evidently a very elaborate essay, of which the greater portion was occupied in a discussion of the seemingly anomalous foot of which we have been speaking. Mr. Horne upholds Chaucer in its frequent use; maintains his superiority, *on account* of his so frequently using it, over all English versifiers; and, indignantly repelling the common idea of those who make verse on their fingers, that the superfluous syllable is a roughness and an error, very chivalrously makes battle for it as "a grace." That a grace it *is,* there can be no doubt; and what I complain of is, that the author of the most happily versified long poem in existence, should have been under the necessity of discussing this grace merely *as* a grace, through forty or fifty vague pages, solely because of his inability to show *how* and *why* it is a grace—by which showing the question would have been settled in an instant.

About the trochee used for an iambus, as we see in the beginning of the line,

> Whēthĕr thou choose Cervantes' serious air,

there is little that need be said. It brings me to the general proposition that in all rhythms, the prevalent or distinctive feet may be varied at will, and nearly at random, by the *occasional* introduction of equivalent feet—that is to say, feet the sum of whose syllabic times is equal to the sum of the syllabic times of the distinctive feet. Thus the trochee *whēthĕr,* is equal in the sum of the times of its syllables, to the iambus, *thoŭ chōose,* in the sum of the times of *its* syllables; each foot being, in time, equal to three short syllables. Good versifiers, who happen to be, also, good poets, contrive to relieve the monotone of a series of feet, by the use of equivalent feet only at rare intervals, and at such points of their subject as seem in accordance with the *startling* character of the variation. Nothing of this care is seen in the line quoted above—although Pope has some fine instances of the duplicate effect. Where vehemence is to be strongly expressed, I am not sure that we should be wrong in venturing on *two consecutive* equivalent feet—although I cannot say that I have ever known the adventure made, except in the following passage, which occurs in "Al Aaraaf," a boyish poem, written by myself when a boy. I am referring to the sudden and rapid advent of a star:

Dim was its little disk, and angel eyes
Alone could see the phantom in the skies,
Whĕn first thĕ phāntŏm's cōurse wăs foūnd tŏ bē
*Hēadlŏng hīthĕr*ward o'er the starry sea.

In the "general proposition" above, I speak of the *occasional* introduction of equivalent feet. It sometimes happens that unskilful versifiers, without knowing what they do, or why they do it, introduce so many "variations" as to exceed in number the "distinctive" feet; when the ear becomes at once balked by the *bouleversement* of the rhythm. Too many trochees, for example, inserted in an iambic rhythm, would convert the latter to a trochaic. I may note here, that, in all cases, the rhythm designed should be commenced and continued, *without* variation, until the ear has had full time to comprehend what *is* the rhythm. In violation of a rule so obviously founded in common-sense, many even of our best poets, do not scruple to begin an iambic rhythm with a trochee, or the converse; or a dactylic with an anapæst, or the converse; and so on.

A somewhat less objectionable error, although still a decided one, is that of commencing a rhythm, not with a different equivalent foot, but with a "bastard" foot of the rhythm intended. For example:

Māny ă | thōught wĭll | cōme tŏ | mēmŏry. |

Here *many a* is what I have explained to be a bastard trochee, and to be understood should be accented with inverted crescents. It is objectionable solely on account of its position as the *opening* foot of a trochaic rhythm. *Memory,* similarly accented, is also a bastard trochee, but *un*objectionable, although by no means demanded.

The farther illustration of this point will enable me to take an important step.

One of the finest poets, Mr. Christopher Pease Cranch, begins a very beautiful poem thus:

Many are the thoughts that come to me
  In my lonely musing;
And they drift so strange and swift
  There's no time for choosing
Which to follow; for to leave
  Any, seems a losing.

"A losing" to Mr. Cranch, of course—but this *en passant*. It will be seen here that the intention is trochaic, although we do *not* see this intention by the opening foot, as we should do—or even by the opening line. Reading the whole stanza, however, we perceive the trochaic rhythm as the general design, and so, after some reflection, we divide the first line thus:

Many are the | thōughts thăt | cōme tŏ | mē. |

Thus scanned, the line will seem musical. It *is*—highly so. And it is because there is no end to instances of just such lines of apparently incomprehensible music, that Coleridge thought proper to invent his nonsensical *system* of what he calls "scanning by accents"—as if "scanning by accents" were any thing more than a phrase. Wherever "Christabel" is really *not rough,* it can be as readily scanned by the true *laws* (not the supposititious *rules*) of verse as can the simplest pentameter of Pope and where it *is* rough (*passim*), these same laws will enable any one of common-sense to show *why* it is rough, and to point out, instantaneously, the remedy for the roughness.

*A* reads and re-reads a certain line, and pronounces it false in rhythm—unmusical. *B,* however, reads it *to A,* and *A* is at once struck with the perfection of the rhythm, and wonders at his dulness in not "catching" it before. Henceforward he admits the line to be musical. *B,* triumphant, asserts that, to be sure, the line is musical—for it is the work of Coleridge,—and that it is *A* who is *not;* the fault being in *A's* false reading. Now here *A* is right and *B* is wrong. *That* rhythm is erroneous (at some point or other more or less obvious) which *any* ordinary reader *can,* without design, read improperly. It is the business of the poet so to construct his line that the intention *must* be caught *at once*. Even when these men have precisely the same understanding of a sentence, they differ, and often widely, in their modes of enunciating it. Any one who has taken the trouble to examine the topic of emphasis (by which I here mean not *accent* of particular syllables, but the dwelling on entire words), must have seen that men emphasize in the most singularly arbitrary manner. There are certain large classes of people, for example, who persist in emphasizing their monosyllables. Little uniformity of emphasis prevails; because the thing itself—the idea, emphasis—is referable to no natural, at least to no well-comprehended and therefore uniform, law. Beyond a very narrow and vague limit, the whole matter is conventionality. And if we differ in emphasis even when we agree in comprehension, how much more so in the former when in the latter too! Apart, however, from the consideration of natural disagreement, is it not clear that, by tripping here and mouthing there, any sequence of words may be twisted into any species of rhythm? But are we thence to deduce that all sequences of words are rhythmical in a rational understanding of the term?—for this is the deduction, precisely to which the *reductio ad absurdum* will, in the end, bring all the propositions of Coleridge. Out of a hundred readers of "Christabel," fifty will be able to make nothing of its rhythm, while forty-nine of the remaining fifty will, with some ado, fancy they comprehend it, after the fourth or fifth perusal. The one out of the whole hundred who shall both comprehend and admire it at first sight must be an unaccountably clever person—and I am by far too modest to assume, for a moment, that that very clever person is myself.

In illustration of what is here advanced I cannot do better than quote a poem:

Pease porridge hot—pease porridge cold—
Pease porridge in the pot—nine days old.

Now those of my readers who have never *heard* this poem pronounced according to the nursery conventionality, will find its rhythm as obscure as an explanatory note; while those who *have* heard it, will divide it thus, declare it musical, and wonder how there can be any doubt about it.

Pease | porridge | hot | pease | porridge | cold |
Pease | porridge | in the | pot | nine | days | old. |

The chief thing in the way of this species of rhythm, is the necessity which it imposes upon the poet of travelling in constant company with his compositions, so as to be ready, at a moment's notice, to avail himself of a well understood poetical license—that of reading aloud one's own doggerel.

In Mr. Cranch's line,

Many are the | thoughts that | come to | me, |

the general error of which I speak is, of course, very partially exemplified, and the purpose for which, chiefly, I cite it, lies yet farther on in our topic.

The two divisions *(thoughts that)* and *(come to)* are ordinary trochees. Of the last division *(me)* we will talk hereafter. The first division (many are the) would be thus accented by the Greek prosodies (māny ăre *thĕ*) and would be called by them αϛτρολογος. The Latin books would style the foot *Pœon Primus,* and both Greek and Latin would swear that it was composed of a trochee and what they term a pyrrhic—that is to say, a foot of two *short* syllables—a thing that *cannot be,* as I shall presently show.

But now, there is an obvious difficulty. The *astrologos,* according to the prosodies' own showing, is equal to *five* short syllables, and the trochee to *three*—yet, in the line quoted, these two feet are equal. They occupy *precisely* the same time. In fact, the whole music of the line depends upon their being *made* to occupy the same time. The prosodies then, have demonstrated what all mathematicians have stupidly failed in demonstrating—that three and five are one and the same thing.

After what I have already said, however, about the bastard trochee and the bastard iambus, no one can have any trouble in understanding that *many are the* is of similar character. It is merely a bolder variation than usual from the routine of trochees, and introduces to the bastard trochee one additional syllable. But this syllable is not *short.* That is, it is not short in the sense of *"short"* as applied to the final syllable of the ordinary trochee, where the word means merely *the half of long.*

In this case (that of the additional syllable), "short," if used at all, must be used in the sense of *the sixth of long.* And all the three final syllables can be called *short* only with the same understanding of the term. The three together are equal only to the one short syllable (whose place they supply) of the ordinary trochee. It follows that there is no sense in thus (˘) accenting these syllables. We must devise for them some new character which shall denote the sixth of long. Let it be (◡)—the crescent placed with the curve to the left. The whole foot (māny ăre thĕ) might be called a *quick trochee*.

We come now to the final division (*me*) of Mr. Cranch's line. It is clear that this foot, short as it appears, is fully equal in time to each of the preceding. It is in fact the cæsura—the foot which, in the beginning of this paper, I called the most important in all verse. Its chief office is that of pause or termination; and here—at the end of a line—its use is easy, because there is no danger of misapprehending its value. We pause on it, by a seeming necessity, just as long as it has taken us to pronounce the preceding feet, whether iambuses, trochees, dactyls, or anapæsts. It is thus a *variable foot*, and, with some care, may be well introduced into the body of a line, as in a little poem of great beauty by Mrs. Welby:

I have | a lit | tle step | sŏn | of on | ly three | years old. |

Here we dwell on the cæsura, *son*, just as long as it requires us to pronounce either of the preceding or succeeding iambuses. Its value, therefore, in this line, is that of three short syllables. In the following dactylic lines its value is that of four short syllables.

Pale as a | lily was | Emily | Gray. |

I have accented the cæsura with a dotted line (......) by way of expressing this variability of value.

I observed just now that there could be no such foot as one of two short syllables. What we start from in the very beginning of all idea on the topic of verse, is quantity, *length*. Thus when we enunciate an independent syllable it is long, as a matter of course. If we enunciate two, dwelling on both equally, we express equality in the enumeration, or length, and have a right to call them two long syllables. If we dwell on one more than the other, we have also a right to call one short, because it is short in relation to the other. But if we dwell on both equally and with a tripping voice, saying to ourselves here are two short syllables, the query might well be asked of us—"in relation to what are they short?" Shortness is but the negation of length. To say, then, that two syllables, placed independently of any other syllable, are short, is merely to say that they have no positive length, or enunciation—in other words that they are no syllables—that they do not exist at all. And if, persisting, we add any thing about their equality, we are merely floundering in the idea of an identical equation, where, $x$ being equal to $x$, nothing is shown to be equal to zero. In a word, we can form no conception of a pyrrhic as of an independent foot. It is a mere chimera bred in the mad fancy of a pedant.

From what I have said about the equalization of the several feet of a *line*, it must not be deduced that any *necessity* for equality in time exists between the rhythm of *several* lines. A poem, or even a stanza, may begin with iambuses, in the first line, and proceed with anapæsts in the second, or even with the less accordant dactyls, as in the opening of quite a pretty specimen of verse by Miss Mary A. S. Aldrich.

The wa | ter li | ly sleeps | in pride | .........
Dōwn ĭn thĕ | dēpths ŏf thĕ | āzūre | lake. |

Here *azure* is a spondee, equivalent to a dactyl; *lake,* a cæsura.

I shall now best proceed in quoting the initial lines of Byron's "Bride of Abydos":

Know ye the land where the cypress and myrtle
  Are emblems of deeds that are done in their clime—
Where the rage of the vulture, the love of the turtle
  Now melt into softness, now madden to crime?
Know ye the land of the cedar and vine,
Where the flowers ever blossom, the beams ever shine,
And the light wings of Zephyr, oppressed with perfume,
Wax faint o'er the gardens of Gul in their bloom?
Where the citron and olive are fairest of fruit
And the voice of the nightingale never is mute—
Where the virgins are soft as the roses they twine,
And all save the spirit of man is divine?
'Tis the land of the East—'tis the clime of the Sun—
Can he smile on such deeds as his children have done?
Oh, wild as the accents of lovers' farewell
Are the hearts that they bear and the tales that they tell!

Now the flow of these lines (as times go) is very sweet and musical. They have been often admired, and justly—as times go,—that is to say, it is a rare thing to find better versification of its kind. And where verse is pleasant to the ear, it is silly to find fault with it because it refuses to be scanned. Yet I have heard men, professing to be scholars, who made no scruple of abusing these lines of Byron's on the ground that they were musical in spite of *all law*. Other gentlemen, *not* scholars, abused "all law" for the same reason; and it occurred neither to the one party nor to the other that the law about which they were disputing might possibly be no law at all—an ass of a law in the skin of a lion.

The grammars said something about dactylic lines, and it was easily seen that *these* lines were at least meant for dactylic. The first one was, therefore, thus divided:

Knōw yĕ thĕ | lānd whĕre thĕ | cyprĕss ănd | myrtlĕ |

The concluding foot was a mystery; but the prosodies said something about the dactylic "measure" calling now and then for a double rhyme; and the court of inquiry were content to rest in the double rhyme, without exactly perceiving what a double rhyme had to do with the question of an irregular foot. Quitting the first line, the second was thus scanned:

Arē ĕmblĕms | ōf dĕeds thăt | āre dŏne ĭn | thēir clĭme. |

It was immediately seen, however, that *this* would not do,—it was at war with the whole emphasis of the reading. It could not be supposed that Byron, or any one in his senses, intended to place stress upon such monosyllables as "are," "of," and "their," nor could "their clime," collated with "to crime," in the corresponding line below, be fairly twisted into any thing like a "double rhyme," so as to bring every thing within the category of the grammars. But farther these grammars spoke not. The inquirers, therefore, in spite of their sense of harmony in the lines, when considered without reference to scansion, fell back upon the idea that the "Are" was a blunder,—an excess for which the poet should be sent to Coventry,—and, striking it out, they scanned the remainder of the line as follows:

—ēmblĕms ŏf | dēeds thăt ăre | dōne ĭn thĕir | clĭme. |

This answered pretty well; but the grammars admitted no such foot as a foot of one syllable; and besides the rhythm was dactylic. In despair, the books are well searched, however, and at last the investigators are gratified by a full solution of the riddle in the profound "Observation" quoted in the beginning of this article:—"When a syllable is wanting, the verse is said to be catalectic; when the measure is exact, the line is acatalectic; when there is a redundant syllable it forms hypermeter." This is enough. The anomalous line is pronounced to be catalectic at the head and to form hypermeter at the tail,—and so on, and so on; it being soon discovered that nearly all the remaining lines are in a similar predicament, and that what flows so smoothly to the ear, although so roughly to the eye, is, after all, a mere jumble of catalecticism, acatalecticism, and hypermeter—not to say worse.

Now, had this court of inquiry been in possession of even the shadow of the *philosophy* of Verse, they would have had no trouble in reconciling this oil and water of the eye and ear, by merely scanning the passage without reference to lines, and, continuously, thus:

> Know ye the | land where the | cypress and | myrtle Are | emblems of | deeds that are | done in their | clime Where the | rage of the | vulture the | love of the | turtle Now | melt into | softness now | madden to | *crime* | Know ye the | land of the | cedar and | vine Where the | flowers ever | blossom the | beams ever | shine Where the | light wings of | Zephyr op | pressed by per | *fume Wax* | faint o'er the | gardens of | Gul in their | bloom Where the | citron and | olive are | fairest of | fruit And the | voice of the | nightingale | never is | mute Where the | virgins are | soft as the | roses they | *twine And* | all save the | spirit of | man is di | vine 'Tis the | land of the | East 'tis the | clime of the | Sun Can he | smile on such | deeds as his | children have | *done Oh* | wild as the | accents of | lovers' fare | well Are the | hearts that they | bear and the | tales that they | *tell.*

Here "crime" and "tell" (italicized) are cæsuras, each having the value of a dactyl, four short syllables; while "*fume Wax,*" "*twine And,*" and "*done Oh,*" are spondees, which, of course, being composed of two long syllables, are also equal to four short, and are the dactyl's natural equivalent. The nicety of Byron's ear has led him into a succession of feet which, with two trivial exceptions as regards melody, are absolutely accurate—a very rare occurrence this in dactylic or anapæstic rhythms. The exceptions are found in the spondee "*twine And,*" and the dactyl, "*smile on such.*" Both feet are false in point of melody. In "*twine And,*" to make out the rhythm, we must force "*And*" into a length which it will not naturally bear. We are called on to sacrifice either the proper length of the syllable as demanded by its position as a member of a spondee, or the customary accentuation of the word in conversation. There is no hesitation, and should be none. We at once give up the sound for the sense; and the rhythm is imperfect. In this instance it is *very* slightly so;—not one person in ten thousand could, by ear, detect the inaccuracy. But the *perfection* of Verse, as regards melody, consists in its *never* demanding any such sacrifice as is here demanded. The rhythmical must agree, *thoroughly,* with the reading flow. This perfection has in no instance been attained—but is unquestionably attainable. "*Smile on such,*" the dactyl, is incorrect, because "*such,*" from the character of the two consonants *ch,* cannot *easily* be enunciated in the ordinary time of a short syllable, which its position declares that it is. Almost every reader will be able to appreciate the slight difficulty here; and yet the error is by no means so important as that of the "*And,*" in the spondee. By dexterity we *may* pronounce "*such*" in the true time; but the attempt to remedy the rhythmical deficiency of the "*And*" by drawing it out, merely aggravates the offence against natural enunciation, by directing attention to the offence.

My main object, however, in quoting these lines, is to show that, in spite of the prosodies, the length of a line is entirely an arbitrary matter. We might divide the commencement of Byron's poem thus:

Know ye the | land where the |

or thus:

Know ye the | land where the | cypress and |

or thus:

Know ye the | land where the | cypress and | myrtle are |

or thus:

Know ye the | land where the | cypress and | myrtle are | emblems of |

In short, we may give it any division we please, and the lines will be good—provided we have at least *two* feet in a line. As in mathematics two units are required to form number, so rhythm (from the Greek αριϑμος, number) demands for its formation at least two feet. Beyond doubt, we often see such lines as

Know ye the—
Land where the—

lines of one foot; and our prosodies admit such; but with impropriety: for common-sense would dictate that every so obvious division of a poem as is made by a line, should include within itself all that is necessary for its own comprehension; but in a line of one foot we can have no appreciation of *rhythm,* which depends upon the equality between *two* or more pulsations. The false lines, consisting sometimes of a single cæsura, which are seen in mock Pindaric odes, are of course "rhythmical" only in connection with some other line; and it is this want of independent rhythm which adapts them to the purposes of burlesque alone. Their effect is that of incongruity (the principle of mirth), for they include the blankness of prose amid the harmony of verse.

My second object in quoting Byron's lines, was that of showing how absurd it often is to cite a single line from amid the body of a poem, for the purpose of instancing the perfection or imperfection of the line's rhythm. Were we to see by itself

Know ye the land where the cypress and myrtle,

we might justly condemn it as defective in the final foot, which is equal to only three, instead of being equal to four, short syllables.

In the foot *"flowers ever"* we shall find a further exemplification of the principle of the bastard iambus, bastard trochee, and quick trochee, as I have been at some pains in describing these feet above. All the Prosodies on English Verse would insist upon making an elision in *"flowers,"* thus *"flow'rs,"* but this is nonsense. In the quick trochee *"mānу ăre thĕ* occurring in Mr. Cranch's *trochaic* line, we had to equalize the time of the three syllables *"any, are, the"* to that of the one *short* syllable whose position they usurp. Accordingly each of these syllables is equal to the third of a short syllable—that is to say, the *sixth of a long.* But in Byron's *dactylic* rhythm, we have to equalize the time of the three syllables *"ers, ev, er"* to that of the one *long* syllable whose position they usurp, or (which is the same thing) of the *two short.* Therefore, the value of each of the syllables *"er, ev,* and *er"* is the *third of a long.* We enunciate them with only half the rapidity we employ in enunciating the three final syllables of the quick trochee—which latter is a rare foot. The *"flowers ever,"* on the contrary, is as common in the dactylic rhythm as is the *bastard* trochee in the trochaic, or the bastard iambus in the iambic. We may as well accent it with the curve of the crescent to the right, and call it a *bastard dactyl.* A *bastard anapœst,* whose nature I now need be at no trouble in explaining, will of course occur, now and then, in an anapæstic rhythm.

In order to avoid any chance of that confusion which is apt to be introduced in an essay of this kind by too sudden and radical an alteration of the conventionalities to which the reader has been accustomed, I have thought it right to suggest for the accent marks of the bastard trochee, bastard iambus, etc., etc., certain characters which, in merely varying the direction of the ordinary short accent (˘), should imply, what is the fact, that the feet themselves are not *new* feet, in any proper sense, but simply modifications of the feet, respectively, from which they derive their names. Thus a bastard iambus is, in its essentiality, that is to say, in its time, an iambus. The variation lies only in the *distribution* of this time. The time, for example, occupied by the one short (or *half of long*) syllable, in the ordinary iambus, is, in the bastard, spread equally over two syllables, which are accordingly the *fourth of long*.

But this fact—the fact of the essentiality, or whole time, of the foot being unchanged—is now so fully before the reader that I may venture to propose, finally, an accentuation which shall answer the real purpose—that is to say, what should be the real purpose of all accentuation—the purpose of expressing to the eye the exact relative value of every syllable employed in Verse.

I have already shown that enunciation, or *length*, is the point from which we start. In other words, we begin with a *long syllable*. This, then, is our unit; and there will be no need of accenting it at all. An unaccented syllable, in a system of accentuation, is to be regarded always as a long syllable. Thus a spondee would be without accent. In an iambus, the first syllable being "short," or the *half* of long, should be accented with a small 2, placed *beneath* the syllable; the last syllable, being long, should be unaccented: the whole would be thus (con$_{2}$trol). In a trochee, these accents would be merely conversed, thus (manly$_{2}$). In a dactyl, each of the two final syllables, being the half of long, should, also, be accented with a small 2 beneath the syllable; and, the first syllable left unaccented, the whole would be thus (happi$_{2}$ness$_{2}$). In an anapæst we should converse the dactyl, thus (in$_{2}$ the$_{2}$ land). In the bastard dactyl, each of the three concluding syllables being the *third* of long, should be accented with a small 3 beneath the syllable, and the whole foot would stand thus (flowers$_{3}$ ev$_{3}$er$_{3}$). In the bastard anapæst we should converse the bastard dactyl, thus (in$_{3}$ the$_{3}$ re$_{3}$bound). In the bastard iambus, each of the two initial syllables, being the *fourth* of long, should be accented below with a small number 4; the whole foot would be thus (in$_{4}$ the$_{4}$ rain). In the bastard trochee we should converse the bastard iambus, thus (many$_{4}$ a$_{4}$). In the quick trochee, each of the three concluding syllables, being the *sixth* of long, should be accented below with a small 6; the whole foot would be thus (many$_{6}$ are$_{6}$ the$_{6}$). The quick iambus is not yet created, and most probably never will be, for it will be excessively useless, awkward, and liable to misconception,—as I have already shown that even the quick trochee is,—but, should it appear, we must accent it by conversing the quick trochee. The cæsura, being variable in length, but always *longer than "long,"* should be accented *above,* with a number expressing the length or value of the distinctive foot of the rhythm in which it occurs. Thus a cæsura, occurring in a spondaic rhythm, would be accented with a small 2 above the syllable, or, rather, foot. Occurring in a dactylic or anapæstic rhythm, we also accent it with the 2, above the foot. Occurring in an iambic rhythm, however, it must be accented, above, with 1½, for this is the relative value of the iambus. Occurring in the trochaic rhythm, we give it, of course, the same accentuation. For the complex 1½, however, it would be advisable to substitute the simpler expression, 3/2, which amounts to the same thing.

In this system of accentuation Mr. Cranch's lines, quoted above, would thus be written:

3/2
Many are the | thoughts that | come to | me
6 6 6 2 2
In my | lonely | musing, |
2 2

3/2
And they | drift so | strange and | swift
2 2 2
There's no | time for | choosing |
2 2 2

3/2
Which to | follow, | for to | leave
2 2 2
Any | seems a | losing. |
2 2 2

In the ordinary system the accentuation would be thus:

Māny arĕ thĕ | thōughts thăt | cōme tŏ | mē
In my | lōnely | mūsĭng, |
And thĕy | drīft sō | strānge ănd | swīft |
Thēre's nŏ | tīme fŏr | chŏōsĭng |
Whīch tŏ | fōllŏw, | fōr tŏ | lēave
Any | sēems ă | lōsĭng. |

It must be observed here that I do not grant this to be the "ordinary" *scansion*. On the contrary, I never yet met the man who had the faintest comprehension of the true scanning of these lines, or of such as these. But granting this to be the mode in which our prosodies would divide the feet, they would accentuate the syllables as just above.

Now, let any reasonable person compare the two modes. The first advantage seen in my mode is that of simplicity—of time, labor, and ink saved. Counting the fractions as *two* accents, even, there will be found only *twenty-six* accents to the stanza. In the common accentuation there are *forty-one*. But admit that all this is a trifle, which it is *not*, and let us proceed to points of importance. Does the common accentuation express the truth in particular, in general, or in any regard? Is it consistent with itself? Does it convey either to the ignorant or to the scholar a just conception of the rhythm of the lines? Each of these questions must be answered in the negative. The crescents, being precisely similar, must be understood as expressing, all of them, one and the same thing; and so all prosodies have always understood them and wished them to be understood. They express, indeed, "short"; but this word has all kinds of meanings. It serves to represent (the reader is left to guess *when*) sometimes the half, sometimes the third, sometimes the fourth, sometimes the sixth of "long"; while "long" itself, in the books, is left undefined and undescribed. On the other hand, the horizontal accent, it may be said, expresses sufficiently well and unvaryingly the syllables which are meant to be long. It does nothing of the kind. This horizontal accent is placed over the cæsura (wherever, as in the Latin Prosodies, the cæsura is recognized) as well as over the ordinary long syllable, and implies any thing and every thing, just as the crescent. But grant that it does express the ordinary long syllables (leaving the cæsura out of question), have I not given the identical expression by not employing any expression at all? In a word, while the prosodies, with a certain number of accents express *precisely nothing whatever,* I, with scarcely half the number, have expressed every thing which, in a system of accentuation, demands expression. In glancing at my mode in the lines of Mr. Cranch it will be seen that it conveys not only the exact relation of the syllables and feet, among themselves, in those particular lines, but their precise value in relation to any other existing or conceivable feet or syllables in any existing or conceivable system of rhythm.

The object of what we call *scansion* is the distinct marking of the rhythmical flow. Scansion with accents or perpendicular lines between the feet—that is to say, scansion *by* the voice only—is scansion *to* the ear only; and all very good in its way. The written scansion addresses the ear through the eye. In either case the object is the distinct marking of the rhythmical, musical, or reading flow. There *can* be no other object, and there is none. Of course, then, the scansion and the reading flow should go hand-in-hand. The former must agree with the latter. The former represents and expresses the latter; and is good or bad as it truly or falsely represents and expresses it. If by the written scansion of a line we are not enabled to perceive any rhythm or music in the line, then either the line is unrhythmical or the scansion false. Apply all this to the English lines which we have quoted, at various points, in the course of this article. It will be found that the scansion exactly conveys the rhythm, and thus thoroughly fulfils the only purpose for which scansion is required.

But let the scansion *of the schools* be applied to the Greek and Latin verse, and what result do we find?—that the verse is one thing and the scansion quite another. The ancient verse, *read* aloud, is in general musical, and occasionally *very* musical. *Scanned* by the prosodial rules we can, for the most part, make nothing of it whatever. In the case of the English verse, the more emphatically we dwell on the divisions between the feet, the more distinct is our perception of the kind of rhythm intended. In the case of the Greek and Latin, the more we dwell the *less* distinct is this perception. To make this clear by an example:

Mæcenas, atavis edite regibus,
O, et præsidium et dulce decus meum,
Sunt quos curriculo pulverem Olympicum
Collegisse juvat, metaque fervidis
Evitata rotis, palmaque nobilis
Terrarum dominos evehit ad Deos.

Now in *reading* these lines, there is scarcely one person in a thousand who, if even ignorant of Latin, will not immediately feel and appreciate their flow—their music. A prosodist, however, informs the public that the *scansion* runs thus:

Mæce | nas ata | vis | edite | regibus |
O et | præsidi' | et | dulce de | cus meum |
Sunt quos | curricu | lo | pulver' O | lympicum |
Colle | gisse ju | vat | metaque | fervidis |
Evi | tata ro | tis | palmaque | nobilis |
Terra | rum domi | nos | evehit | ad Deos. |

Now I do not deny that we get a *certain sort* of music from the lines if we read them according to this scansion, but I wish to call attention to the fact that this scansion, and the certain sort of music which grows out of it, are entirely at war not only with the reading flow which any ordinary person would naturally give the lines, but with the reading flow universally given them, and never denied them, by even the most obstinate and stolid of scholars.

And now these questions are forced upon us: "Why exists this discrepancy between the modern verse with its scansion, and the ancient verse with its scansion?"—"Why, in the former case, are there agreement and representation, while in the latter there is neither the one nor the other?" or, to come to the point,—"How are we to reconcile the ancient verse with the scholastic scansion of it?" This absolutely necessary conciliation—shall we bring it about by supposing the scholastic scansion wrong because the ancient verse is right, or by maintaining that the ancient verse is wrong because the scholastic scansion is not to be gainsaid?

Were we to adopt the latter mode of arranging the difficulty, we might, in some measure, at least simplify the expression of the arrangement by putting it thus: Because the pedants have no eyes, therefore the old poets had no ears.

"But," say the gentlemen without the eyes, "the scholastic scansion, although certainly not handed down to us in form from the old poets themselves (the gentlemen without the ears), is nevertheless deduced from certain facts which are supplied us by careful observation of the old poems.

And let us illustrate this strong position by an example from an American poet—who must be a poet of some eminence, or he will not answer the purpose. Let us take Mr. Alfred B. Street. I remember these two lines of his:

His sinuous path, by blazes, wound
Among trunks grouped in myriads round.

With the *sense* of these lines I have nothing to do. When a poet is in a "fine frenzy," he may as well imagine a large forest as a small one; and "by blazes" is *not* intended for an oath. My concern is with the rhythm, which is iambic.

Now let us suppose that, a thousand years hence, when the "American language" is dead, a learned prosodist should be deducing, from "careful observation" of our best poets, a system of scansion for our poetry. And let us suppose that this prosodist had so little dependence in the generality and immutability of the laws of Nature, as to assume in the outset, that, because we lived a thousand years before his time, and made use of steam-engines instead of mesmeric balloons, we must therefore have had a *very* singular fashion of mouthing our vowels, and altogether of hudsonizing our verse. And let us suppose that with these and other fundamental propositions carefully put away in his brain, he should arrive at the line,—

Among | trunks grouped | in my | riads round.

Finding it an obviously iambic rhythm, he would divide it as above; and observing that "trunks" made the first member of an iambus, he would call it short, as Mr. Street intended it to be. Now farther, if instead of admitting the possibility that Mr. Street (who by that time would be called Street simply, just as we say Homer)—that Mr. Street might have been in the habit of writing carelessly, as the poets of the prosodist's own era did, and as all poets will do (on account of being geniuses),—instead of admitting this, supposed the learned scholar should make a "rule" and put it in a book, to the effect that, in the American verse, the vowel *u, when found imbedded among nine consonants,* was *short,* what under such circumstances, would the sensible people of the scholar's day have a right not only to think but to say of that scholar?—why, that he was "a fool—by blazes!"

I have put an extreme case, but it strikes at the root of the error. The "rules" are grounded in "authority"; and this "authority"—can any one tell us what it means? or can any one suggest any thing that it may *not* mean? Is it not clear that that "scholar" above referred to, might as readily have deduced from authority a totally false system as a partially true one? To deduce from authority a consistent prosody of the ancient metres would indeed have been within the limits of the barest possibility; and the task has *not* been accomplished, for the reason that it demands a species of ratiocination altogether out of keeping with the brain of a bookworm. A rigid scrutiny will show that the very few "rules" which have not as many exceptions as examples, are those which have, by accident, their true bases not in authority, but in the omniprevalent laws of syllabification; such, for example, as the rule which declares a vowel before two consonants to be long.

In a word, the gross confusion and antagonism of the scholastic prosody, as well as its marked inapplicability to the reading flow of the rhythms it pretends to illustrate, are attributable, first, to the utter absence of natural principle as a guide in the investigations which have been undertaken by inadequate men; and secondly, to the neglect of the obvious consideration that the ancient poems, which have been the *criteria* throughout, were the work of men who must have written as loosely, and with as little definitive system, as ourselves.

Were Horace alive to-day, he would divide for us his first Ode thus, and "make great eyes" when assured by prosodists that he had no business to make any such division!

Mæcenas | atavis | edite | regibus |
2 2 2 2 2 2 2 2
O et præ | sidium et | dulce de | cus meum |
2 2 3 3 3 2 2 2 2
Sunt quos cur | riculo | pulverem O | lympicum |
2 2 2 2 3 3 3 2 2
Collegisse | juvat | metaque | fervidis |
3 3 3 2 2 2 2
Evitata | rotis | palmaque | nobilis |
3 3 3 2 2 2 2
Terrarum | dominos | evehit | ad Deos. |
2 2 2 2 2 2 2 2

Read by this scansion, the flow is preserved; and the more we dwell on the divisions, the more the intended rhythm becomes apparent. Moreover, the feet have all the same time; while, in the scholastic scansion, trochees—admitted trochees—are absurdly employed as equivalents to spondees and dactyls. The books declare, for instance, that *Colle,* which begins the fourth line, is a trochee, and seem to be gloriously unconscious that to put a trochee in opposition with a longer foot, is to violate the inviolable principle of all music, *time.*

It will be said, however, by "some people," that I have no business to make a dactyl out of such obviously long syllables as *sunt, quos, cur.* Certainly I have no business to do so. I *never* do so. And Horace should not have done so. But he did. Mr. Bryant and Mr. Longfellow do the same thing every day. And merely because these gentlemen, now and then, forget themselves in this way, it would be hard if some future prosodist should insist upon twisting the "Thanatopsis," or the "Spanish Student," into a jumble of trochees, spondees, and dactyls.

It may be said, also, by some other people, that in the word *decus,* I have succeeded no better than the books, in making the scansional agree with the reading flow; and that *decus* was not pronounced de*cus.* I reply, that there can be no doubt of the word having been pronounced, in this case, de*cus.* It must be observed, that the Latin inflection, or variation of a word in its terminating syllable, caused the Romans—*must* have caused them—to pay greater attention to the termination of a word than to its commencement, or than we do to the terminations of our words. The end of the Latin word established that relation of the word with other words which we establish by prepositions or auxiliary verbs. Therefore, it would seem infinitely less odd to them than it does to us, to dwell at any time, for any slight purpose, abnormally, on a terminating syllable. In verse, this license—scarcely a license—would be frequently admitted. These ideas unlock the secret of such lines as the

Litoreis ingens inventa sub ilici*bus sus,*

and the

Parturiunt montes et nascitur ridicu*lus mus,*

which I quoted, some time ago, while speaking of rhyme.

As regards to the prosodial elisions, such as that of *rem* before *O,* in *pulverem Olympicum,* it is really difficult to understand how so dismally silly a notion could have entered the brain even of a pedant. Were it demanded of me why the books cut off one *vowel* before another, I might say: It is, perhaps, because the books think that, since a bad reader is so apt to slide the one vowel into the other at any rate, it is just as well to print them *ready-slided*. But in the case of the terminating *m*, which is the most readily pronounced of all consonants (as the infantile *mamma* will testify), and the most impossible to cheat the ear of by any system of sliding—in the case of the *m*, I should be driven to reply that, to the best of my belief, the prosodists did the thing, because they had a fancy for doing it, and wished to see how funny it would look after it was done. The thinking reader will perceive that, from the great facility with which *em* may be enunciated, it is admirably suited to form one of the rapid short syllables in the bastard dactyl (pulve$_3$re$_3$m O$_3$); but because the books had no conception of a bastard dactyl, they knocked it on the head at once—by cutting off its tail!

Let me now give a specimen of the true scansion of another Horatian measure—embodying an instance of proper elision.

Integ$_2$e$_2$r | vitæ | sc$_3$el$_3$erisq$_3$ue | purus |
Non e$_2$ge$_2$t | Mauri | jacul$_3$i$_3$s n$_3$e | que arcu |
Nec v$_2$en$_2$e | natis | grav$_3$id$_3$a s$_3$a | gittis |
Fusc$_2$e pha$_2$ | retrâ.

Here the regular recurrence of the bastard dactyl gives great animation to the rhythm. The *e* before the *a* in *que arcu*, is, almost of sheer necessity, cut off—that is to say, run into the *a* so as to preserve the spondee. But even this license it would have been better not to take.

Had I space, nothing would afford me greater pleasure than to proceed with the scansion of *all* the ancient rhythms, and to show how easily, by the help of common-sense, the intended music of each and all can be rendered instantaneously apparent. But I have already overstepped my limits, and must bring this paper to an end.

It will never do, however, to omit all mention of the heroic hexameter.

I began the "processes" by a suggestion of the spondee as the first step toward verse. But the innate monotony of the spondee has caused its disappearance, as the basis of rhythm, from all modern poetry. We *may* say, indeed, that the French heroic—the most wretchedly monotonous verse in existence—is, to all intents and purposes, spondaic. But it is not designedly spondaic—and if the French were ever to examine it at all, they would no doubt pronounce it iambic. It must be observed that the French language is strangely peculiar in this point—*that it is without accentuation, and consequently without verse*. The genius of the people, rather than the structure of the tongue, declares that their words are, for the most part, enunciated with a uniform dwelling on each syllable. For example, *we* say "syl*la*bfi*ca*tion." A Frenchman would say syl-la-bi-fi-ca-ti-on; dwelling on no one of the syllables with any noticeable particularity. Here again I put an extreme case, in order to be well understood; but the general fact is as I give it—that, comparatively, the French have *no* accentuation. And there can be nothing worth the name of verse without. Therefore, the French have no verse worth the name—which is the fact, put in sufficiently plain terms. Their iambic rhythm so superabounds in absolute spondees, as to warrant me in calling its basis spondaic; but French is the *only* modern tongue which has any rhythm with such basis; and even in the French, it is, as I have said, unintentional.

Admitting, however, the validity of my suggestion, that the spondee was the first approach to verse, we should expect to find, first, natural spondees (words each forming just a spondee) most abundant in the most ancient languages; and, secondly, we should expect to find spondees forming the basis of the most ancient rhythms. These expectations are in both cases confirmed.

Of the Greek hexameter, the intentional basis is spondaic. The dactyls are the *variation* of the theme. It will be observed that there is no absolute certainty about *their* points of interposition. The penultimate foot, it is true, is usually a dactyl; but not uniformly so; while the ultimate, on which the ear *lingers,* is always a spondee. Even that the penultimate is usually a dactyl may be clearly referred to the necessity of winding up with the *distinctive* spondee. In corroboration of this idea, again, we should look to find the penultimate spondee most usual in the most ancient verse; and, accordingly, we find it more frequent in the Greek than in the Latin hexameter.

But besides all this, spondees are not only more prevalent in the heroic hexameter than dactyls, but occur to such an extent as is even unpleasant to modern ears, on account of monotony. What the modern chiefly appreciates and admires in the Greek hexameter, is the *melody of the abundant vowel sounds*. The Latin hexameters *really* please very few moderns—although so many pretend to fall into ecstasies about them. In the hexameters quoted, several pages ago, from Silius Italicus, the preponderance of the spondee is strikingly manifest. Besides the natural spondees of the Greek and Latin, numerous artificial ones arise in the verse of these tongues on account of the tendency which inflection has to throw full accentuation on terminal syllables; and the preponderance of the spondee is farther insured by the comparative infrequency of the small prepositions which *we* have to serve us *instead* of case, and also the absence of the diminutive auxiliary verbs with which *we* have to eke out the expression of our primary ones. These are the monosyllables whose abundance serve to stamp the poetic genius of a language as tripping or dactylic.

Now, paying no attention to these facts, Sir Philip Sidney, Professor Longfellow, and innumerable other persons more or less modern, have busied themselves in constructing what they suppose to be "English hexameters on the model of the Greek." The only difficulty was that (even leaving out of question the melodious masses of vowels) these gentlemen never could get their English hexameters to *sound* Greek. Did they *look* Greek?—that should have been the query; and the reply might have led to a solution of the riddle. In placing a copy of ancient hexameters side by side with a copy (in similar type) of such hexameters as Professor Longfellow, or Professor Felton, or the Frogpondian Professors collectively, are in the shameful practice of composing "on the model of the Greek," it will be seen that the latter (hexameters, not professors) are about one third longer *to the eye,* on an average, than the former. The more abundant dactyls make the difference. And it is the greater number of spondees in the Greek than in the English—in the ancient than in the modern tongue—which has caused it to fall out that while these eminent scholars were groping about in the dark for a Greek hexameter, which is a spondaic rhythm varied now and then by dactyls, they merely stumbled, to the lasting scandal of scholarship, over something which, on account of its long-leggedness, we may as well term a Feltonian hexameter, and which is a dactylic rhythm, interrupted, rarely, by artificial spondees which are no spondees at all, and which are curiously thrown in by the heels at all kinds of improper and impertinent points.

Here is a specimen of the Longfellownian hexameter.

Also the | church with | in was a | dorned for | this was the | season
In which the | young their | parents' | hope and the | loved ones of |
    Heaven |
Should at the | foot of the | altar re | new the | vows of their | baptism |
Therefore each | nook and | corner was | swept and | cleaned and the |
    dust was |
Blown from the | walls and | ceiling and | from the | oil-painted |
    benches |

Mr. Longfellow is a man of imagination—but *can* he imagine that any individual, with a proper understanding of the danger of lock-jaw, would make the attempt of twisting his mouth into the shape necessary for the emission of such spondees as "par*ents,*" and "from the," or such dactyls as "cleaned and the," and "loved ones of"? "Baptism" is by no means a bad spondee—perhaps because it happens to be a dactyl;—of all the rest, however, I am dreadfully ashamed.

But these feet—dactyls and spondees, all together—should thus be put at once into their proper position:

> Also, the church within was adorned; for this was the season in which the young, their parents' hope, and the loved ones of Heaven, should, at the foot of the altar, renew the vows of their baptism. Therefore each nook and corner was swept and cleaned; and the dust was blown from the walls and ceiling, and from the oil-painted benches.

There!—That is respectable prose; and it will incur no danger of ever getting its character ruined by anybody's mistaking it for verse.

But even when we let these modern hexameters go, as Greek, and merely hold them fast in their proper character of Longfellownian, or Feltonian, or Frogpondian, we must still condemn them as having been committed in a radical misconception of the philosophy of verse. The spondee, as I observed, is the *theme* of the Greek line. Most of the ancient hexameters *begin* with spondees, for the reason that the spondee *is* the theme; and the ear is filled with it as with a burden. Now the Feltonian dactylics have, in the same way, dactyls for the theme, and most of them begin with dactyls—which is all very proper if not very Greek,—but, unhappily, the one point at which they *are* very Greek is that point, precisely, at which they should be nothing but Feltonian. They always *close* with what is meant for a spondee. To be consistently silly, they should die off in a dactyl.

That a truly Greek hexameter *cannot,* however, be readily composed in English, is a proposition which I am by no means inclined to admit. I think I could manage the point myself. For example:

Do tell! | when may we | hope to make | men of sense | out of the | Pundits |
Born and brought | up with their | snouts deep | down in the | mud of the | Frog pond? |
Why ask? | who ever | yet saw | money made | out of a | fat old |
Jew, or | downright | upright | nutmegs | out of a | pine-knot? |

The proper spondee predominance is here preserved. Some of the dactyls are not so good as I could wish—but, upon the whole, the rhythm is very decent—to say nothing of its excellent sense.

## *NOTES*

1. Verse, from the Latin *vertere,* to turn, is so called on account of the turning or recommencement of the series of feet. Thus a verse, strictly speaking, is a line. In this sense, however, I have preferred using the latter word alone; employing the former in the general acceptation given it in the heading of this paper.

2. A stanza is often vulgarly, and with gross impropriety, called a *verse*.

# The Philosophy of Composition

Charles Dickens, in a note now lying before me, alluding to an examination I once made of the mechanism of "Barnaby Rudge," says—"By the way, are you aware that Godwin wrote his 'Caleb Williams' backwards?[1] He first involved his hero in a web of difficulties, forming the second volume, and then, for the first, cast about him for some mode of accounting for what had been done."

I cannot think this the *precise* mode of procedure on the part of Godwin—and indeed what he himself acknowledges, is not altogether in accordance with Mr. Dickens' idea—but the author of "Caleb Williams" was too good an artist not to perceive the advantage derivable from at least a somewhat similar process. Nothing is more clear than that every plot, worth the name, must be elaborated to its *dénouement* before anything be attempted with the pen. It is only with the *dénouement* constantly in view that we can give a plot its indispensable air of consequence, or causation, by making the incidents, and especially the tone at all points, tend to the development of the intention.

There is a radical error, I think, in the usual mode of constructing a story. Either history affords a thesis—or one is suggested by an incident of the day—or, at best, the author sets himself to work in the combination of striking events to form merely the basis of his narrative—designing, generally, to fill in with description, dialogue, or autorial comment, whatever crevices of fact, or action, may, from page to page, render themselves apparent.

I prefer commencing with the consideration of an *effect*. Keeping originality *always* in view—for he is false to himself who ventures to dispense with so obvious and so easily attainable a source of interest—I say to myself, in the first place, "Of the innumerable effects, or impressions, of which the heart, the intellect, or (more generally) the soul is susceptible, what one shall I, on the present occasion, select?" Having chosen a novel, first, and secondly a vivid effect, I consider whether it can be best wrought by incident or tone—whether by ordinary incidents and peculiar tone, or the converse, or by peculiarity both of incident and tone—afterward looking about me (or rather within) for such combinations of event, or tone, as shall best aid me in the construction of the effect.

I have often thought how interesting a magazine paper might be written by any author who would—that is to say who could—detail, step by step, the processes by which any one of his compositions attained its ultimate point of completion. Why such a paper has never been given to the world, I am much at a loss to say—but, perhaps, the autorial vanity has had more to do with the omission than any one other cause. Most writers—poets in especial—prefer having it understood that they compose by a species of fine frenzy—an ecstatic intuition—and would positively shudder at letting the public take a peep behind the scenes, at the elaborate and vacillating crudities of thought—at the true purposes seized only at the last moment—at the innumerable glimpses of idea that arrived not at the maturity of full view—at the fully matured fancies discarded in despair as unmanageable—at the cautious selections and rejections—at the painful erasures and interpolations—in a word, at the wheels and pinions—the tackle for scene-shifting—the step-ladders and demon-traps—the cock's feathers, the red paint and the black patches, which, in ninety-nine cases out of the hundred, constitute the properties of the literary *histrio*.

I am aware, on the other hand, that the case is by no means common, in which an author is at all in condition to retrace the steps by which his conclusions have been attained. In general, suggestions, having arisen pell-mell, are pursued and forgotten in a similar manner.

For my own part, I have neither sympathy with the repugnance alluded to, nor, at any time the least difficulty in recalling to mind the progressive steps of any of my compositions; and, since the interest of an analysis, or reconstruction, such as I have considered a *desideratum*, is quite independent of any real or fancied interest in the thing analyzed, it will not be regarded as a breach of decorum on my part to show the *modus operandi* by which some one of my own works was put together. I select "The Raven," as most generally known. It is my design to render it manifest that no one point in its composition is referable either to accident or intuition—that the work proceeded, step by step, to its completion with the precision and rigid consequence of a mathematical problem.

Let us dismiss, as irrelevant to the poem, *per se*, the circumstance—or say the necessity—which, in the first place, gave rise to the intention of composing *a* poem that should suit at once the popular and the critical taste.

We commence, then, with this intention.

The initial consideration was that of extent. If any literary work is too long to be read at one sitting, we must be content to dispense with the immensely important effect derivable from unity of impression—for, if two sittings be required, the affairs of the world interfere, and every thing like totality is at once destroyed. But since, *ceteris paribus* [other things being equal], no poet can afford to dispense with *any thing* that may advance his design, it but remains to be seen whether there is, in extent, any advantage to counterbalance the loss of unity which attends it. Here I say no, at once. What we term a long poem is, in fact, merely a succession of brief ones—that is to say, of brief poetical effects. It is needless to demonstrate that a poem is such, only inasmuch as it intensely excites, by elevating, the soul; and all intense excitements are, through a psychal necessity, brief. For this reason, at least one half of the "Paradise Lost" is essentially prose—a succession of poetical excitements interspersed, *inevitably*, with corresponding depressions—the whole being deprived, through the extremeness of its length, of the vastly important artistic element, totality, or unity, of effect.

It appears evident, then, that there is a distinct limit, as regards length, to all works of literary art—the limit of a single sitting—and that, although in certain classes of prose composition, such as "Robinson Crusoe," (demanding no unity) this limit may be advantageously overpassed, it can never properly be overpassed in a poem. Within this limit, the extent of a poem may be made to bear mathematical relation to its merit—in other words, to the excitement or elevation—again in other words, to the degree of the true poetical effect which it is capable of inducing; for it is clear that the brevity must be in direct ratio of the intensity of the intended effect:—this, with one proviso—that a certain degree of duration is absolutely requisite for the production of any effect at all.

Holding in view these considerations, as well as that degree of excitement which I deemed not above the popular, while not below the critical, taste, I reached at once what I conceived the proper *length* for my intended poem—a length of about one hundred lines. It is, in fact a hundred and eight.

My next thought concerned the choice of an impression, or effect, to be conveyed: and here I may as well observe that, throughout the construction, I kept steadily in view the design of rendering the work *universally* appreciable. I should be carried too far out of my immediate topic were I to demonstrate a point upon which I have repeatedly insisted, and which, with the poetical, stands not in the slightest need of demonstration—the point, I mean, that Beauty is the sole legitimate province of the poem. A few words, however, in elucidation of my real meaning, which some of my friends have evinced a disposition to misrepresent. That pleasure which is at once the most intense, the most elevating, and the most pure, is, I believe, found in the contemplation of the beautiful. When, indeed, men speak of Beauty, they mean, precisely, not a quality, as is supposed, but an effect—they refer, in short, just to that intense and pure elevation of *soul—not* of intellect, or of heart—upon which I have commented, and which is experienced in consequence of contemplating "the beautiful." Now I designate Beauty as the province of the poem, merely because it is an obvious rule of Art that effects should be made to spring from direct causes—that objects should be attained through means best adapted for their attainment—no one as yet having been weak enough to deny that the peculiar elevation alluded to is *most readily* attained in this poem. Now the object, Truth, or the satisfaction of the intellect, and the object Passion, or the excitement of the heart, are, although attainable, to a certain extent, in poetry, far more readily attainable in prose. Truth, in fact, demands a precision, and Passion a *homeliness* (the truly passionate will comprehend me) which are absolutely antagonistic to that Beauty which, I maintain, is the excitement, or pleasurable elevation, of the soul. It by no means follows from any thing here said, that passion, or even truth, may not be introduced, and even profitably introduced, into a poem—for they may serve in elucidation, or aid the general effect, as do discords in music, by contrast—but the true artist will always contrive, first, to tone them into proper subservience to the predominant aim, and secondly, to enveil them, as far as possible, in that Beauty which is the atmosphere and the essence of the poem.

Regarding, then, Beauty as my province, my next question referred to the *tone* of its highest manifestation—and all experience has shown that this tone is one of *sadness*. Beauty of whatever kind, in its supreme development, invariably excites the sensitive soul to tears. Melancholy is thus the most legitimate of all the poetical tones.

The length, the province, and the tone, being thus determined, I betook myself to ordinary induction, with the view of obtaining some artistic piquancy which might serve me as a keynote in the construction of the poem—some pivot upon which the whole structure might turn. In carefully thinking over all the usual artistic effects—or more properly *points*, in the theatrical sense—I did not fail to perceive immediately that no one had been so universally employed as that of the *refrain*. The universality of its employment sufficed to assure me of its intrinsic value, and spared me the necessity of submitting it to analysis. I considered it, however, with regard to its susceptibility of improvement, and soon saw it to be in a primitive condition. As commonly used, the *refrain*, or burden, not only is limited to lyric verse, but depends for its impression upon the force of monotone—both in sound and thought. The pleasure is deduced solely from the sense of identity—of repetition. I resolved to diversify, and so heighten, the effect, by adhering, in general, to the monotone of sound, while I continually varied that of thought: that is to say, I determined to produce continuously novel effects, by the variation *of the application* of the *refrain*—the *refrain* itself remaining, for the most part, unvaried.

These points being settled, I next bethought me of the *nature* of my *refrain*. Since its application was to be repeatedly varied, it was clear that the *refrain* itself must be brief, for there would have been an insurmountable difficulty in frequent variations of application in any sentence of length. In proportion to the brevity of the sentence, would, of course, be the facility of the variation. This led me at once to a single word as the best *refrain*.

The question now arose as to the character of the word. Having made up my mind to a *refrain*, the division of the poem into stanzas was, of course, a corollary: the *refrain* forming the close of each stanza. That such a close, to have force, must be sonorous and susceptible of protracted emphasis, admitted no doubt: and these considerations inevitably led me to the long *o* as the most sonorous vowel, in connection with *r* as the most producible consonant.

The sound of the *refrain* being thus determined, it became necessary to select a word embodying this sound, and at the same time in the fullest possible keeping with that melancholy which I had predetermined as the tone of the poem. In such a search it would have been absolutely impossible to overlook the word "Nevermore." In fact, it was the very first which presented itself.

The next *desideratum* was a pretext for the continuous use of the one word "Nevermore." In observing the difficulty which I at once found in inventing a sufficiently plausible reason for its continuous repetition, I did not fail to perceive that this difficulty arose solely from the pre-assumption that the word was to be so continuously or monotonously spoken by *a human* being—I did not fail to perceive, in short, that the difficulty lay in the reconciliation of this monotony with the exercise of reason on the part of the creature repeating the word. Here, then, immediately arose the idea of a *non*-reasoning creature capable of speech; and, very naturally, a parrot, in the first instance, suggested itself, but was superseded forthwith by a Raven, as equally capable of speech, and infinitely more in keeping with the intended *tone*.

I had now gone so far as the conception of a Raven—the bird of ill omen—monotonously repeating the one word, "Nevermore," at the conclusion of each stanza, in a poem of melancholy tone, and in length about one hundred lines. Now, never losing sight of the object *supremeness*, or perfection, at all points, I asked myself—"Of all melancholy topics, what, according to the *universal* understanding of mankind, is the *most* melancholy?" Death—was the obvious reply. "And when," I said, "is this most melancholy of topics most poetical?" From what I have already explained at some length, the answer, here also, is obvious—"When it most closely allies itself to *Beauty:* the death, then, of a beautiful woman is, unquestionably, the most poetical topic in the world—and equally is it beyond doubt that the lips best suited for such topics are those of a bereaved lover."

I had now to combine the two ideas, of a lover lamenting his deceased mistress and a Raven continuously repeating the word "Nevermore."—I had to combine these, bearing in mind my design of varying, at every turn, the *application* of the word repeated; but the only intelligible mode of such combination is that of imagining the Raven employing the word in answer to the queries of the lover. And here it was that I saw at once the opportunity afforded for the effect on which I had been depending—that is to say, the effect of the *variation of application*. I saw that I could make the first query propounded by the lover—the first query to which the Raven should reply "Nevermore"—that I could make this first query a commonplace one—the second less so—the third still less, and so on—until at length the lover, startled from his original *nonchalance* by the melancholy character of the word itself—by its frequent repetition—and by a consideration of the ominous reputation of the fowl that uttered it—is at length excited to superstition, and wildly propounds queries of a far different character—queries whose solution he has passionately at heart—propounds them half in superstition and half in that species of despair which delights in self-torture—propounds them not altogether because he believes in the prophetic or demoniac character of the bird (which, reason assures him, is merely repeating a lesson learned by rote) but because he experiences a phrenzied pleasure in so modeling his questions as to receive from the *expected* "Nevermore" the most delicious because the most intolerable of sorrow. Perceiving the opportunity thus afforded me—or, more strictly, thus forced upon me in the progress of the construction—I first established in mind the climax, or concluding query—that query to which "Nevermore" should be in the last place an answer—that in reply to which this word "Nevermore" should involve the utmost conceivable amount of sorrow and despair.

Here then the poem may be said to have its beginning—at the end, where all works of art should begin—for it was here, at this point of my preconsiderations, that I first put pen to paper in the composition of the stanza:

"Prophet," said I, "thing of evil! prophet still if bird or devil!
By that heaven that bends above us—by that God we both adore,

Tell this soul with sorrow laden, if within the distant Aidenn,
It shall clasp a sainted maiden whom the angels name Lenore—
Clasp a rare and radiant maiden whom the angels name Lenore."
Quoth the Raven "Nevermore."

I composed this stanza, at this point, first that, by establishing the climax, I might the better vary and graduate, as regards seriousness and importance, the preceding queries of the lover—and, secondly, that I might definitely settle the rhythm, the metre, and the length and general arrangement of the stanza—as well as graduate the stanzas which were to precede, so that none of them might surpass this in rhythmical effect. Had I been able, in the subsequent composition, to construct more vigorous stanzas, I should, without scruple, have purposely enfeebled them, so as not to interfere with the climacteric effect.

And here I may as well say a few words of the versification. My first object (as usual) was originality. The extent to which this has been neglected, in versification, is one of the most unaccountable things in the world. Admitting that there is little possibility of variety in mere *rhythm*, it is still clear that the possible varieties of metre and stanza are absolutely infinite—and yet, *for centuries, no man, in verse, has ever done, or ever seemed to think of doing, an original thing*. The fact is, that originality (unless in minds of very unusual force) is by no means a matter, as some suppose, of impulse or intuition. In general, to be found, it must be elaborately sought, and although a positive merit of the highest class, demands in its attainment less of invention than negation.

Of course, I pretend to no originality in either the rhythm or metre of the "Raven." The former is trochaic—the latter is octameter acatalectic, alternating with heptameter catalectic repeated in the *refrain* of the fifth verse, and terminating with tetrameter catalectic. Less pedantically—the feet employed throughout (trochees) consist of a long syllable followed by a short: the first line of the stanza consists of eight of these feet—the second of seven and a half (in effect two-thirds)—the third of eight—the fourth of seven and a half—the fifth the same—the sixth three and a half. Now, each of these lines, taken individually, has been employed before, and what originality the "Raven" has, is in their *combination into stanza;* nothing even remotely approaching this combination has ever been attempted. The effect of this originality of combination is aided by other unusual, and some altogether novel effects, arising from an extension of the application of the principles of rhyme and alliteration.

The next point to be considered was the mode of bringing together the lover and the Raven—and the first branch of this consideration was the *locale*. For this the most natural suggestion might seem to be a forest, or the fields—but it has always appeared to me that a close *circumscription of space* is absolutely necessary to the effect of insulated incident:—it has the force of a frame to a picture. It has an indisputable moral power in keeping concentrated the attention, and, of course, must not be confounded with mere unity of place.

I determined, then, to place the lover in his chamber—in a chamber rendered sacred to him by memories of her who had frequented it. The room is represented as richly furnished—this in mere pursuance of the ideas I have already explained on the subject of Beauty, as the sole true poetical thesis.

The *locale* being thus determined, I had now to introduce the bird—and the thought of introducing him through the window, was inevitable. The idea of making the lover suppose, in the first instance, that the flapping of the wings of the bird against the shutter, is a "tapping" at the door, originated in a wish to increase, by prolonging the reader's curiosity, and in a desire to admit the incidental effect arising from the lover's throwing open the door, finding all dark, and thence adopting the half-fancy that it was the spirit of his mistress that knocked.

I made the night tempestuous, first, to account for the Raven's seeking admission, and secondly, for the effect of contrast with the (physical) serenity within the chamber.

I made the bird alight on the bust of Pallas, also for the effect of contrast between the marble and the plumage—it being understood that the bust was absolutely *suggested* by the bird—the bust of *Pallas* being chosen, first, as most in keeping with the scholarship of the lover, and, secondly, for the sonorousness of the word, Pallas, itself.

About the middle of the poem, also, I have availed myself of the force of contrast, with a view of deepening the ultimate impression. For example, an air of the fantastic—approaching as nearly to the ludicrous as was admissible—is given to the Raven's entrance. He comes in "with many a flirt and flutter."

> *Not the least obeisance made he*—not a moment stopped or stayed he,
> *But with mien of lord or lady*, perched above my chamber door.

In the two stanzas which follow, the design is more obviously carried out:—

> Then this ebony bird beguiling my sad fancy into smiling
> By the *grave and stern decorum of the countenance it wore*,
> "Though thy *crest be shorn and shaven* thou," I said, "art sure no
>     craven,
> Ghastly grim and ancient Raven wandering from the nightly shore—
> Tell me what thy lordly name is on the Night's Plutonian shore?"
>         Quoth the Raven "Nevermore."
>
> Much I marvelled *this ungainly fowl* to hear discourse so plainly
> Though its answer little meaning—little relevancy bore;
> For we cannot help agreeing that no living human being
> *Ever yet was blessed with seeing bird above his chamber door—*
> *Bird or beast upon the sculptured bust above his chamber door,*
>         With such name as "Nevermore."

The effect of the *dénouement* being thus provided for, I immediately drop the fantastic for a tone of the most profound seriousness:—this tone commencing in the stanza directly following the one last quoted, with the line,

> But the Raven, sitting lonely on that placid bust, spoke only, etc.

From this epoch the lover no longer jests—no longer sees any thing even of the fantastic in the Raven's demeanor. He speaks of him as a "grim, ungainly, ghastly, gaunt, and ominous bird of yore," and feels the "fiery eyes" burning into his "bosom's core." This revolution of thought, or fancy, on the lover's part, is intended to induce a similar one on the part of the reader—to bring the mind into a proper frame for the *dénouement*—which is now brought about as rapidly and as *directly* as possible.

With the *dénouement* proper—with the Raven's reply, "Nevermore," to the lover's final demand if he shall meet his mistress in another world—the poem, in its obvious phase, that of a simple narrative, may be said to have its completion. So far, every thing is within the limits of the accountable—of the real. A raven, having learned by rote the single word "Nevermore," and having escaped from the custody of its owner, is driven at midnight, through the violence of a storm, to seek admission at a window from which a light still gleams—the chamber-window of a student, occupied half in poring over a volume, half in dreaming of a beloved mistress deceased. The casement being thrown open at the fluttering of the bird's wings, the bird itself perches on the most convenient seat out of the immediate reach of the student, who, amused by the incident and the oddity of the visitor's demeanor, demands of it, in jest and without looking for a reply, its name. The raven addressed, answers with its customary word, "Nevermore"—a word which finds immediate echo in the melancholy heart of the student, who, giving utterance aloud to certain thoughts suggested by the occasion, is again startled by the fowl's repetition of "Nevermore." The student now guesses the state of the case, but is impelled, as I have before explained, by the human thirst for self-torture, and in part by superstition, to propound such queries to the bird as will bring him, the lover, the most of the luxury of sorrow, through the anticipated answer "Nevermore." With the indulgence, to the extreme, of this self-torture, the narration, in what I have termed its first or obvious phase, has a natural termination, and so far there has been no overstepping of the limits of the real.

But in subjects so handled, however skilfully, or with however vivid an array of incident, there is always a certain hardness or nakedness, which repels the artistical eye. Two things are invariably required—first, some amount of complexity, or more properly, adaptation; and, secondly, some amount of suggestiveness—some under-current, however indefinite, of meaning. It is this latter, in especial, which imparts to a work of art so much of that *richness* (to borrow from colloquy a forcible term) which we are too fond of confounding with *the ideal*. It is the *excess* of the suggested meaning—it is the rendering this the upper instead of the under-current of the theme—which turns into prose (and that of the very flattest kind) the so called poetry of the so called transcendentalists.

Holding these opinions, I added the two concluding stanzas of the poem—their suggestiveness being thus made to pervade all the narrative which has preceded them. The under-current of meaning is rendered first apparent in the lines—

"Take thy beak from out *my heart*, and take thy form from off my door."
Quoth the Raven "Nevermore!"

It will be observed that the words, "from out my heart," involve the first metaphorical expression in the poem. They, with the answer, "Nevermore," dispose the mind to seek a moral in all that has been previously narrated. The reader begins now to regard the Raven as emblematical—but it is not until the very last line of the very last stanza, that the intention of making him emblematical of *Mournful and Never-ending Remembrance* is permitted distinctly to be seen:

And the Raven, never flitting, still is sitting, still is sitting,
On the pallid bust of Pallas, just above my chamber door;
And his eyes have all the seeming of a demon's that is dreaming,
And the lamplight o'er him streaming throws his shadow on the floor;
And my soul *from out that shadow* that lies floating on the floor
Shall be lifted—nevermore.

## *NOTES*

1. *Caleb Williams,* a novel by the English writer and reformer William Godwin (1759–1836), appeared in 1794.

# Longfellow

In our last number we had some hasty observations on these "Ballads"—observations which we now propose, in some measure, to amplify and explain.

It may be remembered that, among other points, we demurred to Mr. Longfellow's *theses,* or rather to their general character. We found fault with the too obtrusive nature of their *didacticism.* Some years ago we urged a similar objection to one or two of the longer pieces of Bryant; and neither time nor reflection has sufficed to modify, in the slightest particular, our convictions upon this topic.

We have said that Mr. Longfellow's conception of the *aims* of poesy is erroneous; and that thus, laboring at a disadvantage, he does violent wrong to his own high powers; and now the question is, what *are* his ideas of the aims of the muse, as we gather these ideas from the *general* tendency of his poems? It will be at once evident that, imbued with the peculiar gift of German song (a pure conventionality) he regards the inculcation of a *moral* as essential. Here we find it necessary to repeat that we have reference only to the *general* tendency of his compositions; for there are some magnificent exceptions, where, as if by accident, he has permitted his genius to get the better of his conventional prejudice. But didacticism is the prevalent *tone* of his song. His invention, his imagery, his all, is made subservient to the elucidation of some one or more points (but rarely of more than one) which he looks upon as *truth.* And that this mode of procedure will find stern defenders should never excite surprise, so long as the world is full to overflowing with cant and conventicles. There are men who will scramble on all fours through the muddiest sloughs of vice to pick up a single apple of virtue. There are things called men who, so long as the sun rolls, will greet with snuffing huzzas every figure that takes upon itself the semblance of truth, even although the figure, in itself only a "stuffed Paddy," be as much out of place as a toga on the statue of Washington, or out of season as rabbits in the days of the dog-star.

Now with as deep a reverence for "the true" as ever inspired the bosom of mortal man, we would limit, in many respects, its modes of inculcation. We would limit to enforce them. We would not render them impotent by dissipation. The demands of truth are severe. She has no sympathy with the myrtles. All that is indispensable in song is all with which she has nothing to do. To deck her in gay robes is to render her a harlot. It is but making her a flaunting paradox to wreathe her in gems and flowers. Even in stating this our present proposition, we verify our own words—we feel the necessity, in enforcing this *truth,* of descending from metaphor. Let us then be simple and distinct. To convey "the true" we are required to dismiss from the attention all inessentials. We must be perspicuous, precise, terse. We need concentration rather than expansion of mind. We must be calm, unimpassioned, unexcited—in a word, we must be in that peculiar mood which, as nearly as possible, is the exact converse of the poetical. He must be blind indeed who cannot perceive the radical and chasmal difference between the truthful and the poetical modes of inculcation. He must be grossly wedded to conventionalisms who, in spite of this difference, shall still attempt to reconcile the obstinate oils and waters of Poetry and Truth.

Dividing the world of mind into its most obvious and immediately recognisable distinctions, we have the pure intellect, taste, and the moral sense. We place *taste* between the intellect and the moral sense, because it is just this intermediate space which, in the mind, it occupies. It is the connecting link in the triple chain.

It serves to sustain a mutual intelligence between the extremes. It appertains, in strict appreciation, to the former, but is distinguished from the latter by so faint a difference, that Aristotle has not hesitated to class some of its operations among the Virtues themselves. But the *offices* of the trio are broadly marked. Just as conscience, or the moral sense, recognises duty; just as the intellect deals with *truth;* so is it the part of taste alone to inform us of Beauty. And Poesy is the handmaiden but of Taste. Yet we would not be misunderstood. This handmaiden is not forbidden to moralise—in her own fashion. She is not forbidden to depict—but to reason and preach, of virtue. As, of this latter, conscience recognises the obligation, so intellect teaches the expediency, while taste contents herself with displaying the beauty: waging war with vice merely on the ground of its inconsistency with fitness, harmony, proportion—in a word with τὸ καλόν [the beautiful].

An important condition of man's immortal nature is thus, plainly, the sense of the Beautiful. This it is which ministers to his delight in the manifold forms and colors and sounds and sentiments amid which he exists. And, just as the eyes of Amaryllis are repeated in the mirror, or the living lily in the lake, so is the mere *record* of these forms and colors and sounds and sentiments—so is their mere oral or written repetition a duplicate source of delight. But this repetition is not Poesy. He who shall merely sing with whatever rapture, in however harmonious strains, or with however vivid a truth of imitation, of the sights and sounds which greet him in common with all mankind—he, we say, has yet failed to prove his divine title. There is still a longing unsatisfied, which he has been impotent to fulfil. There is still a thirst unquenchable, which to allay he has shown us no crystal springs. This burning thirst belongs to the *immortal* essence of man's nature. It is equally a consequence and an indication of his perennial life. It is the desire of the moth for the star. It is not the mere appreciation of the beauty before us. It is a wild effort to reach the beauty above. It is a forethought of the loveliness to come. It is a passion to be satiated by no sublunary sights, or sounds, or sentiments, and the soul thus athirst strives to allay its fever in futile efforts at *creation.* Inspired with a prescient ecstasy of the beauty beyond the grave, it struggles by multiform novelty of combination among the things and thoughts of Time, to anticipate some portion of that loveliness whose very elements, perhaps, appertain solely to Eternity. And the result of such effort, on the part of souls fittingly constituted, is alone what mankind have agreed to denominate Poetry.

We say this with little fear of contradiction. Yet the spirit of our assertion must be more heeded than the letter. Mankind have *seemed* to define Poesy in a thousand, and in a thousand conflicting definitions. But the war is one only of words. Induction is as well applicable to this subject as to the most palpable and utilitarian; and by its sober processes we find that, in respect to compositions which have been really received as poems, the *imaginative*, or, more popularly, the creative portions *alone* have ensured them to be so received. Yet these works, on account of these portions, having once been so received and so named, it has happened, naturally and inevitably, that other portions totally unpoetic have not only come to be regarded by the popular voice as poetic, but have been made to serve as false standards of perfection, in the adjustment of other poetical claims. Whatever has been found in whatever has been received as a poem, has been blindly regarded as *ex statu* [according to its position] poetic. And this is a species of gross error which scarcely could have made its way into any less intangible topic. In fact that license which appertains to the Muse herself, it has been thought decorous, if not sagacious to indulge, in all examination of her character.

Poesy is thus seen to be a response—unsatisfactory it is true—but still in some measure a response, to a natural and irrepressible demand. Man being what he is, the time could never have been in which Poesy was not. Its first element is the thirst for supernal Beauty—a beauty which is not afforded the soul by any existing collocation of earth's forms—a beauty which, perhaps, *no possible* combination of these forms would fully produce. Its second element is the attempt to satisfy this thirst by *novel* combinations, *of those combinations which our predecessors, toiling in chase of the same phantom, have already set in order*. We thus clearly deduce the *novelty*, the *originality*, the *invention*, the *imagination*, or lastly the *creation* of Beauty, (for the terms as here employed are synonymous) as the essence of all Poesy. Nor is this idea so much at variance with ordinary opinion as, at first sight, it may appear. A multitude of antique dogmas on this topic will be found, when divested of extrinsic speculation, to be easily resoluble into the definition now proposed. We do nothing more than present tangibly the vague clouds of the world's idea. We recognise the idea itself floating, unsettled, indefinite, in every attempt which has yet been made to circumscribe the conception of "Poesy" in words. A striking instance of this is observable in the fact that no definition exists, in which either "the beautiful," or some one of those qualities which we have above designated synonymously with "creation," has not been pointed out as the *chief* attribute of the Muse. "Invention," however, or "imagination," is by far more commonly insisted upon. The word ποίησις itself (creation) speaks volumes upon this point. Neither will it be amiss here to mention Count Bielfeld's definition of poetry as *"L'art d'exprimer les pensées par la fiction."*[1] With this definition (of which the philosophy is profound to a certain extent) the German terms *Dichtkunst*, the art of fiction and *Dichten*, to feign, which are used for *"poetry"* and *"to make verses,"* are in full and remarkable accordance. It is nevertheless, in the *combination* of the two omni-prevalent ideas that the novelty and, we believe, the force of our own proposition is to be found.

So far, we have spoken of Poesy as of an abstraction alone. As such, it is obvious that it may be applicable in various moods. The sentiment may develop itself in Sculpture, in Painting, in Music, or otherwise. But our present business is with its development in words—that development to which, in practical acceptation, the world has agreed to limit the term. And at this point there is one consideration which induces us to pause. We cannot make up our minds to admit (as some have admitted) the inessentiality of rhythm. On the contrary, the universality of its use in the earliest poetical efforts of mankind would be sufficient to assure us, not merely of its congeniality with the Muse, or of its adaptation to her purposes, but of its elementary and indispensable importance. But here we must, perforce, content ourselves with mere suggestion; for this topic is of a character which would lead us too far. We have already spoken of Music as one of the moods of poetical development. It is in Music, perhaps, that the soul most nearly attains that end upon which we have commented—the creation of supernal beauty. It may be, indeed, that this august aim is here even partially or imperfectly attained, *in fact*. The *elements* of that beauty which is felt in sound, *may be* the mutual or common heritage of Earth and Heaven. In the soul's struggles at combinations it is thus not impossible that a harp may strike notes not unfamiliar to the angels. And in this view the wonder may well be less that all attempts at defining the character or sentiment of the deeper musical impressions, has been found absolutely futile. Contenting ourselves, therefore, with the firm conviction, that music (in its modifications of rhythm and rhyme) is of so vast a moment in Poesy, as *never* to be neglected by him who is truly poetical—is of so mighty a force in furthering the great aim intended that he is mad who rejects its assistance—content with this idea we shall not pause to maintain its absolute essentiality, for the mere sake of rounding a definition. We will but add, at this point, that the highest possible development of the Poetical Sentiment is to be found in the union of song with music, in its popular sense. The old Bards and Minnesingers possessed, in the fullest perfection, the finest and truest elements of Poesy; and Thomas Moore, singing his own ballads, is but putting the final touch to their completion as poems.

To recapitulate, then, we would define in brief the Poetry of words as the *Rhythmical Creation of Beauty*. Beyond the limits of Beauty its province does not extend. Its sole arbiter is Taste. With the Intellect or with the Conscience it has only collateral relations. It has no dependence, unless incidentally, upon either Duty or *Truth*. That our definition will necessarily exclude much of what, through a supine toleration, has been hitherto ranked as poetical, is a matter which affords us not even momentary concern. We address but the thoughtful, and heed only their approval—with our own. If our suggestions are truthful, then "after many days" shall they be understood as truth, even though found in contradiction of *all* that has been hitherto so understood. If false shall we not be the first to bid them die?

We would reject, of course, all such matters as "Armstrong on Health,"[2] a revolting production; Pope's "Essays on Man," which may well be content with the title of an "Essay in Rhyme," "Hudibras," and other merely humorous pieces. We do not gainsay the peculiar merits of either of these latter compositions—but deny them the position held. In a notice, month before last, of Brainard's Poems,[3] we took occasion to show that the common use of a certain instrument, (rhythm) had tended, more than aught else, to confound humorous verse with poetry. The observation is now recalled to corroborate what we have just said in respect to the vast effect or force of melody in itself—an effect which could elevate into even momentary confusion with the highest efforts of mind, compositions such as are the greater number of satires or burlesques.

Of the poets who have appeared most fully instinct with the principles now developed, we may mention *Keats* as the most remarkable. He is the sole British poet who has never erred in his themes. Beauty is always his aim.

We have thus shown our ground of objection to the general *themes* of Professor Longfellow. In common with all who claim the sacred title of poet, he should limit his endeavors to the creation of novel moods of beauty, in form, in color, in sound, in sentiment; for over all this wide range has the poetry of words dominion. To what the world terms *prose* may be safely and properly left all else. The artist who doubts of his thesis, may always resolve his doubt by the single question—"might not this matter be as well or better handled in *prose?*" If it *may,* then is it no subject for the Muse. In the general acceptation of the term *Beauty* we are content to rest; being careful only to suggest that, in our peculiar views, it must be understood as inclusive of *the sublime.*

Of the pieces which constitute the present volume, there are not more than one or two thoroughly fulfilling the idea above proposed; although the volume as a whole is by no means so chargeable with didacticism as Mr. Longfellow's previous book. We would mention as poems *nearly true,* "The Village Blacksmith," "The Wreck of the Hesperus" and especially "The Skeleton in Armor." In the first-mentioned we have the *beauty* of simplemindedness as a genuine thesis; and this thesis is inimitably handled until the concluding stanza, where the spirit of legitimate poesy is aggrieved in the pointed antithetical deduction of a *moral* from what has gone before. In "The Wreck of the Hesperus" we have the *beauty* of child-like confidence and innocence, with that of the father's stern courage and affection. But, with slight exception, those particulars of the storm here detailed are not poetic subjects. Their thrilling *horror* belongs to prose, in which it could be far more effectively discussed, as Professor Longfellow may assure himself at any moment by experiment. There *are* points of a tempest which afford the loftiest and truest poetical themes—points in which pure beauty is found, or better still, beauty heightened into the sublime, by terror. But when we read, among other similar things, that

> The salt sea was frozen on her breast,
> The salt tears in her eyes,

we feel, if not positive disgust, at least a chilling sense of the inappropriate. In the "Skeleton in Armor" we find a pure and perfect thesis artistically treated.

We find the beauty of bold courage and self-confidence, of love and maiden devotion, of reckless adventure, and finally of life-contemning grief. Combined with all this we have numerous points of beauty apparently insulated, but all aiding the main effect of impression. The heart is stirred, and the mind does not lament its mal-instruction. The metre is simple, sonorous, well-balanced and fully adapted to the subject. Upon the whole, there are few truer poems than this. It has but one defect—an important one. The prose remarks prefacing the narrative are really *necessary*. But every work of art should contain within itself all that is requisite for its own comprehension. And this remark is especially true of the ballad. In poems of magnitude the mind of the reader is not, at all times, enabled to include, in one comprehensive survey, the proportions and proper adjustment of the whole. He is pleased, if at all, with particular passages; and the sum of his pleasure is compounded of the sums of the pleasurable sentiments inspired by these individual passages in the progress of perusal. But, in pieces of less extent, the pleasure is *unique,* in the proper acceptation of this term—the understanding is employed, without difficulty, in the contemplation of the picture *as a whole;* and thus its effect will depend, in great measure, upon the perfection of its finish, upon the nice adaptation of its constituent parts, and especially, upon what is rightly termed by Schlegel *the unity or totality of interest*. But the practice of prefixing explanatory passages is utterly at variance with such unity. By the prefix, we are either put in possession of the subject of the poem; or some hint, historic fact, or suggestion, is thereby afforded, not included in the body of the piece, which, without the hint, is incomprehensible. In the latter case, while perusing the poem, the reader must revert, in mind at least, to the prefix, for the necessary explanation. In the former, the poem being a mere paraphrase of the prefix, the interest is divided between the prefix and the paraphrase. In either instance the totality of effect is destroyed.

Of the other original poems in the volume before us, there is none in which the aim of instruction, or *truth,* has not been too obviously substituted for the legitimate aim, *beauty*. In our last number, we took occasion to say that a didactic moral might be happily made the *under-current* of a political theme, and, in "Burton's Magazine," some two years since, we treated this point at length, in a review of Moore's "Alciphron:" but the moral thus conveyed is invariably an ill effect when obtruding beyond the upper current of the thesis itself. Perhaps the worst specimen of this obtrusion is given us by our poet in "Blind Bartimeus" and the "Goblet of Life," where, it will be observed that the *sole* interest of the upper current of meaning depends upon its relation or reference to the under. What we read upon the surface would be *vox et praeterea nihil* [a word and nothing besides] in default of the moral beneath. The Greek *finales* of "Blind Bartimeus" are an affectation altogether inexcusable. What the small, second-hand, Gibbonish pedantry of Byron introduced, is unworthy the imitation of Longfellow.

Of the translations we scarcely think it necessary to speak at all. We regret that our poet will persist in busying himself about such matters. *His* time might be better employed in original conception. Most of these versions are marked with the error upon which we have commented. This error is in fact, essentially Germanic. "The Luck of Edenhall," however, is a truly beautiful poem; and we say this with all that deference which the opinion of the "Democratic Review" demands. This composition appears to us *one of the very finest*. It has all the free, hearty, *obvious* movement of the true ballad-legend. The greatest force of language is combined in it with the richest imagination, acting in its most legitimate province. Upon the whole, we prefer it even to the "Sword-Song" of Körner.[4] The pointed moral with which it terminates is so exceedingly natural—so perfectly fluent from the incidents—that we have hardly heart to pronounce it in ill taste. We may observe of this ballad, in conclusion, that its subject is more *physical* than is usual in Germany. Its images are rich rather in physical than in moral beauty. And this tendency, in Song, is the true one. It is chiefly, if we are not mistaken—it is chiefly amid forms of physical loveliness (we use the word *forms* in its widest sense as embracing modifications of sound and color) that the soul seeks the realization of its dreams of Beauty. It is to her demand in this sense especially, that the poet, who is wise, will most frequently and most earnestly respond.

"The Children of the Lord's Supper" is, beyond a doubt, a true and most beautiful poem in great part, while, in some particulars, it is too metaphysical to have any pretension to the name. In our last number, we objected, briefly, to its metre—the ordinary Latin or Greek Hexameter—dactyls and spondees at random, with a spondee in conclusion. We maintain that the Hexameter can never be introduced into our language, from the nature of that language itself. This rhythm demands, *for English ears*, a preponderance of natural spondees. Our tongue has few. Not only does the Latin and Greek, with the Swedish, and some others, abound in them; but the Greek and Roman ear had become reconciled (why or how is unknown) to the reception of artificial spondees—that is to say, spondaic words formed partly of one word and partly of another, or from an excised part of one word. In short the ancients were content to read *as they scanned*, or nearly so. It may be safely prophesied that we shall never do this; and thus we shall never admit English Hexameters. The attempt to introduce them, after the repeated failures of Sir Philip Sidney,[5] and others, is perhaps, somewhat discreditable to the scholarship of Professor Longfellow. The "Democratic Review," in saying that he has triumphed over difficulties in this rhythm, has been deceived, it is evident, by the facility with which some of these verses may be read. In glancing over the poem, we do not observe a single verse which can be read, *to English ears, as a Greek Hexameter*. There are many, however, which can be well read as mere English dactylic verses; such, for example, as the well-known lines of Byron, commencing

Know ye the / land where the / cypress and / myrtle.

These lines (although full of irregularities) are, in their perfection, formed of three dactyls and a caesura—just as if we should cut short the initial verse of the Bucolics thus—

Tityre / tu patu / lae recu / bans—

The "myrtle," at the close of Byron's line, is a double rhyme, and must be understood as one syllable.

Now a great number of Professor Longfellow's Hexameters are merely these dactylic lines, *continued for two feet*. For example—

Whispered the / race of the / flowers and / merry on / balancing / branches.

In this example, also, "branches," which is a double ending, must be regarded as the caesura, or one syllable, of which alone it has the force.

As we have already alluded, in one or two regards, to a notice of these poems which appeared in the "Democratic Review," we may as well here proceed with some few further comments upon the article in question—with whose general tenor we are happy to agree.

The Review speaks of "Maidenhood" as a poem, "not to be understood but at the expense of more time and trouble than a song can justly claim." We are scarcely less surprised at this opinion from Mr. Langtree[6] than we were at the condemnation of "The Luck of Edenhall."

"Maidenhood" is faulty, it appears to us, only on the score of its theme, which is somewhat didactic. Its *meaning* seems simplicity itself. A maiden on the verge of womanhood, hesitating to enjoy life (for which she has a strong appetite) through a false idea of duty, is bidden to fear nothing, having purity of heart as her lion of Una.

What Mr. Langtree styles "an unfortunate peculiarity" in Mr. Longfellow, resulting from "adherence to a false system" has really been always regarded by us as one of his idiosyncratic merits. "In each poem," says the critic, "he has but *one* idea which, in the progress of his song is gradually unfolded, and at last reaches its full development in the concluding lines; this singleness of thought might lead a harsh critic to suspect intellectual barrenness." It leads us, individually, only to a full sense of the artistical power and knowledge of the poet. We confess that now, for the first time, we hear unity of conception objected to as a defect. But Mr. Langtree seems to have fallen into the singular error of supposing the poet to have absolutely *but one idea* in each of his ballads. Yet how "one idea" can be "gradually unfolded" without other ideas, is, to us, a mystery of mysteries. Mr. Longfellow, very properly, has but one *leading* idea which forms the basis of his poem; but to the aid and development of this one there are innumerable others, of which the rare excellence is, that all are in keeping, that none could be well omitted, that each tends to the one general effect. It is unnecessary to say another word upon this topic.

In speaking of "Excelsior," Mr. Langtree (are we wrong in attributing the notice to his very forcible pen?) seems to labor under some similar misconception. "It carries along with it," says he, "a false moral which greatly diminishes its merit in our eyes. The great merit of a picture, whether made with the pencil or pen, is its *truth;* and this merit does not belong to Mr. Longfellow's sketch. Men of genius may and probably do, meet with greater difficulties in their struggles with the world than their fellow-men who are less highly gifted; but their power of overcoming obstacles is proportionally greater, and the result of their laborious suffering is not death but immortality."

That the chief merit of a picture is its *truth,* is an assertion deplorably erroneous. Even in Painting, which is, more essentially than Poetry, a mimetic art, the proposition cannot be sustained. Truth is not even *the aim.* Indeed it is curious to observe how very slight a degree of truth is sufficient to satisfy the mind, which acquiesces in the absence of numerous essentials in the thing depicted. An outline frequently stirs the spirit more pleasantly than the most elaborate picture. We need only refer to the compositions of Flaxman and of Retzsch.[7] Here all details are omitted—nothing can be farther from *truth.* Without even color the most thrilling effects are produced. In statues we are rather pleased than disgusted with *the want of the eyeball.* The hair of the Venus de Medicis *was gilded.* Truth indeed! The grapes of Zeuxis as well as the curtain of Parrhasius were received as indisputable evidence of the truthful ability of these artists—but they are not even *classed among their pictures.* If truth is the highest aim of either Painting or Poesy, then Jan Steen was a greater artist than Angelo, and Crabbe is a more noble poet than Milton.

But we have not quoted the observation of Mr. Langtree to deny its philosophy; our design was simply to show that he has misunderstood the poet. "Excelsior" has not even a remote tendency to the interpretation assigned it by the critic. It depicts the *earnest upward impulse of the soul*—an impulse not to be subdued even in Death. Despising danger, resisting pleasure, the youth, bearing the banner inscribed "Excelsior!" (higher still!) struggles through all difficulties to an Alpine summit. Warned to be content with the elevation attained, his cry is still "Excelsior!" And, even in falling dead on its highest pinnacle, his cry is *still* "Excelsior!" There is yet an immortal height to be surmounted—an ascent in Eternity. The poet holds in view the idea of never-ending *progress.* That he is misunderstood is rather the misfortune of Mr. Langtree than the fault of Mr. Longfellow. There is an old adage about the difficulty of one's furnishing an auditor both with matter to be comprehended and brains for its comprehension.

## *NOTES*

1. "The art of expressing ideas by means of fiction."

2. John Armstrong (1709–1779): Scottish physician and poet, author of *The Art of Preserving Health.*

3. John G. C. Brainard (1796–1828): American editor and minor poet, best known for his humor and use of the ballad form.

4. Karl Theodor Körner (1791–1813): German poet and playwright, whose volume of poems, *The Lyre and the Sword,* was translated into English in 1834.

5. Sidney (1554–1586) experimented with classical hexameters in English in his *Arcadia.*

6. S. D. Langtree, the editor of the *Democratic Review* in 1842.

7. John Flaxman (1755–1826): English sculptor. Frederick A. M. Retzsch (1779–1857): German painter and illustrator.

# Emerson

When I consider the true talent—the real force of Mr. Emerson, I am lost in amazement at finding in him little more than a respectful imitation of Carlyle. Is it possible that Mr. E. has ever seen a copy of Seneca? Scarcely—or he would have long ago abandoned his model in utter confusion at the parallel between his own worship of the author of "Sartor Resartus" and the aping of Sallust by Aruntius, as described in the 114th Epistle.[1] In the writer of the "History of the Punic Wars" Emerson is portrayed to the life. The parallel is close; for not only is the imitation of the same character, but the things imitated are identical.

Undoubtedly it is to be said of Sallust, far more plausibly than of Carlyle, that his obscurity, his unusuality of expression, and his Laconism (which had the effect of diffuseness, since the time gained in the mere perusal of his pithiness is trebly lost in the necessity of cogitating them out)—it may be said of Sallust, more truly than of Carlyle, that these qualities bore the impress of his genius, and were but a portion of his unaffected thought.

If there is any difference between Aruntius and Emerson, this difference is clearly in favor of the former, who was in some measure excusable, on the ground that he was as great a fool as the latter *is not*.

## *NOTES*

1. Aruntius or Arruntius (*fl.* 43 B.C.–17 B.C.) was a Roman consul and historian of the First Punic War. Seneca (4 B.C. [?]–65 A.D.), in Epistle 114, discusses Arruntius' imitation of the Roman historian Sallust (86 B.C.–34 B.C.[?]). *Sartor Resartus* (1833) was probably Carlyle's best-known work.

# HAWTHORNE'S "TWICE-TOLD TALES"

We said a few hurried words about Mr. Hawthorne in our last number, with the design of speaking more fully in the present. We are still, however, pressed for room, and must necessarily discuss his volumes more briefly and more at random than their high merits deserve.

The book professes to be a collection of *tales*, yet is, in two respects, misnamed. These pieces are now in their third republication, and, of course, are thrice-told. Moreover, they are by no means *all* tales, either in the ordinary or in the legitimate understanding of the term. Many of them are pure essays, for example, "Sights from a Steeple," "Sunday at Home," "Little Annie's Ramble," "A Rill from the Town Pump," "The Toll-Gatherer's Day," "The Haunted Mind," "The Sister Years," "Snow-Flakes," "Night Sketches," and "Foot-Prints on the Sea-Shore." We mention these matters chiefly on account of their discrepancy with that marked precision and finish by which the body of the work is distinguished.

Of the essays just named, we must be content to speak in brief. They are each and all beautiful, without being characterised by the polish and adaptation so visible in the tales proper. A painter would at once note their leading or predominant feature, and style it *repose*. There is no attempt at effect. All is quiet, thoughtful, subdued. Yet this repose may exist simultaneously with high originality of thought; and Mr. Hawthorne has demonstrated the fact. At every turn we meet with novel combinations; yet these combinations never surpass the limits of the quiet. We are soothed as we read; and withal is a calm astonishment that ideas so apparently obvious have never occurred or been presented to us before. Herein our author differs materially from Lamb or Hunt or Hazlitt—who, with vivid originality of manner and expression, have less of the true novelty of thought than is generally supposed, and whose originality, at best, has an uneasy and meretricious quaintness, replete with startling effects unfounded in nature, and inducing trains of reflection which lead to no satisfactory result. The Essays of Hawthorne have much of the character of Irving, with more of originality and less of finish; while compared with the Spectator, they have a vast superiority at all points. The Spectator, Mr. Irving, and Mr. Hawthorne have in common that tranquil and subdued manner which we have chosen to denominate *repose;* but, in the case of the two former, this repose is attained rather by the absence of novel combination, or of originality, than otherwise, and consists chiefly in the calm, quiet, unostentatious expression of commonplace thoughts, in an unambitious, unadulterated Saxon. In them, by strong effort, we are made to conceive the absence of all. In the essays before us the absence of effort is too obvious to be mistaken, and a strong under-current of *suggestion* runs continuously beneath the upper stream of the tranquil thesis. In short, these effusions of Mr. Hawthorne are the product of a truly imaginative intellect, restrained, and in some measure repressed, by fastidiousness of taste, by constitutional melancholy and by indolence.

But it is of his tales that we desire principally to speak. The tale proper, in our opinion, affords unquestionably the fairest field for the exercise of the loftiest talent, which can be afforded by the wide domains of mere prose. Were we bidden to say how the highest genius could be most advantageously employed for the best display of its own powers, we should answer, without hesitation—in the composition of a rhymed poem, not to exceed in length what might be perused in an hour. Within this limit alone can the highest order of true poetry exist. We need only here say, upon this topic, that, in almost all classes of composition, the unity of effect or impression is a point of the greatest importance. It is clear, moreover, that this unity cannot be thoroughly preserved in productions whose perusal cannot be completed at one sitting. We may continue the reading of a prose composition, from the very nature of prose itself, much longer than we can persevere, to any good purpose, in the perusal of a poem. This latter, if truly fulfilling the demands of the poetic sentiment, induces an exaltation of the soul which cannot be long sustained. All high excitements are necessarily transient. Thus a long poem is a paradox. And, without unity of impression, the deepest effects cannot be brought about. Epics were the offspring of an imperfect sense of Art, and their reign is no more. A poem *too* brief may produce a vivid, but never an intense or enduring impression. Without a certain continuity of effort—without a certain duration or repetition of purpose—the soul is never deeply moved. There must be the dropping of the water upon the rock. De Béranger has wrought brilliant things—pungent and spirit-stirring—but, like all immassive bodies, they lack *momentum*, and thus fail to satisfy the Poetic Sentiment. They sparkle and excite, but, from want of continuity, fail deeply to impress. Extreme brevity will degenerate into epigrammatism; but the sin of extreme length is even more unpardonable. *In medio tutissimus ibis* [you will go most safely in the middle path].

Were we called upon, however, to designate that class of composition which, next to such a poem as we have suggested, should best fulfil the demands of high genius—should offer it the most advantageous field of exertion—we should unhesitatingly speak of the prose tale, as Mr. Hawthorne has here exemplified it. We allude to the short prose narrative, requiring from a half-hour to one or two hours in its perusal. The ordinary novel is objectionable, from its length, for reasons already stated in substance. As it cannot be read at one sitting, it deprives itself, of course, of the immense force derivable from *totality*. Worldly interests intervening during the pauses of perusal, modify, annul, or counteract, in a greater or less degree, the impressions of the book. But simple cessation in reading, would, of itself, be sufficient to destroy the true unity. In the brief tale, however, the author is enabled to carry out the fulness of his intention, be it what it may. During the hour of perusal the soul of the reader is at the writer's control. There are no external or extrinsic influences—resulting from weariness or interruption.

A skilful literary artist has constructed a tale. If wise, he has not fashioned his thoughts to accommodate his incidents; but having conceived, with deliberate care, a certain unique or single *effect* to be wrought out, he then invents such incidents—he then combines such events as may best aid him in establishing this preconceived effect. If his very initial sentence tend not to the outbringing of this effect, then he has failed in his first step. In the whole composition there should be no word written, of which the tendency, direct or indirect, is not to the one pre-established design. And by such means, with such care and skill, a picture is at length painted which leaves in the mind of him who contemplates it with a kindred art, a sense of the fullest satisfaction. The idea of the tale has been presented unblemished, because undisturbed; and this is an end unattainable by the novel. Undue brevity is just as exceptionable here as in the poem; but undue length is yet more to be avoided.

We have said that the tale has a point of superiority even over the poem. In fact, while the *rhythm* of this latter is an essential aid in the development of the poet's highest idea—the idea of the Beautiful—the artificialities of this rhythm are an inseparable bar to the development of all points of thought or expression which have their basis in *Truth*. But Truth is often, and in very great degree, the aim of the tale. Some of the finest tales are tales of ratiocination. Thus the field of this species of composition, if not in so elevated a region on the mountain of Mind, is a table-land of far vaster extent than the domain of the mere poem. Its products are never so rich, but infinitely more numerous, and more appreciable by the mass of mankind. The writer of the prose tale, in short, may bring to his theme a vast variety of modes or inflections of thought and expression—(the ratiocinative, for example, the sarcastic, or the humorous) which are not only antagonistical to the nature of the poem, but absolutely forbidden by one of its most peculiar and indispensable adjuncts; we allude, of course, to rhythm. It may be added here, *par parenthèse,* that the author who aims at the purely beautiful in a prose tale is laboring at great disadvantage. For Beauty can be better treated in the poem. Not so with terror, or passion, or horror, or a multitude of such other points. And here it will be seen how full of prejudice are the usual animadversions against those *tales of effect,* many fine examples of which were found in the earlier numbers of Blackwood. The impressions produced were wrought in a legitimate sphere of action, and constituted a legitimate although sometimes an exaggerated interest. They were relished by every man of genius: although there were found many men of genius who condemned them without just ground. The true critic will but demand that the design intended be accomplished, to the fullest extent, by the means most advantageously applicable.

We have very few American tales of real merit—we may say, indeed, none, with the exception of "The Tales of a Traveller" of Washington Irving, and these "Twice-Told Tales" of Mr. Hawthorne. Some of the pieces of Mr. John Neal abound in vigor and originality; but in general, his compositions of this class are excessively diffuse, extravagant, and indicative of an imperfect sentiment of Art. Articles at random are, now and then, met with in our periodicals which might be advantageously compared with the best effusions of the British Magazines; but, upon the whole, we are far behind our progenitors in this department of literature.

Of Mr. Hawthorne's Tales we would say, emphatically, that they belong to the highest region of Art—an Art subservient to genius of a very lofty order. We had supposed, with good reason for so supposing, that he had been thrust into his present position by one of the impudent *cliques* which beset our literature, and whose pretensions it is our full purpose to expose at the earliest opportunity; but we have been most agreeably mistaken. We know of few compositions which the critic can more honestly commend than these "Twice-Told Tales." As Americans, we feel proud of the book.

Mr. Hawthorne's distinctive trait is invention, creation, imagination, originality—a trait which, in the literature of fiction, is positively worth all the rest. But the nature of originality, so far as regards its manifestation in letters, is but imperfectly understood. The inventive or original mind as frequently displays itself in novelty of *tone* as in novelty of matter. Mr. Hawthorne is original at *all* points.

It would be a matter of some difficulty to designate the best of these tales; we repeat that, without exception, they are beautiful. "Wakefield" is remarkable for the skill with which an old idea—a well-known incident—is worked up or discussed. A man of whims conceives the purpose of quitting his wife and residing *incognito,* for twenty years, in her immediate neighborhood. Something of this kind actually happened in London. The force of Mr. Hawthorne's tale lies in the analysis of the motives which must or might have impelled the husband to such folly, in the first instance, with the possible causes of his perseverance. Upon this thesis a sketch of singular power has been constructed.

"The Wedding Knell" is full of the boldest imagination—an imagination fully controlled by taste. The most captious critic could find no flaw in this production.

"The Minister's Black Veil" is a masterly composition of which the sole defect is that to the rabble its exquisite skill will be *caviare*. The *obvious* meaning of this article will be found to smother its insinuated one. The *moral* put into the mouth of the dying minister will be supposed to convey the *true* import of the narrative; and that a crime of dark dye, (having reference to the "young lady") has been committed, is a point which only minds congenial with that of the author will perceive.

"Mr. Higginbotham's Catastrophe" is vividly original and managed most dexterously.

"Dr. Heidegger's Experiment" is exceedingly well imagined, and executed with surpassing ability. The artist breathes in every line of it.

"The White Old Maid" is objectionable, even more than the "Minister's Black Veil," on the score of its mysticism. Even with the thoughtful and analytic, there will be much trouble in penetrating its entire import.

"The Hollow of the Three Hills" we would quote in full, had we space;—not as evincing higher talent than any of the other pieces, but as affording an excellent example of the author's peculiar ability. The subject is commonplace. A witch subjects the Distant and the Past to the view of a mourner. It has been the fashion to describe, in such cases, a mirror in which the images of the absent appear; or a cloud of smoke is made to arise, and thence the figures are gradually unfolded. Mr. Hawthorne has wonderfully heightened his effect by making the ear, in place of the eye, the medium by which the fantasy is conveyed. The head of the mourner is enveloped in the cloak of the witch, and within its magic folds there arise sounds which have an all-sufficient intelligence. Throughout this article also, the artist is conspicuous—not more in positive than in negative merits. Not only is all done that should be done, but (what perhaps is an end with more difficulty attained) there is nothing done which should not be. Every word *tells,* and there is not a word which does *not* tell.

In "Howe's Masquerade" we observe something which resembles plagiarism—but which *may be* a very flattering coincidence of thought.[1] We quote the passage in question.

> *With a dark flush of wrath* upon his brow they saw the general *draw his sword* and *advance to meet* the figure *in the cloak* before the latter had stepped one pace upon the floor.
>
> *"Villain, unmuffle yourself,"* cried he, "you pass no farther!"
>
> The figure, without blenching a hair's breadth from the sword which was pointed at his breast, made a solemn pause, and *lowered the cape of the cloak* from his face, yet not sufficiently for the spectators to catch a glimpse of it. But Sir William Howe had evidently seen enough. The sternness of his countenance gave place to a look of wild amazement, if not horror, while he recoiled several steps from the figure, *and let fall his sword upon the floor.*—See Vol. 2, p. 20.

The idea here is, that the figure in the cloak is the phantom or re-duplication of Sir William Howe; but in an article called "William Wilson," one of the "Tales of the Grotesque and Arabesque," we have not only the same idea, but the same idea similarly presented in several respects. We quote two paragraphs, which our readers may compare with what has been already given. We have italicized, above, the immediate particulars of resemblance.

> The brief moment in which I averted my eyes had been sufficient to produce, apparently, a material change in the arrangement at the upper or farther end of the room. A large mirror, it appeared to me, now stood where none had been perceptible before; and as I stepped up to it in extremity of terror, mine own image, but with features all pale and dabbled in blood, *advanced* with a feeble and tottering gait to meet me.
>
> Thus it appeared I say, but was not. It was Wilson, who then stood before me in the agonies of dissolution. Not a line in all the marked and singular lineaments of that face which was not even identically mine own. *His mask and cloak lay where he had thrown them, upon the floor.*
>
> Vol. 2, p. 57.

Here it will be observed that, not only are the two general conceptions identical, but there are various *points* of similarity. In each case the figure seen is the wraith of duplication of the beholder. In each case the scene is a masquerade. In each case the figure is cloaked. In each, there is a quarrel—that is to say, angry words pass between the parties. In each the beholder is enraged. In each the cloak and sword fall upon the floor. The "villain, unmuffle yourself," of Mr. H. is precisely paralleled by a passage at page 56 of "William Wilson."

In the way of objection we have scarcely a word to say of these tales. There is, perhaps, a somewhat too general or prevalent *tone*—a tone of melancholy and mysticism. The subjects are insufficiently varied. There is not so much of *versatility* evinced as we might well be warranted in expecting from the high powers of Mr. Hawthorne. But beyond these trivial exceptions we have really none to make. The style is purity itself. Force abounds. High imagination gleams from every page. Mr. Hawthorne is a man of the truest genius. We only regret that the limits of our Magazine will not permit us to pay him that full tribute of commendation, which, under other circumstances, we should be so eager to pay.

## *NOTES*

1. Several critics have pointed out that "Howe's Masquerade" appeared seventeen months before "William Wilson." Hawthorne could not have plagiarized from the latter.

FROM

# TALE-WRITING: NATHANIEL HAWTHORNE

In the preface to my sketches of New York Literati, while speaking of the broad distinction between the seeming public and real private opinion respecting our authors, I thus alluded to Nathaniel Hawthorne:

"For example, Mr. Hawthorne, the author of 'Twice-Told Tales,' is scarcely recognized by the press or by the public, and when noticed at all, is noticed merely to be damned by faint praise. Now, my opinion of him is, that although his walk is limited and he is fairly to be charged with mannerism, treating all subjects in a similar tone of dreamy *innuendo,* yet in this walk he evinces extraordinary genius, having no rival either in America or elsewhere; and this opinion I have never heard gainsaid by any one literary person in the country. That this opinion, however, is a spoken and not a written one, is referable to the facts, first, that Mr. Hawthorne *is* a poor man, and, secondly, that he *is not* an ubiquitous quack."

The reputation of the author of "Twice-Told Tales" has been confined, indeed, until very lately, to literary society; and I have not been wrong, perhaps, in citing him as *the* example, *par excellence,* in this country, of the privately-admired and publicly-unappreciated man of genius. Within the last year or two, it is true, an occasional critic has been urged, by honest indignation, into very warm approval. Mr. Webber, for instance, (than whom no one has a keener relish for that kind of writing which Mr. Hawthorne has best illustrated) gave us, in a late number of "The American Review," a cordial and certainly a full tribute to his talents; and since the issue of the "Mosses from an Old Manse," criticisms of similar tone have been by no means infrequent in our more authoritative journals. I can call to mind few reviews of Hawthorne published *before* the "Mosses." One I remember in "Arcturus" (edited by Matthews [sic] and Duyckinck) for May, 1841; another in the "American Monthly" (edited by Hoffman and Herbert) for March, 1838; a third in the ninety-sixth number of the "North American Review." These criticisms, however, seemed to have little effect on the popular taste—at least, if we are to form any idea of the popular taste by reference to its expression in the newspapers, or by the sale of the author's book. It was never the fashion (until lately) to speak of him in any summary of our best authors. The daily critics would say, on such occasions, "Is there not Irving and Cooper, and Bryant and Paulding, and—Smith?" or, "Have we not Halleck and Dana, and Longfellow and—Thompson?" or, "Can we not point triumphantly to our own Sprague, Willis, Channing, Bancroft, Prescott and—Jenkins?" but these unanswerable queries were never wound up by the name of Hawthorne.[1]

Beyond doubt, this inappreciation of him on the part of the public arose chiefly from the two causes to which I have referred—from the facts that he is neither a man of wealth nor a quack;—but these are insufficient to account for the whole effect. No small portion of it is attributable to the very marked idiosyncrasy of Mr. Hawthorne himself. In one sense, and in great measure, to be peculiar is to be original, and than the true originality there is no higher literary virtue. This true or commendable originality, however, implies not the uniform, but the continuous peculiarity—a peculiarity springing from ever-active vigor of fancy—better still if from ever-present force of imagination, giving its own hue, its own character to everything it touches, and, especially, *self impelled to touch everything*. . . .

The fact is, that if Mr. Hawthorne were really original, he could not fail of making himself felt by the public. But the fact is, he is *not* original in any sense. Those who speak of him as original, mean nothing more than that he differs in his manner of tone, and in his choice of subjects, from any author of their acquaintance—their acquaintance not extending to the German Tieck,[2] whose manner, in *some* of his works, is absolutely identical with that *habitual* to Hawthorne. But it is clear that the element of the literary originality is novelty. The element of its appreciation by the reader is the reader's sense of the new. Whatever gives him a new and insomuch a pleasurable emotion, he considers original, and whoever frequently gives him such emotion, he considers an original writer. In a word, it is by the sum total of these emotions that he decides upon the writer's claim to originality. I may observe here, however, that there is clearly a point at which even novelty itself would cease to produce the legitimate originality, if we judge this originality, as we should, by the effect designed; this point is that at which *novelty becomes nothing novel;* and here the artist, *to preserve his originality* will subside into the commonplace. No one, I think, has noticed that, merely through inattention to this matter, Moore has comparatively failed in his "Lalla Rookh." Few readers, and indeed few critics, have commended this poem for originality—and, in fact, the effect, originality, is not produced by it—yet no work of equal size so abounds in the happiest originalities, individually considered. They are so excessive, as, in the end, to deaden in the reader all capacity for their appreciation.

These points properly understood, it will be seen that the critic (unacquainted with Tieck) who reads a single tale or essay by Hawthorne, may be justified in thinking him original; but the tone, or manner, or choice of subject, which induces in this critic the sense of the new, will—if not in a second tale, at least in a third and all subsequent ones—not only fail of inducing it, but bring about an exactly antagonistic impression. In concluding a volume, and more specially in concluding all the volumes of the author, the critic will abandon his first design of calling him "original," and content himself with styling him "peculiar."

With the vague opinion that to be original is to be popular, I could indeed, agree, were I to adopt an understanding of originality which, to my surprise, I have known adopted by many who have a right to be called critical. They have limited, in a love for mere words, the literary to the metaphysical originality.

They regard as original in letters, only such combinations of thought, of incident, and so forth, as are, in fact, absolutely novel. It is clear, however, not only that it is the novelty of *effect* alone which is worth consideration, but that this effect is *best* wrought, for the end of all fictitious composition, pleasure, by shunning rather than by seeking the absolute novelty of combination. Originality, thus understood, tasks and startles the intellect, and so brings into undue action the faculties to which, in the lighter literature, we least appeal. And thus understood, it cannot fail to prove unpopular with the masses, who, seeking in this literature amusement, are positively offended by instruction. But the true originality—true in respect of its purposes—is that which, in bringing out the half-formed, the reluctant, or the unexpressed fancies of mankind, or in exciting the more delicate pulses of the heart's passion, or in giving birth to some universal sentiment or instinct in embryo, thus combines with the pleasurable effect of *apparent* novelty, a real egoistic delight. The reader, in the case first supposed, (that of the absolute novelty,) is excited, but embarrassed, disturbed, in some degree even pained at his own want of perception, at his own folly in not having himself hit upon the idea. In the second case, his pleasure is doubled. He is filled with an intrinsic and extrinsic delight. He feels and intensely enjoys the seeming novelty of the thought, enjoys it as really novel, as absolutely original with the writer—*and himself*. They two, he fancies, have, alone of all men, thought thus. They two have, together, created this thing. Henceforward there is a bond of sympathy between them, a sympathy which irradiates every subsequent page of the book.

There is a species of writing which, with some difficulty, may be admitted as a lower degree of what I have called the true original. In its perusal, we say to ourselves, not "how original this is!" nor "here is an idea which I and the author have alone entertained," but "here is a charmingly obvious fancy," or sometimes even, "here is a thought which I am not sure has ever occurred to myself, but which, of course, has occurred to all the rest of the world." This kind of composition (which still appertains to a high order) is usually designated as "the natural." It has little external resemblance, but strong internal affinity to the true original, if, indeed, as I have suggested, it is not of this latter an inferior degree. It is best exemplified, among English writers, in Addison, Irving and *Hawthorne*. The "ease" which is so often spoken of as its distinguishing feature, it has been the fashion to regard as ease in appearance alone, as a point of really difficult attainment. This idea, however, must be received with some reservation. The natural style is difficult only to those who should never intermeddle with it—to the unnatural. It is but the result of writing with the understanding, or with the instinct, that the *tone*, in composition, should be that which, at any given point or upon any given topic, would be the tone of the great mass of humanity. The author who, after the manner of the North Americans, is merely at *all* times *quiet*, is, of course, upon *most* occasions, merely silly or stupid, and has no more right to be thought "easy" or "natural" than has a cockney exquisite or the sleeping beauty in the waxworks.

The "peculiarity" or sameness, or monotone of Hawthorne, would, in its mere character of "peculiarity," and without reference to what *is* the peculiarity, suffice to deprive him of all chance of popular appreciation. But at his failure to be appreciated, we can, *of course,* no longer wonder, when we find him monotonous at decidedly the worst of all possible points—at that point which, having the least concern with Nature, is the farthest removed from the popular intellect, from the popular sentiment and from the popular taste. I allude to the strain of allegory which completely overwhelms the greater number of his subjects, and which in some measure interferes with the direct conduct of absolutely all.

In defence of allegory, (however, or for whatever object, employed,) there is scarcely one respectable word to be said. Its best appeals are made to the fancy—that is to say, to our sense of adaptation, not of matters proper, but of matters improper for the purpose, of the real with the unreal; having never more of intelligible connection than has something with nothing, never half so much of effective affinity as has the substance for the shadow. The deepest emotion aroused within us by the happiest allegory, *as* allegory, is a very, very imperfectly satisfied sense of the writer's ingenuity in overcoming a difficulty we should have preferred his not having attempted to overcome. The fallacy of the idea that allegory, in any of its moods, can be made to enforce a truth—that metaphor, for example, may illustrate as well as embellish an argument—could be promptly demonstrated: the converse of the supposed fact might be shown, indeed, with very little trouble—but these are topics foreign to my present purpose. One thing is clear, that if allegory ever establishes a fact, it is by dint of overturning a fiction. Where the suggested meaning runs through the obvious one is a *very* profound under-current so as never to interfere with the upper one without our own volition, so as never to show itself unless *called* to the surface, there only, for the proper uses of fictitious narrative, is it available to all. Under the best circumstances, it must always interfere with that unity of effect which to the artist, is worth all the allegory in the world. Its vital injury, however, is rendered to the most vitally important point in fiction—that of earnestness or verisimilitude. That "The Pilgrim's Progress" is a ludicrously over-rated book, owing its seeming popularity to one or two of those accidents in critical literature which by the critical are sufficiently well understood, is a matter upon which no two thinking people disagree; but the pleasure derivable from it, in any sense, will be found in the direct ratio of the reader's capacity to smother its true purpose, in the direct ratio of his ability to keep the allegory out of sight, or of his *in*ability to comprehend it. Of allegory properly handled, judiciously subdued, seen only as a shadow or by suggestive glimpses, and making its nearest approach to truth in a not obtrusive and therefore not unpleasant *appositeness,* the "Undine" of De La Motte Fouqué is the best, and undoubtedly a very remarkable specimen.

The obvious causes, however, which have prevented Mr. Hawthorne's *popularity,* do not suffice to condemn him in the eyes of the few who belong properly to books, and to whom books, perhaps, do not quite so properly belong. These few estimate an author, not as do the public, altogether by what he does, but in great measure—indeed, even in the greatest measure—by what he evinces a capability of doing. In this view, Hawthorne stands among literary people in America much in the same light as did Coleridge in England. The few, also, through a certain warping of the taste, which long pondering upon books as books merely never fails to induce, are not in condition to view the errors of a scholar as errors altogether. At any time these gentlemen are prone to think the public not right rather than an educated author wrong. But the simple truth is that the writer who aims at impressing the people, is *always* wrong when he fails in forcing that people to receive the impression. How far Mr. Hawthorne has addressed the people at all, is, of course, not a question for me to decide. His books afford strong internal evidence of having been written to himself and his particular friends alone. . . .

I must defer to the better opportunity of a volume now in hand, a full discussion of his individual pieces, and hasten to conclude this paper with a summary of his merits and demerits.

He is peculiar and *not* original—unless in those detailed fancies and detached thoughts which his want of general originality will deprive of the appreciation due to them, in preventing them forever reaching the *public eye*. He is infinitely too fond of allegory, and can never hope for popularity so long as he persists in it. This he will not do, for allegory is at war with the whole tone of his nature, which disports itself never so well as when escaping from the mysticism of his Goodman Browns and White Old Maids into the hearty, genial, but still Indian-summer sunshine of his Wakefields and Little Annie's Rambles. Indeed, *his* spirit of "metaphor run-mad" is clearly imbibed from the phalanx and phalanstery atmosphere[3] in which he has been so long struggling for breath. He has not half the material for the exclusiveness of authorship that he possesses for its universality. He has the purest style, the finest taste, the most available scholarship, the most delicate humor, the most touching pathos, the most radiant imagination, the most consummate ingenuity; and with these varied good qualities he has done *well* as a mystic. But is there any one of these qualities which should prevent his doing doubly as well in a career of honest, upright, sensible, prehensible and comprehensible things? Let him mend his pen, get a bottle of visible ink, come out from the Old Manse, cut Mr. Alcott, hang (if possible) the editor of "The Dial,"[4] and throw out of the window to the pigs all his odd numbers of "The North American Review."

## *NOTES*

1. Seba Smith, William T. Thompson, Charles Sprague, and John Jenkins were all minor writers of the time. George Bancroft (1800–1891) and William Hickling Prescott (1796–1859) were well-known American historians. Richard Henry Dana, Jr. (1815–1882) was the author of *Two Years before the Mast*.

2. Ludwig Tieck (1773–1853): German Romantic writer. Hawthorne did read Tieck later on, but whether he was acquainted with him at this time is not known.

3. A reference to Transcendentalism and to the Brook Farm experiment, which employed the Fourier communal phalanx (though not while Hawthorne was in residence).

4. Probably a reference to Emerson, who edited the Transcendentalist magazine in the early 1840's.

# V. G. Belinskii

1811–1848

Vissarion Grigorievich Belinskii, born in 1811, a journalist and Russia's first literary critic, remains one of the most hotly-contested figures of Russian letters. The Soviet-Marxist school approvingly cites him as the founder of the country's revolutionary-democratic writing and the precursor of Chernyshevsky and Dobroliubov; champions of aesthetics often deride his emphasis on materialism and social consciousness. Shaping an entire generation of Russian writers and largely responsible for the transition in Russian literature from Romanticism to realism, Belinskii struck even his enemies with what Turgenev called his "impetuous, relentless pursuit of truth." Astoundingly, for all of his authority, Belinskii knew no foreign languages; he had to rely on the secondhand descriptions and accounts of his friends for the import and content of the German, French, and English works that he ardently admired and wrote about. But most of his critical judgments remain valid to this day. With all of the polemics his name still conjures, Belinskii is nonetheless a solid—and supremely Russian—literary critic.

Given his background, Belinskii's career is all the more remarkable. The son of a village doctor and the grandson of a priest (neither profession celebrated at the time for its high intellectual standards), he was born in the provincial town of Chembar in the province of Penzensk. Unsatisfied with the education he was receiving in the local secondary school or *gymnasium,* he left after finishing three-and-a-half of a possible four years to become what he passionately desired—a real student in Moscow, even though his father could offer him no financial support. He joined the Department of Philology in Moscow University and was educated at public expense after a year of penury in 1829. While at the university, Belinskii was influenced by the lectures of N. I. Nadezhdin and M. G. Pavlov and their presentation of German idealistic philosophy. The idealistic intellectual interests he shared with some fellow students led to their forming discussion circles, from which were to emerge many future leaders of Russian social and literary thought: Herzen, Ogarev, and, among others, Stankevich. Espousing Kant, Fichte, and Schelling, they—and he—saw art not as a reflection of life or as a moralising force, but as a reflection of divine harmony and what Belinskii termed "the eternal idea." In this climate, Belinskii produced his first literary attempt, a Romantic tragedy à la Schiller, which, although it included a tirade against serfdom, was later (along with some other works of his early period) to make him writhe with embarrassment. His *Dimitri Kalinin,* however, was perceived as not only weak but pernicious: it was forbidden by the censors and led to Belinskii's dismissal from Moscow University in 1832.

With no means of support, Belinskii turned to tutoring and even translation to support himself. Through Nadezhdin, he began to publish small pieces for the journal *Teleskop* and in September of 1834 published his first serious critical article called *Literary Reveries: Elegy in Prose.* In this piece, Belinskii spoke of literature in its ideal sense—forcing him to admit that in Russia there was as yet no literature, but rather a small number of writers. Correctly assessing the relative importance of the poets Lomonosov, Kantemir, and Pushkin, Belinskii wrote:

> We have no literature, I repeat this with ecstasy, with revelling, for in this truth I see the promise of future successes. . . . Look at how the new generation, disillusioned in the genius of immortality of our literary works, instead of bringing immature works into the world, avidly gives itself to study and draws the living water of enlightenment from its very source. . . . The time will come, the intellectual physiognomy of the people will become clearer—then our artists and writers will set a real seal of the Russian spirit onto all their work. But now we need learning! Learning! Learning!

Although Belinskii still preached the "absolute personality" and the possibility of personal development regardless of the social milieu, these views did not prevent him from appreciating Gogol, Koltsov, and Baratynsky, whose works he saw as heralding a new epoch in Russian literature. In 1835 Nadezhdin turned the editorship of *Teleskop* over to him, but when the journal was closed in 1836, Belinskii was once again penniless. Publishing a *Russian Grammar* in 1837 which met with no success, Belinskii became a regular contributor to *Moskovskiy Nabliudatel (Moscow Observer)* from 1838 to 1839. Continuing to identify himself with the ideas of the Stankevich (whose main spokesman now was Bakunin, and whose main passion was Hegel), Belinskii espoused pure art, with the Germans, particularly Goethe, as its chief exemplars. He expressed distaste for the French, whom he saw as being less interested in the eternal than in the gossip of the day. Although Herzen and Ogarev had by now moved on to social and political matters, Belinskii continued to cling to his characteristically Moscow views even after he regretfully moved to Petersburg to become the critical editor for *Otechestvennye Zapiski (Notes of the Fatherland).*

In the second stage of his career, Belinskii increasingly became a social critic. Although he never lost the sense of the worth and unity of a work of art—he wrote in 1844 that one must never approach literature with any preconceptions—he also recognised that what was appropriate for one period could not be produced in another: *The Bronze Horseman* and *The*

*Inspector General* could not have been simultaneous. In his articles and reviews, he developed the "natural school" and began to attack routine, philistine egoism, and the inhumanity he saw directed at one's inferiors, women, and children. From 1840 to 1846, Belinskii published annual surveys of Russian literature as well as individual articles on Derzhavin, Lermontov, Maikov, folk poetry, Marlinsky, and Pushkin, which together amount to a full history of Russian literature.

Although Belinskii held strong social and political beliefs—he studied Mignet's history of the French Revolution and considered himself a *montagnard*—he recognised that in the existing circumstances (the reign of Nicholas I) there was no chance of voicing them. Characteristically, just as his instinctive taste kept him from missing the mark, he understood his place and his limits as a literary critic; did not attempt to discuss music or the visual arts (with the exception of an entirely worthwhile piece on Raphael's *Madonnas*). Everyone who knew him was struck by his lack of vanity and his absence of any frivolity. After Turgenev had spoken with him for over three hours and attempted to change the subject, Belinskii exclaimed, "What! We have not yet settled the existence of God and you want to eat?" Annenkov, in his *Remarkable Decade,* adds that "in his presence, people felt themselves lighter and freer of petty cares."

As his health, always bad, worsened, Belinskii left *Otechestvennye Zapiski* in 1846. He returned from a stay in the south of Russia to contribute to the journal *Sovremennik (The Contemporary)* in 1847, only to have to go away again, this time abroad, for the sake of his health. Being abroad in Salzbrunn allowed him free rein in writing his blistering and perhaps best-known piece, his *Letter to Gogol.* This is the most explicit and concise statement of the Westernizing Russian belief in the traditions of the Enlightenment; it attacks the Slavophile favoring of the paternalistic traditions of autocracy and the Orthodox church. Here Belinskii repeats his conviction that, given the current situation in Russia, the writer was the only spokesman for the best hopes of the people and had no choice but to be involved on the side of the progressives. The *Letter,* along with his *A Glance at Russian Literature* (1847), was to be his last expression of complete involvement in both the art and life of his time: Belinskii died at the age of thirty-seven on May 28, 1848.

FROM

# Thoughts and Notes on Russian Literature

Whatever our literature may be, it has far greater significance for us than may appear: in it, and it alone, is contained the whole of our intellectual life and all the poetry of our life. Only in the sphere of our literature do we cease to be Johns and Peters and become simply people dealing and associating with people.

There is a prevailing spirit of disunity in our society: each of our social estates possesses specific traits of its own—its dress and its manners, and way of life and customs, and even its language. To be convinced of this, it would suffice to spend an evening in the chance company of a government official, a military man, a landowner, a merchant, a commoner, a lawyer, or overseer, a clergyman, a student, a seminarist, a professor, and an artist; seeing yourself in such company you might think you were present at the distribution of tongues. . . . So great is the disunity reigning among these representatives of various classes of the same society! The spirit of disunity is hostile to society: society unites people, caste divides them. Many believe that haughtiness, a relic of Slavonic antiquity, destroys sociability in us. That may be true in part, if it is true at all. Granted that the nobleman is loath to cultivate the society of men of lower station; but then what are men of lower station not prepared to sacrifice in order to cultivate the society of the nobleman? It is their passion! But the trouble is that this *rapprochement* is always an external, formal show resembling a bowing acquaintance; a rich merchant's vanity is flattered by the acquaintance even with a poor nobleman, yet though he has made the acquaintance of the rich nobility he still remains true to the habits, conceptions, language, and way of life of his own merchants' class.

This spirit of particularity is so strong with us that even the new social estates that originated from the new order of things created by Peter the Great lost no time in assuming their specific features. Is it to be wondered at that the nobleman in no way resembles the merchant or the merchant the nobleman when we have sometimes almost the same distinction between the scientist and the artist? We still have scientists who have remained faithful throughout their lives to a noble resolution not to understand art and what it stands for; we still have many artists who do not suspect the vital connection that their art has with science, literature, and life. Bring *such* a scientist and *such* an artist together, and you will find that they will either keep silent or exchange noncommittal phrases, and even these will be more in the nature of work for them than conversation. At times our scientist, especially if he has dedicated himself to the exact sciences, will look down on philosophy and history and those who engage in them with an ironical smile, while poetry, literature, and journalism he simply regards as nonsense. Our so-called "man of letters" looks with contempt on mathematics that eluded him at school.

It may be argued that this is not a spirit of disunity; it is rather a spirit of quasi-education and quasi-learning! Yes, but then did not all these people receive a fairly broad if not very deep elementary education? The man of letters learned mathematics at school, and the mathematicians studied literature. Many of them can on occasion make out quite a good case to prove that the division of the sciences is merely an artificial contrivance and not a thing of intrinsic value, since all sciences comprise a single knowledge of a single subject—Being; that art, like science, is a consciousness of Being but in another form, and that literature should be a delight and luxury of the mind for all educated people alike. But when they have to apply these specious arguments to life, they immediately divide themselves into guilds that eye each other with a certain ironical smile and a sense of their own worth or with a sort of mistrust. . . . How then expect sociability among people of diverse estates, each of which has its own mode of thinking, speaking, dressing, eating, and drinking? . . .

However that may be, it would be wrong to say that we had no society whatever. Undoubtedly there exists with us a strong demand for society and a striving toward society, and that in itself is important! The reform of Peter the Great did not destroy or break down the walls that in old society had divided one class from another; but it had undermined the foundations of these walls and thrown them awry if it had not wrecked them—and now they are leaning over more and more from day to day, crumbling and being buried beneath their own debris and dust, so that to repair them would only give them added weight, which, in view of their sapped foundations, would merely accelerate their inevitable downfall. And if today the estates divided by these walls cannot overstep them as they would a smooth road, they can at any rate jump over them with ease at the spots where they have suffered most from wear and dilapidation. This was previously done slowly and imperceptibly, while now it is being done faster and more perceptibly—and the time is not far off when it will be done swiftly and thoroughly. Railroads will run their tunnels and bridges through and beneath the walls, and the development of industry and commerce will interweave the interests of people of all estates and classes and force them into the close and vital intercourse that must needs smooth down all the sharp and unnecessary distinctions.

But the beginning of this *rapprochement* among the social estates, which in fact represents the inchoation of society, does not by any means belong exclusively to our times: it merges with the beginnings of our literature. A heterogeneous society, welded into a single mass by material interests alone, would be a sorry, humanless society. However great may be the outward prosperity and outward strength of a society, one would hardly regard it as an object of envy if its commerce, industry, shipping, railroads, and generally all its material motive forces constituted the primary, principal, and direct instead of merely the auxiliary means toward education and civilization. . . . In this respect we have no cause to blame fate: social enlightenment and education flowed with us originally through the channel of a small and barely visible brook, but a brook that had sprung from a sublime and noble source—from science and literature itself. Science with us today is only beginning to take root but has not yet taken root, whereas education has taken root but not yet spread its growth. Its leaf is small and scarce, its stem neither high nor thick, but its roots have sunk so deep that no tempest, no flood, no power can tear it up: fell this young wood in one place and its roots will emit shoots in another, and you will sooner tire of felling than this vegetation tire of emitting new shoots and spreading. . . .

In speaking of the progress of society's education, we have in mind the progress of our literature, for our education is the direct effect of our literature upon the ideas and morals of society. Our literature has created the morals of our society, has already educated several generations of widely divergent character, has paved the way for the inner *rapprochement* of the estates, has formed a species of public opinion and produced a sort of special class in society that differs from the *middle estate* in that it consists not of the merchantry and commoners alone but of people of all estates who have been drawn together through education, which, with us, centered exclusively in a love of literature.

If you wish to understand and appreciate the influence of our literature on society, glance at the representatives of its various epochs, speak with them, or make them speak among themselves. Our literature is so young, and of such recent origin, that one may still come across all its representatives in society. The first admirable Russian poem written in regular meter, Lomonosov's *Ode on the Taking of Khotin,* made its appearance in 1739, exactly 107 years ago, and Lomonosov died in 1765, some eighty years ago. There are, of course, no people today who have seen Lomonosov even in their childhood, or who, having seen him, could remember it; but there are still many people in Russia today who have learned to love poetry and literature from Lomonosov's works, and who consider him to be as great a poet as he was considered to be in his time. There is a still greater number of people today who have a lively recollection of the face and voice of Derzhavin, and consider the epoch of his full fame to have been the best time of their lives. Many old men today are still convinced in all sincerity of the excellent merits of Kheraskov's poems, and it was not so long ago that the venerable poet Dmitriev complained in print of the young generation's irreverence toward the talent of the creator of *Rossiada* and *Vladimir*. There are still many old men who are thrilled by memories of Sumarokov's tragedies and are ready, in a dispute, to recite what they consider to be the best tirades from *Dmitri the Pretender*. Others, while conceding that Sumarokov's language is really antiquated, will point out to you with special deference the tragedies and comedies of Knyazhnin as a standard of dramatic pathos and purity of language. Still more often can we meet people who, while saying nothing about Sumarokov or Knyazhnin, will speak with all the greater heat and assurance about Ozerov. As for Karamzin, both the old and elder generations belong to him body and soul, feel, think, and live by him, despite the fact that they have not only read Zhukovsky, Batyushkov, Pushkin,

Griboedov, Gogol, and Lermontov, but even admired them more or less. . . . Then there are people today who smile ironically at the mention of Pushkin and speak with reverential awe and admiration of Zhukovsky, as though homage toward the latter were incompatible with homage toward the former. And how many people are there who do not understand Gogol and justify their prejudice against him by the fact that they understand Pushkin! . . .

But do not imagine that these are purely literary facts: no, if you pay closer attention to these representatives of the different epochs of our literature and different epochs of our society you will not fail to discern a more or less vital relation between their literary and their worldly conceptions and convictions. As far as their literary education is concerned, these people seem to be separated from one another by centuries, because our literature has spanned the gulf of many centuries in the space of a hundred-odd years. And that was why there was a great difference between the society that admired the cumbrous wording of turgid odes and heavy epic poems and the society that shed tears over *Liza's Pond;* between the society that avidly read *Ludmila* and *Svetlana,* was thrilled by the fantastic horrors of *The Twelve Sleeping Maidens,* or basked in romantic languor beneath the mysterious sounds of the *Aeolian Harp* and the society that forgot the *Prisoner of the Caucasus* and *The Fountain of Bakhchisardi* for *Eugene Onegin,* Fonvizin's comedies for *Wit Works Woe,* Ozerov's *Dmitri Donskoy* for *Boris Godunov* (as once Sumarokov's *Dmitri the Pretender* had been forgotten for the former), and then would seem to have cooled to former poets for Pushkin and Lermontov; all the novelists and writers of romance whom they had so recently admired were forgotten for Gogol. . . . Imagine the immeasurable gulf of time that lay between *Ivan Vyzhigin,* published in 1829, and *Dead Souls,* published in 1842. . . . This distinction in society's literary education passed into life and divided people into diversely operating, thinking, and persuaded generations whose lively disputes and controversial relations, originating as they did from principles and not from material interests, represented symptoms of a nascent and developing spiritual life in society. And that great deed is the deed of our literature! . . .

Literature was for our society a vital source even of practical moral ideas. It began with satire, and in the person of Kantemir declared implacable war on ignorance, prejudices, barratry, chicanery, pettifogging, extortion, and embezzlement, which it found in old society not as vices, but as rules of life, moral convictions. Whatever we may think of Sumarokov's gifts, his satirical attacks on corrupt bureaucrats will always earn honorable mention in the history of Russian literature. Fonvizin's comedies rendered a still greater service to society than they did to literature. The same could almost be said of Kapnist's *Slander*. The fable became so popular with us because it belongs to the satirical genre of poetry. Derzhavin himself, pre-eminently a lyrical poet, was at the same time a satirical poet, as for example in *To Felitza, The Grandee,* and other plays. Ultimately there came a time when satire in our literature passed into humor, represented by the artistic portrayal of life's reality.

Of course, it is absurd to suppose that a satire, a comedy, story, or novel could reform a vicious person; but there is no doubt that in opening society's eyes to itself, and being instrumental in awakening its self-consciousness, they cover vice with scorn and disgrace. No wonder many people cannot hear Gogol's name mentioned without a feeling of rancor, and call his *Inspector General* an "immoral" work that ought to be prohibited. Equally, no one is so simple today as to believe that a comedy or a story can make an honest man out of a bribetaker—no, you cannot straighten a twisted tree when it has grown and thickened; but bribetakers have their progeny, as do the non-bribetakers: both, while not yet having cause to regard vivid descriptions of bribery as something immoral, admire them and are, imperceptibly to themselves, enriched with impressions that do not always remain barren in their subsequent lives when they will have become actual members of society. The impressions of youth are strong, and youth believes to be the indubitable truth what has first of all appealed to its emotions, imagination, and mind. And so we see how literature influences not only education but also the moral improvement of society! Be that as it may, it is a fact beyond a shadow of doubt that the number of people who are endeavoring to realize their moral convictions in deeds to the detriment of their private interests and at the risk of their social position has been growing perceptibly with us only lately.

No less undisputed is the fact that literature with us serves as the connecting link between people who are in all other respects *inwardly* divided. The commoner Lomonosov earned important titles by virtue of his talent and learning, and grandees admit him into their circle. On the other hand, it is literature again that drew him closer to poor and socially unimportant people. The poor nobleman Derzhavin himself became a grandee through his talent, and among the men with whom literature brought him in close contact he found not only rich patrons but friends as well. Kamenev, the Kazan merchant, author of the ballad *Gromval,* arrived in Moscow on business and went to make the acquaintance of Karamzin, and through him made the acquaintance of the whole Moscow literary circle. That was *forty years* ago, when merchants got no farther than the vestibules of nobles' houses and even then on matters of business concerned with the sale of their wares or an old debt for payment of which they humbly importuned.

The first Russian magazines, whose very names are now forgotten, were published by circles of young men who had been drawn together on the basis of their common love of literature. Education levels men. And in our days it is no longer a rarity to meet a friendly circle in which you will find a titled gentleman and a commoner, a merchant and a tradesman—a circle whose members have entirely forgotten the outward distinctions that divided them, and entertain a mutual regard for one another simply as men. Here is the true beginning of educated society that literature has established! Is there anyone with a claim to the title of man who does not from the bottom of his heart wish this sociability to wax and grow by the day and the hour like the prodigy heroes of our legends!

Society, like every living thing, should be organic, that is to say, a multitude of people *internally* linked together. Pecuniary interests, trade, shares, balls, social gatherings and dances are also links, but they are external, not vital, organic links, though necessary and useful. People are internally bound together by common moral interests, similarity of views, and equality of education, combined with a mutual regard for one another's human dignity. But all our moral interests, all our spiritual life have hitherto been and will, still for a long time to come, be concentrated in literature: it is the vital spring from which all human sentiments and conceptions percolate into society.

There is *apparently* nothing easier and *actually* nothing more difficult than to write about Russian literature. That is because Russian literature is still an infant, albeit an infant Alcides. It is much more difficult to say anything positive or definite of children than it is of adults. In addition, our literature, like our society, presents a spectacle of diverse contradictions, opposites, extremes, and idiocrasies. This is due to the fact that it did not originate by itself but was originally transplanted from an alien soil. It is much easier, therefore, to speak of our literature in extremes. Say that it is no less rich and mature than any European literature and that we can count our geniuses by the dozen and our talents by the hundred; or say that we have no literature at all, that our best writers are incidental phenomena, or simply that they are worth nothing: in either case you will at least be understood, and your opinion will win ardent supporters.

Love of controversial extremes is one of the characteristics of the still-unsettled Russian nature; the Russian likes to boast beyond measure or be modest beyond measure. Hence we have, on the one side, so many inane Europeans who speak with rapture of the last newspaper story of a dried-up French novelist or sing with gusto a new vaudeville tune the Parisians have long forgotten, and who regard the work of genius of a Russian poet with contemptuous indifference or offensive suspicion; for whom Russia has no future, and everything she has is bad and worthless; on the other side we have so many *kvass patriots* who go out of their way to abominate everything European—even enlightenment, and to love everything Russian—even cheap liquor and fisticuffs duels. Adhere to any of these factions and it will instantly declare you to be a great man and a genius, while the other will hate you and declare you to be a nincompoop. At any rate, though having enemies you will also have friends. By maintaining an unbiased and *sober* view on the subject, you will incur the opprobrium of both sides. One will burden you with its fashionable, parrot-like scorn; the other will most likely declare you to be a troublesome, dangerous, and suspicious character and a renegade, and will play the literary informer against you—before the public, of course. . . . The most unpleasant part of this is that you will not be understood and your words will either be construed as immoderate praise or immoderate obloquy, and not as a faithful assessment of the fact of reality, as it exists, with all its good and evil, its merits and defects, with all the contradictions inherent within it.

This has a special application to our literature, which represents so many extremes and contradictions that in saying anything positive about it one would immediately be obliged to make a reservation the majority of the public, mostly preferring to read than to argue, might well interpret as a negation or contradiction. Thus, for example, in speaking of the strong and salutary influence of our literature on society and, consequently, of its great importance for us, we must make a reservation lest this influence and importance be ascribed a greater value than we had intended and the inference drawn from our words that we have not only a literature, but a rich literature at that, fully capable of standing up to comparison with any European literature. Such a conclusion would be false in every way. We have a literature, and a literature that is rich in talents and works, taking into consideration its means and its youth—but our literature exists for us alone: to foreigners, however, it does not yet represent a literature, and they are fully entitled to disregard its existence, since they are unable, through it, to study and become acquainted with us as a nation and as a society. Our literature is too young, indefinite, and colorless for foreigners to be able to regard it as a fact of our intellectual life. It was only too recently a shy though talented tyro who took pride in copying European models, and passed off copies of pictures from European life as pictures of Russian life. And this was the character of the whole epoch in our literature from Kantemir and Lomonosov to Pushkin. Then, beginning to sense its own powers, it turned from tyro to master, and instead of copying the ready-made pictures of European life, which it artlessly passed off as original pictures of Russian life, it began boldly to paint pictures of both European and Russian life. But as yet it was fully a master only in the treatment of the former, while it still aspired, and not always ineffectually, to become a master in the latter. And this was the character of a period in our literature from Pushkin to Gogol. With the appearance of Gogol our literature addressed itself exclusively to Russian life and Russian realities. It may, because of that, have become more one-sided and even monotonous, but it has on the other hand become more original, independent, and hence more genuine.

Now let us take these periods of Russian literature in connection with their importance, not to us, but to foreigners. There is no need to prove that Lomonosov and Karamzin possess great importance for *us:* but try to translate their works into any European language and you will see whether foreigners will read them, or, if they do, whether they will find them of any interest to themselves. They will say: "We have read all this long ago at home; give us *Russian* writers." They would say the same thing about the works of Dmitriev, Ozerov, Batyushkov, and Zhukovsky. Of all the writers of this period they would have been interested only in the fabulist Krylov; but he is supremely untranslatable into any language in the world, and he can be appreciated only by such foreigners who know Russian and have lived a long time in Russia. Thus, a whole period of Russian literature is sheerly non-existent as far as Europe is concerned.

As for the second period, it may be said to exist for Europe only to a certain degree. Were such works of Pushkin's as *Mozart and Salieri, The Covetous Knight,* and *The Stone Guest* to be worthily translated into a European language, foreigners would be compelled to admit that they are excellent poetical works, but these plays would be practically of no interest to them as creations of Russian poetry. The same can be said of the best creations of Lermontov. No translation can do justice to either Pushkin or Lermontov, no matter how excellent these translations may be. The reason is obvious: though the works of Pushkin and Lermontov reveal the Russian soul, the clear and positive Russian mind and strength and depth of feeling, these qualities are more comprehensible to us Russians than to foreigners, since the Russian nationality is not yet sufficiently fashioned and developed for the Russian poet to be able to place its sharply defined stamp upon his works as a mode of expressing ideas common to the whole of mankind.

The demands of Europeans in this respect are very exacting. Nor is this to be wondered at: the national spirit of European nations is so sharply and originally expressed in their literatures that any work, however great in artistic merit, which does not bear the sharp imprint of nationality, loses its chief merit in the eyes of Europeans. You will find in Marryat, Bulwer-Lytton, or any of the lesser English novelists the same Englishman that you will find in Shakespeare, Byron, or Walter Scott. George Sand and Paul de Kock represent the extremes of the French spirit, and though the former expresses all the beautiful, human, and lofty, and the latter the narrowness and vulgarity, of French nationality, both are obviously the exclusive products of France. A Clauren or an August Lafontaine are as much Germans as Goethe and Schiller. In each of these literatures the writer expresses the good or weak sides of his native nationality, and the national spirit lies like a customs seal both on the productions of genius and on the productions of the literary hack. The French remained supremely national when trying their hardest to imitate the Greeks and Romans. Wieland remained a German while imitating the French. The barriers of nationality are impassable for Europeans. Perhaps it is our greatest blessing that all nationalities are equally accessible to us and that our poets are able in their works so freely and easily to become Greeks and Romans and Frenchmen and Germans and Englishmen and Italians and Spaniards: but that is a blessing of the future, as an indication that our nationality will have a broad and many-sided development. At present, however, it is more a defect than a merit, not so much broadness and many-sidedness as incompleteness and indefiniteness of its own basic principle.

It would therefore be more interesting for foreigners to have good translations of those of Pushkin's and Lermontov's works in which the subject matter is drawn from Russian life. Thus, *Eugene Onegin* would be of greater interest to foreigners than *Mozart and Salieri, The Covetous Knight,* and *The Stone Guest*. And that is why the most interesting Russian poet for foreigners is Gogol. This is not a surmise, but a fact that is borne out by the remarkable success achieved in France by the translation of five of this author's stories published last year in Paris by Louis Viardot. This success is understandable: in addition to his immense artistic talent Gogol strictly adheres to the sphere of Russian *everyday* reality in his works. And that is what mostly appeals to foreigners: through the medium of the poet they want to make the acquaintance of the country that has produced him. In this respect Gogol is the most national of Russian poets, and he has nothing to fear from a translation, though by the very reason of his works being so national the best of translations could not avoid weakening the local color.

But we should not allow even this success to turn our heads. To a poet who would have his genius acknowledged by all and everywhere, and not only by his compatriots, nationality is the primary, but not the sole condition: in addition to being *national* he must at the same time be *universal,* that is, the nationality of his creations must be the form, body, flesh, physiognomy, and personality of the spiritual and incorporeal world of ideas common to all mankind. In other words: the national poet must possess a great *historical* significance not for his country alone—his appearance must be a thing of *world-wide historical significance.* Such poets can appear only in nations that are called upon to play a world-historical role in the destinies of mankind, namely, whose national life is destined to influence the trend and progress of all mankind. And therefore, if, on the one hand, one cannot become a world-historical poet unless possessing great natural genius, on the other hand, one can sometimes fall short of becoming a world-historical poet though possessing great genius, that is to say, to be of importance only to one's own nation. Here the significance of the poet depends not upon himself, upon his activity, trend, or genius, but upon the importance of the country that produced him. From this point of view we do not possess a single poet whom we could be entitled to rank with the first poets of Europe, even in the event of it being obvious that he is in no way inferior to any of them in point of talent.

Pushkin's plays: *Mozart and Salieri, The Covetous Knight,* and *The Stone Guest* are of such excellence that they can without the slightest exaggeration be said to be worthy of the genius of Shakespeare himself; yet this certainly does not mean that Pushkin is equal to Shakespeare. Let alone the great difference of power and scope that exists between the genius of Shakespeare and the genius of Pushkin, such an equivalence would be too bold a hypothesis even if Pushkin has written as much and of equal excellence as Shakespeare. The more so today when we know that the volume and scope of his best works are so poor in comparison with the volume and scope of Shakespeare's works. Rather could we say there are several works in our literature that, for *artistic merit,* could be held up to some of the great works of European literature; but we cannot say that we have poets whom we could hold up against the European poets of the first magnitude. There is a deep significance in the fact that we need acquaintance with the great poets of foreign literature and that foreigners do not stand in need of acquaintance with ours. The relation of our great poets to the great poets of Europe may be expressed thus: of certain plays of Pushkin one can say that Shakespeare would not have been ashamed to own them as his, as Byron would not have been ashamed to own as his certain plays of Lermontov; but we could not, without the risk of committing an absurdity, put it the other way round and say that Pushkin and Lermontov would not have been ashamed to subscribe their names to some of the works of Shakespeare and Byron. We can call our poets Shakespeares, Byrons, Walter Scotts, Goethes, Schillers, and so on, merely as an indication of the power or direction of their talent but not of their importance in the eyes of the educated world. He who is not called by his own name cannot be considered equal to the man by whose name he is called. Byron appeared after Goethe and Schiller, yet he remained Byron and was not called an English Goethe or an English Schiller. When the time comes for Russia to produce poets of worldwide significance, these poets will be called by their own names, and every such poet, while retaining his proper name, will become a common name and be used in the plural, because he will be *typical.*

But saying that a Russian great poet, though richly endowed by nature and equal in talent to the great European poet, cannot at present achieve importance equal to that of the latter, we mean that he can vie with him only in *form* and not in the *substance* of his poetry. The poet receives his substance from the life of his nation, consequently, the merits, depth, scope, and importance of that substance depend directly and immediately upon the historical importance of his nation's life and not upon the poet himself or his talent.

Only a hundred and thirty-six years have elapsed since Russia, by the thunder of the Battle of Poltava, proclaimed to the world her adhesion to European life and her entrance upon the field of world-historical existence—and what a brilliant path of progress and glory has she not achieved in that brief space of time! That is something fabulously great, unprecedented, never before heard of! Russia decided the fate of the contemporary world by "overthrowing into the abyss the idols that hung over kingdoms," and today, having occupied the place she has rightly earned among the first-class powers of Europe, holds with them the destinies of the world on the scales of her might. . . . But this testifies that we have not lagged behind, but have surpassed many countries in politico-historical significance, which is an important but not the sole and exclusive aspect in the life of a nation called upon to perform a great role.

Our political greatness is undoubtedly a pledge of our future great importance in other respects as well; but this alone does not testify to the achievements of such all-round development as necessarily constitutes the fullness and wholeness of life in a great nation. In the future, in addition to the victorious Russian sword, we shall lay the weight of Russian thought on the scales of European life. . . . Then shall we have poets whom we shall be entitled to rank with European poets of the first magnitude. But today let us be content with what we have, neither exaggerating nor diminishing the value of what we possess. By the standard of time our literature has achieved tremendous successes undoubtedly bearing witness to the fertility of the soil on which the Russian spirit grows. Something in our literature, if not our literature itself, is beginning to rouse interest even in foreigners. That interest is still fairly one-sided, since foreigners are able to discover in the works of Russian poets only a local color, the picturesque manners and customs of a country so sharply contrasting to their own countries. . . .

In our country there has long been maintained the custom of denouncing, first, the public for its supposed indifference toward everything native, chiefly toward national talents and national literature; and second, denouncing critics who supposedly are trying to degrade the honored authorities of Russian literature. We placed these charges alongside each other purposely: they have much in common. Let us begin with the first.

The indefatigible defenders of our literature, who modestly call themselves "patriots" and "lovers of justice," complain most of all about the decline of the book trade in Russia, about the miniscule sales of books. But facts indicate something completely different; they make as clear as two times two makes four that in Russia even quite ordinary books sell very well, to say nothing of those that are outstanding. *Three* editions of *A Hero of Our Time* were sold out in the course of *six* years. Lermontov's poems will soon need a third edition, despite the fact that they were originally all printed in journals. *Evenings on a Farm near Dikanka* by Gogol soon will have been printed four times, and there have been three editions of *The Inspector General.* The second edition (1842) of the works of Gogol sold out three thousand copies; *Dead Souls,* of which twenty-four hundred copies were printed in 1842, has long been out of print. Even the tales of Count Sollogub, read by the public in the journals, have already come out in a *second* edition; *Tarantas* will also probably soon appear in a second edition.

Enough of these facts. It is even said that in Russia an edition of the poorest book cannot help making money; that is why the booksellers print so many poor books. The only exceptions to this, apparently, are the essays of Messrs. "lovers of justice," who complain that they cannot get rid of books. But this shows only that it does not pay to hold back talent, intellect, and ideas. In bitterness and despair at the thought that the product of mind and fancy finds no market, these gentlemen have decided to place the blame for the decline of the book trade on the "thick journals" and on the new, supposedly false, school of literature founded by Gogol. These two accusations are worthy of each other. The accusers say that our literature will perish because our journals print multivolume novels, histories, and such in their entirety. They even assure us that the public itself is dissatisfied with this. Of course! It doesn't pay the public to acquire for fifty rubles a year so many works that, if published separately, would cost nearly five times as much! In view of this, how could the public not complain about the journals! Despite that, do you still want books to take their normal course? Publish them as cheaply as possible and in large numbers. The journals won't bother you.

Although books in this country have become much cheaper than they were fifteen years ago, when tiny almanacs published in a dull gray sold for ten rubles each, and poor translations of Walter Scott's novels and original Russian novels sold at twenty rubles and more per copy—despite this, books are still a frightfully expensive commodity. This is known only too well by those who consider it necessary to have the works of all well-known Russian writers in their library. Only last year an edition of Derzhavin's works came out that cost ten rubles at a time when these works ought to have long been selling twice as cheaply. The Smirdin edition of Batyushkov's works costs fifteen rubles. The first eight volumes of Zhukovsky's works can now be acquired only with difficulty for fifty rubles because that edition has been sold out for some time, and a new one still hasn't appeared. The works of Pushkin in a poor edition cost as much as sixty rubles. *Dead Souls* used to sell for ten rubles per copy; now it cannot be bought for less than thirty-five, and there is no mention of a new edition. How can the book trade flourish when the public has nothing to buy, despite all its desire to buy? It will be said that in Russia booksellers and publishers merely ruin themselves by publishing books instead of making a fortune. Yes, but are many of these booksellers good judges of the trade in which they deal? Who is to blame here? Is it really the "Thick Journals"?

Of course, one cannot help agreeing in part that our public is not quite the same as, say, the French in its love for national talent and national literature. In Paris a new edition of Hugo's works (in what quantity it is difficult to say) was released at the same time that the French Academy refused him membership; the public expressed its dissatisfaction over this by buying out the entire edition in a few days. In Russia such manifestations are not yet possible. Almost every educated Frenchman considers it necessary to have in his library all the writers public opinion has accepted as classics. And he reads and rereads them all his life. In our country—why hide the fact?—not many inveterate men of letters consider it necessary to own the old writers. In general we are always more willing to buy a new book than to buy an old one. Most persons, especially those who shout loudest about their genius and glory, read almost nothing by the old writers. This partly arises from the fact that our education is not yet well established, and the needs of the educated have not yet become a habit with us.

But there is yet another, perhaps more essential, reason that not only explains but even partly justifies this moral phenomenon. The French read, say, Rabelais or Pascal, writers of the sixteenth and seventeenth centuries. There is nothing surprising in this, because these writers are still read not only by Frenchmen but also by the Germans and the English, in a word, by people of all educated nations. The language of these writers, especially Rabelais, has become old; but the *content* of their works will always possess a vital interest because it is closely connected with the idea and significance of an entire historical epoch. This testifies to the fact that only *content*—not language, not style—can save a writer from oblivion in the face of changes in the language, customs, and ideas of society.

In this respect, talent, no matter how great, does not constitute everything. Lomonosov was great, a genius; his scholarly works will always have their value. But his poems can interest us only as a historical fact of developing literature, nothing more. To read them is both boring and difficult. One does so only as a duty, not out of desire. Derzhavin was a positively gifted poetical genius; but his era was so little able to provide content for his work that if he is read now it is more for the purpose of studying the history of Russian literature than for purely aesthetic gratification. Karamzin lifted Russian literature from the well-worn, bumpy, and rocky road of Germano-Latin construction, Church Slavic diction and phrasing, and scholastic turgidity of expression onto its real and natural path. He spoke to society in society's language and, it might be said, created both literature and public—a great and immortal service! We quite willingly admit this service and consider it not only our duty but even a pleasure to be beholden to the name of this famous man. But all this does not give content to *Poor Liza, Natalia the Boyar's Daughter, Martha the Mayor's Wife,* and so on; it does not make them interesting for our time and does not make us read and reread them. The same thing can be said for many of our writers. The objection will be raised: "Such were their times; it is not their fault that they were born in their time and not in ours." We agree, agree perfectly; but we are not blaming them; we are just removing the blame from our public. Our role is not accusatory at all, but purely explanatory. It is difficult to quarrel about tastes; but if there is one of our old writers who can be read with true satisfaction, that would be Fonvizin. His works are very similar to notes or memoirs of that era, although they are neither. Fonvizin was an unusually intelligent man. He didn't bother with the pompous, resplendent aspect of his times but considered more their internal, domestic side. Therefore his works are extremely interesting. We shall not speak of Krylov; all of us, once having learned him as children, can never forget him.

Many will take what we have said of Lomonosov, Derzhavin, and Karamzin as the *flagrant délit* of malicious degradation by criticism of our literary greats. Indeed, the evidence is plain, and there is no defense for us. But, as the proverb says, "Fear God and have no other fear!" Fortunately, the public is rapidly ceasing to think that literary greats are degraded by criticism. Now that view has fallen to the share of the so-called critics themselves; it has become the weapon of wounded pride, of forgotten reputations, fallen talents, rejected storytellers—a weapon that is completely worthy of them!

A critic who does not want to extol famous writers, or, still more, does not want to observe them, who when speaking of noted authors does not wish to repeat ready-made, stereotyped, hackneyed phrases, or to echo the opinion of others, but wants to judge according to intelligence, to the limit of his own measure of strength, to judge independently and freely and to evaluate the achievement of every writer, to show this writer's virtues and shortcomings, to point out his real place and significance in Russian literature—what is to be done with such a critic, especially if his opinions strike a responsive chord in the public? There is nothing left to do but to cry out against him as loudly and often as possible that he is degrading the literary greats, defaming Lomonosov, Derzhavin, Karamzin, Batyushkov, Zhukovsky, and even Pushkin! At the same time, one can hint that he is preaching immorality and corrupting the young generation, that he is a renegade at the very least, if not something still worse. This, too, is called "criticism."

Can *such* criticism really still find followers among the public? *What kind* of followers is still another question, but that it does find them is very possible, because our reading public is just as diverse and variegated, uncohesive as our society. Among it are people for whom *The Inspector General* and *Dead Souls* are crude farces, while *The Sensations of Mrs. Kurdyukova* is a most witty work. There are people who, as Gogol said, "love to converse about literature, praise Bulgarin, Pushkin, and Grech, and to speak contemptuously and caustically about A. A. Orlov." Such persons, or rather such perusers (it would be a crime to call them readers), see in criticism either unconditional praise or unmitigated abuse. It is easy for them to understand that type of critic; they would become giddy from any other, for they would be required to think; and that is only more burdensome and difficult for them.

When a review of an author's works appears that is written in the spirit of sincere criticism, that distinguishes unconditional from conditional merits in an author and inadequacies of talent from inadequacies of time, the above-mentioned perusers will not stop to read it. They will be told about him by some critic of *their* faith, some author of all sorts of things, who praises with all his might himself and the old writers who are no longer dangerous to him and who rebukes out of hand everything that is talented in the new generation. In his own way this critic analyzes for his perusers the criticism that has just appeared, extracts from it a line or a word from each page, and exclaims, "Can one thus degrade our honored authorities?" And his perusers believe him because they understand him. He speaks to them in their language, their concepts, their feelings, their taste—*les beaux esprits se rencontrent*. It does not even occur to them, to these perusers, that truth does not degrade talent, just as false opinion cannot harm it; that only undeserved fame can degrade and, consequently, independent judgment of literature can in no way be harmful and is often useful. The inventor of such criticism also assures his perusers that the critic, in the presence of whose name he cannot retain his composure, praises only his friends; and the perusers believe what is printed.

How could they find out that this critic is barely acquainted with the living writers whom he admires? That is a private matter. How could they understand that he had not yet been born when Lomonosov died, could not read or write when Derzhavin died and when Zhukovsky and Karamzin were in their full glory—these men to whose merits and genius he gives full justice, but not through another's voice and not without an accounting? In order to understand, one needs the capacity for understanding. It is much easier to place confidence in the words of someone who merely repeats that, after all, the critic merely praises all his friends.

Generally, together with the surprising and rapid success in intellectual and literary education, a kind of immaturity and lack of determination is perceptible in our country. Truths that in other literatures have long since become axioms and have stopped causing quarrels and requiring proof have not yet been debated in our country and are not yet known to all. For example, you have never written a book, but have been publishing an immensely successful journal: your critics will bellow that your journal is poor *because* you haven't written a book. This "because" is quite original! Yet if the journal is good, what difference does it make whether its publisher has written a book or not? Your business is criticism, and even though you are so successful that you sharply affect others' opinions and prejudices and create enemies for yourself, don't think that your opponents will come to refute your position, to question your conclusions. No, instead, they will begin to tell you that since you have not written anything yourself, you do not have the right to criticize others, that you are young, while you are judging the works of persons already old, and so on. Such devices can put anyone in a difficult position, not because it is difficult to answer them, but precisely because it is too easy to answer them. But who has enough spirit to disprove such opinions, to declare solemnly that you do not have to be a cook in order to judge food properly, nor to be a tailor to express your opinion on the value or worthlessness of a new dress coat unerringly?—just as without being able to write poems, novels, tales, or dramas, nevertheless it is possible to be in a position to judge the works of others sensibly and reasonably; and that if, in the field of gastronomy, it is in its way a talent to have fine taste, then it is all the more so in the sphere of art; and that criticism, in its way, is art.

There are even truths that are trivial just because they are too obvious, as for example the fact that summer is warm and winter cold, that you can get wet in the rain and can dry out before a fire. And yet we must at times defend similar truths with all the force of logic and dialectics. This, however, can only be funny or annoying, depending on the disposition of your spirit, whereas things do occur that you don't want to laugh about. Just recall that a work that grasps certain features of society correctly is in Russia often considered a libel to society or to a class or to a person. Our literature is expected to see only virtuous heroes and melodramatic villains in real life, and not even suspect that many humorous, strange, and ugly phenomena may exist in society. Every person is ready whenever possible to forbid others to live in order that he might live extensively and spaciously.

Scribblers in frieze coats, with unshaven chins, write miserable little books at the order of petty booksellers: what is so bad about that? Why shouldn't the scribbler gain his crust of bread as he best can and knows? But these scribblers ruin the public taste, deface literature, and the calling of the literary man. Let us grant this to prevent them from harming the public taste and the success of literature: we have journals; we have criticism. No, that is not enough: if we had our way, we should forbid the scribblers to write their nonsense and the booksellers from publishing it. And from where, from whom do such ideas come? From the journals, from the literary men! There are some awesome forbidders among them; except for their own works they would forbid all writings in a body. Some would not stop even at this but would want to prevent the sale of all other goods except their own works, even bread and salt.

A humorous writer appeared among us whose talent had so strong an influence on all literature that it gave it a completely new direction. He began to be discredited. They wanted to convince the public that he was a Paul de Kock, a painter of dirty, unwashed, and uncombed nature. He answered no one and just went ahead. In its attitude toward him the public divided into two camps, the more numerous of which was decidedly opposed to him. That, however, did not at all prevent it from buying, reading, and rereading his works. Finally, the majority of the public also stood behind him. What could his censurers do? They began to recognize talent, even great talent, in him, although it was according to them a talent on the wrong road. But at the same time they began to let it be known and hinted directly that he was supposedly debasing everything Russian, insulting the honored class of bureaucrats, and so on. These gentlemen, however, are not at all pleading for the bureaucrats, but for themselves. They would like to silence all contemporary literature so that the public for lack of anything good would willy-nilly be forced to take up their works and would again begin to buy them. All this is printed, and the public reads it, because if nobody read it then it would not be printed. In Russia every opinion finds a place, accommodation, attention, and even followers. What is this if not immaturity and instability of public opinion?

But with all that, truth and good taste march with firm step and take the field for this disorderly battle of opinions. Though every false and empty but brilliant talent without exception enjoys success, there still is no instance of a true talent not being accepted by us and not achieving success. False authorities fall daily. Has it been long since the fame of Marlinsky, that juggler of phrases, was considered colossal? Now they no longer even speak of him, much less praise him; they don't even denounce him. Many such examples could be mentioned. This shows that both our literature and our society are still too young and immature but that there is hidden in them a great, healthy, vital strength promising a rich development in the future.

Somewhere the idea was once expressed that we have more artistic than belletristic works, more geniuses than talents. Like every new and original idea, this one aroused discussion. Actually, this idea at first glance might appear to be a strange paradox; nevertheless, it is basically justified. In order to be convinced of this, one has only to cast a cursory glance at the course of our literature from its beginning to the present time.

The belletrist is an imitator. He lives on another's idea, the idea of a genius. True, the geniuses of the first period of our literature, before Pushkin, were no more than belletrists in respect to the European writers from whom they learned to write and from whom they borrowed both form and ideas. But in our literature their role was quite different. Kantemir imitated Horace and Boileau. Despite that, he was a completely original writer in Russian literature, a subject of amazement for his contemporaries, who thought him a genius, and a subject of respect for posterity, which saw in him one of the outstanding figures of our literature.

There is no point in even speaking of Lomonosov, Derzhavin, and Fonvizin: they were real geniuses, and the second of them was even a real poetic genius. But Sumarokov, Kheraskov, Petrov, Bogdanovich, and Knyazhnin were also considered great poets in their time and even long after their deaths. Sergei Nikolaevich Glinka, that honored and always inspired veteran of our literature, considers them great poets even now. And although our age views them completely differently, it cannot but agree that even the opinion of Sergei Nikolaevich Glinka and his age has its basis too.

The first figures of every literature, especially the imitators, appear even to posterity in such large dimensions as no longer exist for the same talents that arise later, during the period of that literature's successes and development. Sumarokov's contemporaries were convinced that he far outdistanced the fabulist La Fontaine and the tragedians Corneille and Racine and compared him to Mr. Voltaire. Kheraskov was our Homer, Petrov our Pindar. Zephyr gave to Bogdanovich a feather from his wings, and Amor guided his hand when he wrote *Dushenka*. But did these, let us say, *conditional* geniuses engender many imitators? Did Derzhavin himself give rise to many? It is true that in those blessed times millions of triumphal odes were written and printed. But that was because thousands of hands wrote them, and if only one ode came from each hand, the flow would be enormous. Yet have many names of talented belletrists, born of the movement imparted to our literature by its first geniuses, come down to us? Let us grant that Sumarokov, Kheraskov, and Petrov could not possibly have had talented imitators, but did Derzhavin have many? Dmitriev wrote a few odes and Kapnist wrote a few more, that is all; numerically the odes of both these poets are nothing in comparison with the quantitative richness of Derzhavin's odes.

In general it is natural that a belletrist can easily write a great deal more than his model; with us the opposite has always been the case. Makarov and Podshivalov, who wrote very little, especially the latter, functioned independently from Karamzin; whereas the imitators of Karamzin were Vladimir Izmailov, Prionce Shalikov, and, to tell the truth, we don't remember who else—they were so few and wrote so little and spiritlessly! Zhukovsky's influence was enormous. One can learn to translate by studying him even now, and one will always be able to; his poems also will always remain models. Kozlov, Mr. F. Glinka, and partly Mr. Tumansky were echoes of Zhukovsky's muse. The genius of Pushkin gave birth to still more imitators, whose talent cannot be denied and who enjoyed great renown in their time. But taken all together they wrote hardly half as much as Pushkin did alone, although he too did not write very much—and how quickly they outlived their talent and their fame!

Now too, many are writing. One leaves the scene; that is, he is forgotten (with us that happens unusually quickly), and another appears. Taken together they all produce quite an amount (at least comparatively), but individually each writes very little. Moreover, everyone pretends to high artistic value, to creativity. No one wants to be simply a narrator, a storyteller, a belletrist. Almost everyone writes to order, knowing beforehand how much each line, each word, each comma will bring him. But at the same time everyone writes by inspiration. Many sell still-unwritten tales, not because they write too much and receive too many orders, but because they write too little. Some might break out one story a year and look like Napoleon after the Battle of Austerlitz. To succeed in writing two stories in a single year would be equal to conquering the whole world. Therefore we have no belletrists, and the public has nothing to read.

In any year the works that are outstanding in any way (including those that are only tolerable) can be counted on one's fingers. Things are different in France. There they write in spells, and every belletrist who is known at all annually fills up whole volumes, almost tens of volumes, never concerning himself with what the public will take him for, a genius or simply a talent. There the belletrist writes more than the poet-artist. George Sand wrote very much, more than is written here by many people over many years. But the stack of George Sand's works in comparison with those of Eugène Sue or Alexandre Dumas is like a lake compared to the sea, or the sea to an ocean. This is as it should be; creation does not submit to will, and the artist needs time to think over his conception and carry out the thought conceived in his mind. In the real, the true, meaning of the word, we had and have only three belletrists: these are Messrs. Bulgarin, Polevoy, and Kukol'nik. Their indefatigability is amazing.

Of all the types of poetry in this country, we recognize drama, especially comedy, as being weaker than the others. But at least the so-called classical tragedy had its period of development and success in Russia. The tragedies of Sumarokov gave sustenance to our growing theater, and not only delighted contemporaries, but *The False Dmitry* was played in provincial theaters as late as the early twenties of this century. For their time, the tragedies and comedies of Knyazhnin had an undeniable value; it can be said generally if such an intelligent and deft imitator as Knyazhnin was for his time should now appear, our age would gain much. Ozerov was still greater. From all this it is apparent that our classical tragedy developed in the course of three generations. Romanticism appeared and romantic dramas were played—bloody, horrifying, effective, and finally even native dramas that were incoherent and empty. Now they too are written only for benefit performances, and at that more and more rarely. There is hope that they will soon cease altogether. And a good thing, too! It is better to have nothing at all than a great deal of nonsense, whatever its quality!

But in the drama, too, indeed more than elsewhere, the proposition that we have more geniuses than talents (although they are few enough) is borne out. Pushkin, in his *Boris Godunov,* gave us a genuine and genial model for national drama. But perhaps because he was too truthful and too much a genius, it remained without any influence on our dramatic literature. At any rate, not a single dramatic work that has a vestige of talent reflects the influence of *Boris Godunov*. It will be said: "That is because no drama with a vestige of talent has appeared in our country." True! But why then did there appear and do there still appear narrative poems with signs of talent, sometimes even remarkable talent, thereby indicating how strong and fruitful the influence of Pushkin and Lermontov on our literature has been? The best dramatic work in the national spirit after *Boris Godunov* belongs, again, to Pushkin: *Rusalka*. His dramatic poems, *Scene from Faust, Mozart and Salieri, The Covetous Knight,* and *The Stone Guest,* also did not call forth any experiments in Russian literature that were at all fortunate. Nevertheless, all Pushkin's dramatic works are great artistic creations.

Such, too, is the fate of our comedy: it either offers something remarkable or offers something that is less than nothing. There is practically nothing to be said for Russian comedies before Fonvizin. They were either translations or reworkings (in this field the labors of Knyazhnin deserve respect), but as original Russian comedies they were a strange anomaly. *The Brigadier* and

*The Hobbledehoy*, not being artistic creations in the strict sense of the word, were nevertheless creations of genius. By their nature they can be called reliable and accurate satires in the form of comedy. These were imitated, but the imitations were unnatural and awkward. Their belated influence, incidentally, was felt in Osnovianenko's comedy *Elections of the Nobility*, a work that has its inadequacies yet is not without merit.

Between *The Brigadier* and *The Hobbledehoy*, Ablesimov somehow casually blurted out a charming national vaudeville sketch. This was an accident, though a wonderful one. It properly remained without consequence for literature. Kapnist's *Slander* is more remarkable for its aims than for its fulfillment. Now one must go directly to Griboedov's *Woe from Wit*, because the multitude of comedies in prose and verse written during the interval from Fonvizin to Griboedov are not worth mentioning—*Woe from Wit*, this semiartistic, semisatirical comedy, this eminent pattern of mind, wit, talent, genius, of angry, bitter inspiration—*Woe from Wit* remains up to now the sole work in our literature in whose genre not a single talent has decided to test his strength.

From Griboedov's comedy we must move directly to *The Inspector General*. Besides this highly artistic comedy filled with the most profound humor and startling truth, Gogol also wrote a small comedy, *Marriage*, and a few scenes that, by their size, cannot be called comedies, standing in relation to a comedy as a tale does to a novel. All these scenes bear the sharp imprint of the talent of the author of *The Inspector General*, and, like it, remain in our literature to this time as isolated monuments in the midst of a wide sandy steppe where not a tree, not a blade of grass is visible. There were, it is true, two or three attempts that were not completely unsuccessful, but these were too indecisive.

One-sidedness in one's view of things always leads to false conclusions, even though the view is not without profundity and insight. The capacity to have convictions, one of the most wonderful capacities of human nature, leads to fanaticism in the presence of one-sidedness. Literary fanaticism is just as deaf and blind as any other, especially when it exists in the name of theory. German aesthetic theories were so well received in the receptive soil of our recent education that they found for themselves followers who were so zealous and fanatical that they would be looked upon as marvels of theoretical frenzy, even in Germany, especially now. For incorrigible fanatics of this type, French literature and French art are veritable stumbling blocks. Since such fanatics do not understand French literature, and persist in confessing so, they take a great deal of trouble not to recognize its existence. That, however, is not surprising. During the restoration some historians insisted that Napoleon was only a regimental commander under Louis XVIII!

As a matter of fact, from a purely theoretical point of view, without resorting to actual historical observation, not much good can be found in French literature when one is enraptured with German literature. German aesthetics emerged from the scholar's study, and German poetry emerged from

German aesthetics. To be convinced of this, one has only to recall how the genius Schiller wrote. In *Wallenstein* not only was everything thought out by him beforehand; it was also proved and justified. Everything emerged from theory, and the author took *eight* years to write this drama. Schiller wanted to write an epic poem on the life of Frederick the Great, but he did not want to undertake the task until he had philosophically developed a theory of the epic poem for modern times. All these phenomena, somewhat strange if not abnormal, and quite harmful to the genius of Schiller, as well as to other German poets, arose directly from the German social environment—peaceful, contemplative, based on family and study.

On the other hand, all French literature arose from French social and historical life, and is closely tied up with it. Therefore, French cannot be judged according to ready-made theories without falling into one-sidedness and reaching false conclusions. The tragedies of Corneille, it is true, are very awkward in their classical form; and theoreticians have every right to attack this Chinese form, to which the majestic and powerful genius of Corneille yields as a result of the forcible influence of Richelieu, who wanted to be the prime minister of literature also. But the theoreticians would have been cruelly mistaken if behind the awkward classical form of Corneille's tragedies they had glimpsed the awesome internal strength of their pathos. The French of our time say that Mirabeau is indebted to Corneille for the greatest inspiration of his speeches. After this, what wonder that the French quickly forget their romantic tragedies à la Shakespeare, and continue, as they always will, to read old Corneille. Every one of their famous writers was directly connected with the era in which he lived, and has the right to a place in the history of France as well as in the history of French literature.

In Russia all ideas about creation have a somewhat different meaning from those in German literature: they must share their authority and strength with ideas about society and its historical course. We have people who succeeded in understanding that *The Inspector General* is a deeply creative and artistic work and that not one comedy of Molière can bear aesthetic criticism. They are right in that respect, but they are not right in the conclusion they draw from that fact. Actually, not one comedy by Molière can bear aesthetic criticism because they were all *made* rather than *created*. Often they wander off into farce, or at least tolerate farce within themselves (like, for example, the false mufti, dervishes, and Turks in *Le Bourgeois gentilhomme*). The mainsprings of their actions are always artificial and monotonous, the characters abstract; the satire emerges too sharply from forms of poetical invention, and so on. But with all that, Molière had an enormous influence on contemporary society and raised French theater high, a thing that could not be done with mere talent, but required genius. In order to judge his comedies, one must not read them but see them on the stage—and, at that, certainly on the French stage—because their scenic value is greater than their dramatic. The French do not have a right to be proud about this or that specific comedy by Molière, but have a complete right to be proud of his comedies, or better to say the theater of Molière, because Molière gave them an entire theatre. The same may also be said of Scribe. Not one of his dramas nor one vaudeville sketch can be pointed to as a work of art that will always have its value. But it can be stated affirmatively that the theatre of Scribe will always have its value, and now it is priceless; so important is it to the members of contemporary society, of all classes, educated and uneducated, who flock to the theater to see themselves on the stage.

We have a few highly artistic comedies that, by their number, cannot make up a constant repertoire for the theatre. With all their merit, they would become deadly dull to everyone if the theatre presented nothing but them, because one and the same thing without change is always boring.

Let us suppose that the French have not a single artistic comedy. Despite that, there is a theatre that exists for everyone, and in which society is both instructed and entertained aesthetically.

Whose is the advantage?

Let the reader decide; we are not concerned.

What distinguishes genius from talent? The question is very important, the more so since it is always solved very cleverly. We shall not burden ourselves but shall attempt to explain it simply. That both genius and talent are given by nature, that both one and the other, so to speak, are properties of the very organism of man, as light and heat are the properties of flame, there is no point even in stating, since it is a subject concerning which everyone has long been in agreement. The question lies in distinguishing between genius and talent, and the other way round.

Who has not chanced to meet a multitude of people who like to read, to follow literature, and who want to judge it, but who dare to judge a new book only after they have managed to read a discussion of it by a journal that enjoys their absolute confidence, and who feel themselves in a most difficult situation if a review or criticism of a book that is making a big splash doesn't appear in the journal for a long time? Who has not chanced to meet people who are ready to judge anything but who immediately renounce their opinion and agree wholeheartedly with the opinion of their critic as soon as someone takes sharp exception to them?

There are people without opinions, without the capacity for forming an opinion, people who can be firm only through another's opinion, and for whom authority is a requirement of the first order. It must be noted that people of this type have a very strongly developed instinct for feeling another's strength, and always recognize it. Incidentally, these people might be quite intelligent: they recognize proofs; they have the ability to judge. But this capacity of theirs lacks independence, and needs support from authority. The mass consists primarily of such people, and it is always and everywhere controlled by people with more or less independent opinions. This is the reason why the mass does not long fancy the false and ugly, but always sooner or later recognizes the worth of the true and beautiful. Others act for it, and it merely obeys. Without this moral discipline terrible anarchy would reign in people's concepts, instead of unity.

Talent, *as the ability to make, to produce,* concerns more and more a form of creation; and, from this point of view, talent is an internal strength that can exist in man independent of his mind, his heart, and other intellectual and moral sides of human nature. But content is necessary for form. Therefore, this is the particular place where the independent activity of man's spiritual forces gains all its meaning.

If there are people who lack the ability to have their own opinion on things, and who accept another's opinion completely as something they no longer need to think about, then there are others who, while constantly living on another's opinion, have the ability to make it their own, to develop it, to extract new corollaries from it, to discover other ideas through it. This ability so deceives people of this type that they are very sincerely convinced of their own ability to think. They are almost correct about this; with their lively and receptive natures, they themselves do not know and do not understand who transmitted a certain idea to them because everything from without adheres to them almost unconsciously, instinctively. They have only to speak with an intelligent person or to read a good book, and immediately a whole series of new ideas that they cannot help accepting as their own rises within them. These people, controlled by others, have in their turn a great influence on the mass. You often meet them in this world. There is an especially great number of them in the capitals. Generally, the more enlightened and educated a society is, the more such people there are in it.

Finally, there are people (very few of them) who really possess the capacity for the creative independent function of their capacities. They look upon everything in a sort of special, original way; in everything they specifically see what no one else sees without them and what everyone sees after them and is amazed that he did not see it before. These are completely uncomplicated people, not clever at all. They see everything simply, but their simple understanding at first seems complicated to everyone and sometimes seems unintelligent or clumsy. But later it seems so simple that not a single fool fails to wonder why this did not occur to *him*—why, it is so simple! When Columbus was preparing to discover America, everyone looked at him as if he were a mad dreamer; but when he did discover America, almost no one wanted to recognize merit in this accomplishment, because a discovered America seemed to everyone so simple to discover!

In speaking of these three groups of people, we wanted to speak of *the mass*, of *talent*, and of *genius*. . . .

These days talent is no rarity in anything, especially in literature. Mere child's play! It is often confused with genius, and not wisely. A great talent of sorts is needed to distinguish genius from talent in the first place. This reminds us of a passage from a tale by a famous French author of our day, wherein he writes about the hero's literary work as follows:

> He recognized that everything begun by him, after the first ten lines or three or four verses, became so similar to the writers he was reading, that he blushed at seeing himself capable only of imitating. He showed me a few verses and phrases, beneath which Lamartine, Victor Hugo,

> Paul Courier, Charles Nodier, Balzac, and even Béranger could have placed their names. But all these experiments, which could have been called fragments of fragments, in the works of those writers would have served to adorn their individual ideas. But Horace lacked just this individuality. If he wanted to express some kind of idea, you would immediately see (and he himself immediately saw) obvious plagiarism; this idea was not his. It belonged to those writers; *it belonged to everyone but not to him.*

Here is the eternal story of talent! Of course, it does not always occur exactly the way it was presented in the words of the author we cited, but that is always its essence. No matter how great a talent is, he cannot set the seal of his personality on his works, and therefore cannot be original and unique. No matter how great his ability to adopt the ideas of others, he will not long conceal that his inspiration does not gush like a flowing stream from the inner recesses of his nature, but is only "the aggravation of a captive idea." But, on the other hand, no matter how narrow or limited the sphere of talent, if his works contain the sharp imprint of personality that makes work so individual that it is impossible to imitate them, then it is no longer a talent, but a genius. Among such poets of genius in our literature belongs the fabulist Krylov.

# BIBLIOGRAPHY

## GENERAL


Abrams, M. H. *Natural Supernaturalism: Tradition and Revolution in Romantic Literature*. New York: W. W. Norton, 1971.

———. *The Correspondent Breeze: Essays on English Romanticism*. New York: W. W. Norton, 1984.

Baker, Carlos. *The Echoing Green: Romanticism, Modernism, and the Phenomena of Transference in Poetry*. Princeton: Princeton University Press, 1984.

Bloom, Harold. *The Visionary Company*. Revised edition. Ithaca: Cornell University Press, 1971.

———. *The Ringers in the Tower*. Chicago: University of Chicago Press, 1971.

———. *A Map of Misreading*. New York: Oxford University Press, 1975.

———. *Figures of Capable Imagination*. New York: Seabury Press, 1976.

———. *Poetry and Repression: Revisionism from Blake to Stevens*. New Haven: Yale University Press, 1976.

———, ed. *Deconstruction and Criticism*. New York: Seabury Press, 1979.

Blumenthal, Henry. *American and French Culture, 1800–1900: Interchanges in Art, Science, Literature, and Society*. Baton Rouge: Louisiana State University Press, 1975.

Brisman, Leslie. *Romantic Origins*. Ithaca: Cornell University Press, 1978.

Bush, Douglas. *Mythology and the Romantic Tradition*. Cambridge, Mass.: Harvard University Press, 1937.

Buxton, John. *The Grecian Taste: Literature in the Age of Neo-Classicism 1740–1820*. New York: Barnes & Noble, 1978.

Cantor, Paul. *Creature and Creator: Myth-Making and English Romanticism*. Cambridge: Cambridge University Press, 1984.

Clubbe, John, and Ernest J. Lovell, Jr. *English Romanticism: The Grounds of Belief*. Dekalb: Northern Illinois University Press, 1983.

Cook, Michael G. *The Romantic Will*. New Haven: Yale University Press, 1976.

Culler, Jonathan. *The Pursuit of Signs: Semiotics, Literature, Deconstruction*. Ithaca: Cornell University Press, 1981.

Davies, R. T., and B. G. Beatty. *Literature of the Romantic Period 1750–1850*. New York: Barnes & Noble, 1976.

De Man, Paul. *The Rhetoric of Romanticism*. New York: Columbia University Press, 1984.

Elledge, Paul W., and Richard L. Hoffman, eds. *Romantic and Victorian Studies in Memory of William H. Marshall*. Cranbury, N.J.: Fairleigh Dickinson University Press, 1971.

Fogle, Richard Harter. *The Permanent Pleasure: Essays on the Classics of Romanticism*. Athens: University of Georgia Press, 1973.

Hamburger, Michael. *The Truth of Poetry: Tensions in Modern Poetry from Baudelaire to the 1960s*. New York: Harcourt Brace & World, 1970.

Hartley, Robert A., ed. *Keats, Shelley, Byron, Hunt, and Their Circles: A Bibliography. July 1, 1962 to December 31, 1974*. Lincoln: University of Nebraska Press, 1979.

Hartman, Geoffrey. *The Fate of Reading and Other Essays*. Chicago: University of Chicago Press, 1975.

Hoffman, Michael J. *The Subversive Vision: American Romanticism in Literature*. Port Washington, N.Y.: Kennikat Press, 1972.

Hughes, Peter, and David Williams, eds. *The Varied Pattern: Studies in the 18th Century*. Toronto: A. M. Hakkert, 1971.

Jordan, Frank, ed. *The English Romantic Poets: A Review of Research and Criticism*. Third edition. New York: Modern Language Association, 1972.

Krieger, Murray. *Theory of Criticism: A Tradition and Its System*. Baltimore: Johns Hopkins University Press, 1976.

Leavis, F. R. *Revaluation, Tradition, and Development in English Poetry*. London: Chatto & Windus, 1936.

Levin, Joseph M. *Dr. Woodward's Shield: History, Science, and Satire in Augustan England*. Berkeley: University of California Press, 1977.

Lobb, Edward. *T. S. Eliot and the Romantic Critical Tradition*. London: Routledge & Kegan Paul, 1981.

McGann, Jerome J. *The Romantic Ideology: A Critical Investigation*. Chicago: University of Chicago Press, 1983.

MacPherson, Jay. *The Spirit of Solitude: Conventions and Continuities in Late Romance*. New Haven: Yale University Press, 1982.

Rajan, Tilottama. *Dark Interpreter: The Discourse of Romanticism*. Ithaca: Cornell University Press, 1980.

Redpath, Theodore. *The Young Romantics and Critical Opinion 1807–1824: Poetry of Byron, Shelley, and Keats as Seen by Contemporary Critics*. New York: St. Martin's Press, 1973.

Reed, Arden, ed. *Romanticism and Language*. Ithaca: Cornell University Press, 1984.

Reiman, Donald H., ed. *The Romantics Reviewed: Contemporary Reviews of British Romantic Writers*. New York: Garland Press, 1972.

———; Michael C. Jaye; and Betty T. Bennett; eds. *The Evidence of the Imagination: Studies of Interactions between Life and Art in English Romantic Literature*. New York: New York University Press, 1978.

Simpson, David. *Irony and Authority in Romantic Poetry*. Totowa, N.J.: Rowman & Littlefield, 1979.

Thorburn, David, and Geoffrey Hartman, eds. *Romanticism: Vistas, Instances, Continuities*. Ithaca: Cornell University Press, 1973.

Thorpe, Clarence De Witt; Carlos Baker; and Bennett Weaver; eds. *Major English Romantic Poets*. Carbondale: Southern Illinois University Press, 1957.

Thurley, Geoffrey. *The Romantic Predicament*. London: Macmillan, 1983.

## FRIEDRICH HÖLDERLIN

Dilthey, Wilhelm. *Das Erlebnis und die Dichtung: Lessing, Goethe, Novalis, Hölderlin*. Leipzig: B. G. Teubner, 1913.

Feheryary, Helen. *Hölderlin and the Left: The Search for a Dialectic of Art and Life*. Heidelberg: Winter, 1977.

Gadamer, Hans George; Müller, Max; and Staiger, Emil. *Hegel, Hölderlin, Heidegger*. Karlsruhe: Badenia, 1971.

George, Emery Edward, ed. *Friedrich Hölderlin: An Early Modern*. Ann Arbor: University of Michigan Press, 1972.

———. *Hölderlin's "Ars Poetica": A Part-Rigorous Analysis of Information Structure in the Late Hymns*. The Hague: Mouton, 1973.

Harrison, Robin B. *Hölderlin and Greek Literature*. Oxford: Clarendon Press, 1975.

Heidegger, Martin. *Hölderlin's Hymnen "Germanien" und "Der Rhein."* Frankfurt am Main: V. Klostermann, 1980.

Hölderlin, Friedrich. *Hölderlin: His Poems.* Translated by Michael Hamburger, with a Critical Study. 2nd ed. London: Harvill Press, 1952.

Laplanche, Jean. *Hölderlin et la question du père.* Paris: Presses Universitaires de France, 1961.

Nauen, Franz Gabriel. *Revolution, Idealism, and Human Freedom: Schelling, Hölderlin, and Hegel and the Crisis of Early German Idealism.* The Hague: Nijhoff, 1971.

Rehan, Walther. *Orpheus, der Dichter und die Toten: Selbstdeutung and Totenkult bei Novalis, Hölderlin und Rilke.* Dusseldorf: L. Schwann, 1950.

Salzburger, Lore Sulamith. *Hölderlin.* New Haven: Yale University Press, 1952.

Unger, Richard. *Hölderlin's Major Poetry: The Dialectics of Unity.* Bloomington: Indiana University Press, 1975.

Zweig, Stefan. *Masterbuilders: A Typology of the Spirit.* Translated by Edgar and Cedar Paul. New York: Viking Press, 1939.

## HEINRICH VON KLEIST

Angress, R. K. "Kleist's Treatment of Imperialism: *Die Hermanns-Schlacht* and *Die Verlobung in St. Domingo.*" *Monatshefte* 69 (1977): 17–33.

Bennett, Benjamin. "Kleist's Puppets in Early Hofmannstahl." *Modern Language Quarterly* 37 (1976): 151–67.

Bochan, Bohdan. *The Phenomenology of Freedom in Kleist's "Die Familie Schroffenstein" and "Penthesilea."* Bern: Lang Publications, 1982.

Burckhardt, Sigurd. *The Drama of Language: Essays on Goethe and Kleist.* Baltimore: Johns Hopkins University Press, 1970.

Coates, Paul. *The Realist Fantasy: Fiction and Reality since Clarissa.* New York: St. Martin's Press, 1983.

Dyer, Denys. *The Stories of Kleist: A Critical Study.* New York: Holmes & Meier, 1977.

Ellis, John M. *Heinrich von Kleist: Studies in the Character and Meaning of His Writings.* Chapel Hill: University of North Carolina Press, 1979.

Gelus, Marjorie. "Laughter and Joking in the Works of Heinrich von Kleist." *German Quarterly* 50 (1977): 452–73.

Graham, Ilse. *Heinrich von Kleist: Words into Flesh, A Poet's Quest for the Symbol.* Berlin: Walter de Gruyter, 1977.

Lindsay, J. M. "Figures of Authority in the Works of Heinrich von Kleist." *Forum* 8 (1972): 107–19.

Lob, Ladislas. *From Lessing to Hauptmann: Studies in German Drama.* London: University Tutorial Press, 1971.

McGlathery, James M. *Desire's Sway: The Plays and Stories of Heinrich von Kleist.* Detroit: Wayne State University Press, 1983.

Milfull, John. "Oedipus and Adam: Greek Tragedy and Christian Comedy in Kleist's *Der Zerbrochene Krug.*" *German Life and Letters* 27 (1973): 7–17.

Miller, Philip B., ed. *An Abyss Deep Enough: Letters of Heinrich von Kleist, with a Selection of Essays and Anecdotes.* New York: E. P. Dutton, 1982.

Mulligan, John J. "Kleist's *Friedrich von Homburg:* Prince without a Choice." *Forum for Modern Language Studies* (University of St. Andrew's) 16 (1980): 33–45.

Peck, Jeffrey M. *Hermes Disguised: Literary Hermeneutics and the Interpretation of Literature: Kleist, Grillparzer, Fontane.* Bern: Lang Publications, 1983.

Reeve, W. C. "An Unsung Villain: The Role of Hohenzollern in Kleist's *Prinz Friedrich von Homburg.*" *Germanic Review* 56 (1981): 95–110.

Reeves, Nigel. "Kleist's Indebtedness to the Science, Psychiatry, and Medicine of His Time." *Oxford German Studies* 16 (1985): 47–65.

Richardson, Frank C. *Kleist in France*. Chapel Hill: University of North Carolina Press, 1962.

Silz, Walter. *Heinrich von Kleist: Studies in His Works and Literary Character*. Philadelphia: University of Pennsylvania Press, 1962.

Wells, G. A. "The Limitations of Knowledge: Kleist's *Über das Marionettentheater*." *Modern Language Review* 80 (1985): 90–96.

## STENDHAL

Abeel, Erica. "The Multiple Authors in Stendhal's Ironic Interventions." *French Review* 50 (1976): 21–34.

Adams, Robert M. *Stendhal: Notes on a Novelist*. New York: Noonday Press, 1959.

Alter, Robert M., and Carol Cosman. *A Lion for Love*. Cambridge, Mass.: Harvard University Press, 1986.

Bart, B. F. "Hypercreativity in Stendhal and Balzac." *Nineteenth-Century Fiction Studies* 3 (1974–75): 18–39.

Bersani, Leo. *Balzac to Beckett: Center and Circumference in French Fiction*. New York: Oxford University Press, 1971.

Brombert, Victor. *Stendhal: Fiction and the Themes of Freedom*. Chicago: University of Chicago Press, 1986.

Brooks, Peter. "The Novel and the Guillotine; or, Fathers and Sons in *Le Rouge et le noir*." *PMLA* 97 (1982): 348–62.

Buss, Robin. "Quick on the Draw? Stendhal's Lottery Ticket and Some Early Critics of *Le Rouge et le noir*." *Literature and History* 8 (1982): 95–107.

Coe, Richard N. "The Anecdote and the Novel: A Brief Enquiry into the Origins of Stendhal's Narrative Technique." *Australian Journal of French Studies* 22 (1985): 3–25.

Dutord, Jean. *The Man of Sensibility*. New York: Simon & Schuster, 1961.

Ellis, David, ed. *Memoirs of an Egoist*. London: Chatto & Windus, 1975.

Fineshriber, William H. *Stendhal the Romantic Rationalist*. Princeton: Princeton University Press, 1932.

Garber, Frederick. *The Autonomy of the Self from Richardson to Huysmans*. Princeton: Princeton University Press, 1982.

Giraud, Raymond. *The Unheroic Hero in the Novels of Stendhal, Balzac, and Flaubert*. New York: Hippocrene Books, 1969.

May, Gita. *Stendhal and the Age of Napoleon*. New York: Columbia University Press, 1977.

Miller, D. A. *Narrative and Its Discontents: Problems of Closure in the Traditional Novel*. Princeton: Princeton University Press, 1981.

Morris, Robert. *The Masked Citadel: The Significance of the Title of Stendhal's "La Chartreuse de Parme."* Berkeley: University of California Press, 1968.

Mossman, Carol A. *The Narrative Matrix: Stendhal's "Le Rouge et le noir."* Lexington, Ky.: French Forum, 1984.

Paris, Bernard J. *A Psychological Approach to Fiction: Studies in Thackeray, Stendhal, George Eliot, Dostoievski, and Conrad*. Bloomington: Indiana University Press, 1974.

Prendergast, Christopher. *The Order of Mimesis: Balzac, Stendhal, Nerval, and Flaubert*. Cambridge: Cambridge University Press, 1986.

Strickland, Geoffrey. *Stendhal: The Education of a Novelist*. Cambridge: Cambridge University Press, 1974.

Swingewood, Alan. *The Novel and Revolution*. New York: Barnes & Noble, 1975.

Talbot, Emile. *Stendhal and Romantic Esthetics*. Lexington, Ky.: French Forum, 1985.

Tennenbaum, Elizabeth Brody. *The Problematic Self: Approaches to Identity in Stendhal, D. H. Lawrence, and Malraux*. Cambridge, Mass.: Harvard University Press, 1977.

Tillet, Margaret. *Stendhal: The Background to the Novels*. London: Oxford University Press, 1971.

## LEIGH HUNT

Baker, William. "Leigh Hunt, George Henry Lewes, and Henry Hallam's *Introduction to the Literature of Europe*." *Studies in Bibliography* 32 (1979): 252–73.

Blainey, Ann. *Immortal Boy: A Portrait of Leigh Hunt*. New York: St. Martin's Press, 1985.

Blunden, Edmund. *Leigh Hunt's "Examiner" Examined*. London: Cobden-Sanderson, 1928.

Cockshut, A. O. J. *The Art of Autobiography in 19th- and 20th-Century England*. New Haven: Yale University Press, 1984.

Fenner, Theodore. *Leigh Hunt and Opera Criticism: The "Examiner" Years, 1808–1821*. Lawrence: University Press of Kansas, 1972.

Harper, Henry Howard. *Byron's Malach Hamoves: A Commentary of Leigh Hunt's Work Entitled, "Lord Byron and Some of His Contemporaries."* Cedar Rapids, Ia.: Torch Press, 1933.

Johnson, Reginald B. *Shelley—Leigh Hunt: How Friendship Made History*. London: Ingpen & Grant, 1929.

Lulofs, Timothy J., and Hans Ostrom. *Leigh Hunt: A Reference Guide*. Boston: G. K. Hall, 1985.

McCown, Robert A., ed. *The Life and Times of Leigh Hunt: Papers Delivered at a Symposium at the University of Iowa on April 13, 1984, Commemorating the 200th Anniversary of Leigh Hunt's Birth*. Iowa City: Friends of the University of Iowa Libraries, 1985.

Mitchell, Alexander. *A Bibliography of the Writings of Leigh Hunt, with Critical Notes*. London: Bookman's Journal, 1931.

Severn, Derek. "Leigh Hunt vs. the Tories and the Prince Regent." *Cornhill* 1066 (Winter 1970–71): 288–312.

Stam, David H. "Leigh Hunt and the True Sun: A List of Reviews August 1833 to February 1834." *Bulletin of the New York Public Library* 77 (1974): 436–53.

Thompson, James R. *Leigh Hunt*. Boston: Twayne, 1977.

Waltman, John L., and Gerald G. McDaniel. *Leigh Hunt: A Comprehensive Bibliography*. New York: Garland, 1985.

Wells, Stanley. "Shakespeare in Leigh Hunt's Theatre Criticism." *Essays and Studies* 33 (1980): 119–38.

## THOMAS DE QUINCEY

Blakemore, Steven. "De Quincey's Transubstantiation of Opium in the *Confessions*." *Massachusetts Studies in English* 9 (1984): 32–41.

Bruss, Elizabeth W. *Autobiographical Acts: The Changing Situation of a Literary Genre*. Baltimore: Johns Hopkins University Press, 1976.

Buckley, Jerome Hamilton. *The Turning Key: Autobiography and the Subjective Impulse since 1800*. Cambridge, Mass.: Harvard University Press, 1984.

Cockshut, A. O. J. *The Art of Autobiography in 19th- and 20th-Century England*. New Haven: Yale University Press, 1984.

Cook, Michael G. "Modern Black Autobiography in the Tradition." In *Romanticism: Vistas, Instances, Continuities*, edited by David Thorburn and Geoffrey Hartman. Ithaca: Cornell University Press, 1973.

de Luca, V. A. *Thomas De Quincey: The Prose of Vision*. Toronto: University of Toronto Press, 1980.

Dendurent, H. O. *Thomas De Quincey: A Reference Guide*. Boston: G. K. Hall, 1978.

Devlin, D. D. *De Quincey, Wordsworth, and the Art of Prose*. New York: St. Martin's Press, 1983.

Digwaney, Anuradha, and Lawrence Needham. "'A Sort of Previous Lubrication': De Quincey's Preface to *Confessions of an English Opium-Eater*." *Quarterly Journal of Speech* 71 (1985): 457–69.

Goldman, Albert. *The Mine and the Mint: Sources for the Writing of Thomas De Quincey*. Carbondale: Southern Illinois University Press, 1971.

Jordan, John E., ed. *De Quincey as Critic*. London: Routledge & Kegan Paul, 1973.

———, ed. *A Flame in Sunlight: The Life and Work of Thomas De Quincey*. London: The Bodley Head, 1974.

Lever, Karen M. "De Quincey as Gothic Hero: A Perspective on *Confessions of an English Opium-Eater* and *Suspira de Profundis*." *Texas Studies in Literature and Language* 21 (1979): 332–46.

Lindop, Grevel. *The Opium-Eater: A Life of Thomas De Quincey*. London: J. M. Dent, 1981.

Maniquis, Robert M. "Lonely Empires: Personal and Public Visions of Thomas De Quincey." In *Mid-Nineteenth Century Writers: Eliot, De Quincey, Emerson*, edited by Eric Rothstein and Joseph A. Wittreich, Jr. Madison: University of Wisconsin Press, 1976.

Snyder, Robert Lance, ed. *Thomas De Quincey: Bicentenary Studies*. Norman: University of Oklahoma Press, 1985.

Whale, John C. *Thomas De Quincey's Reluctant Autobiography*. Totowa, N.J.: Barnes & Noble, 1984.

## THOMAS LOVE PEACOCK

Able, Augustus. *George Meredith and Thomas Love Peacock*. Philadelphia: University of Pennsylvania Press, 1932.

Brogan, Howard O. "Romantic Classicism in Peacock's Verse Satire." *Studies in English Literature, 1500–1900* 14 (1974): 525–36.

Burns, Bryan. *The Novels of Thomas Love Peacock*. Totowa, N.J.: Barnes & Noble, 1985.

Butler, Marilyn. *Peacock Displayed: A Satirist in His Context*. London: Routledge & Kegan Paul, 1979.

Campbell, Olwen. *Thomas Love Peacock*. London: A. Barker, 1953.

Dawson, Carl. *His Fine Wit: A Study of Thomas Love Peacock*. London: Routledge & Kegan Paul, 1970.

Felton, Felix. *Thomas Love Peacock*. London: George Allen & Unwin, 1973.

Frye, Northrop. *The Critical Path: An Essay on the Social Context of Literary Criticism*. Bloomington: Indiana University Press, 1971.

Helm, W. H. *Thomas Love Peacock*. London: Herbert & Daniel, n.d.

Hoff, Peter Sloat. "The Paradox of the Fortunate Foible: Thomas Love Peacock's Literary Vision." *Texas Studies in Literature and Language* 17 (1975): 481–88.

Kjellin, Hakan. *Talkative Banquets: A Study in the Peacockian Novels of Talk*. Stockholm: Almqvist & Wiksell, 1974.

Madden, Lionel. *Thomas Love Peacock*. Totowa, N.J.: Rowman & Littlefield, 1967.

———. "A Short Guide to Peacock Studies." *Critical Survey* (1970): 193–97.

Mills, Howard. *Peacock: His Circle and His Age*. Cambridge: Cambridge University Press, 1969.

Prickett, Stephen. "Peacock's *Four Ages* Recycled." *British Journal of Aesthetics* 22 (1982): 158–66.

Rudinsky, Norman Leigh. "A Second Original of Peacock's Menippean Caricature Asterias in *Nightmare Abbey*: Sir John Sinclair, Bart." *English Studies* 56 (1975): 491–97.

Walling, William. "'On Fishing Up the Moon': In Search of Thomas Love Peacock." In *The Evidence of the Imagination: Studies of Interactions between Life and Art in English Romantic Literature*, edited by Donald H. Reiman, Michael Jaye, and Betty T. Bennett. New York: New York University Press, 1978.

## ARTHUR SCHOPENHAUER

Bykhovsky, B. *Schopenhauer and the Ground of Existence*. Atlantic Highlands, N.J.: Humanities Press, 1961.

Copleston, F. C. *Arthur Schopenhauer: Philosopher of Pessimism*. London: Burnes, Oates & Washbourne, 1946.

Dauer, Dorothea W. *Schopenhauer as Transmitter of Buddhist Ideas*. New York: Peter Lang Publications, 1969.

Fox, Michael, ed. *Schopenhauer: His Philosophical Achievement*. Totowa, N.J.: Barnes & Noble, 1980.

Hamlyn, David W. *Schopenhauer*. New York: Methuen, 1985.

Knox, Israel. *Aesthetic Theories of Kant, Hegel, and Schopenhauer*. Atlantic Highlands, N.J.: Humanities Press, 1978.

McGill, Vivian J. *Schopenhauer*. New York: Brentano's, 1931.

Magee, Bryan. *The Philosophy of Schopenhauer*. Oxford: Oxford University Press, 1983.

Mann, Thomas, ed. *The Living Thoughts of Schopenhauer*. Stockholm: Bermann-Fischer, 1938.

Miller, Bruce R. *The Philosophy of Schopenhauer in Dramatic Representational Expressions*. Albuquerque, N.M.: American Classical College Press, 1981.

Nietzsche, Friedrich. *Schopenhauer as Educator*. Translated by James W. Hillesheim and Malcolm B. Simpson. Chicago: Regnery Books, 1965.

Simmel, Georg. *Schopenhauer and Nietzsche*. Translated by Helmut Loiskandl, et al. Amherst: University of Massachusetts Press, 1986.

Simpson, David, ed. *German Aesthetic and Literary Criticism: Kant, Fichte, Schelling, Schopenhauer, Hegel*. Cambridge: Cambridge University Press, 1984.

Taylor, Ronald. *The Romantic Tradition in Germany: An Anthology with Critical Essays and Commentaries*. London: Methuen, 1970.

Wallace, William. *The Life of Arthur Schopenhauer*. London: Walter Scott, 1889.

PERCY BYSSHE SHELLEY


Allott, Miriam, ed. *Essays on Shelley*. Totowa, N.J.: Barnes & Noble, 1982.

Allsup, James O. *The Magic Circle: A Study of Shelley's Concept of Love*. Port Washington, N.Y.: Kennikat Press, 1976.

Bloom, Harold. *Shelley's Mythmaking*. Ithaca: Cornell University Press, 1969.

Bradley, A. C. "Shelley's View of Poetry." In *Oxford Lectures on Poetry*. London: Macmillan, 1909.

Brown, Nathaniel. *Sexuality and Feminism in Shelley*. Cambridge, Mass.: Harvard University Press, 1979.

Cameron, Kenneth. *Shelley: The Golden Years*. Cambridge, Mass.: Harvard University Press, 1974.

———, ed. *Romantic Rebels: Essays on Shelley and His Circle*. Cambridge, Mass.: Harvard University Press, 1973.

Chernaik, Judith. *The Lyrics of Shelley*. Cleveland: Press of Case Western Reserve University, 1972.

Duffy, Edward. *Rousseau in England: The Context for Shelley's Critique of the Enlightenment*. Berkeley: University of Calfiornia Press, 1979.

Dunbar, Clement. *A Bibliography of Shelley Studies: 1823–1950*. New York: Garland, 1976.

Fischer, Michael. *Does Deconstruction Make Any Difference? Poststructuralism and the Defense of Poetry in Modern Criticism*. Bloomington: Indiana University Press, 1985.

Fogle, Richard H. *The Imagery of Keats and Shelley*. Chapel Hill: University of North Carolina Press, 1949.

Holmes, Richard. *Shelley: The Pursuit*. London: Weidenfeld & Nicolson, 1974.

Keach, William. *Shelley's Style*. London: Methuen, 1984.

Leavis, F. R. *Revaluation: Tradition and Development in English Poetry*. London: Chatto & Windus, 1936.

Matthews, G. M, ed. *Introduction to Shelley: Selected Poems and Prose*. Oxford: Oxford University Press, 1964.

Perkins, David. *The Quest for Permanence: The Symbolism of Wordsworth, Shelley, and Keats*. Cambridge, Mass.: Harvard University Press, 1959.

Reiman, Donald, and Sharon Powers, eds. *Shelley's Poetry and Prose: Authoritative Texts; Criticism*. New York: W. W. Norton, 1977.

Richards, I. A. "The Mystical Element in Shelley's Poetry." *Aryan Path* 30 (1959): 250–56, 290–95.

Ridenour, George, ed. *Shelley: A Collection of Critical Essays*. Englewood Cliffs, N.J.: Prentice-Hall, 1965.

Robinson, Charles E. *Shelley and Byron: The Snake and Eagle Wreathed in Fight*. Baltimore: Johns Hopkins University Press, 1976.

Scrivener, Michael Henry. *Radical Shelley: The Philosophical Anarchism and Utopian Thought of Percy Bysshe Shelley*. Princeton: Princeton University Press, 1982.

Tennyson, G. B., and Edward Ericson, Jr., eds. *Religion and Modern Literature: Essays in Theory and Criticism*. Grand Rapids, Mich.: William B. Eerdmans, 1975.

Wasserman, Earl R. *Shelley: A Critical Reading*. Baltimore: Johns Hopkins University Press, 1971.

Webb, Timothy. *The Violet in the Crucible: Shelley and Translation*. Oxford: Oxford University Press, 1976.

———. *Shelley: A Voice Not Understood*. Atlantic Highlands, N.J.: Humanities Press, 1977.

Yeats, William Butler. "The Philosophy of Shelley's Poetry." In *Essays and Introductions*. New York: Macmillan, 1961.

JOHN KEBLE

Coleridge, John T. *A Memoir of the Rev. John Keble*. Oxford: J. Parker & Co., 1869.

Donaldson, Augustus B. *Five Great Oxford Leaders: Keble, Newman, Pusey, Liddon, and Church*. London: Rivington's, 1900.

Gilley, Sheridan. "John Keble and the Victorian Churching of Romanticism." In *An Infinite Complexity: Essays in Romanticism*, edited by J. R. Watson. Edinburgh: Edinburgh University Press, 1983.

Martin, Brian W. *John Keble: Priest, Professor, and Poet*. Wolfeboro, N.H.: Longwood-Publishing Group, 1976.

Prickett, Stephen. *Romanticism and Religion: The Tradition of Coleridge and Wordsworth in the Victorian Church*. Cambridge: Cambridge University Press, 1976.

Shairp, J. C. *Studies in Poetry and Philosophy*. Edinburgh: Edmonston & Douglas, 1868.

Waddell, James. "Keble and the Reader's Imagination." *Christianity and Literature* 13 (1985): 39–56.

Warren, William T., ed. *Kebleland: Keble's Home at Hursley, Incidents in His Life, Extracts from His Poetical Works, Keble's Churches, Keble College, Oxford, with Notes on the Neighbouring Villages; Also a Short Life of Richard Cromwell, of Merdon, and Other Character Sketches*. London: Simpkin & Co., 1900.

Wood, Edward L. *John Keble: Leaders of the Church 1800–1900*. Philadelphia: R. West, 1909.

JOHN HENRY NEWMAN

Blehl, Vincent, and Francis X. Connolly, eds. *Newman's Apologia: A Classic Reconsidered*. New York: Harcourt Brace Jovanovich, 1964.

———. *John Henry Newman: A Bibliographical Catalogue of His Writings*. Charlottesville: University Press of Virginia, 1978.

Cameron, J. M. "John Henry Newman and the Tractarian Movement." In *Nineteenth-Century Religious Thought in the West*, edited by Ninian Smart, John Clayton, and Steven Katz. Cambridge: Cambridge University Press, 1985.

Chadwick, Owen. *Newman*. Oxford: Oxford University Press, 1983.

Coulson, John, and Arthur M. Allchin, eds. *The Rediscovery of Newman: An Oxford Symposium*. London: Society for Promoting Christian Knowledge, 1967.

Culler, Arthur D. *The Imperial Intellect*. New Haven: Yale University Press, 1955.

Dessain, Charles S. *John Henry Newman*. Second edition. Stanford: Stanford University Press, 1971.

———. *The Spirituality of John Henry Newman*. San Francisco: Winston Press, 1980.

Earnest, James D., and Gerard Tracey. *John Henry Newman: An Annotated Bibliography*. New York: Garland, 1984.

Elwood, J. Murray. *Kindly Light: The Spiritual Vision of John Henry Newman*. Notre Dame, Ind.: Ave Maria Press, 1979.

Gornall, Thomas. *The Letters and Diaries of John Henry Newman: Liberalism in*

*Oxford, January 1835 to December 1836*. Vol. 5. Oxford: Oxford University Press, 1981.

Griffin, John R. *Newman: A Bibliography of Secondary Studies*. Front Royal, Va.: Christendom Publications, 1980.

Hicks, John. *Critical Studies in Arnold, Emerson, and Newman*. Iowa City, Ia.: The University Press, 1942.

Kenny, Terence. *The Political Thought of John Henry Newman*. London: Longmans, Green, 1957.

Levine, George. *The Boundaries of Fiction: Carlyle, Macaulay, Newman*. Princeton: Princeton University Press, 1968.

Martin, Brian W. *John Henry Newman*. Oxford: Oxford University Press, 1982.

Newsome, David. *Two Classes of Men: Platonism and English Romantic Thought*. London: John Murray, 1974.

Peterson, Linda H. "Newman's *Apologia pro Vita Sua* and the Traditions of the English Spiritual Autobiography." *PMLA* 100 (1985): 300–314.

Robbins, William. *Newman Brothers: An Essay in Comparative Intellectual Biography*. Cambridge, Mass.: Harvard University Press, 1966.

Siebensenuh, William. *Fictional Techniques and Factual Works*. Athens: University of Georgia Press, 1983.

Tillman, Mary Katherine. "The Tension between Intellectual and Moral Education in the Thought of John Henry Newman." *Thought* 60 (1985): 322–34.

Tristram, Henry, ed. *The Living Thoughts of Cardinal Newman*. New York: McKay, 1953.

Weatherby, Harold. *Cardinal Newman in His Age: His Place in English Theology and Literature*. Nashville, Tenn.: Vanderbilt University Press, 1973.

Yearley, Lee H. *The Ideas of Newman: Christianity and Human Religiosity*. University Park: Pennsylvania State University Press, 1978.

## JOHN KEATS

Albrecht, W. P. *The Sublime Pleasures of Tragedy: A Study of Critical Theory from Dennis to Keats*. Lawrence: University of Kansas Press, 1975.

Bate, Walter, ed. *Keats: A Collection of Critical Essays*. Englewood Cliffs, N.J.: Prentice-Hall, 1964.

Bloom, Harold. *The Visionary Company: A Reading of English Romantic Poetry*. Ithaca: Cornell University Press, 1971.

———, ed. *John Keats*. New York: Chelsea House, 1985.

Caldwell, James R. *John Keats's Fancy: The Effect on Keats of the Psychology of His Day*. Ithaca: Cornell University Press, 1945.

Danzig, Allan. *Twentieth-Century Interpretations of "The Eve of St. Agnes": A Collection of Critical Essays*. Englewood Cliffs, N.J.: Prentice-Hall, 1971.

Demetz, P.; T. Greene; and L. Nelson; eds. *The Disciplines of Criticism: Essays in Literary Theory, Interpretation, and History*. New Haven: Yale University Press, 1968.

Dickstein, Morris. *Keats and His Poetry: A Study in Development*. Chicago: University of Chicago Press, 1971.

Hagstrum, Jean H. *The Romantic Body: Love and Sexuality in Keats, Wordsworth, and Blake*. Knoxville: University of Tennessee Press, 1985.

Hirst, Wolf. *John Keats*. Boston: Twayne, 1981.

Jones, James Land. *Adam's Dream: Mythic Consciousness in Keats and Yeats*. Athens: University of Georgia Press, 1975.
Jugurtha, Lillie. *Keats and Nature*. New York: Peter Lang, 1985.
Muir, Kenneth, ed. *John Keats: A Reassessment*. Liverpool: Liverpool University Press, 1958.
Murry, John Middleton. *Keats and Shakespeare*. London: Oxford University Press, 1930.
Patterson, Charles, Jr. *The Daemonic in the Poetry of John Keats*. Urbana: University of Illinois Press, 1970.
Pollard, David. *The Poetry of Keats: Language and Experience*. Totowa, N.J.: Barnes & Noble, 1984.
Rhodes, Jack Wright. *Keats's Major Odes: An Annotated Bibliography of the Criticism*. Westport, Conn.: Greenwood Press, 1984.
Richardson, Joanna. *Keats and His Circle*. London: Cassell, 1980.
Ricks, Christopher. *Keats and Embarrassment*. Oxford: Oxford University Press, 1984.
Rollins, Hyder E., ed. *The Keats Circle*. 2 vols. Cambridge, Mass.: Harvard University Press, 1948.
Ryan, Robert M. *Keats: The Religious Sense*. Princeton: Princeton University Press, 1976.
Schwartz, Lewis M. *Keats Reviewed by His Contemporaries: A Collection of Notices for the Years 1816–1821*. Metuchen, N.J.: Scarecrow Press, 1973.
Stillinger, Jack. *The Hoodwinking of Madeline and Other Essays on Keats's Poems*. Urbana: University of Illinois Press, 1971.
Van Ghent, Dorothy. *Keats: The Myth of the Hero*. Princeton: Princeton University Press, 1983.
Vogler, Thomas A. *Preludes to Vision: The Epic Venture in Blake, Wordsworth, Keats, and Hart Crane*. Berkeley: University of California Press, 1971.
Waldoff, Leon. *Keats and the Silent Work of Imagination*. Urbana: University of Illinois Press, 1985.
Wasserman, Earl R. *The Finer Tone: Keats's Major Poems*. Baltimore: Johns Hopkins University Press, 1953.

## THOMAS CARLYLE

Arac, Jonathan. *Commissioned Spirits: The Shaping of Social Motion in Dickens, Carlyle, Melville, and Hawthorne*. New Brunswick, N.J.: Rutgers University Press, 1979.
Bloom, Harold, ed. *Thomas Carlyle*. New York: Chelsea House, 1986.
Buckley, Jerome Hamilton. *The Turning Key: Autobiography and the Subjective Impulse since 1800*. Cambridge, Mass.: Harvard University Press, 1984.
Clubbe, John, ed. *Carlyle and His Contemporaries: Essays in Honor of Charles Richard Sanders*. Durham, N.C.: Duke University Press, 1976.
———, ed. *Froude's Life of Carlyle*. Columbus: Ohio State University Press, 1979.
Dale, Peter Allan. *The Victorian Critic and the Idea of History: Carlyle, Arnold, Pater*. Cambridge, Mass.: Harvard University Press, 1977.
Dibble, Jerry A. *The Pythia's Drunken Song: Thomas Carlyle's "Sartor Resartus" and the Style Problem in German Idealist Philosophy*. The Hague: Martinus Nijhoff, 1978.
Dillon, R. W. "A Centenary Bibliography of Carlylean Studies, 1928–1974." *Bulletin of Bibliography* 32 (1975): 133–57.

Fielding, K. J., and Roger L. Tarr, eds. *Carlyle Past and Present: A Collection of New Essays*. London: Vision Press, 1976.

Goodheart, Eugene. *The Failure of Criticism*. Cambridge, Mass.: Harvard University Press, 1978.

Harris, Kenneth Marc. *Carlyle and Emerson: Their Long Debate*. Cambridge, Mass.: Harvard University Press, 1978.

Kaplan, Fred. *Thomas Carlyle: A Bibliography*. Ithaca: Cornell University Press, 1984.

Leicester, H. M., Jr. "The Dialectic of Romantic Historiography: Prospect and Retrospect in *The French Revolution*." *Victorian Studies* 15 (1971): 1–17.

Le Quense, A. L. *Carlyle*. Oxford: Oxford University Press, 1982.

Oddie, William. *Dickens and Carlyle: The Question of Influence*. London: The Centenary Press, 1972.

Rosenberg, John D. *Carlyle and the Burden of History*. Cambridge, Mass.: Harvard University Press, 1985.

Rosenberg, Philip. *The Seventh Hero: Thomas Carlyle and the Theory of Radical Activism*. Cambridge, Mass.: Harvard University Press, 1974.

Sanders, Charles Richard. *Carlyle's Friendships and Other Studies*. Durham, N.C.: Duke University Press, 1978.

Seigel, Jules Paul, ed. *Thomas Carlyle: The Critical Heritage*. London: Routledge & Kegan Paul, 1971.

Tennyson, G. B. "Thomas Carlyle." In *Victorian Prose: A Guide to Research,* edited by David de Laura. New York: The Modern Language Association of America, 1973.

## HEINRICH HEINE

Atkinson, Ross. "Irony and Commitment in Heine's *Deutschland ein Wintermärchen*." *Germanic Review* 50 (1975): 184–202.

Block, Haskell M. "Heine and the French Symbolists." In *Creative Encounter: Festschrift for Herman Salinger,* edited by Leland Phelps and A. Tilo Alt. Chapel Hill: University of North Carolina Press, 1978.

Brod, Max. *Heinrich Heine: The Artist in Revolt*. Translated by Joseph Witriol. Westport, Conn.: Greenwood Press, 1976.

Fairley, Barker. *Heinrich Heine: An Interpretation*. Oxford: Clarendon Press, 1953.

———. "Heine's Vaudeville"; "Heine and the Festive Board"; "Heine, Goethe, and the Divan." In *Selected Essays on German Literature,* edited by Rodney Symington. New York: Peter Lang, 1984.

Holub, Robert C. *Heinrich Heine's Reception of German Grecophilia: The Function and Application of the Hellenic Tradition in the First Half of the Nineteenth Century*. Heidelburg: Carl Winter, 1981.

Hueppe, Frederick E. *Unity and Synthesis in the Work of Heinrich Heine*. New York: Peter Lang, 1979.

Kahn, Lothar. "Heine's Jewish Writer Friends: Dilemma of a Generation, 1817–33." In *The Jewish Response to Jewish Culture: From the Enlightenment to the Second World War,* edited by Jehuda Reinherz and Walter Schatzberg. Hanover, N.H.: University Press of New England, 1985.

Kesten, Hermann. "Heinrich Heine and Joseph Roth." *Publications of the Leo Baeck Institute* 20 (1975): 259–73.

Newman, Caroline. "Cemeteries of Tradition: The Critique of Collection in Heine, Nietzsche, and Benjamin." *Pacific Coast Philology* 19 (1984): 12–21.

Prawer, S. S. *Heine's Jewish Comedy: A Study of His Portraits of Jews and Judaism*. Oxford: Oxford University Press, 1983.
———. *Coal Smoke and Englishmen: A Study of Verbal Caricature in the Writings of Heinrich Heine*. London: University of London Press, 1984.
Reeves, Nigel. "The Art of Simplicity: Heinrich Heine and Wilhelm Müller." *Oxford German Studies* 5 (1970): 48–66.
———. *Heinrich Heine: Poetry and Politics*. Oxford: Oxford University Press, 1974.
Sammons, Jeffrey L. *Heinrich Heine*. Princeton: Princeton University Press, 1979.
———. *Heinrich Heine: A Selected Bibliography of Secondary Literature*. New York: Garland, 1982.
Sharp, William. *The Life of Heinrich Heine*. London: Walter Scott, 1888.
Spencer, Hanna. *Heinrich Heine*. Boston: Twayne, 1982.
Stanberry, D. Elaine. *Love's Perplexing Obsession Experienced by Two Geniuses: Heinrich Heine and Percy Bysshe Shelley*. New York: Vantage Press, 1981.
Stein, Jack M. *Poem and Music in the German Lied from Gluck to Hugo Wolf*. Cambridge, Mass.: Harvard University Press, 1971.
Untermeyer, Louis. *Heinrich Heine*. Philadelphia: R. West, 1937.
Wikoff, Jerold. *Heinrich Heine: A Study of Neue Gedichte*. New York: Peter Lang, 1975.

## GIACOMO LEOPARDI

Belmore, H. W. "Two Romantic Poets of Solitude: Leopardi and Morike." *German Life and Letters* 31 (1977): 313–18.
Bickersteth, Geoffrey L. *Leopardi and Wordsworth: A Lecture*. London: Oxford University Press, 1927.
Bini, Daniela. *A Fragrance from the Desert: Poetry and Philosophy in Giacomo Leopardi*. Saratoga, Cal.: Anma Libri, 1983.
Caesar, Michael. "Leopardi Unnamed." *Romance Studies* (1984–85): 143–48.
———. "Poet and Audience in the Young Leopardi." *Modern Language Review* 77 (1982): 310–24.
Carsaniga, Giovanni. *Giacomo Leopardi: The Unheeded Voice*. Edinburgh: Edinburgh University Press, 1977.
———. "Was Leopardi a Scientist?" In *Altro Polo: A Volume of Italian Studies*, edited by Silvio Trambaiolo and Nerida Newbigin. Sydney: University of Sydney Press, 1978.
Caserta, Ernesto. *Giacomo Leopardi: The War of the Mice and the Crabs*. Chapel Hill: University of North Carolina Press, 1976.
Cook, Albert. "Leopardi: The Mastery of Diffusing Sorrow." *Canadian Journal of Irish Studies* 4 (1980–81): 68–81.
del Greco, A. A. *Giacomo Leopardi in Hispanic Literature*. New York: F. Vanni, 1952.
Flint, R. W. "Giacomo Leopardi." *Parnassus* 10 (1982): 42–54.
Garofalo, Silvano. "The Tragic Sense in the Poetry of Leopardi and Unamuno." *Symposium* 26 (1972): 197–211.
Leopardi, Giacomo. *The Moral Essays*. Translated by Patrick Creagh. New York: Columbia University Press, 1983.
Perella, Nicholas James. *Night and the Sublime in Giacomo Leopardi*. Berkeley: University of California Press, 1970.
Robb, Nesca. *Four in Exile: Critical Essays on Leopardi, Hans Christian Andersen, Christina Rossetti, and A. E. Housman*. Millwood, N.Y.: Associated Faculty Press, 1968.

Rosenthal, Alan S. "The Theory and Poetry of Ennui: Leopardi and Baudelaire." *Neophilologus* 60 (1976): 342–56.

## RALPH WALDO EMERSON

Bishop, Jonathan. *Emerson on the Soul.* Cambridge, Mass.: Harvard University Press, 1964.

Bloom, Harold, ed. *Ralph Waldo Emerson.* New York: Chelsea House, 1985.

———, ed. *Ralph Waldo Emerson: Poetry and Later Writings.* New York: Library of America, 1985.

Buell, Lawrence. *Literary Transcendentalism.* Ithaca: Cornell University Press, 1973.

Burke, Kenneth. "I, Eye, Ay—Emerson's Early Essay 'Nature': Thoughts on the Machinery of Transcendence." In *Transcendentalism and Its Legacy,* edited by Myron Simon and Thornton Parsons. Ann Arbor: University of Michigan Press, 1966.

Burkholder, Robert E., and Joel Myerson, eds. *Emerson: An Annotated Secondary Bibliography.* Pittsburgh: University of Pittsburgh Press, 1985.

Carlson, Eric W., ed. *Emerson's Literary Criticism.* Lincoln: University of Nebraska Press, 1979.

Carton, Evan. *The Rhetoric of American Romance: Dialectic and Identity in Emerson, Dickinson, Poe, and Hawthorne.* Baltimore: Johns Hopkins University Press, 1985.

Chapman, John Jay. "Emerson." In *Emerson and Other Essays.* New York: Scribner's, 1898, pp. 3–108.

Cheyfitz, Eric. *The Trans-Parent: Sexual Politics in the Language of Emerson.* Baltimore: Johns Hopkins University Press, 1981.

Ellison, Julie. *Emerson's Romantic Style.* Princeton: Princeton University Press, 1984.

Harris, Kenneth Marc. *Carlyle and Emerson: Their Long Debate.* Cambridge, Mass.: Harvard University Press, 1978.

Hopkins, Vivian. *Spires of Form: A Study of Emerson's Aesthetic Theory.* Cambridge, Mass.: Harvard University Press, 1951.

Hughes, Gertrude. *Emerson's Demanding Optimism.* Baton Rouge: Louisiana State University Press, 1984.

Konvitz, Milton R., ed. *The Recognition of Ralph Waldo Emerson: Selected Criticism since 1837.* Ann Arbor: University of Michigan Press, 1972.

———, and Stephen E. Whicher, eds. *Emerson: A Collection of Critical Essays.* Englewood Cliffs, N.J.: Prentice-Hall, 1962.

Levin, David, ed. *Emerson: Prophecy, Metamorphosis, and Influence.* New York: Columbia University Press, 1975.

Loving, Jerome. *Emerson, Whitman, and the American Muse.* Chapel Hill: University of North Carolina Press, 1982.

McAleer, John. *Ralph Waldo Emerson: Days of Encounter.* Boston: Little, Brown & Co., 1984.

Riese, Teut Andreas, ed. *Vistas of a Continent: Concepts of Nature in America.* Heidelberg: Carl Winter, 1979.

Smith, David L. "Emerson and Destruction: The End(s) of Scholarship." *Soundings* 67 (1984): 379–98.

Whicher, Stephen E. *Freedom and Fate: An Inner Life of Ralph Waldo Emerson.* Philadelphia: University of Pennsylvania Press, 1953.

Winters, Yvor. *In Defense of Reason*. Denver: Alan Swallow, 1943.

Woodbury, Charles J. *Talks with Ralph Waldo Emerson*. New York: Baker & Baker, 1890.

Yoder, R. A. *Emerson and the Orphic Poet in America*. Berkeley: University of California Press, 1978.

## CHARLES-AUGUSTIN SAINTE-BEUVE

Carrington, Samuel M. "Sainte-Beuve, Critic of Ronsard." *Rice University Studies* 59 (1973): 9–16.

Chadbourne, Richard M. "Criticism as Creation in Sainte-Beuve." *L'Esprit Créateur* 14 (1974): 44–54.

———. "Sainte-Beuve's *Livre d'amour* as Poetry." *Nineteenth-Century Fiction Studies* 3 (1974–75): 80–96.

———. *Charles-Augustin Sainte-Beuve*. Boston: Twayne, 1977.

Giese, William F. *Sainte-Beuve: A Literary Portrait*. Westport, Conn.: Greenwood Press, 1974.

Harper, George M. *Charles-Augustin Sainte-Beuve*. Philadelphia: Lippincott, 1909.

Nicolson, Harold. *Sainte-Beuve*. London: Constable, 1957.

Wilson, Norman Scarlyn, ed. *Sainte-Beuve and the French Romantics*. London: Hachette, 1931.

## JOHN STUART MILL

Alexander, Edward. *Matthew Arnold and John Stuart Mill*. New York: Columbia University Press, 1965.

Anschutz, R. P. *The Philosophy of John Stuart Mill*. Westport, Conn.: Greenwood Press, 1986.

Bain, Alexander. *John Stuart Mill: A Criticism with Personal Recollections*. London: Longmans, Green & Co., 1882.

Blanshard, Brand. *Four Reasonable Men: Aurelius, Mill, Renan, Sidgwick*. Middletown, Conn.: Wesleyan University Press, 1984.

Borchard, Ruth. *John Stuart Mill: The Man*. London: Watts, 1957.

Duncan, G. *Marx and Mill: Two Views of Social Conflict and Social Harmony*. Cambridge: Cambridge University Press, 1973.

Eisenach, Eldon J. *Two Worlds of Liberalism: Religion and Politics in Hobbes, Locke, and Mill*. Chicago: University of Chicago Press, 1981.

Ellery, John B. *John Stuart Mill*. New York: Twayne, 1964.

Garforth, Francis W. *Educative Democracy: John Stuart Mill on Education in Society*. Oxford: Oxford University Press, 1980.

Glassman, Peter. *J. S. Mill: The Evolution of a Genius*. Gainesville: University Presses of Florida, 1985.

Goehlert, Robert. *John Stuart Mill: A Bibliography*. Monticello, Ill.: Vance Bibliographies, 1982.

Gouinlock, James. *Excellence in Public Discourse: John Stuart Mill, John Dewey, and Social Intelligence*. New York: Teachers College Press, 1986.

Himmelfarb, Gertrude. *On Liberty and Liberalism: The Case of John Stuart Mill*. New York: Alfred A. Knopf, 1974.

Hollander, Samuel. *The Economics of John Stuart Mill.* Toronto: University of Toronto Press, 1982.

Laine, Michael. *Bibliography of Works on John Stuart Mill.* Toronto: University of Toronto Press, 1985.

Nelson, Allan D. "John Stuart Mill: The Reformer Reformed." *Interpretation: A Journal of Political Philosophy* 13 (1985): 359–401.

Rees, John C. *John Stuart Mill's "On Liberty."* Oxford: Oxford University Press, 1985.

Robson, John M. *The Improvement of Mankind: The Social and Political Thought of John Stuart Mill.* Toronto: University of Toronto Press, 1968.

———, and Michael Laine, eds. *James and John Stuart Mill: Papers of the Centenary Conference.* Toronto: University of Toronto Press, 1976.

Schwartz, Pedro. *The New Political Economy of John Stuart Mill.* Durham, N.C.: Duke University Press, 1973.

Semmel, Bernard. *John Stuart Mill and the Pursuit of Virtue.* New Haven: Yale University Press, 1984.

Thomas, William. *Mill.* Oxford: Oxford University Press, 1985.

Thompson, Dennis F. *John Stuart Mill and Representative Government.* Princeton: Princeton University Press, 1976.

## EDGAR ALLAN POE

Auden, W. H. "Introduction." In *Selected Prose and Poetry of Edgar Allan Poe,* edited by W. H. Auden. New York: Rinehart, 1950.

Bloom, Harold, ed. *Edgar Allan Poe.* New York: Chelsea House, 1985.

Bonaparte, Marie. *The Life and Works of Edgar Allan Poe.* Translated by John Rodker. London: Imago, 1949.

Carlson, Eric W., ed. *The Recognition of Edgar Allan Poe.* Ann Arbor: University of Michigan Press, 1966.

Carton, Evan. *The Rhetoric of American Romance: Dialectic and Identity in Emerson, Dickinson, Poe, and Hawthorne.* Baltimore: Johns Hopkins University Press, 1985.

Davidson, Edward Hutchins. *Poe: A Critical Study.* Cambridge, Mass.: Harvard University Press, 1957.

Eliot, T. S. *From Poe to Valéry.* New York: Harcourt Brace, 1948.

Hammond, J. R. *An Edgar Allan Poe Companion.* London: Macmillan, 1981.

Hoffman, Daniel. *Poe Poe Poe Poe Poe Poe Poe.* Garden City, N.Y.: Doubleday, 1972.

Howarth, William, ed. *Twentieth-Century Interpretations of Poe's Tales.* Englewood Cliffs, N.J.: Prentice-Hall, 1971.

Humphries, Jefferson. *Metamorphoses of the Raven.* Baton Rouge: Louisiana State University Press, 1985.

Huxley, Aldous. "Vulgarity in Literature." In *Music at Night and Other Essays.* London: Fountain Press, 1931.

Irwin, John T. *American Hieroglyphics.* New Haven: Yale University Press, 1980.

Ketterer, David. *The Rationale of Deception in Poe.* Baton Rouge: Louisiana State University Press, 1979.

Lawrence, D. H. "Edgar Allan Poe." In *Studies in Classic American Literature.* New York: Viking, 1923.

Levin, Harry. *The Power of Blackness: Hawthorne, Poe, Melville.* New York: Alfred A. Knopf, 1958.

Regan, Robert, ed. *Poe: A Collection of Critical Essays*. Englewood Cliffs, N.J.: Prentice-Hall, 1967.
Tate, Allen. *The Forlorn Demon*. Chicago: Ayer Publishing, 1953.
Thompson, G. R. *Poe's Fiction: Romantic Irony in the Gothic Tales*. Madison: University of Wisconsin Press, 1973.
Wilson, Edmund. *The Shores of Light*. New York: Farrar, Straus & Giroux, 1952.
Woodberry, George Edward. *Edgar Allan Poe*. Boston: Houghton Mifflin & Co., 1885.
Woodson, Thomas, ed. *Twentieth-Century Interpretations of "The Fall of the House of Usher."* Englewood Cliffs, N.J.: Prentice-Hall, 1969.

## V. G. BELINSKII

Bowman, Herbert E. *Vissarion Belinskii, 1811–1848: A Study in the Origins of Social Criticism in Russia*. Cambridge, Mass.: Harvard University Press, 1954.
Mann, V. "'Gogol' in the Context of Aesthetic Controversies: V. G. Belinskii's Polemic with Konstantin Aksakov." *Soviet Review* 26 (1985): 39–61.
Matlaw, Ralph E., ed. *Belinsky, Chernyshevsky, and Dobrolyubov: Selected Criticism*. Bloomington: Indiana University Press, 1962.
Terras, Victor. *Belinskii and Russian Literary Criticism: The Heritage of Organic Aesthetics*. Madison: University of Wisconsin Press, 1974.

# ACKNOWLEDGMENTS

FRIEDRICH HÖLDERLIN

"On the Process of the Poetic Mind," translated by Ralph R. Read III, is taken from *German Romantic Criticism,* edited by A. Leslie Willson, copyright © 1982 by The Continuum Publishing Company. Reprinted by permission.

HEINRICH VON KLEIST

"On the Marionette Theater," translated by Christian-Albrecht Gollub, is taken from *German Romantic Criticism,* edited by A. Leslie Willson, copyright © 1982 by The Continuum Publishing Company. Reprinted by permission.

STENDHAL

The selections from "Racine and Shakespeare," translated by Guy Daniels, are taken from *Racine and Shakespeare,* copyright © 1962 by The Crowell-Collier Publishing Company. Reprinted by permission.

"Walter Scott and 'La Princesse de Cleves,'" translated by Geoffrey Strickland, is taken from *Selected Journalism from the English Reviews by Stendhal,* edited by Geoffrey Strickland, copyright © 1959 by John Calder, Ltd. Reprinted by permission.

LEIGH HUNT

"What Is Poetry?" is taken from *Selections from the English Poets,* Volume I, by Leigh Hunt, published by Willis P. Hazard (Philadelphia), 1854.

The selections from "Wit and Humor" are taken from *Essays of Leigh Hunt,* edited by Reginald Brimley Johnson, published by J. M. Dent & Co. (London), 1891.

THOMAS DE QUINCEY

"On the Knocking at the Gate in *Macbeth,*" "The Literature of Knowledge and the Literature of Power," and the selections from *Suspiria de Profundis* are taken from *The Collected Writings of Thomas De Quincey,* edited by David Masson, published by A. & C. Black (Edinburgh), 1889–90.

THOMAS LOVE PEACOCK

"The Four Ages of Poetry" is taken from *The Works of Thomas Love Peacock,* Volume III, edited by Henry Cole, published by Richard Bentley & Son (London), 1875.

ARTHUR SCHOPENHAUER

"On Books and Reading," translated by T. Bailey Saunders, and the selections from "The World as Will and Idea," translated by R. B. Haldane and J. Kemp, are taken from *The Works of Schopenhauer* (abridged), edited by Will Durant, copyright © 1928 by Simon & Schuster. Reprinted by permission.

PERCY BYSSHE SHELLEY

"Preface to *The Fall of Islam*," "Preface to *Prometheus Bound*," "On Love," and *A Defence of Poetry* are taken from *The Complete Works of Percy Bysshe Shelley* (10 vols.), edited by Roger Ingpen and Walter E. Peck, published by Charles Scribner's Sons (New York), 1927–30.

JOHN KEBLE & JOHN HENRY NEWMAN

"Sacred Poetry" was originally published in *Quarterly Review*, 1825, and reprinted in *Occasional Papers and Reviews*, by John Keble, published by J. Parker & Co. (Oxford), 1877. "Poetry, with Reference to Aristotle's *Poetics*" is taken from *Essays Critical and Historical*, Vol. 1, by John Henry Newman, published by Basil Montagu Pickering (London), 1872.

JOHN KEATS

The "Selected Letters" are taken from *The Letters of John Keats*, fourth edition, edited by Maurice Buxton Forman, copyright © 1952 by Oxford University Press.

THOMAS CARLYLE

"Signs of the Times," "The Hero as Poet," and the selections from *Sartor Resartus* are taken from *The Complete Works of Thomas Carlyle*, Vols. 1 and 2, published by The Kelmscott Society (New York), 1869.

HEINRICH HEINE

"I Meet August Wilhelm Schlegel," translated by Frederic Ewen, is taken from *The Poetry and Prose of Heinrich Heine*, edited by Frederic Ewen, copyright © 1948 by The Citadel Press. Reprinted by permission. "The Romantic School," translated by Havelock Ellis, is taken from *Prose and Poetry by Heinrich Heine*, edited by Ernest Rhys, copyright © 1934 by J. M. Dent & Sons, Ltd. Reprinted by permission.

GIACOMO LEOPARDI

The selections from *The Zibaldone,* translated by Iris Origo and John Heath-Stubbs, are taken from *Giacomo Leopardi: Selected Prose and Poetry,* edited by Iris Origo and John Heath-Stubbs, copyright © 1966 by Oxford University Press. Reprinted by permission.

RALPH WALDO EMERSON

"Poetry and Imagination" and "Quotation and Originality" are taken from *Letters and Social Aims,* by Ralph Waldo Emerson, published by Houghton Mifflin & Co. (Boston), 1875. "The Poet" is taken from *Essays: Second Series,* by Ralph Waldo Emerson, published by J. Munroe & Co. (Boston), 1844. "Shakespeare; or, The Poet" and "Montaigne; or, The Skeptic" are taken from *Representative Men,* by Ralph Waldo Emerson, published by Phillips, Sampson & Co. (Boston), 1850.

CHARLES-AUGUSTIN SAINTE-BEUVE

"What Is a Classic?" and "Rousseau's *Confessions,*" translated by Francis Steegmuller and Norbert Guterman, are taken from *Sainte-Beuve: Selected Essays,* edited by Francis Steegmuller and Norbert Guterman, copyright © 1963 by Doubleday & Co. Reprinted by permission.

JOHN STUART MILL

"Thoughts on Poetry and Its Varieties" is taken from *Dissertations and Discussions,* second edition, Vol. 1, published by Longmans, Green, Reader & Dyer (London), 1867.

EDGAR ALLAN POE

"The Rationale of Verse," "The Philosophy of Composition," "Longfellow," "Emerson," "Hawthorne's *Twice-Told Tales,*" and "Tale-Writing: Nathaniel Hawthorne" are taken from *The Complete Works of Edgar Allan Poe* (15 vols.), edited by James A. Harrison, published by Thomas Y. Crowell Co. (New York), 1902.

V. G. BELINSKII

The selections from "Thoughts and Notes on Russian Literature," translated by Ralph E. Matlaw, are taken from *Belinsky, Chernyshevsky, and Dobrolyubov: Selected Criticism,* edited by Ralph E. Matlaw, copyright © 1962 by E. P. Dutton & Co. Reprinted by permission.